Control
Sociology's Central Notion

Control
Sociology's Central Notion

Jack P. Gibbs

University of Illinois Press
Urbana and Chicago

HM
24
.G4446
1989
150164
Nov.1990

Publication of this work was supported in part by a grant from
the Faculty Committee for Monograph Subvention at Vanderbilt
University.

This book is printed on acid-free paper.

Library of Congress Cataloging-in-Publication Data

Gibbs, Jack P.
  Control: sociology's central notion.

  Bibliography: p.
  Includes indexes.
  1. Sociology—Methodology. 2. Social control.
I. Title.
HM24.G4446 1989   303.3'3   88-26192
ISBN 0-252-01590-8 (cloth: alk. paper)
ISBN 0-252-06046-6 (paper: alk. paper)

For Walter T. Martin:
mentor, co-author, and dear friend

Contents

Preface

This book is an extensive elaboration of two arguments. First, maximum coherence in any scientific field requires a central notion. And, second, control could be sociology's central notion.

Because a prefatory defense of either argument would be unrealistic, I must be content with a brief explication of a central notion and a stipulation of this book's limits. The stipulation is all the more necessary because the adoption of a central notion (control or otherwise) is only a *necessary* condition for sustained progress in sociology, and the other conditions should be identified here even though beyond the scope of this book.

A central notion is a notion that those individuals trained in some scientific field can use to describe and think about most if not all of that field's subject matter. Such a notion furthers coherence by prompting recognition of conceptual and empirical relations that otherwise would have gone unrecognized. Yet a central notion is not a theory, even though maximum coherence obtains in a field only when *one* theory explains all features or components of the field's subject matter. Nonetheless, up to a point a central notion may be more important than any particular theory, because if a notion is both central and truly *effective* it facilitates the formulation of theories.

As suggested previously, if control should become sociology's central notion, that change would not assure progress in the field. Sustained progress also requires effective consensus as to appropriate criteria for judging the merits of theories, but sociologists have never come even close to an effective consensus. Indeed, there has been a decline in consensus since the 1950s, concomitant with widespread rejection of positivism, the politicization of scholarship, and the growth of apriorism—"a willingness to settle issues by theoretical decree, without even a pretense of evidential appeal" (Crews,

1986:37). Even today many sociologists evidently see no connection between antipositivism and dissensus as to appropriate criteria for assessing theories, perhaps because "positivism" has become merely a derogatory label. Those who rail against positivism persistently fail to identify it with the insistence that the acceptance or rejection of a theory should depend on its predictive power *relative to that of contenders* (for elaboration, see Gibbs, 1972, 1985). While other criteria are conceivable, they are indefensible if they do not suggest how sociology differs (without regard to invidious comparisons) from philosophy, journalism, theology, social work, history, and social criticism.

The emphasis on predictive power is not a departure from the conventional idea that theories should be testable and judged in light of test outcomes, but the toleration of untestable theories throughout sociology's history is indicative of a determination to assess a theory in light of preconceptions, Gouldner's background assumptions (1970), or the presuppositions attributed to the theory (Alexander, 1982, 1983). Such an assessment makes personal opinion sacrosanct and precludes anything like effective consensus when assessing the merits of particular theories. By contrast, the criterion of predictive power is entirely consistent with an emphasis on the importance of tests. No body of data can be used to test a theory unless predictions about the data can be *formally deduced* from the theory, and a positive test outcome is nothing more than an accurate prediction *about the data*. However, the predictive accuracy of a theory is always judged relative to that of contenders; and it is only one of seven dimensions of predictive power, the other six being testability, scope, range, intensity, discrimination, and parsimony (see Gibbs, 1972:66–70).

Just as there is an incontrovertible connection between predictive power and the very idea of testing a theory, so is there between predictive power and explanation. Specifically, an explanatory statement about some phenomenon is inadequate unless it implies predictions, and the adequacy of an explanation is contingent on the accuracy of the implied predictions.

While it is argued that acceptance of control as sociology's central notion would further the predictive power of sociological theories (their scope particularly), truly systematic assessments of predictive power, including tests, are precluded as long as sociologists employ the traditional discursive mode of theory construction (for elaboration, see Gibbs, 1972: e.g., p. 70). That mode is nothing more than the conventions of some natural language, such as English, French, or German. The logical structure of sociological theories will remain obscure (for illustrations, see Gibbs's survey, 1972:80–107) until the discursive mode is largely displaced by a formal mode, meaning a set of rules for stating theories (*not* for arriving at the constituent ideas), with some of the rules transcending the conventions of a natural language. Yet there is no trend toward formal theory construction. As cases in point, the discursiveness of Giddens's recent (1984) structuration theory is perhaps unprecedented; and the willingness of sociologists to take Habermas's (1984) theory of communicative action seriously indicates an unlimited tolerance of discursiveness.

Consistent with the position just taken, the simple illustrative theories in this book are stated formally; but there is no necessary connection between that practice and the two principal arguments about a central notion. However, those arguments cannot be pursued effectively without inflicting an elaborate conceptualization on a traditionally unreceptive audience. Perhaps sociologists are unreceptive because conceptualizations are intrinsically dull. In any case, a competent promotion of a central notion requires a virtual preoccupation with conceptual matters. To illustrate, the relation between social control and deviance is first and foremost a logical (conceptual) consideration. If one accepts the counteraction-of-deviance conception of social control (i.e., social control *is* the counteraction of deviance), a relation between social control and deviance is created by definition; and it becomes illogical to entertain this question: Does social control counteract deviance? That is one of several reasons why social control is conceptualized in this book such that there is no logically necessary connection between it and deviance.

As the foregoing indicates, this book was not written under the illusion that sociologists need only adopt control as their central notion to find a path out of the wilderness in which they now wander; and some notion other than control might contribute more to the coherence of sociology, which is to say that the possibility of alternatives should be entertained. Nonetheless, I do believe that sociology cannot survive indefinitely without far greater coherence than now characterizes the field.

Karen Campbell and Arthur Demarest commented on the initial rough drafts of chapters 1–9, all that I had completed at the time. Walter T. Martin, S. Dale McLemore, Robert Meier, and Mark Stafford were less fortunate; various stages of rough drafts of all chapters were inflicted on them. I am most grateful for their comments and also for those of Sheldon Stryker (a study in diligence). My debt to Bill Form is enormous. For more years than I care to remember, my wife Sylvia tolerated me as I struggled with the manuscript; and she also assisted me in various ways. Finally, the manuscript could not have been finished and published without generous support from Vanderbilt University, the University's College of Arts and Science, and the College's Department of Sociology (including excellent typing by Linda Willingham).

—Nashville, August, 1987

Principal Arguments

The sheer variety of subjects studied by sociologists defies description. They appear to study whatever interests them and rarely advocate a definition of sociology that would narrow the field's subject matter. Consequently, sociological studies are so diverse that only a minority of sociologists can truly understand and appreciate any particular study, a condition that is indicative of the field's fragmentation and a source of even more fragmentation.

Because there is no feasible way to reduce the diversity of sociological studies, greater coherence can be realized only through a central notion, meaning a notion that enables sociologists to describe and think about everything, or virtually everything, that they study. Given such a notion, any sociological study could be truly understood by all sociologists, because they would be able to interpret the findings and conclusions in terms of that notion. Furthermore, when a scientific field has a central notion, everyone in that field has some basis for answering what is perhaps the ultimate question about any study: Why was it undertaken?

Although a central notion does not necessarily reduce the diversity of a field's subject matter or check specialization, it becomes the primary basis of unity in the face of continuing diversification of subject matter and concomitant specialization. Unfortunately, however, sociology's fragmentation does not stem from diverse subject matter alone, especially since the 1960s. Each sociological study now interests and informs an increasingly smaller minority of sociologists if only because of a proliferation of perspectives. That proliferation cannot be described fully in terms of traditional labels, such as conflict versus consensus sociology or macro versus micro sociology; nor do those labels bear directly on several specific issues that divide sociologists, one being a question about whether science is value-laden or value-free.

The proliferation of sociological perspectives will not be ended by a particular theory, which may not interest even a majority of sociologists. Only a central sociological notion will check the fragmentation resulting from the proliferation of perspectives. By definition, a central notion transcends all perspectives, meaning that it permits sociologists to describe and think about any perspective. As for issues, such as value-free versus value-laden sociology, there is no prospect of resolution until the protagonists state their argument in terms that all parties both understand and accept, which requires a central notion.

Chapter 1 is an elaboration of the foregoing, ending with the claim that control could be sociology's central notion. That claim is defended at length in chapter 2. Because the claim's fate depends largely on the way control is conceptualized and the questions asked about it, chapter 3 treats both subjects. In recognition of justified doubts about any proposed central notion for sociology, control or otherwise, chapter 4 examines several issues that emanate from the two principal arguments: first, maximum coherence cannot be realized in any science without a central notion; and, second, control could be sociology's central notion.

Chapter

1

Sociology's Fragmentation

Whatever the scientific field, no mortal can delimit its subject matter carefully without becoming a dreadful bore. Fear of that fate perhaps contributed to the virtual termination long ago of real concern in sociology with the delimitation problem (but see Wallace, 1983), and contemporary sociologists apparently regard the problem as insoluble. In any event, the problem is conspicuous when contemplating the fragmentation of contemporary sociology.[1] One symptom is the admission by candid sociologists that they cannot understand numerous sociological publications, not even why the studies were undertaken. To some extent, those admissions reflect the diversity of subjects studied by sociologists; and that diversity introduces this awful question: What is the field's subject matter? The question may never be answered to any sociologist's satisfaction, let alone so as to reduce the field's subject matter (Boudon, 1981); but the problem will not go away. No field can survive indefinitely without more coherence than now characterizes contemporary sociology (Wiley, 1985); and if sociology's subject matter cannot be delimited so as to reduce its diversity, some other strategy for realizing greater coherence is imperative.

Some Dubious Delimitation Strategies

Although accurate, it is insufficient to say that no delimitation of sociology has commanded a large following. The situation is far worse; there are least five distinct delimitation strategies,[2] and none is defensible.

First Strategy: What Sociologists Study

Just as one may argue (naively) that intelligence is what intelligence tests measure, a field's subject matter can be described as nothing less than everything studied in the field. However, sociology's subject matter is incomprehensible if described in terms of what sociologists actually study (for elaboration, see Boudon, 1981:1). Because a complete list of subjects would run for several pages, a brief illustrative list must suffice: suicide, water witching, voting, homosexuality, migration, strikes, juries, dictionaries, occupations, cities, revolutions, dating, rumors, mental illness, lynchings, marriage, newspapers, incest, religion, unemployment, colonialism, capitalism, old-car enthusiasts, birth order, monotheism, families, nostalgia, robbery, racial prejudice, and wearing beards.

The sheer diversity discourages attempts to delimit sociology's subject matter.[3] No delimitation will compel sociologists to choose certain subjects for study and avoid others; they will continue to study whatever interests them. That incorrigibility is perhaps all to the good, because a rigid delimitation could be stifling. In any event, no delimitation will be accepted unless fairly consistent with what sociologists actually study, and those subjects are so diverse that many appear alien to all definitions of the field. The problem haunts other social sciences, but none (not even anthropology) rivals sociology's diversity. Indeed, introductory texts notwithstanding, one sociologist's interest in a subject (e.g., human fertility) may be viewed by another as unimportant, if not indefensible. In such cases it is as though one sociologist says to another: I do not share your interest and no sociologist should.

Second Strategy: Look to Social Philosophy

The questions posed by sociology's putative founder, Comte, are rarely considered today. Some sociologists are drawn more to questions posed in social philosophy, such as: What is justice? Yet none of those questions interest most sociologists; and if one looks to major names in social philosophy (e.g., Hobbes) for the central sociological question, there is no agreement.

Even if there were agreement, scientific purists in sociology would nurse doubts. They rightly recognize that questions actually define a field's subject matter, and they fear that answers to philosophical questions will be value judgments or metaphysical. True, had sociologists limited their interests to questions suggested by, say, Plato, their field would be less fragmented; but the break with social philosophy now appears irreversible.

Third Strategy: Sociology as a Distinct Social Science

Any delimitation will be questioned if it does not at least suggest a contrast between sociology and other social sciences. Indeed, one strategy is to emphasize the contrast, meaning that sociology's subject matter is delimited by reference to other social sciences. Sorokin excelled in that strategy.

Sorokin presented this schematic version of his argument (1947:7):

"economic: a, b, c, n, m, f
political: a, b, c, h, d, j

religious: a, b, c, g, i,   q
and so on."

The letters designate subclasses of social phenomena (e.g., *m* denotes some subclass of economic social phenomena), and Sorokin indicated that each series of subclasses (*a . . . f*, *a . . . j*, or *a . . . q*) taken together constitutes the subject matter of a particular social science other than sociology. Sorokin further implied that sociology's subject matter comprises two parts, the first being subclasses of social phenomena within the subject matter of all social sciences (in the schematic version, *a*, *b*, and *c*). The second part evidently comprises all other subclasses, because Sorokin suggests that only sociology is concerned with the interrelationship of the subclasses in different classes (e.g., the relation between *n* and *d*).

Sorokin left several questions unanswered. What is a social phenomenon? What classes and subclasses should be recognized? Why assume that the subject matter of all social sciences other than sociology can be delimited? If not, how can sociology's subject matter be determined by reference to other social sciences? For that matter, what is the correct list of social sciences? In particular, Sorokin alludes to a science of religion (1947:7), but why is "religion" not an anthropological subject? Finally, whatever *n*, *m*, *f*, *h*, *d*, and *j* may denote, why assume that economists and political scientists are not interested in the interrelationship between those subclasses?

Sorokin denied (1947:14) that sociology is "an encyclopedic survey of all of the social sciences," but the schematic version of his argument indicates otherwise. If sociology's subject matter comprises all of the ubiquitous subclasses of phenomena (*a*, *b*, and *c* in the schematic context) and the interrelationship between any two of the unique subclasses (e.g., *f* and *h*, *d* and *i*), how could the field be other than "encyclopedic"?

Perhaps Sorokin should have been content to argue explicitly with regard to the schematic context that sociology's subject matter is limited to *a*, *b*, and *c*. To use his own terminology, sociology is the study of generic social phenomena; and in the schematic version of his argument only subclasses *a*, *b*, and *c* appear to be generic. But even if other social scientists would grant sociologists such an exclusive license, what are *a*, *b*, and *c*? It will not do to say that they are superorganic phenomena. Sorokin suggested that sociology's subject matter is superorganic phenomena, but only to say (1947:6) that all social scientists study the superorganic.

Fourth Strategy: Social Relations, Interaction, and the Normative

Although the term *social relation* appears frequently in definitions of sociology, numerous other things are studied by sociologists. Suicide is a case in point. However, sociologists think in terms of causes and consequences; and if one assumes, along with Durkheim (1951), that the character of social relations determines the suicide rate, then sociological studies of suicide are understandable.

So it may appear that sociology can be defined simply as the scientific study of social relations, including causes and consequences; but consider the preoccupation of many sociologists with capitalism and colonialism. Those abstractions are scarcely causes or consequences of social relations.

INTERACTION AND NORMATIVE NOTIONS.   The idea of defining some term (e.g., "capitalism") by reference to social relations suggests that the latter are sociology's elementary units of analysis; but if it is to have conceptual utility, such a unit must be as close to observable things or events as possible. Yet no one will ever see, hear, touch, or smell a social relation; it is always inferred, never observed. Thus, on observing a woman holding a crying child, we may infer that she is the child's mother; but, even so, why does "mother-child" denote a social relation? Any sociological definition that suggests an answer will not bear examination. In particular, if a social relation is defined as "interaction between humans," then armed robbery and forcible rape qualify. Hence, the question: What is the conceptual link between a social relation and human interaction? Should it be argued that a social relation is a certain kind and/or amount of interaction over time, what kind and/or amount? Any answer would reek with arbitrariness. The general point is that sociologists use the term *interaction* blithely; and when defining it or using it in conceptualizations, they do not confront issues or problems (such as those examined in Lamb et al., 1979). Apart from arbitrariness, a strictly "interactional" definition of a social relation would be dubious.[4] To illustrate, most sociologists would grant that, on assuming command, a ship's captain has a social relation with the crew before interacting with them. The point is that putative social relations have a normative quality (authority in this case) that cannot be described strictly in terms of interaction.

Extending the argument, various sociological concepts—authority, law, legitimacy, deviance—are commonly defined by reference to normative notions. Because those notions pertain to what humans believe conduct ought to be (or perhaps will be) and not necessarily to actual behavior, then several major sociological concepts cannot by defined solely by reference to interaction. So the conclusion: a designation of interaction as sociology's subject matter is most questionable.

Accepting the foregoing arguments, one solution is to designate social relations, interaction, and normative phenomena as sociology's subject matter. Yet there is a consideration beyond the failure to distinguish sociology from other social sciences.[5] By any definition of social relations, interaction, and normative phenomena, sociology's subject matter would remain extremely diverse.

NORMATIVE PHENOMENA, NOT NORMS.   As used here, the term *normative phenomena* designates any statement construed as an evaluation or expectation of conduct, be that conduct a particular act or a type of act. Should critics wonder why the term *norm* is not used, it is because no extant definition of that term can be defended. Consider, for example, Blake and Davis's definition (1964:456): "any standard or rule that states what human beings should or should not think, say, or do under given circumstances." Application of that definition requires the identification of standards or rules; but Blake and Davis never defined either term, nor did they recognize that many writers use *standard*, *rule*, and *norm* as synonyms.

The objection to Blake-Davis is avoided by Homans's definition (1961:46): "A *norm* is a statement made by a number of members of a group, not necessarily by all of them, that the members ought to behave in a certain way in certain circumstances." Homans's definition promises more empirical applicability than does that of Blake and Davis because it refers to a norm as a *statement* rather than a standard or rule. Nonetheless, there are several problems, three of which appear insoluble (for a more extensive treatment, see Gibbs, 1981).

Homans's phrase a "number of members" recognizes a collective quality of norms. Such recognition is conventional; but Homans ignored a crucial question: What proportion of social unit members must make or otherwise subscribe to a statement for it to be a norm? To answer "1.0" would make norms virtually peculiar to small groups, but any lesser value is bound to be arbitrary. Yet some answer is needed to solve the sufficient consensus problem; otherwise, empirical applicability is jeopardized.

The second problem is introduced by this question: Why do sociologists concern themselves so much with the notion of norms? The answer seems to be that much of human behavior is governed by norms. Although dubious for several subsequent reasons, the answer is consistent with the widespread resort, especially in sociology and anthropology, to normative explanations (Edgerton, 1985:7–9). However, whereas most definitions of a norm refer to evaluations of conduct, one's overt behavior may be governed by expectations of conduct. Thus, when an individual locks a car, he or she is ostensibly reacting to what someone may do, not what they ought to do. Indeed, some definitions of a norm refer to expectations rather than evaluations, although the choice between the two terms may have been made uncritically. In any event, virtually all definitions of a norm ignore perceived evaluations or perceived expectations of conduct, meaning a social unit member's attribution of evaluations or expectations of conduct to other members. Yet surely in many instances our behavior is governed not by our personal evaluations or expectations but, rather, by what we think significant others believe behavior ought to be or will be. Still another normative property is recognized in some definitions of a norm (see Gibbs's survey, 1981:7–9). Several writers suggest that a norm entails a substantial risk of a sanction (i.e., a punitive reaction) for contrary behavior. To sum up: although most definitions of a norm recognize only one normative property, consistency in normative explanations of human behavior requires recognition of personal evaluations of conduct, personal expectations of conduct, perceived evaluations of conduct, perceived expectations of conduct, and the frequency of punitive reactions to actual behavior. Any definition that recognizes all of those properties would border on the incomprehensible, but to exclude some of them is to embrace extreme arbitrariness.

Insofar as norms consist of evaluations or expectations of conduct (personal and/or perceived), they can be identified in a systematic, defensible way only by soliciting responses of social unit members to such normative questions as: Do you approve or disapprove of smoking marijuana? Although there are numerous alternatives in framing normative questions, none solves the problem of normative contingencies. Briefly, when humans express approval or disapproval of a particular act, they do not react solely to the act itself. Their reaction is commonly contingent also on characteristics of the actor (e.g., age, sex), characteristics of the act's object, and/or situational circumstances; and the same is true even when humans evaluate some type of act in the abstract, as in responding to a normative question. Such contingencies are alluded to in many definitions of a norm (see, e.g., Homans's reference [1961:46] to "circumstances"); but it appears impossible to frame a normative question such that it stipulates all possibilities, especially since the relevant contingencies may not be even approximately the same for all social unit members.

Sociologists persistently ignore all three of the problems with the notion of a norm (Johnson, 1985).[6] Their stance cannot be justified by the argument that they treat norms as purely theoretical entities, nor by the usual bromide— that the notion is heuristic. To the contrary, in the best Durkheimian tradition, most sociologists refer to norms as though they are as real as fireplugs; and few recognize any conceptual problems or issues.

Fifth Strategy: Durkheim's Notion of a Social Fact

In writing *The Rules of Sociological Method* (1938), Durkheim virtually invented a term, *social facts*, to designate sociology's subject matter.[7] Examine Durkheim's definition (1938:13): "A social fact is every way of acting, fixed or not, capable of exercising on the individual an external constraint; or again, every way of acting which is general throughout a given society, while at the same time existing in its own right independent of its individual manifestations."

The definition identifies three distinguishing characteristics of social facts *as a class of ways of acting*: (1) exteriority, (2) constraint, and (3) generality. Lest Durkheim's term *external constraint* be invoked to argue that the first and second characteristics are analytically inseparable, observe that elsewhere (1938:3) Durkheim speaks of "ways of acting, thinking, and feeling, external to the individual, and endowed with a power of coercion, by reason of which they control him." That phrasing clearly indicates that exteriority and constraint are analytically distinct.

EXTERIORITY. Durkheim's insistence that social facts are external to individuals gives rise to puzzles. If social facts are found in ways of acting, how can one observe them apart from the acts of individuals? As for the argument that "social facts" pertain to individuals in general and not to particular individuals, how can one observe the former without observing the latter? True, there are things external to individuals, but the obvious things (e.g., clouds, trees) are not social. As for external things that might be construed as social, such as paintings, they are not acts; rather, they are products of acts. Finally, should someone argue that acts are necessarily external to the actor, Durkheim's reference to "thinking and feeling" makes it clear that a way of acting may be internal behavior. The locus of social facts becomes especially obscure in light of Durkheim's insistence that they exist independently of their individual manifestations. If so, where do they exist? To use one of Durkheim's examples: How can speaking French be a social fact if no one speaks French? Surely it is not just the "idea" of speaking French. Nor can Durkheimians argue that social facts are putative norms (e.g., speaking French is a social fact only in that one *ought* to do it) without implying that norms exist apart from any individual's behavior, which piles one absurdity on top of another.

The exteriority attributed to social facts has an astonishing implication for Durkheim's notion of a collective conscience, which he (1949:79) defined as the "totality of beliefs and sentiments common to average citizens of the same society. . . ." Because all of its elements are internal and must be manifested in the average citizen, the collective conscience is not a social fact.

CONSTRAINTS. To be a social fact, a "thing" must be external to individuals and constrain them.[8] The immediate consideration is Durkheim's identification of the suicide rate as a social fact. Of course, if the suicide rate is *not* a social fact, then *Le Suicide* (1951) is not sociological by Durkheim's own standards. Nonetheless, how can one seriously argue that a suicide rate constrains any individual, let alone all?

Although Durkheim is the foremost name in the sociology of deviance, he conceptualized "social facts" as though deviance simply does not exist. But there is no logical contradiction. If the constraints of social facts are as efficacious as Durkheim suggested, deviance is precluded. Yet if efficacy is irrelevant, then Durkheim's references to constraint are logomachy.

GENERALITY. When introducing the translation of *The Rules*, George Catlin (in Durkheim, 1938:xv) argued that by "general" Durkheim did not "mean that the fact is existent without exception—e.g., that all men are suicides or drunkards—but that it is potentially universal in the sense that, granted given conditions, it will anywhere be set up." Catlin thereby introduces an extremely vague criterion, and there is no obvious connection between Durkheim's conceptualization and Catlin's argument (Durkheim, 1938:xvi) that the constancy of the suicide rate makes it a social fact. For that matter, it is not clear what Catlin means by constancy, and any criterion as to some minimal annual uniformity would be arbitrary.

Durkheim argued (1938:9) that a social phenomenon is "general because it is collective (that is, more or less obligatory) and certainly not collective because general." Therefore, both generality and obligatoriness are required to identify a phenomenon as a social fact, but obligatoriness is puzzling if a phenomenon can be general even though common only among most members of society (Durkheim, 1938:9). More puzzling, Durkheim argued (1938:9) that a phenomenon is "to be found in each part because it exists in the whole, rather than in the whole because it exists in the parts" without considering this question: How many socio-cultural changes commence with alterations in the behavior of a minority of social unit members (perhaps only one) as compared to all members or even a majority? Surely it is difficult to see how socio-cultural changes are manifested in the "whole" *before* in any "part."

CONCLUSION.   If the notion were defensible and if social facts were taken as sociology's subject matter, sociological studies would not be indescribably diverse. Nonetheless, unless one assumes that sociologists will shoulder any burden to avoid even the appearance of reductionism, their uncritical acceptance of the notion of a social fact is baffling, especially given the defects in Durkheim's conceptualizations identified by others (see, e.g., Giddens, 1981:56–57; Pope and Johnson, 1983).

The defects in Durkheim's conceptualizations stem from his superorganicism, especially the denial that major social science terms denote abstractions from human behavior. That denial flourishes in contemporary sociology and anthropology. Thus, culture has been described not as "complexes of concrete human behavior patterns" but as a "set of control mechanisms . . . for the governing of behavior" (Geertz, 1973:44).[9] The ultimate reification is reached when sociologists or anthropologists speak of society or culture as "doing" something.

Should sociologists ever truly recognize the defects in Durkheim's conceptualizations, they might become wary of superorganicism. Until then, the empirical applicability of sociological terminology will remain negligible. The basic problem is not that such terms as *social fact* and *culture* are difficult to define, nor even that they denote very abstract notions. Rather, many sociologists act as though their subject matter has nothing to do with the behavior of individuals, which precludes an empirically applicable vocabulary because it eliminates the possibility of empirical referents.

Major Implications and a Proposed Solution

Given the sheer diversity of subjects studied by sociologists and their disinclination to be bound by a definition of the field (see, e.g., Nisbet, 1969), there is little prospect of a defensible delimitation of sociology's subject matter. Worse, since sociologists will study what they will, no delimitation is likely to reduce the diversity of sociological studies. So until the field has a central notion, no study is likely to be truly understood and appreciated by even a majority of sociologists. A central notion enables those trained in a particular scientific field to describe and think about all or virtually all of the field's subject matter. Hence, once a field has a central notion, the rationale of any study can be understood and appreciated by everyone in the field because its subject, findings, and conclusions can be interpreted in terms of that notion.

Even if a particular delimitation of sociology's subject matter should be accepted and end diversification, diversity has already reached the point where only a central notion can reduce fragmentation, especially if the explosion of research findings continues. Moreover, diversity is conducive to what Hollingsworth (1984) has designated the "snare of specialization," and a central notion alleviates the consequences of that snare.

Other Sources of Fragmentation

Sociology's fragmentation has accelerated since the 1950s not because of the field's diverse subject matter but because of a proliferation of seemingly irreconcilable perspectives. Because contending perspectives have a long history in sociology, a sanguine view of current fragmentation may appear justified.[10] However, as sociology nears its 150th birthday, even optimistic practitioners must be apprehensive. Never before has sociology been so fragmented, not just in North America but also in Europe (see Wiley, 1985; Winkler, 1984).

Consider the ebb and flow of contending perspectives since about 1960: first, the demise of functionalism; second, the appearance and decline of ethnomethodology; third, a move toward Marxist and conflict sociology that now shows sign of declining (see, e.g., Mouzelis, 1984); fourth, a resurgence of historical sociology; fifth, the invasion and retreat of sociobiology; sixth, the emergence of network analysis; and, seventh, "French" structuralism still in the wings after decades (see, e.g., Rossi, 1982). Actually, the fragmentation is far greater than the list suggests (see Wiley, 1985, for an elaborate treatment). Symbolic interactionism has remained a major perspective for decades; functionalism still has a following; and hermeneutics (see Oliver, 1983) may prove to be more than a fad. Most important, no perspective is now remotely dominant (see Wiley, 1979). One reason is that over the past twenty years sociological research has become more oriented toward particular statistical techniques, commencing with causal models and then path analysis. Because many sociologists see issues in substantive terms (e.g., the conflict-consensus debate), no technique will unify the field. Indeed, the gulf between methodological and substantive sociology has grown since 1960 (see Huber, 1979, especially 593, 597).

Descriptions of sociology in terms of contending perspectives underestimate fragmentation because the perspectives themselves rapidly become fragmented. To illustrate, what passes for Marxist sociology includes works variously identified as neo-Marxism, Frankfurt school, historical materialism, conflict sociology, critical sociology, and radical sociology. Perhaps more important, no list of perspectives fully reveals the divergent interests and orientations of sociologists. Thus, not even the majority of sociologists whose interests are "macroscopic" (e.g., the study of capitalism or urbanization) advocate the same perspective; and while well-known reductionists (e.g., Homans) are not Marxists, they are not necessarily ethnomethodologists or even symbolic interactionists. To appreciate the range of orientations better, contemplate Bealer's incomplete list (1979:86) of contending sociological "ontologies": individual-group, individualism-collectivism, existential-sociologism, methodological individualism-metaphysical holism, atomistic-holistic, psychological reduction-social facts, behavioral-ecological, and micro-macro sociology.

Scientific Sociology and the Question of Values

Introductory texts suggest that the most pervasive division in the field is between advocates of "scientific" sociology and their opponents, usually identified as humanists. The suggestion is a gross oversimplification. Divergent conceptions of science abound in sociology, and for that reason alone appeals to science accomplish nothing in sociological debates. Indeed, for more than 20 years attempts to establish a "scientific sociology" (e.g., Wallace, 1983) have been either largely ignored or treated contemptuously.

VALUES. Particularly since the late 1960s, numerous sociologists have denounced the idea that science is or can be "value free" (e.g., Gouldner, 1973). One common interpretation of the denunciation views it as a rejection of science in general and scientific sociology in particular, but to characterize science as value-laden is not to reject science. Moreover, virtually any activity reflects the values of those engaged in it. For example, how could it be denied that eating or jogging is value-free? Now think of science. Surely it is at least in part an activity; as such, it would be unique if free of values. So the value-laden view of science is true but trite.[11] It would not be trite if extended to the claim that most scientists engage in concealed practices (e.g., data fabrication) to promote values, but advocates of value-laden science do not go that far; and they balk at this prescriptive argument: scientists should engage in concealed practices to promote a value of their choosing.

There is still another way to make the value-laden view of science more than trite; advocates could admonish scientists to pursue particular lines of work. Suppose, for example, that a sociologist believes that migrant farm work is exploitative and should be ended. To that end, he or she could admonish demographers to focus on migrant farm worker mortality. There is no scientific reason for that focus, but there is no scientific reason for science. That point lends support to the value-laden view, and there is an immediate implication. There is no scientific reason for not selecting research subjects with a view to promoting particular values or admonishing colleagues to promote those values. The question is, of course: What values? Imagination is not required to understand why no one answers candidly: Promote my values! Nor is there any doubt that sociologists would promote quite different values. The ostensible ideological orientations of these names are telling: Marx, a radical leftist; Weber and Simmel, moderates; Durkheim, a conservative; and Pareto, a reactionary. Because sociologists come in all manner of ideological stripes, the explicit promotion of values would insure the field's irreversible fragmentation, especially since there is no conventional answer to this question: How can debates concerning conflicting values be resolved?

MODELS OF SCIENCE AND HUMANIST SOCIOLOGY. Commentators on the distinction between humanist and scientific sociology typically suggest that some sociologists are "antiscience," and putative humanists do warn sociologists not to take physics as their model of science (see, e.g., Blumer's statement, 1969:23, about physical science).[12] Although the warning suggests a more suitable model, humanists never describe the alternative in any detail (if at all). Yet they do not explicitly reject the idea of assessing theories through tests, even though such an assessment is consistent with taking physics as the model of science.

Critics of humanist sociology never confront this question: After nearly 150 years, what sociological theory is impressive in light of tests? It would be difficult to refute this answer: "None." Even so, it does not follow that humanists reject tests of theories. An alternative interpretation is that humanists construe the track record of sociology's theories as indicating that something is fundamentally wrong with the field (see, e.g., Blumer, 1969).

The Necessity of a Central Notion

To illustrate the importance of a central notion, try to imagine physics without the notion of force. The illustration is controversial because many sociologists appear convinced that their field must be fundamentally different from the so-called natural sciences. Even so, sociology's fragmentation cannot be checked without a central notion. Stating the matter as one of this book's two principal arguments: maximum coherence in a scientific field can be realized only through a central notion. Perhaps an absolutely central notion is never realized in any scientific field; but the more nearly a field comes to a central notion, the greater is its coherence. Thus, returning to the illustration, it may well be that some components of physics' subject matter cannot be described and thought of in terms of force, but physicists do not argue that their field needs no greater coherence.

The Role of a Central Notion

The idea of a central notion is neither radical nor novel. Scientists and philosophers rarely use the term *central notion*, but many of them have come close to a recognition of the idea. Consider, for example, MacIver's argument (in Nisbet and Perrin, 1977:35):

> "Every science has certain ultimate concepts on which the whole system is built, not of course deductively, but in the sense that the unity and the nexus of its subject-matter are discovered to depend on those ultimates. . . . Unless there are certain fundamental concepts which integrate a subject matter there is no science but only a series of detached formulations, conventionally bound together."

Still another tactic to convey the meaning of a central notion: the idea is akin to what Louis Schneider (1975) described as the sociological way of looking at the world.

SOME SOCIOLOGICAL ILLUSTRATIONS. As long as sociologists give even lip service to scientific sociology, all will grant the importance of this question: How and why do social units differ? The social units may be families, corporations, countries, or what have you; and the difference may pertain to any variation (spatial or temporal) that interests sociologists—in the suicide rate, in the intensity of class conflict, etc. In pursuing an answer to a question about a specific subject (e.g., variation in the frequency of terrorism), most sociologists will not be truly satisfied with an answer unless they can relate it to larger concerns, which requires something akin to a central notion.

If empirical associations are discovered only by induction, few will be identified; and the inductive discovery of an empirical association, no matter how uniform, creates little more than a puzzle unless it can be described and thought of in terms of a central notion.[13] Otherwise, the practitioners will doubt the existence of the association, or simply ignore it. For example, suppose a sociologist reports evidence of a close direct relation among cities between some measure of population density and the homicide rate. No matter how reliable the data, many sociologists would regard the relation as either accidental or spurious, because they would find it difficult to describe or think of (1) density in terms of homicide, (2) homicide in terms of density, or (3) both homicide and density in terms of some third notion.

Even if all sociologists do think of their subject matter in terms of cause-and-effect, causation cannot be the field's central notion; and there is a reason beyond the argument that the notion of causation is not peculiar to any particular field.[14] To identify some instance of an empirical association (i.e., a space-time relation) as causal is scarcely a description of it. Rather, the identification is nothing more than the application of a label, and in sociology such application is inherently disputable.

Central Notion, Theories, and Subject Matter

A central notion is not only different from but also more important than any particular theory. When thinking of the field's subject matter in terms of the central notion, the *hope* is not just that such thinking will give rise to theories; additionally, if all of the field's theories stem from thinking in terms of one central notion, the stage is set for a synthesis of theories.

CENTRAL NOTION AND SUBJECT MATTER. The terms used to delimit a field's subject matter do not necessarily denote the field's central notion. Thus, even if interaction, social relations, and normative phenomena constitute sociology's subject matter, it does not follow that any of those terms denote sociology's central notion. Indeed, if two or more classes of phenomena constitute a field's subject matter, there is a need for a central notion to describe and think about those classes.

Whereas a field's subject matter is largely a matter of convention, the utility of *candidates* for the central notion should be continually assessed. "Candidate" is stressed because a notion becomes central only by the discovery that it actually facilitate describing and thinking about the field's subject matter. The subject matter may remain more or less the same for decades, while central notion candidates come and go; however, once a notion comes to be indisputably central, in effect it delimits the field's subject matter. If an event or thing cannot be described or thought of in terms of the central notion, it is regarded as outside the field's subject matter.

Checking Fragmentation

There are few candidates for sociology's central notion, primarily because sociologists are preoccupied with promoting research methods or debating contending perspectives. The idea that sociology's fragmentation can be ended by some research method is so grotesque that it scarcely warrants consideration. As for the argument that competition among perspectives generates better theories, it blithely ignores disagreement among sociologists over appropriate criteria for assessing theories. Gouldner (1970:30) described the predominant reason succinctly but perhaps unwittingly: "Some theories are simply experienced, even by experienced sociologists, as *intuitively* convincing; others are not. How does this happen? . . . The theory felt to be intuitively convincing is commonly experienced as *deja vu*, as something previously known or already suspected. It is congenial because it confirms or complements an assumption already held by the respondent, but an assumption that was seen only dimly by him precisely because it was a 'background' assumption."

Gouldner did little toward either clarifying the idea of a background assumption or identifying particular instances. For example, all sociologists have some conception of the field's subject matter, but is that conception a background assumption or a derivative? In any case, contending perspectives do not necessarily give rise to divergent conceptions of sociology's subject matter. A sociologist may dismiss a particular theory because he or she does not judge it as dealing with fundamental phenomena, and such judgments reflect something akin to a central notion. Those judgments do not contradict the claim that sociology has no central notion. Most sociologists have a sense of the fundamental, but to realize effective consensus sociologists must actively and explicitly promote central notion candidates. Such promotion does not further fragmentation indefinitely. If advocates of a particular notion are productive in the formulation of integrated theories, the raison d'etre of a central notion, their following is likely to grow.

Theoretical fertility is only one consideration in assessing a central notion candidate; scope is another. Given two contenders, X and Y, the challenge is to identify another notion, Z, as supplanting both X and Y. Illustrating formally, if sociologists can describe and think of classes of phenomena a, b, c, and d, in terms of notion X but notion Y is more suitable for describing and thinking about e, f, g, and h, then Z is a superior notion if and only if it facilitates description and thought about all eight classes (a . . . h).

Should the idea of a central notion appear indistinguishable from the idea of a paradigm, consider Masterman's identification (1970) of 21 different meanings of *paradigm* in Kuhn's 1962 study (1970b). Given such ambiguity, one must wonder why sociologists, such as Friedrichs (1970) and Ritzer (1975, 1979), treated the term as though it has profound implications for sociology; and wonderment grows in light of Kuhn's doubts about extending his arguments to the social sciences. In any case, if a paradigm orders "a sociologist's conception of his subject matter" (Friedrichs, 1970:56), the terms of a particular paradigm suggest what the paradigm's creator takes to be sociology's central notion; but Friedrichs's conception of a paradigm is scarcely less vague than Kuhn's original conception (1970b). By contrast, if a paradigm "serves to define what should be studied, what questions should be asked, how they should be asked, and what rules should be followed in interpreting the answers obtained" (Ritzer, 1975:7), that conceptualization goes far beyond a central notion and appears to pertain not to Kuhn's paradigm but to a more conventional sociological term—*perspective*. In any case, Ritzer departed sharply from Kuhn, especially Kuhn's belated equating of *paradigm* and *exemplar* (1970a:272). That equivalence does not greatly clarify, and a central notion is certainly not an "exemplar."

THE CONNECTION WITH PERSPECTIVES. One notion or another is very important for each sociological perspective. Thus, Marxist sociology without "class conflict" would seem absurd, as would symbolic interactionism without "meaning." However, what appears to be a central notion for a particular perspective is not necessarily also central for all of sociology. Moreover, even assuming that they serve any constructive purpose, the terms commonly used to characterize sociological theories, perspectives, or schools (e.g., "element-aristic" and "positivistic organicism" as in Martindale, 1979) do not denote central notions.

Consider the following very brief illustrative list of sociological subjects and try to describe and think about all of them in terms of what appears to be the major notion of any sociological perspective: voting, births, cities, lynchings, migration, rumors, incest, suicide, technology, monotheism, homosexuality, and racial prejudice. Some of those subjects are alien to one sociological perspective or another. Where, for example, does one find studies of migration by ethnomethodologists, of homosexuality by Marxists, of technology by symbolic interactionists? There are none. Certain subjects are alien to a particular perspective simply because they cannot be described and thought of readily in terms of that perspective's major notions.

The proliferation of perspectives virtually precludes an informative answer to two questions. First, in what sense is sociology a discipline? Second, what is the field's raison d'etre? Many sociologists would answer by appealing to some master, such as Durkheim or Marx, each a major figure in some contemporary perspective. Because such an appeal justifies sociology as a discipline only in the eyes of that master's followers, the only hope for justifying sociology as a discipline is a notion accepted as fundamental by sociologists of diverse persuasions.

THE INEVITABILITY OF CONTROVERSY. Unfortunately, a notion may cease to be a viable candidate for the central notion without being replaced. That has happened twice in sociology; the first time was the decline in evolutionary theory more than 70 years ago. The second occasion was the demise of functionalism. Both developments illustrate how a field becomes fragmented when the closest approximation of a central notion ceases to be viable.

The eclipse of a central notion and the appearance of a contender are marked by controversy,[15] but debates do imply a common interest. There are scarcely genuine debates in contemporary sociology about the field as a whole; rather, sociologists simply go their separate ways.

A Particular Candidate and the Value Issue Reconsidered

Recapitulating, sociologists should pursue this question: What is the most promising candidate for their field's central notion? The question is answered here with one word—*control*. The answer's defense must await an elaborate conceptualization of control (chapters 2 and 3); but even at this point consider the answer's bearing on a perennial source of sociology's fragmentation, one identified by three questions. First, to what extent *is* sociology used to promote values? Second, to what extent *can* sociology be used to promote values? And, third, *should* sociology be used to promote values?

Ambiguity surrounds the argument that sociologists promote values; and the argument can be clarified only by this interpretation: sociologists control human behavior. The very idea that someone can attempt to promote values without attempting to control human behavior will not bear examination. Of course, sociologists may have influences on some nonsociologists (e.g., students) that sociologists do not recognize; even so, those influences can be used to promote values only insofar as elites (e.g., foundation directors, employers, high-ranking military officers) are aware of it and control sociologists.

Protagonists in the debate over values commonly speak of sociology as "having consequences," as though no one is aware of the consequences, much less intended them. What purpose does such a view serve when debating whether sociology should be used to promote values? Even granting that sociological works have latent functions (unrecognized and/or unintended consequences), those functions are relevant only in answering the second question: To what extent can sociology be used to promote values?[16] Whatever the answer, "promotion of values" is a euphemism for attempts to control human behavior, and the same is true of "praxis" or even "to make the world a better place" (Nettler, 1980). The point is illustrated by this often-quoted statement (Marx and Engels, 1947:199): "The philosophers have only *interpreted* the world differently; the point is, to *change* it." Only chronic Bolshevik chasers will deny that the admonition has élan, but it appears in a quite different light on recognition that (1) changing the world entails controlling human behavior on a vast scale and (2) coercion is a common means of such control. Hence, sociologists who recoil at the idea of controlling human behavior are inconsistent when they admonish their colleagues to change the world.

Foss's treatment of the value controversy illustrates the resort of sociologists to euphemisms. Early in his book (1977:20) Foss recognizes that ability to control is necessary for the application of sociological knowledge; but subsequently (1977:58) he rejects "imposing" values and concludes: "it is urged that sociology adopt as its primary nonepistemic orientation: the *optimization of alternatives open to every individual* . . . The goal of sociology . . . would not be to impose a specific conception of what is good upon others, but rather to seek a social structure or social structures that optimizes the alternatives open to every individual by which she can actualize her own conceptions of good" (1977:59). Foss uses the word *seek* as a euphemism for "attempt to control."

Returning to the third question: Should sociology be used to promote values? An affirmative answer is nothing less than an endorsement of controlling human behavior on a vast scale. To defend the endorsement, one may argue that human behavior will continue to be controlled on a vast scale (see illustrations in Skinner, 1971) regardless of what social or behavioral scientists do. However, if the promotion of values is sociology's primary mission, it would be paradoxical to deny that interest in control should be paramount. Moreover, it would be a dodge to describe sociology's mission as the promotion of some ideology rather than behavioral control, as though the two are clearly distinct. Surely an "ideology" is not merely *any* set of values, beliefs, or arguments; and Martindale's definition (1979:8) identifies one distinguishing characteristic: "an ideology is a set of arguments advanced with persuasive intent." To persuade someone is to control at least their internal behavior. Moreover, compare the potential empirical applicability of Martindale's definition with that of Humphries and Greenberg (1984:175): "Ideology is not propaganda. Rather, ideology consists of ideas that originate in social experience—particularly the experience of class relations—but without the thinker being aware of it." Imagine someone seriously attempting to apply that definition. It is little more than an endorsement of a robotic sociology maxim: Actors must be unaware!

PROSPECTS FOR RESOLUTION.   Acceptance of control as sociology's central notion would not necessarily resolve the debate over the field's connection with values (or ideology or interests, etc.). Assume two camps of sociologists, one endorsing and the other rejecting this argument: Sociologists should control human behavior. If there are two such camps, there may be no basis for resolving the issue that divides them; but a control language in stating issues is a necessary condition for resolving a debate that traditionally has centered on values. Should the issue continue to be stated in terms of value-laden and value-free, the protagonists are doomed to talk past each other indefinitely.

The foregoing oversimplifies in not recognizing two control arguments. To repeat the *prescriptive* argument: Sociologists should control human behavior. The *empirical* argument is surely different: Sociologists do or can control human behavior. While the same distinction applies to arguments about value-free and value-laden sociology, those arguments (prescriptive and empirical) are much clearer if stated in terms of control. Without clarification of the issue, sociologists will misinterpret their differences; and there will be no prospect for resolving the issue through answers to empirical questions.

Data fabrication is one way to attempt behavioral control, but advocates of value-laden sociology say little about the means that sociologists use to control human behavior; and as long as that is the case, their arguments will defy assessment by appeals to systematic empirical evidence. Yet a focus on arguments about control would pose no less a challenge for advocates of value-free sociology. For example, are they really denying attempts to control students, editors, foundation directors, and government officials?

Because advocates of value-laden sociology are prone to speak of the consequences of sociology rather than behavioral control, they are likely to regard the proposed focus as distorting their argument. Yet it is not at all clear what their arguments really are. Are we to assume, for example, that on completing a sociology course the typical American student has more respect for capitalism, greater trust in the policies of the U.S. government, and is more critical of dissidents? Of course, advocates of value-laden sociology might deny the relevance of such a question, but that denial would underscore the need for them to clarify their arguments.

NOTES

1. Many sociologists (Collins, 1986, being a likely prospect) will dispute the present depressing depiction of sociology. Yet it is significant that in a recent relevant debate (*American Journal of Sociology*, July, 1986, 158–82), the protagonists did not agree even as to the meaning of "theoretical growth"; and the present commentary on the field's deplorable state is not unique (see, e.g., Giddens, 1984:xiii-xvi; Wiley, 1985; and Denzin, 1987).

2. The characterization of sociology as the "science of society" (e.g., DeFluer et al., 1984: especially 7) does not deserve a hearing. The implied macro designation of sociology's subject matter is alien to thousands of studies by sociologists and to at least one perspective: interpretive sociology.

3. The diversity is emphasized by Smelser (1969) in one of the rare thoughtful treatments of the subject since Sorokin (1947). However, Smelser did not delimit sociology's subject matter; rather, he was content to speak of the "core sociological enterprise" without describing its content in any detail.

4. Simmel's vague notion of sociation (1950) may have been an attempt (unsuccessful) to avoid confronting this question: What is the conceptual relation between interaction and social relation?

5. Even if sociologists should strive for a definition that distinguishes their field from other social sciences, the prospects for success are not good. If only because the boundaries of the various social sciences are vague and arbitrary, those sciences should be integrated; but integration requires a common central notion.

6. The same is true of anthropologists. Edgerton (1985:3) does recognize what are here identified as normative contingencies, but he appears to presume that the conceptual problem is avoided by speaking (1985:6) of "rules for breaking rules" without stipulating the procedure and criteria by which rules are to be identified. Edgerton's reference to "rule" rather than "norm" is no mitigation.

7. By contrast, Weber (1978:4) defined sociology as a science concerned with the "interpretive understanding of social action and thereby with a causal explanation of its course and consequences," but later (1978:24) he stated: "Sociology . . . is by no means confined to the study of social action. . . ."

8. As Giddens (1981:57) observed, Durkheim "used 'constraint' and 'coercion' indifferently as synonymous terms."

9. Geertz's conception of culture (1973) is vague in the extreme. Culture can be described and thought of in terms of control, and the notion may never be defensible until so conceptualized. However, for a truly instrumental view of culture, one must look to Swidler (1986) rather than to Geertz.

10. See, for example, Merton's statements (1975). Collins (1975:1) appears even more optimistic: "My contention is that sociology can be a successful science and that it is well on the way to becoming so." Eleven years later (1986), Collins's optimism has diminished only slightly, if at all.

11. The notion of "value-laden" is commonly construed so broadly that statements about it are vacuous. Contemplate Edmondson (1984:1): "Discussions of the problem of objectivity versus value-ladenness take it that values enter sociology at the level of choice of subject-matter, or in terms of specific concepts, claims or judgments, or even in terms of an author's selection of theoretical framework. But the approach to texts I shall take here shows that 'values' operate in a much more systematic and ineliminable manner than any of these discussions show— evaluative positions are properties of communicative processes as a whole."

12. Convention notwithstanding, the crucial question is not whether the "methods" of physics can and should be applied in the social sciences (see Popper, 1957:2,5). Rather, the issue is whether all of the sciences can and should employ a common primary criterion, predictive power in particular, to assess the merits of theories. Viewed that way, the larger issue is the rejection of positivism with nothing coherent as a replacement. Van den Berg's observation (1980:451) on Frankfurt theorists, advocates of so-called critical theory, could be paraphrased so that it applies to sociologists of various persuasions: "they have contented themselves while attacking positivism for its inherent conservatism while vaguely alluding to the obvious superiority of dialectical reason for uncovering the 'essence' of the 'totality,' without ever bothering to specify these concepts. . . ."

13. Describing and thinking about an empirical association in terms of some notion other than the constituent variables commonly precedes and appears necessary for the deduction of that association.

14. Veblen (1898:377) unwittingly supplied an excellent illustration of the distinction between "cause-and-effect" thinking and "central-notion" thinking. "The modern scientist is unwilling to depart from the test of causal relation or quantitative sequence. When he asks the question, why?, he insists on an answer in terms of cause and effect. He wants to reduce his solution of all problems to terms of the conservation of energy or the persistence of quantity. This is his last recourse." A causal answer to a question is not the same as reducing solutions of all problems to the conservation of energy. The latter entails what could be a central notion, and it is not the last recourse; rather, it may be the ultimate goal in an advanced science.

15. Whatever the discipline, any notion's utility is debatable. Examine Kuhn and

Beam's statement (1982:24): "Whatever may be its importance to technology, energy, as such, has no place in the analysis of organization as a social system." Numerous social and behavioral scientists, such as Katz and Kahn (1978) and Adams (1982a, 1975), clearly think to the contrary.

16. The question is commonly neglected in the debate; it is as though sociologists assume that they can have a great impact on the world. To his credit, Nettler (1980) has introduced the question of "competence" into the debate; but even Nettler does not seem to recognize that to "make the world a better place" is to control human behavior.

Chapter

2

The Notion of Control

Sociologists could take control as their central notion without abandoning any major concept or construct; instead, the phenomena would be described and thought of in terms of control. Nor would it be necessary to reject conventional sociological questions, such as: Why does the crime rate vary? What caused the French revolution? Thinking of phenomena in terms of control will promote answers to conventional questions by enabling sociologists (1) to anticipate heretofore undetected empirical associations and (2) to integrate seemingly unrelated propositions. However, the outcome of taking any notion as central depends appreciably on its conceptualization, and Sites's attempt (1973, 1975) to make control sociology's central notion (although he did not use that label) was doomed by his failure to confront conceptual problems. Indeed, a pernicious belief is pervasive in sociology: constructive research and theorizing are possible without confronting conceptual problems (for one manifestation, see Schrag, 1982). Contemplate Tallman's statement (1984: 1121): "Efforts to explicate key concepts in sociology have generally been met with stifling indifference by members of our discipline."

Conceptualization of Control

Defined generically, attempted control is *overt* behavior by a human in the belief that (1) the behavior increases or decreases the probability of some subsequent condition and (2) the increase or decrease is desirable. The commission or omission of an act is overt behavior; and a subsequent condition may be the behavior of an organism or the existence, location, composition, color, size, weight, shape, odor, temperature, or texture of some object or substance, be it animate or inanimate, observable or unobservable. However, the condition may or may not take the form of a change, meaning that one may act or refrain from acting in the belief that such action increases or decreases the probability of change.

An alternative definition of attempted control could be something like this: overt behavior that is intended to have a specific consequence.[1] That terminology has been avoided because the conventional meaning of intentional behavior is far too narrow. An intentional act is commonly thought of as preceded by deliberation in which a specific consequence is consciously anticipated.[2] That conception differs from the present definition of attempted control because of three key terms: *deliberation*, *consciously anticipates*, and *specific consequences*. Think of someone driving a car. To describe his or her gripping the steering wheel as "intentional" would be misleading. Drivers are rarely aware of gripping the wheel, nor do they often consciously anticipate some undesirable consequence of releasing that grip. Thus, much of driving behavior lacks the intentional quality of an assassin firing a gun; but who would deny that drivers grip the wheel in the belief that the behavior decreases the probability of something undesirable?[3] Yet an intentional act is attempted control if undertaken in the belief that it increases or decreases the probability of some subsequent condition.

One counterargument—we have beliefs only when conscious of them—is flawed. If humans could not act without consciously anticipating specific consequences, their survival would be jeopardized. Reconsider the driver holding the steering wheel. The point is not just that "holding" is habitual or unreflective behavior. No one is likely to deny that the driver holds the wheel in the belief that the behavior reduces the probability of any one of seemingly infinite kinds of collisions. To be sure, the phrase "behavior-in-the-belief-that" is cumbersome and unconventional. Moreover, at the cognitive level the idea might be better expressed by the phrase "with knowledge of"; but that phrase is not appropriate at the affective level, certainly far less than speaking of the belief that some anticipated consequences of behavior are desirable and others undesirable.

Successful Control

The concern is with *attempts at control* if only because the success-failure distinction bears on this "repetitional" principle of control (2–1): Individuals tend to repeat those types of attempted control that they perceive as having been more successful than alternatives in the past.[4] While the principle makes operant psychology relevant, it does not belittle vicarious learning.

Many social and behavioral scientists will have misgivings about defining control by reference to beliefs, and some of them explicitly state that control may be intentional or unintentional (e.g., Dahl, 1982:17); but without that reference the distinction between successful and unsuccessful control is lost, along with the repetitional principle.[5] It is maintained here by this definition of successful or effective control: when a human engages in attempted control, it is successful to the extent that he or she perceives the condition in question as having been realized, maintained, or avoided. So conceived, successful control is both perceptual and a matter of degree. For some purposes, it is relevant to consider also the success-failure perceptions of the target of attempted control or of anyone who comes to know of the attempt; but those perceptions can be treated as contingent properties of attempted control rather than a success-failure criterion.

INDEFENSIBLE ALTERNATIVES. As for distinguishing successful and unsuccessful control without reference to cognitive and/or affective facets of internal behavior, the first of four possible criteria is this: behavior is successful control if and only if it has a consequence. But think of an individual backing out of a bank with a gun in hand pointing toward the door and being shot by a police officer. Because there would be no basis for denying that the officer's behavior was caused by the robber's behavior, it follows that the robber "controlled" the police officer.[6] So the overt-behavior-only criterion of control invites absurdities.

Second alternative criterion: an instance of some type of overt behavior is successful control if and only if all known previous instances have been followed by an event of some particular type. The immediate objection is that such invariant associations scarcely exist. Thus, because there are instances in which a police officer shouts "Halt!" but no one nearby ceases moving, then according to the "invariant association" criterion no instance of that act is successful control, not even when someone halts. Moreover, nothing is gained by changing the criterion to "*most* instances." Thus, if in 51 percent of cases in which a police officer shouts "Halt!" no one nearby ceases to move, it would be absurd to identify instances of halting as unsuccessful control. Why would a police officer shouting "Halt!" be an attempt at control in light of the present definition? Because of the inference that the officer acted in the belief that (1) the action increases the probability of an individual halting and (2) the increase is desirable.

Third alternative criterion: an act is successful control if and only if an act has a consequence that the actor perceived as probable. The criterion recognizes only a cognitive facet of internal behavior (perceptions of causation), and consider one illustrative implication of ignoring affective facets. Various surgical operations are virtually certain to produce discomfort, and surgeons know it. Accordingly, accepting the third alternative criterion, should the patient feel discomfort after surgery, then the operation was successful control even if the patient dies. Why? Because the surgery had a consequence—a feeling of discomfort—that the surgeon anticipated. Why is surgery attempted control in light of the definition prescribed here? Surgeons evidently operate in the belief that it increases the probability of some subsequent desirable condition. Would the operation be successful control? Only if the surgeon perceives some anticipated desirable condition as having been at least partially realized. Why the insistence on recognizing both cognitive and affective facets of internal behavior? Because alternatives invite absurdities and make control efficacy less relevant in explaining human behavior, including putative socio-cultural phenomena.

The fourth and final overt-behavior-only criterion: an act is successful control if and only if it is repeated. So a hunter crouches near a water hole for hours and returns to camp without any game but repeats the action the next day; hence, the action on the first day was successful control. Such a ludicrous implication is not the only objection; the criterion in question ignores something essential for human survival—goal persistence despite failures in control attempts (in this case, the failure to make a kill). The notion of a goal relates to internal behavior, both cognitive and affective; and the importance of goal persistence is not limited to human predation. Consider some observations from a psychoanalytic perspective (Tolpin and Kohut, 1980:433): "healthy human children preserve the confidence that they have the power to get what they want despite the fact that, from birth on, actual experience frequently teaches them otherwise." Similar observations can be made about human curiosity and control, especially information seeking as a consequence of control failures or control impotence (see Swann et al., 1981).

The Larger Issue

The present conceptualization presumes that a description of virtually all putative types of overt behavior is bound to distort if no reference is made to internal behavior. We do not literally "see" people saluting, robbing, reaching, signalling, fighting, kissing, eating, or killing, to mention only a few acts. In all instances there are observable ectodermic movements, as when the hand comes into contact with the forehead; but to define those acts only by reference to movement (i.e., ignoring internal behavior) is contrary to the English language and everyday experience.[7] Searle's observation (1983:105) is especially relevant: "If I am asked, 'Why did he raise his arm?,' it sounds odd to say, 'Because he intended to raise his arm.' The reason it sounds odd is because by identifying the action as 'raising his arm' we have already identified it in terms of the intention in action."

That humans continually infer the intentions, beliefs, or perceptions of others, contemplate how readily we are surprised by incomplete acts, as when someone walks to a ringing telephone but never lifts the receiver. We are commonly only dimly aware of inferring internal behavior because inferences are made so often without surprises. Indeed, in defining some type of act many sociologists often ignore the internal component as though it is understood, but incomplete definitions are not the only consequence.[8] Indifference to internal behavior makes sociologists insensitive to the possibility that humans learn how to control in part vicariously by attributing intentions to the behavior of others.

Humans attribute internal behavior to others so much that it is a property of interaction. Moreover, a vast literature indicates that a human's behavior is mediated by his or her intentions and is commonly determined by the human's perception of the evaluative standards of significant others. The bulk of that literature (see, e.g., Brinberg, 1979) is associated with psychology or social psychology, and the indifference of sociologists is conducive to robotic sociology.

Some Anticipated Objections

One likely objection to accepting control as sociology's central notion is that only a very limited range of behavior is attempted control. Extending the argument, humans rarely pursue specific goals consciously and deliberately; rather, human behavior is commonly habitual and unreflective, without rational calculation of any cost-benefit.

The key terms in the argument—*conscious, deliberate, rational, habitual, calculating, cost,* and *benefit*—are not used here, because they suggest a utilitarian and hedonistic quality of behavior that distorts no less than Durkheim's robotic image of humans. However, the present conceptualization of control can be used to describe the actions of crass, utilitarian hedonists; and ignoring them would reflect an indifference to human history, one crowded with calculating and grasping manipulators, whose recognition in classical sociological theory is largely limited to Pareto's ramblings. Thus, the descriptive utility of sociological concepts is negligible when it comes to Richard III or the Wars of the Roses (see, e.g., St. Aubyn, 1983).

Sociological conceptualizations are lifeless also in that they appear removed from an awful fact of human existence—things often go wrong: Sam has lost his job, Debra's husband beats her, Alex is threatened with eviction.[9] Moreover, when trouble comes, people usually do not merely cringe; they attempt to do something about it, to exercise control.

It is pointless to depict social life as governed by putative norms and yet grant that things "go wrong" even for assiduous conformists (perhaps Sam lost his job despite his diligence). For that matter, if norms govern social life, why do sociologists study deviant behavior with gusto? It is no answer to reply, along with Durkheim (1938, 1949), that deviance is normal. The reply only raises doubts about norms governing social life (for elaboration, see Edgerton, 1985). Finally, how can sociologists write about superordinate statuses and power without recognizing that control underlies both?

Should sociologists object that previous illustrations of the inapplicability of sociological concepts are "micro," the objection misleadingly suggests that sociology is relevant for human concerns at the "macro" level. Think of terrorism and nuclear arms control. Those phenomena are surely genuine human concern and macro by any definition. Yet sociologists have had little to say on either subject, leaving thoughtful commentaries on those phenomena to others (e.g., O'Brien, 1986; Dahlitz, 1983).

Sociological concepts, principles, and theories are divorced not just from human concerns; they rarely have real bearing on purposive human phenomenon, micro or macro. If the argument appears exaggerated, examine Donald Black's ostensible conception of an ideal sociological theory (1976:7), as one that "neither assumes nor implies that [the individual] is . . . rational, goal directed, pleasure seeking, or pain avoiding." Because Black's specialty is the sociology of law, his statement is indicative of the indifference to the purposive quality of human behavior that prevails in such sociological specialties as human ecology, demography, and stratification, whose subject matter is inherently less "cultural" or "symbolic" than is law.[10] However, Black's candor is commendable; he has made his predilection explicit, something many sociologists fail to do.

NARROW CONCEPTIONS OF CONTROL. The major anticipated objection—control behavior is rare—reflects more than the robotic image of humans.[11] That objection is consistent with two widespread beliefs about control that most sociologists seemingly accept but seldom acknowledge: first, control is evil; and, second, the targets of attempted behavioral control are particular (specific) individuals.

The first belief is extremely dubious, and the reason has nothing to do with the argument that scientists should have no truck with the notion of evil because it entails value judgments. Rather, by any reasonable standard all manner of human control (i.e., control over human behavior) are benign, normatively neutral, or perhaps even laudatory.[12] Picture an adult rushing into a burning house and forcibly removing a hysterical child; the adult's behavior would be control (indeed, coercive control) but hardly evil. No less important, it is much more accurate to say that "evil requires control" than "control is evil."

Consider one of Liebow's observations on a street corner in Washington, D.C., frequented by some twenty black men in the early 1960s:

"A pickup truck drives slowly down the street. The truck stops as it comes abreast of a man sitting on a cast-iron porch and the white driver calls out, asking if the man wants a day's work. The man shakes his head and the truck moves on up the block, stopping again whenever idling men come within calling distance of the driver" (1967:29).

Many sociologists would regard the behavior of the "labor scavenger" as an evil, one that clearly exemplifies a degrading feature of capitalism and the exploitative character of American race relations. Their indignation may lead them to overlook the obvious—that the evil is an *attempt at control*.

Now consider two widespread and related beliefs: (1) that the *goal* in human control is always to manipulate the behavior of specific individuals and (2) macro human phenomena *cannot* be described or thought of in terms of control.[13] When the owner of a new store places signs on the building's exterior, what could be the goal if not to increase the probability of attracting customers? Yet the owner's goal is not to attract only one particular individual or even only a particular set of individuals. Then think of law and advertising. Human control is the name of the game in those institutions, but the target is commonly an indefinite category of individuals (e.g., all potential offenders, all consumers).

The idea of an attempt at control with indefinite targets takes on special significance because of this conceptual argument: To control someone is to thwart their will. When someone builds a formidable wall around his or her house, it is indisputable that uncountable individuals never had the intention, desire, and/or opportunity to enter the house by stealth or force before the wall's erection. So, the argument would have it (Oppenheim, 1961), the wall makes those individuals "unfree" but does not control them. The argument tends to confuse two questions about a particular act. First, was the act attempted control? Second, if so, who were the targets? Agreement in answers to the second question is not necessary for agreement in answers to the first. Moreover, the home owner may have built the wall in the belief that it decreases the probability of anyone entering the home by stealth or force; if so, the target of the control attempt was an infinite set of individuals.

Some Elaborate Illustrations

Despite the foregoing observations, critics may persist in objecting that control is a rare form of human behavior. To blunt that objection, more elaborate illustrations are needed.

MODES OF DRESS. In dressing for work, a man may never so much as think of his actions as avoiding punishment; yet it would be attempted control if in dressing he believed that should he leave his residence unclothed someone will do something undesirable to him. Do men dress for public appearance in that belief? No one familiar with American life would doubt it; but note the implication—dressing for public appearance is countercontrol in that it is believed to decrease the probability of being controlled, such as being arrested.[14] True, the dresser's beliefs may not pertain to a legal punishment, but that point is conceptually irrelevant.

Should a sociologist stoop to explain "dressing," it would be something like this: The act is conformity. The explanation ignores deviance and reflects an insensitivity to the purposive quality of human behavior. No notion furthers that insensitivity more than norm, which is all the more important because "norm" could be identified as a candidate for sociology's central notion. Sociologists do frequently resort to normative explanations, but deviant behavior poses a problem for all normative explanations (see Edgerton, 1985:4–16). Moreover, sociologists rarely actually study putative norms; instead, they assume that norms exist and ignore this question: For this particular social unit, why are the norms what they are? If the question is defensible, an adequate answer requires reference to control.

Insofar as norms can be defined and identified defensibly,[15] they vary from one social unit to another; hence, an assessment of an explanation of putative American dress norms requires reference to other dress norms. So why is wearing an overcoat a putative American norm of seasonal dress? Suppose someone replies: Because the U.S. is not a tropical country. If the explanation appears absurd, note its consistency with putative dress norms in other countries. However, whatever its merits, the explanation is incomplete without recognition that wearing clothing can be inanimate control, reducing exposure to the elements.

The reference to inanimate control suggests that humans may dress so as to avoid physical discomfort; but thinking of socio-cultural phenomena in terms of control does not necessarily lead to grotesque oversimplifications, such as asserting that all clothing is worn as inanimate control. The very body position of clothing commonly suggests some connection with sex, and only obstinate sociologists will deny that humans are concerned with the control of sexual relations and that some putative norms reflect the concern. Successful control of sexual relations depends on conditions that vary enormously among social units. Insofar as social unit members are concerned with preventing infidelity, premarital promiscuity, or unwelcomed sexual advances, then the relevance of dress depends on, among other things, the frequency with which men and women come into contact outside the marital bond and beyond the view of third parties. That frequency in turn depends on such factors as population density, settlement patterns, household composition, and the spatio-temporal context of sustenance activities. Hence, the argument that clothing has something to do with controlling sexual relations in no way implies invariant modes of dress, or even that in all social units humans wear some clothing.

There are some predictable objections. Polhemus and Procter (1978:10) will be quoted as stating that "climate does not always determine whether or not clothes are worn," without recognition that insofar as climate does determine clothing it does so only through attempts of humans to control conditions. Likewise, critics will be incorrect if they depict the present argument as assuming that humans are naturally prudish.

To describe dress as a means of control is a far cry from a theory, but it is more informative than the conventional reification—"society" or "culture" defines proper clothing. Moreover, clothing facilitates controls that have nothing to do with weather or sexual relations. Human control in military units is facilitated by uniforms that distinguish superordinates and subordinates.

Then consider the "public uniform" of a Victorian male elite in London, complete with cape, gloves, and cane. Veblen would characterize such dress as conspicuous consumption, but such characterization has no more explanatory value than a strictly psychological description (e.g., a mode of dress reflects vanity). Now think of the elite's dress in terms of control. It increases the probability of attention and deference, which is to say control over others (e.g., waiters). A few studies provide evidence that certain kinds of uniforms facilitate effective human control (e.g., Bickman, 1974), although most sociologists evidently do not care because of their preoccupation with structural variables.

A likely objection to the Victorian illustration: in dressing the elite did not intend to control others. "Intent" in the conscious and deliberate sense is not relevant. There is only one immediate empirical question: Did the elite believe that his dress mode increased the probability of a deferential response and that such responses are desirable? If so, when dressing, the elite engaged in attempted control.

Nothing has been said about why the elite wanted to control others, valued control, etc. The goal is to describe an elite's behavior in terms of control rather than pretending to answer this question: Why do individuals want to control behavior? Perhaps that question would have to be answered to explain an elite's mode of dress,[16] but taking control as their central notion would not commit sociologists to motivational questions or explaining individual differences. When sociologists cease chattering about structure and function, the field's generic question becomes: Why is such-and-such type of behavior more frequent in some social units than in others?

So the presumption of the illustration is that male elite dress (a type of behavior) was much more distinctive in Victorian London than, say, a small Iowa town. Why? Describing "dress" as attempted control does not explain the contrast, but describing phenomena in terms of control facilitates and integrates explanations. In the case at hand, one possibility is contrast in population size and, correlatively, that London elites interacted more often with strangers than did small-town Iowa elites. But why would either condition be relevant? Even if uniforms identify the status of strangers, why is identity relevant? Answers are facilitated by recognizing that modes of dress are attempts at control.

The foregoing contradicts conventional sociological wisdom, according to which human conformity to norms becomes an end in itself. To the contrary, humans conform to control others (Edgerton, 1985:9, refers ambiguously to "manipulation of rules"). Granted, once a type of behavior becomes predominant in a social unit, there is something akin to pressure for conformity, but when someone conforms in the belief that to do otherwise invites ridicule, loss, or injury, conformity is attempted control.

The argument extends to Merry's allusion to gossip's "power to control behavior" (1984:271). Even accepting the reification, gossip controls behavior only when humans refrain from some types of conduct because of fear of what others will say about or do to them.[17] Williamson's observation on American history provides a depressing example of a different but related phenomenon: "That the number of lynchings decreased after 1892 might be attributed primarily to a rising caution among black men that led them to avoid occasions that could possibly be twisted into a semblance of rape or an attempt at rape. Almost certainly black men came generally to avoid being alone with white women, were careful not to meet feminine eyes with a level gaze, and lowered the tone of their voice in the presence of white females" (1984:117). Such behavior was no novelty for blacks, who had long since learned to appear simple, docile, and manageable in the presence of whites; but "playing Sambo" was a means of countercontrol.

The argument that putative norms come into being and are perpetuated in connection with control is more informative than the conventional view: norms emerge for obscure reasons and are perpetuated by tradition.[18] Then consider the functionalist view: norms emerge and are perpetuated because they meet a "societal need." Insofar as any collectivity can be said to have needs, the need of one societal division (e.g., the need of capitalists to hire labor at the lowest possible wage) may be inimical to the need of another division (the proletariat's need for more than bare subsistence). Indeed, a putative norm may emerge from a need perceived by individuals in one societal division to control individuals in other divisions.[19] Examine the following commentary (Houts, 1972:107) on a putative British norm—barristers wearing wigs in courts. "In the days of the sixteenth century or thereabouts, the secular courts, called the King's courts, were locked in deadly rivalry with the ecclesiastical courts. The men who performed the function of barrister in the Common Law courts, for the most part, were ecclesiastics with shaved heads. Jealous of their prerogatives and fearful of being overwhelmed, the King's justices ordered that no ecclesiastics would be permitted to appear in King's court; but there were not enough trained and competent nonclerical 'barristers' to handle the pressing needs of the clients with business before his Majesty's courts. The deceptive expedient of the clerics, therefore, was the adoption of the wigs to cover their shaved heads. . . ."

The account is disputable, and ignorance of the conditions in which most putative norms originated precludes constructive arguments. Nonetheless, what is the alternative to Houts's description of wig wearing as *countercontrol*? A barrister just happened to wear a wig and his whimsical act caught on? Hardly informative. Now assume that a vain but distinguished barrister did wear a wig to cover his baldness, and others imitated him in the hope of influencing judges or jurors. Even so, wearing a wig caught on because it facilitated control, and contemporary barristers are unlikely to deny that it is now a means of countercontrol; without it, the barrister would risk negative reactions by court officers.

Critics may argue that descriptions of putative norms in terms of control suggest a rational explanation of them. The argument rests on a dubious premise—explanations of socio-cultural phenomena necessarily assume that human behavior is either rational or irrational. The meaning of *rational* is so vague and definitions of it so divergent that use of the term to criticize theories is indefensible.[20] Nonetheless, some putative norms are commonly viewed as irrational, and they will fuel opposition to control as a candidate for sociology's central notion. One prime example is the ancient Chinese practice of binding the feet of young girls. The practice was extremely painful and resulted in what Westerners view as a hideous deformity. Irrational? Contemplate this quotation: "A Chinese manual for women reasoned that foot-binding was a restraining device: 'Why are feet bound? It is not because they are good looking with their bowed arch, but rather because men feared that women might easily leave their quarters and therefore had their feet bound tightly in order to prevent this.' . . . The possibility of improper behavior was sharply reduced by making it inconvenient for women to get about on tiny feet, in a nation where feminine chastity was to become a vital part of the moral standard" (Levy, 1966:30).

THE IMMEDIATE IMPLICATION.   Consider this version of a control principle (2–2), the "efficacy" principle: Humans tend to employ only those types, kinds, or means of control that they perceive as effective. That version is consistent with the argument that any particular putative norm is present in some social units because at least some members perceive it as facilitating control. More generally, sociological principles should reflect recognition that humans govern their behavior in light of beliefs about consequences, and to that end no notion rivals control.

Another consideration is that humans perceive events in terms of cause and effect, often without experimentation. Thus, no individual may come to perceive a connection between appearing in public naked and punitive reactions through actual experience, but the "how" and "why" of causal perceptions are conceptually relevant. Nevertheless, the present conceptualization of control furthers appreciation that humans perceive events in terms of cause and effect.

ADDITIONAL ILLUSTRATIONS.   Now consider someone speaking to a friend. Observers might disagree about the response anticipated, but that is conceptually irrelevant when identifying "speaking to someone" as attempted control.

Plowing illustrates why there is no fundamental conceptual difference between control of animate things (e.g., growing wheat) and control of inanimate things (e.g., turning a tractor). Why? Humans have beliefs about causal connections and govern their behavior accordingly. However, whereas the farmer believes that plowing is necessary for a crop, the speaker believes that speaking is sufficient for altering the friend's overt behavior. Moreover, unlike some instances of speaking, plowing is *cumulative* control; the farmer believes that a series of different actions (e.g., plowing, planting, weeding) taken together is necessary for a harvestable crop.

When attempted control occurs as a series of similar acts, each act is *repetitional* control. Thus, a homemaker rarely consciously perceives the preparation of a particular meal as necessary or sufficient for maintaining the spouse's domestic behavior; but should the homemaker cease preparing family meals indefinitely for no ostensible reason, no one would be surprised by an eventual marked alteration in the spouse's behavior. Such "surprise potential" always indicates the actor's belief that a repetition of acts maintains or alters the behavior of someone. However, the homemaker is unlikely to believe that repeated preparations of family meals are sufficient to maintain the spouse's behavior; rather, they are only necessary along with a series of other types of acts (e.g., shopping). Accordingly, the preparation of a family meal is more accurately labeled as "cumulative-repetitional."

What has been said of the homemaker applies also to the employee trudging to work without consciously anticipating being fired for doing otherwise. The similarity suggests that cumulative-repetitional control is very common; hence, there is at least one basis for describing and thinking about a remarkable feature of social life—its continuity—in terms of control.

The foregoing types of control are complex notions, but human behavior is too complicated for simple conceptualizations. Moreover, those notions suggest a connection between social relations and human control. The behavioral manifestation of a social relation is a series of acts, and control is often realized only through serial acts; so the notion of cumulative-repetitional control is especially relevant in analyzing social relations.

Finally, consider a judge imposing a prison term on a convicted felon. Surely the judge believes that such a sentence is necessary to incarcerate the defendant, and he or she may believe that the sentence contributes to deterrence. The term *contributes* is strategic because no judge is likely to believe that imposing only one sentence is sufficient to reduce the crime rate; rather, a judge is likely to believe that each sentence is only one of numerous actions by numerous legal officials, which taken together are necessary or sufficient to reduce the crime rate. Such *contributory* control differs from repetitional and cumulative attempted control in that those who engage in it believe that their actions along with those of others increase or decrease the probability of some condition (a kind of control akin to Power's conception [1984] of collaboration and the related notion of mutual intention).

Contributory control is only one subclass of multilateral control. Another subclass, *representational* control, occurs when two or more individuals agree that the outcome of their interactions is to be construed by them as a command or directive to themselves and/or to others. Such control is conspicuous in legislative actions, but it may be a simple agreement between two individuals that either of them speaks or otherwise acts for both.

The foregoing distinctions do not remotely exhaust the possibilities (see, e.g., Burns, 1958), but even a very elaborate typology of control would not be sufficient. The variety of control beggars description, and in the final analysis acceptance, rejection, or creation of particular distinctions should be left to the judgment of sociologists in pursuing their research and theoretical interests.

Illustrative Observations on Homicide

Homicide can be described either as control or as resulting from control failures. Premeditated murder is the ultimate control; and insofar as a homicide is unlawful (not justifiable or "legal"), it represents failure in attempted control. For one thing, the threat of legal punishment did not deter. As for justifiable homicide, the slayer's allegation is that the deceased instigated violence by illegal behavior; and the allegation indicates failures in control over the victim's behavior (e.g., if the deceased was killed in a burglary attempt, he or she had not been deterred by the threat of legal punishment). There is a tautological quality in the foregoing, but a central notion should fuel the imagination through, among other things, tautological thinking. The ultimate consideration is whether such thinking gives rise to empirical propositions that tests subsequently corroborate. Sociological work on homicide has given rise to a few empirical propositions, but they have been reached more by crude induction than by reasoning in terms of some conceptual scheme.

Some Correlates of the Homicide Rate

Numerous investigators have reported a substantial direct relation among American territorial units (urban subareas, cities, metropolitan areas, or states) between the homicide rate and the proportion of residents who are black (see references in Messner and Tardiff, 1986). But the goal is a universal proposition about homicide rates, and the proportion of population black has no bearing on variation in the homicide rate by sex or by age among American whites, let alone on international variation. For that matter, Messner and Tardiff (1986:306) report no statistically significant association between the homicide rate and the percent of population black among Manhattan neighborhoods when several other variables are controlled. Nor is there any reason whatever to expect a substantial direct relation between the annual U.S. homicide rate and the percent of population black over, say, 1947–87.

Another finding is a direct relation among American territorial units between the proportion of families, households, or individuals below the poverty level (or some other aggregate measure of income level) and the homicide rate. However, in some comparisons the association explains less than 30 percent of variation in the rate (see Messner and Tardiff, 1986:317), and there has been a regression analysis in which the association is not even positive (Messner, 1982). Williams (1984) has questioned Messner's report of no positive association (1982); but even if a substantial positive association between some poverty measure and the homicide rate should hold consistently, the premises for deducing the association (thereby explaining it) are obscure; and "poverty" scarcely explains the much higher male homicide rate.

Still other findings suggest that the homicide rate is a function not of poverty but, rather, of income inequality—the amount of variation in family, household, or individual income. However, instances of no statistically significant association between income inequality and the homicide rate have been reported (see, e.g., Messner and Tardiff, 1986); and even if there were no exceptions, the theoretical rationale for anticipating the association is obscure. Whatever the rationale, the association is inconsistent with anthropological reports on nonliterate societies. Those reports indicate that the homicide rate is much greater in some societies than in others, but many nonliterate societies with high homicide rates are labeled as "egalitarian" (i.e., no marked contrasts among households as to wealth), such as the Jivaro and the Yanomamo.

To conclude, the association between the homicide rate and either income variable—inequality or poverty—is extremely problematical. Furthermore, even if either association did hold consistently, it would be a puzzle.

A CONTROL INTERPRETATION. The typical American homicide is not mysterious; police officers quickly identify the slayer and the motive. The vast majority of cases can be described by this phrase: the slayer and the victim were involved in a dispute. The phrase has explanatory implications because a dispute is indicative of ineffective human control by one or both parties over the other.

Even if a survey of the frequency of disputes could be made in each of several populations, a truly close direct association between the dispute rate and the homicide rate will not hold if disputants rely on "third-party mechanisms" for dispute resolution more in some populations than in others. When a disputant requests third-party intervention, control expertise is implicitly attributed to the third party, who traditionally avoids violence.

There may be several types of third parties in a social unit, some American instances being attorneys, priests, ministers, rabbis, counselors, psychiatrists, parents, employers, teachers, judges, and police officers. Comparable statuses do not exist in some societies, but heads of clans or lineages scarcely play a role in American dispute settlement. The general assertion is that social units commonly differ as to the frequency with which disputants turn to a third party, one reason being that in some social units there are few specialists in dispute resolution. So the homicide rate is a function not just of the sheer volume of disputes but also of the frequency of recourse to a third party for peaceful dispute settlement.

Again, homicides represent a failure both in interpersonal control and in the larger control system. If there is anything to the deterrence doctrine, then the failure of the larger system stems from the improbability of a severe punishment for homicide because of infrequent arrests, decisions not to prosecute, not guilty verdicts, and probation. Finally, although the deterrence doctrine is commonly thought of a pertaining to legal punishments, extralegal punitive reactions to homicide (e.g., loss of job) may be even more relevant.

The foregoing arguments culminate in this proposition: The homicide rate of a social unit varies (1) directly with the frequency of disputes, (2) inversely with the frequency which disputants have requested that some third party attempt a peaceful settlement of the dispute, and (3) inversely with the certainty-severity of punitive reactions to homicide. Tests of the proposition will require comparisons of several social units (e.g., cities, age groups); and in addition to the homicide rate three values must be computed for each unit: (1) D, the annual number of disputes (2) T, the annual number of disputes in which at least one of the disputants requested a peaceful third-party intervention to settle the dispute; and (3) ΣCS, a number that represents over all types of actual punishments for homicide the sum of the products of the perceived certainty of the type of punishment (C) and the severity (S) of that type as perceived by at least a sample of social unit members. All three numbers for each unit would have to be combined or somehow treated simultaneously (e.g., $[D/T][1/\Sigma CS]$) to predict ordinal differences in the homicide rates.

Some General Observations

Only systematic tests will corroborate or falsify the proposition; and, if valid, the proposition would throw light on race and income as correlates of homicide, at least in the U.S. Low income scarcely promotes recourse of disputants to a private attorney. True, it is unlikely that a prospective slayer or homicide victim reasons this way: "Well, I do not have the money to hire an attorney, so I will resort to violence." Rather, the use of an attorney for any purpose is less common in low-income categories; and because low-income individuals, especially low-income blacks, are so often reacted to negatively by the police, they are less likely than high-income individuals to turn to the police when a violent outcome of a dispute is anticipated (for a more general but relevant argument, see Hagan and Albonetti, 1982).[21] Finally, to the extent that blacks view legal reactions to violence or its threat as less stigmatizing than do whites, then to that extent blacks perceive those reactions as less punitive.

Although women have a substantially lower homicide rate, there is no reason to suppose that women who commit homicide are subject to more severe punishments, and it is not known whether women turn more to third parties (e.g., husbands, parents, other kin) when involved in a dispute. Casual observations suggests a more likely prospect—that women are involved in fewer disputes largely because men more commonly interact in situations of equality (e.g., strangers in a bar). If all interacting parties perceive one party as having authority over the others, that perception furthers the effectiveness of control attempts by that party and lessens the probability of a dispute. In that connection, women commonly interact more than do men as superordinates (e.g., as a parent) or subordinates (e.g., an employee); both positions are conducive to effective interpersonal control and, consequently, the avoidance of disputes.[22] If the argument is correct, the female homicide rate will increase should women come to interact more as equals with men.

Although systematic tests of the proposition are imperative, isolated observations pertaining to particular populations may provide what is intuitively more convincing evidence. Thus, Hallpike (1977:120) reports numbers indicating an average annual homicide rate of 533.3 per 100,000 (211.1 excluding intertribal cases) for the Goilala tribe of the Tauade speakers in New Guinea. The rate for those nonliterate peoples (subsisting largely by gardening and raising pigs) is thus at least 20 times the U.S. rate, and Hallpike makes a significant commentary on the "basic mode of social control" among those people: "There is no idea of a meeting between disputants and of their case being mediated by some respected arbitrator or council of elders" (188).

Whatever its validity, the proposition was reached by thinking of homicide and disputes in terms of control. It remains to be seen whether such thinking is conducive to propositions about other phenomena, but the sheer number of propositions is not the only consideration. If thinking of phenomena in terms of control generates empirical propositions, it furthers the prospects of deducing those propositions from a general theory.

NOTES

1. Another and much broader alternative would be a definition that permits such expressions as "the environment controls" (or "ideology controls" or "culture controls"). It would be difficult to formulate a clear definition of control that sanctions such expressions; and unless one longs for terminological duplication and ensuing confusion, why speak of the environment as controlling rather than determining or causing? For that matter, how can the environment *attempt* control?

2. Although Goffman (1961a, 1961b, 1974) rarely used the term *control*, virtually all of his observation pertain to attempted control as defined here.

3. Lest the notion of "behavior-in-the-belief-that" be equated with psychologizing

and reductionism, to assert that an individual acted in such-and-such belief is not to assert that the belief explains the act. For that matter, sociologists need not concern themselves with how and why individuals come to have beliefs, nor how and why individuals come to act in accordance with beliefs. Those questions can be left to psychologists, but they should be thought of as connecting sociology and psychology. In any case, beliefs as components of control behavior could be in the subject matter of the sociology of knowledge. The point is not just that humans attempt to control the beliefs of others. What could be more important than beliefs about the kinds of human behavior that increase or decrease the probability of change in some condition? Compared to such beliefs, "knowledge" is a grab-bag notion, and it will never be conducive to disciplinary coherence, nor to testable propositions. Those who think of the sociology of knowledge as no more short of coherence or testable propositions than is the typical sociological specialty should examine Stehr and Meja's book (1984).

4. The principle can be restated to make it a version of the law of effect: The probability of an instance of some kind of control is a direct function of the proportion of previous instances that were successful. Note that throughout this book space limits force an emphasis on general control principles. Such principles are not logically interrelated, and they are only initial steps toward a general theory about control.

5. If the objection is that reference to internal behavior makes the notion of control "psychological," what of Skinner's observations on control? He used the term extensively (e.g., 1983, 1978, 1974, 1971) but never defined it explicitly. Had Skinner defined the term, there is every reason to presume that he would have made no reference to internal behavior (e.g., beliefs, perception, evaluations). The avoidance of such references would have been in keeping with superorganicism, and the same is true of Skinner's frequent references to "environments" or "culture" (e.g., 1978:85, 1974:203) as exerting control. The point is not just that Skinner and superorganicists obliterate the distinction between successful and unsuccessful control; also, they never confront this question: If only to avoid conceptual redundancy, why not speak of causes, determines, or influences rather than control?

6. In robbing the bank the perpetrator undoubtedly acted in the belief that the robbery increased the probability of being shot, but it would strain credulity to argue that the robber believed that being shot is desirable. Hence, absurdities abound when control is defined without reference to both facets of internal behavior, cognitive and affective.

7. "the question of what we can see a person doing raises the most awkward epistemological and ontological issues. To say that we can see a person crossing the street or waiting for a bus or signing a contract . . . is a quite different kind of claim from saying that we can see a metal ball rolling down an inclined plane. All that we can actually *see* . . . is the person's movement" (Maze, 1983:6).

8. When sociologists attempt (in the tradition of Watson and Skinner) to cleanse their field's vocabulary of terms pertaining to internal behavior, the outcome is inevitably bizarre definitions. Consider, for example, Scott's definition of a *sanction* (1971:65): "It is the reinforcement of behavior produced by the behavior of other organisms of the same species." The definition promises little empirical

applicability if only because researchers are likely to regard it as unintelligible. Confusion is compounded by Scott's earlier reference (1971:46) to a reinforcement as "any event or process possessing stimulus properties for a particular organism which, when it follows the occurrence of a particular repeatable act, increases the rate at which that act subsequently occurs." So sanctions in the negative and conventional sense—punishments—can only *increase* the rate at which some type of act occurs?

9. For a rare manifestation of sensitivity on the part of sociologists to this awful fact of human existence, see Emerson and Messinger (1977).

10. The need to recognize the purposive quality of human behavior may not be the same in all social and behavior sciences, specialties, or investigations; but Gibbs and Martin's praise (1959:33–34) of Sumner's dismissal of purposes was misguided even in connection with human ecology.

11. The "robotic" image of humans reflects an indifference to the purposive quality of human behavior, and it is widespread in both sociology and anthropology largely because of pervasive functionalism. Gluckman's debate with Paine (see Merry's commentary, 1984:274) over gossip illustrates the issue in anthropology.

12. Skinner (e.g., 1971, 1974, 1978, 1983) has confronted the control-as-an-evil argument much more than have sociologists, and he concludes that it stems from the perception of control as negative (i.e., as punitive or aversive). Skinner rightly emphasizes that much of control is not perceived as control because "we do not feel the control exerted when our behavior is positively reinforced" (1978:4). Stating Skinner's argument in words that he chooses not to use, attempts to influence human behavior are especially unlikely to be perceived as control if also perceived as positive (i.e., pleasant or rewarding).

13. Even when sociologists analyze control phenomena (as defined here) at the macro level, they commonly do not make use of the term *control* (see, e.g., Griffin et al., 1986). The reason is not just the belief that targets of control attempts are necessarily particular (identifiable) individuals. Sociologists are not prone to recognize that various kinds of collective behavior (e.g., strikes, social movements, legislation, revolutions, and wars), organizations, and even what is loosely identified as institutions are nothing less (or more) than innumerable control attempts by diverse individuals. Insofar as those control attempts are synchronized or coordinated (as they often are), the "controllers" are collectivities rather than isolated individuals. However, only in that sense can one speak of, for example, an organization attempting to control anything (Pfeffer and Salanick, 1978:39).

14. What Skinner (1971:30) has labeled the "literature of freedom" is a vast instruction in countercontrol. Many of the observations made by Goffman (1963) on behavior in public places can be described as countercontrol, and the notion itself is suggested by his term "proper management of personal appearance." More important, perhaps, Durkheim makes essentially the same point about dress as that made here, but he ignored the implications (1938:2–3): "if in my dress I do not conform to the customs observed in my country and in my class, the ridicule I provoke, the social isolation in which I am kept, produce, although in attenuated form, the same effects as a punishment in the strict sense of

the word." Yet Durkheim evidently could not bring himself to recognize the possibility that he dressed one way rather than another in the belief that it decreased the probability of others ridiculing or ostracizing him.

15. As argued in chapter 1, sociologists conveniently ignore several seemingly insoluble problems in defining and identifying norms.

16. There is no connection between the proposal to make control sociology's central notion and the belief that references to motives or motivation are necessary to explain human behavior. All that need be said on that issue is that motives or motivation can be described or thought about in terms of control.

17. The argument applies not just to isolated acts but also to an indefinite repetition of some type of act, as in putative role performance. Goffman's observations are especially relevant (1961b:87): "in performing a role the individual must see to it that the impressions of him that are conveyed in the situation are compatible with role-appropriate personal qualities effectively imputed to him: a judge is supposed to be deliberate and sober; a pilot, in a cockpit, to be cool; a bookkeeper to be accurate and neat in doing his work." However, rather than analyze role performance in terms of control and countercontrol, Goffman writes of image and self-image; but contemplate the implications of his phrase "the individuals must see to it." Why must the individual see to it?

18. Sociologists have surprisingly little to say about the origination and perpetuation of putative norms, and they shun the point of view suggested by the biologist Lewontin. He (1977:284) quotes Dawkins as saying: "The idea of hell-fire is, quite simply, *self-perpetuating*, because of its own 'deep psychological impact.' " Lewontin then says: "He shrugs off without analysis the much more plausible and clearly causal hypothesis that hell-fire is not *self-perpetuating*, but is perpetuated by some people because it gives them power over other people" (284).

19. Here and elsewhere, the use of the term *norm* is not contrary to the argument advanced in chapter 1—that the very notion of a norm is a thicket of difficulties. So the term is used in this book to refer only to behavior, internal and/or overt, that one social scientist or another has identified as a norm.

20. Sociologists, including Max Weber (especially 1978), use the terms *rational* and *irrational* (or *logical, illogical, nonrational, nonlogical*) in a blasé manner. Far from attempting to solve the related conceptual problems, sociologists appear ignorant of repeated demonstrations that conventional definitions of those terms will not bear examination. Consider Barry Barnes's conclusion, one reached after a lengthy and careful examination of several alternative definitions: "We possess no rationality criteria which universally constrain the operation of human reason, and which also discriminate existing belief systems, or their components, into rational and irrational groups" (1974:41).

21. The observation appears inconsistent with Baumgartner's contention (1985) that middle-class residents of a New York City suburb are less likely to complain to legal officials about the conduct of their personal associates, such as relatives or neighbors. However, Baumgartner *did not* (1) express the frequency of the complaints in question as a ratio to the frequency of disputes, (2) emphasize recourse of disputants to a private attorney, or (3) devote much attention to the resolution of disputes that were not between personal associates. Nonetheless,

Baumgartner's emphasis on the reliance of middle-class individuals on "avoidance" suggests that both the frequency and duration or intensity of disputes may be relevant.

22. The argument is consistent with research on ingratiating behavior (Bohra and Pandry, 1984) and with observations by Evans-Pritchard on disputes among the Azande: "A man quarrels with and is jealous of his social equals. . . . Offence is more easily taken at the words or actions of an equal than of a superior or inferior" (1977:104–5). Although Evans-Pritchard did not emphasize the relation between social inequality and authority, some of his observations do suggest a relation, one instance being: "A noble is socially so separated from commoners that were a commoner to quarrel with him it would be treason" (104–5).

Basic Types of Control, Power, and Major Questions

A simple control typology is provided in this chapter to clarify control's generic meaning and demonstrate that control is a very broad notion. The generic definition of control in chapter 2 makes the notion so inclusive that research and theory should focus initially on one of three basic types— inanimate, biotic, and human (human control over human behavior).

Inanimate Control

Attempted inanimate control is overt behavior by a human in the belief that (1) the behavior increases or decreases the probability of an inanimate thing's existence or a change in the thing's characteristics and (2) the increase or decrease is desirable. An inanimate thing may be a solid object (e.g., a rock), an observable substance (e.g., a body of water), or an unobservable substance (e.g., a volume of gas); and a characteristic may pertain to any property, such as location, shape, size, weight, color, composition, texture, or odor.

When the first primate threw a rock at a predator, he or she engaged in inanimate control to facilitate biotic control, driving off an animal. Such use of inanimate things is rare among animals, and the primate altered only the rock's location. The next and more important stage in inanimate control was the modification of inanimate objects, such as stripping a twig preliminary to inserting it into a nest and pulling out insects to eat, as chimpanzees do. From that stage onward, inanimate control increasingly became technological.

Technology

Appreciable agreement is realized in identifying *some* things as technological, but what do they share in common that makes them distinctive? Little is gained by replying that they are tools or machines. The meaning of either word is too vague for consensus in answers to several questions. Are these tools or machines: shoes, maps, gasoline, bolts, buckets, sails, eyeglasses, pencils, houses, sweaters, ropes, and gates? If so, why? If not, why not? If only some qualify, which ones?

PROPOSED DEFINITION. For reasons just suggested, *tool* and *machine* are unsuitable terms for defining technology. The following definition encompasses all commonly recognized tools and machines but much more: technology includes all inanimate objects or substances made or modified by humans, excluding human food (classes of substances or objects consumed by some or all humans solely for nutrition).[1] Not all features of an object or substance need be made or modified for it to be technological. If a piece of flint is chipped, the flint's ensuing shape alone makes it technological. Likewise, when preparing a field for planting, it is the holes or furrows that make the field technological. Once made or modified, an inanimate thing's subsequent use is conceptually irrelevant; and some things used for a human purpose are not technological (e.g., throwing an unmodified rock at an animal).

The proposed definition facilitates classifying things without disagreement or without leaving the rationale obscure. Thus, in addition to unquestioned tools and machines, technology includes, among other things, shoes, maps, gasoline, bolts, buckets, sails, eyeglasses, pencils, houses, sweaters, ropes, and gates.

ANTICIPATED OBJECTIONS. For obscure reasons, a few writers accept a "material" definition of technology but only if it limits technology to things "used to realize physical goals." Although that phrase is less ambiguous than "useful purpose" (Oswalt, 1976:24), difficult questions are raised. Used by whom and how many? Must the use be uniform? If not, what criteria determine predominant use?

As the questions indicate, the phrase "material things used to realize physical goals" is ambiguous; and the suggested designation of symbolic artifacts as nontechnological is especially debatable. A painting is surely symbolic; but if hanging a painting in a room is not the pursuit of a physical goal, what is it? Then what of symbolic artifacts (e.g., traffic lights) that are used to control human behavior? Likewise, what is the purpose of displaying paintings in an art gallery if not to attract people physically? The general point: a definition of technology that excludes instruments of behavior control greatly diminishes the notion's utility.

If technology is defined in terms of use rather than origin, the distinction between analytic and synthetic statements about it becomes blurred. In particular, many technological items appear efficient in that they reduce the amount of time and/or human energy to realize physical goals; but if technology is so defined, the claim that technology is efficient becomes tautological.

Other definitions suggest that technology includes not only material things but also (1) knowledge pertaining to those things and (2) the way goods or services are produced, including the organization of production (e.g., corporations, the division of labor, assembly lines). To identify various kinds of knowledge or beliefs as technological makes the notion of technology extremely broad; and there is an obvious alternative—identify them as "technical knowledge." Moreover, if production organization is identified as technology, then a well-known argument—the latter determines the former—becomes confusing, for it suggests that technology determines technology. Such confusion is promoted by the rejection of a material definition of technology. "A final reason that advanced technologies have more division of labor is that a high degree division of labor is *part* of an advanced technology" (Stinchcombe, 1983:89). The argument blurs the distinction between a conceptual link and an empirical association. Similarly, granted that "No tool exists apart from social organization, or from ideas and beliefs" (White, 1973:13), why establish the connection by definition?

CONTENDING DEFINITIONS. Subsequent quotations demonstrate, Frisbie and Clarke (1979) notwithstanding, great diversity in definitions of technology.

Barbour: "Technology may be defined as the organization of knowledge for the achievement of practical purposes. It is a set of skills, techniques, and activities for the shaping of materials and the production of objects for practical ends. . . . We will be using the term technology to refer to a broad set of human activities, and not simply to the machines and tools that constitute the hardware of technology" (1980:35).

Lenski and Lenski: " 'Technology' refers to the information, techniques, and tools with which people utilize the material resources of their environment to satisfy their many needs and desires" (1974:38).

Gendron: "A technology is any systemized practical knowledge, based on experimentation and/or scientific theory, which enhances the capacity of society to produce goods and services, and which is embodied in productive skills, organization or machinery" (1977:23).

Hannay and McGinn: "technology can be characterized as that form of cultural activity devoted to the production or transformation of material objects, or the creation of procedural systems in order to expand the realm of practical human possibility. . . . As for . . . content . . . let us define *a technology* as the complex of knowledge, methods, and other resources used in making a particular kind of product or in creating a particular procedural system" (1980:27).

Oswalt: "An artifact is the end product resulting from the modification of a physical mass in order to fulfill a useful purpose. . . . Technology may be defined as all the ways in which people produce artifacts. . . ." (1976: 24, 33).

Richter: "for present purposes it will be most convenient to abandon the conception of technology-as-knowledge, and to define technology to encompass tools and practices deliberately employed as natural (rather than supernatural) means for attaining clearly identifiable ends" (1982:8).

White: "Technology consists of tools and weapons and techniques of using them" (1975:17).

Weinstein: "*technology* refers primarily to a system of knowledge intended to have practical bearing—know-how" (1982:xi).

ISSUES AND PROBLEMS.   Although never demonstrably invalid, definitions are not beyond criticism, especially as regards prospective empirical applicability. A definition is empirically applicable to the extent that independent investigators agree in applying it to identify particular events or things; and given negligible agreement, the definition serves no purpose unless it pertains to a purely theoretical notion.

Only actual attempts to apply a definition can be conclusive, but judgments about prospective empirical applicability need not be sheer opinion. No definition is empirically applicable if unintelligible or inconsistent, and Barbour's definition illustrates inconsistency. The first sentence limits technology to knowledge, but the second creates doubts, and the last refers to an activity. Then some definitions can be misleading. As one case, Richter's definition indicates that technology includes "tools," but he subsequently states: "It is possible to have not only technologies that do not entail tool using, but also technologies that consist essentially of refraining from doing certain things" (1982:12).

Vague terminology and dubious distinctions abound in definitions of technology. Examine these phrases from the contending definitions (*supra*): "aspects of the pattern of activities," "form of cultural activity," "procedural systems," and "the capacity of society." Those phrases are vague, and their rationale is obscure. Yet even Gendron's reification—"the capacity of society to produce"—is a minor offense compared to two common practices in writing on technology: (1) a failure to recognize conceptual problems (e.g., Susskind, 1973:1) and (2) recognition but with no attempted resolution (e.g., Winner, 1977:8–12).

The major contrast between definitions of technology is the material-nonmaterial emphasis, but two definitions may emphasize the nonmaterial and yet otherwise differ sharply. Thus, Weinstein and Gendron would limit technology to knowledge, whereas Oswalt would limit it to "ways" of producing artifacts. As for definitions (e.g., Lenski and Lenski) that are not exclusively "material" or "nonmaterial," the inclusion of objects or substances, overt behavior, and internal behavior (e.g., knowledge) makes technology such an unmanageably broad notion that fruitful theories are unlikely.[2] Then note again that a broad definition tends to blur the distinction between analytical and synthetic statements. Contemplate Brooks's statement: "Technology must be sociotechnical rather than technical, and a technology must include the managerial and social supporting systems necessary to apply it on a significant scale" (1980:65). Is the statement analytic or synthetic?

Biotic Control

Although social scientists often appear indifferent to it, starvation has been common throughout history (Sorokin, 1975); and even if human starvation should cease, the importance of the food quest would remain. The quest is a study in biotic control, but that basic type of control is becoming increasingly important for additional reasons.

A Definition and a Typology

Attempted biotic control is overt behavior by a human in the belief that (1) the behavior increases or decreases the probability of an organism's existence or a change in any of the organism's characteristics but including behavioral changes only in the case of nonhuman organisms and (2) the increase or decrease is desirable. An organism is a living plant or animal (human or nonhuman); and a characteristic pertains to any property, such as size, shape, weight, color, texture, composition, or odor. The definition applies to a human killing a turtle or planting seeds, but various kinds of biotic control (e.g., dentistry, cutting lawns, training animals) are not food quests. However, virtually all kinds can be assigned to one of six subtypes.

GATHERING FOOD.   Whatever Adam and Eve's indiscretion, biotic control became onerous. Short of Eden, all environments are potentially lethal for humans, meaning that they can gather enough food in the wild state to survive only by moving about, commonly over several miles.

The spatial mobility required to gather food is a variable in the "starvation equation." Movement without technology requires human energy; and if the calories burned exceeds the food's caloric value, starvation is imminent.

HUNTING AND FISHING.   Anthropologists commonly describe the pursuit of small, slow animals as food gathering. However, the distinction between hunting or fishing and gathering food is clear only if the former is defined as the pursuit of undomesticated animals regardless of their size or mobility.

Hunting and fishing are generally much more technologically intensive than food gathering, and there is an obvious reason. Some animals are so swift, powerful, and/or dangerous that successful control of them virtually requires technology (e.g., spears, nets). So hunting or fishing may have been the first major impetus for technological innovation.

DOMESTICATION OF PLANTS. An indescribable variety of activities has entered into plant domestication. The earliest activity may have been only protective, perhaps driving animals from wild plants. In any case, humans can facilitate wild plant growth several ways, such as watering, fertilizing, and weeding.

Plant domestication is not limited to farming or forestry; it also includes experimental work (other than genetic engineering) undertaken to modify the shape, size, weight, color, composition, growth rate, or adaptability of plants, including trees. Moreover, numerous varieties of inanimate control (e.g., plowing) and human control (e.g., hiring farm laborers) enter into contemporary plant domestication, but the basic types of control are often closely integrated. Designating control behavior as (for example) inanimate-biotic, human-biotic, inanimate-human-biotic, or human-inanimate-biotic introduces a complexity; but sociology's conceptual apparatus must recognize that a human's actions are often manifold, processual, and functionally integrated.

DOMESTICATION OF ANIMALS. Whenever and wherever the first human controlled an animal without killing it, the first step was taken in animal domestication. The second step was to extend control over and protect an animal long enough for its reproduction.

No one questions that plant domestication was conducive to sedentary spatial organization and substantial population density. However, animal domestication was also a major evolutionary step. Several populations came to specialize in pastoralism, and in some cases extensive plant domestication may have required earlier animal domestication. Meat is a major protein source for many human populations, and animal domestication was probably the impetus for technological innovations (inanimate control). Various technological items are used in animal domestication—ropes, saddles, harnesses, wagons, carts, etc.; and the division of labor is another important correlate of animal domestication. Only a few occupations have evolved with animal domestication, such as the veterinarian, but the eventual result was extensive product specialization in manufacturing (e.g., barbed wire, saddles). Perhaps most important, applied scientific research (e.g., immunology) devoted to animal domestication is beyond estimation, and selective breeding of animals is an ancient form of biotic control. Finally, keeping pets is a puzzling but distinctive human practice.

Try to imagine feudalism or the Spanish conquest of Mexico without the horse. Although those episodes suggests that the horse's domestication had an enormous impact on human history, the first domesticator did not anticipate feudalism or Mexico's conquest; rather, those episodes were clearly unintended consequences of biotic control. Nonetheless, the horse's domestication is another reason to argue that all major episodes in human history stem from control attempts.

SOMATIC CONTROL. As the proportion of the labor force in agriculture declines, biotic control appears to become less important. Yet the necessity of food remains, and biotic control has gone far beyond domestication.

Millions of Americans make a living by altering the shape, size, weight, or functioning of human organs. Surgeons are obvious practitioners of such *somatic control*; but health care in general qualifies, and the number of related occupations (e.g., dentists, nurses, dieticians, and physical therapists) is astonishing. Finally, humans employ various means to promote or prevent births (see, e.g., Stinchcombe, 1983: 193–97), which makes somatic control all the more diverse and important.

GENETIC ENGINEERING. For thousands of years humans have altered the shape, size, weight, color, composition, and behavior of animate things through selective breeding. That kind of biotic control only narrows the gene pool of particular sets of organisms. Now, however, humanity has reached the penultimate biotic control—the direct alteration of genetic material, which could be a step toward the literal creation of life from inanimate substances.

Control is the only candidate for sociology's central notion that facilitates describing and thinking about modes of producing genetic change, which is all the more important because sociologists have a terrible record when it comes to anticipating change. They have no notion that facilitates describing and thinking about all logically possible future worlds; instead, they try to make do with such time-bound notions as bureaucracy and capitalism.

Control over Human Behavior: Internal Control or Self-control

Any adult has asked himself or herself a question something like these: What must I do to eat less? If I find a new job, will I be less depressed? How can I stop smoking? Such questions pertain to self-control, but an explicit definition is needed. Attempted self-control is overt behavior by a human in the belief that (1) the behavior increases or decreases the probability of some particular kind of subsequent behavior by the individual and (2) the increase or decrease is desirable.

Some Issues

Those who equate reality with "the observable" will question the very idea of self-control; but "observable" is no more the touchstone of reality than "experienceable," and the latter justifies the notion of self-control. No one is likely to deny ever striving to modify their behavior—to drink less, to act more decisively, etc. But self-control is not just avoiding vices, overcoming fears, and the like, all of which illustrate the "challenge" view of self-control.[3] Much of human behavior is self-control primarily because humans believe that acts are functionally interrelated, as when an act is perceived as necessary for a subsequent act. For example, an individual acts in the belief that dialing increases the probability that he or she will speak on the telephone. True, one act may be believed to follow another with absolute certainty, but such beliefs simply pertain to maximum probability (i.e., 1.0.). Moreover, although humans rarely use the term *probability*, let alone literally calculate probabilities, no sense of "self" would develop without beliefs as to consequences of their behavior. Consider Blumer's statement about that term: "It means merely that a human being can be an object of his own action" (1969:12). To be an object of one's action is to engage in self-control, but self-control is not an exclusively "mental" phenomena. It entails overt behavior and in some cases even the use of material objects, such as watches (see Landes, 1983). After all, "setting" an alarm clock is overt behavior in the belief that it increases the probability of some subsequent behavior.

SOME ALTERNATIVE CONCEPTUALIZATIONS.   The pursuit of a definition of self-control that makes exclusive reference to overt behavior could reflect a concern with empirical applicability rather than an epistmemological dogmatism, such as that displayed by Watson and Skinner in psychology.[4] Nonetheless, the pursuit results in definitions that are vague or arbitrary, if not grotesque. Consider Thoresen and Mahoney's explicit overt-behavior-only definition: "A person displays self-control when in the relative absence of immediate external constraints, he engages in behavior whose previous probability has been less than that of alternatively available behaviors" (1974:12). Subsequently, the authors write: "Thus the individual who has usually smoked at parties is exhibiting self-control if—in the absence of externally controlled factors such as physical illness or the unavailability of cigarettes—he refrains from smoking at a party" (14). The illustration promotes understanding of the definition but only because withdrawal discomfort can be attributed to the ex-smoker (i.e., the illustration is that of self-control as "challenge"). Moreover, the definition is astonishing in light of another illustration: after decades of unblemished conduct, a male professor rapes a coed in his office.

Although "behavioristic" conceptualizations of self-control are conducive to absurdities, the present definition of self-control is compatible with the behavioral view Blankstein and Polivy (1982:2) attribute to Skinner: "an individual engages in self-control when she or he arranges the environment so that only certain controlling stimuli are present."[5] While Blankstein and Polivy do recognize that "behavior is a function of the environment, but the environment itself is controlled by the organism" (3), they conveniently ignore Skinner's failure to emphasize the need for conceptual recognition of internal behavior.[6] For that matter, the greatest sensitivity to self-control's importance has been displayed not by a psychologist or a sociologist but by an economist, Thomas C. Schelling (1984).

Attributions of Self-Control

The experiential reality of self-control lies in (1) making choices, (2) acting overtly in a manner consistent with a choice, (3) being unable to make a choice, or (4) being unable to act overtly in a manner consistent with a choice. The last two experiences pertain to lack of self-control, but any conceptualization of self-control should clarify that notion. No adult is likely to deny having thoughts something like these: "I do not know what I will do." "I do not know what I ought to do." Such thoughts are a far cry from overt behavior in the belief that it increases or decreases the probability of some subsequent desirable act.

Just as individuals may experience a lack of self-control, so may they attribute lack of it to others.[7] Imagine someone talking into a telephone without lifting the receiver. Insane? But "insane" is one of several English words that suggest an attribution of a lack of self-control. Adults believe acts are functionally interrelated; hence, when an individual repeatedly behaves contrarily, observers conclude that the individual is mentally impaired (or a gifted comedian).

Avoiding Ambiguities

The present conceptualization would be incomplete without recognition of at least some ambiguities, two of which can best be introduced as questions. First question: What constitutes internal behavior? If only cognitive or mental phenomena (thinking, perceiving, etc.) and affective or evaluative phenomena (feeling, emotion, etc.) are designated, what is loosely called "physiological functioning" would be excluded. It may appear that such instances as heartbeat are not even subject to control, but research on "biofeedback" (see Yates, 1980) indicate that some individuals can alter some physiological functions within a broad range. However, granted that any biofeedback technique is attempted self-control, what of dieting to lose weight or exercising to alter body contours? Stated more generally, what is the distinction between self-control of internal behavior and somatic control of body structure? Since the weight, size, or shape of a body part is scarcely "behavior," a human's attempt to alter those structural properties of his or her body is somatic control. Correlatively, a human's attempt to control his or her physiological functioning is an attempt at self-control.

Second question: Are the means of attempted control relevant in identifying the self-control of internal behavior? A simple negative answer must suffice, but some of the many implications require an all too brief consideration. The negative answer justifies identifying psychopharmacology (see Pope, 1985) as the study of a subsubtype of self-control, the subtype being "chemical self-control." Only an incorrigible Durkheimian or Skinnerian would deny the potential significance of psychopharmacology for the behavioral and social sciences, especially on recognizing that, the label notwithstanding, drugs are not taken or administered to alter or maintain only internal behavior (see Gabe and Lipshitz-Phillips, 1984). Yet one may protest: Preparing or ingesting any chemical substance is inanimate control. That it is; however, control behavior is commonly a series of acts, no two of which are the same type (or subtype or kind) of control. Hence, if the final act in a series determines the identification of the type or subtype of control, all preceding acts identify the subtype or subsubtype. Thus, "chemical self-control" (e.g., ingesting a tranquilizer) signifies inanimate control in attempted self-control, and using an alarm clock to wake up is an instance of "mechanical self-control." However, Skinnerian derision notwithstanding, the alternative to inanimate control in self-control is not just "willing it." Virtually any kind of successful control of one's physiological functioning without inanimate control requires some kind of overt behavior, even if only remaining still.

Finally, the notion of self-control is rich with paradoxes that can be illustrated only briefly. Whereas suicide may appear to stem from a lack of self-control, it is actually (by definition) the deceased's last successful attempt at self-control.

External Control Over Human Behavior: Proximate Control

Attempted proximate control is overt behavior by a human in the belief that (1) the behavior *directly* increases or decreases the probability of a change in the behavior of one or more other humans and (2) the increase or decrease is desirable. The "directly" signifies no intermediary (third party) in proximate control. Thus, should X order Y to order Z, X's action in relation to Z would not be proximate control. But proximate control is not necessarily dyadic. There are situations in which an individual controls numerous individuals simultaneously, as when an officer shouts an order to an infantry platoon.

The Ubiquity of Proximate Control

Although commands and requests are conspicuous instances, there are various other kinds of proximate control, even though such words as *command*, *order*, *instruct*, and *direct* are treated here as synonyms, as are *request*, *plea*, *beg*, and *implore*. Thus, an explicit offer of an exchange or a promise is not a command or a request, but it is attempted proximate control, as are direct threats.

Coercive control is a very distinctive kind of proximate control. It entails the use of a purely physical force or process, as when (1) holding or shoving someone, (2) using an inanimate object to restrain or move someone by purely mechanical principles, (3) administering an inanimate substance (e.g., a chemical) to immobilize or kill a human, or (4) using some inanimate object (e.g., a knife) to terminate or limit someone's behavior. Weber (1978:34–35) notwithstanding, "psychological coercion" is a misnomer; and control through the threat of coercion is not coercive control (i.e., the threat of coercion is not coercion). As defined here, coercive control is not realized through symbols or any kind of communication; it is strictly mechanical or chemical (hence, its distinctiveness).

The variety of proximate control is so great that some kinds can be described by a phrase but not by one word or term. For example, no one is likely to identify "inviting a friend to dinner" as a request, let alone a command; nonetheless, it is attempted proximate control. The same is true of numerous other phrases, such as: "hailing a cab," "signaling for a turn," and "saying hello."

Some Issues

Although no dictionary definition justifies it, sociologists will deny that the phrases describe control attempts. So why the denial? One answer that sociologists have a narrow conception of control over human behavior because they think of control as an evil. Thus, sociologists do not think of a dinner invitation as attempted control; and many would bristle at Burns's statement: "the way in which persons deal with others always consists in an attempt to control them. . . ." (1958:137).

One defense of the control-as-evil argument is that attempts at control over human behavior are commonly resisted. But even if all attempts are resisted, the rationale for making resistance a criterion is obscure, and there would be an astonishing implication. Because a control attempt can be resisted only if recognized, secretive control becomes a logical impossibility. So evil or resistance to control is conceptually irrelevant. Granted, of all human behavior, control attempts may be *commonly* the most evil and/or dangerous; but that is another rationale for making control sociology's central notion.

ANOTHER ISSUE. Given the variety of proximate control, this objection is likely: But most of interaction is proximate control. Perhaps so, and that is still another rationale for identifying control as sociology's central notion.[8] However, the argument is not really radical, if only because numerous theorists have described interaction in terms that identify it as control in light of the present conceptualization. Consider Parsons's observation on interaction: "Part of ego's expectation . . . consists in the probable reaction of alter to ego's possible action, a reaction which comes to be anticipated in advance and thus to affect ego's own choices" (1951:5). Because ego's actions are manifested in overt behavior, ego is attempting to control alter's behavior.

Despite what has been said, some sociologists will claim that most interaction is not proximate control. In particular, because "saying hello" appears unreflective and habitual, critics will deny that it is a control attempt. The denial implies that control is always conscious and deliberate, terms that are alien to the present conceptualization. Moreover, if in saying hello we do not act in the belief that the behavior increases the probability of a response and the increase is desirable, why are we surprised and miffed by no response?

Whereas control is a more inclusive notion than interaction because of inanimate and biotic control, the conceptual link between control and action is more complicated. The best known definition of action, Weber's, promises negligible empirical applicability and creates doubts about action's sociological significance: "We shall speak of 'action' insofar as the acting individual attaches a subjective meaning to his behavior—be it overt or covert, omission or acquiescence. Action is 'social' insofar as its subjective meaning takes account of the behavior of others and is thereby oriented in its course" (1978:4).[9] In suggesting that "social action" can be entirely internal behavior, Weber jeopardized the term's empirical applicability and promoted indifference to it.

External Control Over Human Behavior: Sequential Control

The limits of effective proximate control are suggested when one tries to imagine an army in which all social relations are dyadic (i.e., no component of the army exceeds two members). That arrangement would not preclude commands, but there would be no chain of command. Yet there is a chain of command in all armies, and a chain of command is sequential control, not proximate control.

Attempted sequential control is a command or request by one human to another in the belief that (1) it increases the probability of a subsequent command or request by the other human to still other humans and (2) the increase is desirable. For simplicity, the definition pertains to the minimum conditions, at least three individuals and at least two commands or requests; and further discussion is limited to a chain of commands, by far the most common sequential control.

The Near Ubiquity of Sequential Control

Most external control over human behavior is of the proximate type; but the amount of sequential control is beyond reckoning, one reason being the limits of effective proximate control. The sheer number of prospective controlees is the most conspicuous consideration, but the relation between sheer numbers and the limits of effective proximate control is contingent on, among other things, communication technology. Whatever the relation, why are there effective limits? One can shout a command to thousands of individuals, perhaps millions, depending on technology; but that is the case only if there is one command that applies to everyone, for example: Fire toward the hill! If each of numerous commands applies only to some individuals, the commands cannot be given simultaneously by one individual. Yet success in a major battle requires that numerous and diverse commands be given more or less simultaneously; hence, sequential control is an essential feature of military organization.

A variety of simultaneous commands implies differentiation in the activities of the controlees (e.g., some fire guns, others repair equipment, still others transport ammunition) and coordination or synchronization of activities (e.g., an aerial bombardment followed by a land attack). Because hundreds of different activities cannot be carried out simultaneously unless there are hundreds of individuals, proximate control tends to give way to sequential control as the number of controlees increases. Yet sequential control is conspicuous in military units not because of uncritical conformity to tradition, nor does it stem from some structural property. Rather, sequential control stems from the human concern with effective control. Any doubts can be ended by attempting to command an army in battle or managing an airline through proximate control alone. That point will be lost on sociologists who eschew concern with control because they view it as reducing sociology to psychology. They seek to avoid reductionism by pursuing "structural" questions, such as: What is the relation between an army's size and the number of its organizational components (e.g., regiments, batallions, companies)? Even if there is a relation, sooner or later sociological structuralists must confront this question: Why does it obtain? An adequate answer requires reference to a human concern with control effectiveness.

External Control Over Human Behavior: Social Control

Whereas sociologists have devoted little attention to proximate or sequential control, they have used the term *social control* extensively throughout this century; but it is a major sociological term only in that sense. There is no well-known theory on the subject, and no major line of work on it in sociology's literature other than, possibly, deterrence research (Gibbs, 1986).[10] The sad history (see Cohen, 1985:2–9) is hardly puzzling; from the outset sociologists failed to realize a defensible conceptualization, the immediate reason being their indifference to conceptual problems.

Principal Conceptualizations

E.A. Ross published the first book on social control in 1901, and he established the tradition of ignoring conceptual problems. Consistent with his book's subtitle, *Survey of the Foundations of Order*, Ross wrote as though social control is anything that maintains social order. After quoting Ross's definition of social control as "concerned with that domination which is intended and which fulfills a function in the life of society," Pitts commented: "Yet when he [Ross] described social control in action, he fell back upon all the forms of the Durkheimian *conscience collective* that constrain the individual: public opinion, law, belief systems, education, custom, religion. . . ." (1968:382). So, despite his definition, Ross treated social control as though internal behavior is irrelevant.

Ross suggested that social control's locus is in institutions—education, religion, law, etc.—meaning that institutions maintain social order. Because the terms *social order* and *institution* denote vague notions, they cannot be used to clarify the meaning of *social control*. Then there are objections to Ross's logic. Given that institutions are components of social order, to say that the former contribute to the maintenance of the latter is to imply that social order maintains social order. And what of social control within and over institutions? Presume a demonstration that Catholicism's confessional somehow promotes conformity to putative norms. Even so, why do priests and the laity engage in the confessional? Surely it is not instinctual, and it does not tax credulity to suppose that social control is required to maintain that practice. Then consider Mount's argument. He points out that we are led to think of the family as "propping up the established order"; but he introduced his monograph with this conclusion: "The family is the enduring permanent enemy of all hierarchies, churches and ideologies" (1982:1). Finally, Ross made this question illogical: Does social control contribute to the maintenance of social order? By definition, if something does not maintain social order, it cannot be social control.

ENTER TALCOTT PARSONS.   In the early fifties, sociologists began defining social control by reference to deviant behavior (or deviance). The change can be traced largely to statements by Talcott Parsons, like those that follow (1951:297, 321): "The theory of social control is the obverse of the theory of the genesis of deviant behavior tendencies. It is the analysis of those processes in the social system which tend to counteract the deviant tendencies. . . . . . . Every social system has, in addition to the obvious rewards for conformative and punishments for deviant behavior, a complex system of unplanned and largely unconscious mechanisms which serve to counteract deviant tendencies."

Although Parsons's counteraction-of-deviance conception of social control is now conventional (see, e.g.,Cohen, 1985:1), it is a thicket of problems. The immediate problem stems from the common definition of deviant behavior, something like this: behavior that is contrary to the norms of some social unit. Because Parsons defines social control by reference to deviant behavior and because the latter is in turn conventionally defined by reference to norms, then problems in conceptualizing norms (chapter 1) create problems with the counteraction-of-deviance conception of social control; it refers to something (deviance) that cannot be identified readily. The problems are not solved by defining deviant behavior as that which is subject to social control and then defining social control by reference to deviant behavior (see Black, 1976:9,105).

Even if there were no problems with the notions of norms and deviance, Parsons's definition precludes identifying some highly organized manipulations of human behavior on a massive scale as social control. Think of American advertising, an industry in which thousands attempt to manipulate the behavior of millions. Yet their efforts are not social control in light of the counteraction-of-deviance conception unless a failure to buy a particular product is deviant, and extending the notion of deviance to such behavior raises doubts about the notion itself. If buying a Ford is deviant from the viewpoint of Chevrolet advertisers and vice versa, then deviance becomes an all inclusive notion, for in a large social unit virtually any act is disapproved by someone.

Finally, think of Hitler's efforts to further electoral support of the Nazi party. If an attempt to sway the electorate is the "counteraction of deviance," then that notion is unmanageably broad. Should it be argued that Hitler perceived himself as counteracting deviance, the argument makes deviance so relative that virtually any behavior qualifies, meaning that someone disapproves of it.[11] Thus, even if most citizens disapprove of terrorism, terrorists view themselves as counteracting deviance; but advocates of the counteraction-of-deviance conception of social control are prone to identify terrorists as objects rather than *agents* of social control. Yet if an organized attempt to overthrow a government is not social control, what is it? The general point (see Burke, 1980:59, for elaboration) is that the counteraction-of-deviance conception of social control erroneously presupposes an indisputable and empirically applicable answer to this question: What and who is deviant?

Parsons's statement amounts to a denial that social control has any necessary connection with internal behavior. Thus, if the custom of wearing a wedding ring promotes marital fidelity and if adultery is deviant, then the custom is social control regardless of anyone's intention, perception, or beliefs. Likewise, the billions spent annually on U.S. prisons and jails is not social control without a demonstration that incarceration does in fact "counteract" crime.[12] Finally, like Ross's conception, Parsons's conception precludes the distinction between successful and unsuccessful social control; and it makes this question illogical: Does social control counteract deviance?

THE SOCIAL QUALITY OF SOCIAL CONTROL.　Despite its shortcomings, the counteraction-of-deviance conception does imply an answer to an important question: What is social about social control? To illustrate, the counteraction-of-deviance conception suggests a rationale for *not* identifying the behavior of a typical bank robber as social control, nor the behavior of a traveler when soliciting directions from a stranger. Surely those behaviors are attempts at control, but it could be argued that they are not social control because neither counteracts what is commonly considered to be deviance.

The foregoing takes on added significance in assessing the few instances in the current sociology literature where social control is not defined in terms of reactions to deviance. Such definitions do not clearly identify the social quality of social control. As an instance, examine Goode's statement: "We lay bare its [social control] most important meaning when we focus on how social behavior moves (or fails to move) people to act in ways other people want them to act" (1978:1). Yet any definition is preferable to a common practice in sociology—to use the term *control* or write on "social control" without defining either term (e.g., Dubin, 1986; Hogan, 1985; Janowitz, 1975), let alone confronting conceptual issues and problems.[13] One related practice is to publish an edited book bearing the title of social control without the slightest indication as to the sense in which the individual papers bear on the subject (see, e.g., Suttles and Zald, 1985).

THE FUNDAMENTAL ISSUE.   Of definitions that do not refer to the counteraction of deviance, most are consistent with a statement made by Buckley: "Our perspective embraces the view so well argued by Homans: 'social control' is not a separate part of a system—something 'set up' by or imposed upon a system—but is inherent in the interrelations and interactions of elements that make up the system" (1967:164–65). Buckley's argument seems to reduce to this: the system is social control. But he did express misgivings: "The notion of 'social control' has not had a very successful career in sociology because of difficulties of conceptualization. It has perhaps most often been made virtually synonymous with sociology itself, concerned, for example, with the problem of social order in the broadest sense" (164). Buckley's misgiving is paradoxical because he perpetuates the very conceptual tradition he decries.

Parsons's conception of social control appears different from Buckley's perspective; but both view intention as irrelevant, meaning that social control may or may not be intentional.[14] That view has had a large following from Ross to the present (see, e.g., Carlton, 1977:14); and the reason is implied by Buckley: "The notion of 'control' implies some end or goal, but the sociocultural system . . . can only metaphorically be said to have a goal" (1967:176). So what became of the solution? Define control so that it has no necessary connection with ends, goals, or any kind of internal behavior.

Proposed Alternative

Attempted social control is overt behavior by a human, the first party, in the belief that (1) the overt behavior increases or decreases the probability of a change in the behavior of another human or humans, the second party in either case; (2) the overt behavior involves a third party but not in the way of sequential control; and (3) the increase or decrease is desirable. An understanding of the definition can be furthered by considering five inclusive types of attempted social control.

REFERENTIAL SOCIAL CONTROL. In attempted referential social control the first party always makes reference to a third party in the belief that the reference is necessary for success. The first illustration is a boy's statement to his brother: "Give me back my candy or I'll tell mother." As in all social control, there are three parties; in this case, the boy is the first party, the brother the second party, and their mother the third party.

The illustration erroneously suggests a narrow range of behavior; that the reference to the third party must be explicit and verbal.[15] A nonverbal and implicit reference is well illustrated by the discovery of a European administrative officer in the former Congo (Hallett, 1965:21) that the lenses in the glasses of his black assistant were ordinary glass. When the officer asked "Do things really look different to you when you put them on?," the assistant replied astutely: "No, monsieur. I look different. These *bashenzi*—those ignorant natives—this way they have more respect for me." So it appears that the glasses were worn to prompt other blacks to identify the assistant with Europeans and thereby make them more compliant; hence, in this "associational" subtype of referential control, the assistant was the first party, Europeans the third party, and other blacks in the region the second party.

Impersonation is an implicit and nonverbal means of referential control. To illustrate, when a robbery gang member dresses like a uniformed police officer to enter a bank before or after business hours, he or she is the first party, the bank guard is the second party, and "police" the third party. So the third party may be an indefinite category of individuals, not known by name to the first party and/or the second party. However, both the second and third party may be an indefinite category, as in Hitler's statement (quoted in Waite, 1977:367): "My enemy is Germany's enemy: always and only, the Jew." Note that the first party (Hitler) expressed a negative evaluation of the third party (Jews); hence, the subtype of referential social control is "disassociational." In seeking the electoral and financial support of German gentiles (the second party), Hitler adopted this Machiavellian principle of referential control: to control someone, attack his or her enemies or praise his or her friends.

The third party need not be a living human being, the illustration being this statement: "Your mother would die again if she knew of your addiction." Then when first party threatens the second party with "God's wrath," the third party is a supernatural being.[16] Finally, the third party may be fabricated by the first party, as in Rock's description of a creditor's tactic when writing to debtors: "One mail order firm invented a debt-collector because the word 'debt collector' flourishes a threat" (1973:23).

Despite the illustrations, referential social control is not an exclusively micro phenomenon. Law is surely a macro phenomenon, and just as surely it is a study in referential social control. In American courts attorneys commonly address a judge something like this: "Your Honor, my argument is consistent with a Supreme Court ruling." As for criminal statutes, they threaten a punishment for a designated kind of behavior (e.g., burglary), but it is judges and wardens who impose legal punishment. So in enacting a criminal statute, legislators make implicit reference to what a third party will do to a violator (second party).

The first party need not make reference to what the third party will do, is doing, or has done to the second party (or anyone else). Instead, the reference may be to what will happen, is happening, or has happened to the third party; or what the third party will think or feel, is thinking or feeling, or has thought or felt.

ALLEGATIVE SOCIAL CONTROL. In attempted allegative social control, the first party always communicates an allegation about the second party to the third party in the belief that (1) the allegation will increase or decrease the probability of the third party doing something to the second party and (2) the "something" will change or maintain the second party's behavior. The allegation may be any kind: what the second party has done or may do, who the second party is, what could happen to the second party, etc. In any case, the first party perceives the allegation as an appeal to the third party's normative standards or interests and as necessary to elicit some action by the third party toward the second party.

Suppose that a boy makes this statement to his mother about his brother: "Fred took my candy." As for interpretation, no one should study social control in any context (be it a family or a country) without thorough knowledge of that context. If the mother has commanded Fred to do things in the boy's presence, an experienced observer would entertain this conclusion: the boy believes that his mother can make Fred return the candy. Finally, while the allegation may be false, credibility is essential for success in allegative control.[17] In the illustration, the boy's attempt at control will fail if the mother does not believe his allegation.

Lest the illustrative case suggest that allegative control is limited to the nuclear family, consider actions in tort law. The plaintiff or the plaintiff's attorney, the first party in either case, makes allegations about the defendant (second party) to a judge or jury (third party). For that matter, a criminal trial is a study in allegations, and the police often investigate in response to allegations that they construe as complaints (indeed, they commonly require complaints).

Although both allegative and referential control entail judgments by the first party about authority, normative standards, and credibility, the two are distinct. Whereas in referential control the first party does not presume that the third party will become involved directly, that presumption is essential in allegative control. However, one and the same act can be both allegative and referential control. To illustrate, although Hitler engaged in Jew-baiting to gain the support of German gentiles (referential control, with Jews as the third party), he may have acted also in the belief that it would provoke violence against Jews that would drive some of them from Germany (allegative social control, with Jews as the second party).

VICARIOUS SOCIAL CONTROL. In all instances of attempted vicarious social control the first party attempts to punish the third party, reward the third party, or somehow rectify the third party's behavior, always presuming that such action will influence the second party's behavior. Because the first party does not make reference to the third party, vicarious control differs from referential control. Likewise, because the first party does not presume that the third party will do something to the second party, vicarious control differs from allegative control.

Vicarious control is conspicuous in the administration of criminal law. In imposing a prison sentence on a convicted felon, a judge may believe that it is necessary to deter others; if so, the judge is the first party, the convicted felon the third party, and all potential offenders the second party. Vicarious control is the basis of the general deterrence doctrine, which enters into criminal justice policy throughout most of the world (see Morris, 1966:631).

After decades of research, the deterrence doctrine's validity remains disputable (see Gibbs, 1986); nonetheless, imposing legal punishment to deter others is attempted vicarious control. However, some critics argue that legal punishments should be retributive, meaning that criminals should be punished solely because they deserve it. The argument suggests that general deterrence may not be even one aim of those who prescribe or impose legal punishments; and Durkheim (1949:89) asserts that legal punishments simply express the "outrage to morality," meaning that legal punishments are expressive rather than instrumental. Retributivists (including Durkheim) have ignored an instrumental quality of what may appear to be purely retributive punishments. A punishment may be imposed in the belief that it will terminate or prevent a complaint; if so, the punished individual is the third party, as in the case of general deterrence; but those demanding punishment are the second party. Such placative vicarious control is illustrated by Dillon's statement: ". . . Rosemary Harris . . . reports that in order to prevent a disturbance in trade relations with neighboring groups, precolonial trading towns such as Ikom, on the Upper Cross River of Nigeria, sometimes executed their own citizens for killing outsiders" (1980:659). However, one and the same action may be both placative and deterrent as in the case of Henry VIII's harsh response to the "Evil May Day" riot against foreigners in London (1517). "But Henry wished to show the foreign merchants that they could safely come to London and carry on their business there; and, even more important, he would not tolerate anarchy in his realm, or any defiance of his royal authority and laws" (Ridley, 1984:107).

Vicarious control is limited neither to the legal sphere nor to punishment. The first party may reward the third party in the hope that the second party will emulate the third party. Thus, an employer may give a very productive employee a special award in the hope that other employees will work harder.

MODULATIVE SOCIAL CONTROL. Influence is an empirical association between the overt behavior of one or more individuals and subsequent behavior of other individuals. So there is a logical connection between influence and successful external human control: the latter is a subclass of the former. Such conceptualization of influence is essential for understanding modulative social control. In all instances the first party attempts to use the third party's influence on the second party's behavior but not in the belief that making any allegation about or reference to either party is necessary for success.

Advertising executives offer celebrities money to praise products in radio or television commercials. The offer is attempted proximate control, but it makes no sense unless the executive (first party) perceives the celebrity (third party) as having an influence over potential consumers (second party) that the first party does not have. Note that the executive need make no allegation about consumers to the celebrity; so his or her action is not allegative social control. Nor does the executive communicate with potential consumers directly, let alone make reference to the celebrity; so the action is not referential social control. Finally, in vicarious social control the first party assumes that "doing something to the third party" will have an influence on the second party's behavior, which is not the case in modulative social control (rather, the third party must do something).

The political sphere is replete with modulative control, although attempts are commonly made to conceal it.[18] Political leaders often contemplate this question: Whom shall I appoint? One common answer: Appoint an influential person. Thus, the President may appoint a black or a woman with a view to furthering electoral and congressional support, the assumption being that the appointee will, among other things, praise the adminstration. As a quite different example, during the Korean War, Chinese officers reportedly moved "natural" leaders from one group to another in prisoner camps, thereby diffusing and supposedly reducing leadership influence (see Schein, 1956:153). A much more common instance occurs when a judge orders lengthy detention of a juvenile offender on the presumption that the isolation will diminish the offender's "bad" influence on his or her siblings and friends.

Modulative control may take the form of the first party increasing the third party's influence, as when a representative of a political party subsidizes a popular writer. Likewise, mill owners have been known to make financial contributions to the ministry of fundamentalist preachers, who admonish mill-hands to accept their fate passively but work diligently (Pope, 1942). As the last two examples suggest, co-optation is a common kind of modulative social control.

In modulative control, the first party perceives the third party as having an influence that the first party lacks, and that feature clarifies the distinction between modulative social control and sequential control. As a chain of command, sequential control operates by this logic: if X can order Y to order Z, then X can order Z.[19] However, when X orders Y to order Z because X presumes that he or she cannot substitute himself or herself for Y, it is modulative social control.

The most frequent kind of modulative social control cannot be described without using the term *agent* or *representative*. Owners and managers of American business firms must look beyond their employees to experts such as lawyers, public relations consultants, and advertising agents. However, when anyone solicits the services of an attorney, they are in effect saying: "By virtue of your expertise, you have an influence over others that I lack."

PRELUSIVE SOCIAL CONTROL. Success in attempting to control numerous individuals is unlikely unless the first party considers alternative means, but a systematic assessment of relative efficacy may require substantial time and expertise. Indeed, limited resources may prompt the first party to confront this question: Which social unit members should be controlled the most? The task of preventing or promoting certain behaviors can require so much time and resources that the first party must exclude entire categories of individuals from the control context, be it a country, a jury, or a building. Finally, regardless of the control type—inanimate, biotic, or human—there are situations in which success is improbable unless something is done to facilitate the control.

All of the foregoing control actions may be so demanding that the first party cannot undertake them. If so, the first party often turns to a third party to do what the first party cannot do; in doing so, the first party engages in prelusive social control. In all instances the first party attempts to increase the probability that the third party will (1) assess the efficacy of alternative or means of control, (2) by surveillance or monitoring identify influential individuals or those who appear inclined to act contrary to the desires of the first party, (3) act so as to exclude certain categories of individuals from participation in some social unit or restrict their spatial movement, and/or (4) take any other action that facilitates the first party's subsequent attempts at external human control.

Because the third party's activities are not necessarily actual control attempts, prelusive social control may appear to be a misnomer. However, like other activities, control can be so highly organized that preliminaries are perceived by the participants as a part of the activity, just as recruiting players is a part of professional football, although distinct from actual games.

Prelusive social control is illustrated dramatically in Orwell's *1984* and Huxley's *Brave New World*. There are also all manner of actual instances, for example: advertising executives paying psychologists to conduct research on the effectiveness of advertisements, governmental agents planting informants to identify members of some organization as "subversives" (see Marx, 1974), and legislators enacting laws that bar designated categories of individuals (e.g., "communists") from entering the country. Exclusion from organizations is an especially common form of prelusive social control. Personnel officers (third parties) are instructed to be selective in recruiting or admitting members (employees or otherwise), meaning to bar particular categories of individuals. True, some exclusionary practices are not followed to reduce the need for control; but the purpose is only rarely obscure, and Etzioni's observations identify the benefits: "The role of selection should be especially emphasized because the liberal-humanist tradition, which prevails in the social sciences, tends to underplay its importance and to stress that of socialization. Actually, various studies indicate that a small increase in the selectivity of an organization often results in a disproportionately large decrease in the investments required for control. . . . One reason is that in most organizations a high percentage of the deviant acts are committed by a small percentage of the participants; hence, if these are screened out, control needs decline sharply" (1968:399).

Reconsideration of a Previous Question

The foregoing conceptualization answers this question: What is social about social control? It involves three parties but not through a chain of commands or requests. Should critics allege that the distinction between social control and other kinds of human control is arbitrary, they will have ignored a previous claim: When it comes to controlling numerous humans simultaneously, social control is more effective than proximate or sequential control.

The most effective defense of any conceptualization is to show that it leads to impressive theories. The present conceptualization cannot be so defended at present, but neither can contending conceptualizations. In particular, the counteraction-of-deviance conception has prevailed for more than thirty years; but, excluding the deterrence doctrine, there is no well-known theory of social control (for an even bleaker commentary, see Cohen, 1985:6). The doctrine is excluded because it antedates the counteraction-of-deviance conception of social control, and it has been ignored by advocates of that conception.

Control and Power

As the following definitions indicate, in the social sciences the notion of power is a conceptual swamp.

Dahl: "power terms . . . refer to *subsets of relations among social units such that the behaviors of one or more units . . . depend in some circumstances on the behavior of other units. . . . . . .* The closest equivalent to the power relation is the causal relation. For the assertion, '*C* has power over *R*' one can substitute the assertion, '*C*'s behavior causes *R*'s behavior' " (1968:407,410).

Emerson: "Thus . . . the power to control or influence the other resides in control over things he values. . . . In short, *power resides implicitly in the other's dependency.* . . . If the dependence of one party provides the basis for the power of the other, that power must be defined as a potential influence. . . ." (1962:32).

McFarland: "Power . . . may be taken to mean intended influence (i.e., intended social causation): *C*'s behavior exercises *power* over *R*'s behavior if and only if *C*'s behavior causes changes in *R*'s behavior *that C intends*" (1969:13).

Nagel: "A power relation, actual or potential, is an actual or potential causal relation between the preferences of an actor regarding an outcome and the outcome itself. . . . In social power relations, the *outcome* must be available indicating the state of another social entity—the behavior, beliefs, attitudes, or policies of a second actor" (1975:29).

Oppenheim: "To have power is to be capable of exercising power, that is, to be able to subject others to one's control or to limit their freedom" (1961:100).

Russell: "Power may be defined as the production of intended effects" (1938:35).

Walter: "One has power over another with respect to a particular act if he can control (cause) the act or make it punishable to perform or to withhold it" (1969:35).

Weber: "'Power' (*Macht*) is the probability that one actor within a social relationship will be in a position to carry out his own will despite resistance, regardless of the basis on which this probability rests" (1978:53).

Major Conceptual Issues and Problems

Whereas some authors depict power as intentional (e.g., McFarland and Russell), others (e.g., Emerson, Nagel, Oppenheim, Walter, and Weber) are ambiguous about it, and still others (e.g., Dahl) imply that it is conceptually irrelevant. Although no definition is demonstrably valid or invalid, failure to grant or deny intention's relevance is an obfuscation. Of course, intentionality is only one facet of internal behavior; and while a power definition may refer to other facets, it should clearly indicate whether internal behavior is relevant at all.

With few exceptions (e.g., Sites, 1973:1), social scientists who use both the term *power* and the term *control* define the former by reference to the latter. However, in the foregoing definitions only Emerson, Oppenheim, and Walter use the term *control*;[20] and none of them explicitly define it or stipulate the connection between power and control. There are at least four possibilities: (1) control is a subclass of power, (2) power is a subclass of control, (3) control and power are synonyms, or (4) no logical connection exists between the two. Treating the terms as synonyms only sanctions conceptual redundancy, and the fourth possibility is inconsistent with most conceptualizations.

Note again that Dahl's definition of power implies denial of the relevance of intention. If one individual's behavior causes another's behavior, then the former has power over the latter regardless of either individual's intention, perception, or belief. Moreover, because Dahl did not use the term *control*, his definition leaves the logical connection between power and control obscure.

Nothing is gained by avoiding the term *control* in defining power, and it is no solution to say that power is control. That syntax creates either a conceptual redundancy or an ambiguity. If it makes power a subclass of control, there is no suggestion how power differs from other subclasses; and to equate power with "resource control" is merely a contribution to conceptual obscurantism (see Spaeth, 1985).

Toward a Solution

Power can be defined such that neither control nor power is a subclass of the other. Specifically, power can be taken as the capacity or ability for control. That conceptual strategy was employed in only one of the seven illustrative definitions, Oppenheim's; and even his definition leaves a crucial question unanswered: How much control must an individual exercise before he or she has the capacity to control? Any answer would be arbitrary. The problem takes on special significance in examining Weber's definition of power. He did not even suggest how "probability" is to be identified in particular cases, let alone stipulate the level of probability necessary for a power relation. Perhaps that is the reason why in translating Weber (1962:117) Secher used the term *opportunity* rather than *probability*.

WRONG'S CONCEPTUALIZATION. In a thoughtful conceptualization, Wrong defines power as "the capacity of some person to produce intended and foreseen effects on others" (1979:2). So defined, power is not a strictly behavioral phenomenon, rather, it is a capacity. However, the definition does not speak to another version of a previous question: How much intended and foreseen effects must a person produce to have such capacity? So, despite the divergent terminology, Wrong's definition and Oppenheim's definition are subject to the same objection.

Wrong's definition may appear to make control the behavioral side of power—the actual production of intended and foreseen effects; but he rarely used the term *control*, and his summary diagram suggests that the only place for the notion in his elaborate conceptual scheme is the category of unintended influence. That syntax is contrary to the way that the vast majority of English-speaking people use the term *control*; and in various ways Wrong makes it appear that power is intended influence, thereby suggesting that power is actual behavior rather than a capacity. In any case, Wrong and everyone else who has offered a similar definition[21] ignored this question: If *Y* or someone else punishes *X* because of *X*'s previous attempt to control *Y*, in what sense did *X* have power over *Y*? Virtually any adult is capable of producing intended behavioral effects by threatening violence (e.g., pointing a pistol at someone), but it would be questionable to identify that capacity as power.

PROPOSED DEFINITION. The following brief definition is offered as an alternative to Wrong: Power is the perceived capacity for effective control, including the capacity to avoid or preclude retaliation as a reaction to an attempt at control. The definition avoids conceptual redundancy; it does not equate power and control,[22] and the logical connection between power and control is such that one is not a subclass of the other.

The key term in the definition—*perceived capacity* could be construed as redundant, the argument being that any capacity (or ability) must be perceived. Far from rejecting the argument, the term *perceived capacity* has been used to underscore the perceptual character of power. In particular, unlike control, power is not a particular overt act, nor a series of overt acts. As such, a previous question—How much control must an individual exercise before he or she has the capacity to control?—need not be answered. The question can be best confronted by allowing theorists and researchers to recognize types of power consistent with their interests. Unless qualified, the term *power* relates to what researchers themselves perceive as an actor's capacity (or incapacity) for control. Another type of power is "subjective," meaning that it relates to the actor's perceptions of his or her capacity for control.[23] Still another type is "respondent" power, in which case the perceptions are those of actual objects of the actor's previous control attempts. Finally, in the case of "reputational" power the perceptions are those of potential objects of the actor's control attempts.[24] Similar distinctions can be introduced in connection with inanimate, biotic, or self-control, meaning that the perceived capacity to control is not limited to external human control.

Immediate Implications for Research and Theory

Compared to others, the proposed definition of power is conducive to a greater concern with empirical referents and two research questions. First, what are the consequences or postcedent correlates of power (whatever the type)? Second, why do some individuals come to be perceived by themselves and/or others as having greater or less power than the typical individual? Because the first question does not lend itself to a finite answer and because Spector (1986) has provided an excellent illustration of the possible consequences of subjective power of employees (their perceptions of the control they exercise), attention focuses on the second question. The proposed definition suggests this answer: An individual is perceived as having power in direct proportion to the frequency that he or she actually exercises effective control. That proposition does not contradict the widespread belief that power is a correlate of income, occupational position, or property ownership, to mention three possibilities (see Pitcher and Hong, 1986), nor is the proposition inconsistent with the argument that alter perceives ego as having power over him or her to the extent that alter depends on ego (Emerson, 1962). If valid, the belief and argument simply give rise to this question: Why is power a correlate of those things? Of course, variables such as income may not be correlated with the exercise of effective control, but that question will remain unanswered as long as social scientists tolerate uncritical use of the term *power*.

Social scientists commonly speak of power as though it is never symmetrical, as when X is perceived as controlling Y only in a particular context (e.g., at work) but Y is perceived as controlling X in some other context. Then the vague notion of a "power structure" suggests that power is necessarily transitive. Thus, if X is perceived as controlling Y and Y is perceived as controlling Z, then X is perceived as controlling Z.

If power is asymmetrical and transitive by definition, it is rare phenomenon. Of course, the extent to which control is perceived as symmetrical and intransitive may well vary considerably from one social unit to another, but social scientists will not examine the possibility as long as they are allowed to use the term without defining it and make empirical claims about power (e.g., glib statements about some "power structure") without supporting data.

Close reading of some definitions of power (e.g., Oppenheim's, Wrong's) will reveal that the proposed definition is not radical, especially if it is granted that "ability" and "capacity" are synonyms. Moreover, the proposed definition is consistent with two of the few lines of research where investigators have attempted to establish the empirical referents of power. In several community studies (various references in Waste, 1986), "power possessors" have been identified by asking residents questions worded something like this: Who has influence over . . . ? Responses can be thought of in terms of the perceived capacity to control. Then in several studies (see, e.g., Tannenbaum et al., 1974) investigators have asked employees (e.g., factory foremen) questions something like this: "How much does . . . have to say about . . . ?" Again, responses can be thought of in terms of the perceived capacity to control; but the suggestion is not that the measurement of perceived control (in communities or organizations) has been perfected (on problems in the case of organizational control, see Markham et al., 1984).

Six Major Questions about Control

Whether or not control becomes sociology's central notion, sociologists could pursue two goals: (1) explaining variation among social units and over time in the prevalence of basic types or specific means of control (e.g., coercion) and (2) identifying the consequences of such variation. Because the goals are too general to guide research, specific questions are needed.

Six Questions

Many sociologists are interested in variables that appear uncontrolled by anyone. Think of 1988 American statistics pertaining to the crude death rate, income inequality, the robbery rate, the degree of urbanization, occupational differentiation, and number of voluntary associations. Imagine, for example, someone saying: so-and-so acted in the belief that the action would result in a 1988 U.S. crude death rate of 9.6. Yet precise effective control is one thing, but indefinite control attempts are quite another. Thus, although no one effectively and precisely controls the crude death rate, generations of federal and state legislators have voted for laws and related governmental programs in the belief that their votes increased the probability of a decline in the crude death rate.

Although precise effective control of the crude death rate may never be realized, that consideration introduces the first of the six major questions: *What is the efficacy of each major means of attempted control?* There are two presuppositions. First, even though the efficacy of any means of control appears contingent on various conditions, it is meaningful to speak of efficacy in general. Second, sociologists can agree in identifying major means of attempted control, at least enough for continuity in research and theory. Neither presupposition reduces the difficulty of assessing the efficacy of control attempts.[25] Thus, there are horrendous problems in estimating the extent to which an immediate goal of legal "gun control" (e.g., reducing the number of pistols possessed per capita) or an ultimate goal (e.g., reducing the homicide rate) is realized (see, e.g., Lester, 1984), but those problems make the sociological study of control both challenging and important.

SECOND MAJOR QUESTION. As suggested by the first presupposition, any efficacy measure is virtually certain to vary from one condition to another. Such variation is the subject of the second major question: *What determines the efficacy of a given means of control?*

The typical sociological generalization is alien to the spirit of the second major control question. Consider this illustration: Class conflict is inevitable in a capitalist society. If valid, the generalization precludes a capitalist society free of class conflict; but it does not identify the conditions that are necessary and sufficient for the reduction or intensification of class conflict, let alone means to realize those conditions. Moreover, even when a sociological generalization suggests a means, its efficacy is commonly ignored. That is the case because the independent variables in virtually all sociological propositions and theories are such that they cannot be manipulated readily (if at all). The point is not limited to macro theories in which the independent variable is (for example) the division of labor or urbanization. In micro theories, the independent variable is commonly some attitude, value, or cognitive condition that cannot be manipulated readily (again, if at all).

THIRD MAJOR QUESTION.   Admittedly, there have been social units in which no attempt was ever made to control the crude death rate, and attempts never have been made to control all variables that have interested one sociologist or another. Consider primacy in the urban size hierarchy—the ratio of the size of the largest urban unit (city, urban area, or metropolitan area) to the size of smaller urban units (e.g., the second and third combined). In high primacy countries (e.g., Thailand, Denmark), the largest urban unit dwarfs the second largest, and there is enormous international variation in degree of primacy (see, e.g., Mehta, 1964). Nonetheless, American legislators may not even know of primacy, let alone vote on some bill in the hope that passage would increase or decrease the probability of the U.S. becoming a high-primacy country. The point is not merely that legislators refrain from using the term *primacy*. Whoever the actors may be, the question is always: How can their behavior (overt or internal) be described or interpreted in light of the prescribed control terminology? To the extent that sociologists do not agree on such descriptions or interpretations, the conceptual scheme lacks empirical applicability and is a failure.

The foregoing does not undercut the proposal to make control sociology's central notion. Granted that attempts to control certain phenomena (e.g., the mortality rate) are not universal and granted that still other phenomena (e.g., extramarital sex) are more subject to control in some social units than in others, such observations only give rise to the third major question: *As regards attempts to control phenomena, why is the variety of phenomena and the intensity of the attempts much greater in some social units than in others?* Although a complete answer is inconceivable, research and theory can focus on this version of the question: If some particular phenomenon (e.g., human fertility) is subject to control attempts more in some social units than in others, why such contrasts?

FOURTH MAJOR QUESTION.   Whereas attempts to control national weather are extremely rare, attempts to reduce the national armed robbery rate appear fairly common. That contrast introduces the fourth major question:

Why are some types of phenomena more subject to attempts at control than are other types?

Pursuit of an answer will further recognition that the major questions are interrelated; specifically, a defensible answer to the fourth major question is unlikely without extensive attention to the first ("efficacy") question. Thus, the rarity of attempts to control the weather on a national scale is hardly baffling if one considers the effectiveness of possible means.

FIFTH MAJOR QUESTION.   Suppose that functionalists demonstrate what they evidently only assume—that most consequences of human behavior are neither anticipated nor recognized. The demonstration would indicate that various phenomena never have been subject to control attempts, because humans never attempt control without beliefs about behavioral consequences. So we have the primary rationale for the fifth major question: *What are the consequences of control attempts and why are some of them unanticipated and/or unrecognized?*

Because sociologists cannot identify behavioral consequences confidently, there is no immediate prospect for constructive work on the fifth question; but the initial step can focus on a largely ignored subject—beliefs about behavioral consequences. Whatever the actual consequences, whether they are unanticipated and/or unrecognized depends on beliefs about consequences.

SIXTH MAJOR QUESTION.   The most speculative answers will be to the final major question: *What is the future of inanimate, biotic, and human control?* That question directs attention to a possible evolutionary trend, one first suggested by Lester Frank Ward's emphasis (1903) on "telesis," toward ever greater control (inanimate, biotic, and human). If such a trend is demonstrated, it will become even more dubious to deny control's importance, but there is an issue. The belief that the unanticipated consequences of human behavior are the most important is commonly associated with two other beliefs (see Sieber, 1981): first, unanticipated consequences are preponderant; and, second, control attempts at the macro level often result in the very opposite of the intended goal.

Because scientific propositions are conditional (e.g., if X increases, then Y increases), "futurology" may appear inherently conjectural. Thus, given evidence that some feature of inanimate control causes some feature of biotic control, a related prediction about biotic control in, say, 2000 would necessarily assume continuance of some trend in inanimate control (e.g., 1960–85). If the assumption proves invalid, then the prediction must be set aside. Nonetheless, the market for prophecies cannot be glutted, as witness the popularity of futuristic novels, such as Orwell's *1984* and Huxley's *Brave New World*.

Sociologists could do worse than pursue this question about those novels: Are the implied prophecies realistic? Because statements about the possible and impossible are the most reliable guides to the future, answers to the sixth major question about control will hinge largely on answers to the previous major questions.

NOTES

1. Convention is not the only justification for excluding food. If food is technological by definition, a crucial question becomes confusing: How do humans use technology to obtain food?

2. If the trend in definitions of technology continues, the term will become virtually meaningless. Consider Winner's commentary: "In the twentieth century . . . *Technology* has expanded rapidly in both its denotative and connotative meanings. It is now widely used in ordinary and academic speech to talk about an unbelievably diverse collection of phenomena—tools, instruments, machines, organizations, methods, techniques, systems, and the totality of all these and similar things in our experience" (1977:8). Perhaps worse, entire books on technology have been written without the slightest recognition of conceptual problems or issues (see, e.g., Alcorn, 1986).

3. This view ignores even the distinction between capacity for denial and management of stress. Yet so many types of self-control can be recognized that there is no immediate prospect of a defensible typology (see Klausner, 1965, especially 9–48). Accordingly, even though the "challenge" view of self-control has generated virtually a publishing industry in self-help manuals (see the survey in Blankstein and Polivy, 1982:183–99), it pertains to only one of many kinds of self-control.

4. In what is now a hoary philosophical debate, some protagonists suggest a close connection between the notions of self-control and free will. The present conceptualization has no bearing on the debate, nor does it reflect acceptance of Parsons's voluntarism (see Scott, 1971). Just as the experience of making a choice can be thought of as determined, so can the experience of controlling one's behavior. Likewise, the proposed definition of self-control has no *necessary* bearing on philosophical subtleties, such as Mele's question: "Do we exhibit self-control *whenever* we act as we judge best?" (1985:169). The last two words are so ambiguous as to preclude a defensible answer.

5. Granted its merits, this view tends to blur the distinction between internal (or self-control) and external control. Many control terms, such as *personal control* (e.g., Pitcher and Hong, 1986), are ambiguous because they also blur the internal-external distinction. Thus, social psychologists speak of an individual's sense of control as being "low" or "high" (e.g., Seeman and Seeman, 1983) without recognizing contrasts concerning self-control, external human control, inanimate control, biotic control, and control immunity-vulnerability (the extent to which an individual perceives his or her behavior as controlled by others). Perhaps most important, social psychologists persistently fail to emphasize the distinction between the perceived capacity to control and actual control behavior.

Such contrasts cannot be described in terms of alienation (Seeman, 1983), nor in terms of the distinction between internal and external locus of control as known in psychology (see Lefcourt's survey, 1984, and criticisms by Rothbaum et al., 1982).

6. Nonetheless, Skinner has used the term "self-control" frequently (e.g., 1971, 1974, 1978, 1983), and he appears to regard control notions as important. There are even instances where he alludes to internal behavior in connection with control, one being: "No mystic or ascetic has ever ceased to control the world around him; he controls it in order to control himself. We cannot choose a way of life in which there is no control. We can change only the controlling conditions" (1974:190).

7. There are even situations where an individual acts toward another in the belief that such action increases the probability of the other loosing self-control. Otherwise, various games of insult, such as "playing the dozens," would make no sense (see Goffman, 1961b:59).

8. If interaction is defined as an instance where a human responds to the behavior of another human, not all instances are control attempts. In particular, some instances of Goffman's (1961b:7) "unfocused interaction" may not be control attempts, but it does not follow that all instances of his "focused interaction" qualify. Unfortunately, like all others, Goffman's typology of interaction does not speak to two questions. First, if alter responds to ego's behavior, did ego act in the belief that his or her behavior increased the probability of a response by alter? Second, in responding to ego's behavior, did alter act in the belief that the response increased or decreased the probability of some response by ego? An affirmative answer to the first question would make ego's behavior attempted control; but there would be no interaction without a response by alter, and the response might not be consistent with ego's expectations. However, an affirmative answer to the second question would make alter's response a control attempt, but alter's response would be interaction despite a negative answer to the second question.

9. Despite Weber's preoccupation and that of his disciples (especially Parsons) with the term *action*, one is hard pressed to think of kinds of behavior that *clearly* would not qualify as action, especially on recognition that one may attach a subjective meaning to a putative reflex. So the distinction between action and behavior is inconsequential, and the two terms are used in this book as interchangeable.

10. Of the few possible exceptions, the most immediate doubts pertain to the theorist's conception of control. For example, Hirschi's "control" theory of delinquency (1969) reduces to the claim that the probability of a juvenile engaging in delinquency varies inversely with the juvenile's attachment to persons, commitment of conformity, involvement in conventional activities, and belief in the moral validity of societal norms. The claim may be valid; but even granting that the four conditions make a juvenile vulnerable to control, they are not control in the sense defined here. Indeed, Hirschi does not offer a conceptualization of control, and he appears to use the term as the loose equivalent of *influence*, a very common practice in sociology.

11. Black (1984c) appears indifferent to the problem in his observations on crime

as social control. Even if social control refers "to how people define and respond to deviant behavior" (Black, 1984b:5), it does not follow that all instances of self-help or "expression of a grievance by unilateral aggression" or conduct "intended as a punishment or other expression of disapproval" are reactions to deviant behavior, certainly not unless deviance is simply any behavior that someone (perhaps only one person) disapproves. Yet Black (1984c:4) quotes observations by anthropologists on wife beating as though the husbands are reacting to deviance. That would be the case only if deviant behavior is defined as any act that elicits a punitive reaction, and even advocates of the reactive conception of deviance stop short of such a definition (for elaboration, see Gibbs, 1981).

12.   Requiring such a demonstration is more defensible than merely assuming that imprisonment can be identified as social control without any definition.

13.   The practice commonly results in uninformative reifications, as illustrated by, of all people, Garfinkel's statement: "Every society exerts close controls over the transfers of persons from one status to another" (1967:116). Worse, when someone writes at length on social control without explicitly defining the term (e.g., Simpson, 1985), there are usually puzzling statements about the subject. Thus, in a well-known essay Janowitz never defines the term *social control* or confronts conceptual issues and problems, but he characterizes coercive control as the "opposite" of social control (1975:84).

14.   Denial of the relevance of internal behavior in defining control is not peculiar to sociology or Skinnerian psychology. Consider Dahl's statement: "Thus control need not be intentional; it may also be unintentional" (1982:17). Why, then, does Dahl even refer to "intentions" in defining control?

15.   Although Goffman rarely used the term *control* in some of his publications, his books provide numerous illustrations of referential social control, especially the implicit and/or nonverbal kinds. See particularly the chapters (4 and 6) on "fabrications" in Goffman's *Frame Analysis* (1974).

16.   Supernatural referential control is by no means employed only by nonliterate peoples, the ignorant, or fundamentalists. Despite Nazism's pagan trappings, Hitler frequently invoked God's will (see Schweitzer, 1984:69–71).

17.   The seriousness of an allegation may be as important as its credibility. As Black observed: "Reports of violence occasionally may even be fabricated in order to ensure that the police will handle cases that the callers fear—possibly with justification—would otherwise be dismissed as trivial. . . ." (1984c:18). Curiously, however, Black (1984b:6, 1976) denies any concern with the "subjective aspect" (e.g., intention, belief) of social control or law.

18.   An attempt to conceal anything is attempted human control.

19.   This formula applies to control in bureaucracies despite Dunsire's argument about the discontinuous transmission of orders from the top of a hierarchy: "it is well-nigh impossible, and will usually be unwise, for chief executives to give direct instructions to operating personnel" (1978:7). Dunsire simply identified a perennial tension in bureaucracies.

20.   It may appear that Emerson defined power in terms of control, but his conceptualization is extremely disorganized.

21.   Unfortunately, social scientists use the term *power* so ambiguously that conceptual comparisons are debatable. Thus, Bacharach and Lawler treat power as a perceptual phenomenon but only to suggest that "power perception" is somehow different from "potency attributed to an adversary" (1976:124).

22.   The definition makes the intention issue moot. As the perceived capacity to control, power is neither intentional nor unintentional. Lest the distinction between control and power appear to be logomachy, note that it makes the following phrase meaningless: "to use power effectively. . . ." (Ridgeway and Berger, 1986:604). Ridgeway and Berger do not indicate what constitutes "use of power," and it is difficult to imagine an instance that would not be attempted control.

23.   The notion of subjective power is akin to what sociologists (e.g., Pitcher and Hong, 1986) refer to as "personal control"; but their conceptualization of that term is superficial, and they persistently ignore the distinction between *perceptions* of personal control and actual control *behavior*.

24.   The determinants of subjective, respondent, and reputational power are left an open question. However, only the notion of control makes it possible to identify one of those determinants, as suggested by Moltoch and Boden: "through purposive control over the very grounds of verbal interchange, conversational procedures become mechanisms for reifying certain versions of reality at the expense of others. . . ." (1985:273).

25.   For that matter, neither presupposition will reduce the opposition of numerous sociologists to taking the question seriously. The opposition stems not just from the belief that the unanticipated consequences of human behavior are preponderant and, hence, more important (see, especially, Boudon, 1982). Additionally, numerous sociologists appear convinced that humans have little control over features of social life. Sieber's book (1981) is the best known statement of that conviction, but Mayhew's argument is more explicit: "*intention-free* mechanisms and/or conditions are the most powerful determinants of sociological phenomena. . . . And this means that social life is largely beyond human control" (1984:274).

Chapter

4

Additional Arguments

Because wholesale rejection of terminology, theories, and traditional research is unrealistic, a new central notion must conserve much of the field's heritage. That consideration entails several additional arguments.

Control and the Sociological Vocabulary

A central notion must be useful in all conceptualizations; hence, it should be defined without using the field's major terms. For example, Nisbet and Perrin (1977) focus their survey of sociology on the "social bond," but that notion is not used in defining what they treat as the field's major terms—symbolic interaction, social unions, norms, social authority, social roles, social status, social values, norms, alienation, anomie, and deviance. Rather, they treat those terms as denoting elements of the social bond (1977:39). So "social bond" is not used to define the terms; just the reverse is true.

Illustrative Use of the Term Control

In subsequent chapters a few sociological concepts and constructs are defined in terms of control, but the proposal to make control sociology's central notion should not stand or fall on those definitions.[1] There are various ways that any term can be defined by reference to control, and the choice should be left to specialists in sociology's subfields. Hence, all subsequent "control" definitions are only illustrative; and this argument is more important: Sociologists will confront seemingly insoluble conceptual problems until their terminology is based largely on a central notion, be it control or something else.

One illustration must suffice. *Marriage* is a sociological term if only because it pertains to a social relation, but anthropologists have devoted more attention than sociologists to the conceptual problems. Goodenough's definition (1970) is well-known; but di Leonardo (1979) alleges that it reflects a dubious assumption—universal male dominance. Yet both Goodenough and di Leonardo seem to recognize that marriage is a power relation. Recall that power is the perceived capacity to control, and in the case of marriage the capacity pertains to three broad classes of behavior: (1) sexual, including access to and exclusion of others; (2) production and property possession; and (3) parental, including control of offspring. Hence, there are 64 quadripartite possibilities, one being that the male has power over the female's sexual and parental behavior but not her production behavior and the female has no power over the male as regards any of the three classes of behavior. Designating only one possibility as marriage would be arbitrary and ethnocentric, especially because none of the possibilities appear universal.[2] That argument is suggested by di Leonardo (1979) but without confronting the implication—arbitrariness can be avoided only by defining marriage such that the term denotes any one of 63 possibilities. Each possibility can be recognized as a type of marriage; but if marriage is so conceptualized, there is only one meaningful immediate question about it: Why does the type of marriage vary?

The Variety Problem

If a notion is truly central, then it necessarily bears on the field's descriptive vocabulary as well as its theoretical terms. Examine these illustrative descriptive words: persuade, direct, influence, request, command, dominate, lead, beg, deprive, build, ask, coerce, exchange, resist, buy, destroy, modify, threaten, restrain, alter, seduce, move, convince, and sell. All of the words refer to inanimate, biotic, or human control; and the list could be extended for pages. So adoption of a control terminology could reduce sociology's vocabulary and give it greater coherence. The connection between some sociological terms and control is not obvious because sociologists tend to define terms without reference to human behavior. *Occupation* is an example. Sociologists commonly use that term as though it denotes a structural position, but occupations do not exist apart from control behavior.

The point is not merely that occupations can be described and thought of in terms of control; in addition, control notions can be used to explain occupational phenomena. Consider the fairly uniform prestige hierarchy of occupations from one country to another (see Marsh, 1971). The conventional sociological explanation appeals to common structural features of complex societies; but the appeal is hardly informative, and Marsh rightly points out that it is too imprecise for empirical falsification. His findings indicate a substantial direct relation between the prestige of an occupation and the amount of control exercised by incumbents. There is a tendency to think of that amount in terms of number of subordinates, but biotic and inanimate control are probably also relevant.

Some Qualifications

Sociologists are not admonished to substitute control terms for all of their ostensible "empirical" terms; rather, virtually all of the latter denote phenomena that can be described and thought of by reference to control. The exceptions are those terms (e.g., social structure) whose meaning is so vague that they have no specific empirical referents.[3] However, obfuscation haunts the terminology of the social sciences and the humanities, not just sociology.[4] Thus, the historian Landes argues that for the West to grow rich it was necessary "to unleash innovation" (1986:46). Perhaps so, but the phrase cannot be clarified sufficiently without recourse to a control terminology.

The ultimate goal lies beyond the claim that describing and thinking about phenomena will promote conceptual coherence and the anticipation of empirical relations. That goal is a unified theory, but it cannot be realized without some notion that applies to all special theories.[5] To illustrate application of the control notion, consider a theory (Gibbs, 1982c) that implies, among other things, a direct relation between the amount of role conflict in a population and the population's suicide rate. By definition, when confronted with a role conflict an individual's control over others is impeded and vice versa. Accordingly, we have this implied postulate: A population's suicide rate is inversely related to the effectiveness of human control in that population. The postulate creates the potential for subsuming the theory about suicide rates (along with numerous other special theories) under a broad theory of human control.

A Crippling Problem

Sir Fred Hoyle did sociology a service by pointing to one of its crippling problems. As the following quote (in Lenski, 1975:140) indicates, the service was rendered snidely; even so, it is noteworthy.

> "Physicists would describe most of what happens in everyday life as 'noise'. . . [or] activity without information content. 'Signal' consists of genuine information. A signal-to-noise problem in physics consists in digging out genuine information from activity without content. . . . The protagonists of studies in the humanities fail to appreciate the extent to which their problems are of the signal-to-noise kind. . . . Students of sociology might indeed be described as the ultimate students of noise, literally and figuratively.

Hoyle conveniently ignored this question: What is the noise criterion? Surely noise is not simply any phenomenon outside the field's subject matter. Thus, when formulating a theory about crime, a sociologist is not likely to consider all the field's subject matter as relevant; but it would be trite to say: Consider relevant phenomena. Nonetheless, "noise" merely means something that is irrelevant for the purpose at hand, and it is when a scientist struggles to formulate a theory that a relevance criterion or "noise screen" is most needed. Scientists are never totally bereft of a criterion, but it may be extremely vague or implicit. Candid sociologists will admit that their relevance criterion is obscure, thereby confirming Hoyle's indictment; but his conception of noise is vague. As suggested previously, a relevance criterion is a "noise screen," and the most inclusive but least idiosyncratic criterion is a central notion.

Connections between Control Notions and Collective Variables

To acknowledge again, numerous collective variables (aggregate, macro, or structural) appear uncontrolled, and even attempts to control them are rare. The acknowledgment does not undermine the claim that sociology's subject matter can be described and thought of in terms of control; that claim stands if only because of the following versions of four of the six major questions about control (chapter 3). First, given an uncontrolled collective variable, why is it uncontrolled and how could it be controlled? Second, when repeated attempts to control a particular collective variable fail, why? Third, given a collective variable that is subject to attempts at control in some social units but not in others, why the contrast? And, fourth, if some collective variables are more subject to control attempts in all social units than are other collective variables, why such differences? Pursuit of the four questions will further the integration of control studies and traditional sociology.

Collective Variables and Control Efficacy

The context of a control attempt may determine its success or failure. Identifying the connection between such contexts and collective variables is one way to describe and think about those variables in terms of control.

IMPEDIMENTARY VARIABLES AND CONTROL.   If a particular collective variable is negatively correlated with the "success rate" for a particular kind of attempted control, the correlation would indicate that some type of context impedes that kind of control. Given the paucity of systematic sociological research on control, any identification of a collective variable as "impedimentary" would be conjecture. Nonetheless, several variables are obvious possibilities, one being social differentiation, including stratification and the division of labor. There is a clear-cut rationale for assuming that social differentiation impedes various kinds of human control. Effective human control commonly requires that the would-be controller know what and whom the control targets value, fear, hate, love, respect, etc.; and as social differentiation increases, it becomes more difficult to acquire such knowledge about all social unit members.

The argument can be stated as a control principle (4–1): The greater the social differentiation in a social unit, the less the effectiveness of external human control in that unit. Like all others, the principle is not identified as an axiom, postulate, or proposition because such identification should be made when the principle enters into a theory; only then can evidence be brought to bear on it. Such theories are beyond the present work, but the generalization illustrates thinking about a collective variable in terms of control. For that matter, the control variable in the principle is itself a collective variable, a property of a social unit.

FACILITATIVE VARIABLES AND CONTROL. Just as some collective variables may vary inversely with some measure of control efficacy, so others may vary directly; and the latter relation would suggest that some contexts facilitate control. Again, however, the paucity of systematic research makes conjecture inevitable when identifying instances.

The most obvious candidate is "normative consensus," but that notion should not be equated with "norm." Sociologists traditionally describe norms so as to suggest that any particular norm (e.g., premarital chastity) is either present or absent in a given social unit, but any presence-absence criterion would be inherently arbitrary or grossly unrealistic (see chapter 1 and Gibbs, 1981:7–21). Because normative consensus is quantitative, the arbitrariness problem is avoided; but both normative consensus and norms do pertain to evaluations and/or expectations of conduct, and in soliciting answers by social unit members to normative question no one has devised a procedure that solves the problem of normative contingencies. Until a procedure is devised to take those contingencies into account, normative consensus must be treated as a construct. Even so, an argument can be made to justify the supposition that normative consensus facilitates human control. If maximum normative consensus prevails, would-be controllers have a reliable basis for inferences as to what and whom members of the social unit fear, hate, love, respect, etc.; and to the extent controllers and controlees share predispositions (such as values), commands or requests will be perceived as warranted (justified and legitimate). So we have this control principle (4–2): The greater the normative consensus in a social unit, the greater the effectiveness of external human control in that unit.

Problematic Variables and Control

A collective variable may have control implications even if no attempt ever has been made to control the variable and even if it is neither impedimentary nor facilitative.[6] The values of a collective variable are abstractions from particular events; and to the extent those events stem from successes or failures in control attempts, there is a connection between the variable and control. Such collective variables are designated as "problematic" because there is currently no methodology to ascertain the extent that control attempts determine a collective variable's values.

Fertility rates illustrate the point. Even if no attempt is made to control the crude birth rate of a particular social unit (e.g., a city), who would argue that all births in that unit occur independently of control successes or failures? The use of a contraceptive device or practice is attempted biotic control. If contraception is never attempted, a population's birth rate is largely a function of its fecundity, rate of voluntary abortions, and rate of heterosexual intercourse. Voluntary abortion is biotic control, and sexual intercourse requires attempts at human control. True, little is known about the extent to which birth rates are determined by successes or failures in control, and a great deal remains unknown about the relative importance of the various means of birth control; but that situation reflects the failure of demographers to emphasize the importance of control as a determinant of fertility rates. There is no well-known theory of differential fertility in which the primary independent variable pertains to success or failure in attempts at biotic control (primarily sexual abstinence, contraception, and abortion); but consider Nardi's argument: "We know that people in all cultures and epochs have regulated fertility. In fact, there are many data to suggest that fertility regulation is a virtually universal phenomenon. . . ." (1981:31). Furthermore, there is growing evidence (see, e.g., Tsui and Bogue, 1978) that from a global perspective programs to promote birth control have become much more common and effective.

The arguments pertaining to problematic collective variables cannot be reduced to a meaningful generalization, but everything is secondary to the claim that collective variables can be described and thought of in terms of control. The claim is debatable, and no amount of additional illustrations would be conclusive; nonetheless, the claim itself indicates that the proposal to make control sociology's central notion is not really radical. The intent obviously is not to end the sociological concern with collective variables.

Logical Connections

The percentage of the labor force in agriculture would be important for present purposes even if it did not frequently enter into sociological research. That percentage illustrates a logical connection between a collective variable and biotic control.

A logical connection between occupational composition or industry composition (both collective variables) and control is not limited to biotic control. Consider the percentage of the labor force classified occupationally as "operatives in manufacturing." Such a figure pertains to individuals engaged in a major subtype of inanimate control—transformational. Likewise, the connection between the percentage of "managers" (regardless of industry) and external human control is a logical relation.

Census figures on occupations, industries, and class of worker categories (e.g., employer, employee, and self-employed) are indicative of the total number regularly engaged in each basic type of control (inanimate, biotic, and human) and some subtypes (e.g., inanimate transformational). To illustrate, security guards in manufacturing would be identified as engaged in human control rather than inanimate control; all mechanics, regardless of industry, would be identified as engaged in inanimate control; and in all industries supervisors would be identified as engaged in human control.

Sociologists make extensive use of statistics on occupations, industries, and class of worker statistics because those data have been available in published form (e.g., census reports) for numerous countries over more than a century. So macro research on control (see, e.g., Adams, 1982b) is feasible, and the point is stressed because systematic exploratory research on control is needed as a step toward theories.

COLLECTIVE VARIABLES AND OBJECTS OF CONTROL. Previous illustrations are largely limited to categories of controllers, but various published data pertain to objects of control. A short illustrative list must suffice: employees, prisoners, patients, children, students, probationers, and parolees.

Data on nonhuman control objects are even more extensive, especially statistics on production or consumption. Again, a very short illustrative list must suffice: number of sheep sheared, tons of coal mined, bushels of wheat harvested, acres of corn cultivated, and tons of steel produced.

COLLECTIVE VARIABLES AND MEANS OF CONTROL. Any description of a control attempt should speak to this question: *How* was it attempted? The answer would designate some means of·control (e.g., corporal punishment, a command). Currently, there is no adequate typology of means, and the same is true of what might be construed as synonyms, such as manipulative tactics (commencing with Lumley, 1925, and ending with Buss et al., 1987); but a typology is not necessary to illustrate a connection between some collective variables and means of control.

Money is a means of human control if only because it serves as a medium of exchange and exchange requires human control. Should sociologists grant that money is a means of control but deny its importance, their denial would ignore the extensive use of "income" variables in sociological research.[7] Such variables are virtually always collective; but sociologists use them without offering an interpretation, which indicates that they do not think about income in terms of some notion. Hence, crude induction is the usual rationale in sociology for anticipating an empirical relation between monetary variables (e.g., median family income) and other variables; and given such a relation, sociologists are commonly unable to explain it. Consider the frequent reports of an relation among social units (e.g., countries or families) between income and fertility rates. In attempting to explain that relation, sociologists may refer to social class; but that reference explains nothing.

CONTROL VARIABLES AS COLLECTIVE VARIABLES.   If it were possible to identify all attempts at human control in a given social unit and classify each as proximate, sequential, or social, then the percentage of attempts in each of the three subtypes could be computed readily. Because each percentage for a particular social unit would be a collective variable, some collective variables pertain directly to control.

Collective control variables are extremely rare in sociological research, but it does not follow that control is somehow inherently micro. They are rare because it is often the case that enormous resources are required to gather the requisite data for even a few social units.[8] However, data are not necessary to describe and think of collective variables in terms of control, and terms that denote collective control variables can be treated as constructs.

Some Possible Losses

It is not claimed that all collective variables can be described and thought of in terms of control, at least not constructively.[9] While judgments along that line should be made by sociologists in the relevant substantive specialties, a few illustrative possibilities can be identified.

Consider population size, such as the number of city residents or group members. That variable has preoccupied many sociologists, commencing primarily with Simmel (especially 1950:87–177); but only one thing can be said of it in connection with control. Beyond some minimum number, all else being equal, an increase in population size makes it more difficult for any one member to control all of the behavior of other members. Yet there is no basis to assume that the minimum number is remotely the same for all social units regardless of the kind of behavior or how control is attempted. The argument questions not the importance of control but, rather, the importance of population size. Vast sociological research on the relation between size and other features of human populations (including organizations; see Beyer and Trice, 1979) has revealed nothing even approximating a consistent empirical association, let alone a close one. Even if Nolan's finding (1979) of a nonmonotonic association among countries between population size and percentage employed by governments (local and national) should hold in further research, there is no coherent basis to explain the relation.

What has been said of population size applies also to population density, especially gross density (e.g., residents per square mile). There is no basis to assume that density always either impedes or facilitates human control; and despite the astonishing amount of attention devoted to the subject, there is no evidence of even one uniform correlate of population density, especially when socio-economic variables are controlled (see Levinson, 1979, and Choldin, 1978).

A STANDARD OF MEANINGFULNESS.   Sociologists only rarely confront this question: In what sense are collective variables meaningful and why assume that they have any identifiable correlates? To understand the question, think of the ease with which a collective variable can be *created*. "Fras" is the combined number of traffic lights, elections, widows, and burglaries in a particular territorial unit during a year as a ratio to the total residents at the beginning of the year. Numerous "fras" values can be computed, they would be real, and they would likely vary; but who would pursue an explanation of the variation? Lest the illustration be dismissed as absurd, some collective variables may not be recognized as absurd only because they are conventions in certain specialties. Urban primacy is only one of many possibilities (see Mehta's report, 1964, of an attempt to identify correlates).

Adopting a central notion does entail abandoning variables that cannot be described and thought of in terms of that notion, but the use of the notion as a standard of meaningfulness compensates for such losses. For example, if control is the central notion, there are three reasons why the official robbery rate is meaningful: (1) individuals direct other individuals to record instances of robbery, (2) some individuals attempt to prevent robberies, and (3) robbery itself is a kind of control.

Logico-empirical Connections between Collective Variables

Arguments about the unanticipated consequences of human behavior notwithstanding, virtually all collective variables (i.e., aggregate, macro, or structural) can be described and thought of in terms of control. True, with or without a central notion, the goal is always to identify correlates of collective variables, and correlates are commonly also collective variables; but sociologists are less likely to anticipate and explain empirical associations between collective variables if they work without a central notion. The use of a central notion to those ends is illustrated by Figure 4–1.

Central Notions, Intervening Variables, and Explanation

Whatever variables I and II are, an empirical association between them may be anticipated by thinking of both variables in terms of the field's central notion;[10] and thinking is conducive to recognizing a logical connection between variables. Recognition of those connections furthers conceptual unification, but a logical connection does not insure an empirical association between variables (e.g., robbery is a subclass of crime—a logical relation—but there may be no correlation whatever between the robbery rate and the total crime

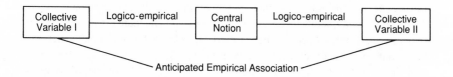

Figure 4–1.   Diagram of Types of Associations

rate). So the connection between the central notion and components of the field's subject matter is logical and/or empirical (hence, the "logico-empirical" designation in Figure 4–1), but a central notion is not necessarily an intervening variable in the ordinary sense. An intervening variable is illustrated as follows: $X \longrightarrow Y \longrightarrow Z$, where $\longrightarrow$ signifies causation. In such a case, X causes Z indirectly, through the intervening variable, Y; but to describe the sequences as causal would not suggest a logical (conceptual) connection between X and Y or between Y and Z.

EXPLANATION AND A SPECIAL PROBLEM WITH COLLECTIVE VARIABLES. Many scientists and philosophers have argued that a particular thing or event is explained adequately when and only when (1) a claim is made as to the cause or causes of all such things or events and (2) compelling research findings support that claim. Because causation cannot be observed, evidence must be in the form of observations of space-time associations; but many philosophers and scientist reject Hume's argument that evidence of a space-time association between variables is the only possible justification for inferring causation. They seem to regard such evidence as necessary but not sufficient. What else is required to justify a causal inference? Advocates of causal explanation either commonly avoid the question or answer obscurely (for elaboration, see Gibbs, 1982d), and no answer will be complete without reference to mechanisms or media through which alleged causes have effects. Mechanisms are most relevant when there is a discernible distance between the alleged cause and the alleged effect, and "action-at-a-distance" poses a problem in physics or any other field (see Maze, 1983:14).

When a causal relation between collective variables is asserted, action-at-a-distance may not appear to be a problem because the variables have the same spatial context (e.g., "Chicago's 1980 homicide rate" and "Chicago's 1980 median family income" both refer to the same territorial unit); and it is difficult to think of a "distance" between them. However, contemplate a negative correlation coefficient for U.S. metropolitan areas between median family income and the homicide rate. Regardless of the coefficient's magnitude, one must wonder: How could the relation be causal? The question introduces a sociological instance of the action-at-a-distance problem.

There is a special need to identify a causal mechanism in the case of collective variables because they are so far removed from specific acts by particular individuals that a substantial statistical association between them may be puzzling. Think of the population size of cities, the residential density of neighborhoods, and the number of positions in an organization; then try to describe any of those variables in terms of specific acts. Because any description would be debatable at best, there is no basis for explaining a statistical association between those collective variables and other variables.[11] However, the argument is not that sociologists should compute only correlations among individuals and abandon so-called ecological correlations (actually, aggregate correlations), and the problem of causal mechanisms would not be avoided by recourse to individual correlations. As a case in point, the individual correlation between income and homicide (slayer or victim) would hardly be less puzzling than the correlation at the aggregate level (e.g., per capita income and the homicide rate among cities).

One may understand and perhaps even explain a particular empirical association in terms of some notion but be unable to extend that notion to all other associations in the field; if so, the notion could not be central for the field. To illustrate, Cohen and Felson's findings (1979:598) indicate that between 1960 and 1971 the percentage of U.S. houses unattended (no one in) between 9 a.m. and 10 a.m. increased from 29 percent to about 44 percent. They then report (1979:600) that (1) the percentage of all burglaries classified as "residential daytime" increased from 15.6 percent in 1960 to 31.7 percent in 1970 but (2) a negligible 1960–70 increase in the percentage classified as "residential nighttime" (24.4 percent to 25.8 percent). No one is likely to doubt the possibility of some kind of causal connection between the two changes, or to regard it as puzzling. Although the association could be described and thought of in terms other than "failures in control by home occupants and success in countercontrol by burglars," any noncontrol notion is less applicable than the notion of control in regard to empirical associations between sociological variables in general. That contrast is crucial because Cohen and Felson prefer the notion of opportunity; but all aspects of that notion can be described in terms of control, while the reverse is not true, meaning that control is the broader notion.

A different kind of illustration of the problem is provided by Judith Blau and Peter Blau's analysis (1982) of variation in murder, rape, robbery, and assault rates (1971) among 125 U.S. metropolitan areas (SMSAs). In their commentary on statistical evidence of an association between income inequality and crime rates, the Blaus (1982:126) invoke such diverse notions that their explanation is incoherent. A partial list of the notions includes spirit of democracy, alienation, despair, conflict, relative deprivation, proportion divorced or separated, anomie, and pent-up aggression. Most of those notions are so vague that a systematic test of the Blau explanation would not be feasible even if it were coherent.

Causal Mechanisms and Central Notions

Generalizing the criticism of Blau and Blau, advocates of "sociological structuralism" cannot identify casual mechanisms readily. Their identification is greatly facilitated by a central notion, especially when a theorist is thinking about possible relations among collective variables; and describing or thinking of two variables (collective or not) in terms of some notion may enable a theorist either to anticipate conditions in which there is no relation or to describe an "ideal" condition (no exceptions to the association in question).

One may grant that describing and thinking of variables in terms of some notion facilitates the identification of a connecting causal mechanism but then argue that the notion need not be, and commonly cannot be, the same for all sociological variables. If valid, that argument precludes a central notion. There are two immediate counterarguments: first, no notion can be used effectively without an elaborate conceptualization and a sophisticated methodology of empirical application; and, second, sociology does not have the resources to develop several notions. Moreover, sustained use of a particular notion in a field engenders so much confidence that plausible observations can be made without recourse to research. Thus, if someone describes robberies as attempts at proximate control, surely research is not needed to substantiate that description; by contrast, if robberies are described in terms of class conflict, the unconscious, the collective conscience, or social structure, the description is bound to be sheer verbiage or extremely debatable.

There is a dilemma in contemplating causal mechanisms. Suppose that an empirical relation ostensibly holds between X and Y. The question becomes: If the relation is causal, what is the mechanism? Suppose the answer is that: X and Y are related through Z. Even if accepted, the answer suggests two additional questions. First, What mechanism connects X and Z? Second, What mechanism connects Z and Y? Such questions become an infinite regression, and for that reason alone scientists in each field must agree, expressly or tacitly, that an empirical relation is explained satisfactorily when the connecting mechanism is a fundamental phenomenon in the field's subject matter. Such a phenomenon can be described and thought of only in terms of the field's central notion.

If various notions are used to explain empirical relations, a proliferation of special theories is inevitable. A central notion holds forth the promise of integrating special theories; and, once it becomes truly central, the notion in effect defines the field's subject matter. If some event or thing cannot be described and thought of in terms of that notion, it is outside the field's subject matter. So a central notion eventually limits the field's subject matter. The argument extends even to the idea that a field is actually defined in terms of the questions pursued. Consider Kitcher's contention that "Not every collection of questions constitutes a field. The questions must form a family, that is, they must hold out the promise of a unified collection of answers" (1985:114). Extending that contention, "unified answers" require a central notion.

Reductionism

Because control is hardly "structural," the proposal to make it sociology's central notion raises the specter of reductionism. However, conceptions of reductionism are so divergent and vague that debates of the issue are sterile. Examine DiTomaso's use of the term: "Theoretical *reduction* can take two forms (see, e.g., Suppe, 1977:54–55): (a) the replacement of one theory by a closely related and more comprehensive theory, where the second specifies the conditions of applicability of the first, or (b) the absorption of one theory into a more inclusive or comprehensive theory, where the second replaces the first. My concern is with the latter. Whereas theoretical *reduction* may be a proper goal of scientific development, theoretical *reductionism* is arbitrary or inappropriate. *Sociological* reductionism can be defined as the arbitrary reduction of all social phenomena to the level of structure. It assigns ontological preference to structure and maintains, by definition, that any nonstructural phenomenon is not social" (1982:14–15).

Why does replacing one theory with or absorbing it into a more comprehensive theory constitute reductionism? Whatever the answer, DiTomaso's definition of "sociological reductionism" suggests that social phenomena are at one level and structure is somehow at a lower level. One alternative interpretation is even more startling. If DiTomaso means that defining social phenomena in structural terms is reductionism because it limits the phenomena to structure, the definition of any phenomenon must be reductionism because any definition can be thought of as limiting something.

Still another conception of reductionism equates it with determinism. Thus, Davis writes of "the reductionism implicit in 'materialism'," having earlier declared: "the type of reductionism represented by technological or economic determinism is equally differentiated from functionalism" (1959:761). That argument contradicts the idea that reductionism in sociology necessarily takes the form of a psychological or biological explanation of a social phenomenon, for technology is hardly psychological or biological. Moreover, why is functionalism not a kind of determinism and, hence, reductionism? In any case, if writers have license to apply the term *reductionism* to any determinism that they reject, the term is purely pejorative. The same argument extends to the use of the term antireductionism, as exemplified by Ellis's astonishing claim: "Purposeful explanations for phenomena usually are closely linked with antireductionism" (1977:57).

So the term *reductionism*, like *positivism*, has become merely a derogatory label. Indeed, some writers suggest a connection between reductionism and reification or even anthropomorphism. Consider Grabosky's characterization of theories about penal severity as "handicapped by their obvious reductionism—the tendency to attribute personal characteristics to collectivities. . . ." (1984:171).

THE ISSUE RAISED BY HOMANS.   Rather than speak of reductionism, Homans (1964b) argues that sociological theories must "bring men back in." He calls for sociological explanations based on psychological principles, and critics may see similarities between Homans's prescription and this book's principal arguments. Actually, they are quite different.

Although Homans frequently refers to psychology, it is not clear which psychological concept or construct could be sociology's central notion. Indeed, he does not explicitly advocate describing and thinking about sociological variables in psychological terms; rather, he argues that "sociological uniformities" can be explained adequately only if deduced from psychological principles. Whatever the argument's merits, there is a difference between deducing relations between collective variables from psychological principle and describing or thinking about those relations in terms of control. Control is a *relational* phenomenon rather than psychological; furthermore, the presumption is not that sociologists will ever formulate a theory about control from which they can deduce empirical relations between all collective variables.

Homans's equating explanation and deduction is conventional; but he also argues that explanations of sociological phenomena are inadequate unless based on psychological principles (again, 1964a, 1964b, 1974), thereby suggesting some necessary connection between deduction and psychological principles. But what is psychological about, for example, the classical syllogism? Actually, Homans's insistence on deduction is only one of his criteria of an adequate explanation; additionally, the premises must be psychological principles. Nonetheless, although most sociologists reject Homans's sociology as "reductionistic," Homans provided sociology with the most meaningful conception of reductionism.

The Question of Importance and Related Issues

Critics of this book are likely to protest something like this: But the French revolution was unplanned, no one invented monogamy, and the rarity of miscegenation in the U.S. is not due to legal proscriptions; hence, since the very things that interest sociologists are uncontrolled, why be concerned with control? Such a protest suggests this argument: The unanticipated or unintended consequences of human behavior are more important than the anticipated or intended consequences (see Schneider, 1975:35–58; Sieber, 1981; and Boudon, 1982), and the proposal to make control sociology's central notion would terminate the sociological study of unanticipated consequences.

Rebuttal commences with this control principle (4–3): Every major episode in human history and all meaningful properties of social units stem from attempts at inanimate, biotic, or human control. To illustrate, even if the American Civil War stemmed wholly from slavery, southerners did not practice slavery in the belief that it increased the probability of secession; accordingly, insofar as the war was a consequence of slavery, it was an unanticipated consequence. Nonetheless, slavery is blatant human control; hence, again insofar as the war was a consequence of slavery, it stemmed from human control. The issue is not whether slavery caused the war.[12] Suppose that the war was a consequence of efforts by southern elites to dominate the federal government. How could such hegemony be realized without attempts at human control? Then accept this argument: The cotton gin was necessary for a genuine slave economy in the South. Even so, it does not follow that Whitney anticipated that consequence. In any case, no one invents or uses a cotton gin accidentally. Finally, consider the frequent comments of historians on the "martial spirit" of the antebellum South. From a superorganicist's perspective, that spirit simply reflected a cultural value, something unplanned, unanticipated, etc. However, contemplate Joel Williamson's observations: "The militant South, the military South . . . sprang from the necessity of controlling a potentially explosive black population. . . . Black-belt white Southerners of military age were conditioned to leap into the saddle at the mere suspicion of a black revolt, and, apparently, after Nat Turner they had an abundance of exercise in that drill. . . . It was no accident that the Southern landscape was dotted with preparatory schools run rigidly along the military model. . . ." (1984:19, 21, 20).

Some Implications of Control Principle 4–3

Those who accept the principle may not fully grasp the implications, one of which is illustrated also by slavery and the American Civil War. Even if slavery did cause the war, it may appear that the "control" character of slavery is irrelevant, meaning that the consequences would have been the same had slavery been accidental. But examine that argument in light of two questions. First, would southern "slavers" have urged war to protect their economic interests had they been unaware that they controlled slaves? Second, would the abolitionists have urged war had they perceived slavery as accidental?

The contention is not that all major episodes in human history and all meaningful properties of social units are controlled. Nonetheless, even if no major episode in human history or meaningful property of a social unit has been planned, control principle 4–3 would remain important for two reasons. First, it may be that humans will increasingly come to recognize the consequences of their control attempts; and, if so, unless one presumes colossal human indifference, major episodes in human history and properties of social units will increasingly become subject to attempts at control (as suggested by Ward's argument about "telesis," 1903). Second, even if all major historical episodes or social unit attributes are unanticipated consequences of control attempts, their explanation cannot be considered as complete without reference to those attempts.

Some Other Historical Events or Episodes

Major sociological terms (e.g., *anomie*, *social class*) are so far removed from particular events that their empirical referents are obscure at best. Furthermore, most of those terms denote a sequence of heterogenous events, some of which are unique in a given space-time context and perhaps absolutely unique. To illustrate, no revolution is a "thing" or even a class of homogeneous events. Thus, no account of the French revolution ignores the summoning of the Estates-General; and whether construed as an event or a sequence of events, the summoning was unique.

The point is not merely that sociology's terminology is too far removed from events; additionally, human events can be described and thought of in terms of control. How could it be denied, for example, that the summoning of the Estates-General was successful control by Louis XVI? But sociologists do not emphasize control in explaining the French revolution, because they assume that revolutions are never intended (see, e.g., Skocpol, 1979:17). Hence, revolutions must be explained "structurally," whatever that may mean. Examine Skocpol's statement (1979:65): "as everyone knows, the summoning of the Estates-General served not to solve the royal financial crisis but to launch the Revolution." Given that statement, Skocpol cannot object to this one: The French revolution was launched by an attempt at control. Of course, Louis XVI did not intend to launch the revolution, but the summoning of the Estates-General was not accidental.

Major historical episodes may take the form of, or stem from, either control successes or control failures. The French royal financial crisis is no exception; it stemmed from failures in control attempts by a series of monarchs and their ministers. Indeed, successful political revolutions are a sequence of control failures by state officials, including military officers and perhaps monarchs; and it is ludicrous to assume that revolutionaries, whatever their original intentions, ever triumph without some success in control. The issue can be understood better by contemplating two contending questions as points of departure in explaining the French revolution. First, why did Louis XVI lose so much control over events after the Estates-General? Second, what "structural variables" determined the French revolution? The first question is both more meaningful and more manageable.

What has been said of failures in control attempts applies to wars.

Sociologists have devoted so little attention to warfare that the field scarcely has any theories on the subject, but that situation is not surprising. It taxes credulity to characterize wars as superorganic, crescive, etc., the very notions that sociologists commonly employ when analyzing macro phenomena. The point is not just that warfare is highly organized coercive control attempts, or that a conquest is the outcome of successful and unsuccessful control attempts. For that matter, even in speculating about the determinants of a military outcome, it is a grievous error to ignore control successes or failures before the first battle. Think of the Spanish conquest of the Inca Empire. Pizzaro's force invaded when the Inca Empire was in disarray after a long civil war. The Inca emperor Huascar precipitated and lost the war to his half-brother, Atauhualpa, by attempting to abolish the imperial or royal ancestor cult, an attempt that resulted in Huascar's losing effective control over numerous nobles (see Conrad and Demarest, 1984:134–39).

Related Phenomena

Any attempt at control is virtually certain to have unintended and unrecognized consequences. Examine, for example, Laura Lake's argument:

> "in the process of attempting to implement federal laws, political relations and institutions are changed in profound ways. For example, federal preemption in a policy area that was formerly the sole responsibility of states may strain federal-state relations. States reacting to such preemption may, for example, initiate constitutional lawsuits and politically resist federal authority. These responses in turn redefine federalism" (1982:1).

No one would question that many consequences of implementing federal laws are unintended even if eventually recognized; but, whatever the unanticipated or unrecognized consequences, implementation is an attempt at control.

A PARTICULAR KIND OF UNINTENDED INFLUENCE. Even when parents monopolize the socialization of a child, their influence on the child's personality may be largely unintended; but how could that influence be substantial if parents did not frequently attempt to control the child's behavior over several years? Also relevant: How could parents have so much unintended influence if children did not attempt to control parents? Although there has been little systematic research on control of parents, there are some illustrative findings: (1) children initiate approximately 50 percent of parent-child interactions and (2) intentional behavior can be identified before the infant's first birthday (see Bell and Harper, 1977:64).

Appearances to the contrary, the foregoing argument is not conventional; far from it. Definitions of socialization (chapter 17) commonly do not emphasize control, and control notions have no place in the prevailing conception of socialization.[13] Likewise, the preoccupation of psychoanalysts with the unconscious blinds them to the significance of extensive control attempts in the family context.

MORE ON REVOLUTION. The preoccupation of many sociologists with unanticipated consequences is not limited to a concern with collective variables. It is also manifested in their explanations or interpretations of major historical episodes. Contemplate some of Theda Skocpol's concluding statements in her highly praised book: "Before social revolutions could occur, the administrative and military power of these states had to break down. When this happened in France 1789, Russia 1917, and China 1911, it was *not* because of deliberate activities to that end, either on the part of avowed revolutionaries or on the part of politically powerful groups within the Old Regimes. Rather revolutionary political crises, culminating in administrative and military breakdowns, emerged because the imperial states became caught in cross-pressures between intensified military competition or intrusions from abroad and constraints imposed on monarchical responses by the existing agrarian class structures and political institutions" (1979:285).

Skocpol's statements exemplify robotic sociology by depicting humans as unwitting actors at best. Insofar as she recognizes individuals, they are described as ineffectual; and her second sentence denies that in any of three countries avowed revolutionaries engaged in deliberate activities to promote an administrative or military breakdown. Then in describing administrative and military breakdowns, Skocpol writes as though the monarchs and their officers were thumb-twiddling spectators. To the contrary, ruling class members made various attempts to control the events or episodes identified by Skocpol as sequences in each revolution. Those attempts commonly failed; but surely this question is relevant in explaining any revolution: Why did attempts to preserve the Old Order fail? Rather than entertain that question, Skocpol resorts to gross reifications, as exemplified by the last sentence in the quoted passage. Even accepting those reifications, imagine someone doing what Skocpol failed to do—demonstrating that the breakdowns were caused as she describes them.

Toward the Integration of the Social and Behavioral Sciences

Although efforts to integrate the social and behavioral sciences have waned over recent decades, the disciplinary boundaries remain arbitrary. Unfortunately, however, not even the merger of anthropology, economics, political science, psychology, and sociology into one academic department would solve the immediate problem: no journal interests and informs even a majority of social and behavioral scientists. The same is true within each discipline, meaning that the literature of one specialty (e.g., deviance in sociology) rarely interests or informs other specialists (e.g., demographers in sociology).

Because specialists often go their own way in the same academic department, there can be no organizational path to integration of the social and behavioral sciences; but there is an alternative strategy. This question should be paramount when promoting or assessing a candidate for each discipline's central notion: Could the notion be central for all social and behavioral sciences? The answer is affirmative in the case of control, and that answer introduces the strongest argument for making control sociology's central notion.

Anthropology

The only unquestioned distinction between anthropology and sociology lies in the auditor's office of universities.[14] Should it appear that an interest in the "products" of human behavior is peculiar to archaeologists, what of sociologists (e.g., Frisbie and Clarke, 1979) with an abiding interest in technology? Like archaeologists, those sociologists are concerned with inanimate control.

Now consider research in physical anthropology as another problem. Much of that research does appear more relevant for biologists than for sociologists (or cultural anthropologists, for that matter); but that would not be the case if the research focused on this question: What is the relation between the biological characteristics of humans and their capacity for control?

If control cannot be central for anthropology, it cannot be central for sociology; the arguments are exactly the same for the two fields. Just as many sociologists have championed antireductionism and emphasized the unanticipated consequences of human behavior, so have many anthropologists (see, e.g., White, 1949). The counterargument is also the same for both fields—that antireductionism and preoccupation with the superorganic notion blinds one to the purposive quality of human behavior, a quality that would be difficult to ignore if control were the central notion.

Political Science

Although control is the name of the game called politics (see McDonald, 1965), political scientists rarely use the term *control* (Oppenheim, 1961, and Dahl, 1982, are notable exceptions). If they have a candidate for the central notion, it appears to be *power* (see Krislov, 1982, and Lane and Stenlund, 1984:318). Accordingly, the prospect for greater integration of political science and other social sciences hinges particularly on the conceptualization of power.

The history of the conceptualization of power in political science parallels that in sociology, meaning two indistinguishable quagmires.[15] However, the definition in chapter 3—power is the perceived capacity for control—resembles several definitions in the political science literature (see citations in Lane and Stenlund, 1984).

Economics

Critics notwithstanding, the laissez-faire theory of classical economics is not merely prescriptive; it asserts that the highest levels of productivity and consumption are realized when the concentration of control over economic transactions is minimal—no governmental regulation or monopolies in particular. Therefore, valid or invalid, it is a theory about the consequences of control. And what do its critics offer as alternatives? They argue that monopolies are inevitable without governmental regulation and that central planning eventually becomes necessary to sustain a productive economy. Therefore, valid or invalid, the opposing theories are also theories about control. Finally, Marx's "law" of capitalist crisis (Itoh, 1978, refers to Marx's theory of crisis) surely implies this argument: Capitalists cannot control the fate of capitalism.

Now consider Boulding's statement: "The key to the theory of economic behavior is the concept of *optimization* through choice. The organism is perceived as examining the set of images of possible futures, ordering these on a value scale—that is, a scale of better or worse—and then selecting that one which is 'best,' that is, first in the value order" (in Wiegele, 1982:131). Boulding's statement is incomplete. Regardless of the value selected, it cannot be realized without the organism attempting inanimate, biotic, and/or human control.

To exchange something is to control someone. The connection goes unrecognized by economists and sociologists because they think of exchange but not control as benign. Moreover, because parties to economic transactions in a large market commonly do not even know each other, their market behavior may not appear to be attempted control. However, as argued in chapter 2, one may act in the belief that the action increases the probability of someone responding without knowing (or caring) who will respond. Finally, the notion of control is not limited to exchange; to produce a good or service is to engage in inanimate, biotic, and/or human control.

Much of macro economic phenomena are unanticipated consequences of human behavior and in that sense uncontrolled, but the major control questions (chapter 3) apply to economics. What is the efficacy of attempts to control the economy? How could the economy be controlled? What features of the economy are not subject to control in any social unit and, if so, why? Why is the economy more subject to attempts at control in some social units than in others? Why do humans fail to anticipate and/or recognize some economic consequences of their behavior? What does the future hold for control of the economy? In answering, economists might employ terms and methods that are alien to sociology, but sociologists would grasp the questions if control should become the central notion of both fields. The argument is not trite; no scientist can truly appreciate the questions pursued by another unless they share some notion.

Psychology

Diverse subject matter makes it difficult to describe and think of psychology in terms of control. Self-control appears to be the most directly relevant subject; but there is no well-known theory on it, and contemporary work by psychologists on "locus of control" (see Lefcourt's survey, 1984) has less bearing on self-control than it may appear. Nonetheless, control notions have important implications for all of psychology's broad divisions or specialties (see Hyams et al., 1982:177).

EXPERIMENTAL AND CLINICAL PSYCHOLOGY.   Virtually all experimental work in psychology has some bearing on this version of a major control question: How can human behavior be controlled? The bearing is most obvious in operant psychology; but many operant psychologists appear reluctant to speak of control, perhaps because Skinner's candid admission to an interest in human control provoked shrill criticism.

Operant psychology takes on added significance because it has a following among sociologists (e.g., Homans, Akers). Their attempts to apply operant principles have scarcely captured sociology; but they did *not* use control notions extensively, and those notions facilitate the sociological application of operant principles. Moreover, the prospects of integrating sociology and psychology through the notion of control are not limited to operant principles.

The reluctance of clinical psychologists to emphasize the connection between their work and human control is conspicuous but feckless. Although many clinicians engage exclusively in diagnostic work, diagnosis is a prelude to control attempts. Likewise, whatever the "behavior problem," a clinician's goals cannot be realized without human control, not even if the clinician seeks only to promote the patient's self-control. Rogerians and other specialists in "undirected" therapy claim that they help rather than control, but the claim will not survive scrutiny (see Skinner's commentary, 1974:185). All that has been said of clinical psychology applies *a fortiori* to psychiatry and social work.

Why have psychologists not made control their central notion? The answer is not that they have some other central notion, but the defensive stance of psychologists with an interest in behavior modification (e.g., Krasner, 1982) is suggestive. The stance is hardly surprising in light of charges that behavior modification is inherently evil and/or dangerous, charges that are consistent with the prevailing image of control in the social and behavioral sciences.

PSYCHOANALYSIS.   Because ineffective control rarely attracts attention, clinical psychology and psychiatry will interest few social scientists until radically new therapies are devised. That development is improbable without a distinct alternative to psychoanalytic theory; but since psychoanalysis has yet to be truly interred in the cemetery of ideas, the prospects for an integration of psychoanalysis and the social sciences deserves a brief hearing. After all, a multitude of social scientists have identified Freud as being a rival, a charlatan, or a genius. Moreover, sociologists, anthropologists, and political scientists should be willing to entertain integration if only because of the bearing of the widespread belief that social order requires socialization practices that produce a personality type, one which "fits" the culture and social structure.

Sociologists and anthropologists criticize Freud's assumption that psychosexual stages and related phenomena (e.g., the Oedipus complex) stem from instincts rather socialization. However, "socialization" is such a grab-bag notion that it makes the criticism in question unconstructive; and neither psychoanalysts nor social and behavioral scientists have really confronted this question: How could parents have an appreciable influence over their children's personalities without extensive attempts at behavioral control in the family context (parents over children and children over parents)? The point is that one need not be even a neo-Freudian to argue that parents have a great deal of influence on their children's personalities.

OTHER LINES OF WORK.   What is the appropriate methodology for inferring beliefs about the consequences of acts? The question bears directly on the methodology for the study of control—inanimate, biotic, or human; and there are some particularly relevant lines of work in psychology. The first line is the study of perception, including imputations, especially in connection with attribution theory, which is concerned with the how and why of perceptions of causation and dispositions (for a recent brief survey, see Hampson, 1985). Those studies are directly relevant when inferring control attempts; and they also bear on this question: Given an act, why are beliefs attributed to the actor by those who react? Whatever the answer, the attributions alone make human control a social phenomenon, and the outcome may depend appreciably on the perceptions of the control targets.

Identifying an act as attempted control requires inferences as to what the actor believes are desirable possible consequences, but sociologists need not explain why a possible consequence is believed desirable. Nonetheless, studies of the relation between the affective dimensions of internal behavior (e.g., attitudes, values) and overt behavior are relevant for inferences about control, even though the principal question is not the hoary issue whether overt behavior and attitudes are consistent. Rather, it is: What must an observer do to justify an inference that the actor not only perceives some consequence of his or her action but also perceives it as being desirable or undesirable (albeit perhaps unavoidable)?

NOTES

1. The fact that various important phenomena are ignored entirely should not be misconstrued. Thus, were it not for this note, critics might ask "But what about cooperation and control?," as though the two are clearly independent. To the contrary, cooperation requires control, involves control, or is necessary for success in various kinds of control. Doubts can be reduced by a careful reading of Axelrod's extensive analysis of cooperation (1984), even though he did not use a control terminology. Had he offered a careful conceptualization of cooperation, the relevance of control notions would have been even more obvious.

2. Conceptual problems are not avoided by this kind of definition of marriage (or "married"): a social relation is a marriage if and only if it is perceived as such by the related parties and/or other social unit members. Unless the phrase "perceived as such" pertains to the literal use of the term *marriage* by social unit members, it is hopelessly vague; but if it does so pertain, the definition would apply only in English-speaking populations and presume consensus in the use of the term.

3. Merton's theory of anomie and deviance (1957) is surely a candidate. It defies anything like systematic tests if only because Merton never even suggested how the disjunction of culturally approved goals and institutionalized (legitimate) means to those goals is to be measured in testing the theory (see Gibbs's commentary, 1985:42–46). Yet the very idea of "means" makes control relevant; and Merton's argument can be restated as follows: If individuals are deprived of access to socially approved means of control and/or those means are not stressed, those individuals will resort to deviant means of control.

4. The point is not just that virtually all phenomena of interest to social scientists can be described in terms of control; they can be described with greater clarity. Consider Nigel Davies's observation on human sacrifice: "all over the world, wherever one looks at the record, the sacrificial victims were taken from the same categories of people: war captives, slaves, women, and children—that is to say, precisely those who had few, if any rights of their own" (1984:22). The term *rights* has virtually no descriptive utility. Davies is clearly making observations on the control of human behavior, and those observations would have been less ambiguous had he used a control terminology.

5. To be sure, contemplation of an ultimate goal is hardly realistic until sociologists confront immediate problems and issues, such as the cavalier conceptualizations that haunt the field. Consider an illustration from Collins: " 'Society' is just an abstract way of talking about people encountering each other" (1975:54). Collins shows no awareness that the same could be said about any label for various other types of social units, such as community. But if society and community are both just abstract ways of talking about people encountering each other, how could they be different?

6. As a case in point, numerous sociologists appear fascinated with Durkheim's suggestion that societal reaction to deviance is more or less constant over time. He is conventionally interpreted as implying, among other things, that the annual size of the prison population varies very little (despite massive evidence to the contrary;

see, e.g., Cohen, 1985:45). Such assumed stability is attributed to Durkheim's equivalent to Adam Smith's invisible hand—society; and it illustrates the propensity of sociologists to view collective variables as unrelated to the purposive quality of human behavior. However, after reviewing work on the subject (see, e.g., *Journal of Criminal Law and Criminology*, Winter, 1981, 1772–812) and conducting research on trends in California's prison population, Berk et al. concluded that the "Durkheimian framework . . . may have diverted attention from what we suspect is at the core of these processes: a concern for maintaining resources sufficient to establish or continue the uneasy peace that is usually found inside prison walls. It may also have diverted attention from the conscious efforts correction officials constantly make to achieve this aim" (1983:580).

7. Paradoxically, Skinner (e.g., 1978:11) has devoted more attention to money as a means of control than has the typical contemporary sociologist (but see Smelt, 1980). Yet Weber (1978), Simmel (1978), and Marx (e.g., 1975-III:322–26) displayed real interest in money (Pareto's work on income distribution is also relevant). That interest will not be extended until control becomes sociology's central notion.

8. Note, however, that the anthropological literature has been used to classify parental control in numerous social units (predominantly non-Western and/or nonliterate) according to such general distinctions as extreme permissiveness, low control, firm control, and restrictive control. Two points should be made in connection with such studies (e.g., Rohner and Rohner, 1981): first, substantial inter-coder agreement is commonly reported in such analyses of control even though the observations in the literature used by the coders were not made for that purpose; and, second, studies of control need not employ the terminology introduced in chapters 2 and 3.

9. Nor is the point that the notion of control becomes most useful when describing or thinking about quantitative collective variables. It may well be that the notion is most useful when describing or thinking about qualitative social phenomena. Sorcery or witchcraft are cases in point, and it is significant that many of the observations on those two phenomena are couched in terms of control (see, e.g., Cawte, 1974).

10. Coleman's proposed strategy (1986) for establishing macro-micro relations and the present strategy are similar. However, he does not make use of the idea of a central notion, and his frequent reference to a theory of action only perpetuates Parsons's uncritical use of the term *theory*.

11. The problem is not peculiar to population size or density; it haunts all collective variables and all "macro" social theories. To illustrate, examine Woodward's statements (1983:811) made in reviewing Mahler's book (1980): "dependency theory is not theory, particularly in Mahler's version. It does not, nor does Mahler, explain how and why this pattern of association between international economic ties and lower welfare, greater repression, and less development occurs." The statements extend to "modernization" and "developmentalist" theories (see Nolan, 1983), and it may well be that what passes for dependency theory is more nearly a perspective (see Ragin, 1983:125). Doubts about all such theories or perspectives will flourish as long as mechanisms linking the structural variables remain unidentified.

12. "The war was about slavery. Slavery had caused it: If slavery had vanished before 1861, the war simply would not have taken place" (Catton, 1981:4).

13. The socialization research of Cook-Gumperez (1973) is a rare illustration of a concern with control; but she never defines socialization or control clearly, let alone such as to reveal the conceptual link between them.

14. The same could be said of all of the other social sciences, and attempts of sociologists (e.g., DeFleur et al., 1984:14) to distinguish their discipline from the other social sciences have been unproductive.

15. Lane and Stenlund (1984) identify ten different types of definitions of power.

Part

II

Some Conspicuous Features
of Control

Sociologists commonly state their basic question like this: How is social order possible? A more fundamental question is never contemplated: How are humans possible? Perhaps sociologists do not construe the second question as distinctively sociological. However, while a physiologist would answer the second question by stipulating conditions necessary to sustain human life, such as a certain minimum caloric intake, it does not follow that sociologists have nothing to add. For one thing, the idea of a minimum caloric intake gives rise to a third question: How do humans realize the conditions necessary for survival? The question cannot be answered satisfactorily without resort to control notions; and those notions are even relevant in contemplating a fourth question: How did a line of primates evolve into *Homo sapiens sapiens*? That question is the subject of chapter 5.

Since numerous arguments are made in chapter 5 to underscore the importance of inanimate control and biotic control for human survival, those two basic types of control are the subjects of simple illustrative theories in chapters 6 and 7. Lest the emphasis on inanimate and biotic control be construed as vulgar materialism, some qualifications are in order at the outset. Depending on the physiographic features of the environment (e.g., soil quality, weather) and the size of the human population, a certain amount of inanimate and biotic control is necessary to maintain that population. Yet it is not claimed that each human population realizes only that minimum amount, and diverse kinds of inanimate and biotic control could realize the minimum. Hence, an appeal to "human survival" fails as an answer to this question: Why do two human populations differ appreciably as to the kind and/or amount of inanimate and biotic control?

It is pointless to presume that a simple answer to the question can be given; and a complex answer must be pursued through a series of narrow theories, each limited to a particular feature of inanimate or biotic control. The illustrations of such theories in chapters 6 and 7 presuppose that both inanimate control and biotic control have some connection with the division of labor; but, contrary to the impression created by Durkheim, the division of labor is not a collective variable somehow apart from human behavior. To counter that impression, the theory in chapter 8 identifies a particular organizational context as at least necessary for a high degree of division of labor, and that context is described in terms of human control.

Chapter

5

Hominid Evolution

Most sociologists are indifferent to the origin of *Homo sapiens sapiens*. Although a theory about human society need not explain human origins, denials to the contrary, sociologists do study human behavior; hence, their disinterest in hominid evolution is paradoxical. Indeed, one strategic question about any candidate for sociology's central notion is this: To what extent is the notion useful in describing and thinking about hominid evolution?

Six Distinctive Human Characteristics

Humans differ from other animals in at least six conspicuous ways. First, humans would win the decathlon in an animal olympics because the versatility of their physical capacities is unique. Second, of all wingless animals, humans move greater distances and more uniformly by bipedal locomotion in an upright position. Third, the size of the human brain—absolutely and/or relative to total body weight—exceeds that of other animals. Fourth, humans evidently have a unique capacity for using arbitrary symbols to think and communicate (see, especially, White, 1973:1). Fifth, in comparison to other animals, human behavior appears to be shaped more by experience and learning than by hereditary or genetic predispositions (including instincts). Sixth, of all animals with hands, no species rivals *Homo sapiens sapiens* when it comes to dexterity without a diminution of the power grip.

The Relevance of Sociological Notions

The six contrasts are potentially relevant for an explanation of something that sociologists seldom consider—social differences between humans and other animals (e.g., much greater food sharing among humans than is typical of other animals). That potential will not be realized unless the contrasts can be described and thought of in terms of sociology's central notion. For that matter, even assuming that the distinctive human characteristics developed because they somehow furthered reproduction (increasing fertility and/or decreasing mortality), some notion is needed to identify the intervening processes or mechanisms. Only a few illustrations are needed to indicate why major sociological notions are not adequate for that purpose.

CONFLICT.   Once social conflict becomes lethal, then physical versatility, bipedalism, learning capacity, and dexterity might provide a reproductive advantage; but what of the capacity to use arbitrary symbols in communication? It would facilitate the organization of hominids in conflict with other primates or other hominids, but organization commonly requires cooperation. Moreover, there is no evidence of extensive lethal conflict among the earliest hominids.

If there is any relation between evolutionary stages and homicide rates, it appears that homicide first became common among relatively sendentary humans who domesticate plants, such as various New Guinea tribes (Hallpike, 1977), which is to say long after the appearance of the six distinctively human characteristics in question. For that matter, despite isolated instances of cannibalism among chimpanzees, apparently the nearest living "relatives" of early hominids, it grossly distorts to describe chimpanzee existence as persistently Hobbesian (Tanner, 1981).

NORMS.   The life of early hominids probably was far from idyllic if only because they evidently lacked effective weapons to cope with predators during most of the initial two or three million years. Hence, selection favored hominids who organized themselves to frustrate predators.

The alternative to organization ostensibly based on instincts (as among social insects) is normative behavior. If norms are construed as evaluations of conduct rather than merely behavioral uniformities, they are necessarily abstract and learned appreciably by communication through arbitrary symbols. Accordingly, assuming a large brain to be necessary for such communication, that distinctively human characteristic makes "normative" organization possible; and from the earliest hominids to *Homo sapiens* (unequivocal humans) normative organization somehow gave large-brained primates a reproductive advantage, although the average brain size of the earliest hominids evidently was not substantially greater than that of contemporary apes (see Johanson and Edey, 1981).

Granted that an adequate but completely anormative explanation of distinctive human characteristics is unlikely, norms have no obvious bearing on the bipedal locomotion, physical versatility, or dexterity. Those characteristics are conducive to intensive exploitation of the environment, but such exploitation is a matter of inanimate and biotic control, not norms.

INTERACTION AND SOCIAL RELATIONS.   Although the notions of interaction and of social relation often enter into definitions of sociology's subject matter, neither can be used readily to describe and think about all of the six distinctive human characteristics. When it comes to the frequency, duration, and regularity of interaction, there is no obvious contrast between early hominids and all other animals. True, in comparison to other animals, the medium of human interaction is predominantly a language based on arbitrary symbols and a phonetic code, which evidently requires a large brain. However, because a large brain did not appear until long after bipedalism and considerable physical versatility, it is by no means clear how "linguistic" interaction explains those two characteristics.

Social relations may transcend close genealogical ties (e.g., mother-child) and somehow connect individuals who interact only rarely. Such social relations increase the effective population size, which would be an advantage in coping with predators. However, for social relations to transcend genealogy and persist despite infrequent interaction, they must be formed and maintained by symbols; and that requirement suggests links between human social relations and three of the distinctively human characteristics—large brain, use of arbitrary symbols, and extensive learning (White, 1973:9–12). Nonetheless, there is no reason to suppose that early hominid bands transcended genealogy, and there is no obvious connection between social relations and either bipedal locomotion or physical versatility (but see Lovejoy's complicated argument in Johanson and Edey, 1981:309–40).

OTHER NOTIONS.   Because social conflict, norms, interaction, and social relations cannot be used readily to describe and think of all of the six distinctive human characteristics, nothing would be gained by considering other and less basic sociological notions as alternatives. It must suffice to assert that all other major sociological terms (e.g., stratification, status, institution, role, socialization, bureaucracy, group, and community) are even less useful.

In the present context, reference to "functions" would beg the question. That question is not whether the six distinctive human characteristics "functioned" to increase the reproductive advantage (lowering mortality and/or raising high fertility) of a particular primate line; rather, the question is how. Consider this schematic version of bipedal locomotion (B) and reproductive advantage (R).

$$B \longrightarrow X \longrightarrow R$$

Again, the question is how bipedal locomotion gave bipedalists a reproductive advantage, and the answer, X, must be a term that also serves to describe and think about sociology's subject matter. The term cannot be *function* because it is actually part of the question.

Control

The notion of control has far greater potential than any major social science notion when it comes to describing and thinking about the six distinctive human characteristics, but the claim is not that control explains those characteristics. Although a truly defensible explanation may never be realized, its pursuit is facilitated more by the notion of control more than by other notions.

BIPEDALISM AND VERSATILITY. The anatomical changes (e.g., broadening and shortening the pelvis, straightening of leg bones, arching the foot) that accompanied bipedal locomotion were such that the earliest hominids could walk or run long distances before becoming exhausted.[1] That increase in endurance or stamina enabled hominids to expand the range of their biotic control over a larger area, and the importance of that expansion cannot be exaggerated.

It is extremely unlikely that the earliest hominids were the voracious "killers" described by Robert Ardrey (see commentary by Johanson and Edey, 1981:65; Leakey and Lewin, 1978:128, 251–82). Lacking great size, strength, fangs, claws, or lethal weapons, those hominids could not bring down swift or dangerous animals, let alone persistently defend kills from large carnivores. So there is reason to assume that the earliest hominids hunted small animals, gathered wild vegetation, and scavenged the remains of large animals. Such control scarcely requires any technology; but even a small band of hominids (say 20 members) would have to search for food over a large area, especially in the savannas of East Africa, where hominids probably originated. The movement required depends on the field of vision, which is greater with upright posture. So upright posture and bipedalism facilitated biotic control over widely scattered plants and small animals; and the posture facilitated another kind of biotic control—avoiding predators by detecting their presence at a great distance.

Bipedalism did more than expand the long-range mobility; it also freed the hands to carry food, and carrying food to a protected location (e.g., a cave) promoted food sharing. Without food sharing, hominids would not have become big game hunters, because success in that kind of hunting (biotic control) is too problematical to insure the survival of isolated individuals with a meager technology. Hence, bipedal primates came to have a reproductive advantage, but it is scarcely less important that social individuals were selected.

Had the earliest hominid food been limited to ground plants or to slow, small animals, the mobility required for survival would have been even greater. Therein lies the significance of physical versatility—running, climbing, swimming, etc. No plant and few small land animals were beyond the control of early hominids. Moreover, versatility made the early hominids less vulnerable to predation, and the capacity of hominids to throw objects (inanimate control) led to more than baseball.

THE OTHER DISTINCTIVE HUMAN CHARACTERISTICS. The reproductive advantage promoted by food sharing is furthered by the capacity to communicate the location of food sources and water. While organisms can exploit a large area by dispersing and by carrying food to one place for sharing, an individual may find more food than he or she can carry; and transporting water was probably beyond the technology of early hominids. Merely appearing with food in hand or with thirst satiated communicates all too little, and the ability to communicate "where" and "how much more" could have been a life or death matter for a hominid band. Similarly, insofar as large numbers facilitate a defense against predators, dispersion in the food search is a disadvantage; and it can be overcome only through an ability to communicate the presence of predators, the kind of predators, and a defense strategy. Because arbitrary symbols make communication all the more flexible, they can be used both in predation defense and in organized hunting. Accordingly, assuming some complex association between cranial capacity and the use of arbitrary symbols in communication, hominids with the larger brain size had a reproductive advantage throughout hominid evolution.

The foregoing emphasis on communication is fully consistent with the larger thesis: a line of primates evolved into *Homo sapiens* because the changes gave that line a reproductive advantage through an increase in the range and scope of control. The initial increase was largely limited to biotic control, but control eventually changed such as to give a reproductive advantage to hominids with larger brains and the correlative capacity to use arbitrary symbols and to learn. That advantage stemmed in part from greater control of hominids over their fellows; but large brain and the correlative ability to learn perhaps played an even more decisive role in inanimate control, especially the invention and perfection of tools and weapons, even though a genuine stone technology evidently appeared some two million years after the first hominids.

The "control" argument is furthered by considering the human hand. Both the power grip and the precision grip are essential for creating and using various technological items. Because technology is the product of inanimate control and because the efficiency of biotic control (including predation defense) largely depends on the technology employed, hominids with the most dexterous and powerful hands had a reproductive advantage. However, the hand's evolution was a very long process, and the changes may have furthered hominid biotic control long before there was any hominid technology. In particular, once bipedalism freed the hand to carry food, dexterity in itself could have given bipedal primates a reproductive advantage.

Dexterity is also relevant in considering the consequences of increasing brain size. At birth, the human brain is only about 25 percent of its adult size. That neoteny enables human females to give birth with relative safety and without the great loss of mobility that an even wider pelvis would cause. Moreover, because some 75 percent of brain growth is postnatal, human behavior is much more learned than instinctive, which is all the more important given the postulated role of language in hominid evolution. But the human infant cannot survive without extensive care for several years. Dexterity facilitates infant care (holding, carrying, feeding), a special kind of human control. Bipedalism increased the reproductive advantage of dexterity all the more because it enabled hominids to carry infants, thereby permitting an increase in fertility without a proportional increase in child mortality.

Hominid Evolution: Major Stages

Paleoanthropologists describe hominid evolution largely in terms of major stages, the postulated appearance or disappearance of particular primate species. Accordingly, control is not sociology's central notion unless it can be used to describe and think about the major evolutionary stages that led to *Homo sapiens sapiens*.

Attempts to identify major stages continue to be controversial, despite more than a century of studies of primate fossils. The controversies stem more from grossly incomplete evidence than from the arguments of creationists. Quite literally, the evidence comes in bits and pieces—a skull fragment here, a tooth there—that are commonly difficult to date precisely. Even if all fossils could be examined and dated precisely, it might be difficult to identify decisive turns in the line leading to *Homo sapiens sapiens*. As a case in point, long before any animal remotely resembled humans, the ratio of brain size to body size commenced increasing; and since a large brain is a truly human characteristic, it could be said that human genesis began at least 600,000,000 years ago (see Wenke, 1980:85).

Australopithecus

Some 4,000,000 years ago East Africa came to be inhabited by a new animal, a featherless biped who walked and ran upright over great distances. *Australopithecus* was the link between apes and humans; but contemporary humans are not descendants of ancient gorillas, orangutans, or chimpanzees. Those apes are "cousins" of humans; the last common ancestor disappeared perhaps about 15,000,000 years ago.[2] The "hominid path" from that distant ancestor evidently led to *Australopithecus*.

There were at least two lines of Australopithicenes, and observations here are limited to the line that evidently led to contemporary humans.[3] The average height of early australopithecines could have been less than four feet, and the average weight somewhat less than 80 pounds. Those dimensions do not clearly distinguish australopithecines from contemporary pongids or humans (think of gibbons, gorillas, African pygmies, and the Masai); but in comparison to the average contemporary human, the australopithecines had a flatter skull, a much longer jaw, probably a less dexterous hand, larger teeth, and probably much more body hair. More important, the cranial volume of early australopithecines averaged about 450 cc, within the contemporary ape range but only about one-third the human average. So it was the bipedal locomotion and upright posture that marked the australopithecines as a major turning point in primate evolution, the first hominid.

The relatively small brain of the early australopithecines is consistent with speculation that they made crude stone weapons or tools (because bone and wood deteriorates rapidly, little can be said on that subject) if at all only shortly before ceasing to be a distinct species, about 1,500,000 B.C. Moreover, it is extremely doubtful that the australopithecines ever truly mastered the use of fire.

The character of australopithecine social life is mostly conjecture. They probably traveled and hunted in small bands, but the character of cooperation within the band and typical band size are unknown. Even the extent of the sexual division of labor is a matter of speculation, especially since the predominant kind of sexual relation is unknown (see Tanner and Zihlman, 1976, and Zihlman, 1978).

CONTROL. Nothing known about *Australopithecus* refutes the previous argument that an increase in the intensity (range and scope) of biotic control was the first major step in primate evolution toward *Homo sapiens sapiens*. That increase required bipedal locomotion and dexterity to forage over great distances and carry the food back to some "sharing" point.

Unfortunately, paleontological evidence cannot reveal whether or not the use of arbitrary symbols in communication commenced with *Australopithecus*. Nonetheless, intensive biotic control requires more than bipedal locomotion and dexterity; it also requires that the discoverer of a large food source communicate its location to others. We may never know the extent to which the australopithecines communicated with arbitrary symbols, but their survival without at least some such symbols and communication is difficult to imagine. Here were animals without exceptional speed, great strength, fangs, or claws, but they reproduced perhaps for over two million years without using stone tools extensively. So there must have been something about australopithecine technology that has not and perhaps cannot be discovered. Several commentators (e.g., Tanner and Zihlman, 1976:598–603; Leakey and Lewin, 1978:130–42) have pointed to a major possibility—the carrying bag, a technological item that would not be discovered among fossils. The creation and use of a carrying bag is inanimate control, and the notion of control is essential to describe the carrying bag's significance. Not even a very dexterous individual can transport numerous nuts, roots, berries—the very foods that most likely sustained the early australopithecenes. So the carrying bag would have expanded the intensity of biotic control enormously. Moreover, carrying food to a particular place (a cave or some other defensible space) promoted food sharing; and food sharing is an effective basis of human control, for the message is simple: conform or risk starvation.

The carrying bag also may have resulted in a quantum jump in the sexual division of labor. Since australopithecenes evidently survived primarily as gatherers, the carrying bag could have made women the principal producers (Tanner and Zihlman, 1976). That development in turn freed men to engage extensively in hunting, which set the stage for even more intensive biotic control once the australopithecenes possessed weapons and tools. So women perhaps deserve the principal credit for the survival of *Australopithecus*.

Homo erectus

One candidate for "first unequivocal human" (i.e., *Homo sapiens*), designated by paleoanthropologists as *Homo erectus*, appeared perhaps as early as 1,500,000 B.C.[4] As the name suggests, those creatures walked and ran erect; but so did *Australopithecus*. Yet *Homo erectus* had a cranial volume on the average nearly twice that of the early australopithecines and within the lower range of contemporary humans.

The average height of *erectus* probably was about five feet, with an average weight of around 100 pounds. However, recent findings suggest a much larger size, especially height; but, in any case, *erectus* probably had a more powerful build (thicker bones relative to body size) than do contemporary humans. The hands of *erectus* were only slightly less dexterous (if at all) relative to contemporary humans, but *erectus* had a smaller head, a flatter skull, a much more prominent brow ridge, a much longer jaw, larger teeth, a less prominent chin, and probably more body hair. Hence, in numerous respects *erectus* was intermediate between *Australopithecus* and contemporary humans.

CONTROL. Given the brain size of *Homo erectus*, it is not surprising that they made a variety of stone tools (choppers, daggers). Contemporary humans would regard those tools crude, but not if they tried to make similar objects. For that matter, only stone tools remain intact over thousands of years, and *Homo erectus* probably worked bone and wood with appreciable skill.

Homo erectus mastered fire; and that mastery, along with their construction of crude shelters, enabled them to move into cold climates. Mastery of fire was essential for warmth and to cook meat from big animals, the primary food source in a cold climate. Cooking food is not just a matter of taste. Various uncooked foods are difficult to chew, swallow, and digest; hence, the mastery of fire by *Homo erectus* probably increased their scope of biotic control.

Whereas the australopithecenes were largely if not entirely limited to the warm parts of Africa and Asia, *Homo erectus* inhabited various parts of Europe, South Asia, and even northern parts of contemporary China. However, it does not follow that *erectus* "invaded" cold climates with a suitable technology. In Europe they had to cope with the early Ice Ages, and their coping may have stimulated major technological innovations.

Although little is known about their social organization, *erectus* may have been something more than a "small band animal." Like many contemporary huntergatherers (e.g., those occupying the Kalahari Desert), the members of a typical *erectus* band probably numbered around 25; but several bands may have coordinated their hunting enterprises periodically, thereby setting the scene for social units larger than immediate kindred, perhaps something like clans or lineages. But that is speculation, and the same is true of virtually all observations on the social organization of *Homo erectus*.

It is reasonable to assume that the sexual division of labor among *erectus* was more conspicuous than among the australopithecenes; but the assumption is reasonable only because the technology and hunting enterprises of *erectus* were not drastically different from those of some contemporary hunting and gathering peoples, where there is often a conspicuous sexual division of labor. Yet that reasoning ignores a possible major contrast. As remarked by Wenke: "In basic patterns of subsistence and social organization . . . *Homo erectus* appears to have been very similar to modern hunters and gatherers; yet there is something alien about these creatures. We look for artifacts expressing ritual or complex symbolism, but not a single figurine, wall painting, or rock carving can be securely attributed to *Homo erectus*" (1980:163).

Many controversies that preoccupy paleoanthropologists are not relevant for the present thesis—that the major anatomical changes in primate evolution leading to *Homo sapiens sapiens* were such as to expand control (all basic types). *Homo erectus* is additional evidence that an increase in brain size was necessary for more effective inanimate control, the creation of stone tools in particular. Effective inanimate control increased the reproductive advantage of large-brained hominids indirectly, by increasing the intensity of their biotic control, especially in predator defense, killing big game, and making food more digestible.

The Neanderthals

Relative to modern humans, Neanderthals (circa 150,000 B.C.–35,000 B.C.) had larger cheekbones, a much more prominent brow ridge, less of a chin, bigger teeth, a larger nose, and probably somewhat more body hair. So on the whole Neanderthals were intermediate between *erectus* and contemporary humans; but they had a more powerful body build than either *erectus* or contemporary humans, and their average cranial volume was somewhat larger on the average than that of contemporary humans.

The differences between Neanderthals and *erectus* with respect to social life and technology appear far less than suggested by the cranial contrast. The tools of the Neanderthals exceeded those of *erectus* both in effectiveness and in variety, but there is no compelling evidence of a major technological innovation. Although the Neanderthals probably made greater and more sophisticated use of bones, wood, and especially stone (flint), they evidently did not exploit a substantially greater variety of raw materials or domesticate plants.

Although behavioral changes are difficult to detect from material remains, there is no convincing evidence that social life changed drastically with the appearance of Neanderthals. Like *erectus*, Neanderthals hunted in bands; and there is no evidence that the scale of their social organization was appreciably greater than that of *erectus*. Neanderthal social life may have resembled that of contemporary hunters and gatherers somewhat more than did the social life of *erectus*; but there is no basis to argue that pair bonding, clans, exogamy, and a clear-cut sexual division of labor commenced with Neanderthals.

The major unanswered question about Neanderthals: Given the great increase in cranial volume over *erectus*, why is there so little evidence of technological and social changes of a corresponding magnitude? The only plausible answer is that the Neanderthals' tenure was very short, perhaps no more than 100,000 years. Given that short span, it is significant that Neanderthals evidently had a greater capacity for complex symbolism than did *erectus*, the most obvious manifestation being Neanderthal ceremonies for the dead, as suggested by evidence of floral arrangements in a grave (see Leakey, 1982:57).

Neurological changes—inferred from an increase in cranial volume—influence both the capacity for symbolic behavior and for technological innovations; but, evidently, changes in symbolic behavior are manifested much more quickly and fully. If so, human art and symbolism in general will not change drastically without a "neurological leap" comparable to that manifested in the Neanderthals. Changes in technology are slower, and the full technological manifestation of even major genetic alterations may be delayed for an enormous time. To illustrate, the inspiration to place flowers in a grave is one thing but building an airplane is quite another, largely because the latter requires thousands of innovations in a particular sequence.

Contrary to what has been said about the big brains of Neanderthals, they may not have been the link between *erectus* and the first *Homo sapiens sapiens*, the Cro-magnons. While Neanderthals were not limited to Europe, it could be that they evolved from *erectus* only in Europe as a response to a cold environment and the concomitant predominance of big animals as a food source. If so, Cro-magnon may have evolved from Neanderthals in Europe but elsewhere from *erectus*. In any case, the relatively sudden disappearance of Neanderthals is puzzling.

CONTROL. Whatever the fate of Neanderthals, it would not refute the thesis that an increase in brain size was necessary for greater biotic, inanimate, and behavior control. True, there is no evidence that the Neanderthal technology was radically different from that of *erectus*; but, again, the technological consequences of an increase in brain size may be fully manifested only after a very long period, and the survival of the Neanderthals in the Ice Age was in itself a monumental technological achievement.

It would be difficult to exaggerate the importance of evidence of the Neanderthal's symbolic capacity. There is no way to demonstrate that the capacity promoted behavioral control; nonetheless, there is a basis for presuming that the Neanderthals advanced the use of arbitrary symbols.

The Cro-magnons

Between some 35,000 and 50,000 years ago Neanderthals began to give way to Cro-magnons, but it would be misleading to suggest that humans evolved from Cro-magnons. Rather, since there is no evidence of any significant physical difference between Cro-magnons and at least some contemporary humans, Cro-magnons never became extinct.

There is a striking resemblance between the technology of Cro-magnons and that of some contemporary hunting-gathering people. The stone tools of the Cro-magnons were generally more effective than those of Neanderthals, and they expanded the variety of technological items enormously with such inventions as the spear thrower. The capacity for symbolic expression, first manifested among the Neanderthals, was extended by Cro-magnons to impressive carvings, dramatic paintings on cavern walls, and a sense of style in tools.

Because various fundamentals of human social organization (e.g., food sharing, pair bonding, sexual division of labor) may have been present before the Cro-magnons, it is questionable to attribute any particular social invention to them. The bulk of their technology can be described as extensions of a trend that commenced with *Home erectus*. There is no evidence of a basic neurological difference between Neanderthals and Cro-magnons. The contrast in cranial volume was not great, and other contrasts (e.g., Cro-magnons were taller, Neanderthals had a more massive brow) appear important largely because Cro-magnons and contemporary humans differ so little.

Because there is no evidence of any appreciable biological change in *Homo sapiens sapiens* over the last 35,000 years or so, the vast social and technological changes during the past 10,000 years indicate that human history is genetically determined only in a very distant sense. Specifically, even granting that airplanes or television could not have been invented by *Australopithecus*, the biological preconditions antedate the Cro-magnons.

CONTROL. All things considered, the Cro-magnons extended a trend that commenced with *Australopithecus* some four million years ago. That trend is an ever increasing intensity of biotic control.[5] The intensification, especially the killing of large animals, required an increase in the effectiveness of inanimate control. However, the emphasis on inanimate control should not be construed as belittling behavior control. It is conceivable that, perhaps largely independently of technological change, the development of a truly human language increased behavioral hominid control, which in turn facilitated biotic control (e.g., predator defense and predation). That possibility takes on special significance in the case of Cro-magnons, because of doubts about the nature of Neanderthal language. If a truly human language appeared only with the Cro-magnons, then the present account greatly underestimates the evolutionary significance of the Cro-magnons. Nonetheless, to argue that the Neanderthals survived without an effective means of communication (truly human or not) taxes credulity.

Even if Cro-magnons originated with a massive genetic mutation that made them neurologically quite different from Neanderthals (despite the similarity in brain size), the control thesis would not be refuted. Indeed, whether or not a genetic mutation provides a reproductive advantage depends on the answer to this question: Did the mutation expand the capacity for control? Thus, even if the first truly human language developed among Cro-magnons, that change would not have resulted in a reproductive advantage unless it furthered the capacity for human control and, indirectly, biotic control.

Some Illustrations of Other Developments

Several developments in hominid history are best ignored because a description of them in terms of control entails enormous conjectures. However, a few such developments should be examined briefly if only to indicate what must be known to go beyond conjecture.

The Absence of Estrus

The human female is more receptive to sexual advances by males when not ovulating than is typical of primates in general.[6] The difference may appear very important, meaning that it must have all manner of consequences; yet it is difficult to identify those consequences.

There is no widely accepted explanation of the "loss" of estrus in hominid evolution. One explanation (Campbell, 1976:178–79) attributes it to an environmental change that led to a fission of hominid bands into much smaller groups, with only one adult male in most groups. The argument seems to be that when a male and female are together for a long time, a continuous sexual interest between them develops. The periods of the female's sexual receptivity gradually became longer and longer, until she became more or less continuously receptive (see Campbell, 1976:178).

One can imagine a long-run aridization of the early hominids' environment so intense that it eliminated those hominids who did not enlarge their range of biotic control and disperse in very small groups; but the correlative explanation of estrus loss in those terms leaves at least two questions unanswered. What was the character of control of sexual relations before disbanding? If pairbonding existed before disbanding, why would the isolation of adult couples bring about the end of estrus?

Disbanding or dispersion would end estrus if before disbanding there was negligible "exclusionary" control over sexual relations, such that virtually all males had an opportunity for sexual intercourse with any ovulating female. Once dispersed, males would have been no less inclined to seek frequent sexual gratification, and females who were sexually receptive more or less continuously would have been selected. The other females, those sexually receptive only when ovulating, would have had two reproductive disadvantages. First, males would have been less likely to share food with those females or protect them from predators. Second, because of the dispersion of males, women who were sexually receptive only when ovulating would have been less likely to be impregnated and continue contributing to the gene pool, thereby over several generations eliminating females who were genetically predisposed to estrus. Of course, selectivity would operate only if there were substantial variation among females with regard to estrus before disbanding, and dispersion itself would work against the survival of the population unless inanimate control were such that isolated male-female pairs could effectively fend off predators.

The foregoing is conjectural (for a contrary view, see Zihlman, 1978:10), and at least three kinds of evidence are needed to go beyond conjecture. First, there must be evidence of an aridization of the hominid environment that for several hundred years substantially reduced the availability of hominid food. Second, evidence must be found of greater dispersal of hominids shortly after the outset of aridization. And, third, among hominid artifacts at that time there must have been a weapon or device that would be an effective defense against predation when used by only two adults. Because there is evidence that hominids commenced making effective weapons about two million B.C., the argument suggests that they were promiscuous before that date. To be sure, the suggestion is speculation, but no notion—control in this case—can be central unless it fuels speculation.

Facial Features

The facial features of early hominids evidently were conspicuously different from those of contemporary humans. For example, relative to contemporary humans, the typical hominid had larger teeth and a very prominent brow. Why? Raw meat and tough vegetables are difficult to swallow and digest without extensive chewing; and in addition to large teeth (a persistent trait of early hominids), the chewing requires powerful muscles, which in turn require large head bones. So this conjecture: the persistence of early hominid facial features stemmed from characteristics of biotic and inanimate control among early hominids. Being without domesticated plants or animals, early hominids could not limit their consumption to readily digestible food; and until the mastery of fire they could make food more digestible only by chewing or pulverizing it.

Because hominids mastered fire to some extent before the Neanderthals, the contrasts in the facial features of Neanderthals and Cro-magnons may appear puzzling. However, the effectiveness of inanimate control was substantially greater among Cro-magnons, who may have invented devices for starting a fire effectively and quickly (see Campbell, 1976:390). Moreover, Neanderthals may have used their front teeth extensively as a built-in tool, like pliers, to hold one end of wood, bone, or hide and leaving a hand free to cut, scrape, or puncture the material. Given the variety of items in the typical Cro-magnon tool kit, teeth came to be used less as a tool substitute; and powerful muscles attached to large head bones contributed less to inanimate control and survival.

The Loss of Body Hair

Humans are the least hairy of primates, but early australopithecines may have been very hairy animals. The loss of hair in the course of hominid evolution can be described in terms of biotic and inanimate control.

In coming to occupy a particular ecological niche in the savannas of East Africa, hominids engaged in a kind of biotic control—hunting and gathering food (including scavenging) over great distances—that required extend periods of physical exertion and exposure to intense sunlight. The "biological" solution was the development, through selectivity, of more sweat glands and the concomitant reduction of hair cover that inhibits evaporative cooling of the body (see Campbell, 1976:254; Carrier, 1984).

But what of the even more hairless human female? An answer requires recognition again that females played a crucial role in the food quest of early hominids (see, especially, Tanner and Zihlman, 1976), a "gathering" role that required considerable physical exertion under intense sunlight. Selection thus favored females without thick body hair, even though that skin covering protects against skin lacerations that are particularly prone to become infected. However, because females specialized in food gathering, they may have been less exposed to dangerous encounters with animals and skin lacerations than big-game hunters (males); and the risk was perhaps even greater for males because of their role in predator defense.

Genetic Change and Control

Previous observations have ignored a necessary condition for any qualitative change in animals or plants, be that change anatomical, physiological, or behavioral. That necessary condition is a genetic mutation or a new combination of genetic materials brought about by any of several different ways, (e.g., exposure to intense radiation), several of which may be unknown.

All distinctly human behavior, whether shooting craps or praying, stemmed from genetic mutations or new combinations of genetic materials. Observe, however, that genetic mutations alter only the potential range of one or more features of the organism's offspring, and the environment may be such that the new possibilities are never realized. Indeed, far from furthering reproduction, a genetic change may have lethal consequences (the fetus is not born alive) or results in deformities that reduce the probability of reproduction.

Appearance to the contrary, genetic change can be described and thought of in terms of control, at least in the case of hominid evolution. Whatever the major changes and whenever or wherever they took place, some of them furthered hominid evolution by expanding the capacity of some line of primates and some subsequent hominids for control over the environment. Those primates and subsequent hominids became more numerous because their control over the environment increased the ratio of births to deaths.

It may appear that "controlling the environment" is equivalent to "adapting to the environment," but the latter phrase is a monument to vagueness (see Bargatzky, 1984). To say that a population has adapted to an environment is to say nothing more precise than that births exceed deaths in that population. Whatever adaptation may be, it is commonly thought of as an end product or state; hence, it is hardly meaningful to point to the activity of a particular animal and say: That is adaptation to the environment. By contrast, one can point to all manner of specific means of controlling the environment, such as clothing, houses, cultivation, and pesticides; and whatever is meant by adaption, humans "adapt" to an environment by controlling features or parts of it.

NOTES

1. Lovejoy is described in Johanson and Edey (1981:309) as ridiculing the idea that bipedalism increased mobility or the efficiency of movement, but he persists in comparing bipedalism and quadrupedalism among animals in general rather than among primates exclusively. The most strategic comparison would be between the first truly bipedal primates and the quadrupeds from which the bipeds evolved. Finally, it is not claimed that bipedalism was the only characteristic that contributed to speed, endurance, and/or stamina in running (see, especially, Carrier, 1984).

2. As noted by Tisdall (1981:90), some findings in biochemistry suggest that the

divergence of hominids and apes may have been much later, perhaps as recently as 5,000,000 B.C. However, any estimate as to the timing of the divergence is most controversial.

3. According to Johanson and White's version (1979) of hominid evolution, the first australopithicenes—*afarensis*—diverged into two lines between 2,000,000 and 3,000,000 B.C. One of the lines led to *Homo sapiens* possibly through *Homo habilis* (see note 4) and certainly through *Homo erectus*. The other line led through *Australopithecus africanus* to *Australopithecus robustus* and came to an end. When is another question (possibly as late as 1,000,000 B.C.), as it is for most divisions of *Australopithecus* or *Homo*. The possibility of the co-existence of various divisions is a major issue, and still another of the many issues is the proper use of the term *boisei* in designating and "locating" (both spatially and temporally) divisions of *Australopithecus* (see Walker et al., 1986).

4. Still another and earlier candidate is conventionally designated as *Homo habilis*, a division that originated about 2,500,000 B.C., concomitant with the appearance of conspicuous stone tools or weapons (see Leakey and Lewin, 1978). Even if *Homo habilis* is recognized as a distinct species in hominid evolution (see Leakey, 1982), not enough is known to identify incontrovertible qualitative differences between them and all divisions of *Australopithecus* or *Homo erectus*. The general problem is that a description of hominid evolution in terms of distinct species or even sharp discontinuities may be far less realistic than a description in terms of purely quantitative trends (e.g., a larger and larger brain).

5. Lest the point appear irrelevant for contemporary humans, the intensification of biotic control has long since reached the point of a paradox. Although the intensification was necessary to support a global human population of several billion, the very intensity of current biotic control makes human survival problematical. To illustrate briefly, because humans do not control the weather, some major sudden change in global climate (e.g., a sudden and sharp drop in temperature) could result in a catastrophic decrease in the efficacy of biotic control because the flexibility of biotic control has declined for millenia concomitant with its increasing specialization.

6. The absence of estrus is not identified as a distinctive human characteristic because some observations (e.g., Tisdall, 1981:107–22) suggest that estrus is not uniformly present in all nonhuman primates. However, it may well be that no one characteristic (e.g., bipedalism) categorically distinguishes hominids from all other primates, past and present. Indeed, it is more realistic to think of a "hominid" as a distinctive configuration of traits, some of which are found among some other primates. So the present focus on isolated traits is an oversimplification.

An Illustrative Theory About Inanimate Control

Although inanimate control is not limited to technology, therein lies its primary significance. Technological items are created through inanimate control, and their use or maintenance is necessarily inanimate control. Moreover, technological items are commonly used in biotic and human control.

The Paucity of Technological Theories

Whatever their theoretical orientation, sociologists grant the importance of technology (see DeFleur, 1982). Perhaps they recognize that, antimaterialism in the humanities notwithstanding, making numerous and diverse things is a truly distinctive human characteristic. Yet there is *not one* well-known theory about technology. As described by Winner: "William Ogburn's cultural lag thesis, whereby social and cultural institutions are seen to drag behind technological development by a number of years, is still, unfortunately, just about the most profound general view that we have" (1977:77).

The paucity of theories indicates that social scientists cannot think of technology readily in terms of its behavioral correlates, but the difficulty is paradoxical because technology creates a surplus of human time and energy. Bereft of technology, humans could survive (if at all) only by devoting virtually all time and energy to quests for essentials. Viewed that way, humans engage in elaborate religious ceremonials, organized games, warfare, etc., because technology makes those activities possible; but such reasoning smacks of vulgar technological determinism, and it is sterile. In particular, granted that humans would never engage in religious ceremonials without a time-energy surplus, the surplus alone scarcely generates a religious fervor, let alone determines whether humans will be monotheists. The surplus creates only a potential for "nonessential" activities, and there is no basis for assuming that it determines also the content of those activities.

Even an accurate description of the behavioral correlates of a particular technological innovation is no substitute for a theory. Consider one of many of Marx's suggestions of technological determinism: "The handmill gives you society with the feudal lord; the steam-mill, society with the industrial capitalist" (1963:109). Valid or not (see Weber, 1978:1091), the statement merely asserts a connection between events in European history; and it cannot be deduced from any identifiable premises in Marx's theory. Moreover, Marx did not answer several parallel historical questions, such as: What technological changes produced the transition from slavery to feudalism? Even if Marx had demonstrated conclusively that the steam engine ushered in capitalism, there are two reasons why the demonstration would not constitute a theory. First, it would not justify a generalization beyond 18th-century Europe. And, second, even in that space-time context the demonstration would not imply anything about other technological items and institutions.

The second reason takes on special significance because in any country the number of types of technological items (e.g., tires, cameras, syringes) is beyond counting, and a theory about each type is unrealistic. Paradoxically, a theory about technology as a whole is more feasible, but only if general properties of technology can be identified. Such a theory follows; but it is only a simple illustration, and it is not so much an explanation of technology as it is an explanation of the relation between technology and the division of labor.

Properties of Technology and the Division of Labor

The initial problem is that seemingly infinite properties of technology can be identified. Because each technological item has a color, any set of items can be described in terms of color variety. Intuitively, color variety is not a significant property, but intuition is not enough. A central notion is needed to justify a focus on some properties while ignoring others, and the present focus is on technological efficiency and technological complexity.

Technological Efficiency

Most technological items are essential to realize some physical goal or to reduce the time and/or human energy required. To understand the first possibility, try to imagine space travel without vehicles. All such human limitations are described by a control principle, the "principle of indispensability" (6–1): Some types of attempted control are ineffective without the use of a particular type of technological item.

The term *efficiency* is used here to denote a reduction in the time and/or energy required to realize a physical goal. If someone requires 60 minutes to fell a tree with an axe, whereas doing it without technology (i.e., by gnawing, pushing, etc.) or without an animal would have required 1,200 minutes, then the axe's *gross temporal efficiency* (GTY) in that case was: GTY$=1-(60/1200)=.950$. Now suppose that felling the tree with an axe requires 450 calories of human energy beyond the metabolic (i.e., calories burned at full rest), whereas 22,500 calories are required without any technology or an animal; as such, the axe's *gross energy efficiency* (GEY) in that particular situation was: GEY$=1-(450/22,500)=.980$.

The examples just given pertain to gross technological efficiency, in that the amount of human time, human energy, animal energy, and inanimate energy (e.g., coal, hydroelectricity) invested in the axe's production, distribution, and maintenance have been ignored. When such amounts enter into the formula, the computed value pertains to *net technological efficiency* (NTY). To illustrate, suppose that in addition to the 60 minutes required to fell the tree some 120 minutes were invested in the axe's construction, and further suppose that the axe becomes irreparable after about 6,000 minutes use in felling trees. As such, the 60 minutes consumed 1 percent (60/6000) or 72 seconds of the 120 minutes invested in the axe. So the total direct and indirect human time in felling the tree was 61 minutes and 12 seconds; hence, the axe's *net temporal efficiency* was: NTY$=1-(61.2/1200)=.949$.

Now assume that the equivalent of 1,800 calories of human, animal, and inanimate energy were required to produce, transport, and maintain the axe. If so, 1 percent (60/6000) or 18 calories were required to fell the tree beyond the 450 burned in the 60 minutes of chopping. Accordingly, the approximate *net energetic efficiency* of the axe was: NEY$=1-(468/22,500)=.979$.

In the illustrative case the gross-net contrast is negligible, but in some countries (the U.S. being one) the contrast in the realization of various physical goals appears enormous. The exact amount cannot be even estimated because the time or energy required to realize physical goals without technology is conjectural. A more precise sense of the gross-net contrast requires observations on food production. On average, about 26,040 kilocalories (kcal) of human energy is invested per hectare in spinach production, and the kcal yield (per hectare) is 2,912,000 (Pimentel and Pimentel, 1979:91). Hence, *gross food production efficiency* (GFPY) in growing spinach is: GFPY$=2,912,000/26,040=112.00$; but when the inanimate energy used is considered in addition to human energy, *net food production efficiency* (NFPY) in growing spinach is 0.23. So American spinach production is inefficient in that the total energy (human, animal, and inanimate) invested far exceeds the food's caloric value. Such a situation is peculiar to countries where agriculture is highly mechanized. Thus, the net energetic efficiency of rice production is approximately 7.00 for the Iban of Borneo but about 1.55 in California (Pimentel and Pimentel,

1979:75–77).[1] The contrast primarily reflects the more extensive use of inanimate energy in California rice production.

THE INITIAL POSTULATE.   Even if technology is efficient in the gross sense and/or indispensable, neither property can be expressed numerically. However, arguments can be made in support of *Postulate 6–1*: Among countries, the greater the gross efficiency and indispensability of technology during T_{0-1}, the greater the per capita inanimate energy use over T_{0-1}.

The postulate asserts that *if it were possible* to measure the gross efficiency and indispensability (a composite value representing both) of all technological items in each of several countries at any point during any particular year (T_{0-1}) and the amount of inanimate energy used per capita in each country throughout that year, there would be a close direct relation between the two sets of values. The amount of inanimate energy used is not a measure of the two technological properties (gross efficiency and indispensability); rather, it is an asserted correlate of those two properties. Although the postulate is testable only in principle, without the temporal quantifier (T_{0-1}, signifying *any* year) it would be so ambiguous as to preclude falsification. Not even a simple equation (e.g., $X=3Y$) that asserts an empirical relation can be refuted without a stipulation of the relation's temporal character; and some asserted relations are vacuously true without such a stipulation. Thus, if it is asserted that an increase in X is followed by a decrease in Y, then an increase in X (whatever X may be) is virtually certain to be followed by a decrease in Y (whatever Y may be) *some time and some place*. While temporal quantifiers in the theorems (conclusions) are essential for tests, they should appear also in the premises to indicate how the theorist thinks of the relation.[2] The failure of sociologists to stipulate temporal quantifiers (or something akin) when stating a theory reflects an indifference to the need for systematic tests.

The compound construct in Postulate 6–1, "gross efficiency and indispensability of technology," cannot be defined completely; and although it pertains to a quantitative phenomenon, an empirically applicable formula cannot be stated. Hence, direct tests of the postulate are precluded even though the constituent concept—per capita inanimate energy use—can be linked to an empirically applicable formula (*infra*).[3] Yet once the postulate is linked with other premises (*infra*), all of the premises can be tested indirectly through direct tests of the conclusions (theorems). So, contrary to the tenets of operationalism, a theory can be tested systematically even though some of its constituent terms denote vague notions, unobservable phenomena, or things not subject to measurement. But unless stated formally (i.e., in accordance with rules that transcend the conventions of a natural language), such a theory's logical structure will be so obscure that all purported tests are debatable.

Technological Complexity and the Division of Labor

When social units are arranged in order of estimated per capita inanimate energy use (e.g., U.S., 1980; U.S., 1900; and Cheyenne Indians, 1840) and casual observations are made on other technological contrasts, in high-energy social units (e.g., U.S., 1980) there appears to be a much greater variety of technological items. Variety is indicative of technological complexity; but the theoretical implications are richer if complexity is defined in terms of control: a social unit's technological items are complex to the extent that the typical member cannot effectively control (create, operate, and maintain) each type of item.[4] To illustrate, suppose there are 37,000 distinct types of technological items in a particular social unit, but the typical member cannot effectively control more than 740. *Technological complexity* (TC) would be: $TC = 1 - (740/37,000) = .980$.

Several terms in the definition of technological complexity (e.g., typical member, effectively control, type of technological item) offer little in the way of empirical applicability if left undefined, but empirically applicable definitions cannot be formulated. Moreover, even if there were no objections to the formula for measuring technological complexity, the resources required to apply it would be prohibitive. Nonetheless, in light of previous observations, a defensible statement can be made about a correlate of technological complexity. *Axiom 6–1*: Among countries, the greater the gross efficiency and indispensability of the technology during T_{0-1}, the greater the technological complexity during T_{0-1}. The statement is identified as an axiom because it links two constructs (by contrast, a postulate links a construct and a concept).

The definition of technological complexity suggests one of two limiting factors—no human can master infinite varieties of inanimate control. Population size is the other limiting factor; but it is relevant only insofar as social unit members engage in different types of inanimate control, especially the technological items they attempt to master. Because an occupation can be virtually defined by reference to the technological items used, the variety of occupations in a social unit tends to set a limit on technological complexity; and such variety is a correlate of the division of labor. The relation is stated formally as *Axiom 6–2*: Among countries, the greater the technological complexity during T_{0-1}, the greater the degree of division of labor during T_{0-1}.

THE DIVISION OF LABOR AND OCCUPATIONAL DIFFERENTIATION. Were it not for the division of labor, technological complexity would be limited by the typical human's ability (mental and physical) to master the creation, use, and maintenance of technological items. Such mastery is successful inanimate control, and there is surely a limit as to the variety of "things" (e.g., tools and machines) that any human can control effectively. Hence, unless increases in the division of labor are proportionate with increases in technological complexity, the typical social unit member's attempts at inanimate control become ineffective. The assumption is that humans typically do not attempt control without anticipating success; and although "tolerance-for-failure" may vary somewhat, the variance does not preclude the relation asserted in Axiom 6–2. Again, however, nothing whatever is gained by characterizing the assumption as one of "rationality."

The division of labor is a complex notion if only because it refers both to differentiation in sustenance activities (i.e., individual differences in production behavior) and to the concomitant functional interdependence. Neither dimension of the division of labor, differentiation or interdependence, can be defined completely or expressed numerically (however, see Ervin, 1987); but general observations justify the assumption that the two dimensions vary directly, and in the case of countries an argument can be made for assuming that differentiation in sustenance activities and occupational differentiation also vary directly. *Occupational differentiation* refers to the number of occupational categories in a population and the evenness or uniformity of the distribution of population members among the categories. So we arrive at *Postulate 6–2*: Among countries, the greater the division of labor during T_{0-1}, the greater the occupational differentiation during T_{0-1}.

Other Correlates of the Division of Labor

A wide variety of sustenance activities can be realized in a population if (1) each member changes his or her sustenance activity every few minutes but with negligible differences among members *or* (2) each member engages in the same sustenance activity (e.g., driving a cab) throughout the day but with substantial differences among members. Casual observations suggest that the second way prevails; and individual differences constitute one of the two dimensions of the division of labor, the other being functional interdependence. So we have *Axiom 6–3*: Among countries, the greater the degree of division of labor during T_{0-1}, the greater the variety of sustenance activities during T_{0-1}.

While Axiom 6–3 indicates *how* a variety of sustenance activities is realized, it does not answer this question: In contemporary countries, why do individuals rarely vary their sustenance activity throughout the day? The answer lies in two generalizations. First, all sustenance activities involve inanimate, biotic, and/or human control. Second, when humans attempt control, they perceive the means employed as increasing the probability of success. Now contemplate someone driving a cab for ten minutes, then tailoring for ten minutes, then practicing surgery for ten minutes, and so forth. Each activity is an attempt at control, and control efficacy is likely to be perceived as substantially greater if the individual engages only in that activity. Should it be alleged that the argument depicts humans as rational, invoking that term introduces an obscure consideration and invites sterile debates.

INDUSTRY DIFFERENTIATION. Once individual differences in sustenance activities become conspicuous and seemingly permanent, individuals come to be identified as to industry, meaning as to the type of object or service they produce or to which production they contribute (as in the case of a secretary employed by a manufacturing firm). Stated more abstractly, industry differentiation is a theoretical correlate of variety of sustenance activities. *Industry differentiation* is the number of industry categories in a population and the evenness or uniformity of the distribution of population members among the categories. So we arrive at *Postulate 6–3*: Among countries, the greater the variety of sustenance activities during T_{0-1}, the greater the industry differentiation during T_{0-1}.

Like occupational differentiation, industry differentiation is a concept, meaning that its definition is construed as complete (i.e., all possibly relevant properties are identified). However, since both concepts pertain to a quantitative phenomenon, neither can be expressed numerically (i.e., applied empirically) without a formula and data instructions.

Three Transformational Statements

All of these terms denote quantitative properties of countries: gross efficiency and indispensability of technology, technological complexity, degree of division of labor, variety of sustenance activities, per capita inanimate energy use, occupational differentiation, and industry differentiation. The first four terms are constructs, meaning that they have not been defined such that the definition is regarded as complete, nor can the defined term be linked directly with an empirically applicable formula. By contrast, per capita inanimate energy use, occupational differentiation, and industry differentiation are defined such that the definition is regarded as complete, and subsequently each term is linked directly with an empirically applicable formula. As such, the three terms are concepts, and they must enter into additional statements to realize tests of the theory.

FIRST TRANSFORMATIONAL STATEMENT. A theory about quantitative phenomena is not systematically testable unless it includes transformational statements, each linking a concept and a "referential," a symbol denoting a formula and related instructions for obtaining specified kinds of data.[5] Even if the theorist stipulates a formula and related data instructions, nothing is gained if investigators regard the stipulations as unintelligible. Moreover, compliance with the instructions must be feasible, meaning, among other things, consistent with the field's resources. Feasibility is particularly relevant in contemplating *Transformational Statement 6–1*: Among countries, the greater the per capita use of inanimate energy over T_{0-1}, the greater the RPCIEU over T_{0-1}. Observe that referentials (here, RPCIEU or referential of per capita inanimate energy use) are not defined, because such an acronym means nothing more or less than what it designates—a formula and related instructions for its application. So in that sense a concept is considered as directly linked to a formula.

The referential formula is: RPCIEU = $\Sigma[k(E1-E2)]/P$, where $E1$ is the total amount of some type of inanimate energy source (e.g., barrels of petroleum) produced in or imported by the country during a particular year, $E2$ is the total amount of the same type of inanimate energy source exported by or left unused (stored) during that year, k is a constant that expresses the energy source in question as the equivalent of some standard amount of a particular inanimate energy source (e.g., kilograms of coal equivalent), and P is the country's total population at some point during the year.[6] Enormous resources would be required to apply the formula to even one country. Fortunately, some international statistical agencies report values that were supposedly computed by applying the RPCIEU formula, and those values can be used to test the theory, provided that: (1) all values were reported by the same statistical agency (e.g., the United Nations Statistical Office) and (2) the energy equivalent standard (e.g., kilograms of coal equivalent) is the same for all countries.

SECOND TRANSFORMATIONAL STATEMENT.   Occupational differentiation has been defined as a function of (1) the number of occupations in a population and (2) the uniformity of the distribution of population members among the occupations. Appearances to the contrary, any one of several formulas could express occupational differentiation (so defined); but, whatever the formula, it must be linked with the concept in a statement that becomes part of the theory. In this case we have *Transformational Statement 6–2*: Among countries, the greater occupational differentiation during T_{0-1}, the greater the RAOD during T_{0-1}.

RAOD (referential of adjusted occupational differentiation) designates this formula: $(1-[\Sigma X^2/(\Sigma X)^2])/[1-(1/Nc)]$, where X is the number of population members in a given occupational category (e.g., professional) and Nc is the number of occupational categories. If the RAOD formula is empirically applicable, then the values computed for a particular country and point in time (e.g., India, some 1981 date) by two or more independent investigators should differ negligibly, if at all. That outcome is improbable unless the investigators apply the formula to more or less the same occupational data. Accordingly, to maximize the formula's empirical applicability, the requisite kind of occupational data must be identified.

Because enormous resources would be required to gather occupational data on even one country, the data are to be obtained from published national census reports or published reports of international statistical agencies (e.g., the U.N.'s Statistical Office). In computing RAOD values, all occupational data are to be obtained from one of the two sources, not both; and, whatever the source, the formula is to be applied to X values in the longest (most detailed) list of occupational categories for each country. It is recognized that international variation in the number of occupational categories in census reports is arbitrary, but the RAOD formula "adjusts" for the number.

In some cases instructions for gathering data rather than (or as an alternative to) using published data furthers the theory's testability. Whatever the case, traditional sociology notwithstanding, idiosyncratic tests (if any at all) are virtually inevitable when a theorist fails to state instructions for obtaining or gathering the data.

THIRD TRANSFORMATIONAL STATEMENT. Because occupational differentiation and industry differentiation are similar concepts, the latter can be linked to a referential without preliminary comments. *Transformational Statement 6–3*: Among countries, the greater industry differentiation during T_{0-1}, the greater RAID during T_{0-1}.

The formula previously used in connection with RAOD applies to RAID (referential of adjusted industry differentiation), with the X values denoting the number of individuals in a particular industry (e.g., retail trade). All of the instructions pertaining to the requisite data also apply, but the RAID census data pertain to industry composition. Although the temporal quantifier is the same (during T_{0-1}) for RAOD and RAID, in tests of the theory the RAOD data and the RAID data for a country need not pertain the same date during the year;[7] but the calendar year must be the same for both sets of data and the energy data, though not necessarily the same for any two countries.

Derivation of Theorems

Given the foregoing axioms, postulates, and transformational statements, three theorems, which follow, can be derived by applying the sign rule (Gibbs, 1972:190). In applying the rule, a plus sign $(+)$ is an attribute of a statement if its constituent relational term is "greater . . . greater" or "varies directly with," and a negative sign $(-)$ if "greater . . . less" or "varies inversely with." A theorem's sign is negative if and only if an odd number of statements that imply the theorem have a negative sign. As one of at least two alternatives, it is assumed—as a sufficient condition—that all of the relations asserted in the premises are so close as to determine the direction of the relation $(+ \text{ or } -)$ in a theorem. Should it be demanded that the assumption extend to both a sufficient and necessary condition, the demand calls for the demonstration of a unique derivation of each theorem (that it can be deduced only from the stipulated premises). Regardless of the science, a unique derivation can never be demonstrated.

Theorem 6–1 (from Transformational Statement 6–1, 6–2; Axiom 6–1, 6–2; Postulate 6–1, 6–2): Among countries, the greater the RPCIEU over T_{0-1}, the greater the RAOD during T_{0-1}.

Theorem 6–2 (from Transformational Statement 6–2, 6–3; Postulate 6–

2, 6–3; Axiom 6–3): Among countries, the greater the RAOD during T_{0-1}, the greater the RAID during T_{0-1}.

Theorem 6–3 (from Transformational Statement 6–1, 6–3; Postulate 6–1, 6–3; Axiom 6–1, 6–2, 6–3): Among countries, the greater the RPCIEU over T_{0-1}, the greater RAID during T_{0-1}.

A fuller understanding of the derivation of the theorems is conveyed by the diagram of the theory in Figure 6–1.[8] Observe that Axioms 6–1 and 6–2 enter into the derivation of Theorems 6–1 and 6–3 even though the construct "technological complexity" is not linked to any concept. There is no obvious concept that can be linked to technological complexity and also to a referential that denotes an empirically applicable formula. Finally, while other statements can be derived from the axioms and postulates, none of them would be testable.

Tests of the Theorems

Table 6–1 provides the referents necessary for tests of the three theorems above. If only because there is more than one set (column) of values in that table, systematic tests require epistemic statements, statements that link each referential (RPCIEU, RAOD, or RAID) with a particular set of values.

Epistemic Statement 1: Among the countries in Table 6–1, the greater the RPCIEU over T_{0-1}, the greater the value in column 1.

Epistemic Statement 2: Among the countries in Table 6–1, the greater the RAOD during T_{0-1}, the greater the value in column 2.

Epistemic Statement 3: Among the countries in Table 6–1, the greater the RAID during T_{0-1}, the greater the value in column 3.

The epistemic statements are not tautologies or logically necessary truths. While they indicate that someone has applied the formulas in question to the designated kinds of data for the designated countries, an error could have been made. For that matter, two of the referentials, RAOD and RAID, refer to any value during the year, whereas the reported value refers to some particular date during that year. Most important, the referential in each epistemic statement represents the "true" referent, the value that would be computed if the formula were applied without a mistake to the correct kind of data. Whatever the country, that "true" value cannot be known with absolute certainty; hence, epistemic statements force recognition of doubts about any test of any theory, especially when (as here) the referents have not been computed by two or more independent investigators. When two or more investigators have applied a particular referential formula independently to a particular unit (a country in this case), to the extent that the two sets of referents are positively correlated, the formula can be considered as empirically applicable.

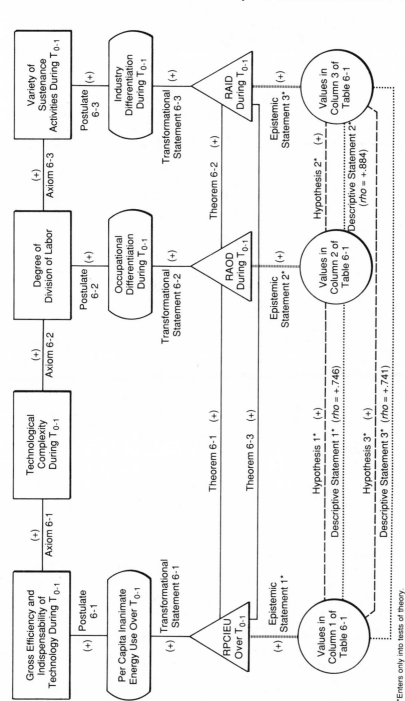

Figure 6-1. Diagram of a Theory and Particular Tests

*Enters only into tests of theory.

Table 6–1. RPCIEU Referents (Per Capita Inanimate Energy), RAOD Referents (Occupational Differentiation), and RAID Referents (Industry Differentiation): 28 Countries, circa 1962–71*

Country and Year	RPCIEU (Per Capita Inanimate Energy Use)[1] Col. 1	RAOD (Occupational Differentiation)[2] Col. 2	RAID (Industry Differentiation)[2] Col. 3
Algeria, 1966	379	.732[b]	.669[d]
Australia, 1971	5,359	.886[c]	.931[e]
Bulgaria, 1965	2,573	.832[a]	.742[d]
Chile, 1970	1,287	.928[b]	.903[e]
Columbia, 1964	492	.795[c]	.792[d]
Costa Rica, 1963	251	.806[b]	.783[e]
Ecuador, 1962	174	.713[b]	.696[d]
Greece, 1971	1,470	.838[b]	.857[e]
Guatemala, 1964	183	.626[b]	.611[d]
Hungary, 1970	3,185	.800[b]	.894[e]
Indonesia, 1964	114	.581[b]	.557[d]
Iran, 1966	414	.777[b]	.811[d]
Ireland, 1966	2,413	.873[b]	.908[d]
Japan, 1970	3,215	.914[b]	.922[e]
South Korea, 1966	511	.727[b]	.715[d]
Liberia, 1962	123	.401[b]	.735[d]
Libya, 1964	269	.833[b]	.833[d]
Mexico, 1970	1,241	.879[b]	.838[e]
New Zealand, 1966	2,640	.879[c]	.932[d]
Nicaragua, 1963	269	.705[b]	.692[d]
Paraguay, 1962	97	.716[b]	.723[d]
Poland, 1970	4,270	.833[b]	.766[d]
South Africa, 1970	2,168	.924[b]	.941[e]
Spain, 1970	1,485	.856[c]	.915[e]
Sweden, 1965	4,458	.870[c]	.909[d]
United Kingdom, 1971	5,507	.869[c]	.864[d]
United States, 1970	11,077	.909[c]	.887[d]
Uruguay, 1963	794	.905[c]	.899[d]

*Data on industry composition and occupational composition from United Nations (1973: Tables 10–11); and data on per capita use of inanimate energy (in kilograms of coal or coal equivalents) from United Nations (1967–75 Table 142 each year).

1. In kilograms of coal equivalent.
2. Formula: $(1-[\Sigma X^2/(\Sigma X)^2])/[1-(1/Nc)]$, where Nc is the number of categories (occupational or industry).

(a) Six occupational categories; (b) seven occupational categories; (c) eight occupational categories; (d) eight industry categories; (e) nine industry categories.

Hypotheses and Descriptive Statements

Any theory is systematically testable only insofar as it generates predictions, each of which is labeled as a hypothesis. In this case, each hypothesis predicts the direction of the association between two particular sets (columns) of values in Table 6–1, and the truth of a hypothesis depends on a corresponding descriptive statistic. Hypothesis 1 is derived (by the sign rule) from Theorem 6–1 and the two epistemic statements, 1 and 2: Among the countries in Table 6–1, the greater the value in column 1, the greater the value in column 2. Now consider Descriptive Statement 1: The rank-order coefficient of correlation (*rho*) between the values in column 1 and the values in column 2 of Table 6–1 is +.746. The sign of the coefficient (+) in the descriptive statement is consistent with the hypothesis,[9] and the coefficient's magnitude is substantial. So Theorem 6–1 can be retained until such time that the theory is replaced by one with greater predictive accuracy as regards variance in RAOD values.

Hypothesis 2 is derived from Theorem 6–2 and two epistemic statements, 2 and 3: Among the countries in Table 6–1, the greater the value in column 2, the greater the value in column 3. Descriptive Statement 2 is: The rank-order coefficient of correlation (*rho*) between the values in column 2 and the values in column 3 of Table 6–1 is +.884. Again, the sign of the coefficient (+) in the descriptive statement is consistent with the hypothesis, and the coefficient's magnitude is substantial. So Theorem 6–2 can be retained, again until such time that the theory is replaced with a theory having greater predictive accuracy as regards the association between RAOD and RAID values.

Hypothesis 3 is derived from Theorem 6–3 and two epistemic statements, 1 and 3: Among the countries in Table 6–1, the greater the value in column 1, the greater the value in column 3. Descriptive Statement 3: The rank-order coefficient of correlation (*rho*) between the values in column 1 and the values in column 3 of Table 6–1 is +.741. The sign (+) of the coefficient is as predicted (Hypothesis 3); and the coefficient's magnitude is substantial and consistent with a principle of discriminatory power (a dimension of predictive power explicated in Gibbs, 1972:69, 299, 359): the greater the number of intervening variables, the less the correlation. So Theorem 6–3 can be retained until such time that the theory is replaced with one of greater predictive accuracy as regards variance in RAID values.

Should the correlation coefficients be judged inessential or irrelevant for the corroboration or falsification of the hypotheses and related theorems, the judgment would be a tacit rejection of predictive power—predictive accuracy in particular—as to the appropriate criterion for assessing theories (even isolated empirical generalizations, for that matter). To be sure, tests of a theory can be reported in a less formal mode than that employed here, but such a mode is likely to obscure the bearing of the data on the theory.

Although the test findings are such that the theory need not be rejected or even modified, the most desirable step cannot be undertaken. That step would be a comparison of the theory's predictive power with that of contending theories, but it cannot be undertaken because the contending theories about the division of labor—Smith's (1952) and Durkheim's (1949)—are not testable. For that matter, those theories are so discursive that they cannot be assessed in terms pertaining to any dimension of predictive power other than testability, the others being predictive accuracy, discrimination, scope, range, parsimony, and intensity (see Gibbs, 1972:63). Yet a comparison of theories does not lead to an irresolvable dilemma of identifying one dimension of predictive power as more important than the others, because the ultimate goal is a theory that exceeds all contenders as regards all dimensions of predictive power.

In recognition that test findings for social science theories are commonly incongruent over time, it should be noted that tests of the three theorems have been reported previously for a set of 19 countries and 1960 or 1961 data (Gibbs, 1972:299). The three rank-order coefficients of correlation in that series of tests are $+.904$ (Descriptive Statement 1), $+.949$ (Descriptive Statement 2), and $+.837$ (Descriptive Statement 3). Hence, the earlier findings provide even more support for the theory.

Conclusion

Because no one can be certain about future tests, all that can be said is that the findings justify retaining the theory. However, the same is true of any theory when, as in the present case, the contending theories cannot be assessed in terms of predictive power.

While their signs are as predicted (all $+$), the coefficients do not remotely approach unity (1.00); but such a magnitude was not expected if only because of doubts about the data (e.g., extremely gross occupational and industry categories). Moreover, there is a theoretical rationale for expecting near unity correlations only if the countries are ecologically autonomous, no international trade especially. Once international trade reaches a substantial level, some countries are highly specialized in the global division of labor; and that specialization results in less industry and occupational differentiation than would be expected on the basis of per capita inanimate energy use (for elaboration, see Gibbs, 1972:243 and 260).[10] Hence, the more substantial correlation coefficients in earlier tests are not surprising because international trade increased between the two data points (i.e., circa 1960 and circa 1970). In any case, the theory extends to an identification of a condition in which the predicted association will be negligible: a substantial amount of international trade per capita for each country. Consistent with that identification, in the earlier tests (circa 1960 data, 19 countries) the rank-order coefficient of correlation between RPCIEU referents (energy) and RAID referents (industry differentiation) among the six countries having the greatest international trade per capita is only $+.14$ (Gibbs, 1972:302). So although crude data and the inevitability of international trade preclude a unity correlation, only in one particular condition does the correlation approaches zero. Accordingly, the theory extends to predictions about the conditions in which the variables in question will and will not be associated, and there can be no other realistic requirement.

The Notion of Control

When reacting to this chapter, superorganicists are likely to make this argument: But no individual or group attempts to control the degree of division of labor. Perhaps so, but the argument in no way contradicts a principle previously enunciated—all major episodes in human history and all meaningful structural features of human societies stem from control attempts. The related major claim underlying the present theory is that beyond some low level an increase in the division of labor stems from the inability of the typical human to control (create, use, and maintain) a wide variety of technological items effectively. If the claim be doubted, a manager of any large manufacturing firm should be asked: Why is work in this firm not organized such that all employees master the same kinds of tools and machines? To be sure, such uniformity may not be literally impossible, depending on the variety of tools and machines; but it is unlikely that the manager would doubt that efficient use of tools and machines requires some division of labor.

Even though the term *control* does not appear in any premise, the theory is nothing less than a theory about control, as is any theory about technology. To make the point again: creating, using, or maintaining any technological item is inanimate control; and technological complexity is literally defined in terms of control. Granted, because the division of labor is "structural," it appears far removed from control; but occupational activities are nothing less than inanimate control, biotic control, and/or human control. Contemplate this brief illustrative list of occupations in English-speaking countries, with parenthetical designations of the predominant control: police officer (human), farmer (biotic), physician (biotic-human), welder (inanimate), cab driver (inanimate-human), blacksmith (inanimate-biotic), and radiologist (inanimate-biotic-human).

Nonetheless, some critics will argue that individuals never act in the belief that the act increases or decreases the division of labor. The basis of the argument is that the division of labor entails occupational diversity and functional interdependence, both of which are distinct from control activities in particular occupations. Yet managers in large organizations create positions that eventually come to be occupations, and who would assert that managers never recognize such a potential "contribution" to occupational diversity? Then in developing countries governmental policy is commonly to shift employment from the agricultural sector, which is an attempt to increase occupational diversity. However, diversity is not just a matter of number of occupations.

An even distribution of individuals among occupations also furthers diversity; and insofar as competition sets a limit on the number in a particular occupation (e.g., farmer), the limit exists only because occupational activity is perceived by those engaged in it as a means. Individuals pursue an occupation in the belief that it increases the probability of acquiring use-value objects or exchange-value objects, including money. Beyond some point, as more individuals enter a particular occupation, the incumbents come to perceive their control as ineffectual (i.e., the acquisition of objects becomes more and more problematical); and they commonly change to a less populated occupation, thereby contributing to occupational diversity. Likewise, labor force novices often choose a "modern" occupation because they perceive it as a more effective means for acquiring objects. So "structural constraints" are relevant only because occupational activities are control activities.

Functional Interdependence and Exchange

Functional interdependence is manifested in exchange, and to buy, sell, or barter anything is to control someone. True, some exchanges are described as reciprocities rather than as buying, selling, or bartering; but unless one is determined, along with Levi-Strauss, to use the term *exchange* so loosely that it borders on the meaningless, then an exchange is always a control act by two parties, each party being either an individual or a set of individuals acting in coordination.

The foregoing argument is consistent with this maxim: The economy is secondary to and dependent on political order. No one is likely to produce a commodity or enter into exchanges without expecting something in return. Because that expectation can be nullified by theft or robbery, then to the extent that government is necessary to prevent those acts, it is also necessary for exchange. However, government is a vast coordination and synchronization of control attempts backed by coercion; and because no one produces objects for exchange without perceiving themselves as having the capacity to control others (some kind and degree of power), any condition that furthers the perceived capacity to control furthers exchange and the division of labor.

Beyond the Theory

One of the various lines of work beyond the present theory bears on the theory's validity. The theory's premises stem from various assumptions about some preponderant features of control, notably: (1) the use of inanimate energy reduces the amount of human energy required to realize physical goals; (2) humans realize various physical goals that could not be realized without inanimate control, the use of inanimate energy in particular; and (3) not even the most gifted human can master all of a nation's technology.[11] Those assumptions are not analytical truths, and critics should undertake research to refute them. However, one advantage of taking control as sociology's central notion will be the facilitation of plausible assumptions, and theories of human behavior entail so many assumptions that an assessment of all of them through systematic research is not feasible. For that matter, the pivotal assumptions are commonly the very ones that cannot be so assessed.

Possible Directions for Expanding the Theory

Durkheim, Marx, and Adam Smith were preoccupied with the division of labor, which is a testimonial to its importance (see Garnsey, 1981). Because they had quite different perspectives, their ideas about possible correlates of the division of labor (e.g., the character of law, features of the class system, level of production) suggest various ways to expand the present theory.

DURKHEIM. He asserted (1949) that increases in the division of labor cause increases in the ratio of "restitutive" laws to "repressive" laws. The assertion is untestable, and its rationale is obscure. Systematic tests are precluded if only because Durkheim failed to clarify the distinction between the two types of laws, and the distinction is empirically applicable only if repressive law is equated with criminal law and restitutive law is treated as residual. Even so, Durkheim scarcely had any basis for denying (1949:111) Tarde's suggestion that the distinction between tort law and criminal law is not clearcut. More serious, if restitutive law is simply all noncriminal law (contract law, tort law, etc.), there is no clear rationale for arguing that increases in the restitutive-repressive ratio are caused by increases in the division of labor; and sociologists tend to ignore contrary observations (see Sheleff, 1975).

Had Durkheim spoken of regulatory rather than restitutive law, his argument would have been both more testable and more compelling, despite conceptual problems with the notion of regulatory law (chapter 17). That is the case because the volume of regulatory law can be estimated either by (1) counting the rules promulgated by governmental agencies to control economic transactions and the activities of economic organizations or (2) counting the number of such agencies (in the case of the U.S., the FDA, the SEC, etc.). One reason why Durkheim did not couch his argument in terms of regulatory law is suggested by his conceptual statements about restitutive law, such as: "it [a restitutive sanction] does not necessarily imply suffering for the agent, but consists only of *the return of things as they were*, in the reestablishment of troubled relations to their normal state. . . ." (1949:69).[12] The statement hardly clarifies, and it erroneously suggests genuine recognition by Durkheim of the purposive quality of human behavior. Those who enact laws surely have goals, but that is precisely the quality of law that Durkheim was at great pains to ignore.

In creating regulatory law, legislators are concerned with solving or avoiding perceived problems, such as strikes, lockouts, fraudulent occupational practices, unemployment, and boycotts. Those problems stem directly or indirectly from the division of labor; and although Durkheim did recognize the connection (1949), he did not emphasize that legislators or other sovereigns (not "society") create regulatory laws to solve problems. His opposition to utilitarianism was so intense that he created the impression that laws simply appear.

Although sociologists rightly appreciate Durkheim's imagination, they persistently underestimate his vagueness. The point is not just that he failed to stipulate how his principal theoretical variables (including the division of labor) are to be measured; worse, the logical structure of his theory is so obscure that restatements of it (e.g., Gibbs, 1982b:96–100) are inherently debatable. Even if agreement on the premises of Durkheim's theory about the division of labor could be realized, the rationale for most of them would be obscure. That point was made in connection with restitutive law; now consider another illustration. In asserting a causal relation between density and the division of labor, Durkheim vacillated between the "material" meaning of density (e.g., possibly residents per square mile) and its "social" or "moral" meaning (e.g., possibly frequency of interaction). If he really meant the former, it was a colossal error (think of India and the United States); and he ignored responses to population pressure other than an increase in the division of labor, one being emigration. On the other hand, if Durkheim meant social or moral density, it is not clear why an increase in interaction would cause the division of labor to increase. For that matter, in light of Durkheim's assertion of a direct relation between material density and moral density (1949:257), the distinction is inconsequential in contemplating tests of the theory.

ADAM SMITH. Even granting Adam Smith's claim that humans are predisposed to "truck and barter" (1952), that propensity does not explain vast international differences in the degree of the division of labor. There is even a basis for questioning Smith's argument that the division of labor is a function of the "size of the market." The notion of a market suggests that the relevant evidence would pertain to industries, but the market for agricultural products is large even though that industry is known for a low degree of division of labor. For that matter, even if there is a direct relation among industries between market size and intra-industry division of labor, the relation could be evidence that the division of labor expands market size by increasing production efficiency and lowering commodity prices.

The last observation directs attention to Adam Smith's major contribution. He never tired of suggesting that increases in the division of labor result in greater productivity; and, unlike Durkheim, Smith made it obvious that the increases do not happen independently of human goals. Time and again, he suggested that owners or managers of large companies pursue higher levels of productivity through the creation of a division of labor; as such, the idea of an "invisible hand" appears more consistent with Durkheim's thinking than with Smith's. In any case, there is no incompatibility between the present theory and Smith's emphasis on organization, productivity, and the division of labor.

MARX. If various commentators have rightly depicted Marx as a technological determinist, the present theory is more consistent with him than with Durkheim or Adam Smith. However, because Marx's observations on the relation between technology and the division of labor are vague generalities, they provide no basis for expanding the present theory. The same is true of his ideas about the consequences of the division of labor, but in that connection the present theory could be expanded so as to be a partial reformulation of Marx.

Contemporary Marxism notwithstanding, Marx's theory badly needs reformulating. As one of several arguments to justify reformulation, Marx's prophecies about the growth of class consciousness and class conflict as capitalism "matured" were gross overestimations at best. He never grasped the consequences of prolonged increases in the division of labor, an inevitable error given Marx's inclination to describe the division of labor as though a capitalist phenomenon and one analyzable in terms of the mental-manual distinction. That inclination led Marx to disregard the possibility that up to some point increases in the division of labor contribute to class concreteness (e.g., visibility, consciousness) but reduce class concreteness beyond that point. Once the proletariat are distributed among thousands of occupations, the social reality of classes becomes debatable. That possibility should be entertained in expanding the present theory, even though those who write on class and the division of labor (e.g., Garnsey, 1981:354) commonly ignore it.

Technological Complexity

The most immediate need in expanding the present theory is suggested by Figure 6–1. No postulate connects the construct "technological complexity" and a concept, and without that connection there is no way to assess the validity of Axiom 6–1 and Axiom 6–2 independently. However, the call is not for a purported measure of technological complexity. Even if a measure could be devised, the resources required to apply it would be prohibitive. A more likely prospect is a postulate that identifies an empirical correlate of technological complexity other than technological efficiency-indispensability or the division of labor.

Regardless of how complex a technology becomes, an ever finer division of labor makes it possible for individuals to operate and maintain the technology without special talents or skills; but creating components for a very complex technology is another matter. To that end, a fairly large number must undergo lengthy formal education. Accordingly, the theory could be expanded by adding a postulate that asserts a direct relation between technological complexity and percent of the labor force having graduate degrees (for a step in that direction, see Grandjean, 1974).

Possible Modification Needs

If tests of the theory ever yield compelling negative evidence, the theory should be modified in order to salvage it. To that end, it is desirable to identify the especially questionable premises.

As suggested by Postulate 6–1, inanimate energy use has been taken as the principal empirical correlate of gross technological efficiency and indispensability. However, it could be argued that the most strategic consideration is the efficiency of inanimate energy use itself. Inanimate energy use commonly requires its conversion from one source or form to another (e.g., coal→ steam→electricity); and no technology can be efficient if a large proportion of the energy is lost in those conversions. The argument takes on added significance because over the past century the greatest change in energy technology has been not the total inanimate energy used per capita but a decrease in the proportion of energy lost in conversions (much of the decrease being due to perfections of the combustion engine and to turbine innovations).

In light of the foregoing, it may prove necessary to abandon an heretofore implicit assumption—that there is a close direct relation among countries between per capita inanimate energy use and the efficiency of energy converters. Of course, the relation may be direct but not so close that either variable can be ignored. If so, the concept in Postulate 6–1 will have to be redefined so that it incorporates both per capita inanimate energy use *and* the conservation ratio of energy converters. Yet the suggestion is not that only the efficiency of energy converters is relevant. International variation in weather (temperature particularly) may reduce the association between per capita energy consumption and technological efficiency (especially that of tools and machines in general), and the association may be reduced further by affluence (see Lacy, 1985). Finally, but perhaps most important, the theory does not recognize that those who make decisions as to the nature of the production process may accept or reject technological items partially with a view to controlling producers, be they employees, slaves, or some other kind of subordinates (for references to research along that line, see Staples, 1987). Nonetheless, note that such "use" of technology can be described in terms of control.

NOTES

1. Such comparisons do not mean less efficiency, gross or net, for American agriculture per producer or per hectare. However, not even that clarification will satisfy defenders of American agriculture, who (e.g., Duncan and Webb, 1980:3–6) argue that noncommercial energy sources are underestimated for less developed countries. Their arguments about the reliability of energy statistics

are debatable, and contrasts between gross and net efficiency values for American agriculture are telling without international comparisons.

2. Note 7 provides a rationale for all of the theory's temporal quantifiers, a subject best introduced after the formulation.

3. Note the distinction between a concept and a construct. A *construct* is a term that a theorist may or not define when using it to formulate a theory. If left undefined, the term is a "theoretical primitive"; and, unlike an "empirical primitive," the term does not enter into the explicit definition of any other term. Should the theorist define the term, his or her designation of it as a "construct" signifies that he or she does not regard the definition as complete, let alone clear. If the term denotes a quantitative phenomenon or property, the theorist does not link the term (in the theory) directly to what the theorist identifies as an empirically applicable formula. By contrast, a *concept* is a term that a theorist must define when using it in formulating a theory, and the theorist regards the definition as complete and clear. Accordingly, if the term refers to a qualitative phenomenon or property, the theorist regards his or her definition of the term as empirically applicable (a construct is not so regarded even when it denotes a qualitative phenomenon or property). On the other hand, if a concept denotes a quantitative phenomenon or property, it is empirically applicable only in the sense that the theorist links it (in the theory) directly to a formula that the theorist claims to be empirically applicable, provided that his or her related application instructions are heeded.

4. The definition bears on Winner's proposed curtailment of technological complexity: "that as a general maxim, technologies be given a scale and structure of the sort that would be immediately intelligible to nonexperts" (1977:326). Winner's proposal would entail a return to a prehistorical technology.

5. So an axiom links constructs; a postulate links a construct and a concept; and a transformational statement links a concept and a referential. Should the notion of a transformational statement appear pretentious, without the stipulation of formulas and requisite kinds of data tests of a theory comprising quantitative variables will be idiosyncratic. The specification of kinds of data (including designations of procedures or sources) implies that all such data are sufficiently reliable, which is an empirical claim. Nonetheless, if researchers are allowed to select the appropriate kind of data, some negative evidence is virtually inevitable. Should the theorist claim that the evidence is irrelevant because the "wrong" test procedure was employed, the theory becomes unfalsifiable. Finally, the suggestion is not that all variables in sociological theories must be quantitative, but even in the case of qualitative variables tests will be idiosyncratic if the theorist does not stipulate requisite kinds of data.

6. Were there no danger in a greater departure from convention, the theory would have been stated even more formally by a sharper separation of two major parts. The "intrinsic" part comprises synthetic statements—all axioms, postulates, propositions (statement linking concepts), transformational statements, and theorems. The "extrinsic" part comprises analytic statements—definitions of the constructs, concepts, and unit terms (countries in the present case); referential formulas along with definitions of the constituent variables; and instructions for gathering or otherwise obtaining requisite data. Should the advantage of

distinguishing the two parts be doubted, examine any well-known sociological theory carefully and attempt to identify each constituent statement as being either synthetic or analytic. Distinguishing the two types of statements (for illustrative instances, see Gibbs, 1972:81–83) is not a problem if one gives only lip service to testability.

7. Were it not for three problems, the temporal quantifiers would have been stipulated so as to express the only empirically applicable conception of a causal relation, that of antecedent and postcedent correlates (see Gibbs, 1982d). Specifically, the temporal quantifiers would be such as to imply that the maximum correlations would obtain if the temporal sequences (lags) were thus: per capita inanimate energy use over T_{0-1}, RPCEIU over T_{0-1}, gross efficiency and indispensability of technology during T_{1-2}, technological complexity during T_{2-3}, degree of division of labor during T_{3-4}, occupational differentiation during T_{4-5}, RAOD during T_{4-5}, variety of sustenance activities during T_{3-4}, industry differentiation during T_{4-5}, and RAID during T_{4-5}. Again, however, three problems preclude temporal quantifiers other than those shown in Figure 6–1. First, there are perhaps insurmountable difficulties in defining causation and in stipulating related criteria of causal evidence, most of which the advocates of causal models or path analysis conveniently ignore (for elaboration, see Gibbs, 1982d). Second, the temporal sequence just stipulated (0–1, 1–2, 2–3, 3–4, 4–5) is *ordinal*, and crude induction is the only basis to determine the appropriate interval between the periods or points in time (i.e., the appropriate "lag"). Third, the requisite data are not compiled and published on even a yearly basis; hence, the appropriate temporal intervals cannot be identified through experimentation with alternatives. Note, finally, that the theory could be stated such that it applies to any country over time; but even in that case no temporal lags could be stipulated, and the reasons are the same as those in international comparisons.

8. Should it appear strange that referentials rather than concepts are the constituent variables of theorems, quantitative concepts are empirically applicable only when linked to formulas (a construct is not so linked). So theorems are the only statements in a theory that are testable in something approximating a direct sense, and that is the case because only theorems comprise referentials. Note also that theorems cannot be derived systematically without transformational statements. The only alternative to such statements is the murky language of operational definitions or indicators (see Gibbs, 1972, Subject Index, p. 415). Unless a theorist uses something akin to that language, idiosyncratic tests of the theory (if any) are inevitable; but the language makes the theory's logical structure obscure.

9. *Rho* is the association measure rather than Kendall's *tau* only because readers are more likely to be familiar with *rho*. The rationale for a measure of ordinal statistical association is advanced in chapter 7, p. 159.

10. This consideration is one of two reasons for stipulating *countries* as the unit term rather than simply *territorial units*. The latter designation would encompass not only countries but also metropolitan areas, urban areas, and cities, which are much more likely to be specialized in the territorial division of labor than are countries. The other reason is that Postulate 6–1 and an *implied* postulate

(the greater the per capita inanimate energy use, the greater the technological complexity) are more likely to hold for countries. In particular, per capita inanimate energy use is negligible among what anthropologists loosely identify as *tribes* or *peoples* (e.g., the Comanche, the Eskimos); hence, it is possible that the efficiency of the technology of tribes or peoples varies more or less independently of inanimate energy use (see Oswalt, 1976).

11. Although the three assumptions are stated in terms most appropriate for the theory in question, each can be stated as a control principle, as follows. First, the principle (6–2) of energy conservation: Any technological item used to pursue a physical goal reduces the energy expenditure of at least one member of the social unit. Second, the principle (6–3) of indispensability: If technology changes so as to decrease the expenditure of human energy, at the same time it is used more and more to realize physical goals that could not be realized by human energy alone. Third, the principle (6–4) of limited technological mastery: The variety of items in a social unit's technology never increases indefinitely without reaching a point where the typical social unit member cannot effectively control all types of technological items.

12. Few commentators on Durkheim's notion of restitutive law recognize the vagueness of the notion, let alone attempt to clarify it. Worse, many statements pertaining to the notion are gross oversimplifications, one instance being Alexander's pronouncement: "modern law is restitutive, not repressive" (1982-II:132).

Chapter

7

An Illustrative Theory About Biotic Control

Contemplate this control principle (7–1): The amount, kind, and efficacy of biotic control depends primarily on the amount, kind, and efficacy of inanimate control. The principle is illustrated readily by a wealth of evidence that the crop yield of cereals depends appreciably on the instruments used to break the soil; thus, adoption of the heavy plow in Northern Europe evidently revolutionized agriculture. Such illustrations notwithstanding, there will be three difficulties in reducing the principle to credible and testable propositions. First, the variety of biotic control (e.g., herding cattle, growing orchids, reducing human weight) is astonishing, and currently biotic control cannot be described readily as a totality in terms of any abstract property (something comparable to technological complexity). Second, the efficacy of particular kinds of biotic control (e.g., hunting swift animals) depends not so much on some abstract property of inanimate control (e.g., gross technological efficiency) as on particular technological items, such as the bow and arrow. And, third, the kinds of animals or plants that are controlled depends not just on technology but also on physiographic features, such as soil quality or precipitation, and on geological history (e.g., the absence of domesticated horses as of 1492 in America and Australia was not a consequence of a similarity in regional technology).

The Stirrup and Feudalism: An Illustrative Case

A general theory relating inanimate, biotic, and human control cannot be formulated readily because it appears that no empirical association between any two kinds of control holds universally. For example, while the Metal Age of inanimate control eventually furthered the human use of horses through the adoption of nailed horseshoes, unshod horses are useful in a dry climate or rocky terrain. Because of such contingencies, an impressive theory about the relation between inanimate control and biotic control is unlikely without numerous exploratory case studies. Fortunately, the path has been marked by historians, notably Lynn White.

The Stirrup and Cavalry in European History

White (1962:3) described feudalism as a social organization designed to create and maintain cavalry suited for mounted shock combat. Men on horse-back were equipped to charge and scatter infantry. The rider grasped a shield with his left hand, held a heavy lance at rest between the upper right arm and body, and smashed into his foes with the combined mass of man and horse. With nothing more than a saddle for lateral support, a mounted warrior maintains his seat with difficulty even when swinging a heavy sword. The solution came with the adoption of the stirrup by European cavalry in the 8th century A.D., long after the saddle. Quoting White: "The stirrup, by giving lateral support in addition to the front and back support offered by pommel and cantle, effectively welded horse and rider into a single fighting unit capable of violence without precedent. The fighter's hand no longer delivered the blow; it merely guided it. The stirrup thus replaced human energy with animal power, and immensely increased the warrior's ability to damage his enemy. Immediately, without preparatory steps, it made possible mounted shock combat, a revolutionary new way of doing battle" (1962:2).

OTHER ELEMENTS OF FEUDALISM. White's argument is not vulgar technological determinism, and it does more than illustrate how inanimate control innovations further the effectiveness of biotic control (in this case, over a horse). Feudalism required the fusion of the ancient custom of swearing allegiance to a leader (vassalage) and the leader's grant of estates (benefices) to his vassals (White, 1962:5), meaning a distinctive kind of human control conventionally identified as a "property relation." The control argument survives the conceptual complexities and issues in defining elements of feudalism, such as those identified by Weber (1978:1070–110).

Sociologists may be aware that property relations undergirded feudalism; but few probably know that the relations were used by Charles Martel of the Franks to create and maintain cavalry, meaning to control human behavior. After all, would a Frank suddenly equip himself for mounted shock combat, at a cost approximately equal to the plough-teams of ten peasant families (White, 1962:29), merely because the stirrup made such combat feasible? It is most improbable that a multitude of Franks equipped themselves for such combat and then waited for Martel to organize them. Martel undoubtedly gave his fellow Franks some incentive to serve in a new kind of cavalry—the prospect of land; but he could attempt human control on that scale only after seizing Church estates (control in itself).

Beyond the Illustrative Case

Should sociologists resist analyzing studies like White's on the grounds that they are not interested in the unique, they will ignore the possibility that defensible theories require case studies. Actually, sociological theories about change, including Marx's, scarcely explain the emergence of feudalism; and that is the case because sociologists rarely view major socio-cultural changes as products of attempts at control.

The argument is not a tacit endorsement of the "great man" theory of change. Feudalism probably would have taken place without Charles Martel; he did not invent the stirrup, and his men were not the first to use it in battle. Moreover, had the agricultural technology of northern Europe not generated a food surplus, Martel's promise of land would have been an ineffective means of control; and had the Church fathers used coercive countercontrol to resist Martel's land grab, his enterprise might have failed. Yet, granting all of that, feudalism could not have originated without a series of changes in inanimate, biotic, and human control.

Primary Biotic Control: A Simple Illustrative Theory

One major turning point in human evolution had to do with biotic control—the change in predominant dependence from hunting and gathering to the domestication of organisms, plants especially. That change is all the more puzzling because plant domestication apparently occurred in widely scattered places between about 10,000 and 4,000 B.C.

The change to plant domestication was the most important step in the evolution of human sustenance activities, but it took place long after technological innovations (e.g., the spear thrower) increased hunting efficiency (the ratio of calories of food realized through hunting as a ratio to human energy expended). Such innovations probably reduced the human mortality rate and created the first demographic transition,[1] and they may have been necessary for plant domestication (e.g., less spatial mobility, more control over wild herbivores, less time devoted to hunting). For that matter, at some times and places in human history animal domestication may have increased food production efficiency even more than did plant domestication. Finally, perhaps for hundreds of years after plant domestication commenced, humans may have remained dependent on hunting; and even today fishing is a major food source for several countries.

An Axiom

Just as efficiency may well be technology's most important property, so is it in the case of primary biotic control—hunting, fishing, foraging, animal domestication, and plant domestication. However, the notion of technological efficiency can be described more accurately than can the efficiency of primary biotic control (EPBC). In particular, EPBC can be defined as the amount of biotic materials (plants or animals) produced per unit of human energy invested in production, but there is no appropriate metric to express that amount. It cannot be expressed as nutritional calories because many products of biotic control are either indigestible or do not necessarily become human food (e.g., lumber, race horses, lawns), and neither weight nor bulk is a suitable metric for all biotic materials. Therefore, EPBC must be treated as a construct.

EPBC is substantially a direct function of gross technological efficiency, whether reckoned in terms of energy and/or time. Other than a few varieties of food gathering, primary biotic control entails the use of technological items. True, EPBC is not solely a function of gross technological efficiency because variation in physiographic features (e.g., soil quality) and production techniques (e.g., crop rotation, "team" hunting) increase yields independently of technology. Nonetheless, EPBC depends appreciably on the technology employed; and since some of the tools and machines (e.g., tractors) cannot be created without technology, indispensability as well as efficiency is relevant. So we arrive at *Axiom 7–1*: Among countries, the greater the gross efficiency and indispensability of technology during T_{0-1}, the greater the efficiency of primary biotic control during T_{0-1}.

Sociologists have come to think of Marx in terms of capitalism, class, class conflict, and alienation so much that many of them will not recognize the Marxist character of Axiom 7–1. But how could it be denied that the axiom pertains to what Marx loosely identified as mode of production? However, for reasons described in chapter 12, it is doubtful whether Marx's terminology is suited for stating theories; and it is not needed to assert a relation between properties of inanimate control and properties of biotic control.

Two Postulates

Formal theory construction facilitates the synthesis of theories if only because it makes the key constructs and concepts conspicuous. By contrast, it is often very difficult to identify common components of two discursively stated theories; typically, even their key constructs and concepts are submerged in a sea of verbiage.

If two or more theories have been stated in accordance with the same mode of formal theory construction and at least one particular property term (construct, concept, or referential) appears in those theories, all of the theories can be integrated. Moreover, when someone uses a particular property term, he or she can borrow any premise from any theory where that term appears. That possibility is exploited here. Because the construct "gross efficiency and indispensability of technology" is a constituent of the theory in chapter 6, one of that theory's postulates appears again in the present theory; and it is here repeated. *Postulate 6–1*: Among countries, the greater the gross efficiency and indispensability of technology during T_{0-1}, the greater the per capita inanimate energy use over T_{0-1}.

ANOTHER POSTULATE.   Although Axiom 7–1 asserts that EPBC (efficiency of primary biotic control) is a function of both technology's energy efficiency and technology's temporal efficiency, the latter is more meaningful in the present context because in some kinds of biotic control "time" and "people" are substitutable within certain limits. For example, if one individual must work thirty hours to harvest a corn field, then ten similar individuals could harvest it in approximately three hours. To appreciate the implications, consider two ratio variables for a country: Th/Aw and Aw/Tw, where *Th* is the total number of hours required each year to produce all of the nation's agricultural products, *Aw* is the number of workers regularly engaged in agricultural work, and *Tw* is the total number of workers (agricultural and nonagricultural). As the efficiency of agricultural technology increases, the Th/Aw ratio declines, but over generations the Aw/Tw ratio tends to decline even more.

The greater decline in the Aw/Tw ratio is puzzling, but no explanation is needed to state an important empirical generalization about EPBC as *Postulate 7–1*: Among countries, the greater the efficiency of primary biotic control during T_{0-1}, the greater the concentration of primary biotic control during T_{0-1}. The postulate is sociologically significant if only because (1) the concentration of primary biotic control can be presumed to vary inversely with the percentage of all population members regularly engaged in agriculture, hunting, forestry, or fishing; and (2) research findings indicate that the percentage has all manner of correlates (e.g., degree of urbanization, literacy rate).[2] Elaborating on the second point: Although the theory formulated here is illustrative and all too simple, it demonstrates how thinking in terms of control can lead to theories about important structural variables.

Two Transformational Statements

Most census agencies tabulate the number of economically active individuals (or labor force participants) in the industries of agriculture, forestry, hunting, and fishing. That practice is fortunate because those four "animate" industries taken together correspond closely to the notion of primary biotic control. Accordingly, we have *Transformational Statement 7–1*: Among countries, the greater the concentration of primary biotic control during T_{0-1}, the less the RAI during T_{0-1}. RAI (referential of animate industries) denotes this formula: $(A + F + H + G)/E$ where each of the first four letters denotes the number of individuals in a particular industry—A in agriculture, F in forestry, H in hunting, G in fishing—and E is the total number of economically active individuals. For any country, all five numbers must be obtained either from national census reports or from a publication of an international statistical agency. Individuals tabulated by census officials as "unemployed" must be either excluded from or included in *each* of the five numbers (i.e., *A*, *E*, *F*, *G*, and *H*).

ANOTHER TRANSFORMATIONAL STATEMENT. Even when two theorists use the same concept, they may differ sharply in devising a corresponding referential formula; and even if they devise the same formula, they may stipulate different requisite data and/or acquisition procedures. Nonetheless, if tests of a particular theory yield impressive support, subsequent theorists will borrow that theory's transformational statements when using its constituent concepts. Test outcomes make the transformational statements more credible; and, short of sheer opinion, those outcomes are the only warrant for credulity. Indeed, one pernicious myth in sociology is that the "validity" of definitions, formulas, measures, or procedures must be demonstrated independently of tests of theories; but only their empirical applicability can be so demonstrated.

For all manner of reasons, no premise should be borrowed uncritically. Yet in formulating the present theory consistency requires *Transformational Statement 6–1*. Repeating: Among countries, the greater the per capita inanimate energy use over T_{0-1}, the greater the RPCIEU over T_{0-1}. The RPCIEU (referential of per capita inanimate energy consumption) formula and data instructions are exactly as stated in chapter 6.

A Derivation

Axiom 7–1, Postulates 6–1 and 7–1, and Transformational Statements 6–1 and 7–1 imply (in accordance with the sign rule) *Theorem 7–1*: Among countries, the greater the RPCIEU over T_{0-1}, the less RAI during T_{0-1}. The theorem's derivation is better understood by inspecting Figure 7–1.

Note that the theory ends with the theorem, and the remainder of the diagram pertains to an illustrative test.[3] Should the theory be construed as merely an assertion of an inverse relation among countries between per capita energy use and the proportion of the economically active in animate industries, that simplification obscures the theory's logical structure and ignores the need for a special language to denote formulas and for stipulations of requisite data. Finally, although the same theorem might be deduced from a radically different theory, it is virtually certain that the two theories would differ as regards dimensions of predictive power other than predictive accuracy, such as parsimony (ratio of theorems to premises) and scope (number of constructs, concepts, and referentials).

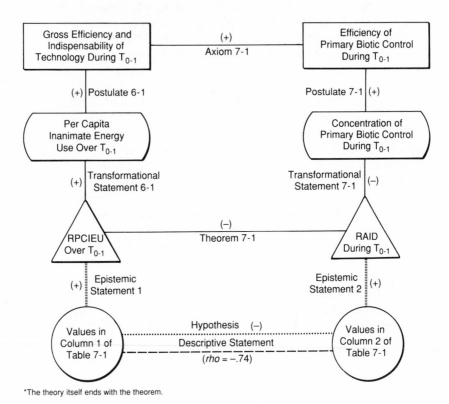

*The theory itself ends with the theorem.

Figure 7–1.   Diagram of a Theory and a Particular Test*

A Test of the Theorem

Table 7–1 provides the necessary referents for a test of Theorem 7–1 as it applies to 104 countries. Even though there is only one theorem, a truly systematic test requires the deduction of a hypothesis pertaining to two sets of referents. The premises for that deduction include, in addition to the theorem, two epistemic statements, as follows.

> *Epistemic statement 1*: Among the countries in Table 7–1, the greater the RPCIEU over T_{0-1}, the greater the value in column 1.
>
> *Epistemic statement 2*: Among the countries in Table 7–1, the greater the RAI at any point during T_{0-1}, the greater the value in column 2.

Table 7–1. Statistics for 104 Countries, 1970

Countries	Per Capita Inanimate Energy Use: RPCIEU Referents* Col. 1	Percentage of Economically Active in Animate Industries RAI Referents** Col. 2	Per Capita Imports, U.S.Dollar Values*** Col. 3
Afghanistan	34	82	7
Algeria	342	56	88
Argentina	1,703	15	70
Australia	5,440	8	358
Austria	3,408	16	478
Barbados	1,104	23	492
Bolivia	229	58	32
Brazil	474	44	31
Bulgaria	3,941	42	216
Burma	58	64	6
Burundi	15	86	6
Cameroon	91	82	41
Canada	8,389	8	627
Chad	25	91	17
Chile	1,299	25	99
Colombia	606	45	41
Congo	194	45	48
Costa Rica	421	45	183
Cuba	1,067	33	156
Cyprus	1,380	35	392
Czechoslovakia	6,522	16	258
Denmark	5,723	12	894
Dominican R.	321	61	68
Ecuador	297	54	46
Egypt	275	55	24
El Salvador	192	57	61
Ethiopia	33	85	7
Finland	4,071	25	572
France	3,956	14	376
Gabon	897	72	160
Germany, D.R.	6,051	12	284
Germany, F.R.	5,419	9	491
Ghana	173	55	48
Greece	1,222	46	223
Guatemala	212	63	54
Guyana	1,093	32	191
Haiti	34	77	12

Table 7–1. Continued

Countries	Col. 1	Col. 2	Col. 3
Honduras	247	67	88
Hungary	3,152	25	242
India	181	68	4
Indonesia	120	70	8
Iran	1,020	46	58
Iraq	633	47	54
Ireland	3,145	27	535
Israel	2,561	11	489
Italy	2,793	21	279
Ivory Coast	228	81	90
Jamaica	1,325	27	281
Japan	3,342	21	181
Jordan	306	39	80
Kenya	135	80	35
Korea, R.	815	58	62
Kuwait	9,411	1	845
Lebanon	665	47	230
Liberia	454	74	99
Libya	537	43	278
Madagascar	71	86	25
Malawi	46	87	19
Mali	21	91	9
Malta	978	8	488
Mauritania	144	85	48
Mauritius	189	31	95
Mexico	1,047	47	46
Morocco	180	61	44
Netherlands	4,943	6	1,030
New Zealand	2,895	12	443
Nicaragua	418	56	108
Niger	25	91	14
Nigeria	52	67	19
Norway	4,844	14	954
Panama	683	43	250
Paraguay	140	53	28
Peru	619	46	46
Philippines	301	70	35
Poland	4,269	38	111
Portugal	754	37	183
Romania	3,013	52	97
Rwanda	11	91	8
Saudi Arabia	845	61	89
Senegal	139	76	49

Table 7–1.   Continued

Countries	Col. 1	Col. 2.	Col. 3
Sierra Leone	134	73	45
Singapore	1,402	8	1,189
Somalia	39	82	16
Spain	1,514	34	140
Sri Lanka	153	52	31
Sudan	130	80	21
Sweden	6,430	9	871
Switzerland	3,546	7	1,048
Syria	502	49	57
Thailand	247	77	36
Togo	67	75	33
Tunisia	261	46	59
Turkey	479	69	26
Uganda	74	86	12
U.S.S.R.	4,424	32	48
United Kingdom	5,336	3	391
United States	11,020	4	194
Upper Volta	13	89	9
Uruguay	930	17	80
Venezuela	2,319	26	160
Yugoslavia	1,459	53	141
Zaire	81	78	25
Zambia	495	69	114

*Total commercial energy consumption in kilograms of coal or coal-equivalents per capita. Figures from United Nations (1976:Table 2).

**Animate industries: agriculture, forestry, fishing, and hunting. Percentage figures from United Nations (1980:Table II.21).

***Figures from United Nations (1979:Table J).

The Hypothesis and the Descriptive Statement

According to the sign rule, the theorem and the two epistemic statements imply a statement about Table 7–1, one designated here as Hypothesis 1: Among the countries in Table 7–1, the greater the value in column 1, the less the value in column 2.

Hypothesis 1 is a prediction in that it was deduced and could be false. A judgment as to its truth or falsity requires a statement, one that supposedly describes the nature of the actual relation between the values in column 1 and the values in column 2 of Table 7–1. Descriptive Statement 1: The product-moment coefficient of correlation (r) between the values in column 1 and the values in column 2 of Table 7–1 is $-.74$.

The coefficient's negative sign is consistent with the hypothesis, and its magnitude is substantial by any reasonable standard.[4] So the test outcome justifies retaining the theorem and, because there is only one theorem, the theory as a whole.

Extension of the Theory to Third Order

The immediate reason for doubting the theorem's validity is that it asserts a second-order (bivariate) relation. When such a relation pertains to human behavior, it is never even approximately invariant, let alone close, in all conditions. Stated more abstractly, any second-order theory is virtually certain to be such that it needs to be extended to a third-order theory, which asserts that at least one designated second-order relation is contingent on the magnitude and/or amount of variation in a designated third variable. The point is not to belittle second-order theories; each may be a necessary step toward a third-order theory. In any case, a formal mode of theory construction is needed all the more when stating third-order theories.

A third-order theory identifies a condition in which a designated second-order relation will be greater (closer) than it is in at least one other condition. Such conditions are described in terms of characteristics of the units of comparison—countries in the present second-order theory. Stated otherwise, a third-order theory stipulates how "sets of units" are to be created so that one set more nearly approximates some stipulated ideal condition.

Ecological Autonomy

The second-order theory entails two arguments about macro control phenomena. First, no country's population can survive unless a certain minimal proportion of members engage in primary biotic control. Second, that proportion depends on the efficiency of primary biotic control, which in turn depends on technological efficiency and indispensability.

No one is likely to dispute either argument; but they do not provide a direct answer to this question: Why do sustained increases in the efficiency of primary biotic control eventually result in a decrease in the proportion of the economically active population in animate industries? The question is all the more important because it bears on the evolution of human productivity through major stages (e.g., hunting-gathering → domestication → manufacturing → services). However, the idea is not that a theory should answer all questions. A theory necessarily leaves at least one question unanswered: If the theory's premises are true, why are they true? If that question must be answered, then a complete theory is impossible.

Nonetheless, Postulate 7–1 in the present theory may be substantially more valid for some countries than others. That postulate asserts an inverse relation between primary biotic control's efficiency and its concentration, meaning that as efficiency increases there is a reduction of the proportion of workers regularly engaged in that kind of control. Sustained increases in technological efficiency require a decrease in the proportion of the economically active regularly engaged in primary biotic control and an increase in the proportion regularly engaged in inanimate control (manufacturing especially). However, the necessity of that relation can be questioned. A country may export a huge volume of biotic products and import technological items on a vast scale; conversely, a country may specialize in the production of technological items and import a large volume of biotic products. In either case, the proportion of the economically active in animate industries would differ appreciably from that predicted on the basis of the theory.

In light of the foregoing, some exceptions to Postulate 7–1 are possible unless all countries are ecologically autonomous. No country is fully ecologically autonomous, but some are more so than others, and Postulate 7–1 would hold better without any international variation in the degree of ecological autonomy. So we arrive at the third-order theory's first premise, *Axiom 7-III–1*: Among *sets* of countries, the greater the uniform ecological autonomy of countries in a set over T_{0-1}, the greater the direct relation among the countries in that set between the efficiency of primary biotic control and the concentration of primary biotic control over T_{0-1}.

Two Postulates

While complete isolation insures ecological autonomy, various kinds of contact between two populations might have no discernible influence on either population's industry composition or technology; but all of the relevant kinds of contact cannot be specified. Accordingly, since a complete and empirically applicable definition of ecological autonomy is not feasible, the term is left essentially undefined and treated as a construct. Nonetheless, ecological autonomy is a matter of degree; and one of its many possible correlates is identified in third-order theory's second premise, *Postulate 7-III–1*: Among sets of countries, the greater the uniform ecological autonomy of countries in a set over T_{0-1}, the less the mean and standard deviation of monetary values of imports per capita in that set over T_{0-1}. Tradition in sociology notwithstanding, the second variable is not a "measure" of the first variable; rather, the second is an asserted epistemic correlate of the first.

While the compound concept (second variable) in the postulate could also denote exports, only imports need be considered. Even so, there is no feasible metric for expressing amount of imports other than monetary value, and to realize international comparability the total value must be expressed in some standard currency (e.g., U.S. dollars, French francs).

Observe that the second variable in Axiom 7-III–1 (a *relational* construct) is the bivariate relation asserted in Postulate 7–1 of the second-order theory; and that relation enters into the derivation of an implied proposition in the second-order theory (Fig. 7–1), one that asserts a direct relation among countries between per capita inanimate energy use and the concentration of primary biotic control. Presuming that the closeness of the relation in the implied proposition is contingent on the association asserted in Postulate 7–1, we arrive at the third premise in the third-order theory, *Postulate 7-III-2*: Among *sets* of countries, the greater the direct relation among countries in a set between the efficiency of primary biotic control and the concentration of primary biotic control over T_{0-1}, the greater the direct relation among countries in that set between per capita inanimate energy use and concentration of primary biotic control over T_{0-1}. The assertion made by the postulate is simpler than it appears, because the statement is of this form: the relation between X and Y depends on the relation between W and Z.

Two Transformational Statements

Given the monetary value of imports per capita for each country in a set, no special instructions are needed to compute the mean and standard deviation of those values. However, the mean and the standard deviation are to be expressed as one composite value, which is their product (i.e., the mean multiplied by the standard deviation). Denoting that product as referential of the average and variance in per capita imports (RAVPCI), we have the fourth third-order theory's premise, *Transformational Statement 7-III-1*: Among sets of countries, the greater the mean and standard deviation of monetary values of imports per capita of countries in a set over T_{0-1}, the greater the RAVPCI over T_{0-1} for that set.

Although special instructions are not necessary to compute RAVPCI referents, some observations on import data are in order. International statistical agencies compute and report per capita annual imports in terms of a standard currency for numerous countries. The RAVPCI formula can be applied to such values in any of those reports. Alternatively, the values can be computed by investigators when conducting a test of the third-order theory; but with a view to maximizing comparability, each of the kinds of statistics that enter into the computation must be from a particular report of a particular international statistical agency, meaning that all statistics of the same kind must be taken from the same report (publication).

SECOND TRANSFORMATIONAL STATEMENT. The third-order theory anticipates variation in the correlations reported in tests of the second-order theory. That is the case because each test will pertain to a particular set of countries, and it is unlikely that the RAVPCI referents (the product of the mean and standard deviation of per capita monetary values of imports) for any two sets will be even approximately the same. The more immediate point is that any correlation between RPCIEU referents and RAI referents itself becomes a referent (for that set of countries), one that can be used in testing the third-order theory. Described another way, the referential of inanimate energy use and animate industries (RIEUAI) denotes instructions for computing the correlation between RPCIEU referents and RAI referents for any set of countries. For reasons advanced subsequently, the rank-order coefficient of correlation (*rho*) is prescribed rather than the product-moment correlation coefficient (*r*). So we have *Transformational Statement 7-III–2*: Among *sets* of countries, the greater the direct relation per capita inanimate energy use and the concentration of primary biotic control over T_{0-1}, the greater the RIEUAI over T_{0-1} for that set.

Because a RIEUAI referent is a bivariate correlation coefficient for a particular set of countries, it requires instructions as to RPCIEU referents and RAI referents. Those instructions have been given in connection with the second-order theory and need not be repeated, but note that previous instructions as to the requisite data for the RPCIEU and RAI referential formulas also apply.

Derivation of a Theorem and the Creation of Sets

By the sign rule, the five premises discussed previously imply *Theorem 7–III–1*: Among *sets* of countries, the greater the RVAPCI over T_{0-1} for a set, the greater the RIEUAI over T_{0-1} for that set. All such theorems assert that the relation between two designated variables depends on the magnitude and/or variance in a third variable, and at least one theorem of that form must be present in any third-order theory. Understanding the theorem's derivation will be furthered by inspection of Figure 7–2.

CREATION OF SETS.   Tests of a third-order theory require special instructions for creating sets of units (countries in this case). Instructions are difficult because of variation in the number of units that investigators will examine in tests, especially when limited research resources make it necessary to obtain the requisite data from publications; and the present test procedure must stipulate such data. One consequence: it is realistic to prescribe only the minimum number of sets and the minimum number of units in each set. Although any third-order theorem could be tested with only two sets and two countries in each set, it is more realistic to stipulate *three* as the minimum number of sets and the minimum number of countries in each set.

Special instructions are needed when data are available for more than nine countries. This rule maximizes the number of countries in each set, thereby reducing the effect of extreme cases (units) in any particular set: The number of sets is the smallest factor greater than 2 of the number of countries. To illustrate, given 27 countries, three sets of units would be created with nine countries in each, because 3 is the smallest factor of 27 greater than 2. Applying the rule to the 104 countries in Table 7–1, there are four sets, each comprising 26 countries. Had the total number of countries been such as to have no factor

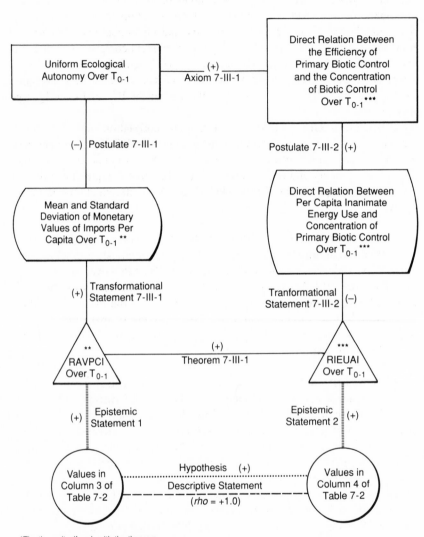

Figure 7–2. Diagram of a Third-Order Theory and a Particular Test*

*The theory itself ends with the theorem.

**A property or characteristic of a set of countries, one which refers not just to the amount of ecological autonomy of the countries in a set but also to the uniformity in that amount within the set.

***Relation among the countries in a set of countries.

greater than 2, it would be reduced by random reduction of countries to the first lesser number with a factor greater than 2.

Given the number of sets and countries in each set, a procedure is needed to assign particular countries to each set. When testing Theorem 7-III–1, countries are to be ranked according to per capita monetary value of imports, and the value ranges are to be identified so that each range encompasses the number of units desired in each set (26 in this case).

Such a creation of sets is appropriate for testing the third-order theory because the sets differ as to approximation of an ideal condition—absolute ecological autonomy. The amount of intraset variation in ecological autonomy is also relevant, but that can be taken into account by computing the standard deviation of the per capita import values for each set.

When the foregoing procedure was applied to the 104 countries in Table 7–1, the four sets of countries (26 in each set) are as shown in Table 7–2. Because the four sets were created by reference to the magnitude of import values, each set represents a quartile. Note, however, that the RAVPCI referent for each set of countries refers not to the mean or to the standard deviation of the of import values (columns 1 and 2) but to their product (column 3).

An Illustrative Test

The statistics in column 3 and 4 of Table 7–2 are sufficient to test the theorem, but a systematic test requires the deduction of a hypothesis and the formulation of a descriptive statement, as follows.

Epistemic Statement 1: Among the sets of countries in Table 7–2, the greater the RAVPCI over T_{0-1}, the greater the value in column 3.

Epistemic Statement 2: Among the sets of countries Table 7–2, the greater the RIEUAI over T_{0-1}, the greater (more positive or less negative) the value in column 4.

Hypothesis (from Theorem 7-III–1, Epistemic Statement 1, and Epistemic Statement 2): Among the sets of countries in Table 7–2, the greater the value in column 3, the greater (less negative) the value in column 4.

Descriptive Statement: The rank-order coefficient of correlation (*rho*) between the values in column 3 and the values in column 4 of Table 7–2 is $+1.00$.

INTERPRETATION OF THE TEST OUTCOME.   Because a third-order theory extends a second-order theory, it is more complex; and the same is true of tests of a third-order theorem. Nonetheless, a brief assessment of the test will suffice: No set of countries is an exception to the hypothesis; hence, the test outcome clearly justifies retaining the third-order theory.

The test can be better understood by recognizing again that Set IV (Table

Table 7–2.   Statistics for Four Sets of Countries*

Countries Grouped by Per Capita Amount of Imports in U.S. Dollar Values, 1970	Per Capita Dollar Value of Imports, 1970			
	Mean of Set Col. 1	Standard Deviation of Set Col. 2	Product of Columns 1 and 2: RAVPCI Referents Col. 3	rho_{be}** RIEUAI Referents Col. 4
Set I: First quartile, 26 countries with per capita dollar values ranging from 258 to 1,189	582	277	161,214	−.433
Set II: Second quartile, 26 countries with per capita dollar values ranging from 88 to 250	151	54	8,154	−.606
Set III: Third quartile, 26 countries with per capita dollar values ranging from 35 to 80	52	12	624	−.733
Set IV: Fourth quartile, 26 countries with per capita dollar values ranging from 4 to 33	17	9	153	−.809

*See Table 7–1 for data sources and the values that enter into the statistics in this table.
**Rank-order coefficient of correlation (N=26 for each set) between (1) percent of the economically active in agriculture, forestry, fishing, or hunting and (2) per capita consumption of commercial energy in kilograms of coal or coal-equivalents (see Table 7–1 for each value that enters into the correlations.)

7–2) is the closest to an ideal condition—no imports and, inferentially, the greatest ecological autonomy. It is among Set IV countries that the correlation between RPCIEU referents (per capita inanimate energy use) and RAI referents (percentage of the economically active in agriculture, fishing, forestry, or hunting) is most negative. While the correlation is negative for each set, the Set IV coefficient is nearly twice that of Set I; and there is a consistent increase in the correlation from Set I to Set IV.

Beyond the Illustrative Test

Why does the correlation coefficient for Set I (column 4, Table 7–2) not approach zero? The volume of international trade has not reached the level necessary to preclude the relations asserted in the second-order theory. That answer is speculative, of course; but if international trade continues to increase and the third-order theory is valid, the correlation coefficient in question (Set I) will eventually approach zero. Indeed, if the trade trend continues, future tests of the second-order theory will support it less and less.

Why is the Set IV correlation (column 4, Table 7–2) not closer to unity (–1.00)? All countries in the set had some imports; hence, none of them were absolutely ecological autonomous. But that answer suggests the possibility of a perfect theory and an ideal test. To the contrary, no sociological theory will recognize all relevant variables; and test data never will be completely reliable, which is the primary reason for assessing a theory's predictive power (accuracy particularly) relative to that of contenders.

MEASUREMENT ERROR.   *Rho* was used as the measure of *intraset* association to minimize the effect of measurement error.[5] Even if there is, say, a ten percent random error in each X value and each Y value, the ordinal X-Y association could be unity. If there is a great difference between any two measured values of the same variable (e.g., each X value is at least ten percent greater or less than any other X value) but only moderate measurement error (e.g., no more than plus or minus five percent for any X value), then the rank of any measured value and the rank of the true value will be identical. Hence, *rho* will be greater than r to the extent there is: (1) perfect monotonic association between the true values of the two variables, X and Y; (2) random measurement error for all X and Y values; and (3) substantial variation in the true X and Y values.

Even if using *rho* did reduce the effect of measurement error, it is unlikely that the effect was entirely eliminated. However, the test procedure could have been stated with a view to reducing the effect of measurement error even more. Subsets could have been created in each of the four sets (Table 7-2) in order to maximize variation in per capita energy use and/or percentage of the economically active in animate industries for some subsets and minimize variation in others.

PHYSIOGRAPHIC VARIATION.   Even if the effects of measurement error were entirely eliminated, not even an approximation of a unity correlation (−1.00) for any set of countries (Table 7–2) would be expected. Again, it may well be impossible to state a sociological theory such as to recognize all relevant variables. The only realistic demand is for an identification of the relevant variables that were excluded, for one reason or another. The second-order theory and the third-order theory excludes an entire class of variables, all pertaining to physiographic features (e.g., soil quality, precipitation).

Physiographic features are relevant in light of three arguments. First, an isolated population cannot survive unless a certain minimal proportion of its members engage in primary biotic control. Second, the proportion depends on the efficiency of primary biotic control. Third, that efficiency depends both on technology and on physiographic features (e.g., soil quality). The last contingency was not considered in formulating either theory because all of the relevant physiographic features cannot be identified or measured with confidence. The tests of the second-order theorem and the third-order theorem indicate that variation in physiographic features is not crucial;[6] but that was probably not the case in the 18th century, before a rapid global increase in technological efficiency. In any case, the scene is now set for a theory of biotic control that incorporates physiographic variables.

Beyond the Present Theories

Although the two theories (second order and third order) are simple, they have implications for all basic types of control. Unfortunately, however, the theories have no bearing on several important features of biotic control.

Extension to Inanimate and Human Control

Previous tests of the two theories entailed the assumption that the amount of time invested in biotic control is reflected in occupation-industry composition, and there is a similar assumption about inanimate control and human control.[7] Moreover, it is possible to anticipate a relation among countries between technological efficiency and the percentage of the economically active in certain occupations and industries presumed to be associated with inanimate or human control.

INANIMATE CONTROL.   The anticipated relation between technological efficiency and the percentage of the economically active in "inanimate" occupations-industries (e.g., mechanics regardless of industry, laborers in mining) is somewhat complex. Up to some unascertained point, per capita inanimate energy use varies directly with the percentage, and beyond that point it varies inversely with the percentage. The direction of the relation reverses because inanimate energy use can reach such a level that the human time needed to produce technological items (tools, cars, etc.) declines, and at that point the percentage of economically active in inanimate occupations-industries commences to decline.

If the direction of the relation does change once a certain level of per capita inanimate energy use is reached, that level cannot be deduced; hence, exploratory research is needed. A scatter plot of numerous countries, 1980s data, should reveal the approximate level where the relation becomes inverse. Alternatively, researchers can assume that (1) at the turn of the century virtually all countries were well below the level at which the relation in question changes and (2) over 1900–80 several countries came to exceed it; if so, the 1900 *linear* correlation between energy values and the percentages in inanimate industries should be substantially greater than the 1980 correlation.

HUMAN CONTROL. A corresponding anticipation about human control could be simpler because the international relation between per capita inanimate energy use and the percentage of the economically active in the predominantly "human control" occupation-industries (e.g., all managers regardless of industry, security guards in manufacturing) is expected to be direct at all use levels. The expectation is based on assumption that human time invested in human control increases at a greater rate than does the technology that reduces the amount of such time.

Important though it is, the expected relation does not bear on the fundamental question. That question has been suggested by the previous allusion to the apparent expansion of human control in Western countries over several centuries (see Adams, 1975, 1982a, 1982b). The ultimate theory about control must explain that expansion, but the immediate need is more research to confirm it.

Still more research is needed to assess the assumption that the time invested in human control expands at a greater rate than does the technology that reduces the time. If that assumption should prove invalid, then employment opportunities in human control industries (e.g., education) will eventually decline; and it is difficult to imagine alternative employment opportunities (especially without a sharp reduction in annual average hours of working time per worker), because at that point the percentage of the economically active in biotic or inanimate industries will be negligible. So countries throughout the world may eventually confront a crisis like Marx envisioned for capitalism but for a different reason. True, if humans must be controlled whether employed or unemployed, then time invested in human control will never be neglible; but that "solution" has the ring of *1984* or *Brave New World*.

Future Work on Biotic Control

Even ignoring the possibility of transplanting the organs of nonhuman animals to humans, the potential for reducing mortality through human-to-human transplants or prosthetic implants is enormous. Yet there is no basis for even an approximate estimate of the reduction, the immediate reason being that the technological changes necessary for maximum reduction cannot be envisioned. Whatever those changes, they are not likely to be correlates of per capita inanimate energy use. The amount and kind of human-to-human transplants or prosthetic implants will depend not just on technological developments but also on legal regulation, which is to say on the control of biotic control. Considering the prospects of successful xenografts (e.g., apes to humans), the future of biotic control is doubly problematical.

Although sociologists are currently not trained to anticipate technological change, they should at least attempt to anticipate the issues, problems, and concomitant legal regulation of somatic control. Most important, sociologists should be concerned with a particular consequence of a sharp reduction in the mortality rate through transplants or implants—a quantum jump in the population growth rate (assuming no substantial reduction in fertility rates).

GENETIC ENGINEERING. Another future line of work on biotic control pertains to the newest and most rapidly expanding industry in high-energy countries: genetic engineering (see, e.g., Zimmerman, 1984; Stableford, 1984). Even if the percentage of the economically active in that industry could be computed, the significant questions about genetic engineering would not be answered by analyzing employment trends; and the major independent variable in a theory about genetic engineering is not likely to be inanimate energy use.

There are at least two significant questions. First, how much and soon will genetic engineering expand the human life span? And, second, how much and soon will it increase the efficiency of primary biotic control? Expansion of the human life span by altering genes may appear to be only a remote possibility; but if genetic engineering is used effectively to that end, then only a massive reduction in fertility will prevent unprecedented population growth. Yet genetic engineering could further the production of food enormously by creating new life forms. Should that prospect appear unrealistic, note that genetic engineering and selective breeding are quite different ways of altering life forms.

BIRTH CONTROL. Still another line of future work on biotic control will focus on sexual restraint, contraception, and voluntary abortion. In no well-known theory about differential fertility is birth control treated as the principal independent variable. The subject's neglect probably reflects realistic recognition by demographers that programs (governmental or otherwise) to increase or decrease births commonly have been unsuccessful, at least until recently (see Tsui and Bogue, 1978). Even so, the impact of birth control at the individual level (i.e., independently of programs) on the fertility rate can no longer be ignored; and many recent programs of birth control, as in the People's Republic of China (see Greenhalgh and Bongaarts, 1987), have altered thinking about program effectiveness.

The most significant question about birth control is this: What will be its eventual impact on global population growth? While any answer must entail conjecture, some answers are more defensible than others. All answers should go beyond an assessment of current birth control to the possibility of new developments. Moreover, birth control technologies and practices are one thing, while the identification of conditions under which they will be used is quite another. Likewise, birth control can be extensive without reducing the birth rate, meaning that birth control may be used as to prevent only "untimely" conceptions or births (see Keyfitz, 1971). So the most significant question about birth control will be extremely difficult to answer.

Significance of Future Work on Biotic Control

The questions posed for the sociological study of transplants, implants, genetic engineering, and birth control are significant because they bear on a truly global concern. Conceivably, within a few decades the world's population will be so large that billions of people will live on the very edge of starvation. The question is, of course, whether the world's population will outstrip the resources necessary for life. That hoary question entails conjecture about future population trends and changes in the production of material necessities. So in light of what has been said about transplants, implants, genetic engineering, and birth control, the future global population trends and their consequences depend on the future of biotic control.

The argument stops short of claiming that humanity's fate depends solely on transplants, implants, genetic engineering, and birth control. That fate also depends on the future of inanimate control, especially since those forms of biotic control are essentially control through technology. Nonetheless, it is not ludicrous to argue that humanity's fate will depend on those forms of biotic control if an effective substitute for fossil fuels is not discovered before 2200. In any event, biotic control is virtually certain to create more and more social issues. Two of those issues have yet to really surface, and they can best be introduced as questions. First, whose life span should be expanded? Second, who should be social parents and who should be biological parents? Whatever the answers, they will pertain to the control of control; and the two questions are only a few of a multitude about biotic control that will trouble humanity for centuries (see Carpenter, 1982).

Many of the immediate problems pertaining to biotic control illustrate a myth—the certainty of success in biotic control. As instances, the current outcome of the "war on cancer" and the current exponential increase in deaths from AIDS indicate ineffective control over various lethal biotic phenomena. No sociological theory will answer etiological questions about human diseases, but *sociological* theories could bear on this question: What conditions facilitate research on human diseases? That question will be pursued extensively in sociology only if control becomes the field's central notion.

NOTES

1. Actually, the first demographic transition may have been a fertility increase without a concomitant increase in infant mortality, all through selection of dexterous bipedals who could carry children and food more effectively.
2. Whatever the type of control, its "concentration" is a property of a social unit.

An empirical relation between concentration and specialization is expressed as control principle 7–2: The greater the concentration of some type of control, the greater the specialization within that type. To illustrate, given the long-run decline in the percentage of the American labor force in agriculture (greater concentration), data on American agriculture should show a concomitant increase in the percentage of agriculturalists affiliated with only one principal product.

3. Were it not for the problems described in note 7 of chapter 6, the temporal quantifiers would be such as to imply that the maximum correlations obtain if the temporal sequences (lags) are thus: per capita inanimate energy use over T_{0-1}, gross efficiency and indispensability of technology during T_{1-2}, efficiency of primary biotic control during T_{2-3}, concentration of primary biotic control during T_{3-4}, RPCEIU over T_{0-1}, and RAI during T_{3-4}. Should the theory be stated so as to apply longitudinally (any country over time), the same problems (note 7, chapter 6) would preclude lagged temporal quantifiers.

4. All observations made in chapter 6 on tests and predictive power apply here; but in this case, unlike chapter 6, there are no real contending theories. The theory in this chapter and that in chapter 6 are not contenders, the reason being that they are integratable (they share a construct and a concept in common). Two considerations led to the use of *r* rather than Kendall's *tau*. First, readers are more likely to be familiar with *r*. Second, the tests are only illustrative, and *r* is sufficient to indicate that the theory's predictive accuracy is impressive. However, when comparing the theory and contenders, *tau* should be used in all tests. Because of doubts about data reliability, accuracy should be assessed in terms of ordinal predictions; and *tau* is more appropriate than *r* or even *rho*.

5. Here and subsequently, *rho* has been used rather than *tau* only because readers are more likely to be familiar with *rho*.

6. There is no basis to assume that the theory's predictive accuracy could be furthered by introducing variables that are ostensible components of dependency theory. The word "ostensible" is used because the theory is vague in the extreme (see Ragin's commentary, 1983, and *American Journal of Sociology*, January, 1984, 932–51), and the predictive accuracy of conventional versions is unimpressive (see, e.g., Nolan, 1983). The same comments apply to dependency theory in connection with the technology-division of labor theory in chapter 6.

7. All types of control are governed by control principle 7–3, the "specialization imperative": Beyond some point an increase in the diversity of control is followed by an increase in control specialization. Stating the principle in a more testable form: The greater the variety of things controlled in a social unit, the more the social unit members differ as to the things that they attempt to control. The specialization principle is viewed as a consequence largely of as control principle 6–4 (chapter 6, note 11), the principle of limited technological mastery.

An Illustrative Theory About Human Control

No theory can answer all of the major questions about control (chapter 3), and a general theory about each basic type of control (inanimate, biotic, or human) is only a distant possibility because of the diversity of subtypes. The variety of human control (i.e., attempts to control human behavior) far exceeds that suggested in chapter 3 or the tactics of manipulation identified by Buss et al. (1987); but it must suffice to illustrate the seemingly infinite kinds or means of human control within each major type (e.g., proximate) or subtype (e.g., allegative social control): command, request, coerce, threaten, placate, offer, promise, and praise. While such distinctions must be entertained, the quest for a theory about each specific kind of control would be unrealistic. The alternative is a theory about one or more basic properties of human control. An illustration of such a theory is provided in this chapter, but it is a simple illustration if only because limited to the relation between one property of human control—its concentration within the sphere of sustenance activities — and the division of labor.

The Concentration of Human Control

Whatever the type or kind of human control considered, there are two polar extremes: (1) a social unit in which *only one* member attempts to control *all* behavior of *all* other members and (2) a social unit in which no member attempts to control no more than one type of one member's behavior.[1] "Concentration of human control" is at the maximum in extreme (1) but at the minimum in extreme (2). As those extremes suggest, one dimension of concentration is the extent to which attempts at human control are limited to particular social unit members, perhaps only one; but that partial definition promises very little empirical applicability. Think of a legislative body in a social unit. Even though the body cannot be equated with "a member," it is nonetheless control concentration; but there is no methodology for expressing the amount, especially in light of another illustration. Should the legislative body be displaced by a singular sovereign, whether monarch or dictator, he or she would not attempt to control all of anyone's behavior. Yet both the variety of behavior controlled and the proportion of social unit members engaged in control are concentration dimensions.

The empirical inapplicability of "concentration of human control" makes it necessary to treat the term as a construct. It denotes one of numerous properties of control at the macro level (i.e., a collective variable), many of which are not limited to human control; but space limitations preclude more than even a brief treatment of only one property. Concentration of human control has been selected primarily because it contradicts what appears to be a widespread belief among sociologists—that control is a micro phenomenon.

Control over Sustenance Activities and Modes of Production

Research on the concentration of human control is feasible only if limited to human control over particular types of behavior. No type is more important than a sustenance activity (an expenditure of human energy in the production of a thing or benefit); and observations on controls over those activities facilitate thinking about production modes and the division of labor, two macro phenomena.

The Familial Mode of Production

As stressed in chapter 6, functional interdependence is one of the two basic dimensions (along with differentiation in sustenance activities) of the degree of division of labor; and it is reflected in the exchange of things and benefits. When the exchange in a territorial unit (e.g., a country or community) is only among members of the same household, the familial mode of production prevails in that unit.

There is a complex relation between modes of production and the division of labor in that each mode facilitates the division of labor and at the same time imposes an upper limit on it. The familial mode of production facilitates the division of labor because human control in households tends to be concentrated. Such terms as *patriarchal, matriarchal, avunculate, paternalism,* and *genontocracy* are indicative of that tendency. However, regardless of the persons who exercise control, they assign some kinds of sustenance activities to particular household members and coordinate or synchronize those activities. Such control is in itself differentiation, and it furthers functional interdependence.

Even if any two members of each household differ sharply as to their sustenance activities, the sheer variety of activities within a household is very limited because there are so few members. Accordingly, when the familial mode of production prevails in a territorial unit, the unit's division of labor is limited by the number of members in the largest household. For that matter, when the familial mode prevails, there is negligible variation in the character of sustenance activities among households because household activities are largely limited to essentials—acquiring and preparing food, caring for children, repairing tools, etc. Because there is little variation among households, the variety of sustenance activities throughout the territorial unit is negligible.

The Symbiotic Mode of Production

To the extent that members of different households exchange things or benefits, then the locus of sustenance activities is "public." Such an exchange implies that those involved differ as to their sustenance activities, the variety of which is limited only by the territorial unit's population size. Once things or benefits are exchanged at the public level, it becomes more feasible for an individual to specialize in some type of sustenance activity; but occupations do not appear until functional interdependence has gone far beyond the household level. In particular, such occupations as tailor, blacksmith, baker, barber, and cobbler evidently emerged with the symbiotic mode of production.

To understand the symbiotic mode, think of ego and alter as members of different households but residents of the same community. In producing some thing or benefit for alter, ego engages in a public sustenance activity; and alter is expected to compensate ego with some other thing, some other benefit, or money. So there is an exchange, and it has a normative quality. However, ego may not feel obligated to continue the relation; he or she may even commence producing for an impersonal market. Should ego cease producing completely, he or she would suffer some loss (e.g., fewer material possessions) but not because someone outside of his or her household has attempted to control him or her punitively. More generally, the "symbiotic producer" makes decisions as to what he or she will produce, when, where, and how, without regard to the probability that someone outside of his or her household will react punitively. The point is that the symbiotic mode cannot be described fully without reference to control: to the extent that population members engage in public sustenance activities and no one outside any member's household attempts to control that member's sustenance activities other than through terms of exchange (making offers or rejecting offers), then the symbiotic mode of production prevails.

The symbiotic mode avoids the limits imposed on the division of labor by household size because all residents of a territorial unit are potential consumers of anything produced by any resident. Hence, to use Adam Smith's notion (1952), market size expands with the transition from the familial to the symbiotic mode of production, and the expansion permits specialization. Accord-

168 / *Control: Sociology's Central Notion*

ingly, whereas familial production virtually precludes distinct occupations, the symbiotic mode may be such that there is only one individual in each of several particular occupations (e.g., baker, blacksmith) and everyone in the territorial unit depends on that individual.

Just as the familial mode limits the division of labor, so does the symbiotic mode. Many types of objects or substances can be produced only if several individuals synchronize or coordinate their activities regularly (imagine an isolated individual attempting to build a passenger jet). But the point is not that the symbiotic mode precludes the control of one individual over the sustenance activities of others, even though they are members of different households. By offering favorable terms of exchange, one individual may exert some control over production in several households; nonetheless, there are of numerous types of objects that cannot be produced without much greater synchronization-coordination of activities than is characteristic of symbiotic production.

Formally Coordinated Production

In high-energy countries the predominant mode of production is neither familial nor symbiotic. The sustenance activities of most individuals are "public" but controlled by persons outside the individual's household. That is the case because most economically active residents of high-energy countries are predominantly employees; and no employee works when, where, and how he or she happens to see fit. At least one person (proprietor, manager, director, dean, etc.) believes that an employee should conduct himself or herself in a particular manner, and in that sense the employee's conduct is subject to more or less continuous control. If the employee does not conform to expectations, he or she is subject to a punitive reaction (e.g., dismissal).

To the extent that sustenance activities are public and subject to control independently of household affiliation, the mode of production is formally coordinated. The sustenance activities of employees exemplify the formally coordinated mode of production. True, they appear to produce objects or benefits for an impersonal market, which suggests a symbiotic quality; but an employee actually produces for and is controlled by an employer.

As an illustration of the transition from the symbiotic to the formally coordinated mode of production, consider Landes's observation on the shift of the textile industry from the "cottage" to the "factory" system early in England's Industrial Revolution: "No longer could the spinner turn her wheel and the weaver throw his shuttle at home, free of supervision, both in their own good time. Now the work had to be done in a factory, at a pace set by tireless, inanimate equipment, as part of a large team that had to begin, pause, and stop in unison—all under the close eye of the overseers, enforcing assiduity by moral, pecuniary, occasionally even physical means of compulsion. The factory was a new kind of prison; the clock a new kind of jailer" (1969:43).

To better understand the formal coordination of sustenance activities, compare (1) the relation between two individuals working at different points on an assembly line and (2) the relation between a physician and a photographer in a small town. One of the assemblers depends on the other, and that relation requires a coordination of activities. The coordination is "normative" in that a third party (the factory owner or a supervisor) believes that the two assemblers ought to behave in stipulated ways. If the assemblers do not conform to the third party's expectations, the third party reacts punitively.

Functional interdependence on an assembly line differs in several respects from that between a physician and a photographer in a small town. The sustenance activities of the physician and the photographer are not synchronized or coordinated by a third party, and their functional interdependence has no necessary normative basis. They may depend on each other, but typically either party can seek the service in question elsewhere without risking a punitive reaction. Nonetheless, the physician and the photographer perform different activities in a system through which various objects and benefits are produced for the general public, and such differentiation is a division of labor. It is different from Adam Smith's pin factory (formally coordinated), but it is a mistake to conceptualize the division of labor so that it is limited to associations—companies, corporations, or otherwise.

The Question of Measurement

The predominance of formally coordinated production, like the other two modes, is a matter of degree; but there is no method for the numerical representation of the predominance of any one of the three modes, let alone one that could be applied to large territorial units. The problem is not alleviated by the argument that the concentration of control over sustenance activities increases with the transition from the familial to the symbiotic mode of production and from the symbiotic to the formally coordinated mode. But that argument is important because it suggests this generalization: The greater the concentration of control over sustenance activities, the greater the degree of division of labor.

Only the predominance of the formally coordinated mode of production can be inferred systematically. In the case of Western capitalist countries the formally coordinated mode is predominant to the extent that those regularly engaged in sustenance activities are employees of a company, corporation, or other organizations. However, greater generality is realized if the argument is made in connection with a particular type of association, one far less time-bound and space-bound.

Sustenance Associations

A sustenance association is an association in which all of the members coordinate and/or synchronize some or all of their sustenance activities as members in the collective production of some thing or benefit. Numerous associations are not sustenance associations, even though the members engage in the same kind of sustenance activities. Thus, if farmers create some association (e.g., "Patrons of Husbandry") to further a mutual pecuniary or aesthetic interest, neither that goal nor their activities as members makes the social unit a sustenance association, for the farmers do not engage in and coordinate or synchronize their sustenance activities as members. Conceivably, a member could resign from the association without altering any of his or her sustenance activities (as a farmer); and even though the activities of the members may further their well-being, they are not collectively producing things or benefits for others. Likewise, if a businessperson joins the Rotarians with the intention of furthering his or her financial interests, that intent does not make the Rotarians a sustenance association. True, the members expend energy to attend meetings, but they do not necessarily produce anything as members.

Companies and corporations in the U.S. are conspicuous sustenance associations because all employees engage in sustenance activities as a condition of their employment. But a particular family also qualifies if all of its members coordinate or synchronize their sustenance activities in the collective production of some thing or benefit.

The definition does not stipulate that sustenance association members participate as an exclusive means of livelihood. In high-energy countries individuals commonly work for only one employer and scarcely engage in sustenance activities outside of that organizational context. Even when some employees have one or more other jobs, it would be ludicrous to deny that a company or corporation is a sustenance association merely because one employee moonlights; and any designation of a maximum proportion would be arbitrary. Accordingly, the extent to which association members engage in sustenance activities outside that organizational context is conceptually irrelevant.

Finally, sustenance association members need not coordinate or synchronize their sustenance activities continuously (companies or corporations are commonly inactive over weekends and holidays), but extended periods of inactivity do pose a conceptual problem. In some populations, especially nonliterate ones, particular kinds of sustenance activities may cease for months. Given long intervals of inactivity, one would argue that the organizational context is so transitory that an association does not exist; but any stipulation as to necessary periods of collective activity would be arbitrary. So the crucial consideration is the expectations of participants as to when periods of activity or inactivity will end. A set of individuals who at least occasionally coordinate or synchronize their sustenance activities constitutes a sustenance association only if those individuals agree as to when they will end and resume coordination-synchronization.

Formal Version of the Theory and a Test

All of the preceding arguments enter into a theory about the concentration of control over sustenance activities and the degree of division of labor. The theory's logical structure can be clarified only by stating it formally, and that statement is also necessary for systematic tests; but tests are pointless unless predictive power is the criterion for assessing theories.

Principal Constituent Statements

All of the foregoing arguments reduce to an axiom and a postulate. However, the theory comprises also a postulate from chapter 6, two transformational statements (one from chapter 6), and a theorem derived from the five premises (the axiom, the two postulates, and the two transformational statements).

THE AXIOM. The fundamental assertion is *Axiom 8–1*: Among countries, the greater the concentration of control over sustenance activities during T_{0-1}, the greater the degree of division of labor during T_{0-1}.[2] The axiom pertains to differences among countries because a close direct relation between the two variables may not hold intranationally, such as among Canadian metropolitan areas. Intranational units are commonly components in an extensive territorial division of labor; so some of them (e.g., Detroit) specialize in production, with one consequence being below average occupational differentiation. However, control over sustenance activities would not necessarily be less concentrated in such a metropolitan area than in other metropolitan areas. It is simply a case where some empirical relation may hold much more for units of a particular type.

Axiom 8–1 expresses this argument: A high degree of division of labor requires extensive coordination and synchronization of sustenance activities.[3] That is the case because beyond some point the division of labor increases primarily through highly coordinated and synchronized activities in the collective production process, such as on an assembly line. Coordination-synchronization in turn requires control in the form of directives, supervision, management, and planning, which constitute a concentration of control over sustenance activities. Increases in that concentration can be described, as it has been here, in terms of evolutionary trends in three modes of production; but those modes need not be recognized in stating the axiom.

TWO POSTULATES. Again, extensive coordination-synchronization of sustenance activities requires concentration of control over those activities. Sustenance associations are a manifestation of that concentration; but it is not just a matter of the number of sustenance associations, nor even the percentage of the population who engage in sustenance activities as a sustenance association member (e.g., employer or employee). The average size of sustenance associations is also relevant; control tends to become more concentrated as the size of a sustenance association increases (see Scott, 1987:241), with the change in concentration reflecting a concern on the part of some association member with control efficacy. There is a tendency for owners or managers to delegate authority as the number of members increases, but the proportionate increase in the diffusion of authority is less than the proportionate increase in sustenance association size. Accordingly, two features of sustenance associations in a territorial unit must be recognized: first, the proportion of the population who engage regularly in sustenance activities as a sustenance association member; and, second, the average number of members in the associations. The term *scope of sustenance associations* is used to denote both features considered simultaneously.[4] So we arrive at *Postulate 8–1*: Among countries, the greater the concentration of control over sustenance activities during T_{0-1}, the greater the scope of sustenance associations during T_{0-1}.

The second postulate is borrowed from the theory in chapter 6; and it is again identified as *Postulate 6–2*: Among countries, the greater the division of labor during T_{0-1}, the greater the occupational differentiation during T_{0-1}. No explication or defense of the postulate is needed beyond what was said in chapter 6. Note, however, that all previous comments on the form of Axiom 8–1, especially the temporal quantifiers and its cross-sectional character (see notes 2 and 3), apply to the two postulates and subsequent premises.

TWO TRANSFORMATIONAL STATEMENTS. Scope of sustenance associations is a concept in that it can be defined completely and a formula for numerical representation can be stipulated. However, enormous resources would be required to gather the requisite data for even a few communities, and the resources required for only one country is prohibitive. So the referential formula must be applicable to data in national census reports or publications of international statistical agencies. Those data appear as "class of worker" statistics, the number of economically active in each of the following categories: employees (*Ee*), employers (*Er*), self-employed (*Se*), and unpaid family workers (*Uf*). The formula for expressing RSSA (referential of the scope of sustenance associations) in connection with class of worker statistics is: *RSSA* = (*Ee* + *Uf*)/(*Er* + *Se*). The formula's rationale can be illustrated two ways. First, if every economically active individual is self-employed, the formula would yield a zero value; and the inference would be that no sustenance association exists. Second, by contrast, if all but one economically active individual are employees and that one remaining individual is an employer, the RSSA referent (value) would indicate that all of the economically active population engage in sustenance activities as members of one huge association.[5] So we have *Transformational Statement 8–1*: Among nonMarxist countries, the greater the scope of sustenance associations during T_{0-1}, the greater the RSSA during T_{0-1}.

The transformational statement is limited to non-Marxist countries because in Marxist countries the vast majority of the economically active may be classified for census purposes as state employees. If so, that classification would not reflect the reality of control over sustenance activities in those countries.

The theory on technology and the division of labor (chapter 6) is the source of *Transformational Statement 6–2*: Among countries, the greater the occupational differentiation during T_{0-1}, the greater the RAOD during T_{0-1}. As before, RAOD (referential of adjusted occupational differentiation) designates this formula: $(1 - [\Sigma X^2/(\Sigma X)^2])/[1 - (1/Nc)]$, where X is the number of individuals in an occupational category and Nc is the number of categories. The RAOD formula applies to data reported by either a national census agency or an international agency, but in any one test the formula is not to be applied to data from both sources (i.e., national census reports for some countries but a report of an international agency for others). Finally, when data pertaining to the same country are reported for two or more lists of occupational categories, the most detailed list must be used.

DERIVATION OF A THEOREM. The theory comprises five premises—one axiom, two postulates, and two transformational statements. In accordance with the sign rule, those premises imply *Theorem 8–1*: Among nonMarxist countries, the greater the RSSA during T_{0-1}, the greater the RAOD during T_{0-1}.

Figure 8–1 offers a pictographic representation of the theory.[6] Because a theory's logical structure may be more evident in a pictographic representation than in a verbal version, the diagram should be examined particularly with a view to understanding the theorem's derivation. Note that the theory ends with the theorem, and the other parts of the diagram (the epistemic statements, the hypothesis, and the descriptive statement) pertain only to a particular test.

A Particular Test

All of the data necessary for a test of the theory appear in Table 8–1. Because the data sources and computational formulas are identified in the table footnotes, only four statements are needed to report the test, and each is distinct from the theory itself.

Epistemic Statement *1*: Among the countries in Table 8–1, the greater the RSSA during T_{0-1}, the greater the value in column 1.
Epistemic Statement 2: Among the countries in Table 8–1, the greater the RAOD during T_{0-1}, the greater the value in column 2.

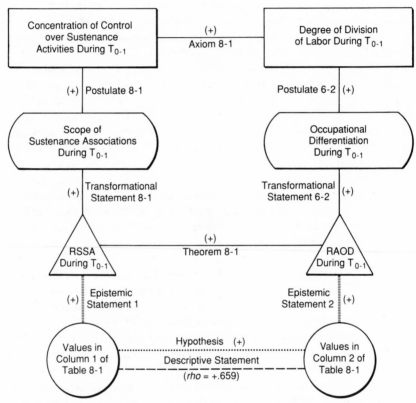

*The theory itself ends with the theorem.

Figure 8–1.   Diagram of a Theory and a Particular Test*

Hypothesis 1: (from Theorem 8–1, Epistemic Statement 1, and Epistemic Statement 2): Among the countries in Table 8–1, the greater the value in column 1, the greater the value in column 2.

Descriptive statement 1: The rank-order coefficient of correlation (*rho*) between the values in column 1 and the values in column 2 of Table 8–1 is +.659.

Both the sign and the magnitude of the correlation coefficient justify retaining the theorem and, hence, the theory. However, there are doubts because the theory formulated in chapter 6 is a contending theory about the degree of division of labor, and it appears to explain more variance in the referents of occupational differentiation (reconsider tests of the hypothesis corresponding to Theorem 6–1).[7] A more dispositive conclusion must await tests of hypotheses corresponding to Theorem 6–1 and Theorem 8–1 based on data for the same countries and years, with contending variables controlled in each test. Of course, it may prove that the scope of sustenance associations explains a significant amount of variation in occupational differentiation independently of inanimate energy use; if so, a combination of the present theory and that in chapter 6 will warrant consideration. The problem is, of course, that simple combinations of theories or even the expansion of the number of independent variables reduces parsimony.

Future Research Needs

Although the one previous test, limited to twelve Latin American countries (Gibbs and Browning, 1966), yielded even more positive results, in both tests the correlation coefficient indicates that the rank of several countries are far removed from that which would be predicted, assuming the theorem to be absolutely valid. The theorem's predictive accuracy might increase considerably if the occupational data were based on much more detailed categories. An examination of that possibility should be the immediate goal of future research; but regardless of the occupational data employed in future tests, investigators should contemplate two theoretical rationales for anticipating that the correlation between the RSSA and RAOD referents will never approach unity. One rationale is suggested by the previous argument for restricting tests to countries. Even though countries are more ecologically autonomous than are intranational territorial units, the global division of a labor may have long since reached the point where for at least some countries territorial specialization has reduced the increase of occupational differentiation but without a concomitant proportionate reduction in the increase of the scope of sustenance associations. If so, the relation anticipated by the theorem should be closer among countries characterized by relatively uniform low values of

Table 8–1.   Scope of Sustenance Associations and Occupational Differentiation in
22 Countries, 1962–71

Country and Year	Scope of Sustenance Associations (RSSA)* Col. 1	Adjusted Occupational Differentiation (RAOD)** Col. 2
Algeria, 1966	3.1	.732
Australia, 1966	6.3	.886[a]
Chile, 1970	3.4	.928
Colombia, 1964	2.2	.795
Costa Rica, 1963	4.0	.806
Ecuador, 1962	1.3	.713
Greece, 1970	1.6	.838
Guatemala, 1964	2.0	.626
Iran, 1966	1.5	.777
Ireland, 1966	3.0	.873
Japan, 1970	4.3	.914
Korea, South, 1966	2.5	.727
Liberia, 1962	1.4	.401
Libya, 1964	1.8	.833
Mexico, 1970	2.4	.879
New Zealand, 1966	6.6	.879
Nicaragua, 1963	3.3	.705
Paraguay, 1962	1.1	.716
Sweden, 1965	9.0	.870
Turkey, 1965	2.4	.530[b]
United States, 1970	13.3	.909
Uruguay, 1963	3.4	.905

*Scope is defined in terms of the size and proportionate participation in sustenance
associations. $RSSA = (MEr + FEr + MEe + FEe + MU + FU)/(MEr + FEr + MSe + FSe)$, where
M=males, F=females, Er=employers, Ee=employees, U=unpaid family workers, and
Se=self-employed workers. Source of data: United Nations, *Demographic Yearbook, 1972.*
For reasons indicated in text, three "communist" countries (Hungary, Poland, and
Yugoslavia) were excluded even though requisite data for those three countries are reported
in the course.
**Formula: $(1 - [\Sigma X^2/(\Sigma X)^2])/[1 - (1/Nc)]$, where X is the number of individuals in a given
occupational category and Nc is the number of occupational categories. Source of data:
United Nations, *Demographic Yearbook, 1972.*
Qualification of years: [a]1971, [b]1970.

international trade per capita, and data are available to examine that possibility (see chapter 7).

Still another consideration is more nearly a possible defect in the theory itself, Postulate 8–1 in particular. The theory implies that associations are necessary and sufficient for extensive and complex coordination or synchronization of sustenance activities. Even so, in some instances the relation between an employer and employees (as distinguished in census data) may be largely exploitative, meaning that the putative employer does not coordinate or synchronize the activities of employees;[8] rather, the putative employer merely claims some portion of the employees' production by virtue of their using the employer's property (e.g, land). If so, then a relatively high RSSA referent (scope of sustenance associations) is necessary but not sufficient for a relatively high RAOD referent (occupational differentiation).[9] That association would not completely invalidate the theory, but *rho* would not be a suitable statistic for tests of the theorem.

Beyond the Theory

To repeat, a sustenance association may be created to exploit the participants rather than to coordinate and synchronize sustenance activities, in which case it would not further the division of labor.[10] Recognition of that possibility may suggest that the theory contradicts Marx. He never tired of characterizing capitalism as exploitative, and he often wrote as though suggesting that the division of labor originated with capitalism.[11] Savor Marx's indignation: "The division of labor reduces the worker to a degrading function; to this degrading function corresponds a depraved soul; to the deprivation of the soul is befitting an ever-increasing wage-reduction" (1963:132). Yet Marx clearly suggested that capitalism furthered the division of labor through the formal coordination of production in large sustenance associations.

Despite agreement just identified, the present theory departs from Marx in several respects; but space limitations make it necessary to treat only two divergences very briefly. First, the present conceptualization of the division of labor is completely contrary to Marx's astonishing suggestion that the division of labor can be described in terms of the mental-manual distinction. And, second, the theory is inconsistent with one of Marx's prophecies: "in communist society, where nobody has one exclusive sphere of activity but each can become accomplished in any branch he wishes, society regulates the general production and thus makes it possible for me to do one thing to-day and another to-morrow, to hunt in the morning, fish in the afternoon, rear cattle in the evening, criticize after dinner, just as I have a mind, without ever becoming hunter, fisherman, shepherd or critic" (Marx and Engels, 1947:22). While only a misanthrope would deny the intrinsic desirability of the arrangement envisioned by Marx, the temporal division of labor cannot insure a wide variety of sustenance activities; and an extreme variety is essential for what Marx clearly assumed—a greater material standard of living under industrial communism than under capitalism.

The Most Conspicuous Shortcoming

The theory suggests an extremely narrow conception of human control. Obviously, human control is not limited to the coordination and synchronization of sustenance activities, nor is the concentration of human control limited to sustenance activities. The concentration of political control is scarcely less important; but the theory does not even suggest a way to estimate the degree of concentration, let alone explain variation.

Whether sociologists go beyond the theory depends on how seriously they take the notion of control concentration. In weighing that notion's importance, sociologists should contemplate this version of Lord Acton's maxim: The concentration of human control corrupts and absolute concentration corrupts absolutely. That version is relevant in critiques of both capitalist and Marxist countries, and it bears on Orwell's *1984*. Perhaps Orwell's dark prophecy is unrealistic, but our knowledge of control is too limited for that judgment.

More on Associations and the Division of Labor

The theory is very narrow not just because it is limited to human control within sustenance associations. More serious, a multitude of important questions about human control in that context (see, especially, Clegg and Dunkerley, 1980) are not even suggested by the theory.

SOME UNANSWERED QUESTIONS. The theory's basic assertion will remain disputable until sociologists answer two questions, the first pertaining to the origins of particular occupations. Has there been a trend in recent centuries toward greater origination of incipient occupations in sustenance associations? A negative answer would make the theory suspect.

The second unanswered question arises from the theory's depiction of the division of labor as contingent on the scope of sustenance associations. While size is only one dimension of scope, the theory assumes a direct relation among sustenance associations between number of employees and number of occupations or positions. To date, the evidence does not indicate anything like a uniform close relation (see Scott, 1987:241–49). The relation's problematical character is consistent with this argument: The relation between any two structural variables is not even approximately invariant if only because it holds only through control as the intervening mechanism. Nonetheless, the theory will not be complete until extended to this question: To what extent and how is the relation between the size of an association and internal differentiation contingent on features of control?

TECHNOLOGICAL COMPLEXITY RECONSIDERED.   Although the theory in chapter 6 asserts a direct relation between technological complexity and the division of labor, there is an underlying argument: An individual's control effectiveness declines as the variety of controlled objects increases. If employers, managers, and supervisors are insensitive to that relation, the formally coordinated mode of production would not further the division of labor. However, tests of the organizational theory of the division of labor reported in this chapter do not provide evidence of that sensitivity, and a quite different line of research is needed.

The investigators would examine the relation between the number of occupations and technological complexity over time and among sustenance associations. Unlike research at the international level, investigators would use measures of technological complexity, one pertaining to the variety of kinds of tools or machines and the other to the average time required to master each kind.

Control in Sustenance Associations

Tannenbaum et al. (1974) compared 50 industrial plants located in five countries. In each plant a large sample of personnel were asked "How much influence do the following groups or persons actually have on what happens in this plant?" about (1) the plant manager and executive board, (2) other managers or supervisors, and (3) workers. There were five possible responses commencing with "little influence" and ending with "a very great deal of influence."

Unfortunately, the research did not extend to an analysis of actual control attempts, rather, the data pertain to "power," the perceived capacity to control. Even so, the research illustrates one way of gathering data on power, and there were several noteworthy discoveries. For example, the average "influence score" for all three categories of "possible influentials" was much greater for American plants; so American workers seemingly did not perceive intraplant power differentials as a zero-sum game. Moreover, Tannenbaum et al. claimed that their findings contradict Michels's "iron law of oligarchy." But that claim is disputable. Indeed, because Michels (1959) had little to say about the correlates of variation in control concentration among organizations or associations, one must surely wonder why he has received so much attention and why critics (e.g., Beetham, 1981) do not emphasize the ambiguity of his claim.

A PERENNIAL QUESTION.   Who effectively controls corporations—owners or managers? Had Tannenbaum et al. focused on that question, their research would have received much more attention. The question even bears on Marx's prophetic arguments about capitalism. Of Marx's several so-called laws of capitalism, only one appears empirically defensible: As capitalism develops, control of the economy becomes increasingly concentrated (described by Marx as the centralization of capital; see Popper, 1966:167). Consider that as early as 1975 about 3 percent of U.S. employing organizations accounted for 55 percent of the employed (Scott, 1987:9), one of many statistics that appear to corroborate Marx. Yet generations of diffusion of corporate ownership among stockholders can be construed as a deconcentration of control over the economy (see, however, Dye, 1983). Perhaps most important, more than 50 years ago critics of Marx commenced arguing that corporate control was shifting from owners (stockholders or otherwise) to managers, evidently because only managers have the technical expertise required to control large corporations effectively. "Managerialism" questioned the cherished Marxist belief that private productive property will be socialized. Indeed, should managers prevail, the *de jure* socialization of productive property will be considerably less than a proletarian triumph, whether in capitalist or in Marxist countries.

The owners-or-managers question has attracted considerable attention (see, e.g., Dhingra, 1983; Kerbo and Fave, 1983; and the literature cited by Scott, 1987:272–77; Herman, 1981:1–16; and Hill, 1981:71–76), but the conclusions reached have been neither clear not indisputable. The research findings (Scott, 1986; Kerbo and Fave, 1983; and Herman, 1981) do suggest a long trend away from "owner-controlled" corporations, but the sense and extent to which managers now control remains debatable. The inconclusive outcome of research was inevitable if only because the owners-or-managers question has been pursued without a defensible conceptualization of control and a related methodology of application.

Granted that the owners-or-managers question entails complexities that economists are best qualified to treat, sociologists have yet to make a well-known contribution to research on the question, nor are they likely to unless control becomes the field's central notion. For that matter, the counteraction-of-deviance conception of social control is not conducive to research on the question.

Beyond Sustenance Associations

The typical organization is the context of intensive human control, and commonly a small proportion of members virtually monopolize that control. So it hardly exaggerates to characterize control in organizations as an "especially acute problem" (Etzioni, 1968: 396). Organizational control (i.e., control over members and/or nonmembers in the context of some organization) takes on added significance because the study of human control in larger social units, even communities, requires enormous resources.

ORGANIZATIONS AND TYPES OF CONTROL.   Casual observations on prisons, clubs, universities, families, military units, corporations, and churches suggest vast differences in types or kinds of organizational control. An explanation of such differences requires a theory. Appearances to the contrary, the most relevant observations, those of Etzioni (1968), do not constitute such a theory.

Etzioni discusses coercive organizations, utilitarian organizations, and normative organizations, defining those types in terms of the predominant means of human control (physical, material, and symbolic, respectively). Hence, the relation between control and types of organizations is conceptual rather than empirical. Conceptualizations are needed; but Etzioni's means of control and related organization types are too broad to be really meaningful (e.g., symbolic control may be proximate, sequential, or social control), and the same is true of other typologies of control in organizations or bureaucracies (see Rothschild-Whitt, 1979, especially 513).

CONTROL ORGANIZATIONS. There are two major classes of organizational control: first, attempts by members to control other members; and, second, attempts by members to control nonmembers (e.g., clients, consumers, the public at large).[12] The first kind, endogenous control, is present in all organizations, but there are various organizations (e.g., clubs, families) in which the second kind, exogenous control, is virtually absent. Yet the ratio of exogenous control to endogenous control may be so great that the organization appears to have been created to control nonmembers. Law-enforcement agencies, advertising firms, and legislative bodies are conspicuous instances of such "control organizations."

Consistent with the counteraction-of-deviance conception of social control, there is a substantial sociological literature on the police, prisons, and mental hospitals, all control organizations. Yet since 1960 that literature has come to pertain largely more to the impact of reactions to alleged deviance on the alleged deviant than with the organizations themselves. Hence, there is a theory of secondary deviance (Lemert, 1972) but no theory of control organizations. Worse still, no particular question about control has shaped the literature on control organizations, and Goffman's *Asylums* is not an exception.

Beyond Organizations and the Ordinary

Regardless of the subject, a theory should not be limited to extreme cases; but observations on those cases can be strategic in work toward a theory. Two contexts of extreme kinds of human control should be recognized: (1) those that have no connection with any organization and (2) those that are organizational in one sense or another.

INEXPLICABLE SUBMISSIONS TO CONTROL. Submission to control is so ubiquitous that sociologists rarely recognize that it is a control phenomenon. Nonetheless, some instances of submission are puzzling, especially those in

Stanley Milgram's experiment (1974) on "obedience to authority." Milgram reported that several American adults administered what they ostensibly perceived as very painful electrical shocks to other experimental subjects, confederates who feigned expressions of great pain. The wonder is not that the naive experimental subjects inflicted pain but that they did it without being threatened in any sense (e.g., with physical harm or financial loss). Rather, they inflicted pain ostensibly because they were directed to do so by someone whose "authority" was nothing more than being identified as the person immediately in control of an experiment and being dressed to fit (perhaps) the layperson's stereotype of a scientist.

How did sociologists respond to Milgram? The silence was nearly total (see Gamson et al., 1982, as one rare exception). Milgram's study is not cited even in a recent sociology paper (Hamilton and Biggart, 1985) entitled "Why People Obey." Since "authority" is supposedly an important sociological notion, why have sociologists ignored Milgram's work? Sociologists rarely do any research on authority (Gamson et al., 1982, is again the exception); rather, they analyze it as an *idea.*

If control were taken as the sociology's central notion, sociologists would be far less inclined to ignore experiments like Milgram's; and the central notion would supply the basic vocabulary for a conceptualization of authority, commencing with its identification as a type of power. More specifically, authority is the perceived capacity for external human control through means other than explicit coercion, threats, promises, offers, or requests. There are numerous alternatives (see Dunsire's commentary, 1978:21–27); but the proposed definition has two advantages over most contenders: (1) it relates to a larger conceptual scheme and (2) it promises more empirical applicability.

EXTREME CASES OF ORGANIZATIONAL CONTROL.   Given a German official, officer, or enlisted person who participated directly in the extermination of Jewish prisoners during World War II, why did he or she do it? Before Milgram's experiment, this answer might have appeared naive: In response to a command. Milgram's findings make the answer all the more plausible if it is assumed that, all else being equal, control-through-authority in purely dyadic interaction (i.e., no organizational context) is generally less effective than is endogenous organizational control. Extending the assumption, exogenous organizational control is intermediate in general effectiveness. When organization members attempt to control nonmembers, the latter perceive the former as representing the organization and as thereby having power (capacity for control).

Even if the extension of the assumption appears plausible, it may not apply to the Holocaust. The extent to which the German exterminators of Jews obeyed orders independently of coercive threats (explicit or implicit) is a debatable question, and the same is true of the obedience of doomed Jews.

However, even if coercive threats pervaded the Holocaust, the effectiveness of organizational control (endogenous and exogenous) in the Holocaust is puzzling, so much so that the Holocaust represents the kind of extreme case that warrants attention in working toward a general theory of human control. Indeed, all of Nazism constitutes a strategic phenomenon, but sociologists have played a minor role in the vast research on the subject (see, especially, Deak, 1984). Their seeming disinterest in the "Jonestown massacre" is also telling, because that episode was another extreme case of organizational control, primarily endogenous. The indifference of sociologists is additional evidence that the field's principles, theories, and conceptualizations have little bearing on actual human behavior.

NOTES

1. The case where no social unit member attempts to control the behavior of any other member is not relevant because control concentration (as it applies to human control) presupposes some control. Also note that "control concentration" and "amount of control" are logically distinct.

2. Both temporal quantifiers (T_{0-1} in each case) refer to any point or period during any year (but the same historical year, whatever it may be) for the country in question.

3. Accordingly, if the axiom were directly testable, the closest relation between the two variables would hold when each division of labor value is for a later time than the corresponding control concentration value. But the appropriate time lag is unknown, and for various reasons (note 6) census data are not suited for exploratory research on the question.

4. Although the concept "scope of sustenance associations" may appear to have some bearing on economic development, the latter is too much of a sponge notion to be important. In any case, since the concept pertains to a quantitative phenomena (a continuum), the arbitrariness entailed in distinguishing levels of development (e.g., Field and Higley, 1980:25) is avoided.

5. Observe that RSSA referents are assumed to be correlates of the two variables recognized in defining the concept "scope of sustenance associations."

6. The relation between the two variables in the theorem should hold also over time for any country (i.e., longitudinal-synchronic), but short-run variation (e.g., 1970–80) in the values of the variables is substantially less than international variation (i.e., cross-sectional). The contrast takes on significance because tests of theorems cannot be feasible unless census data are used to compute the values, but those data are so crude and unreliable that only differences in values of a huge magnitude (e.g., one value is 10 percent greater than another) should be taken as indicating a true ordinal difference. Were it not for the problems described in note 7 of chapter 6 (in connection with the theory pertaining to the division of labor), the temporal quantifiers would be such as to imply that the maximum correlations would obtain if the temporal sequences (lags) were thus: scope of sustenance associations at T_{0-1}, concentration of control over sustenance

activities at T_{1-2}, degree of division of labor at T_{2-3}, occupational differentiation at T_{2-3}, RSSA at T_{0-1}, and RAOD at T_{2-3}. Although the theory could be stated so that it applies longitudinally (any country over time), the same problems (note 7 of chapter 6) would preclude the stipulation of temporal lags. All of the observations on temporal considerations and data problems made here apply in more or less the same way to the theories introduced in chapter 6 and chapter 7.

7. All comments in chapter 6 on assessing theories in terms of predictive power apply also to this case.

8. The point is illustrated by Field and Higley's statements about the aristocracy in societies of "Level 1" development (about 100 percent of the work force in agricultural or artisan occupations): "For the most part, the members of aristocracies did not participate in, or closely regulate, the ongoing agricultural, artisan and other work. They were usually content merely to levy their incomes from the work of others" (1980:21).

9. Dependency theory can be construed as suggesting still another reason for a relatively high RSSA referent but a relatively low RAOD referent, but as indicated in chapter 7 (note 6) the theory is so vague that interpretations of it are little more than sheer opinion.

10. There is an implied argument that sociologists appear reluctant to recognize: any set of individuals is "organized" only to the extent that their activities are coordinated or synchronized. So the present theory is only a special case of control principle 8–1, the "sequential imperative": Beyond some point, an increase in the coordination and synchronization of activities in a population is preceded by an increase in the amount of sequential control.

11. The suggestion is misleading despite Marx's frequent allusions to a "social" division of labor as precapitalist. Whatever Marx meant by that term, the social type of division of labor did not end with capitalism, nor did the implied alternative type—"asocial"—commence with capitalism.

12. Dunsire suggests three kinds, at least in connection with bureaucracies: control through or by a bureaucracy, control over bureaucracy, and control *in* a bureaucracy (1978:vii). All three kinds of "organizational control" can be examined by extending research on the police (see, especially, Punch, 1983). In any case, this chapter is clearly a superficial treatment of organizational control; but note that unless one sees merit in ambiguity and conceptual redundancy, it is pointless to equate environmental effects or constraints on organizations with the "external control of organizations" (see Pfeffer and Salanick, 1978).

Part III

Control and Contending Sociological Perspectives

A perspective consists of beliefs shared by some or all practitioners in a scientific field as to: (1) the field's subject matter, (2) appropriate questions about that subject matter, (3) the general *substantive* nature of preferred answers, and (4) formal criteria (e.g., parsimony, predictive accuracy) for assessing answers. Space limitations preclude clarification beyond one observation on the distinction between the third and fourth belief. Suppose that two sociologists agree as to their field's subject matter and appropriate questions about it; but one prefers answers that imply genetic determinism, while the other prefers answers that imply technological determinism. As such, the two differ as to the kind of answers they are likely to regard as credible, but credibility suggests formal criteria for accepting or rejecting answers. Indeed, several alternative "genetic" answers to the same question are conceivable, and an advocate of genetic determinism must invoke formal criteria in choosing among those alternatives. The same may be said of the contending perspective, in which case an advocate must choose among alternative "technological" answers to a question. Yet an advocate of one determinism and an advocate of the other may subscribe to the same formal criteria for judging the adequacy of answers, as when both demand causal answers and employ the same criteria of causal evidence.

Perspectives flourish in sociology, and the number of contenders has increased exponentially since the 1950s. Some sociologists may be sanguine about the increase; their argument parallels Mao's admonition: Let a hundred flowers blossom. However, extending Mao's admonition to sociology could lead to irreversible fragmentation; and, mixing metaphors, a hundred-flower garden could resemble a weed patch.

It is not claimed that acceptance of control as sociology's central notion would eliminate contending perspectives, and fragmentation will not be reduced if the notion of control is far more compatible with some perspectives than with others. Indeed, no notion is likely to be accepted as central if clearly incompatible with any perspective in the field. Yet a demonstration of compatibility is not enough. It must be argued that taking control as sociology's central notion would enhance the merits and diminish the shortcomings of each perspective, and that argument is pursued throughout Part III.

Given that several books have been written on each of the perspectives identified in chapters 9–16, an extensive treatment of them is not feasible. So each chapter is limited essentially to four things: (1) the principle merits of the perspective, (2) an argument that those merits would be enhanced by treating control as the perspective's central notion, (3) the perspective's principal shortcomings, and (4) an argument that the shortcomings would be diminished by treating control as the perspective's central notion.

Functionalism

A sense of functionalism's importance is conveyed by these names of putative functionalists: Durkheim, Freud, Malinowski, Marx, Pareto, Parsons, and Radcliffe-Brown. Yet other perspectives in sociology's history are no less important. Functionalism is unique in that functionalists have been at great pains to deny their preference for a *distinctive kind of explanation*, and even critics of functionalism commonly ignore its explanatory distinctiveness.

A Distinctive Type of Explanation

None of the usual dictionary definitions (e.g., Morris, 1969:533) are consistent with a common use of the term *function* by sociologists—to denote a special kind of effect. That usage has been recognized by others, and Goode prescribes replacement of a functional language with a strictly causal language (1973:63–64). Yet he writes (85) of translating "function" into a causal language when it is used as a verb, which is curious because sociologists commonly use the term as a noun, as in the phrase "the function of." When the term is so used, it is meaningless unless equivalent to effect; but "function" may be used to denote a special kind of effect—one that explains its alleged cause.[1] Otherwise, the term only obfuscates. The argument may appear consistent with Goode, but he writes as though sociologists have never used "function" to denote an effect that explains its cause.

Elaboration of the Argument

Whatever variables X and Y may be, there are two interpretations of the assertion that Y is a function of X. First, X is a necessary and/or sufficient cause of Y; as such, Y is an effect of X and X somehow explains Y. Second, X is a necessary and/or sufficient cause of Y; as such, Y is an effect of X but Y somehow explains X. The second interpretation, Y explains X, makes a functional explanation distinctive—a phenomenon is explained in terms of its effects. If the term *function* does not have that special explanatory meaning, it is a redundant synonym of "effect." Moreover, Bredemeier (1955:173) notwithstanding, the explanation is not special in the sense that X causes Y and then Y causes X (i.e., reciprocal causation).

Consider two illustrative assertions. First, the function of a tribal exogamy rule is to insure the tribe's survival. Second, the effect of a tribal exogamy rule is the tribe's survival. Whereas the "effect" assertion implies an explanation of tribal survival, the functional statement implies an explanation of the exogamy rule (it preserves the tribe). However, both assertions would be clarified by these three amplifications: (1) the rule of tribal exogamy insures a high rate of marriage between tribal members and members of other tribes, (2) such intermarriage prevents frequent intertribal war, and (3) infrequent tribal war is necessary for survival of the tribe.[2] The three amplifications comprise four variables, diagrammed as follows:

$$A \rightarrow B \rightarrow C \rightarrow D$$

A is the rule of tribal exogamy, B a high rate of tribal intermarriage, C infrequent tribal warfare, and D tribal survival.

Because the three amplifications appear to be nothing more than causal assertions, they suggest why functionalists may have misgivings about substituting "effect" for "function." If the term *function* is not used, there is no way to create the impression of an explanation of the cause and not merely the assertion of an effect. Contemplate Davis's statement: "To speak of the *function* of an institution *for* a society or *for* another institution in that society is a way of asking what the institution does within the system to which it is relevant" (1959:772). Why is it that Davis speaks of "what the institution does" rather than simply "the effects of the institution"? When one purports to describe what an institution *does*, the description creates the impression of explanation.

A Conspiracy of Silence

One peculiar feature of functionalism in sociology is the widespread failure of commentators to emphasize the nature of a functional explanation (see, e.g., papers reprinted in Demerath and Peterson, 1967). In the best known critique of functionalism in the sociological literature, Merton (1957) writes of functional analysis or functional orientation rather than functional explanation. Most remarkable, in a major article on functionalism, Davis (1959) not once uses the term *functional explanation*; instead he discusses functional analysis and argues that it is not even a special method. The closest Davis comes to recognizing a distinctive mode of explanation is his denial that

"in functionalism data are explained *solely* in terms of their consequences
. . . ." (759). His denial is at least a tacit admission that functionalists do
explain social phenomena at least partially in terms of consequences. Moreover, there are several well-known functional explanations, including the
Davis-Moore theory of stratification (1945), where it is difficult to see how
anything other than alleged consequences enter into the explanation. The same
is all the more true for Davis's explanations of the incest taboo (see Bredemeier,
1955:173).

Unlike Davis, many commentators have not equated functionalism with
sociological analysis in general, but their failure to focus on the distinctive
character of a functional explanation is puzzling. Thus, in writing four volumes
on the theoretical logic of sociology, Alexander (especially 1982-I:55–63)
treated functionalism at length but without emphasizing the distinctive character of functional explanations (the same is true of Abrahamson, 1978; Barber,
1956; Fallding, 1963; Mulkay, 1971; and authors in Martindale, 1965). Why
have sociologists either been so silent on the subject or have equivocated
(see Turner and Maryanski, 1979)? Even if they accept Davis's astonishing
suggestion (1959:760–61) that the only alternative to functionalism is reductionism, why their reluctance to recognize that its mode of explanation makes
functionalism distinctive?

The most defensible answer pertains to criteria of an adequate explanation formulated by philosophers of science, especially Hempel (1965). Sociological explanations in general are so defective when judged by those criteria
that sociologists appear reluctant to criticize functionalism on those grounds
(see, e.g., van den Berghe, 1963). That interpretation is consistent not only
with Davis's silence about explanation but also with the inclination of critics
to allege that functionalism is conservative, ignores conflict, and assumes
normative consensus (see commentaries in Merton, 1957:37–46; Demerath
and Peterson, 1967:441–98). Those criticisms have no connection with formal
criteria emphasized by various philosophers of science.

Hempel's Critique of Functionalism

Throughout a chapter that sociologists tend either to ignore or cite
perfunctorily, Carl Hempel (1959) is concerned with the explanatory import
of "functional analysis." He introduced his strategy this way (283):

> "Suppose . . . that we are interested in explaining the occurrence of a
> trait *i* in a system *s* (at a certain time *t*), and that the following functional
> analysis is offered:
>
> (a) At *t*, *s* functions adequately in a setting of kind *c* (characterized
>   by specific internal and external conditions)

(b) s functions adequately in a setting of kind c only if a certain necessary condition, n is satisfied

(c) If trait i were present in s then, as an effect, condition n would be satisfied

(d) (Hence,) at t, trait i is present in s"

Subsequently (1959:284), Hempel points out that "statement (d) could be validly inferred if (c) asserted that *only* the presence of trait i could effect satisfaction of condition n." Hence, if a valid deduction is necessary for an adequate explanation, then an explanation in the form depicted by Hempel is clearly inadequate. Moreover, a valid deduction is insufficient without evidence that the premises are empirically valid, but even the identification of the premises of functional explanations in sociology is debatable. No ostensible premise in any well-known functional explanations in sociology has ever been subjected to anything approaching systematic tests, and the meaning of the constituent terms of those premises are so vague as to preclude systematic tests. To summarize, in sociology functional explanations are not logically valid, and there is no systematic evidence that their premises are empirically valid[3]; or in Hempel's terms (1959:286): "the information typically provided by a functional analysis of an item i affords neither deductively nor inductively adequate grounds for expecting i rather than one of its alternatives."

Possible Miscomprehension of Hempel's Critique

Given that several assessments of functionalism in the sociological literature ignore Hempel's critique (e.g., Cancian, 1960; Turner and Maryanski, 1979; and Alexander, 1982-I), perhaps many sociologists simply do not comprehend him. Yet Hempel's illustration of a functional explanation's form is no distortion, and it clearly fits the previous illustrative functional explanation of tribal exogamy. Specifically, s is a tribe; c is the potential for intertribal war, including the existence and proximity of other tribes; n is a low level of intertribal war; and i is the rule of tribal exogamy. If that example is deemed inappropriate, then consider Merton's functional analysis of the Hopi rain ceremonial (1957:64–65). In that case, s is again a tribe, c is (evidently) the spatial scattering of tribal members, n is reinforcement of group identity, and i is the rain ceremonial.

Observe how the illustrations are vulnerable to Hempel's paramount objection, that being: if i is sufficient but not necessary for n, there is no basis for explaining and predicting the presence of i from knowledge that n is present. That objection applies to the tribal exogamy illustration unless there is evidence that only tribal intermarriage reduces intertribal warfare (e.g., intertribal trade is irrelevant). As for the Hopi rain ceremonial, Merton does not even suggest that no other institution or practice reinforces group identity.

POSSIBLE SOURCES OF MISCOMPREHENSION. Sociologists are so accustomed to discursive arguments that many of them perhaps do not understand Hempel's formal exposition. However, there is no other systematic way to clarify an argument. Yet Hempel's exposition has shortcomings.

Hempel's illustration suggests that a functional explanation comprises, at a minimum, five variables and four statements. In the illustrative case, the variables are s, c, n, t, and i; the four statements (three premises and conclusion) are (a), (b), (c), and (d). Those numbers are not an essential feature of a functional explanation. Consider the following reduction of Hempel's illustration to three statements and two variables.

(1) s functions adequately if i is present in s
(2) s now functions adequately

---

(3) (Hence,) trait i is now present in s

Hempel's paramount objection to the logic of a functional explanation applies to this three-statement illustration as well as his own; and the reason is the same in both cases: i is a sufficient but not a necessary condition. So t, c, and n are not essential to explicate Hempel's paramount objection. Whatever s may be, the argument could be that it functions adequately at all times (i.e., all t's) if item i is present; and there is surely no reason why an i is sufficient only through some n. The inclusion of c and n is perhaps more realistic, but it is not essential to show why the logic of functional explanations is commonly invalid.

In various ways Hempel indicates that an explanation (whatever the kind) cannot be adequate unless at least one premise is taken as a law or a valid nomothetic generalization. Yet all premises in Hempel's illustration can be construed as limited to a particular s and perhaps to a particular time point (t). The major premise of the three-statement illustration is also limited to a particular s, but that is not the case in this version of that premise: (1') any instance of s functions adequately if item i is present in that instance. Given that change, then with a view to predicting and explaining the presence-absence of i in a particular instance s (e.g., particular tribe) statement (2) must be altered as follows: (2') X is now an instance of s. Those two statements, (1') and (2'), may appear to imply (3'): item i is now present in X. However, if that implication is claimed, then Hempel's paramount objection applies.

Hempel's failure to include at least one nomothetic premise in his illustration scarcely distorts. Insofar as the premises of functional explanations (or "analyses") in sociology can be identified at all, they commonly appear finite—limited to particular things or events at particular points in time. Shils and Young's analysis (1953) of the coronation of Elizabeth II (see Birnbaum's critique, 1955) is an obvious possibility; but the space-time limits of their premises are actually ambiguous, and the same is all the more the case for Merton's analysis (1957:72–82) of the political machine and boss.

Finally, some sociologists may be confused by the conditional form of Hempel's statement (*c*). That form is alien to functional explanations because the presence or absence of the *explanandum* (item *i* in Hempel's illustration) is not an issue. Thus, the presence of a rain ceremonial among the Hopi, of a political boss in Boston, and of social inequality are the *explananda* (the points of departure or givens) in functional explanations.

Functionalism and Types of Explanation

Hempel's critique suffers from his failure to confront this question: Given convincing evidence that item *i* is both necessary and sufficient for *n* and that *n* is both necessary and sufficient for *s* to function adequately, what would be the rationale for accepting those relations as an adequate explanation of item *i*? Apparently, such evidence would blunt Hempel's paramount objection. Nonetheless, not even empirically valid premises and a logically valid deduction would answer this question: How can the effects of an entity possibly explain that entity? There is an answer, but Hempel did not consider the question.

The justification of a functional explanation is best introduced in the context of an argument—there are only three broad possibilities in the way of explaining any human entity, be it an act, practice, institution, or some other socio-cultural phenomenon. First possibility: the entity serves some purpose of the humans who engage in it and those humans perceive the connection (for elaboration, see Halfpenny, 1983:74–75). Second possibility: the entity is *caused* by something removed from those purposes. Third possibility: only those social units (clans, countries, etc.) in which the entity is present *survive*. For reasons indicated subsequently, a functional explanation is indefensible if it is not an argument about selective survival, the third type of explanation.

Before an extensive commentary on selective survival, it is desirable to indicate why that notion, rather than cause or purpose, makes a functional explanation unique. It is not adequate to say that in a functional explanation an entity's effects explain the entity, although that consideration is the crucial distinction between a functional explanation and a causal explanation. In addition, an entity's effects can explain the entity only through selective survival.

Functionalists avoid the notion of purpose or any notion pertaining to internal behavior by a seemingly exclusive focus on "latent" functions. Whereas a *manifest* function is an entity's consequence (effect) that was intended and/or subsequently recognized, a *latent* function is a consequence that was neither intended nor subsequently recognized (Merton, 1957:51).

Why should sociologists be preoccupied with latent functions? Manifest functions have something to do with internal behavior, such as purpose; but because internal behavior is not a property of aggregate, structural, or macroscopic phenomena (rates, institutions, etc.), it is therefore not within sociology's subject matter. Yet sociologists are indifferent to the purposive quality of human behavior not simply because they are interested in the latent functions; rather, many sociologists are determined to avoid reductionism at all cost, and the preoccupation with latent functions both reflects and reinforces their indifference to the purposive quality of human behavior.

Selective Survival

The term *selective survival* is rarely employed in functional explanations, but no particular term, not even *function*, is used in all functional explanations. Rather, functionalists are prone to speak of a socio-cultural phenomenon (e.g., a particular institution) as contributing to this or that (e.g., boundary maintenance), insuring something (e.g., socialization), or as serving such and such (e.g., to prevent conflict). The terminology suggests that the phenomenon in question fulfills some need of a social unit; but the explanation is unfalsifiable unless it extends to the claim that the *explanandum* in question is necessary for the survival of those social units in which it is present, and functionalists rarely make that claim explicit.

Of the few commentators who rightly view functionalism as a distinctive kind of explanation (e.g., Halfpenny, 1983; Cohen, 1978; Isajiw, 1968), only Dore (1961) emphasizes selectivity as the explanatory mechanism.[4] However, he uses the term *evolutionary selection* without recognizing that the first word entails issues and creates problems that can be avoided by speaking simply of selective survival.

A selective survival explanations can appear compelling, such as the answer to this illustrative question: Why are there organized bodies of armed individuals (military or police) in Mexico? Because Mexico is a country, and without at least one such body any country will eventually disintegrate because of violent secession or be absorbed through conquest. Plausible or not, the presence of such bodies in all other countries is consistent with the explanation. The explanation would be even more plausible if there were systematic evidence of a very low survival rate for countries in which organized bodies of armed individuals are absent.

A MORE COMPLEX ILLUSTRATION.   Selective survival explanations are not limited to any particular type of social unit or socio-cultural phenomena. Suppose findings indicate that, relative to other types of retail establishments, there are very few rural shoe stores. Why such a locational pattern? The argument that an urban location is necessary for sufficient sales would have to extend beyond a precise definition of all of the terms to answers of three explanatory questions. First, to what extent do owners of urban shoe stores believe that a rural location precludes sufficient sales? Second, over the past decade how many shoe stores have located in a rural place? And, third, during that period what percentage of urban and rural shoe stores failed because of insufficient sales?

A defensible answer to the third question would require conceptualizations and a methodology, and there should be some consistency between the answers to the first and second questions. If the vast majority of owners ostensibly believe that a rural location precludes sufficient sales, that finding would suggest a purposive explanation of the locational pattern; but that would be the case only if the answer to the second question is "none" or "very few." Now suppose that (1) very few owners ostensibly believe that an urban location is necessary for sufficient sales, (2) that during the preceding decade numerous shoe stores were established in a rural place,and (3) the vast majority of rural shoe stores failed because of insufficient sales. Those findings would point to a location pattern resulting from selective survival.

Finally, the argument does not require categorical answers (none, all) to the three questions (*supra*). Suppose that (1) about 50 percent of shoe stores owners ostensibly believe that a rural location precludes sufficient sales, (2) during the past decade about 50 percent of all new shoe stores located in rural places, and (3) the failure rate of rural shoe stores is (say) twenty times that of urban stores. Those findings would suggest a combination of two types of explanation, purposive and selective survival.[5] The idea of combining the two types of explanations forces recognition that a strictly functional explanation of organized bodies of armed individuals in Mexico would be premature. All manners of general observations suggest at least a partially purposive explanation.

Even though a functional explanation is not credible unless couched in terms of selective survival, virtually any phenomenon is subject to that kind of explanation. However, regardless of the phenomenon, empirically applicable criteria of survival are imperative; and the foregoing illustrations do not mean that secession or conquest are the only ways that countries cease to survive, or that "failure" is sufficiently precise to analyze the survival of business firms. A careful definition of survival and stipulation of related criteria are essential, but the terminology need not apply to both organisms and socio-cultural phenomena (Turner and Maryanski, 1979, notwithstanding). No one doubts that some marriages *end* in divorce, or that numerous 19th-century occupations will disappear in this century. Finally, no claim to novelty is made in this attempt to promote selective survival as an explanatory mechanism. The argument has been adopted (at least tacitly) in a line of organizational research (e.g., Carroll, 1985); but the research is commonly described as exemplifying the "ecological perspective" rather than what it is—defensible functionalism.

HEMPEL NOTWITHSTANDING. The logic of treating selective survival as the rationale of a functional explanation is hardly obscure. Briefly, when some pattern is taken as the *explanandum*, a functional explanation consists of the argument that exceptions to the pattern have a very low survival rate. To illustrate formally, suppose that approximately 99 percent of class X organisms are also members of class Y (a pattern). Hence, the question: Why is there such a high degree of association in class membership? Now suppose that class X members who become class Y members survive 99 years on the average, whereas none of those that never become class Y members survive beyond one year. Given those suppositions, the X-Y association is not puzzling.

Despite the case that can be made for identifying selective survival as the rationale for a functional explanation, Hempel (1959) did not emphasize it, nor did Nagel (1956) in another well-known critique of functionalism in the social sciences. The reason cannot be that the rationale is wholly alien to functionalism. For example, Malinowski defined function as "the satisfaction of a need" (1944:159) and defined need as "the system of conditions in the human organism, in the cultural setting, and in the relation of both to the natural environment, which are sufficient and necessary for the survival of group and organism" (90).

Two considerations could have made Hempel reluctant to emphasize selective survival as functionalism's explanatory mechanism. Most major figures in the history of functionalism only rarely used the term *survival*, and there are even doubts about Malinowski. Because he identified so many cultural traits as meeting some need or another, it is doubtful whether he meant that each trait is literally necessary for survival. Even when Malinowski describes magic as fulfilling "an indispensible function within culture" and as satisfying a "definite need which cannot be satisfied by any other factors of primitive civilization" (1926:136), the appropriate interpretation is debatable. Finally, note that Merton refers to "adaptation" or "adjustment," not survival (1957:51).

Still another consideration is the uncritical way that functionalists have used the term *survival*. Far from clarifying the term's meaning, they use it to define other terms, such as *need*. The idea that social units or collectivities have needs may well be the most ludicrous notion in the social sciences. Even if a need is simply a necessary or sufficient condition for a social unit's survival, that conceptual redundancy serves no purpose. Surely it does not clarify the meaning of survival; and as Hempel rightly points out (1959:294), a defensible definition is difficult, especially if its meaning is to extend beyond organisms. Again, however, survival need not be defined such that the definition applies to organisms as well as socio-cultural phenomena.

Whatever Hempel's reasons for not emphasizing selective survival, his phrase "functions adequately" (1959) cannot be defended. The phrase's meaning is vaguer than that of survival; and even if item i is necessary (not just sufficient) for a particular *s* to function adequately, how could that possibly imply that any *s* would cease to exist without *i*? The point is that Hempel's language is not conducive to recognition of the very mechanism—selective survival—that would make functional explanation defensible.[6] To be sure, if *i* does make *s* function adequately, then *i* is likely to be present in any *s*. Should that be the case, however, the ubiquity of *i* could be due not to selective survival but to the pragmatic human concern with instrumentality, the very concern that functionalists are determined to ignore (for a more elaborate similar argument, see Dore, 1961).

Purposive Explanation as a Sociological Heresy

Many sociologists categorically reject purposive explanations of human behavior.[7] The rejection is consistent with but not peculiar to functionalism. The hostility to purposive explanations is so widespread in sociology that one can speak of rules that function (latently, of course) to maintain it.

FIRST RULE: EMPHASIZE THE IRRATIONAL.   Functionalists never tire of suggesting that only their mode of explanation can account for irrational actions, but the objection is not just to the practice of leaving the meaning of "irrational" (or nonrational or nonlogical) obscure. Additionally, in analyzing institutions functionalists write as though obliged to heed this rule: always attribute something grossly unrealistic to the institution. So what is the "purpose" of the Hopi rain ceremony? Obviously, to make it rain. Just as obviously, the ceremony does not have that effect; ergo, the ceremony requires a functional explanation. The argument ignores a third possibility—a strictly causal explanation; and functionalists avoid one absurdity (the ceremony does make it rain) only to embrace another—the suggestion that the Hopi tribe would not survive without the rain ceremonial. The suggestion is made by describing the rain ceremony as adaptive, contributing to the maintenance of the Hopi system, or some other beguiling phrase. In any case, the validity of the functional explanation is no more obvious than the meteorological effectiveness of the rain ceremony.

When functionalists argue that an institution's manifest functions are fictions, they thereby suggest that participant purposes are irrelevant. But surely the purposes themselves cannot be denied. It would not be incongruous for a Hopi to say that he or she participates in the rain ceremony to renew old acquaintance, because it is a way to meet prospective lovers, or because failure to participate would invite ridicule. Why are such purposes irrelevant in explaining the ceremonial? Functionalists never really confront such a question.

Consider the argument in the way of this question: Why are American anthropologists so adept at describing exotic institutions as irrational but so rarely offer a similar description of American institutions? If the difficulty is doubted, try to describe the rationality of professional football, Christmas, the

July 4 celebration, golf, and trials. Generalizing the point, social unit members think of the social unit institutions as rational because they participate in them purposefully. In any case, to argue that institutions can be explained without considering participation is to suggest that institutions exist independently of participation in them.

SECOND RULE: ACCEPT PURPOSIVE EXPLANATIONS ONLY IN REAL LIFE. One likely reaction to the foregoing: the very diversity of purposes in participating invalidates a purposive explanation of an institution. By what logic does that argument follow? Confronted with that question, the response could be: Purposes have to do with manifest functions. The proper rejoinder question: Why is a manifest function explanation less valid than a latent function explanation?

The truth is that the hostility of sociologists to purposive explanation has less to do with functionalism than with the determination to avoid any hint of reductionism, psychological explanations in particular, at all costs. But why is it that the determination does not extend to everyday life? The rule seems to be: Reject purposive explanation in scientific work but accept them in everyday life. So we hear one sociologist ask another: "Why is Fred walking toward the cafeteria?" Reply: "He forgot to bring his lunch today." Sociologists accept such explanations in real life with monotonous regularity but only to reject them in professional work. Puzzling is hardly the word for it.

THIRD RULE: TOLERATE INCONSISTENCY. Sociologists commonly make one of two arguments to reject a particular purposive explanation. First, the explanation does not indicate why the individuals in question pursued one goal rather than another. Or, second, the explanation does not indicate why the individuals in question pursued the goal by one means rather than another.

When such criticism is made, the critics do not recognize that they are calling for an infinite regression in explanation; and two questions suffice to indicate that the criticism extends to causal and functional explanations. First, if X is the cause of Y, why does X cause Y? Second, if Y is necessary for the survival of type X social units, why is it necessary?

The Codification of the Indefensible

Robert Merton's codification of functionalism (1957) differs in a fundamental way from the present critique. Although Merton goes further than Davis (1959) toward recognizing that functionalism is distinctive, he does not speak of "functional explanation," much less selective survival.

The Famous Distinction

Quoting Merton: "*Manifest functions* are those objective consequences contributing to the adjustment or adaptation of the system which are intended and recognized by participants in the system; *Latent functions*, correlatively, being those which are neither intended nor recognized" (1957:51). Although sociologists routinely invoke the latent-manifest distinction, it is a thicket of ambiguities, problems, and issues.

CONSEQUENCES. The term *consequences* enters into virtually all of Merton's key conceptualizations, but he never really confronts these two questions: First, what is a *consequence*? Second, *what* has consequences? Considering the first question, it is puzzling that Merton did not use the term *effect*; and the difference is important because Merton's terminology may imply that observations on consequences somehow have more explanatory significance than observations on effects. Whatever the terminological rationale, Merton implicitly presumed that observers can agree in identifying consequences of macro phenomena (e.g., institutions) but also in their judgments as to whether a consequence makes for or lessens the "adjustment or adaptation of a given system." To the contrary, sociologists can do little more than agree about space-time conjunctions of particular things or events.

Merton's failure to confront the second question (What has consequences?) is troublesome. At one point he writes of "unintended consequences of action" (1957:51), but elsewhere he indicates that the objects of functional analysis may be "social roles, institutional patterns, social processes, cultural patterns . . . social norms, group organization, social structure, devices for social control, etc." (50). The point is not just that observations on the consequences of such phenomena are inherently debatable; further, Merton failed to recognize the distinction between direct and indirect consequences. Individuals are likely to intend and recognize the direct consequences of their actions; hence, those consequences are predominantly manifest. Correlatively, the consequences of aggregate, macro, or structural phenomena (e.g., an institution) are virtually by definition indirect consequences of particular acts and less likely to be intended and recognized by the actors; hence, those consequences are predominantly latent. So the import of Merton's latent-manifest distinction depends on the unit of analysis. If particular acts, the preponderant consequences are manifest; if aggregate, macro, or structural phenomena (e.g., institutions), the preponderant consequences are latent.

OTHER PROBLEMS. Two questions survive Merton's latent-manifest distinction. First, what of consequences that system participants do not intend but come to recognize? Second, what of consequences that system participants intend but do not recognize even though the sociologist observer does recognize them? Those questions force recognition that the classes in Merton's scheme are not inclusive. The excluded classes are relevant if only because those consequences may make for or lessen the system's adjustment or adaptation.

Taking Merton's definitions literally, manifest functions exist only insofar as objective consequences were intended and subsequently recognized by all system participants. One implication is that the consequences of particular acts are virtually certain to be latent functions, for only the actor intends those consequences. Again, though, perhaps Merton really thought only of the consequences of institutions, but how could an institution's consequences be intended by all system participants? Such problems would have been avoided had Merton indicated that all system participants need not be considered, but another set of problems would surface in the way of two questions. First, which system participants are relevant? Second, of the relevant participants, how many must intend and recognize a consequence for it to be manifest? Merton never confronted such questions.

The Rationale for the Distinction

According to Merton, the latent-manifest distinction was devised to "preclude the inadvertent confusion, often found in the sociological literature, between conscious *motivations* for social behavior and its objective consequences" (1957:60). However, since Merton did not document the confusion or describe its supposedly disastrous impact, his rationale for the latent-manifest distinction is neither clear nor convincing.

THE QUESTION OF IMPORTANCE.   Merton's argument is that the distinction "serves further to direct the attention of the sociologist to precisely those realms of behavior, attitude and belief where he can most fruitfully apply his special skills" (1957:65). The statement clearly suggests that some realms are more strategic for sociology than others; and Merton subsequently warns sociologists against confining their studies to manifest functions, which he equates "very largely with determining whether a practice instituted for a particular purpose does, in fact, achieve this purpose" (65). Moreover, if sociologists confine their studies to manifest functions, Merton asserts that their inquiries will be set by practical men of affairs (e.g., captains of industry, trade union leaders) rather than by the "theoretic problems which are at the core of the discipline" (65). The assertion is curious in several respects. Are we to believe that sociology will be supported indefinitely if it has no bearing on the interests of "practical men"? Why are instrumental questions (What social practices work?) not a theoretic problem? Why does Merton warn sociologists only against an exclusive concern with manifest functions?

Most important, manifest functions could make for or lessen a system's adaptation or adjustment, the ultimate concern in functional analysis. Are the system participants indifferent to such adaptation or adjustment, or is it that the system simply has greater wisdom than the participants?

A RELATED THEORETICAL ISSUE.   Merton writes as though consequences are objectively given and the only question is whether system participants recognize them. Yet to characterize a consequence as objectively given really means that a sociologist either recognizes or does not recognize it. Hence, if a system participant recognizes some event or thing as being a consequence of his or her act but the sociologist observer does not recognize it, there may or may not be a latent consequence of the act (depending on the judgment of the sociologist observer); but there will be no manifest functions. Finally, there is even no place in Merton's scheme for failures to realize goals as perceived by the system participants.

In light of the foregoing, Merton's latent-manifest distinction contradicts Thomas and Thomas's dictum: "If men define situations as real, they are real in their consequences" (1928:572). The distinction suggests a quite different dictum: Consequences are not real until sociologists say they are.

Postulates of Functional Analysis

Despite present criticisms of Merton, no one has written a more insightful critique of functionalism. That is particularly true of his treatment of the postulates of functional analysis.

THE POSTULATE OF FUNCTIONAL UNITY.   Merton (1957:25–30) rightly points out that some distinguished functionalists (e.g., Radcliffe-Brown and Malinowski) assumed that a society is a functional unity. Also rightly, Merton argues that the assumption is a vast exaggeration at best.

Unfortunately, Merton ignores this question: Why is the functional unity postulate necessary for a functional explanation? Because Merton scarcely speaks of functional explanation, he does not see that the explanatory mechanism—selective survival—requires something akin to the assumption of functional unity. A particular component (e.g., an institution) of a society could hardly be necessary for the society's survival if not closely integrated with numerous other components.

THE POSTULATE OF UNIVERSAL FUNCTIONALISM.   Merton cites some anthropologists (e.g., Malinowski) as holding that "all standardized social or cultural forms have positive functions" (1957:30). That postulate of universal functionalism is clarified by another famous distinction drawn by Merton: "*Functions* are those observed consequences which make for the adaptation or adjustment of a given system; and *dysfunctions*, those observed consequences which lessen the adaptation or adjustment of the system" (51). Hence, functionalism entails the assumption that the consequences of all societal components (e.g., institutions) are functions rather than dysfunctions. Merton's distinction does clarify, and one of his conclusions is a model of prudence: "although any item of culture or social structure *may* have functions, it is premature to hold unequivocally that every item *must* be functional" (31).

Although Merton writes as though the function-dysfunction remedies a defect in functionalism, it more nearly eliminates functionalism as a mode of explanation. If a socio-cultural component may have dysfunctions as well as functions, how can one justifiably assume that the component is necessary for the social unit's survival. Merton does not pose the question, evidently because he does not view functionalism as a mode of explanation. However, wittingly or unwittingly, he supplies a rationale for modifying and thereby retaining the postulate of universal functionalism. He advances the "provisional" assumption that "persisting cultural forms have a *net balance of functional consequences. . . .*" (1957:32). Whatever the merits of that assumption, there is no prospect whatever for a defensible method of computing a value that describes the "functions" of a particular socio-cultural component and another that describes its "dysfunctions." But suppose it does become possible to compute those values; and further suppose that in a particular case the ratio of the function value is 1.25, meaning that the component is 25 percent more functional than dysfunctional. How could that ratio possibly explain anything? The question would stand even if all socio-cultural components have positive functional values. In particular, to say that each component makes for the system's adaptation or adjustment is not to say that any component is necessary for the system's survival.

THE POSTULATE OF INDISPENSABILITY. In describing the assumptions that underly this postulate, Merton comes close to recognizing that functionalism entails a distinctive mode of explanation: "First, it is assumed that there are certain *functions* which are indispensable in the sense that, unless they are performed, the society (or group or individual) will not persist. . . . Second . . . it is assumed that *certain cultural or social forms* are indispensable for fulfilling each of these functions" (1957:33).

If functionalism is a mode of explanation and selective survival the mechanism, then the two assumptions are essential. But Merton does not make that point; instead, he argues (1957:33–34) that "just as the same item may have multiple functions, so may the same function be diversely fulfilled by alternative items." The argument is plausible; but, unlike Hempel (1959), Merton does not recognize that functional equivalents preclude a formally adequate functional explanation. If *X* exists because it "promotes" the survival of some type of social unit, then to admit alternatives amounts to a denial that *X* is really necessary for any unit's survival. Even granting the possibility of functional equivalents and the notion's importance, Merton failed to acknowledge that his argument implicitly condemns functional explanations.

Two Final Considerations

Just as Merton treats functionalism more as a mode of analysis rather than as a mode of explanation, so does he rarely speak of functional theories. The rarity is understandable because the arguments pursued by functionalists are so ambiguous that it dignifies to label them as theories. However, Merton does not castigate functionalists for failing to state explicit, systematic theories, and that failure is another reason why so many sociologists do not view functionalism as a mode of explanation. It is only when the likes of Hempel (1959) puts functionalist arguments in some explicit logical form (i.e., premises and conclusions) that their explanatory character become obvious.

THE QUESTION OF EVIDENCE. Time and again Merton castigates functionalists for failing to support their postulates with evidence; but he never confronts this question: What research is needed to test a functional postulate, theory, or explanation? At a minimum, researchers must attempt to determine whether or not the socio-cultural component under consideration is present in all social units of the specified type (e.g., tribes, urban countries). Unless the component is present in virtually all of the relevant social units examined in the research, how could it possibly be necessary for their survival? The component need not be present in all social units to retain the functional explanation (the exceptions may be near extinction), but the survival rate must be demonstrably far less for the exceptions.

One likely objection is that the requisite research has been described as though limited to two binary variables: (1) the presence-absence of some socio-cultural component and (2) the survival-extinction of social unit. Alternatively a functional explanation can be interpreted as requiring three variables: (1) the presence-absence of some socio-cultural component, (2) an intervening variable, and (3) the survival-extinction of a social unit. The intervening variable is described as a functional requisite, functional prerequisite, or functional requirement, meaning in any case a condition necessary for some type of social unit to persist, such as "integration."

Sociologists disagree when identifying the kinds of conditions in question, even their appropriate generic label. Thus, Levy (1968) refers to the conditions as functional requisites, reserving the term *functional prerequisite* for statements about change; but most other writers use one of the two terms exclusively, and Merton (1957:52), among others, uses the term *functional requirement*. Whatever the label and whatever the condition considered, claims about conditions being necessary for the survival of social units are commonly concealed tautologies. Thus, if it is claimed that integration is a functional requisite, functional prerequisite, or functional requirement, the claim ignores the point that some degree of integration is a *logical* property of social units. Accordingly, in that case, what appears to entail three variables reduces to two. Consider, a functional argument in this form: $C \to R \to S$, where C is some socio-cultural component (e.g., a particular type of ceremony), R is some system requisite (e.g., integration), and S is the survival of the system. If R is a logical property of the system, then the argument is really $C \to S$. Even so, one can imagine research designed to test the assertion that a particular socio-cultural component satisfies the requisite, prerequisite, or requirement in question. For example, Merton states that ceremonials "may fulfill the latent function of reinforcing the group identity" (1957:64), which suggests that group identity is greater immediately after a ceremonial. Merton cites no corroborating research, nor is that surprising. For all practical purposes, there has been no research on the relation between socio-cultural components and alleged functional requisites, prerequisites, or requirements; and invoking those terms solves none of the problems identified here.

A Case of Closet Functionalism

The most noteworthy feature of contemporary functionalism is the resort of sociologists to implicit functional explanations, meaning without using the term *function* or describing the phenomenon in question as contributing to some larger system. Functionalism is suggested largely because the explanation emphasizes effects, consequences, or postcedent correlates rather than causes, determinants, or antecedent correlates.

An Illustrative Instance

An illustration of a concealed functional theory in sociology is provided by Mizruchi's observations on "abeyance," defined as a "holding process that occurs within and between social organizations of various types, some institutionalized and other not" (1983:1). Examine his introduction: "The basic idea that organizations may be created to absorb and control the potentially dissident in our society has been with me for three decades" (ix). Mizruchi supports his theory by observations on monasteries, medieval Beguinages, Bohemian communes, compulsory apprenticeship settings and schools, and the WPA writers' and artists' projects of the 1930s. How are those entities explained? "Control of the consequences of too many people and too few places is viewed as a problem that is not only economic but moral as well, since dissident behavior may be perceived as a threat to the normative system of a society. The precise point at which sanctioning agents respond remains problematic. Certain structures emerge, either by design or by spontaneous social processes, to contain the temporary surplus of people" (Mizruchi, 1983:11).

If the explanation is causal rather than functional, why was Mizruchi not content to assert that a surplus population causes the appearance or expansion of such "structures"? Given that Mizruchi described abeyance as "typically unplanned and unrecognized" (1983:2), how could his explanation be characterized as purposive rather than functional?

THE QUESTION OF EXPLANATORY ADEQUACY. Mizruchi never identified his theory as "functional," but that is hardly strange since the identification would fuel criticisms. In any case, let us assume that independent investigators agree in answering two questions about at least one period in the history of several countries. First, if a surplus or marginal population increased beyond some critical magnitude, did an abeyance structure emerge or expand? Second, did the emergence or expansion reduce the surplus population to a point below the critical magnitude?

Mizruchi does not confront either question. Rather, he selected periods and countries when ostensibly large increases in the surplus population and the emergence or expansion of abeyance organizations or institutional patterns coexisted, a selection procedure that precluded negative evidence. But suppose that the two questions are not answered affirmatively in all cases. If so, there would be a third but no less crucial question: Where an abeyance structure did not emerge or expand, or where the surplus population remained above the critical magnitude for (say) a decade or more, did the country disintegrate? In the best tradition of functionalism, far from presenting the requisite data, Mizruchi ignores the question.

Functionalism and Control

Sociological perspectives gain adherents because each perspective has some meritorious features. Sociology's central notion should preserve those merits.

The Principal Merit and Shortcoming of Functionalism

It is not puzzling that functionalism had many adherents in sociology for some fifteen years, *circa* 1950–65. The notion of "function" may have come closer to being central for sociology than any other notion before or since 1950; in any case, much of sociology's subject matter can be described and thought of functionally.

Any socio-cultural phenomenon can be analyzed in light of this question: What are its principal functions? Whatever functionalism's shortcomings, the question did provide a sense of direction for sociologists.

Although not emphasized by well-known functionalists, answers to the "principal functions" question (*supra*) are in no sense a test of a theory; but the answers could be conducive to theories. Unfortunately, many functionalists came to regard a list of a phenomenon's alleged functions as an explanation, and they never developed a corroboration-falsification methodology.

THE SHORTCOMING. Commencing primarily with Weber, many sociologists have worried over this question: What kind of explanation of socio-cultural phenomena is appropriate? The question implicitly denies the possibility of one kind of explanation for all sciences—physical, biological, social, etc; and numerous sociologists seem to doubt that the kind of explanation commonly attributed to the physical or natural sciences—nomological-deductive with covering laws (Hempel, 1965:331–489)—is feasible for sociology. In particular, they doubt whether the premises of a sociological theory can be valid even though spatially and temporally unlimited (see, e.g., Maynard and Wilson, 1980:311).

Although numerous social and behavioral scientists appear to share the humanist belief that explanations of socio-cultural phenomena must be somehow different from those in the physical sciences, they have not gone far beyond that belief (see Crews's comment, 1986, on Quentin Skinner); and it is not informative for a sociologist to warn against taking physics or the natural sciences as the model of science (see, e.g., Blumer, 1969:23, and Scheff, 1984:178). The response should be: What model do you have in mind? Attacks on positivism are not an answer, nor is the answer found in arguments opposing "value-free sociology."

Functionalism as it came to be practiced in the social sciences is surely not an answer. By any conventional standard in the philosophy of science, functional explanations or theories in sociology are indefensible. The premises are not explicit; and insofar as the premises can be surmised, there is nothing approaching systematic evidence (e.g., reported tests) to corroborate them. For that matter, typically the putative premises are not generalizations that transcend the particular and the unique; and, even when the premises are explicit generalizations, logically valid deductions are precluded because the *explanandum* does not appear to be necessary for survival of the type of social unit in question. All such defects stem from the belief that a socio-cultural phenomenon can be explained by arguing that it meets some need of a system, an argument that creates the illusion of an adequate explanation.

Control and the Principal Merit of Functionalism

Should control become sociology's central notion, it would provide the field with something akin to functionalism. Indeed, functionalism's merit would not be lost.

Consider this question as it applies to any component of sociology's subject matter: How does the component impede or facilitate inanimate, biotic, and human control? That question is a more meaningful research directive than this one: What are the component's principal functions? The control question is more meaningful if only because it promises substantially greater empirical applicability. Consider the phrases that have been used frequently to describe the function of a socio-cultural component: what it does, the contribution it makes to the larger system, the correspondence between it and some need, how it makes for adjustment or adaptation. Those phrases are not just very vague; they are conducive to tautologies. Thus, Parsons's (1980) list of the functions of law includes the very terms that are commonly employed in defining law (e.g., sanctioning); as such, the list is trite.

Compared to alternatives, Merton's conceptualization of "functions" is a monument to clarity. Even so, there is no basis to assume that researchers can ever agree in describing how a particular socio-cultural component makes for or lessens the adjustment or adaption of a given system (Merton, 1957:51). True, a methodology for using the terms *facilitating control* and *impeding control* is wanting, but those terms have greater potential for empirical application than do Merton's terms.

Should it be argued that observations on functions have more explanatory significance than do observations on control, the identification of an alleged "function" in itself explains nothing. Moreover, if one longs for observations that appear to have enormous theoretical significance, reconsider a previous challenge: Try to imagine humanity or social life without inanimate, biotic, and human control.

No description of a type of behavior, an institution, or an organization is complete unless it speaks to this question: What role does the phenomenon play in inanimate, biotic, and human control? Consider the mass sacrifices and alleged related cannibalism of the Aztecs. Descriptions commonly do not emphasize that the ceremonies were human control on a massive scale. Hence, the descriptions scarcely have no bearing on various possibilities, one being that the ceremonies furthered the control of Aztec nobles (*pipiltin*) over the masses and/or tributary peoples. As for the accounts of cannibalism, even if they were fabrications by apologists for the Spanish conquest, the accounts were surely attempts at human control. On the other hand, to explain the cannibalism as meeting some need for protein is to make an implicit argument about biotic control among the Aztecs.

True, to say that human sacrifice and cannibalism have control implications is not an answer to this question: But why did the Aztecs come to employ those "means" of control rather than alternatives? The answer commences with the argument that an answer to the "how" question is an essential for answering the "why" question. So the conclusion: human sacrifice or cannibalism in a social unit (Aztec or otherwise) cannot be explained adequately without ascertaining how those practices facilitate and impede control (inanimate, biotic, and human) in general. That the two practices are in themselves control poses no contradiction, paradox, or dilemma. While the conclusion perhaps suggests that pursuit of a "how" question ends in a function explanation (i.e., selective survival), the question does not preclude a purposive explanation; and there is no reason why a strictly causal explanation of a human phenomenon cannot be couched in terms of control, not even if the phenomenon is itself a control practice.

MAKING THE INCREDIBLE MORE CREDIBLE.   Selective survival (as an explanatory mechanism) and the notion of control are more than compatible. It does not tax credulity to suppose that some social units would cease to exist without certain types of control (inanimate, biotic, and/or human). Evidence of such indispensability would set the scene for an explanation of particular types of control, and the explanation would be in keeping with functionalism. Now consider a more complex possibility. If certain types of control are necessary for the survival of a certain type of social unit and a particular kind of socio-cultural condition is necessary for that type of control, selective survival would explain both the control and the condition.

Merton (1957) emphasized functional equivalents evidently because he doubted that any one socio-cultural component is necessary for any social unit's survival. To illustrate formally, suppose that any one of five institutions—V, W, X, Y, and Z—is sufficient for the survival of a particular type of social unit, but none is necessary. If so, the presence of any of the five in any social unit is not explained by selective survival (because none is necessary), but the selective-survival explanation can be combined with the purposive type. Suppose that institution Z is present in an instance of the type of social unit in question. Then suppose convincing evidence that the social unit members perceive Z as facilitating some type of control more than would any of the four alternatives—V, W, X, or Y. Finally, suppose there is evidence corroborating this generalization: Given a set institutions, if most social unit members perceive a particular institution as facilitating control more than do the other institutions, that particular institution will be present in that social unit.

Given all of those suppositions, why would they not amount to an adequate explanation of the presence of Z in that particular social unit? True, the perception of Z as facilitating control more than does V, W, X, or Y is not explained; but that consideration has nothing to do with the original question: Why is Z present in this social unit? Nor would the explanation require rejection of the notion of a latent function, for the members of the social unit might be totally ignorant of the possibility that Z is necessary for the social unit's survival.

The proposal to make control sociology's central notion would not preclude a combination of any two or all three types of explanations—causal, selective survival, and purposive; but the proposal takes on special significance in contemplating a purposive explanation. A purposive explanation can be stated in terms of control without using the term purpose, and a control language has one major advantage over that term. Whereas "purpose" refers to internal behavior, "control" pertains to both overt and internal behavior. Nonetheless, taking control as sociology's central notion would facilitate something that functionalists appear reluctant to entertain—a combination of a purposive explanation and a selective survival explanation.

NOTES

1. Of various commentators in sociology, only Dore (1961) emphasizes "the effect explains the cause." Halfpenny recognizes that interpretation, but as only one of several equally tenable alternatives (1983:77).

2. Alleged effects of intertribal marriage other than intertribal peace could be considered. Thus, White explains the incest taboo by arguing (1973:40–41) that it extends cooperation from *within* families to *among* families. Even though White used the term *positive biological survival value* (41), he seemed unaware of giving a functional explanation.

3. The same is true of all illustrations in this chapter. Indeed, the exogamy illustration has been offered because it appears plausible (as functional explanations commonly do) until considering a report of no association between exogamy and peaceful relations among social units (see Kang, 1979). Hallpike writes of a New Guinea tribe: "The Tauade are aware . . . that they frequently fight other tribes with whom they have numerous marriage links" (1977:203).

4. Paradoxically, Skinner appears more sensitive to the nature of a "selective survival" explanation than do most sociologists or anthropologists, even though he does not use the term. Contemplate his felicitous sentence: "A practice that makes a culture more likely to survive survives with the culture" (1978:53). By comparison, Cohen's extensive analysis of functionalism (1978:249–96) is a monument to ambiguity, and even his identification of Marx's theory as "functionalist" is disputable (see *Theory and Society*, July, 1982).

5. A combination of a purposive explanation and a selective survival explanation is likely to be especially strategic when considering the origin of institutions or practices. Thus, White (1973:4) purports to explain the incest taboo by arguing that it resulted in an extension of cooperation from *within* families to *among* families. Even granting that *only* the incest taboo could have so extended cooperation (dubious, needless to say) and that interfamily cooperation is necessary for the larger social unit to survive, how could the incest taboo have had those effects before it became an institution or practice? It makes no sense to assume a *de facto* incest taboo, meaning that social unit members disapprove of certain kinds of sexual relations or marriages without being aware of it. Hence, White's explanation pertains to the persistence of the taboo, not its origin. The only alternative to a causal explanation of the taboo's origin is a purposive explanation—that humans commenced attempting to prevent certain kinds of sexual relations or marriages. Such attempts were control attempts. Those who made the attempts may or may not have anticipated such possible consequences as tribal survival; nonetheless, it taxes credulity to suppose that the taboo's origin had nothing to do with attempts at control, and its persistence certainly does.

6. For that matter, without the notion of selective survival, the rationale for a functional explanation cannot be intelligible and plausible. As a case in point, Isajiw (1968) equates a functional explanation with "telecausality," one characteristic of which is described as the "repetition or multiplicity of coincidences" (58), such as when all of numerous known instances of Y are preceded by an instance of X. Isajiw makes this statement about such a sequential relation: "Note that no necessity (uniqueness of bond, continuity of action) is implied between X and Y, since the argument states only that Y is preceded by X repetitively. It states that since X keeps reappearing as a productive cause of Y, it can occur only if Y is its effect. It does not say that X occurs because it is produced by Y, but it says that X occurs because it keeps producing Y. In that sense Y determines

X" (58–59). Insofar as Isajiw's statement is intelligible, it appears incredible. A cause may occur simply because it keeps producing an effect? Again, an explanation of a cause in terms of its effects is intelligible and plausible only if it entails the notion of selective survival.

7.   The term *teleological explanation* is not used here because critics commonly allege that in such an explanation a future state or condition is the cause of a current state or condition. Such an allegation creates the impression that a teleological explanation reverses what is commonly taken to be the necessary temporal sequence of causation (the cause precedes the effect), thereby suggesting that all teleological explanations are patently absurd. Hence, the term *purposive explanation* is used here to emphasize the point that a purpose (whether described as an intention or a belief about the consequences of behavior) is not a future state or condition. Obviously, the purpose of an overt act precedes that act (see Nagel, 1961).

Interpretive Sociology and Some of Freud's Arguments

The term *interpretive sociology* denotes a very broad perspective (for strategic references, see Denzin, 1987). Its adherents are identified with symbolic interactionism, phenomenological sociology, ethnomethodology, humanistic sociology, subjectivism, sociological impressionism, *verstehen* sociology, or dramaturgical sociology. Each label need not be defined, because it is a particular belief about preferred answers to questions that distinguishes interpretivism from other perspectives. Stating that belief as the defining argument: An adequate answer to a sociological question requires recognition that human behavior is determined by past experience and the immediate environment or situation through mechanisms involving conscious internal behavior (e.g., perception, valuations). Because of that belief, the label *interpretive sociology* has a descriptive advantage over *methodological individualism*, but the latter label does rightly suggest that interpretivists are more concerned with human behavior or social action than with society, culture, or social structure.

Toward Further Clarification of the Perspective

The first part of interpretive sociology's defining argument is elaborated in Wagner's comment (1973:71) on Schutz's thesis: "This thesis means . . . that the assumption of an equal effect of situational elements and conditions upon any individual exposed to a given situation—the basic assumption of any rigidly situational approach from Kurt Lewin to George Homans—does not hold: The unique past experiences of an individual are brought into any new situation and may become important factors in his definition of this situation as well as in his decision to adopt a certain course of action and response in the unfolding process circumscribed by 'the situation'." Wagner wrote in connection with phenomenological sociology, but no interpretivist is likely to demur (see, e.g., McHugh, 1968:8; Blumer, 1969:2). If Lewin and Homans reject Schutz's thesis, as Wagner suggests, they are behaviorists (chapter 15), not interpretivists.

Wagner's "definition of the situation" and "decision to adopt" pertain to the second part of interpretive sociology's defining argument, but it is more accurate to say that interpretivists emphasize internal behavior, *meaning* in particular.[1] That emphasis is the major difference between interpretivists and Skinner, and the inclination of sociological structuralists (e.g., Mayhew, 1980, 1981) to equate interpretive sociology with "psychology" is indefensible. Skinnerians, like sociological structuralists, eschew terms that denote internal behavior, especially "mentalistic" notions, such as the processes emphasized by interpretivists (e.g., Blumer, 1969:5).

Two Illustrative Violations of Interpretive Principles

Interpretive sociology can be further clarified by examining its defining argument in connection with this question: Why has the division of labor increased in England since 1700? Now consider the answer implied by Durkheim (1949): Because there has been an enormous increase in England's density since 1700. Although sociological structuralists could have no a priori objections to that answer, interpretivists would reject it even in the face of a positive correlation between density and the division of labor over time in England (or elsewhere). Durkheim's answer does not even suggest the relevance of past experience, much less mechanisms by which past experience and current conditions (level of density in this case) determine human behavior.

Consider one more example. Assume unquestioned evidence that in a particular U.S. election a significantly greater proportion of self-identified Catholics voted the Democrat ticket than did self-identified Protestants. So the question: Why that behavioral difference? One possible answer is that the unemployment rate was much greater for Catholics than for Protestants. Interpretivists would not regard the answer as an adequate explanation, not even given a substantial correlation between unemployment and voting Democrat at the individual level and the aggregate level. There are two reasons. First, interpretivists would insist that (1) unemployment is a current condition and (2) the correlation does not reveal the nature of the connection between the past experience of Catholics and their current voting behavior. Second, interpretivists would insist that human responses to current conditions are contingent on how the responders perceive those conditions, meaning that past experiences determines human behavior through perception. Furthermore, to label a person "unemployed" (or "Catholic" for that matter) implies nothing about how he or she perceives unemployment; hence, an explanation of behavior, voting or otherwise, in terms of "objective" conditions cannot be adequate. It is not just a matter of how the unemployed perceive their unemployment. Whether or not one is unemployed depends on how he or she perceives his or her current condition and the perceptions of those who interact with him or her. The argument applies both to cognition and to the evaluative (affective) facets of perception. In brief, possible correlates of unemployment (e.g., voting, suicide) depend on the meaning of "being unemployed" for the unemployed and those who interact with them.

The Principal Merit of Interpretive Sociology

No sociological perspective has a more obvious principal merit than interpretivism. Few sociologists are likely to deny that most human behavior is determined by past experience and the immediate situation, nor that a human's response to a situation (or condition) depends on how he or she perceives it. Indeed, there are only two alternatives: (1) human behavior is genetically determined or (2) human responses to the external environment are no different from those of inanimate objects. Think of the argument in connection with Galileo's rolling balls down an incline. What would he have concluded had some balls rolled faster with each successive roll but some slower, some rolled faster at noon regardless of previous rolls, some rolled slower at midnight but only on the first roll, and some did not roll at all on Sundays? If it is agreed that Galileo would have been baffled, that would be a step toward recognizing that the subject matter of the social and behavioral sciences is intrinsically more complex than that of physics.

Granted that sociologists are unlikely to reject the defining argument of interpretivism, many of them appear indifferent to it (see Blumer's commentary, 1969:2–3). The indifference of sociological structuralists (chapter 11) reflects two of their convictions. First, structural concepts (e.g., the division of labor) refer to superorganic phenomena, and only those phenomena constitute sociology's subject matter. Second, because structural concepts supposedly refer neither to individuals nor to human behavior, the past experience of humans is sociologically irrelevant.

The Principal Shortcoming of Interpretive Sociology

Although the defining argument of interpretivism is defensible, even the loose way that sociologists use the term *theory* does not justify identifying more than a few statements of any interpretivist as a theory, much less a testable theory.[2] There are even doubts as to whether interpretivists have nomethetic statements as a goal. "Rather than seeking to emulate the natural sciences in the search for universal, transhistorical concepts and laws, the task of sociology is the analysis of specific social structures and how they work within the context of their historical development" (Maynard and Wilson, 1980:311). So, granted some exceptions and particularly among symbolic interactionists (see, especially, Stryker's survey, 1981), it appears that the vast majority of interpretivists will be forever content with description or ad hoc interpretations. As for the well-known "theoretical" statements in interpretive sociology's literature, they have become little more than aphorisms, the classic one being in Thomas and Thomas: "If men define situations as real, they are real in their consequences" (1928:572). The statement is not a testable proposition, because it implies no particular prediction about anything, McHugh (1968) notwithstanding.

Interpretivists commonly pursue interests that culminate in a solipsist epistemology rather than substantive theories (e.g., Berger and Luckman, 1966). One consequence is that interpretivists alienate other sociologists by lecturing them about the reality of everyday life, as though the audience has never experienced it. Arguments about the nature of reality are inherently sterile, and interpretivists pursue related theses so vague as to jeopardize their perspective's merits. Thus, Berger and Luckman (1966) maintain this thesis: Reality is socially constructed. The thesis is so vague that no imaginable evidence would refute it; and the same thesis was maintained by Durkheim (especially 1965), who otherwise opposed the defining argument of interpretive sociology.

Some Common Misconceptions

Critics of interpretive sociology depict Weber, Mead, Schutz, Simmel, Goffman, and Garfinkel as incapable of formulating testable theories. By contrast, interpretivists view those figures as staunch empiricists who refused to equate empiricism and quantification.

Both the critics and interpretivists err. To be sure, interpretivists are prone to write gibberish, one example coming from Schutz: "The Acts of the cogito in which the Ego lives, the living present in which the Ego is borne along from each Here and Now to the next—these are never caught in the cone of light. They fall, therefore, outside the sphere of the meaningful. On the contrary (and this also emerges from our argument): The actual Here and Now of the living Ego *is the very source of the light*, the apex from which emanate the rays spreading out conelike over the already elapsed and receding phases of the stream of duration, illuminating them and marking them off from the rest of the stream" (1967:70).

Yet the vast majority of statements in interpretive sociology's literature are intelligible. On the other hand, consider Goffman's observation that "in all societies, seemingly, an individual can find himself dissolving into laughter or tears or anger, or running from an event in panic and terror, in a word, 'flooding out' " (1974:350). The statement appears to be a generalization; but, like so many others made by interpretivists, it is an existential proposition,

214 / *Control: Sociology's Central Notion*

because it claims nothing more than the present, past, or future existence of at least one instance of some class of things or events. The objection is not just that such propositions are unfalsifiable (consider claims about UFO's), but also that they are uninformative to the point of being trite.

When an interpretive generalization or theory appears to be something more than a existential proposition, its validity is usually extremely questionable (see, e.g., Felson, 1981).[3] Consider Schutz again: "The structure of the social world is meaningful, not only for those living in that world, but for its scientific interpreters as well. Living in the world, we live with others and for others, orienting our lives to them. In experiencing them as *others* . . . we *understand* the behavior of others and assume that they understand ours" (1967:9).

Schutz evidently never read a suicide note proclaiming that the world is not meaningful, nor did he ever encounter a hermit or a misanthrope; and, most remarkable, Schutz himself apparently never felt misunderstood. Lest Schutz appear to be the only interpretivist who taxes credulity, contemplate Berger and Luckman's generalization: "The reality of everyday life is shared with others" (1966:27). If the statement is more than a tautology or simply verbiage, Louis XIV surely would have found it amusing.

Given the tendency of interpretive sociologists to write obscurely and state incredible or trite generalizations, it is not surprising that their extreme critics dismiss them caustically; but those critics (e.g., Mayhew, 1980, 1981) err when they depict interpretivists as mystics. Yet interpretivists persist in equating a mixture of vague arguments, isolated existential propositions, and anecdotal observations with a theory. Indeed, what passes for theory among them is commonly nothing more than vaguely stated empirical generalizations about the "how" of everyday activities. Such generalizations are the products of crude induction but bereft of qualifications as to who, when, and where.

The Basic Problem

Because the defining argument of interpretive sociology suggests a special sensitivity to the complexities of human behavior and social life, it may appear that interpretivists rarely formulate testable theories only because they are cautious. A more compelling argument is that interpretivists work primarily with a notion that precludes replicable observations on human behavior. The notion is "meaning,"[4] and that term or any well-known definition of it promises negligible empirical applicability. There are at least nine distinct meanings of *meaning*; hence, the observations of interpretivists on human behavior are bound to be ambiguous as long as meaning is their primary notion. But interpretivists are prone to disregard the various "meanings of meaning," and they confront the problem only to leave it unresolved. Thus, Schutz (1967:12) recognized Gomperz's identification of nine distinct meanings of meaning and took Weber to task for his use of the term, but Schutz then reneged on his promise (1967:19) to "arrive at an adequate analysis of the concept of meaning."

Despite divergent definitions of meaning, all suggest that it refers to internal behavior; and for that reason alone the term *meaning* promises negligible empirical applicability. Sociologists observe overt behavior, not meaning; and any notion pertaining only to internal behavior is conducive to solipsism. However, the solipsistic tendency in interpretive sociology stems not from Husserl's impact on Schutz's restatement of Weber; the preoccupation of interpretivists with meaning has diverse sources. For that matter, any notion—be it motive, purpose, drive, value, or attitude—that pertains only to internal behavior hinders an empirically applicable vocabulary.

Interpretive Sociology and Control

No major interpretivist has used the term *control* frequently, and only Goffman's writings can be translated readily as observations on human control. So interpretivism may appear incompatible with the proposal to make control sociology's central notion. To the contrary, acceptance of the proposal would reduce the shortcomings of interpretivism, and interpretivists are best qualified to remedy defects in the present conceptualization of control.

The Principal Shortcoming Reconsidered

As long as *meaning* is interpretive sociology's primary notion, the perspective will verge on solipsism; and attempts to corroborate the empirical claims made by interpretivists will become infinite regressions. Consider one of Douglas's arguments in a study preoccupied with meaning: "since there exist great disagreements between interested parties in the categorizations of real-world cases, 'suicides' can generally be said to exist and not exist at the same time. . . ." (1967:196). Douglas failed to justify his generalization about disagreements; and he ignored this question: What definition and methodology promises the greatest agreement between investigators when identifying suicides? If the focus is on the meaning, as Douglas would have it, agreement cannot be furthered.

To be sure, no one "observes" suicides; they must be inferred. However, if meaning rather than intention is made pivotal, an infinite regression ensues. Suppose that someone labels a particular death as suicide and to justify that inference points to a note in which the deceased supposedly wrote: "I cannot go on living." Even if the deceased did write the note, how would we know what he or she meant by the statement? Indeed, had the deceased used the word "suicide," how could one know its meaning for the deceased? To make the point another way—one never really confronted by ethnomethodologists—any word, term, phrase, expression, or action is "indexical," Garfinkel's reference to "indexical expressions" notwithstanding (1967:5,11).

There is no basis to argue that sociological descriptions can avoid infinite regressions because sociologists agree as to an act's ultimate meaning. The sheer variety of meanings of meaning precludes any ultimate connotation, and arbitrariness will haunt any attempt to narrow the meaning of meaning. So in retrospect, interpretivists were unfortunate in their implicit choice of meaning as their primary notion.

While the divergent meanings of meaning make it unsuitable as a central notion for any social or behavioral science, there is another reason. Whatever the social or behavioral science, the empirical applicability of its central notion will be negligible unless it pertains to both overt behavior and internal behavior. The notion of meaning does not qualify.

CONTROL AS THE ALTERNATIVE NOTION. If interpretivists had taken control as their primary notion at the outset, they would have never become preoccupied with internal behavior. That is the case because control is defined in terms of internal and overt behavior; hence, taking control as sociology's central notion is not conducive to extreme behaviorism or to extreme subjectivism. The notion of control circumvents conventional dualisms by making it necessary to treat internal and overt behavior as integrated, as they are in any act. To illustrate with a question: What is the meaning of eye contact between two humans? Given the way that interpretivists use the term *meaning*, the question is unanswerable. Now contemplate Argyle's claim that residents of big cities quickly learn these "laws" of looking: "Never make eye contact with a panhandler, or you will be pursued for handouts; with a religious fanatic, or you will be caught in a diatribe; with a belligerent lover, or you will become the object of a menacing tirade; with a lost visitor, or you will feel responsible to help" (1980:65). Argyle's failure to speak of control is irrelevant. He clearly suggests that big city residents avoid eye contact in the belief that avoidance reduce the probability of a subsequent undesirable condition; so their behavior is attempted control, countercontrol in particular.

The connection between "behavior-in-the-belief" and "meaning of behavior" is debatable, but that is precisely the point. Moreover, the conceptualization of control (chapter 3) recognizes all of the internal behavior, cognitive or affective, that sociologists need consider, and sociologists need not explain individual differences as regards beliefs.[5] If there must be disciplinary lines, explanations of individual differences are best left to psychologists. Sociologists can take beliefs as givens, and none of the major questions about control (chapter 3) refer to individual differences.

Interpretivism repels many sociologists because of its predominant focus on micro phenomena, but sociology needs a notion that can be used to describe and think about phenomena at both levels, micro and macro. Meaning is not such a notion, but control is; and it offers an *anormative* basis (hence, an alternative to Sciulli, 1986) for analyzing the idea of voluntary action.

ONE ILLUSTRATION. Some interpretive sociologists have not avoided a control terminology (see, e.g., Molotch and Boden, 1985), nor is extreme subjectivism a feature of interpretive sociology generally. The caveat is illustrated by "affect-control" theory, especially Heise's summary statement (1979:viii): "The theory . . . relates to common social actions, like those of a doctor toward a patient, a judge toward a thief . . . a mugger toward a victim. According to the theory, all such events have an underlying basis in the psychology of affect. In particular, people in such relationships theoretically act to maintain established feelings, and when an event occurs that strains these feelings, the individuals anticipate and implement new events to restore normal impressions. Events cause people to respond affectively. In turn, people expect and construct new events that will cause established sentiments to be confirmed."

Self-control has been conceptualized (chapter 3) such that it encompasses "affect control," but all interpretive sociologists should recognize that to implement or construct an event is to attempt inanimate, biotic, or external human control. Humans rarely make the attempt in the belief that their internal behavior (affective or cognitive) will be altered or maintained; but what Heise designates (1979:86–89, 127–32) as reidentification, reconceptualization, or reinterpretation both results from and leads to control attempts. That recognition facilitates the integration of the affect-control theory and the law of effect (see, e.g., Griffith and Gray, 1985).

A Special Reliance on Interpretivism

The conceptualization of control in chapters 2 and 3 does not extend to a methodology of application; and ignorance of the most appropriate methodology is admitted, even though it is scarcely less important than the conceptualization.[6] Without that methodology, sociologists are not likely to realize sufficient agreement in identifying instances of control.

Interpretivists are qualified to develop a methodology for applying the present conceptualization of control, including observations procedures and inference rules.[7] In particular, they are sensitive to problems in classifying, describing, and interpreting human behavior (see, especially, Cicourel, 1964, 1973). Lest it appear that a bone has been tossed, consider two arguments about some conditions that are essential for progress in sociology. First, sociologists cannot obtain defensible data unless their conceptualizations are accompanied by a methodology of application. Second, methodological expertise in sociology is virtually equated with knowledge of statistics, which is not particularly relevant in developing methods for applying conceptualizations. Interpretivists would accept both arguments readily (see, e.g., Blumer, 1969:21–47), but their tirades against quantification and positivism scarcely constitute a methodology.

The Use of Control Terms as Constructs

While the need for empirically applicable control terminology cannot be exaggerated, some control terms can be constructs rather than concepts. A construct is a term that a theorist may leave undefined (i.e., a *theoretical primitive term*) and, if defined, the theorist does not regard the definition as empirically applicable. By contrast, a concept is a defined term, and the theorist regards the definition as complete and empirically applicable. However, a concept that pertains to quantitive phenomenon cannot be empirically applicable, even indirectly, unless linked with a formula; and if application of the formula is precluded for some reason (e.g., limited research resources), the concept must be treated as a construct. That is likely to be the case when attempting macro applications of control terms.

Self-control as a Case in Point

The term *self-control* can be used effectively as a construct in formulating theories. Such a theory is beyond this book, but use of the self-control notion to arrive at a testable empirical generalization can be illustrated. The illustration is needed all the more because interpretivists, although appreciative of self-control's importance, rarely state testable empirical generalizations.

Feelings of shame or guilt are common correlates of disapproved behavior, whether designated as deviant or not; but the intensity of those feelings varies considerably among social unit members. Why the variation? It is not informative to reply that the intensity of shame or guilt is a direct function of the extent to which the member has internalized the putative norm that proscribes the behavior in question. The problem is not just the difficulty in defining and identifying norms (chapter 1); additionally, there is this paradoxical question: Granted that individuals who have internalized a norm will feel shame or guilt if they engage in the proscribed behavior, why would they engage in it?

Now consider a quite different argument, one pertaining to variation in the intensity of shame or guilt feelings among participants in some type of behavior, excluding those who are ostensibly free of such feelings. Among such participants, intensity of shame or guilt is a direct function of the extent to which the participant accepts responsibility for his or her behavior. Acceptance of responsibility for one's behavior is the moral dimension of self-control because individuals who deny responsibility commonly describe their behavior as beyond their control. So we arrive at a generalization: the more an individual believes that his or her disapproved behavior is beyond his or her control, the less he or she feels shame or guilt for that behavior.

Tests of the generalization should be based on data gathered especially for that purpose; but in reporting a survey of beliefs supposedly held by a sample of male homosexuals or bisexuals in three countries, Weinberg and

Williams (1975) unwittingly supplied data for an illustrative test. The nature of the data is suggested by Table 10-1, and because the test is only illustrative, a detailed commentary is not necessary. It will suffice to say that the generalization anticipates an inverse relation between the values in the first column of Table 10-1 and the values in the third column (those values are aggregate values and an individual correlation cannot be computed).

Table 10-1. Survey Statistics on Beliefs by Males About Self-control and Homosexuality by Sexual Orientation and Nationality*

Sexual Orientation[1]	Country	Percent Who Report Believing that Homosexuality Is Beyond One's Control		Percent Who Report "High" Guilt, Shame, or Anxiety Regarding Homosexuality	
		%	Rank[2]	%	Rank[2]
Bisexual	United States	40.8	6	33.2	1
	Netherlands	74.4	4	24.8	2
	Denmark	76.0	3	16.0	3
Homosexual	United States	58.3	5	15.5	4
	Netherlands	85.3	2	7.4	6
	Denmark	89.9	1	8.8	5

*Figures from separate panels of a table in Weinberg and Williams (1975:307–8).
1. Classified in accordance with the Kinsey scale.
2. Rank-order coefficient of correlation between the two columns of rank values: −.77.

Because the rank-order coefficient of correlation between the two sets of ranks in Table 10-1 is −.77, it appears that, consistent with the generalization, those individuals who view their homosexuality as beyond their control are less inclined to feel intense shame or guilt. Although the finding is limited to one type of behavior and only six populations, the generalization does illustrate thinking of phenomena in terms of self-control as a construct.

Control and Freud's Theories

If only because of their interest in socialization, some sociologists pursue questions about personality; and as long as Mead and Cooley have followers sociologists will be interested in the "self," a notion that bears on personality. Indeed, should sociologists continue to pursue the "social order question," they must confront this argument: social order requires that socialization produce personality types consistent with putative societal norms and values. Apart from social order, self-control could be a strategic notion if there is ever a revival of interest in national character. Fallows's observation is pertinent: "Several American psychologists have recently claimed that the Japanese approach may in fact equip children for more happiness in life than American practices do. Americans are taught to try to control their destiny; when they can't, they feel they've failed. Japanese children, so these psychologists contend, are taught to adjust to an externally imposed social order, which gives them 'secondary control'—that is, a happy resignation to fate" (1986:35).

Freud's Towering Presence

If interested in socialization and personality, social and behavioral scientists face an embarrassing recognition. After nearly a century, Freud's personality theory remains best known, despite myriad objections to it.[8] The theory defies a test procedure acceptable to the protagonists, and no procedure has yielded impressive positive evidence. For that matter, Freud never formulated a defensible conceptualization of personality, and he said very little as to how his postulated mechanisms (e.g., projection, introjection) or libidinal stages (oral, anal, phallic) generate particular personality traits. Indeed, how could the enormous variety of commonly recognized traits result from regression to or fixation at one of only three stages? Finally, Freud's insistence on the instinctive (or phylogenetic) basis of human behavior makes his theory incompatible with conventional ideas about socialization.

Objections to the theory notwithstanding, there are scarcely truly distinct and viable contenders; and no social scientist can dismiss Freud's theory as irrelevant simply because he or she has no interest in personality or psychopathology. Freud, his disciples, and numerous commentators have created the impression that his theory explains socio-cultural phenomena, such as religion. Moreover, for decades one sociologist or another has attempted to do something with Freud's ideas (e.g., Chodorow, 1985; Golding, 1982); and in that connection interpretivism takes on added significance because interpretive sociologists share some interests with Freud's disciples (see, e.g., Golding, 1982), despite Freud's biological orientation.

Parental Control and Control of Parents

Granted Freud's towering presence in Western intellectual history, his personality theory is unlikely to endure without more stress on socio-cultural factors and testability. Yet to call for greater stress on those factors is all too vague, and it is a myth that the "culturalists" in psychoanalysis (see Anthony's survey, 1980) have reformulated Freud so as to make his theory more testable. By contrast, it is not vague to argue that Freud failed to emphasize the control relation between parents and children; and should his theory be restated so as to correct that omission, it would be more testable. However, it must suffice for present purposes to illustrate how control notions could enter into the restatement.

Freud never granted the possibility that his postulated libidinal stages (or phases) stem not from instincts but from parental control over children and the attempts of children to control their parents.[9] To simplify, assume that power is the most appropriate notion for analyzing the parent-child relation, and recall that power has been defined as the perceived capacity for control. Children obviously come to perceive their parents as having that capacity.[10] It is less obvious that children come to perceive themselves as having the capacity to control their parents, but only because social scientists seem to regard power as asymmetrical. Yet to deny by definition the possibility of X having power over Y in some contexts and Y having power over X in other contexts is to diminish the theoretical utility of the notion of power.

The immediate consequences of viewing power as asymmetrical or symmetrical is the sheer variety of possibilities. If $X \rightarrow Y$ signifies that X is perceived as having the capacity to control some of Y's behavior, $X \leftarrow Y$ signifies that Y is perceived as having the capacity to control some of X's behavior, $X \longrightarrow Y$ signifies no perceived control by X or Y over the other's behavior, and $X \leftrightarrow Y$ signifies mutual control, then there are 64 possibilities in a triad, with Z as the third member. One possibility is $X \leftarrow Y \rightarrow Z$, meaning that X, Y and/or Z perceives Y as capable of controlling some of X's behavior and some of Z's behavior, whereas neither X nor Z is perceived as having such a control capacity. If the "power perceiver" (X, Y, or Z) is treated as a contingency, there are 192 possibilities. Some of those possibilities are shown in Figure 10–1, which pertains to a familial triad, where F = father, M = mother, B = boy, and G = girl.

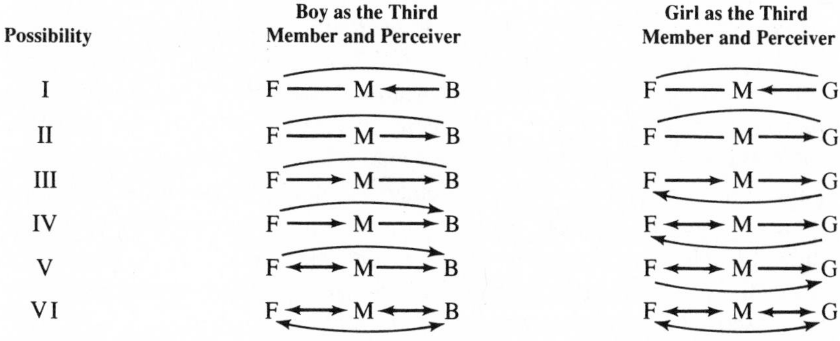

Possibility	Boy as the Third Member and Perceiver	Girl as the Third Member and Perceiver
I	F ——— M ◄— B	F ——— M ◄— G
II	F ——— M —► B	F ——— M —► G
III	F —► M —► B	F —► M —► G
IV	F —► M —► B	F ◄—► M —► G
V	F ◄—► M —► B	F ◄—► M —► G
VI	F ◄—► M ◄—► B	F ◄—► M ◄—► G

Figure 10–1. Some Illustrative Power Relations in a Family

Freud's Libidinal or Psychosexual Stages

The major argument: Freud's stages can be described and thought of in terms of the familial power relations.[11] Although Figure 10–1 serves to explicate, it is merely illustrative.

THE ORAL STAGE AND POSSIBILITY I.   The idea of an infant perceiving himself or herself as controlling his/her mother may appear far-fetched; but it is consistent with Freud's characterization of the oral stage (approximately the first 18 months of life) as one of omnipotence, primarily because the infant's hunger is so commonly gratified (see Silverman, 1980:152–57).[12] However, although Freud (1957-XIV:88, 134–35, 249–50) suggested a link between the oral stage and infantile narcissism, a broader generalization can be stated as a control principle (10–2): As an individual comes to perceive himself or herself as capable of total and asymmetric control over everyone, that individual becomes narcissistic.

The meaning of *narcissistic* may be too vague for identifying a personality type; but if control is made central in restating Freud's theory, a connection between *narcisstic* and *domineering* is suggested. Narcisstic individuals act as though they exert control over everyone, and they are extraordinarily frustrated by failures in control attempts.[13] Finally, it does not strain credulity to argue that inordinate success in control during the oral stage leads to fixation or regression and subsequent delusions of grandeur or megalomania (see Freud, 1957-XIV:98–100).

THE ANAL STAGE AND POSSIBILITY II.   Freud's emphasis on erogenous zones notwithstanding, the correlates of his postulated anal stage (about age 1.5 to 3) could stem from the child's perceived ascendance of the mother's power (i.e., the transition from possibility I to II in Figure 10–1). A shift in the focus of the mother's control from toilet training to something else (e.g., speech habits) might have the same impact on the child's personality.

Freud's suggested (e.g., 1955-XVII:127) connection between the anal stage and compulsive or obsessional neuroses extends to the notion of a rigid personality type, an individual who controls his or her behavior by inflexible rules. But if all children go through an anal stage, why are some adults much more compulsive or obsessive than others? Perhaps because toilet training is more exacting, intense, and punitive for some children than others; but Freud did not emphasize that possibility, nor is it consistent with his allusions to the instinctive or phylogenetic basis of the libidinal stages. Nonetheless, whatever its consequences, toilet training is a series of control attempts.

During the anal stage the child first fully recognizes his or her vulnerability to control, especially by the mother. In coping with parental control through punishments and rewards, the child's efforts at self-control are uniquely intensified and determine personality traits. Yet compulsive behavior is not self-control, because it is experienced as "ego alien"; indeed, many adults seek psychiatric treatment because they perceive themselves as lacking self-control. Moreover, some children do not develop self-control to the point that they regularly avoid punishments and realize rewards. Parental control of toilet behavior may be so erratic that the child cannot cope; if so, he or she will suffer anxiety throughout life and frequently resort to overt behaviors that symbolize safety. The overt behavior stems from superego drives (self-control imperatives) that are unconscious because the ego cannot make them consistent with any reality principle. Because the drives are unconscious, they are not self-control; nonetheless, they originate in early failures by the child at self-control or countercontrol; and the outcome is a very rigid personality—punctual, systematic, undeviating, and xenophobic.

THE PHALLIC STAGE AND POSSIBILITY III.   Freud implicitly identified the phallic stage (about ages 3–6) as the context for the most important determinant of adult behavior.[14] During that stage a boy allegedly comes to (1) long for sexual relations with his mother, (2) hate his father as a rival, (3) suffer from castration fear, and (4) repress his infantile sexuality as a step in superego development. Freud designated that sequence of events as the Oedipus complex and attributed much of adult male neuroses to it.

It is puzzling that Freud frequently attributed a particular neurosis to specific events, such as a boy witnessing adult copulation, seeing a naked female, or being threatened by his mother or nurse that his father will castrate him (e.g., Freud, 1964-XXIII:78–80). Such attributions suggest that accidental events are sufficient for neurosis; yet time and again Freud suggested that the Oedipus complex is universal for all boys. But how can accidental events result in a universal? Even though emphasizing accidental events in particular cases, Freud never claimed that those events are necessary for the Oedipus complex; but if being threatened by castration is not necessary for castration fear, why is the fear supposedly universal? The answer appears to be "phylogenetic" or "instinctive" (see, e.g., Freud: 1964-XXIII:99), not just in connection with castration fear but also with other facets of the Oedipus complex and libidinal stages.

The claim is not that Freud contradicted himself.[15] Perhaps he meant that certain accidental events make the Oedipus complex more traumatic (see, e.g., Freud, 1964-XIII:191). Thus, even if all boys come to fear castration regardless of experience, seeing a naked female accentuates the fear.

Although Freud was preoccupied with the Oedipus complex, he had little to say about specific personality traits as correlates. For that matter, Freud attributed various personality traits and neuroses (e.g., anxiety, perversion) to the Oedipus complex without explaining such diverse manifestations. His arguments cannot be an adequate explanation of such diversity unless expanded to conditions that he never emphasized, nor can the conditions be the kind of problematical events stressed by Freud in analyzing particular clinical cases, because his explanations of those cases appear ad hoc.

If a boy perceives his father as having power over the boy's mother and his mother as having power over him (possibility III in Figure 10–1), the boy's envy of his father becomes more understandable. However, the Freudian tradition of confusing conjecture and evidence should not be perpetuated. In this case the conjecture extends to a generalization about a correlate of a triadic power relation in any context, familial or otherwise. If *Z* is controlled by *Y* and perceives *X* as having power over *Y*, *Z* will envy *X*.

Nothing has been said to contradict or affirm Freud's arguments about infantile sexuality and castration fear. Those features of the Oedipus complex can be left an open question. If a boy does long for sexual relations with his mother and perceives his father as an effective sexual rival, then the boy's envy of his father may well be intensified; but envy can be anticipated without assuming infantile sexuality. Similarly, a perceived threat of castration is a power perception, but the boy could come to the perception without that threat over him. The early rough-and-tumble behavior of father and son is sufficient for the boy to perceive the father's coercive control capacity, and systematic research (see Johnson's literature survey, 1982:5) indicates that fathers are more likely to punish their sons.

The control argument makes it possible to predict variations in features of the Oedipus complex from knowledge of familial power relations. Briefly illustrating, whereas possibility III in familial power relations (Figure 10–1), could generate envy of the father by the boy, possibility IV could generate both envy and hatred. What of possibilities V and VI? The question cannot be answered at present, and the same is true of the other 58 possibilities in the case of the boy as the third triad member and perceiver. But that admission does not negate the claim that the principal features of the Oedipus complex are contingent on familial power relations in potentially demonstrable ways.[16] If personality is shaped appreciably by familial power relations, the variety of those relations is consistent with the variety of personality traits.

The control argument is important for two reasons. First, it suggests how the Oedipus complex results in diverse neuroses and personality traits but without ad hoc attributions of significance to accidental events.[17] Second, it anticipates systematic variation in features of the Oedipus complex among social units (countries, social classes, etc.) and over time. The second reason entails a credible assumption—familial power relations vary appreciably.

The Contrast between the Sexes

Freud assumed that men and women differ psychologically in fundamental ways, much of which he attributed to a sexual contrast in the Oedipus complex (he did not use the term *Electra complex*). In describing the female counterpart of the Oedipus complex, Freud argued that the girl's maternal hostility commences with the belief that her mother gave the girl too little milk, and the hostility is augmented by the mother forbidding the girl pleasurable genital activity. However, because Freud did not indicate why his argument is limited to girls, the basic sexual contrast appears to be the girl's penis envy. According to Freud, the girl holds her mother responsible for her "disability," and the girl turns to the father as a substitute love object. Freud is obscure as to the reason for that outcome, but he does state: "In the absence of fear of castration the chief motive is lacking which leads boys to surmount the Oedipus complex. Girls remain in it for an indeterminate length of time; they demolish it late and, even so, incompletely. In these circumstances the formation of the super ego must suffer. . . ." (1964-XXII:129). Freud acknowledged that feminists take exception, but their reaction is hardly surprising. His argument implies that the superegos of women are somehow inferior; and Stoller (1980:594) speaks of Freud's "belief that women were less moral, more envious, more insincere, more narcissistic than—and therefore inferior to—men. . . ."

A "control" interpretation differs from Freud's in several respects. For one thing, he ignored possibility III (Figure 10–1) in familial power relations, wherein the "daddy's girl" status gives the girl a basis for controlling her father, meaning that she initiates or tolerates much of their cuddling (speculation, but Johnson's literature survey [1982:5] indicates that fathers flirt more with daughters than mothers with sons). Again, however, the control argument neither contradicts nor affirms Freud's claim about infantile sexuality. Whether a girl suffers from penis envy and longs for a sexual relation with her father, she has a special relation with him. The girl may view her mother as a rival, as Freud claimed; but the girl's power relations alone could generate hostility. As in the boy's case, the mother's control of the girl generates ambivalence; but in the girl's case there is another source of hostility. The mother's control is inconsistent with the girl's perception of having power over the father and the father's power over the mother (i.e., the girl perceives power as intransitive).

The more general and important point is the possibility that boys and girls perceive familial power relations differently. Their perceptions may or may not be realistic; in any case, the sexual perceptual difference could vary appreciably among social units and over time. The difference has yet to be demonstrated systematically, but it is much more amenable to research (see, e.g., Hadley and Jacob, 1976) than are Freud's conjectures.

Socio-cultural Relativity

Freud ignored the possibility of persons other than parents or children playing major roles in familial power relations. That is not surprising given certain features of European marriages and households in Freud's lifetime.

The marriages were frequently neolocal, and the residential unit was more oriented to the nuclear family than the extended family. Most important, the typical European family at that time is thought of today as patriarchal; the husband-father largely monopolized ultimate control (see, e.g., van Dam, 1980:583). So it is hardly puzzling that Freud was insensitive to this question: What if the *biological father* exercises negligible control over other nuclear family members? Such a condition was approximated among the Nayars, and even the patriarchal-matriarchal distinction suggests that the father's power is not a universal constant. Yet Freud never recognized the possibility that his arguments are valid only if patricontrol is universal, a special case of a more general criticism—Freud ignored socio-cultural differences. Again, however, it is vacuous to argue that Freud should be restated so as to recognize socio-cultural relativity. Even the term *family constitution* is far too vague, but it is strategic because of Malinowski's critique of Freud.

MALINOWSKI'S ARGUMENTS.   The Trobriand Islands are of special relevance in assessing Freud's theory because Trobriand descent is matrilineal and authority over a woman and her children is exercised by her brother (the avunculate). The husband-father is more nearly the wife-mother's sexual companion and friend of his children; he is supposedly not even identified as genitor. Hence, so Malinowski argued: "in the matrilineal society of the Trobriands the wish is to marry the sister and to kill the maternal uncle" (1955:76).

Malinowski's claim that the Trobriand boy's hostility is directed toward his uncle contradicts Freud's theory, and there is a crucial implication. If Trobriand boys' hostility stems from the uncle's authority rather than sexual rivalry, then even in Freud's Europe the father's authority may have created the hostility Freud attributed to the Oedipus complex.

The immediate problem in assessing Malinowski's argument is the vagueness of Freud's theory. Although Freud did emphasize sexual rivalry, he never explicitly denied the relevance of the authority relation. Of course, Oedipal hostility could stem from both sexual rivalry and the authority relation; and it is unfortunate that Malinowski did not really answer this question: To what extent did a Trobriand boy view his maternal uncle as a sexual rival?

REACTIONS TO MALINOWSKI.   Given the import of Malinowski's argument, reactions to it have been strange. Unsurprisingly, most anthropologists evidently accept the argument, but why have numerous psychoanalysts accepted it (Spiro's claim, 1982:1) without attempting to alter psychoanalytic theory? Strangest of all, only Spiro's critique of Malinowski became well-known.

Spiro characterized Malinowski's observations as incomplete, inconsistent, or irrelevant. To illustrate (Spiro, 1982:30): "No where in any of his writings does Malinowski provide an on-the-ground description of the relationship between the boy and his uncle. Instead, he states jural norms and formulates abstract generalizations." Malinowski's arguments fare little better, but one example must suffice (Spiro, 1982:19): "Malinowski's finding concerning the absence of conscious incestuous desires for the mother in Trobriand adult sons not only is consistent with Oedipal theory, but—contrary to his assumption—is required by it." Like Freud and his disciples, Spiro would have it both ways; whether or not a boy expresses incestuous desires for his mother, his behavior corroborates Freud's theory.

Spiro failed to recognize that the observations in the typical contemporary anthropological report are no more defensible than Malinowski's. Moreover, Spiro uses the same kind of observations (e.g., alleged myths, customs, reports of dreams) to refute Malinowski; and he appears indifferent to the point that Freud never remotely answered this question: What is evidence of the presence of the Oedipus complex in a social unit? Until that question is answered to the satisfaction of both defenders and critics of Freud, assessments of "Oedipal theory" are pointless.

THE NECESSITY OF A CONTROL TERMINOLOGY. Whatever the evidence of the Oedipus complex, it will be difficult to demonstrate an association between that evidence and features of family life as described in conventional terms. Thus, to label a family as *patriarchal* is an extremely vague characterization. The same is true even of statements that a woman's brother has *authority* over her sons, and the term has been used here only in keeping with convention.

An empirically applicable definition of patriarchal or authority requires a control terminology and recognition that amount of control is a quantitative variable. It is arbitrary to say that once some kind of control reaches a particular level the family is patriarchal or matriarchal, but arbitrariness is preferred to the uncritical use of the terms. Moreover, the terms *patriarchal* and *authority* should be abandoned eventually and replaced by a concern with questions about family members. First, how much does each member attempt to control other members? Second, how effective are those attempts? And, third, how does each member perceive the capacity of other members for control? For some purposes the questions may focus on certain means of control (e.g., corporal punishment) over certain kinds of behavior (e.g., where a child sleeps); but such considerations are secondary to two general arguments: (1) authority is a control phenomenon and (2) research along the lines indicated is feasible (see, e.g., Hadley and Jacob, 1976). True, in testing a theory dyads could be classified as to the predominant kind of power relation, in which case the distinctions would be qualitative (i.e., X does not perceive Y as capable of controlling Z). Nonetheless, a control terminology is necessary to define power relations.

NOTES

1. McHugh (1968:8): "According to this view, the same events or objects can have different meanings for different people, and the degree of difference will produce comparable differences in behavior."

2. The most obvious possible exception is Expectation States Theory or EST (e.g., Berger et al., 1974; Ridgeway and Berger, 1986; and the brief survey by Fararo and Skvoretz, 1986). However, the "theory" appears to be more nearly a vast effort to answer this question: How does interaction generate and depend on the expectations of those involved? Indeed, Berger's characterization (in Berger et al., 1974:3) of EST as a "theoretical research program" is telling, as is this statement by Fararo and Skvoretz (1986:592): "expectation states theory . . . formulates (*sic*) discrete theories. . . ." So inconclusive debates as to relevant evidence (see *American Journal of Sociology*, July, 1986, 162 and 178) are hardly surprising. In any case, the research findings reported in connection with EST do bear on this control principle (10–1): Variation in the means of attempted control and submission to or rejection of control attempts are a function of the expectations of those involved in that particular interactional situation. To the extent that "expectations" in Expectation States Theory have no phenomenological basis (see Fararo and Skvoretz's commentary, 1986:593), the theory is obscure.

3. Presuming, of course, that the statement is empirically contingent, but the logical status of statements made by interpretive sociologists is commonly obscure. Consider Goffman's statement: "Games, then, are world-building activities" (1961b:27). To all such statements, the only reasonable response is something like this: "Yes, you can say that." But surely one must wonder at the same time: Isn't this mere phrase-making? Where is this taking us? What is the ultimate goal of sociologists who specialize in such statements? Why is training in sociology necessary to make such statements? Couldn't philosophers or journalists make them just as well? Yet such statements are not peculiar to interpretive sociology; they are an art form among French structuralists (e.g., Foucault).

4. Observe that *meaning* is the key term in Blumer's statement (1969:2) of the three premises of symbolic interactionism, and the term appears frequently in Stryker's especially informative commentary on developments in symbolic interactionism (1981:15).

5. Note, however, that values can be described or thought of in terms of control, one tenable assumption being that values are reflected in what people attempt to control and the way they make those attempts.

6. There are two taxonomic questions when observing any act in conducting research on control. First, was the act control? And, second, if the act was control, what type? The conceptualization of control in chapters 2 and 3 may have to be modified to realize sufficient agreement in answers to the questions (especially the second) by independent observers, but note that the terminology of many observations in the literature precludes application of the conceptualization. Consider Black's summary (1984c:5) of van den Steenhoven's observations: "Netsilik Eskimo parents may subtly encourage their children to destroy an offender's cache of food, so that what appears to be mischief or vandalism

may actually be a carefully orchestrated act of revenge." It appears that such an act by an Eskimo parent was a control attempt, but the phrase "subtly encourage" is far too vague to permit an identification of the type of control. Unfortunately, the literature of sociological and anthropological field studies, even the classics (e.g., Whyte, 1955; Liebow, 1967) is replete with similar phrases or terms, such as: *persuaded them, convinced her, led the group to do it, deal with*. In that connection, acceptance of an empirically applicable notion as central furthers the integration of research and theory, because the notion's conceptualization provides researchers and theorists with a common language.

7.   Various procedures for research on control are not so identified because those who developed them did not employ a control terminology (e.g., Eve, 1986; Wilson, 1980), but a few investigators (e.g., Manderschied et al., 1982) have developed methods for observing and recording control behavior. Unfortunately, however, no one has taken the lead in developing methods for research on control at the macro level.

8.   The term *personality* is used to characterize Freud's theory (or theories, as the case may be) with doubts about its appropriateness, especially since in recent years those who write from a psychoanalytic perspective and psychiatrists in particular (see, e.g., Greenspan and Pollock, 1980) rarely discuss personality. For that matter, the term *personality* has the unfortunate consequence of suggesting that Freud's theory should interest only psychologists or psychiatrists.

9.   The most appropriate term is *character of familial control* because it prompts recognition that any family member can learn from or otherwise be influenced by the control attempts of any other member. The point takes on added significance in light of the finding (see Currie, 1985:206) that violent children are especially likely to come from violent families, especially ones in which the father displays severe violence against the mother.

10.   Freud dimly recognized that children perceive the capacity for control, but he did not grasp the implications. For example, he argued (1959-IX:220) that children come to adopt "what may be called a *sadistic view of coition*. They see it as something that the stronger participant is forcibly inflicting on the weaker. . . ." Yet Freud never confronted this question: Could that conception of coition (call it sadistic or not) stem from the child's perception of the father as having the capacity to control the mother?

11.   Should it be claimed that "environmentalist" versions of Freud (see Anthony's survey, 1980:210–35) take control and familial power relations into account, those versions are as vague and vacuous as the "culturalist" versions.

12.   As evidence of a possible connection between omnipotence and control phenomena, contemplate Stein's argument: "Since it is impossible to avoid making some mistakes in an active practice of medicine, a . . . physician develops the belief that he is omnipotent and omniscient, and therefore incapable of making mistakes. . . . The feelings of omnipotence become generalized to other areas of his life. . . . in 1964 and 1965 physicians had a fatal-accident rate four times as high as the average for all other private pilots. . . . The trouble, suggested an FAA official, is that too many doctors fly with 'the feeling that they are omnipotent' " (1967:701). The suggestion is that the "control" character of an occupation has an impact on the nonoccupational behavior of incumbents. To

be sure, such speculation takes us far from Freud, but that is precisely the point (for an illustrative line of research on personality and control, see Strube and Werner, 1985).

13. See Freud's commentary (1961-XXI:218) on the narcisstic libidinal type. However, it is not claimed that the present characterization of the narcisstic personality type is entirely consistent with Freud. For that matter, his observations on the traits of particular personality or character types are commonly vague and inconsistent (in the case of the narcisstic type, compare Freud in the *same* volume, 1961-XXI: 83 and 218).

14. Some writers on psychoanalytic theory use the term *genital* and others use the term *phallic* even when referring to some early years of life (for illustrations, see Greenspan and Pollock, 1980-I, passim), and even the same writer (e.g., Parens, 1980:462–64) may use the two terms in a confusing way.

15. Yet Freud made himself vulnerable to all manner of justified criticisms. Illustrating briefly, an army of scholars has described his arguments about, among other things, the primal horde and the Moses-monotheism connection (Freud, 1964-XXIII:7–137) as seas of conjecture. Then there are numerous and startling reversals or inconsistencies in Freud's conclusions. Two examples must suffice. Freud based his first general theory of neuroses on the postulation of actual pedophiliac practices (the "seduction" hypothesis), only to conclude shortly after that the traumatic childhood experiences reported by his adult patients were sexual fantasies (see, e.g., Anthony, 1980:205–6). Then in 1925, Freud declared that the postulated Oedipal conflict began about age four, but by 1940 the commencement age had become two (see van Dam, 1980:575). Such reversals and inconsistencies give rise to this question: How can any of Freud's conclusions be accepted?

16. The same is true for the onset age, duration, and even the existence of Freud's three libidinal stages, except they must be thought of in terms of various types or kinds of control rather than only in terms of familial power relations. There is no basis whatever to assume that the success/failure ratio of control attempts is even approximately uniform from one infant to the next over the first 18 months of life, or even that the average of that ratio varies negligibly from one putative "culture" to the next. A denial of enormous variation in the character of control in toilet training would be an even greater absurdity. The argument that the character of each libidinal stage is contingent on related control properties is all the more plausible in light of observations made even by psychoanalysts in recent decades, many of which generate doubts about the onset age, duration, and even the sequence of Freud's libidinal stages (see, e.g., Greenspan and Pollock, 1980-I:444, 448, 575).

17. More important, it is possible to describe and think about neuroses, psychoses, and personality traits in terms of control without any reference to the Oedipus complex or the libidinal stages. Mirowsky and Ross (1983) have provided an illustration in their research on paranoia. Brenner unwittingly supplied illustrations in his formula for anxiety prevention or defense—"if I do 'A,' (the defense), then 'B' (the danger) will not happen"—and for depressive affect—"If I do 'A,' then 'B' will change. It will stop happening, or it will stop making me suffer

so, or both" (1975:17). Even if the formulas operate at the unconscious level, the very idea of doing implies an attempt at control of something. That point is not made by Brenner, because those who write from the psychoanalytical perspective are prone to describe overt behavior in vague and very abstract terms—mastering, shaping the environment, adapting, etc. If those terms mean anything at all, they refer to a series of control attempts of one kind or another. Of course, psychoanalysts may use the term *control* infrequently because they want to avoid the suggestion that the behavior in question is intentional in the conscious and deliberate sense, but control has not been conceptualized that way in this book.

Formalism: Sociological Structuralism and Network Analysis

Sociologists rarely recognize the extreme diversity of their field's subject matter, let alone attempt to reduce it; and "formalism" is the only perspective that manifests a concern with the problem. It can be described as an implicit delimitation of sociology's subject matter that ostensibly ignores the substantive features of human behavior.[1] One of two versions should be labeled *sociological structuralism*, because its advocates argue that sociologists should be concerned exclusively with social structure. Whereas structuralists depict social structure as somehow removed from human behavior, advocates of "network analysis" recognize human behavior but largely in connection only with social interaction or social relations, concepts that emphasize form rather than content. The two formalisms may be reconcilable; but in light of several contrasts, especially terminology and research focus, they are treated here as though distinct perspectives.

Some Distinctive Features of Sociological Structuralism

Like other sociological perspectives, structuralism has roots in the distant past, but a coherent interpretation of structuralism requires a particular focus on the publications of contemporary advocates, especially Peter Blau. Even that focus does not avoid the need to stress possible misinterpretations.

Three Likely Misinterpretations

Although *structuralism* is an appropriate label for Blau's brand of sociology, the term is also used, even by some sociologists, to denote the works of a circle of scholars who never claimed to be sociologists, notably Claude Levi-

Strauss and Michel Foucault. In recognition of the predominant nationality of the circle's early members, their views are commonly identified as "French structuralism." There are various differences between French structuralism and sociological structuralism, but nothing would be gained by suggesting that the former is not sociological (especially in light of Rossi, 1982). Sociology's fragmentation is now such that virtually any point of view in the social and behavioral sciences or the humanities could be construed as sociological for one reason or another. Moreover, when it comes to characterizing the content of French structuralism, any statement is debatable. Levi-Strauss apparently subscribed to something like this principle: All socio-cultural phenomena stem from the "deep structure" of the human psyche. Vague though the principle is, one would be hard-pressed to demonstrate that it guided Foucault's work (see, especially, his *Discipline and Punish*, 1977). Foucault's only discernible principle is something like this: Socio-cultural phenomena are explained when they are described evocatively.

French structuralism is the apogee of antipositivism (see Clarke, especially 1981:1); but since the term *positivism* is now little more than a derogatory label, it is again necessary to indicate the sense in which the term is used in this book. Positivism is nothing more or less than the insistence that predictive power be taken as the primary criterion when assessing the merits of empirical or scientific theories. That criterion cannot be fully applied without systematic tests of the theory in question, and systematic tests in turn require that the theory be stated so that statements can be deduced from its premises by explicit rules. Those statements are potentially falsifiable predictions only to the extent that their constituent terms are empirically applicable.

The ideas, arguments, and observations of French structuralists are stated so discursively that it would be a travesty to identify any of their statements as a theory, let alone a testable theory. Even more telling, French structuralists display an indifference if not hostility to the idea of systematically stated and testable theories. After all, the very idea smacks of positivism, and French structuralists have ably demonstrated the end product of antipositivism—the license to say what one will as long as someone finds it interesting.

Unlike French structuralists, sociological structuralists have not embraced antipositivism. To the contrary, of well-known sociological theorists, Blau (especially 1977) has few rivals when it comes to the systematic statement of theories; and he obviously regards tests as essential for assessments of a theory (e.g., Blau et al., 1984).

STRUCTURALISM-FUNCTIONALISM. Structure-function was once a staple in the sociological vocabulary, but it is not a meaningful term. By contrast, though rarely used by sociologists, "structuralism-functionalism" is meaningful, because it can be construed as a combination of two perspectives, sociological structuralism (as described in this chapter) and functionalism (as described in chapter 9). But, as such, "structuralism-functionalism" would be a totally inappropriate characterization of Blau's brand of sociology. Blau's explanations appear to be "causal," meaning that he purports to identify the causes of the *explanandum*, not its alleged effects.

Any term pertaining to structuralism-functionalism is likely to suggest some erroneous connection between Parsons (especially 1951) and Blau. Although Parsons never tired of using the term *structure*, he used it as a sponge concept (without an explicit and coherent definition), evidently to create the impression that Parsonian sociology is macro, when in reality many of his key terms were explicated only in connection with individuals or dyads (Parsons's ego and alter). Even the extent to which Parsons's explanations are genuinely functional is debatable. The point commonly overlooked in commentaries on Parsons is that he offered sociologists a smorgasbord, with dishes to attract all but positivists and Marxists. Hence, Parsons's penchant for discursive theories and his peculiar eclecticism set him apart from Blau.

LOOK NOT TO SIMMEL.   Although Blau occasionally refers to Simmel as an intellectual ancestor, the reference does not clarify sociological structuralism. Blau's emphasis on the importance of population size (or number of group members) is consistent with Simmel, but that consistency does not really link Blau and Simmel. More important, Simmel's abiding interest (e.g., 1950:40–57 and 181–303) in forms of human association or interaction—domination, subordination, cooperation, conflict, etc.—is a reason for thinking of Simmel's sociology as "formalism"; but that interest is much more in keeping with network analysis than with Blau's structural concepts or his research.

Most important, Simmel's work hardly suggests any distinct conception of sociology's subject matter; rather, it suggests an enormous range of interests, perhaps unrivalled among major figures in sociology's history.[2] That diversity is alien to sociological structuralism, Blau's version or any other.

Blau's Sociological Structuralism

Throughout his career Blau has been concerned with formulating theories more than a perspective; hence, direct quotations would not fully reveal his conception of sociology's subject matter or questions about it. Nonetheless, Blau's works (e.g., 1977, Blau and Schwartz, 1984) indicate that he would use the term *social structure* to designate sociology's subject matter. The problem is that sociologists use the term in diverse ways (see Homans's survey, 1975), each of which is either so vague as to preclude empirical application or so broad as to include virtually all collective features of human behavior. As an illustration of the latter, examine Blau's definition: "Social structure refers to the patterns discernible in social life, the regularities observed, the configurations detected" (1975b:3). Now consider unquestioned patterns in official U.S. suicide rates, such as the increase among white females up to about age 50 and then a gradual decline (Gibbs, 1982c). If that variation does not qualify as a component or feature of social structure by Blau's definition, then the definition is ambiguous; but if it does qualify, one must surely wonder what collective feature of human behavior would not qualify. The meaning of the phrase "collective features of human behavior" is obscure unless this: any attribute or property of the behavior of two or more humans considered together. As such, if the phrase is equated with the term *social structure*, the term denotes a hodgepodge.

Another complication stems from Blau's claim that "social structures are observable aspects of social life" (1977:2). On the same page he admits that "social structures are not empirical phenomena in the raw but abstractions from them in terms of a conceptual scheme"; and still later: "Social structure is . . . not an object that can be observed directly" (244). Such contradictory statements make the meaning of social structure all the more confusing, and Blau's claim that social structures are observable is symptomatic of superorganicism.

Superorganicists ignore this question: If terms pertaining to collective phenomena denote observable entities, why are their definitions always controversial and difficult? Blau's admission that social structures are abstractions is relevant because arbitrary distinctions abound in definitions of highly abstract notions. Such distinctions can be avoided by a vague definition and/or one so broad that it delimits a hodgepodge, and Blau opted for that strategy.

Because Blau's structuralism is a sociological version of superorganicism, what has been said of his definition of social structure extends to definitions of society and culture by superorganicists. The defects of those definitions are not obvious because superorganicists do not consider problems and issues in identifying and delimiting the boundaries of societies or cultures. In particular, they have ignored the difficulties encountered by human ecologists in delimiting natural areas, communities, or neighborhoods (see Micklin and Choldin, 1984:239–45).

BLAU'S KEY STRUCTURAL CONCEPTS.   Blau's definition of social structure (*supra*) is inconsistent with his other conceptual statements, most of which suggest a much narrower notion. That is especially true of the statements in Blau's preface to his "macrosociological" theory of social structure (1977:ix) as follows: "Social structure is conceptualized in terms of these elemental properties: different social positions, the number of their incumbents, and the implications of differentiation among positions for social relations. Of major substantive concern are the influences of social differentiation on social integration. Social differentiation is defined by the distributions of a population among social positions. Inequality and heterogeneity are the two generic forms differentiation assumes, depending on whether the positions among which people are distributed constitute a rank order, as socio-economic status and power do, or are unordered categories, like religion and sex. A fundamental characteristic of social structures is the degree to which various forms of inequality and heterogeneity intersect or the extent to which social differences along various lines are correlated. Variations in this structural condition govern largely the strength of the integration of the different segments of society."

Blau distinguishes two social positions, groups and status (1977:7): "All characteristics of people that influence their role relations are designated either as group membership or as status; if such characteristics classify people categorically, the nominal categories are defined as groups; if they classify them in rank order, they are defined as status." Blau neither defines "role relation" nor stipulates a procedure for judging whether a given characteristic influences role relations. Moreover, consider his earlier statement (1977:4): "The defining criterion of a distinction in social positions is that the role relations among incumbents of the same position differ, on the average, from those between incumbents of different positions." So it appears that role relations identify positions, but Blau's earlier statement indicates that positions influence role relations. By definition a characteristic that identifies members of a group or status incumbents is something that influences their role relations.

Even ignoring the foregoing contradiction, Blau's conceptual statements about a group and his illustrations are puzzling. Blau writes that (1977:7): "The term *group* . . . includes any category of people who share an attribute that influences their role relations. . . . This criterion unequivocally distinguishes groups from arbitrary categories of unconnected aggregates. . . ." But because national origin and language are two examples (1977:8) of the "nominal parameters" that enter into the identification of groups, Blau's conceptualization lumps "groups" in the interactional or organizational sense (e.g., primary groups and associations) with such aggregates as "English-born" and "English-speaking."

Now consider income, power, and intelligence as examples of the graduated parameters that in Blau's scheme (1977:8) identify statuses. First off, any related category is bound to be extremely arbitrary. Moreover, definitions of power and intelligence are notoriously divergent, and none promises sufficient empirical applicability. For that matter, if "intelligence" categories are statuses, what of weight, popularity, and friendliness? So it is difficult to think of graduated categories of humans that would not be statuses.

How do social structures differ? Blau's statement about elemental properties suggests this answer: number of positions, inequality, heterogeneity, and intersection. To Blau's credit, he stipulated formulas for, or at least illustrated, the measurement of all four properties, but many of his structural concepts (he did not recognize the concept-construct distinction) cannot be defined in terms of those four properties.[3] Finally, note that in Blau's scheme even with only two sets of mutually exclusive positions (e.g., a set of income categories and a set of educational categories), seven values would be needed to describe the social structure—one value denoting the total number of position sets, one value denoting the total number of positions, two values pertaining to intraset heterogeneity (one for each set), two values pertaining to intraset inequality, and an intersection value for each pair of sets of positions (only one pair in this case).

SOME AMBIGUITIES. It is not clear whether Blau regards the nature (or "content") of positions as properties of social structure. Imagine two communities, in one of which there are three religious groups but no racial differentiation, and in the other there are three distinct racial groups but no religious differentiation. Because Blau admits to a "quantitative conception of social structure," the two communities could have social structures with identical quantitative properties (the same number of sets of positions, the same number of positions, and the same distributional forms) despite sharp contrasts as to the nature of the positions.

Because Blau speaks frequently of broad kinds of heterogeneity or inequality (e.g., sex, religion, income), it appears that he does recognize the nature of positions. But how would he recognize the difference if in one community there are only Jews, Catholics, and Muslims, while in another community only Methodists, Baptists, and Presbyterians? The general point is that Blau never entertains this question: What concepts and measurement methods should be used to describe the nature of positions (i.e., their qualities or content)? The question becomes all the more important and difficult when contemplating cross-cultural comparisons, a kind of research Blau has not undertaken. Indeed, Blau admits that his theory "ignores cultural differences, and another theory is required to deal with them" (1977:245). But even the admission is ambiguous. Does Blau mean that the nature of positions are entirely irrelevant?

Another ambiguity in Blau's scheme is more complicated. Although he makes frequent reference to social relations, it is not clear whether they are components of social structure. His definition of social structure creates one of two reasons for doubt, and the other is this statement (Blau, 1977:246): "The theory . . . explains patterns of social relations in terms of properties of social structure. . . ."

Blau's use of the term *social relations* is all the more confusing because he also refers to *role relation*, *association*, and *interaction* as though all four are logically interrelated but without defining them so as to make their meaning distinct or to clarify logical connections. In particular, at various points Blau writes as though each of the following three pairs of terms are synonyms: (1) social relation-role relation, (2) social relation-association, and (3) association-interaction. Even if social relation and association are not synonyms in Blau's conceptual scheme, at no point does he confront this question: What kinds and amounts of association or interaction constitute a social relation or role relation?

For that matter, Blau does not recognize that his statements about and method for measuring position "intersection" are inconsistent with his observation (1977:3) that the component parts of social structure are linked through social relations. To illustrate, suppose that in a particular community two percent of all economically active Protestants are physicians and of all physicians 80 percent are Protestants. Those figures would bear on the intersection of those two positions, but in no sense do they describe the social relation between physicians and Protestants, physicians and non-Protestants, non-physicians and Protestants, or non-physicians and non-Protestants. Similarly, excluding rates of intermarriage (see Blau et al., 1984), it is disputable whether any of the measures in Blau's research describe social relations.

The defects in Blau's conceptual scheme stem from the reifications that are inherent in sociological structuralism and the way that structuralists treat the notion of social structure (for elaboration see Maynard and Wilson, 1980). Like other structuralists, Blau does not fully recognize that his major terms denote abstractions from human behavior; consequently, the statements into which those terms enter are vague and riddled with contradictions.

QUESTIONS ABOUT SOCIOLOGY'S SUBJECT MATTER. A multitude of terms appear in the axioms or theorems of Blau's theory (1977), some being: *discrimination, social mobility, elite, superordinate role, fertility, immigration, group pressures, segregation, social resources, conflict, friendship, ideology, urbanization, efficient means of transportation, physical propinquity, density, cohesion, division of labor, linguistic heterogeneity, authority, and power*. Blau does not even suggest how some of those terms can be defined by reference to social structure properties, and it is difficult to see how they could be so defined. Accordingly, if social structure is sociology's subject matter, then many of the variables in Blau's theory are not sociological.

Should sociologists adopt Blau's structuralism, they would be committed to this thesis (Blau, 1977:x): "that the structures of objective social positions among which people are distributed exert more fundamental influences on social life than do cultural values and norms. . . ." Why should sociologists be content to demonstrate that structural variables explain more variation in, say, the homicide rate than do cultural values or norms? Surely there is an alternative: consider any independent variable, whatever its nature, that contributes substantially to an explanation of variation in the dependent variable. To do otherwise is to pay a very high price for the purity offered by sociological structuralism.

Mayhew's Version of Structuralism

Although Bruce Mayhew (especially 1980, 1981) does more than Blau toward formulating structuralism's epistemology, his attempted summary of its distinctive features is more confusing than informative. He makes the

Table 11-1.   From Mayhew (1980: Table 1).

	Difference in assumptions and concerns corresponding roughly to:	
Psychologism		Sociologism
Individual (individualism)	(Unit of analysis)	Social Network (structuralism)
Inside (subjectivism)	(Location of observer)	Outside (objectivism)
Essentialist	(Construction of phenomena)	Analyst
Ideal	(Prime movers are)	Material
Voluntarism (free will)	(Dynamic assumed)	Mechanism (impersonal constraint)
Ideographic (interpretation: humanist)	(Understanding mode)	Nomothetic (explanation: naturalist)
Consensus	(Basis for association)	Conflict
The present	(Time frame for study)	All history and prehistory
Parochial	(Location of inquiry)	Cross-cultural

attempt by listing contrasts between "psychologism" and "sociologism," as shown in Table 11-1.

Given Mayhew's concern with individualism and structuralism, his shift to "psychologism" and "sociologism" is puzzling; and his observations on particular sociologists is a study in inconsistencies. Thus, he identifies Durkheim with sociologism but only to recognize that Durkheim is not a conflict theorist (1980:336). Then he identifies Homans with psychologism, only to recognize that Homans's style of explanation is nomothetic (1980:336); and Homans's commitment to operant psychology is contrary to what Mayhew's tabular scheme implies—that Homans advocates voluntarism and subjectivism. Then it scarcely helps to be told (Mayhew, 1980:337) that "many" Marxists are structuralists but some structuralists are not Marxists. Finally, there are some blatant contradictions, such as (Mayhew, 1981:633): "The claim by some structuralists that supra-individual social facts are a reality *sui generis* is an essentialist position."

The Seeming Indifference to Human Behavior

If structuralists "do not study human behavior" (Mayhew, 1980:339), then their perspective reduces the diversity of sociology's subject matter enormously; but Mayhew's claim is disputable. What do structuralists study if not human behavior? Consider one version of Mayhew's answer (1980:338): "in this *structuralist* conception of social life, sociologists are studying a communication network mapped on some human population. That network, the interaction which proceeds through it, and the social structures which emerge in it are the subject matter of sociology." Communication is not behavior? Interaction is not behavior? Unless Mayhew answers in the negative, his claim that structuralists do not study human behavior is logomachy.

Mayhew's claim that structuralists do not study human behavior is far more radical than it may appear. Consider this statement (Mayhew, 1980:359): "humans and their actions are—from the structuralist point of view—biological phenomena." Must structuralists label human behavior as biological phenomena to justify their purported indifference to it? Then examine another startling statement (Mayhew, 1980:347): "Structuralists find symbols stored in either the biological memory banks of humans or in the external memory banks of material culture: writing in books . . . numbers in computers . . . paintings on cave walls . . . etc." How can use of the term *memory banks* possibly justify denying that writing books and painting cave walls are human behavior?

Mayhew's views have not been described to ridicule them. Although his views are so radical that many other structuralists might deny them, Mayhew has rendered a service by indicating how structuralism can be a truly distinctive sociological perspective. For that matter, Mayhew has made explicit what many sociologists choose to leave implicit.

Sociology's Subject Matter and Questions about It

However narrow the delimitation of sociology's subject matter, questions about the subject matter's causes or consequences will generate diverse theories and lines of research. In that connection, Mayhew suggests that structuralists should not ask questions about the consequences that pertain to individuals or human behavior (1980:339–40). What questions would Mayhew have sociologists pursue? His answer is obscure for two reasons, commencing with his ambiguous identification of sociology's subject matter. Mayhew often refers to social networks as *sociology's subject matter*, but he also writes of *social organization* and *social structure* as though they are alternative designations. Yet those three terms are not synonyms. Only the term *social organization* is commonly used to denote a process; and while sex structure and age structure (Mayhew, 1980:359) may be dimensions of social structure, they are not "networks" dimensions. So it would appear that Mayhew's question for sociology must be formulated this way: How are social networks, social organization, and social structure related to other forms of organization? Mayhew (1980:338) indicates that "forms of organization" includes, in addition to social organization, the organization of information (symbols) and the organization of material (tools) without any further clarification. There is even a problem with

Mayhew's statement (1980:338) that structuralists are concerned with aggregate properties of population as well as emergent (purely structural) properties of organization itself. Rates of human behavior (e.g., robbery, suicide, migration) are properties of populations, but Mayhew has dismissed the study of human behavior as alien to structuralism.

Network Analysis

Unlike Mayhew, network analysts appear more concerned with developing methodologies and conceptualizations than with becoming explicit arbiters of "good" sociology; and they see themselves as unifying the social sciences (see, e.g., Berkowitz, 1982:158–59) rather than purging sociology of closet psychologists and misguided humanists.[4] Moreover, the constructs or concepts of network analysts differ conspicuously from Blau's. Yet there are some similarities, such as the references to Simmel as the most notable ancestor and the emphasis on the form rather than the content of social relations or interaction; and those similarities are the basis for characterizing network analysis and sociological structuralism as alternative versions of formalism.

The essential difference is only suggested by the more extensive use of graph theory in network analysis than in Blau's structuralism. Even if diagrams have less utility in network analysis than matrix representations (Knoke and Kuklinski, 1982:38), diagrams have more illustrative utility in network analysis than in Blau's structuralism. Expressed otherwise, network analysis is much more "topological," but the basic difference is that a line drawn in a network diagram typically signifies some kind of social relation. By contrast, although Blau uses the term *social relation* frequently, he emphasizes mensurable features of social structure that have no real bearing on social relations. The suggestion is not that Blau's structuralism must be inferior to network analysis; rather, they are different in that the latter ostensibly deals more directly with social relations, whereas Blau offers more in the way of analyzing the composition and statistical interrelations of population categories. Hence, his mode of representation is "tabular" not "graphic."

Conceptual Considerations

If distinctive terminology is indicative, network analysis will become sociology's most fully developed perspective. Consider this illustrative list: asymmetric path, bonded-ties, centrality, clique, clustering, connectedness, context diversity, continuous distance, degree of a point, density, duality, emanations, intensity, multiplexity, network cohesion, network closure, network isolation, network resilience, nodes, paths, path distance, range, reachability, structural balance, structural equivalence, and transitivity. The list is only illustrative and excludes several terms pertaining to the techniques of network analysis, such as *adjacency matrix, block-modeling, cluster analysis, dendogram, digraph, path distance matrix,* and *signed graph.*

Unlike other special sociological vocabularies (e.g., Parsons's), several network concepts are defined with impressive precision; and network analysts are concerned with measurement procedures to a point described by Fararo and Skvoretz as a "preoccupation" (1986:594). However, although more than superficial knowledge of mathematics is necessary to read many publications in its literature (e.g., Burt, 1982), network analysis is not "mathematical sociology" (see Berkowitz's commentary, 1982:159, but also Freeman, 1984).

The terminology of network analysis suggests a very distinctive version of formal sociology because it has nothing to do with any particular kind of human behavior. To illustrate, suppose that each line connecting points or nodes in a network signifies "friend," while those in another network signifies "enemies." Despite the contrast, both networks could be described in terms of "density."

The formal quality of network terminology will fail to impress only those sociologists who never worry about this question: How can a field with an indescribably diverse subject matter ever have a unified theory? Even if sociology's subject matter were reduced to social relations, their variety cannot be exaggerated; and although concepts could be developed to classify social relations, such work is not conducive to empirical questions. By contrast, contemplate this question: What is the association between density and centrality? The measures of density and centrality could be such that the question is indisputably empirical, and a question in the same form can be posed about virtually any two major network terms.

CONCEPTUAL PROBLEMS. The most immediate conceptual problem stems from the procedure employed by network analysts to gather "relational data." It is primarily survey research in which the survey questions are couched in the natural language of the respondents. Thus, in the case of English-speaking respondents, the key words or phrases in network survey questions are commonly like these: *friend, neighbor, kin, relative, those you respect, those you see often, close, important* (see, e.g., Marsden, 1987). Although those words or phrases may appear to have a perfectly clear meaning, it does not follow that they have the same meaning for even the majority of English speakers (see Fischer, 1982b). So doubts about the nature of "relational data" in network analysis are inevitable, and at bottom the problem is conceptual. That problem is illustrated by this question: If ego describes alter as being a friend, other than uncritical convention what justifies the conclusion that they have a social relation? That the problem haunts all survey research, whatever the perspective, is not a mitigation. Moreover, because network analysts have no conceptual basis for identifying social relations by reference to actual interactions, switching from survey research to observational research would not solve the problem.

Another problem is that network analysts make extensive use of sociological concepts and constructs. That usage contributes to the integration of network analysis and general sociology, but sociology's conceptualizations are disasters. Because no definition of any major sociological term (e.g., *social relation, status, social integration, social class, social resources*) appears logically defensible and sufficiently empirically applicable, network analysts are using defective tools. That is particularly true for the central network term—*social relation*. As argued in chapter 1, there is no defensible definition of that term in the sociological literature, and network analysts have not improved on those definitions. Their occasional use of the terms *connection* or *tie* may reflect recognition of conceptual problems with the notion of social relation, but merely switching to an undefined term is no solution. What has been said of social relations applies to all other terms that network analysts have borrowed from general sociology, such as *status, social resources, strong ties, weak ties,* and *social constraint*. Consider *status*. Network analysts commonly leave the term undefined, which may well be no worse than accepting any well-known definition. Because those definitions are merely loose metaphors (e.g., a status is a position), it is hardly surprising that network analysts often speak of *position, node,* or *point* rather than status; but those terms have a clear meaning only in connection with a graph, and what they signify sociologically is obscure.

To sum up, network analysis has not clarified sociological terminology; and as long as network analysts use borrowed terms uncritically, their work will suffer.[5] Critical usage could commence with recognition that many of the borrowed terms (e.g., *social resources, social support*) should be identified as constructs rather than concepts. Such identification would acknowledge that the term in question cannot be defined such that the definition is considered as complete and empirically applicable, but network analysts appear indifferent to the concept-construct distinction.

Although network analysts employ an impressive array of terms, scarcely any two of the major network concepts are logically (mathematically) independent. Consider *density* and *reachability* as illustrations. Density refers to the relative number of pairs of points directly connected in a network graph. Suppose the network comprises 10 points; there would be 45 unique pairs of points $N(N-1)/2$, some or all of which may be connected (see Freudenberg, 1986:30). Now suppose that 18 of the 45 pairs are directly connected; if so, that particular network's density would be .40, meaning that in 40 percent of the cases (pairs) there is a direct connection between the two points. "Reachability" appears to be a quite different concept; it refers to the path distance (average number of connections) between any two points in a network.

However, given maximum "density," then maximum "reachability" is logically necessary because each point is connected directly with any other point. Yet the two concepts are not totally redundant because as density declines reachability becomes problematic; but beyond some amount any further decline in density is necessarily associated with a decline in reachability.

Network analysts are aware that their major concepts are not entirely logically independent; and much of their work has been devoted to creating measures that are mathematically independent, such as a measure that expresses the actual amount of centrality relative to the maximum possible given the density level. Nonetheless, while some logical interrelations among a field's concepts are actually desirable, "partial redundancy" is the third major conceptual problem in network analysis.

Substantive Theory

Granted the potential of network analysis, it is far from being realized. Although it might be premature to demand a genuine network theory, network analysis is largely a terminology and a methodology in search of significant empirical questions (see, e.g., Marsden, 1987). Some works have come to be known as "network theories"; but even the authors suggest doubts about that identification, as when Granovetter (1983) refers to his "strength of weak ties" as a theory, as hypotheses, and as an argument.

INDEFENSIBLE QUESTIONS AND OBSCURE THEORIES.   Although "community" may appear a particularly appropriate subject for network analysis, the notion is so vague and defined so diversely that there is no warrant to take questions or arguments about it seriously. Yet that is precisely what Claude Fischer (1977, 1982a) did in a now well-known application of network terms and techniques. Fischer confronted the "decline-of-community" argument, which has been popular among sociologists for generations. While Fischer rightly treated the argument as an empirical question, an incontrovertible answer is precluded. The point is not just that those who make the argument never quite define "community" (a point Fischer recognized). Even if Fischer had employed network terms to arrive at an empirically applicable definition of "community," advocates of the decline-of-community argument never fully speak to two questions. First, in exactly what ways have human communities declined? Second, whatever has supposedly declined, how can it be demonstrated? Without a detailed answer, it is pointless to assess the validity of the decline-of-community argument.

The most striking pursuit of obscure empirical questions by network analysts is found in the work of Laumann and Pappi (1976). When introducing their study of a German city (Altneustadt), they turned to Talcott Parsons for their major questions. The choice is startling if only because Parsons habitually confused conceptual schemes with substantive theory and was notoriously indifferent to research. Be that as it may, Laumann and Pappi write (1976:2) that they "wholeheartedly endorse his [Parsons's] assumption that social systems must be treated as open-ended rather than closed systems." The assumption illustrates Parson's talent for concealing triteness, and the postulates articulated by Laumann and Pappi scarcely do more than the assumption when it comes to identifying answerable questions. Consider their third postulate (1976:8): "given a plurality of relationship-specific structures predicated on different principles of organization, structural contradictions are possible features of any complex social system." Now consider the prospects of agreement among researchers when attempting to answer what Laumann and Pappi (1976:1) identify as the central integrative question: "How does a social system as a whole establish priorities among competing sets of ends (or goals) requiring the expenditure of its scarce resources (means), given the existence of competing standards for evaluating these alternatives among its component standards?"

Confusion is compounded when Laumann and Pappi (1976:11) switch to a discussion of community decision making in connection with "ruling elite vs. pluralist models." Given the vagueness of those two models, it is idle to suggest that their merits can be assessed defensibly. To be sure, Laumann and Pappi write clearly when describing their commendable analysis of social networks of a German city, but one comes to their book's end wondering what the findings corroborate or refute.

What has been said of Laumann and Pappi applies also to Burt's (1982) use of network terms and techniques in stating and bringing evidence to bear on a "structural theory of action." The immediate problem is that none of the distinctive network terms (e.g., *density, centrality, connectedness*) enter into the theory itself. They are not in the theory's diagrammatic representation (Burt, 1982:9); rather, in that diagram the arrows connect action, actor interests, and action. There is some correspondence between the diagram and what Burt describes as "the premise underlying a structural theory of action, namely, actors are purposive under social structural constraints, implies a very general scope of substantive issues within a causal cycle" (9). Nonetheless, while Burt claims (1982:11) to have chosen a deductive approach to theory construction, at no point does he identify any other premises and no theorems or conclusions whatever. True, Burt's book fairly bristles with formulas and data; but at no point is it possible to ascertain what conclusions (theorems or otherwise) are being tested, let alone how they were deduced from the theory.

SOME PARADOXES.   Although network terms are truly distinctive, they are not central in the theories pursued by network analysts. More specifically, no network theory purports to answer questions such as suggested by the illustration: What is the empirical relation among network populations between density and centrality, between centrality and connectedness, between connectedness and reachability, and why do those relations hold? The question is far less conventional than any of the following: Why does the crime rate vary? Why is there evidence of an inverse relation among countries between per capita income and fertility rates? With few exceptions (e.g., Fischer, 1977, 1982a) network analysts appear unconcerned with such questions; yet it is not clear what they prefer as alternatives.

Network constructs and concepts are so "formal" that theorists cannot think in terms of them readily, and the connection between those terms and actual human behavior appears tenuous. Quoting Boissevain: "Analytical rigour in this field easily leads to methodological refinements remote from human beings" (1985:558). Koepping's criticism is more specific: "network-analysis by itself is of limited value if we aim at explaining or even predicting either behavioural correlates through structural elements or of gauging the value-system of a group of people from inferences from structural features alone" (1983:126). So it may well be that as long as the network analysts think of connections between points as denoting any and all kinds of social relations, they will be unable to formulate impressive theories.

Principal Strengths and Weaknesses of Formalism

Despite its connection with Simmel, formalism is a relatively new perspective. Even so, its principal strength and weakness are already conspicuous.

Principal Strength

Recall Blau's suggestion that sociology's subject matter is nothing more or less than "social structure." Extant definitions of that term appear broad if only because vague; but should sociologists accept social structure as their subject matter, it would reduce the diversity of their studies; and the reduction would be enormous if only Blau's major concepts are employed.

A great reduction in the diversity of sociological studies would also ensue should social relations become sociology's exclusive subject matter, and most network analysts evidently assume that the lines, connections, or paths in a network graph signify social relations. That assumption alone unifies network studies to an uncommon degree among sociological perspectives.

The Principal Weakness

No theory in formalism is remotely as well known as Durkheim's theory of the division of labor or Marx's theory of capitalism. To demand such a theory would be premature, but the formalism's principal weakness precludes the prospects of a theory that will interest most sociologists. The weakness is the same for both structuralism and network analysis: there is no notion in either version of formalism that remotely enables sociologists to describe and think about all phenomena that interest them.

MANIFESTATIONS IN STRUCTURALISM. Given the sheer number of theories formulated by Peter Blau, sociological structuralism may appear very fertile; but Blau remains the only major theorist in that version of formalism. Furthermore, despite Blau's enormous talent and productivity, his theories have not attracted anything like the following enjoyed by Parsons in the 1950s. The reason has been suggested by comments (chapter 4) on Blau and Blau's analysis (1982) of variation in violent crime rates among U.S. metropolitan areas. Consider again their interpretation of a statistical association between income inequality and those rates. Even though Blau and Blau refer to a "general sociological theory," they never state it, let alone deduce the association in question from the theory. Rather, in a clearly ex post facto manner, Blau and Blau purport to explain the association by invoking some eight notions (e.g., spirit of democracy, pent-up aggression, anomie). No corresponding measures are presented, and none of the notions appear in Blau's list (1977) of key structural properties. The defects of the explanation illustrate the weakness in question: there is no notion in sociological structuralism that enables a theorist to describe and think about the connection between structural properties and behavioral rates or between one structural property and another. To underscore the obvious, the notion of social structure cannot be used to describe and think about its elemental properties. Just the reverse is true; and, even more obvious, one cannot describe and think of social structure in terms of social structure.

Most of Blau's theories appear "deductive"; but there are several objections to Blau's mode of theory construction, commencing with his implicit rules of deduction. Consider Axiom O in Blau's theory of social structure: "The members of a society associate with others not only in their own but also in different groups" (1977:42). Now examine Theorem 1.11: "For any dichotomy of society, the proportion of group members intermarried is an inverse function of group size" (42). Blau describes the theorem as being "from" the axiom, one of many instances where he makes questionable use of the logic of classes. Even if "members of a society *associate* with others in different groups," it does not follow that intergroup marriages ever occur.[6] Moreover, the theorem illustrates the proliferation of analytical statements in Blau's theories. Thus, if one dichotomy is larger than the other and if there is any intermarriage between the two, it is mathematically necessary for the smaller dichotomy to have the higher intermarriage rate. Blau recognizes the analytical quality of such statements; but sociologists are likely to find them uninteresting, if not pretentious (see Porpora, 1983).

Blau evidently relies exclusively on crude induction for his premises; and that exclusive reliance is conducive to dubious generalizations, as in Blau's Axiom 1.2 (1977:43): "The prevalence of associations declines with increasing status distance." What of the *association* between master and servant? True, Blau qualifies some of his statements by adding *ceteris paribus*; but that qualification makes generalization untestable because in sociological research (observational) all other things are never equal, and it suggests that *everything* is relevant. More important, however, Blau relies on crude induction because he has no notion that enables him to describe and think about all of the variables in his theories.

MANIFESTATIONS IN NETWORK ANALYSIS.   Formalism's principal weakness is more conspicuous in network analysis than in structuralism. The reason for the contrast is suggested by the frequent use of the terms *line, connection,* and *path* in network analysis. Those terms have a clear meaning in reference to a particular graph, but in actual research graph lines (or connections or paths) surely signify something. Comments by network analysts clearly indicate that typically the lines signify social relations between whatever is represented by the graph points; otherwise, network analysis would have no real bearing on sociology.

Even if network analysts should formulate a defensible definition of a social relation, progress in their theoretical works requires a notion that enables them to describe and think about social relations. Such a notion has nothing to do with a line, connection, or path. Similarly, major network concepts, such as density and centrality, may enable one to describe and think about networks; but no social relation has a density or centrality.

Formalism and Control

Few if any other sociological perspectives are so bereft of anything like a central notion as is formalism. As long as that remains the case, formalism's theories will be neither numerous nor impressive.

Preserving Formalism's Strength

Again, formalism's principal strength lies in its implied designation of sociology's subject matter—social relations (see Fararo and Skvoretz, 1986), a designation that could greatly reduce the diversity of sociological studies. Although some sociologists might reject that designation as all too narrow, it is clearly compatible with the proposal that control be taken as sociology's central notion. Control is not identified in this book as sociology's subject matter; rather, if social relations are so identified, they can be described and thought of in terms of control.

Control takes on special significance because of doubts about attempting to explain a given social relation in terms of other social relations. All social relations can be described in terms of human control, but the reverse is not the case; and it may well be that the notion of inanimate control or biotic control can be used effectively in explaining features of some social relations.

Diminishing Formalism's Principal Weakness

This book's second principal argument fails if formalists are unable to describe and think of their interests in terms of control or the use of the notion does not diminish formalism's weaknesses. The same applies to all sociological perspectives, but it is necessary to examine the two versions of formalism separately.

STRUCTURALISM. Consider a measure of "heterogeneity" (one of Blau's major concepts) as applied to the religious composition of two communities, *A* and *B*. Suppose the measure's values cannot be less than .00 or greater than 1.00, with the latter indicating that no two population members have the same religious affiliation. Now suppose that the religious heterogeneity value (RHV) is .17 for community *A* but .71 for community *B*. What would that difference mean? To reply that religious heterogeneity is more than four times greater in *B* than in *A* would hardly be informative. Informative answers to various what-does-it-mean questions would indicate that the field has a central notion; but structuralists rarely confront such questions, much less answer informatively.

Now contemplate two possible counterarguments by structuralists. First, to pose a what-does-it-mean question is to license "psychologizing." Second, an informative answer to such a question requires nothing less than a theory. The rejoinder is best given by answering the previous question about the contrast between a RHV of .17 for community *A* and a RHV of .71 for community *B*. For one thing, the contrast suggests that attempts to control behavior on a large scale by appeals to any one particular religious belief or doctrine are more likely to fail in community *B*. Still another answer is that the concentration of control over religious behavior is greater in *A* than in *B*.

Lest the illustration appear idiosyncratic, suppose that the two values refer to income inequality rather than religious heterogeneity. What would that contrast mean? One answer is that there is much greater concentration of power (perceived capacity to control) in *B* than in *A*.

"Control" answers to what-does-it-mean questions will be conjectural and dubious until sociologists make extensive efforts to describe and think about their subject matter in terms of control. Answers to such questions may point the way to fruitful theories; but the road to fruitful theories is not paved with unique answers to each what-does-it-mean question, such as "complexity" in one answer, "higher standard of living" in another, and "greater cohesion" in still another. Nonetheless, insofar as structuralists can answer what-does-it-mean questions informatively, each answer tends to be unique.

NETWORK ANALYSIS. The previous comments apply to network analysis no less than to structuralism. To illustrate, suppose that the centrality value for one network is .28 but .63 for another. What does the contrast mean? To reply that the probability of a connection between any two members is much greater for one population than the other is not informative. Then consider this question as it applies to either network graph: What do the lines mean? To answer "social relations" would be scarcely informative, not even if sociologists possessed a defensible definition of a social relation. The question is what the lines mean, not what they signify; and one cannot describe or think about social relations in terms of social relations.

Network analysts could answer what-does-it-mean questions much more readily if network lines were interpreted in terms of control. That is the case even if the network lines denote some type of social relation. The question then becomes: What kinds and amount of human control are entailed in that type of social relation?[7] In answering that question, network analysts have an advantage over structuralists. Because network analysts rely more on survey data than on census data, they can word their survey questions so that the questions bear on control, for example: Who have you borrowed money from during the past year? Are you an employee and, if so, who is your employer and who is your immediate supervisor? Who last came to you for advice and followed your advice? Ignorance as to the most appropriate survey questions for "getting at" control is admitted, but the proposal to make control sociology's central notion does not require specification of research procedures.

Once network analysts commence describing and thinking about network lines (whether signifying social relations, interaction, or otherwise) in terms of control, then their major constructs or concepts can be so described and thought of. Briefly illustrating, suppose the network lines denote asymmetrical control (e.g., X controls Y but Y does not control X) and suppose again that the centrality value for one population is .28 but .63 for another. What would the contrast mean? That control concentration in one population is more than twice that in the other population. By itself, the answer would not be significant; but a series of such answers—all couched in terms of control—would further the detection and explanation of relations among network properties.

Whatever the relational phenomenon in question, its empirical association with another phenomenon can best be explained in terms of control. Consider the generalization suggested by Freudenburg's findings (1986): a decline in a community's acquaintanceship density reduces the effectiveness of deviance control. Freudenburg actually used the term *control* when interpreting his findings; and he implicitly invokes control notions when arguing that the decline in density acquaintanceship results in this sequence: (1) more anonymity, (2) a decrease in the probability of an offender being apprehended, and (3) an erosion of deterrence. Control appears less relevant when contemplating Freudenburg's argument (1986:32) that a decline in a community's acquaintanceship density disrupts socialization mechanisms, but that is not the case on recognizing that socialization is an intolerably vague notion unless defined in terms of control.

Freudenburg may well be correct in asserting that people who know a child's parents are more likely to inform them about the child's misbehavior; but he fails to make the corollary argument: when informing the parents, those people engage in allegative social control; and they also engage in a more immediate attempt to control the child's behavior—referential social control—when they threaten to inform the parents. Either type of social control is likely to be effective when the people know the parents and the child is aware of it. Finally, although Freudenburg argues convincingly (1986:33) that a decline in a community's acquaintanceship density reduces the informal care of the needy, he does not recognize that to care for someone is to control them and to solicit care is to attempt control. So all of Freudenburg's arguments and findings can be subsumed under this generalization: as community residents come to know one another less, both the frequency of control attempts and their effectiveness decline.

NOTES

1. "Structuralists conceive of sociology much in the fashion of Simmel . . . as being concerned with the forms of human association abstracted from their *specific* content" (Mayhew, 1980:345). Earlier (344), Mayhew describes structuralists as being concerned with network properties: "That such concerns do not require paying attention to the concrete behaviors (actions) of individuals is easily discerned from Figure 4. Each of the networks in Figure 4 can channel wide varieties of individual action. These networks can map the flow of rumors, or business transactions, or moves in chess games, or any number of other concrete activities *without in anyway altering the structural properties of each communication system.*" Figure 4 (Mayhew, 1980:343) is made up of six configurations of points, with each of the four points in a configuration connected by a line with at least one other point in the same configuration (the configurations are unconnected).

2. Simmel can be designated as one of the ancestors of three sociological perspectives identified in this volume—interpretive sociology, formalism, and conflict sociology.

3. Consider Blau's definition of the division of labor: "It is equivalent to occupational heterogeneity" (1977:276). While that definition is couched in structural terms, it ignores functional interdependence among social unit members, the other primary dimension of the division of labor. One may assume that functional interdependence and occupational heterogeneity are closely related, and the assumption may be realistic; but it is an assumption nonetheless, one not somehow given by a definition. No less important for present purposes, it is not clear how functional interdependence can be defined or described in terms of Blau's elemental properties of social structure.

4. Yet network analysts often appear as obsessed with the notion of structure as are Blau and Mayhew, and Wellman's claim (1983) that network analysis is superior to other "sociological analyses" actually generates doubts as to whether

various kinds of phenomena, the normative in particular, can be analyzed in network terms. In any case, network analysts often unwittingly create grave doubts about the significance of the very idea of "structural." Freudenburg, for example, is at great pains to identify the density of acquaintanceship as a "community-level social structural characteristic" (1986:29); but his subsequent statement creates doubts as to whether there is really anything special about such characteristics: "The density of acquaintanceship may be thought of as the average proportion of the people in a community known by the community's inhabitants." The characteristic is social, but why is it "structural"?

5. The point is illustrated by Berkowitz's defense (1980) of the "relational" as opposed to the "aggregate" approach in analyses of elites, in which he fails to emphasize that neither approach solves the problems in defining elites (chapter 14). However, the suggestion is not that network analysts treat their own terminology uncritically. To the contrary, they appear more sensitive to conceptual problems than do advocates of other perspectives, especially when it comes to recognition that some conceptual problems call for techniques or procedures for boundary delimitation (see, e.g., Laumann et al., 1983).

6. Blau's structural propositions actually pertain to opportunities for interaction (or social relations), and the shortcoming is not just that statements about the opportunities identify (at most) only necessary conditions. More seriously, sociological structuralism cannot answer this question: Why are some kinds of interaction more closely related with a given structural property (e.g., population size, heterogenity) than are other kinds of interaction? To illustrate, in reporting tests of Blau's theory, South and Messner made this statement about statistical associations among U.S. metropolitan areas: "The rate of interracial marriage is positively affected by the degree of racial income inequality, whereas interracial crime rates are more strongly influenced by relative group size and racial residential segregation" (1986:1409). Sociological structuralism cannot explain such contrasts because it offers no notion to describe and think about kinds of interaction. Because proposing marriage and criminal acts are both attempts at control, their frequency is appreciably a function of the probability of success as perceived by would-be controllers. To be sure, those perceptions are influenced by recognition of opportunities, some of which can be described structurally; but it would be absurd to assume that the relevant opportunities are the same for marriage proposals and crime attempts. So there is a basis for expecting that the two interracial rates are not associated even more or less the same with each structural property. No less important, because no one structural property represents even a fraction of all relevant opportunities, there is no basis to expect a close association between any property and the rate of interaction in question; and that is precisely what South and Messner (1986) report. The general point is that the notion of control facilitates anticipation not just of empirical associations but also in some cases a negligible association.

7. A "control" definition of a social relation is formulated in chapter 18.

Materialism

Materialism is a partial perspective at most, despite its connection with Marxism. The nature of the connection is debatable, and materialism itself is diversely interpreted. Definitions in philosophy are ignored here in preference for a more sociologically relevant definition. Briefly, materialism is the belief that socio-cultural phenomena can be explained in terms of conditions distinct from and external to human behavior. Materialists differ in identifying those conditions; some emphasize natural resources, others climate, and still others technology. Yet most versions are consistent with Brubaker's characterization: "Sociological materialism, neglecting values and norms, conceives of action as essentially instrumental and social order as emerging from the rationally adaptive responses of individuals to external conditions" (1985:509).

No version of materialism ever has commanded even a majority of sociologists, and currently materialism scarcely has any following (see, however, Leavitt, 1986).[1] Nonetheless, the perspective's total extinction is unlikely. While sociologists publicly reject the quest for an ultimate cause or prime mover, the quest will continue under one guise or another.

Some Initial Issues Concerning Marx's Theory of Human Society

A Marxism-materialism connection is suggested by the common identification of Marx as a technological determinist (see, e.g., Shaw, 1978), but some definitions of technology do not justify that identification. If technology is defined (contrary to chapter 3) as some kind of human behavior, then it is not external to human behavior. Be that as it may, the scope of Marx's theory of human society (*infra*) is unrivalled. Unfortunately, however, any version of the theory is only one of numerous possibilities.

Some Contending Points of Departure

The familiar allegation that Marx's theory is a vast value judgment (i.e., prescriptive) rather than scientific overlooks the differences among scientific theories suggested in Table 12-1. Some scientific theories are instrumental in that they can be construed as directions for bringing about a change, but they are empirical (susceptible to falsification) because the directions could be invalid. In Table 12-1 that change would be the emergence of condition Y; and instances of statements IID, IIE, IIID, and IIIE could be construed as directions for producing that condition (note that in the case of ID and IE, X is only antecedently necessary for Y). Type C statements would be directions for avoiding Y, but no less instrumental and empirical. By contrast, all type B statements would be noninstrumental but empirical, and all type A statements would be empirical despite being ambiguous as to the instrumental-noninstrumental distinction. Yet none of the 15 types of statements are *prescriptive*, for each expresses some empirical claim (some instrumental, others not). To illustrate, surely the following four statements make different types of claims. First, convince those without property that they are being exploited, and the country's economic system will change. Second, capitalism is an evil. Third, I favor socialism. And, fourth, in any city the burglary rate varies directly over time with the unemployment rate.

So the prescriptive-scientific dichotomy oversimplifies, especially when applied to Marx's theory of human society. Marx formulated a bewildering mixture of statements, some prescriptive, others instrumental-empirical, and still others noninstrumental-empirical. Hence, it is not just a matter of different versions of Marx's theory; there may well be several theories differing along the lines suggested by Table 12-1. What follows is a brief version of Marx's noninstrumental-empirical theory.

THE STERILITY OF EXEGETICAL MARXISM.   Much of Marxist sociology is a vast effort to interpret Marx correctly. To be sure, an interpretation is needed; otherwise, short of pointing to a massive stack of publications, there is no way to present Marx's theory or theories (as the case may be).[2] Nonetheless, should it be agreed that Marx formulated several distinct theories, there is no basis to anticipate further agreement in identifying them (e.g., possibly a prescriptive theory about industrial communism, a noninstrumental theory about socio-cultural evolution); and even assuming consensus in identifying Marx's theories, the constituent statements are scattered over literally hundreds of Marx's publications—books, newspaper columns, letters, etc. Then in the unlikely case of agreement in assigning each of Marx's statements to a particular theory, the logical relations among the statements are bound to be obscure.

	The statement does not assert anything about the possibility of creating an instance of condition X by deliberate human activity.	The statement asserts that an instance of condition X cannot be created by any kind of deliberate human activity.	The statement asserts that some stipulated kind of deliberate human activity is necessary for an instance of condition X to exist.	The statement asserts that some stipulated kind or kinds of deliberate human activity is sufficient for an instance of condition X to exist.	The statement asserts that some stipulated kind or kinds of deliberate human activity is necessary and sufficient for an instance of condition X to exist.
The statement asserts that X is antecedently necessary for Y.	Type IA	Type IB	Type IC	Type ID	Type IE
The statement asserts that X is antecedently sufficient for Y.	Type IIA	Type IIB	Type IIC	Type IID	Type IIE
The statement asserts that X is antecedently necessary and sufficient for Y.	Type IIIA	Type IIIB	Type IIIC	Type IIID	Type IIIE

Table 12-1. A Typology of Empirical Statements about Any Two Conditions, *X* and *Y*

So the conclusion: Marx stated his theory or theories so discursively that diverse interpretations are inevitable. Contemporary Marxists and their opponents commonly write as though there can be a demonstrably correct version of Marx, although more than a century of experience indicates otherwise. Hence, a few comparisons of the following brief version of Marx's theory of human society with particular contenders are made, but only to clarify.

The Structure of Marx's Theory of Human Society

The initial three premises and four principal variables in Marx's theory of human society are suggested by Figure 12-1. The immediate issue is whether Marx formulated only such a theory. That interpretation is contrary to frequent allusions to "Marx's theory of capitalism." One objection is that the allusion confuses a theory with (1) Marx's interpretation of historical events in Europe over (circa) 1500–1850 and (2) his implicit extrapolations of what he perceived as trends in those events.[3] Writers who imply that Marx "explained" capitalism and deduced predictions about its future avoid this question: Given that a formally adequate explanation or a deduced prediction requires explicit premises, where did Marx state them? Any answer other than "no where" would distort; and the counterfactual quality of this reply makes it ineffectual: Had Marx made his premises explicit, they would constitute a theory about capitalism. Finally, even if Marx did state a theory of capitalism, it is only a special case of what is suggested by Figure 12-1.

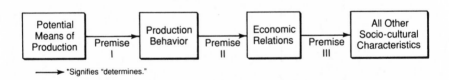

Figure 12-1.   A Representation of Marx's Theory of Human Society

What has been said of Marx's putative theory of capitalism extends to his assertions about evolutionary stages (see Laibman, 1984), such as this sequence: primitive communism → slavery → feudalism → capitalism → socialism → industrial communism. The sequence excludes the "Asiatic" mode because it is so disputable (see, e.g., Gellner, 1985); and the first three transitions may reflect nothing more than crude induction, meaning what Marx took as historical facts (but note that Laibman, 1984, writes of theories of transition).

The foregoing is less critical than it appears, because it implies that evidence commonly offered to refute Marx does not bear on his theory about human society. Consider Marx's "maturity" law or thesis—that socialism emerges initially in countries where capitalism has developed the fullest. Granted that the law does not hold (see, e.g., Popper, 1966:349), no premise in Figure 12-1 is invalidated by the histories of Britain, Russia, China, and Cuba.[4] Likewise, a transition from primitive communism to feudalism without slavery *intervening* would refute Marx's claim about societal evolution, but not any premise in Figure 12-1.

Premise I

Marx's formulation is so garbled that commentators disagree even as to the number of principal variables in his theory. Thus, whereas the present version identifies four, Cohen (1978) seems to identify only three: productive forces, relations of production, and superstructural. In any case, Premise I should be translated as follows: Change in the potential means of production in a society causes change in the character of production behavior. Like any premise in any version of Marx, Premise I is debatable; and one of the two major reasons is the same for all of the other premises.

THE PREMISE'S DETERMINISTIC CHARACTER. Critics are likely to dismiss Figure 12-1 as vulgar Marxism. Potential means of production are depicted as ultimate causes, and change in each variable is assertedly necessary and sufficient for a change in the following variable. Not even the ambiguity of Marx's related statements permits an interpretation of *only* necessary causation or *only* sufficient causation. However, to make Marx appear plausible, many of his epigones have diluted him by offering confusing equivocations. Their slogan might well be: Better to be ambiguous than appear implausible.

A truly deterministic version of Marx's theory may be incompatible with any dialectical version. To be sure, many of Marx's arguments are dialectical in one sense or another, but it is an illusion to suppose that exegetes agree in offering dialectical versions of Marx's theory. Even the logical structure of any purported dialectical version is disputable, and those versions are murkier than anything Marx ever wrote (see, e.g., Lefebvre, 1968). There are even doubts as to whether the meaning of the term *dialectic* can be clarified and defended (see, e.g., Popper, 1940). Contemplate Mirkovic's contentment (1980:5, 36) in writing on the dialectic and sociological thought with two brief quotes of Lenin—"In brief, dialectics can be defined as the doctrine of the unity of opposites" and "Dialectic in the proper sense is the study of contradictions in the very essence of object"—and with this: "In very general terms, dialectical thought could be described tentatively as a mode of viewing historical reality in its totality, in terms of its immanent contradictions leading to qualitative change and transformation of the existing social relations." Finally, sociologists should read the literature cited in van den Berg's critique (1980) of "critical theory" and Habermas's more recent (1984) contribution to that literature; and then they should confront this question: Would it be wise to abandon vulgar, materialist, or even positivistic versions of Marx for any version of critical theory?

POTENTIAL MEANS OF PRODUCTION.   Premise I is debatable if only because other terms could be used to denote the two variables. "Potential means of production" is less debatable than "production behavior" because Marx did speak frequently of means of production; but in making observations clearly pertaining to some kind of ultimate cause, Marx used a bewildering variety of other terms such as *labor power*, *labor process*, *factors of production*, *instruments of labor*, and *objects of labor*. He may have regarded some of those terms as synonyms, but we shall never really know. For that matter, the list could be expanded to include terms that Marx may have construed as denoting subclasses of the means of production (e.g., material means of production, material powers of production) or a more inclusive class (e.g., forms of production, mode of production, and productive forces). In any case, no social science theorist rivals Marx when it comes to the sheer variety of arcane terms, and for that reason alone divergent interpretations of him are inevitable.

Even if everyone should agree that "potential means of production" appropriately denotes Marx's postulated ultimate cause, the immediate question is no less controversial: What are the means of production? Shaw (1978:10) notwithstanding, the question cannot be answered by quoting Marx. The answer must be an interpretation of Marx, and no one has done more along that line than G. A. Cohen (1978) to clarify Marx's terminology.

Cohen concludes (55) that there are two subclasses of the productive forces, labor power and means of production, with the latter encompassing instruments of production (tools, machines, premises, instrumental materials), raw materials, spaces, and certain means of subsistence. The metaphysical character of "labor power" is rivalled only by Marx's notion of value (see Heilbroner, 1983); and even accepting Marx's various statements about it as somehow constituting an intelligible definition, there is no basis to analyze labor power without observations on laboring activity, which Cohen (1978:42) excludes from productive forces. Yet he admits (1978:42): "Marx never provides a list of productive forces, and our discussion of them is based partly on scattered remarks and partly on theoretical considerations." Such candor in exegetical Marxism is all too rare.

Unfortunately, using the term *potential means of production* and avoiding the term *productive forces* does not clear a path through Marx's terminological jungle. Even if Cohen's list of the means of production is complete and even if "space" should be included, the empirical applicability of several of his key terms is extremely dubious; and the same may be said of Marx's terminology (struggle through Marx, 1906:197–206). Thus, Cohen states that "certain means of subsistence figure among instruments of production and raw materials" (1978:55), but that passage surely does not clarify means of subsistence. For that matter, Cohen (1978:52) rejects Marx's denial that food is a subsistence means, having earlier (1978:40) used the word *unnatural* in dismissing Marx's designation of "uncaught fish" as a means of production. Likewise, Cohen (1978:40) speaks of Marx's distinctions in connection with raw materials as "flawed" and his criterion as "inappropriate." When a careful and sympathetic critic creates such doubts about Marx's terminology, surely one must wonder about any version of Marx.

The alternative to listing all means of production is some general conception. Cohen (1978:33–34) follows Marx in rejecting the idea that any condition is a means of production if it facilitates or enables production; but that rejection hardly clarifies, nor does Cohen's insistence (1978:33) that a condition must be *materially* necessary for production. After all, a hoe is not truly materially necessary in corn production (one can imagine an alternative tool or even no tool), but if a hoe is not a means of production in horticulture, what is it? Moreover, consider Cohen's general statement (1978:34): "Only what contributes materially within and to productive activity as Marx demarcates it counts as a productive force." Does a factory worker's automobile contribute to production when he or she drives it to work? If not, why not? The distinction between direct and indirect use provides no answer, because it is extremely vague. To illustrate, if the use of a machine to shape wood is direct use, then the fuel that powers the machines is used indirectly; but surely fuel is a means of production in that context. However, if the fuel but not the factory worker's automobile is described as direct use, then the direct-indirect distinction becomes incomprehensible. Finally, no conceptual problem is solved by Cohen's quote (1978:34) of Marx's disparagement of treating as indirect means of production "everything that furthers production, everything which tends to resolve an obstacle, to make production more active, speedier, easier."

The only realistic possibility for an empirically applicable conceptualization requires an alteration of Marx's terminology, to speak of potential means of production, defined as any nonhuman animal, object, or substance that has been made, modified, or moved by humans (i.e., by inanimate or biotic control). Not all objects or substances are potential means of production; otherwise, even distant galaxies would qualify. Rather, an object or substance becomes a potential means of production when humans exert some kind of control over it.

PRODUCTION BEHAVIOR. The term is disputable because Marx did not use it, nor have other interpreters; but it is essential because Marx and his interpreters do not maintain a distinction between two distinct classes of phenomena, the subclasses of which are: (1) the degree of the division of labor; (2) the bases of the division of labor; (3) the coordination and synchronization of sustenance activities; (4) the context of coordination and synchronization, such as an organization or associations; (5) power over access to potential means of production; (6) power over those who do have access; (7) power over the ends to which potential means of production are used; (8) power over whatever can be described as products of the potential means of production. The two distinct classes are actual production behavior (items 1–4) and economic relations, the interests or claims that any one of various parties may have in that behavior (items 5–8).

The term *production behavior* is used rather than *relations of production* because the latter is less likely to be confused with economic relations. But that choice does not avoid another problem. It is not clear where Cohen (or Marx for that matter) "locates" everything identified here as production behavior.[5] The variable cannot be identified as relations of production because Cohen (1978:63) describes the latter (as did Marx) in terms of ownership. "Work relations" could be construed as having something to do with production behavior as defined here, but the meaning of the term is obscure; and Shaw's argument that "work relations" and "ownership relations" are the two components of production relations has no rationale (1978:28).

Production behavior has no obvious place in Cohen's conceptualization of the means of production, and there is no basis to subsume it under "labor power." Marx used the term *labor power* to denote not laboring but, rather, the capacity to labor; therefore, actual production behavior is excluded. For that matter, the notion of labor power has been interpreted by Marx and his followers in diverse ways; and the term's empirical applicability is jeopardized when Cohen extends its meaning to productively applicable knowledge, including scientific knowledge that is open to productive use (1978:45). Such knowledge is treated here as beliefs pertaining to inanimate control, biotic control, or human control in the context of production, distribution, or exchange.

Production behavior encompasses all attempted inanimate control, attempted biotic control, and attempted human control in the implementation or execution of some procedure for the production, distribution, or exchange of things or benefits. The third component—attempted human control—includes not only instruction and supervision but also attempts to control humans in an exchange context (e.g., the behavior of anyone engaged in "sales"). However, the third component does not include attempts at human control through the design and imposition of a production procedure and related decisions as to: (1) what will be produced, distributed, or exchanged; (2) where; (3) when; (4) how; (5) who will be allowed, induced, or forced to participate in production, distribution, or exchange; (6) inducements to realize the human energy and skills required for production, distribution, or exchange (e.g., wages or salaries for employees, coercive threats for slaves, shelter for serfs); and (7) the term and conditions under which whatever is produced or distributed will be exchanged. All of those phenomena (1–7) are subsumed under "economic relations," the second variable in Premise II (Figure 12-1).

Here, as elsewhere, the contrasts between Cohen's version of Marx (or any other) and the present version do not imply that only the latter is correct. It is even admitted that some contending versions appear truer to Marx in one sense or another; but the present version has a clearer logical structure, offers more in the way of empirical applicability, and will prove to have greater predictive accuracy. The last two claims cannot be assessed readily, but the first claim can. By comparison, Marx's statements are so garbled that no candid reader can confidently identify even the number of principal variables.

The present version of Marx's theory will tax credulity because of, among other things, the idea that potential means of production cause production behavior. Because all means of production have been shaped, made, modified, and/or moved by human behavior, then it may appear that, contrary to Figure 12-1, production behavior determines potential means of production. That is the reason why Marx's theory cannot explain behavior before the existence of objects or substances that have been made, modified, or moved, a perennial problem with "materialism." Yet Marx's theory is more credible in light of this question: Would production behavior in an automobile factory be what it is without processed metals? The question suggests that the potential means of production determines production behavior in this sense: humans adapt their behavior to existing potential means of production. To be sure, the present formulation is not strict materialism, but neither is Marx in the original, nor in Cohen's version. For that matter, a strictly materialist version would postulate physiographic determinism (see Shaw's reference, 1978:65, to Plekhanov's geographic determinism).

Premise II

What was said about vulgar Marxism in connection with Premise I applies to Premise II, but there are even greater doubts about II because of Marx's argument that economic relations constrain changes in productive forces. How can productive forces both determine and be determined by economic relations? That question is best considered after some observations on economic relations.

FURTHER DESCRIPTION OF ECONOMIC RELATIONS. Again, the term *economic relations* is preferred over the term *relations of production* because the latter is likely to be confused with production behavior, but Marx used both terms without clarifying the distinction. A description of what is subsumed here under economic relations already has been given (the seven numbered classes of phenomena), but the description may appear alien to Marx because it excludes the term *ownership*. Actually, Marx's conceptualizations suffer because of his preoccupation with capitalism. He described capitalists as owning the means of production; but because the same could be said for feudal lords and slavers, the term *ownership* is not useful in conceptualizing economic relations. Insofar as ownership can be defined coherently, the definition cannot be more than a list of what different persons can and cannot do with regard to designated things (including humans and animals) or types of acts having no concrete objects (e.g., singing a particular song) in some designated space-time context without any discernible risk of punishment.

So a description of economic relations requires extensive observations as to who designs and imposes procedures pertaining to production, distribution, and exchange—the what, the where, the how, the who, the whom, and inducements for participation. Those observations must extend to a description of categories of individuals in connection with production, distribution, and exchange, such as employers, employees, and the self-employed in the case of American economic relations.

ESPECIALLY CONTROVERSIAL CONSIDERATIONS.   Marx provides no basis for interpreting Premise II other than this: Change in the character of production behavior causes change in the character of economic relations. Marxists are likely to reject that interpretation for two reasons. First, they perceive it as making Marx's theory vulnerable. Second, the premise does not recognize Marx's idea that economic relations "fetter" production productive forces (see the "Fettering" entry in Cohen's subject index, 1978:366).[6] That claim enriches the theory, but it is ambiguous and inconsistent with many of Marx's suggestions of an asymmetrical or nonreciprocal causal relation between productive forces and economic relations.

Because Marx provided no coherent alternative to stating Premise II in terms of simple causation, the term *determines* must be used in the translating the premise. Although that term admits the possibility of an unidentified mechanism, one that somehow delays the effect of a change in production behavior, the very idea of economic relations "resisting" anything is one of Marx's many impenetrable anthropomorphic reifications. Granted, individuals who design and impose procedures of production, distribution, and exchange are likely to defend those procedures, but Marxists eschew that terminology.

Whatever the basis of resistance to change in economic relations, Premise II does not claim that violence by the unpropertied class (slaves, serfs, or industrial proletarians) is necessary to change economic relations. Although that omission may prompt some of Marx's defenders to reject Premise II, Marx equivocated about the necessity of violence (see Popper, 1966), though many writers fail to emphasize the equivocation (see, e.g., commentary by Alexander, 1982-II:458–60).

PLAUSABILITY. Space limits preclude extensive observations that would further understanding of Premise II and make it more plausible. Hence, as in the case of Premise I, one illustration must suffice.

Although not writing in defense of Marx, Leslie White made a pertinent argument: "Slavery as an institution will exist and endure only when the master can derive profit and advantage by exploiting the slave. This is possible only when a family group is able to produce considerably more than it requires for its continued existence" (1949:128). Because production per family group is a feature of production behavior, White's argument suggests that slavery, a type of economic relation, is not present unless production behavior generates a surplus.

White's argument ignores this question: Does slavery always appear when family groups commence producing a surplus? Then consider the validity of White's statement (1949:129) about the "end" of slavery: "Modern industrial technologies could not be operated by ignorant, illiterate human chattels. Also, the slave owner suffered a handicap which does not affect the employer of free labor. . . ." But slavery disappeared in many European countries long before "modern industrial technologies," and serfs rather than free laborers supposedly replaced slaves. Nonetheless, White's argument is entirely consistent with Premises I and II, and it is unfortunate that contemporary Marxists do so little to add more support through descriptive research.

Premise III

This premise must be translated something like this: Change in the character of economic relations causes change in all socio-cultural characteristics other than potential means of production and production behavior. Like I and II, Premise III asserts simple causation, and there are two major conceptual issues. First, many interpreters would make the dependent variable less residual by assigning more socio-cultural phenomena to the previous principal variables. Second, no other interpreter has used the phrase "all other socio-cultural phenomena" in stating the theory.

CLASS. Although classes are socio-cultural phenomena, numerous interpreters of Marx seem to equate economic relations and class relations. If that conceptual link is accepted, classes cannot be identified as "other socio-cultural phenomena." True, Marx often alluded to a social class as a position in economic relations; hence, definitions of social class in terms of income, education, or even occupation are not Marxist. Yet it is one thing to define a class by reference to economic relations but quite another to equate them.

The locus of class phenomena in Marx's theory is all the more controversial because of shifts in the fortunes of various Marxist schools. Whereas "mechanists" argue that socialism and postindustrial communism occur only as a consequence of production changes, activists advocate the promotion of class conflict and revolutionary activity. Hence, such mechanists as Plekhanov (e.g., 1940, 1947) and Bukharin (e.g., 1925) were more prone to emphasize the materialist quality of Marx's theory than were the activists, such as Lenin and Stalin. What with Plekhanov's demise, Lenin's triumph, Stalin's eventual seizure of power, and Bukharin's reported execution on Stalin's order, interpretations of Marx increasingly became less materialist. In sociology, materialist Marxism was supplanted by an emphasis on anomie, class, and class conflict, so much that Marxists evidently came to regard research on the correlates of technology or production as irrelevant. In brief, Marx's theory came to be depicted as a theory without anything akin to Premises I and II in Figure 12-1.

OTHER PROBLEMS AND ISSUES.   Several terms used by Marx to describe economic relations also designate phenomena supposedly caused by economic relations, and the paradox becomes especially conspicuous in the case of legal terminology (Cohen, 1978:218). Marx often used the terms *ownership* and *property* to describe economic relations; but he also asserted that law, which necessarily includes property law and defines the privileges that constitute ownership, is determined by economic relations. Taken as a purely conceptual problem, the solution is to define economic relations in terms that are more nearly behavioral than legal. Thus, Cohen (1978:219) advocates use of the term *power* rather than *right*. Whatever its merits, Cohen's strategy provides no alternative to Premise III. That assertion of direct and simple causation is all the more an issue because Marx suggested that law preserves economic relations, which makes it appear that the causal association is reciprocal. Nevertheless, if the theory is to be consistent and comprehensible, it is necessary to depict economic relations as the nonreciprocal and *eventual* cause of all socio-cultural characteristics, including law, other than potential means of production and production behavior.

The most glaring problem is the phrase used to denote that second variable in Premise III—"all other socio-cultural characteristics." The residual nature of the variable taxes credulity. There is an alternative—"superstructural" phenomena—but Marx came no closer to a definition than references to particular phenomena that he evidently thought of as superstructural. True, he emphasized some phenomena more than others, ideology especially; but if superstructure is equated with ideology, then difficult questions erupt, such as: How can all features of law, especially the actual imposition of a punishment, be described as ideology? For that matter, if superstructure is equated with ideology, it would be a conceptual redundancy.

Some of the syntactical gymnastics commonly displayed in conceptualizing "superstructure" are illustrated by Cohen (1978:45–46):

"science is neither superstructural nor ideological. The superstructure consists of legal, political, religious, and other non-economic *institu-*

tions. It probably (*sic*) includes universities, but it does not include knowledge, for knowledge is not an institution. Ideology, on the other hand, is also not an institution but, like science, a set of ideas. Yet science is not ideology, since it is a defining property of ideology that it is unscientific."

By roughly equating the superstructure with noneconomic *institutions*, Cohen avoids treating the last major component of Marx's theory as residual, thereby possibly making the theory appear less "vulgar" and more plausible. Be that as it may, Cohen's conceptualization of "superstructural" creates a problem. Even granting a distinction between noneconomic institutions and ideology, what is ideology if not superstructural? Cohen does not confront the question. Then even if a distinction can be drawn between noneconomic institutions and knowledge, what is the locus of knowledge in Marx's theory? Cohen (1978:45) does give a partial answer: "scientific knowledge which is open to productive use is a productive force." But surely not all knowledge, scientific or otherwise, is open to productive use. So it appears that Cohen's "superstructure" excludes some socio-cultural phenomena other than those pertaining to production or economic relations; and although that exclusion may appear realistic, it negates the most distinctive and attractive feature of Marx's theory—its seeming inclusiveness.

Some Caveats

Marx's interpreters should be preoccupied with the question: How can the theory be restated so as to maximize its empirical validity? Unfortunately, however, the present version of Marx's theory (Figure 12-1) cannot be defended by appealing to empirical validity.

UNTESTABLE PREMISES.   No claim about empirical validity can be made because the premises in Figure 12-1 are not testable in any sense. Doubts can be reduced by contemplating three questions corresponding to the three premises in Figure 12-1. First, which specific features of the potential means of production determine which specific features of production behavior? Second, which specific features of production behavior determine which specific features of economic relations? And, third, which specific features of economic relations determine which specific features of other socio-cultural characteristics?

If Marxists protest that Marx answered the three questions, they could contribute enormously to the social sciences by supplying the relevant quotes.[7] Note, however, that the answers must be nomothetic generalizations, not statements limited to particular space-time contexts. To illustrate, consider Marx's statement: "The handmill gives you society with the feudal lord; the steam-mill, society with the industrial capitalist" (1963:109). Surely Marx should have said "gave" rather than "gives," as his statement is a claim about two historical causal connections and not a nomothetic generalization.

The foregoing commentary is not a denial that the premises depicted in Figure 12-1 are nomothetic generalizations. They are nothing less, but they are untestable because they make no claims whatever about an empirical association (causal or otherwise) between *specific features* of potential means of production, production behavior, economic relations, and other socio-cultural phenomena.

It would be a gross illusion to suppose that a testable version of Marx's theory can be realized by changing the terms of Marx's premises (e.g., relations of production rather than production behavior) or by defining the terms in some particular way.[8] It would be another illusion to suppose it possible to deduce a testable statement from any one of the premises or from any combination of them. It would be still another illusion to suppose that Marx's theory can be made testable by avoiding assertions of simple (direct and unlimited) causation.

AN EXTREME STRATEGY.   The only obvious way to escape the foregoing dilemmas is to abandon any pretense of formulating a version of Marx's theory or theories (as the case may be). Instead, sociologists would formulate theories about the interrelations among such variables as technological efficiency, technological complexity, degree of division of labor, sexual basis of labor, size of production associations, concentration of control over production, degree of stratification, types of religion, and types of marriage. Each theory would be in the Marxist tradition; but a theorist need not claim that his or her theory restates Marx, and that is the case for the illustrative theories in chapters 6, 7, and 8.

Granted, such theories would have only a very loose connection with Marx, but that is minor defect compared to the sterility of exegetical Marxism and the narrowness of contemporary Marxism. Again, contemporary Marxist sociologists appear preoccupied with class and class conflict to the point of denying that a theory about, say, technology or the division of labor is "Marxist."

Control and Marxist Sociology

If a central notion candidate proves incompatible with even one brand of sociology, it is doomed. Far from being alien to Marxist sociology, the notion of control is needed by that brand for several reasons.

A Route Out of Marx's Terminological Jungle

The basic types of control—inanimate, biotic, and human—are compatible with Marx's arguments because of various strategic conceptual links. Try to think of production instruments apart from inanimate control; and, Marx's seeming indifference to it notwithstanding, biotic control has been a major component of production throughout human history. But the suggestion is not that a control terminology should be used to define Marx's terms; rather, if it does not replace those terms, confusing and sterile debates will continue.

A control terminology exceeds Marx's terminology in regard to both conceptual richness and logical connections. Because inanimate control encompasses the creation, use, and maintenance of technology as well as locational control, a control terminology can be used to describe any material facet of production. Then the notion of biotic control facilitates description of some essential components of production largely ignored by Marx. Most important, Marx failed to clarify *production relations* and *economic relations* because he did not perceive that in the final analysis those terms pertain to external human control.[9] Their meaning can be clarified only by defining them such that they can be used to answer this question: Who controls whom, where, when, how, and with regard to what? Finally, if Marx's theory is to be extended to recognition of personality or character types (as in Weber's "ideal" capitalist), the notion of self-control could be essential.

BEYOND THE PREMISES.   Although the premises suggested by Figure 12-1 are untestable for reasons previously described, they could guide research. However, Figure 12-2 could serve even better if only because the basic types of control can be defined more precisely than can Marx's principal terms.

Figure 12-1 is less complex than Figure 12-2 because it asserts a simple causal sequence, but that is precisely its most disputable feature. By contrast, it would be premature to deny any of the alternative causal possibilities in Figure 12-2; and the diagram suggests complexities that Marx never recognized, particularly the possibility that changes in human control or biotic control are not always caused by changes in inanimate control. Indeed, one complexity is not even recognized in Figure 12-2: that subtypes of control may determine other subtypes within the same type, as when the domestication of the horse led some Plains Indians to virtually abandon plant domestication. Harris has provided another illustration: "In the New World the wheel was invented by the American Indians, perhaps for pottery and certainly as a toy, but its further development was halted by the lack of animals suitable for hauling heavy loads" (1977:29). So the absence of a certain kind of biotic control (over traction animals) precluded various kinds of inanimate control. Nonetheless, in some predominant sense one basic type of control may directly or indirectly determine the other two; and the determinacy (e.g., possibilities

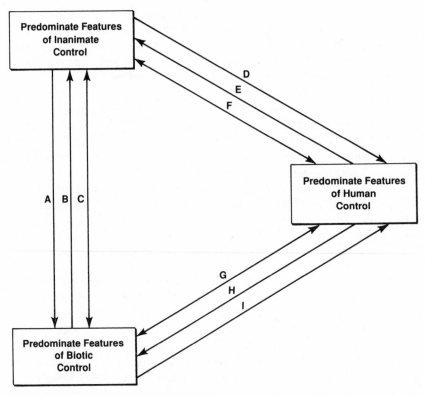

*All arrows signify the direction of causation, with a double-headed shaft (◄────►) signifying reciprocal causation. A, B, C are mutually exclusive possibilities, and the same is true of D, E, F and G, H, I.

Figure 12-2.   Major Possibilities Concerning Causal Connections among Basic Types of Control*

A and *D* in Figure 12-2) could be universal, the very thing that makes Marx's theory attractive. Or there could be an evolutionary trend in the nine possibilities, perhaps commencing with *A* and *D* but ending with *E* and *H*.

SOME CLARIFICATIONS. Contemporary Marxist materialists, if any are left, may voice this objection: Inanimate control is actual behavior, not tools or machines; hence, no control theory can be true to Marx because it will ignore the purely "material" determinants of behavior. That objection reflects a misunderstanding. Granted that inanimate control is behavior, there is no reason to ignore the behavior's products. To the contrary, technology and inanimate control are inseparable; and a control theory could exemplify technological determinism, even more than Marx's theory.

Now consider a puzzling question about Marx's theory: How can instruments of labor determine production behavior when they were created by human behavior? That question would not haunt a control theory; after all, tools are created through inanimate control. True, should a particular technological item be necessary for some particular kind of control, in that sense it determines that control behavior. Even so, technology itself is ultimately determined through the control by which technological items are produced.

Finally, whereas some of Marx's terms (e.g., raw materials) suggest physiographic determinism, a control theory would be free of such ambiguity. Physiographic variables are not control; but a control theory would admit the possibility of physiographic determinism and answer this question: How do physiographic variables (e.g., climate, mineral deposits) determine human behavior? They make the success of some kinds of control problematic, difficult, or impossible.

Other Needs for the Notion of Control

Marxist sociologists have long since ignored infrastructural variables, thereby creating the impression that Marx's arguments constitute nothing more than a theory about class. That impression will persist until Marxists return to this question: How do potential means of production directly or indirectly determine the character of social classes and class conflict?[10] The question receives insufficient attention because Marxists have no notion that enables them to describe and think about potential means of production, production behavior, economic relations, and classes.

MARXISM AS AN IDEOLOGICAL WEAPON. To repeat, critics who dismiss Marx's arguments as a vast value judgment ignore two points. First, directions for promoting or preventing change constitute a control theory. Second, some of Marx's arguments can be construed as a control theory.

The second point is unrelated to Gouldner's contention that: "Scientific

Marxism was an ideology that intellectuals could and did use against their artisan competitors; it served to justify intellectuals' presence in a workers' movement in which they were all too obviously aliens" (1985:138). Although Gouldner's contention may further understanding of Marx and Marxism, contemporary Marxists are unlikely to welcome it, because it creates the impression that Marx was a conniving manipulator. But why are contemporary Marxists reluctant to interpret Marx's arguments as a control theory—a specification of the action that would end capitalism and promote socialism? After all, Marxists have used Marx's arguments as ideological weapons so effectively that nearly a third of the world's population lives under Marxist regimes. The oppressiveness of those regimes may make contemporary Marxists in capitalist countries reluctant to claim that the regimes corroborate Marx's arguments as a control theory. Be that as it may, appeals to praxis scarcely make Marx's arguments an explicit control theory, and Ernesto (Che) Guevara's death is grisly evidence that idiosyncratic action is not an effective substitute for that theory.

Socio-cultural Evolution, Two Determinisms, and Cultural Materialism

Materialism suffers because some social scientists are attracted more to Marx the ideologue than to Marx the materialist, whereas others reject the materialist because of the ideologue. So other versions of materialism are needed.

Socio-cultural Evolution

Both creationists and their critics debate as though the meaning of the term *evolution* is clear, but it is difficult to define (see Giddens, 1984:228–33). Consider this definition: "A process of change in a definite direction, particularly from a simple to a more complex state" (Lenski and Lenski, 1974:493). The word *particularly* rather than *necessarily* means that a steady gain in the weight of a human throughout his or her adult life would be evolution.

Virtually all theories about socio-cultural evolution are materialist in one sense or another, but they lost their large following long ago. Leslie White (1973:47) dates the decline as commencing about 1890, and the last renowned "evolutionist" in American sociology, William G. Sumner, published his best known work, *Folkways*, in 1906. Several things contributed to the decline, notably oversimplified theories (e.g., Morgan's *Ancient Society*), two world wars that mocked the idea of human progress, abuses of evolutionary ideas by Social Darwinists, and the eventual rise of functionalism as an effective contender. Yet evolutionary theory never disappeared completely, surviving more in anthropology (e.g., White, 1949; Steward, 1955) than in sociology.

RENEWAL OF SOCIOLOGICAL INTEREST IN EVOLUTIONARY THEORY. Gerhard and Jean Lenski's attempt (1974) to revive interest in evolutionary theory is the best known and most commendable since sociology turned to functionalism. However, the Lenskis made a curious statement about socio-cultural evolution (1974:79): "it is technological advance and its consequence." They identified that statement as a definition, but subsequently it becomes a causal argument: "This evolving system of technology, with its increasing power and effectiveness, has been largely responsible for all the other basic evolutionary patterns—the growth and spread of the human population, the increased production of goods and services, the increased cultural diversity, the growth in size and the increased structural complexity of societies and communities, and the accelerating rate of sociocultural change" (83). The Lenskis' technological determinism is also obvious in two propositions (1974:110) that appear to be their premises.

"1. Technological advance is the chief determinant of that constellation of global trends—in population, language, social structure, and ideology—which defines the basic outlines of human history.

2. Subsistence technology is the most powerful single variable influencing the social and cultural characteristics of societies, individually and collectively—not with respect to the determination of each and every characteristic, but rather with respect to the total set of characteristics."

Similar statements once abounded in the anthropological literature (e.g., White, 1959); but the Lenskis (1974) did something rare: they presented systematic evidence of technology's correlates. Most of that evidence comes from the assignment of 694 human societies listed in the Ethnographic Atlas (various issues of *Ethnology*) to one of eleven types or subtypes: simple hunting-gathering, advanced hunting-gathering, fishing, simple horticultural, simple herding, advanced horticultural, advanced herding, simple agrarian, maritime, advanced agrarian, and industrial. Each type is defined largely in terms of predominant mode of subsistence, with the presence or absence of particular kinds of technological items distinguishing the four agricultural types (e.g., simple horticulturalists lack metallurgy, plow, and iron, while advanced agrarians have all three).

Having classified the 694 societies, the Lenskis then demonstrated that at least some of the types and/or subtypes differ appreciably as regards socio-cultural phenomena.[11] Thus, the percentage of societies having slavery varies from 10 in the hunting-gathering type to 84 in the herding type, while the percentage of societies in which there is a "belief in a Supreme Creator who is active and supports human morality" varies from 2 in the hunting-gathering type to 80 in the herding type (Lenski and Lenski, 1974:107,106).

CRITICAL COMMENTARY. The Lenskis undertook the kind of research required to maintain or refute technological determinism, something contemporary Marxists in sociology neglect.[12] Nonetheless, the work of the Lenskis is subject to several criticisms.

If the two propositions are the premises, the findings cannot be deduced from them; and there are no obvious alternative premises.The criticism is not blunted by the Lenski admission (1974:108) that "Technological factors are obviously incapable of explaining *all* social phenomena," because they do not stipulate the kind of finding that would falsify their theory. Recall that the slavery range is 74 percentage points, from 10 percent for hunting-gathering societies to 84 percent for herding societies. By contrast, the range is only 1 for polyandry. What is one to make of such contrasts? Are the slavery findings more consistent with the theory than the polyandry findings?

True, the Lenskis could claim that, despite the unanswered questions, their findings do reveal an evolutionary pattern. Specifically, they appear to assume that their diagrammatic or tabular arrangements of societal types (commencing with hunter-gatherer and ending with industrial) represents an evolutionary path, but they treat the notion of an evolutionary path ambiguously. Their notion of general evolution (1974:84) suggests that the first instance of each type appeared in the sequence indicated by their figures and tables (hunting-gathering . . . industrial), one implication being that hunting-gathering societies appeared before any horticultural society. However, their notion of *specific* evolution (1974:84) appears more relevant, because the argument appears to be (see Lenski and Lenski, 1974:96) that societies change in a particular path or sequence (e.g., if a particular society is hunter-gatherer, it has never been simple horticultural). Yet few anthropologists now believe in invariant paths or sequences in socio-cultural change, one reason being evidence that some Plains Indian tribes changed from horticulture to hunting, after adopting the horse. True, the Lenskis speak only (1974:96) of "common paths of evolutionary development," but that terminology precludes the possibility of compelling evidence.

Even granting the ostensible assumptions of the Lenskis as to "technological advance," such differences imply nothing about temporal sequences. Furthermore, if the Lenski arrangement of societal types represents nothing more than an ordinal scale of technological advancement, then a regular increase in some variable (e.g., the percentage of societies having slavery) would be evidence of technological determinism but not of unidirectional change in technology.

Finally, the Lenskis placed fishing, herding, and maritime societies in a special panel of their tables and in an irregular position in their diagrams, thereby indicating that those types somehow do not fit into the "common evolutionary path." Yet they never confronted this question about the path: Does it represent an assumption about general evolution, an assumption about specific evolution, or simply an ordinal scale of technological advancement?

Leslie White's Technological and Cultural Determinism

If technological determinism is materialism, then Leslie White (1899–1975) was more unambiguously a materialist than was Marx; and this quote (White, 1959:18–19) clearly asserts technological determinism: "we have distinguished four kinds of components of cultural systems: technological, sociological, ideological, sentimental, or attitudinal. . . .The technological factor is the basic one; all others are dependent upon it." That White was an anthropologist is irrelevant, for a defensible distinction between sociology and anthropology has never been drawn.

WHITE'S CULTURAL DETERMINISM AND SUPERORGANICISM. White could be described as a cultural rather than technological determinist. No one ever devoted more attention to the notion of culture, and White's superorganicism was more extreme than that of Durkheim. Examine some of White's statements.

"Culture put young children to work in textile mills for fifteen hours a day, begat sweat shops that consumed the lives of impecunious women who had no alternatives but starvation or prostitution." (1975:11)

"Cultural systems act and react upon one another, band with band . . . nations with nations." (1975:17)

"Culture and cultural vectors grow by themselves . . . culture is a process *sui generis*, a stream in which cultural things and events produce other cultural things and events. . . ." (1975:67)

"Our cultural system is wrestling with the question of mass transit systems in metropolitan areas. . . ." (1975:71)

"Each vector strives to have its own interest served, regardless of the welfare of other vectors or of the society as a whole. . . ." (1975:80)

"A cultural system divided against itself cannot behave in a rational manner." (1975:98)

"Thus we explain the behavior of peoples in terms of their cultures. . . ." (1949:125)

"while the culturalogist is quite willing to admit that it is people who 'enamel their fingernails' or drink milk, he desires to point out that whether they do or not is determined not by themselves but by their culture." (1949:144)

"Behavior varies because cultures differ. You will do, or taboo, what your culture calls for." (1949:153)

The quotes demonstrate that White never balked at reifications, some grotesquely anthropomorphic. Thus, "culture" puts children to work, has objectives, grows, produces things, wrestles with questions, strives to have its own interests served, can be divided against itself, and may not behave in a rational manner. Even White's assertion that culture determines human behavior will not bear examination. Reexamine the next-to-last quote. If "enameling fingernails" is not a cultural trait unless the people enamel their fingernails (how could it be otherwise?), then it is tautological to describe that behavior as determined by the culture.

"Cultural tautology" is common in the social science literature, but the argument is not just that White indulged in tautologies. When he comes close to an explanation comprising a genuine nomothetic generalization, the term *culture* is superfluous. "In some cultural settings, warfare is non-existent; the mode of life as culturally defined has no place for it. In other situations there is only occasional skirmishing between tribes. Where rich hunting or fishing grounds are at stake, we can expect military conquests" (White, 1949:132). The first sentence appears partially tautological, but the last one does not. Note, however, the term *culture* does not appear in the last sentence, and it would serve no purpose.

CONCEPTIONS OF CULTURE. To his credit, White confronted several conceptual issues, commencing with this conception: culture exists in the mind and consists of ideas (1973:23–26). White rejects that conception because (1) it does not explain the ideas, (2) is ambiguous as to "whose mind," and (3) precludes the notion of material culture (1973:23). He then argues that conceiving of culture as learned behavior admits the possibility of a subhuman species having a culture and surrenders anthropology's subject matter to psychology (24). Still another conception—culture as an abstraction—is rejected by White because the meaning of "abstraction" is unacceptably ambiguous (25). Finally, White rejects the numerous definitions of culture that require that more than one individual be involved in a class of events or things for that class to be cultural. He argues that classes of phenomena should be distinguished "in terms of their *properties*, not in terms of their *number*" and "as far as human beings and human behavior and culture are concerned, there is no such thing as an individual apart from other individuals" (33).

Although White created the impression that his opponents agree in their definitions of culture, there are now even *surveys of surveys* of definitions (e.g., Weiss, 1973); and they reveal bewildering contrasts. Those contrasts reflect far more than idiosyncratic choices of terms; the definitions differ primarily because of the very kind of conceptual issues White recognized. However, like many sociologists and anthropologists, White ignored this question: If culture is real, perceptible, and does things, why is it that definitions of culture are so starkly divergent?

White (1973:29) defines culture as "that class of things and events dependent upon symbolizing, products of symboling, considered in an extrasomatic context." Numerous statements by White (1949, 1959, 1973, 1975) clearly indicate that symboling is learned behavior and that ideas are products of symboling; yet White balked at recognition of learned behavior or ideas in defining culture. But why did he use the arcane term "extrasomatic context"?

Although White never defined the term explicitly, the following passage is revealing: "The growing infant and child becomes humanized, culturized, as a consequence of cultural influences exerted upon him from the world outside his own organism. From his standpoint the origin and locus of culture are definitely extrasomatic" (1959:13). So culture appears to be the very thing that White denies it is—learned behavior. Moreover, because it is difficult to think of human events or things that are not "dependent upon symboling" or "products of symboling," culture is a virtually inclusive class of human events or things, meaning a hodgepodge.

"Culture" would be less of a hodgepodge had White stipulated that the symboling in question must be collective or shared; but he eschewed that limitation, having overlooked the possibility of a number being a class property. Consider one implication. There are numerous American communities, perhaps entire counties, in which over several generations no woman has murdered her mother. When such a murder occurs, is it a trait of that community's culture? Given White's definition and his denial of a collective quality, an affirmative answer is clearly suggested. White himself emphasized that the reckoning of kinship requires "symboling"; and if matricide is "not dependent on symboling," then that phrase has no meaning.

The suggestion is not that a definition of culture can be such as to avoid problems and resolve issues. To the contrary, *any* definition will be (1) inclusive to the point of being meaningless, (2) arbitrary in the extreme, or (3) so vague as to promise only negligible empirical applicability. Space limitations preclude an elaborate defense of that conclusion, but consider Weiss's definition of culture, one reached after contemplating literally hundreds of alternatives: "all human nongenetic, or metabiological, phenomena" (1973:1382). Even assuming, erroneously, that the terms *nongenetic* or *metabiological* are empirically applicable without an elaborate definition, by Weiss's own admission the first term denotes a residual category; and that category is hardly less of a hodgepodge if designated as "metabiological."

WHITE'S TECHNOLOGICAL DETERMINISM. Given the foregoing, White's statement is astonishing: "The 'discovery' of culture may one day rank in importance in the history of science with the heliocentric theory of Copernicus or the discovery of the cellular basis of all living forms" (1949:405). However, White's technological determinism can be distinguished from his cultural determinism because technological arguments do not require the term *culture*.

Although various statements by White suggest technological determinism, it is not logically possible to falsify any of those statements. Thus, his claim (1959:18–19) that ideology depends on technology is vacuous because it does not even suggest an answer to this question: Which particular component or feature of technology is the regular antecedent of any particular component or feature of ideology? So White, like Marx, at most only set the scene for research on correlates of technology.

Harris's Cultural Materialism

Marvin Harris refers to cultural materialism as a scientific research strategy, meaning: "an explicit set of guidelines pertaining to the epistemological status of the variables to be studied, the kinds of lawful relationships or principles that such variables probably exhibit, and the growing corpus of interrelated theories to which the strategy has thus far given rise" (1979:26). The quote introduces a perspective, one relevant for sociology even though Harris is an anthropologist.

THE BEHAVIORAL, THE MENTAL, THE EMIC, AND THE ETIC. Repeatedly, Harris asserts that cultural materialism is concerned primarily with behavioral and etic phenomena rather than mental and emic phenomena. By behavioral Harris (1979:31) evidently means "all the body motions and environmental effects produced by such motions," and by mental he evidently means "all the thoughts and feelings that we human beings experience within our minds." So the "behavioral" evidently includes both overt behavior and its environmental effects, and the term *mental* evidently denotes both cognitive processes and dispositional states (e.g., motives, values).

The issue is Harris's suggestion that a concern with the "mental" precludes progress in the social sciences. While the suggestion is clear, the rationale is not. Harris (especially 1979:59) appears concerned with causal primacy and evidently assumes that overt behavior determines internal behavior. Whatever the assumption's merits, Harris scarcely defends it; rather, he alludes to the need for extreme caution in "making inferences about what is going on inside people's heads. . . ." (39). Granted that need, Harris erroneously assumes that social or behavioral scientists literally *see* humans saluting, kissing, or turning left, meaning that those scientists do not and need not make inferences as to mental states. Moreover, Harris never recognizes that mental notions enter into the very language that social and behavioral scientists use to describe overt acts. Perhaps he assumes that his *The Nature of Cultural Things* (1964) provides a strictly "overt behavior" language, but no one, not even Harris, has employed his esoteric language in research. An observer would require thousands of pages to describe a brief political speech (several pages pertaining to the movement of the speaker's hands alone); and the product would be the most grotesque document in the history of science.

Harris's treatment of the emic/etic distinction is confusing. Just before introducing the two terms, Harris makes this argument about participants (humans under observation by social or behavioral scientists): "the thoughts and behavior of the participants can be viewed from two different perspectives: from the perspective of the participants themselves and from the perspective of the observers" (1979:31). Judging from subsequent statements (Harris, 1979:32–45), the quote bears on the emic/etic distinction, with emic referring to any participant's communication of his or her perspective and etic referring to an observer's perspective. However, when introducing the two terms (1979:32), Harris immediately muddies the conceptual water with these statements: "Emic operations have as their hallmark the elevation of the native informant to the status of ultimate judge of the adequacy of the observer's descriptions and analyses. The test of the adequacy of emic analyses is their ability to generate statements the native accepts as real, meaningful, or appropriate. In carrying out research in the emic mode, the observer attempts to acquire a knowledge of the categories and rules one must know in order to think and act as a native. . . . Etic operations have as their hallmark the elevation of observers to the status of ultimate judges of the categories and concepts used in descriptions and analyses. The test of the adequacy of etic accounts is simply their ability to generate scientifically productive theories about the causes of sociocultural differences and similarities."

Harris's statements stop short of what is needed—explicit definitions; and they are far removed from Pike's original conceptualization of the emic and etic (1967). Conceptual clarity is lessened more when Harris refers to the emic mode, etic accounts, the emics of the situation, etic behavioral components, emic components, etic outputs, and etic inputs. Harris acknowledges (1979:39) "misunderstandings" but contributes to them by attempting to treat the emic/etic distinction and the mental/behavioral distinction as logically independent (38). Whatever an "emic" is—an account, a perspective, an interpretation, a description, an explanation, or what have you—it must be communicated by a participant. How could the communication be other than behavior? To illustrate suppose that a sociologist conducts an investigation to identify the incest norms of an English-speaking social unit and makes this summary statement: "Ninety percent of the social unit members stated that they disapprove of marriage between cousins." Would that statement pertain to the mental-emic, mental-etic, behavioral emic, or behavioral-etic? Harris's commentary on the distinctions provides no basis for an answer.

A CORNUCOPIA OF EXPLANATIONS.   In *Cultural Materialism* and *Cannibals and Kings*, Harris purports to explain numerous phenomena, such as the origins of agriculture, the origins of war, infanticide among early peoples, Yanomamo aggressiveness, the origins of male supremacy, the Oedipus complex, the origin of pristine states, the rise and fall of pre-Columbian states in Mesoamerica, Aztec cannibalism, taboos on pork, the origin of the sacred cow complex, hydraulic societies and early oriental despotism, the origin of capitalism, marriage rules, the origins of neolithic modes of production, the rise of chiefdoms, matrilineality, and feudalism. Given such an illustrative list, it is not surprising that some of Harris's explanations take up less than a page; but it is surprising that not one is deduced from explicit premises. However, Harris (1979:62–63) does formulate four "human biopsychological selective principles," as follows:

"1. People need to eat and will generally opt for diets that offer more rather than fewer calories and proteins and other nutrients.

2. People cannot be totally inactive, but when confronted with a given task, they prefer to carry it out by expending less rather than more energy.

3. People are highly sexed and generally find reinforcing pleasure from sexual intercourse—more often from heterosexual intercourse.

4. People need love and affection in order to feel secure and happy, and other things being equal, they will act to increase the love and affection which others give them."

The role of those principles in Harris's explanations is obscure, especially because he acknowledges (1979:63) so many exceptions that any rigorous deductive explanation is precluded. Furthermore, the four principles are perhaps secondary to this statement (Harris, 1979:55–56): "The cultural materialist version of Marx's great principle is as follows: The etic behavioral modes of production and reproduction probabilistically determine the etic behavioral domestic and political economy, which in turn probabilistically determine the behavioral and mental emic superstructure." Harris identifies his version as the "principle of infrastructural determinism"; and his statements (especially 1979:53) clearly justify this summary: infrastructure components probabilistically determine the structure, which in turn probabilistically determines the superstructure. Because Harris's principle is limited to the behavioral-etic components of both the infrastructure (mode of production and mode of reproduction) and the structure (domestic economy and political economy), one must surely wonder about the mental-emic components (if any) of the infrastructure and structure.

Harris's term *probabilistically determines* reflects more than caution; he admits that cultural materialism "does not deny the possibility that emic, mental, superstructural, and structural components may achieve a degree of autonomy from the etic behavioral infrastructure" (1979:56). Yet the admission has little import because Harris makes few assertions about the causal relation between specific infrastructural components and structural components, or between specific structural components and superstructural components, and there are some contradictions. As one case, Harris (e.g., 1977:41 and 1979:91) insists that warfare has promoted female infanticide, but in his scheme (1979:52–53) war is a structure component and infanticide is an infrastructure component.

Harris does not speak this question: What is the mechanism by which structural or superstructural components are explained in terms of infrastructural components? Should he reply that the mechanism is strict causation, one must wonder how, for example, the adoption of maize can *directly* cause complex chiefdoms or even rapid population growth (see Harris, 1979:93).

Alternatively, Harris may have entertained selective survival as the explanatory mechanism. That possibility is suggested by his frequent reference to "selection" and a long section in *Cultural Materialism* (1979:60–62) on the subject; but he consistently stops short of any declaration in this form: the reason that X (e.g., the taboo on pork, the sacred cow complex) exists is that no society survives unless X is present. Without something like that declaration, an explanation of X in terms of selectivity is not defensible.

Given Harris's emphasis on the behavioral-etic, he seems to have eschewed purposive behavior as an explanatory mechanism. However, many of his statements suggest that X exists because the participants recognize X's advantages, and his frequent references to cost/benefit are ambiguous precisely because that term applies both to purposive behavior and to selective survival. Consider one of Harris's frequent implicit recognitions of human behavior's purposive quality: ". . . Sahlins proposes that nothing but the whimsical feeling that 'dogs are like people' prevents Americans from eating them. But the reason Americans feel that way about dogs surely is related to the practical disadvantages of a dog-meat industry" (1979:255). Practical disadvantages? So Harris appears to be a closet utilitarian, and the quote is not isolated instance. Elsewhere, Harris attributes (1979:84) the absence of marriage classes among the Eskimo to their impracticality.

To summarize, Harris explains diverse socio-cultural phenomena without deductions from explicit nomothetic premises. Moreover, defensible theories require some reference to explanatory mechanisms, but Harris skirts that issue.

The Relevance of Control

Each theory examined in this chapter commences with a distinction between basic categories of phenomena, one of which is supposedly an ultimate cause. Hence, the conceptualization of basic categories (e.g., infrastructure, structure, superstructure) is crucial. The categories must be exhaustive and mutually exclusive; and the terms denoting the categories must be empirically applicable, meaning that independent investigators agree in assigning particular events or things to those categories. Even sociologists who appreciate the importance of empirical applicability may not recognize the advantages of a conceptual scheme that permits confident classification of all events or things. Materialists have never had such a conceptual scheme, even though they need it more than do advocates of any other perspective.

Although Harris's identification of basic categories is more careful than was Marx's, the empirical applicability of his terminology is extremely doubtful. Moreover, it appears that Harris really has no clear idea as to the content of specific components of the infrastructure: "As a cultural materialist, I hold that infrastructure should consist of those aspects of a sociocultural system which enable one to predict a maximum number of additional components up to the behavior of the entire system if possible" (1979:64). So Harris proposes to conceptualize infrastructure by crude induction, which makes his principle of infrastructural determinism vacuously true.

Whereas Harris's category of ultimate causes is so broad as to defy definition, in the case of White and the Lenskis the category is too narrow, ostensibly limited to technology. Reconsider how Harris (1977:29) unwittingly questioned technological determinism by arguing that the absence of a certain kind of biotic control (over traction animals) in the New World precluded an entire line of technological change associated with the wheel.

A theory about control could be in keeping not just with Marx but also the Lenskis, White, and Harris. The theory could be based on something lacking in Harris's theory—an empirically applicable conceptual scheme (chapters 2 and 3). In the case of White's theory and the Lenski theory, the category of ultimate causes is limited to technology, but both could be supplemented by the identification of various kinds of biotic and human control.

THE PARAMOUNT EXPLANATORY ISSUE. The theories in question share two things with regard to explanatory mechanisms. First, none of the theorists address the subject fully, if at all; and, second, it appears that none of the theorists would explain a socio-cultural phenomenon by reference to human behavior's purposive quality. There is no indication whether White took strict causation or selective survival as his explanatory mechanism, whereas Harris appears to lean toward selective survival but frequently alludes to purposive behavior. So only the Lenskis come close to an explicit explanatory mechanism, which is clearly (1974:70–75) selective survival. Specifically, if a particular space-time relation holds between socio-cultural variables, it holds because exceptions are eliminated. But the Lenskis leave a host of questions about selectivity unanswered.

In writing on socio-cultural continuity, innovation, and extinction, the Lenskis emphasize intrasocietal selection, the selection of elements within a society (1974:70). However, they use the term *selection* in this vacuous sense: in any society sooner or later some socio-cultural phenomena disappear and others appear. But to infer selectivity is surely not informative, especially since no reference is made to its possible purposiveness.

When it comes to intersocietal selection, the Lenskis do something that functionalists (chapter 9) avoid—they clearly identify selective survival as their explanatory mechanism (1974:71–72): "While the selective process goes on within societies, eliminating first one, then another, of the elements of sociocultural systems, a similar process is taking place in which societies themselves are the units whose survival is in question." Yet in stating their two basic propositions and in commenting on their related research findings the Lenskis (1974:110, 104–9) did not refer to intersocietal selection. For that matter, some of their findings generate doubts. There is enormous variation from one type of society to the next in the percentage of societies where "leather working is wholly or largely a female type of activity." Are we to assume that in some types of societies (e.g., hunting-gathering) but not others such female activity is necessary for societal survival? Surely that assumption is debatable, but the criticism is not that the Lenskis subscribe to it; instead, they simply ignore the issue.

It cannot be said that the Lenskis or Harris explicitly and categorically rejected purposiveness as explanatory mechanism. For example, the Lenskis state: "the major transformations of human social life have hitherto never corresponded to the consciously held objectives of the historical participants" (1974:75). But they (1974:75) equivocate as to "the significance of man's conscious, rational faculty" by stating "we should never minimize this factor, neither should we exaggerate it." As for Harris, he allows that "Cultural materialism does not view inventors or any other human beings as zombielike automata whose activities are never under conscious control" (1979:59). That statement suggests moderation, but it scarcely clarifies. Yet many of Harris's casual observations and even some of his "selective principles" seem to underscore the purposive quality of human behavior, as when commenting on the transformation to plant domestication he argues that (1979:86) hunter-gatherers "cannot fail to note the relationship between seeds, shoots, and mature plants." Then consider Harris's contention that "dowry" should not be confused with "groom-price" in patrilineal societies: "it [dowry] is not considered compensation for the loss of the groom's productive and reproductive services. Rather, it is intended to help cover the cost of maintaining an economically burdensome woman. . . ." (1977:59). So Harris invokes "emics" and/or the "mental" when needed.

TOWARD A RESOLUTION OF THE ISSUE THROUGH THE NOTION OF CONTROL. Explanatory mechanisms pose an unresolvable issue if it is assumed that *only one* is relevant for sociology. Otherwise, the issue is really a problem, meaning that sociologists often do not know which mechanism is most relevant. The problem may be particularly acute in the case of materialist theories, but it is by no means peculiar to them; indeed, it haunts all of the social sciences.

There are four reasons why taking control as sociology's central notion would be entirely compatible with all explanatory mechanisms. First reason: the notion forces and facilitates recognition of the purposive quality of human behavior and its importance. Generally, control behavior is purposive behavior and vice versa, but there are advantages in taking control rather than "purpose" to be sociology's central notion. The former can be conceptualized much more precisely by focusing on basic types of control. Furthermore, "purpose" is internal behavior, which alone has no environmental impact; but control behavior is both overt and internal behavior simultaneously.

Second reason: the notion of control is compatible with explanatory mechanisms other than purposiveness. Consider strict causation. Superorganicists notwithstanding, a space-time relation between macro, aggregate, or structural variables actually pertains to a relation between types of behavior; and surely one type of human behavior may cause another type. To say, for example, that some people weep profusely in some situations because of their socialization is to suggest strict causation. So in explaining a relation between variables, sociologists should speak in terms of "control behavior." That term is preferred over "behavior in general" because even though virtually all of human behavior is control behavior, the latter can be conceptualized much more precisely.

Variables may be linked through selectivity rather than strict causation, but selectivity operates through control behavior. As for individual selectivity, the probability of reproduction for an individual (a matter of both mortality and fertility) clearly depends on the amount of effective control that he or she exercises and/or the amount of effective control exercised over him or her by others. As for socio-cultural phenomena—norms, institutions, culture complexes, or what have you—they influence the probability of survival of individuals or populations by impeding or facilitating control (as illustrated in chapter 4).

Third reason: the notion of control bears on a question about ultimate causes. How can the nonhuman components of the environment (e.g., climate, terrain, natural flora) cause human behavior? The question's difficulty is one reason why materialist theories are ambiguous when it comes to physiographic determinism. One of Harris's statements is illustrative: "The ecology of the Artic . . . does more than constrain the Eskimos from hunting in the nude; it determines that they must put something warm on" (1979:222). Must? How so? Selectivity is one answer (nude Eskimos are eliminated); but as long as selective survival is the only way to answer questions about environmental variables, theorists will treat those variables ambiguously (if at all). Progress with the notion of physiographic determinism requires recognition that the "environment" determines human behavior primarily through the attempts of humans to control the environment. Thus, whatever else it may be, wearing warm clothing is virtually always an attempt at inanimate control. Moreover, environmental features can make certain types of control difficult if not impossible, and humans may perceive that relation. Harris (1979:105) unwittingly supplies an illustration: "Rainfall agriculture leads to dispersed, multicentered forms of production. Hence it is doubtful that any pristine state ever developed on a rainfall base." He did not add: because would-be rulers are likely to perceive the difficulty of controlling a widely dispersed population.

Fourth and final reason: an adequate explanation of some if not all socio-cultural phenomena may require more than one explanatory mechanism, and the notion of control makes it possible to describe and think of all three mechanisms operating simultaneously. Reconsider Harris's failure to recognize that potential rulers may perceive the difficulty of controlling a dispersed population. Such perception could stem from strict causation, meaning that a dispersed population *causes* some members to perceive the population as dispersed. However, whether a potential ruler perceives the difficulty as surmountable or insurmountable, a description of his or her action or inaction would necessarily entail reference to a purposive quality. Finally, assume that a potential ruler in a region of rainfall agriculture fails to perceive control difficulties or underestimates them, with the consequence being that he or she makes an attempt at regional control and fails. Each such failure would be an event in a selective process. The illustration suggests how describing and thinking in terms of control is conducive to recognition that the presence or absence of a particular socio-cultural phenomenon is commonly problematical because of the difficulty in predicting perceptions of potential controllers and/or the success of control attempts.

NOTES

1. Mukerji (1983) describes "materialism" as a cultural characteristic, theme, force, or value system rather than a theory or even a philosophy.
2. Alexander (1982-II) describes Marx's work as comprising several theories—on commodity forms, on class struggle, on revolution, on ideology, on class consciousness, etc. Such attribution of multiple theories to Marx is conventional, but identifications of those theories are markedly divergent.
3. Turner and Beeghley: "all of Marx's predictions and propositions are historically specific: they apply only to capitalist society as it existed in Europe during the 19th century. Thus, for example, neither his 'general law of capitalist accumulation' nor his prediction of increasing impoverishment of the proletariat is intended to be trans-historical or abstract in the sense that it could be applied to in any society in diverse historical epochs" (1981:171).
4. Statements about evidence refuting Marx are not made in the naive belief that Marxists will accept them. Marxist social scientists appear determined to deny the relevance of whatever is offered as evidence invalidating Marx's arguments. The point is illustrated by McQuarie's commentary on Popper's critique of Marx, especially: "many of the 'laws of motion' of capitalist society stated in the three volumes of *Capital* are not concrete predictions but are rather abstract laws pertaining solely to the interaction of variables within the theoretical model" (1977–78:480). Likewise, in defending Marx's "theory of immiseration," Lebowitz declares: ". . . Marx's argument was in fact no more than a methodologically sound working *assumption*" (1977–78:431). Such statements illustrate why antipositivism is a boon to Marxists.
5. Cohen does speak of work relations as "*material* relations of production and, being material, they fall outside the economic structure. . . ." (1978:35) and subsequently indicates that the economic structure consists entirely of social

relations of production; but the meaning of "work relations" is hardly clarified by characterizing them as material rather than social.

6. The *possibility* of reciprocal causation is a problem even in the case of Premise I (Figure 12-1). Consider Marx's statement: "every big mechanical invention is followed by a greater division of labour, and each increase in the division of labour gives rise in turn to new mechanical inventions" (1963:139).

7. There are even doubts as to whether the three questions are sufficient, because Figure 12-1 is only the simplest of three possible versions of a "Marxist" theory. For illustrative purposes, assume that each of the four sets of variables in Figure 12-1 comprises only two variables, such that $P1$ and $P2$ refer to potential means of production, $B1$ and $B2$ refer to production behavior, $E1$ and $E2$ refer to economic relations, and $C1$ and $C2$ refer to all other socio-cultural characteristics. Even with that maximum simplification and assuming simple causation, there would be 16 possible versions of an "interset" theory, two being: $P1 \rightarrow B1 \rightarrow E1 \rightarrow C1$ and $P2 \rightarrow B1 \rightarrow E2 \rightarrow C1$. Now contemplate two illustrative representations of 16 possibilities in the way of an "intraset" theory: $P1 \rightarrow P2 \rightarrow B1 \rightarrow B2 \rightarrow E1 \rightarrow E2 \rightarrow C1 \rightarrow C2$ and $P2 \rightarrow P1 \rightarrow B2 \rightarrow B1 \rightarrow E2 \rightarrow E1 \rightarrow C2 \rightarrow C1$. Finally, a "mixed" theory (some causal relations interset and some intraset) would be so complicated, even with only two variables in each set, that the number of possibilities cannot be calculated readily. So it appears impossible to reformulate Marx's theory through an empirical assessment of all possibilities (i.e., inductively), even assuming agreement as to the sets of variables. Should followers of C. Wright Mills (especially 1959a) dismiss the foregoing as "abstracted empiricism," the real issue is the choice between systematic empiricism and (at most) casual empiricism.

8. As a case in point, Cohen (1978) perpetuated a Marxist tradition: never stipulate what would be negative evidence. Even the premises of Cohen's version are left implicit. As for Cohen's identification (1978:278–96) of Marx's theory as "functionalist," his conception of a functional explanation (1978:249–77) is incomprehensible. Cohen (1978:278) admits that Marx failed "to say . . . what kind of explanation he is hypothesizing"; and it is grotesque when Cohen suggests (1978:278) that the theory is functionalist because Marx used such relational terms as *correspond to*, *rises on*, and *is conditioned by*. Such uncritical selection of relational terms is merely characteristic of a discursive theory, functional or otherwise.

9. The following suggests that Cohen would agree: "By *ownership* is here meant not a legal relationship but one of *effective control*" (1978:35). But the quote suggests that a legal relationship has nothing to do with control.

10. The question presumes the possibility of direct causation rather than causation through production behavior and/or economic relations, which contradicts Figure 12-1. However, that presumption introduces only one of a multitude of debatable questions concerning Marx's theory.

11. Similar findings were reported by Hobhouse et al. (1930) in a publication not cited by the Lenskis.

12. In the fifth edition of *Human Societies* (1987:92) the Lenskis avow "rejection" of technological determinism. The second edition has been used here because it

is less ambiguous and equivocal with regard to implying technological determinism (or "materialism"). Although the Lenskis' subsequent rejection of technological determinism perhaps makes their position appear more tenable, at the same time it makes their argument and claims more obscure.

Chapter

13

Conflict Sociology and Social Class

If trends in sociological perspectives could be expressed numerically, the comparisons probably would indicate that conflict sociology became dominant in the 1970s and declined in the 1980s. No connection between Marxist sociology and conflict sociology fully explains that change. The conflict perspective had a large following in early American sociology (see Coser's commentary, 1956:15–20), but its orientation was predominantly reformist, not Marxist. Even today there is a conflict sociology apart from Marxism, one that emphasizes the processual character of conflict; and Marxist "materialists" view both conflict and class as derivative phenomena.

The Consensus-Conflict Debate

Even more than interpretive sociology (chapter 10), conflict sociology is "the opposition." However, a perspective that exists only in opposition to conventional sociology can have no enduring distinctive features.

Consensus or Dissensus

Although the "consensus-conflict" debate did not become intense until after about 1965 (concomitant with the decline of functionalism), it has a long history. Bernard (1983) traces the debate from antiquity, and he classifies 14 individuals, commencing with Plato and ending with Dahrendorf, as being either a consensus theorist or a conflict theorist. The consensus-conflict dichotomy is conventional but misleading.

THE OPPOSITE OF CONSENSUS.   The opposite of consensus is dissensus, not conflict. Moreover, the empirical association between the cooperation-conflict continuum and the consensus-dissensus continuum is debatable, and it may well be that the relation is contingent on, among other things, the types of social units in question (e.g., nuclear families versus countries). True, it is difficult to think of conflict without some dissensus (i.e., some contrast in the values or other normative orientations of the conflicting parties), but it may well be that dissensus is at most only sufficient for conflict. Two populations could battle for land precisely because they do agree that might makes right.

If someone complains that the illustration is mere sophistry, the complaint also applies to the theories that Bernard treats as exemplifying the consensus-conflict debate. Had systematic empirical evidence been demanded as a basis for assessing those theories, the debate would have been abandoned long ago.

The Ultimate Sterility

Although it would strain credulity to assert that a society can exist despite maximum dissensus, many sociologists accept the idea that a society can be "based" on conflict. Consider Dahrendorf's statement about the conflict model of society, which Bernard (1983:3) quotes without reservation: "From the point of view of this model, societies and social organizations are held together not by consensus but by constraint, not by universal agreement but by coercion of some by others."

Dahrendorf's statement does not deny the possibility of a social unit being "held together" by the coercive acts or threats of *one* individual. Otherwise, the statement is somewhat misleading; but if that possibility is not denied, the statement is no more credible than the assertion that some societies are free of dissensus, conflict, and coercion.

Casual observations indicate that (1) no society ever has approached maximum consensus or dissensus and (2) the extent to which social order is based on conflict varies substantially. Although sociologists are likely to accept both generalizations, the consensus-conflict debate has not given way to this question: What theory best explains societal variation in the extent to which consensus or conflict is the basis of social order?

None of the 14 theories that Bernard examines even address the variation question, and Bernard's classification of each theory and theorist as being either "consensus" or "conflict" is disputable. Thus, Bernard (1983:63) characterizes Hobbes as "probably one of the most confusing cases in the history of the consensus-conflict debate," but he concludes (1983:193), contrary to an army of predecessors, that Hobbes was a *consensual* theorist.

Bernard does not recognize that the "grand" theories of sociology and social philosophy are so vague and discursive that they are open to virtually any interpretation. Yet many sociologists do not merely tolerate those theories; they more nearly venerate them. A genuine concern with systematic evidence is not necessary to participate in perennial assessments of the theories,[1] and those who demand the derivation of testable predictions as an essential step in an assessment can be dismissed as "positivists."

Given the way sociologists assess theories, the consensus-conflict debate could continue indefinitely.[2] The debate's intractability evidently makes it all the more attractive to sociologists (see Alexander, 1982, especially I:5–35); but it is one of sociology's sterile legacies, and conflict sociology will suffer as long as tied to that debate.

Conceptual Problems

Sociologists often write at length on conflict without defining the term or recognizing conceptual problems. As a case in point, Bernard (1983) published some 229 pages on the consensus-conflict debate without even posing the question: What is conflict? More remarkable, in writing the longest book on conflict sociology Collins (1975) never conceptualized "conflict."

Coser's Definition

Because Lewis Coser (especially 1956:7) is one of those rare sociologists who appreciate the importance of conceptualization, his definition deserves special attention: "Social conflict . . . will provisionally be taken to mean a struggle over values and claims to scarce status, power and resources in which the aims of the opponents are to neutralize, injure or eliminate their rivals" (8). Surprisingly, Coser never recognized three problems with that definition, nor did he formulate an unprovisional alternative.

FIRST PROBLEM.   Coser's definition limits conflict to a struggle over "values and claims to scarce status, power and resources." But if two parties are engaged in a struggle wherein each aims to eliminate the other, why deny that the struggle is conflict apart from whatever caused it?

The phrase that makes Coser's definition appear too narrow is objectionable also because there are doubts as to its empirical applicability. There is no reason to assume even appreciable agreement among independent investigators not only as to what a particular struggle is "over" but also as to the meaning of the terms "values, claims, status, power, and resources." Therefore, deleting "over values and claims to scarce status, power and resources" would both broaden Coser's definition and further its empirical applicability.

SECOND PROBLEM.   Coser's definition is conventional in that the *definiendum* is *social conflict* rather than *conflict*. Sociologists may use the latter term inadvertently or, as here, to avoid cumbersome locutions (e.g., social conflict sociology); but there is agreement on two points. First, not all instances of conflict constitute social conflict. Second, even when sociologists use the term *conflict*, they commonly mean *social conflict* (as in this book).

Coser's definition provides no answer this question: What is *social* about social conflict? To illustrate, when a purse-snatcher and the victim struggle to possess the purse, that struggle could be social conflict by Coser's definition. Yet the illustration is alien to all examples in Coser's book (1956).

THIRD PROBLEM. There are doubts about the empirical applicability of several terms or phrases in Coser's definition. In the case of the term *struggle*, the question is whether it denotes all kinds of "opposing wills." If so, any argument between two individuals would satisfy that part of Coser's definition. Now the second unanswered question: Does the term struggle denote only a series of related but discontinuous acts? If not, instances of purse-snatching might qualify as conflict along with numerous other kinds of isolated acts.

There are also doubts about the meaning of "neutralize." It can be construed as meaning either "resulting in a physical disability" or as "resulting in social impotence"; and unless the former means total, it is not a subclass of the latter. However, because total physical disability or social impotence is extremely rare, it appears that the meaning of "neutralize" must be a matter of degree (i.e., to reduce physical ability and/or social competence).

The point is not that Coser employed the wrong terms in defining conflict, nor to do what Coser failed to do—define several of his key terms. Rather, there is only this point: until those key terms are defined, the empirical applicability of Coser's definition is not promising.

Forms of Social Conflict

Writing on conflict without defining the term is ludicrous in light of the variety of phenomena that one sociologist or another has identified as conflict or manifestations of it. An illustrative list follows: assassinations, boycotts, coups, demonstrations, discrimination, dissent, factionalism, insurrections, irredentism, lockouts, looting, mutiny, prejudice, protests, purges, rebellion, repression, revolts, revolutions, sectarianism, schisms, social banditry, sabotage, separatism, squatters, strikes, subversion, terrorism, treason, uprisings, and war. The list excludes particular historical manifestations of conflict (e.g., Luddism, apartheid); and it also excludes various phenomena that have a problematical connection with conflict, such as censorship, desertion, disinheritance, divorce, grievance, and homicide.

The suggestion is not that conflict must be defined such that it includes all phenomena denoted by the illustrative lists; rather, there are two arguments. First, given the variety of manifestations of conflict, the term *conflict* cannot be left undefined but taken as empirically applicable. Second, because even a relatively narrow definition of conflict will encompass very diverse phenomena, a defensible general theory on the subject may require what appears to be an extremely narrow definition of social conflict. In light of the second argument, extant theories on conflict were ill advised.

Two Conflict Theories: Sans Marx

Lewis Coser (1956) will be long remembered for stating a theory of conflict that stems from Simmel and exemplifies functionalism. However, while rejecting the Marxist dictum—that a theory of conflict must be a theory about class conflict—Coser eschewed (1956:22) the inclination of functionalists, Parsons in particular, to depict conflict as a "disease in need of treatment."

Coser's Propositions

Coser (1956) modestly identified Simmel as the source of sixteen propositions about conflict, but only someone who has read Simmel can appreciate Coser's accomplishment. Even Simmel's admirers rarely speak of his theory or theories (as the case may be). Simmel's writing (e.g., 1950) is a bewildering mixture of rhetoric, empirical generalizations, anecdotes, implicit definitions, and illustrations, with digressions on digressions.

So it is not surprising that Coser evidently was unable to reduce several of Simmel's arguments to an explicit, one-sentence proposition. Thus, Coser (1956:48) commences his treatment of Proposition 4 (below) with a quote from Simmel that runs for four sentences and some 125 words, but Coser never purports to reduce that quote to an explicit proposition. In such cases, one sentence has been selected from several alternatives as the suggested proposition. In several other cases, rather than purport to restate Simmel in the way of an explicit proposition, Coser wrote a paragraph. Given such a case, unless two sentences in the paragraph could be taken as a dual proposition, one of three choices was made: first, select one sentence as the suggested proposition; second, treat the entire paragraph as a proposition; or, third, treat the epigraph as the proposition. All such cases are identified parenthetically in the following list of propositions (from Coser, 1956:38, 47, 48, 50, 59, 64, 71, 80, 85, 95, 110, 118, 121, 132, 133, 139) as "suggested," "dual," and/or "epigraphic."

Proposition 1: "Conflict serves to establish and maintain the identity and boundary lines of societies and groups."

Proposition 2 (dual): "(1) Conflict is not always dysfunctional for the relationship within which it occurs; often conflict is necessary to maintain such a relationship. . . . (2) Social systems provide for specific institutions which serve to drain off hostile and aggressive sentiments."

Proposition 3 (suggested, dual): "In realistic conflict, there exist *functional alternatives as to means*. . . . In nonrealistic conflict . . . there exists only *functional alternatives as to objects*."

Proposition 4 (suggested): "Conflict can occur only in the interaction between subject and object; it always presupposes a relationship."

Proposition 5 (suggested): "Antagonism is usually involved as an element in intimate relationships."

Proposition 6 (suggested): "A conflict is more passionate and more radical when it arises out of close relationships."

Proposition 7 (suggested): "Conflict may serve to remove dissociating elements in a relationship and re-establish unity."

Proposition 8 (suggested): "The absence of conflict cannot be taken as an index of the strength and stability of a relationship."

Proposition 9 (suggested): "Conflict with another group leads to the mobilization of the energies of group members and hence to increased cohesion of the group."

Proposition 10 (epigraphic): "Conflict with another group defines group structure and consequent reaction to internal conflict."

Proposition 11 (suggested): "Rigidly organized struggle groups may actually search for enemies with the deliberate purpose or the unwitting result of maintaining unity and internal cohesion."

Proposition 12: "Conflicts in which the participants feel that they are merely the representatives of collectivities and groups, fighting not for self but only for the ideals of the group they represent, are likely to be more radical and merciless than those that are fought for personal reasons."

Proposition 13 (epigraphic): "Conflict binds antagonists."

Proposition 14: "In view of the advantages of unified organization for purposes of winning the conflict, it might be supposed that each party would strongly desire the absence of unity in the opposing party. Yet this is not always true. If a relative balance of forces exists between the two parties, a unified party prefers a unified opponent."

Proposition 15 (epigraphic): "Conflict establishes and maintains balance of power."

Proposition 16 (epigraphic): "Conflict creates associations and coalitions."

THE PARAMOUNT CRITICISM.   An issue haunts the foregoing, and it transcends the parenthetical identifications. Indeed, it transcends Coser's frequent use of "may," which precludes falsification of the proposition.

Coser wrote (1956) when functionalism was the dominant sociological perspective; and some of the propositions (notably 1, 2, 7, 9, 10, 13, 15, 16) appear to be explanations of conflict, not simply assertions of conflict's effect. Why, otherwise, did Coser use the term *serve* rather than *effect* or *consequence*? As suggested in chapter 9, such a term is characteristic of a functional statement and creates the impression of an explanation.

If there were evidence that in each case conflict is at least the necessary cause for the effect attributed to it and that the alleged effect is at least necessary for the survival of the type of social unit or social relation in question, the propositions could be valid explanations. Such evidence would take the form of a demonstration that in the absence of conflict instances of the social unit or social relation disappear or never appear.

Unfortunately, much in keeping with functionalism, Coser presented no findings to support the propositions. Moreover, there is no prospect of testing the propositions. Most of the constituent terms (e.g., *identity of societies, boundary lines of societies, strength and stability of a relationship, cohesion of the group, group structure,* and *balance of forces*) defy anything like a complete and clear definition, and in no instance does Coser stipulate a measurement formula or research procedure.

Collins's Conflict Sociology

Randall Collins (1975) wrote of "conflict theory" and formulates 17 postulates and over 400 propositions, but his book could be construed as a general treatise on sociology and/or a statement of a conflict perspective. Doubts about identifying the book—what it is or was intended to be—are harbingers of difficulties in evaluating it.

AN AMORPHOUS THEORY. Collins's book is evidence that explicit premises are not sufficient to clarify a theory's structure. Collins's statements are identified as postulates and propositions, and he clearly indicates that some of them were derived. Otherwise, however, the theory has no coherence.

Contrary to convention, Collins indicates that some of his postulates are derived from other postulates. Worse, the rules of derivation are not identified, and the derivations were not made by any conventional logic (e.g., the classical syllogism). Such defects are illustrated by two of Collins's postulates, as follow (Collins, 1975:153):

> "XIII. *Cicourel's multimodality principle.* All human communications take place in several modalities (visual, aural, emotional) simultaneously.
> XIV. *Garfinkel's indexicality principle.* Social interactions can be carried out smoothly to the extent that mutually accepted implications do not have to be verbally explicated (from XIII)."

Garfinkel is not the only one who should be puzzled by the cryptic "from XIII" at the end of Postulate XIV.

Collins's theory is all the more amorphous because there is no discernible rationale for the labels he applies to the constituent statements. In particular, there appears to be no difference between the statements with regard to the character of the constituent terms. Two terms may differ sharply as to empirical applicability, but there is no hint of that contrast in Collins's postulates or propositions. The situation is unfortunate because, otherwise, tests of propositions could bring evidence to bear indirectly on the postulates from which the propositions were supposedly derived, even if most of the terms in the postulates are not empirically applicable. Collins may have contemplated direct tests of each postulate (i.e., without derivations), but he made no stipulations as to requisite data or research procedures. Indeed, although attributing some of his statements to others (e.g., Cicourel, Garfinkel), Collins offers no systematic supporting evidence.

A THEORY WITH NO SUBSTANTIVE FOCUS. The title of Collins's book suggests that his theory pertains to conflict, but the term *conflict* or derivatives (conflicts, conflictual) appears at least once in only 14 of the 419 postulates and propositions. In recognition that Collins may have used synonyms and antonyms of conflict extensively, a separate count was made. Only six obvious instances—anger, fighting, hostility, peace, conquest, faction—were found, and one or more of them appears in only 13 of the 419 postulates and propositions.

The substantive focus of Collins's theory is all the more obscure because there is no hint of any particular source or cause of conflict. In particular, although Collins cites Marx often, the term *class* or *class conflict* appears in only one postulate or proposition. As for related terms (e.g., *occupations*, *occupational, income, wealth, stratification, stratified*), one or more appears in only 71 of the 419 postulates and propositions.

If the theory does not pertain to conflict, what is its substantive focus? It appears that Collins simply compiled statements—some micro, some macro, some phenomenological, some structural, some about humans, some about animals—without regard to any logical connection. Four examples (Collins, 1975:73, 152, 158, 219) must suffice.
"Postulate I. Each individual constructs his own subjective reality.
Postulate IX. All animals have autonomic emotional (hormonal, neural, postural, gestural) responses to certain gestures and sounds made by other animals.
Postulate XV. Human beings have strong drives for sexual gratification.
Proposition 5.42. The more things people have to talk about with each other, the longer they can talk."

Granted the possibility that Collins's work is a treatise on sociology rather than a conflict theory, it nonetheless suggests a major problem with the conflict perspective. Apart from its Marxist connection, the perspective appears to have little coherence.

Conceptions of Social Class

Numerous sociological studies of class have scarcely considered conflict, and there are even a few conflict studies that do not emphasize class. Nonetheless, the two subjects are treated together if only because of the Marxist attribution of conflict to irreconcilable class interests.

An Ancient Problem

The sterility of the "consensus-conflict" debate is rivalled by the century-old struggle with the notion of class. The concern with class is a struggle in that only a hopeless ideologue can be content with his or her thinking on the subject, commencing with misgivings about any extant definition. To the extent that one of those definitions is empirically applicable, it appears arbitrary; and to the extent that it avoids arbitrariness, the definition promises negligible empirical applicability.[3] Indeed, were it not for their perennial indifference to conceptual problems, sociologists might have long ago abandoned the notion of class.

There is one obvious reason for the staying power of the class notion—it is commonly construed as the cornerstone of Karl Marx's legacy (see Wright, 1985:6–8). Yet Marx wrote less than two printed pages toward completion of "The Classes," the last chapter in volume III of *Capital* (Marx, 1909). So why do thousands of publications create the impression that Marx conceptualized class carefully and formulated a related theory when he actually did neither? Whatever the answer, an army of exegetes (e.g., Dahrendorf, 1959:8) have written as though they know what Marx would have said had he completed the last chapter of *Capital*.

Even if all exegetes should agree as to what Marx would have said, their version is not likely to clarify his conception of class; and anyone who argues that it needs no clarification is deluded. Some of Marx's most ardent disciples freely grant that he never systematically conceptualized class (see, e.g., Wright, 1985:6). Why, then, is there an enormous literature on Marx in the English language alone? Marx offered a rationale for anticipating the end to capitalism, even vague directions for expediting it, and a justification for delighting in that prospect. So it is hardly surprising that Marx has attracted so many disciples and opponents as to rival Darwin and Freud.

Marxist Conceptions of a Class

It is difficult to identify any kind of argument about conceptual matters that has not been made in connection with Marx's conception of class. Even the assertion that Marx never formulated an explicit definition of a class can be challenged (see Anderson, 1974:50) by quoting Marx (1926:133): "In so far as millions of families live in economic circumstances which distinguish their mode of life, their interests, and their culture, from those of other classes, and make them more or less hostile to other classes, these peasant families form a class."

Because Marx does not declare that only such families can constitute a class, his statement could be construed as describing only a sufficient condition, and perhaps one that cannot be generalized beyond peasants. Be that as it may, in seeking an empirically applicable definition of a class, no one is likely to take Marx's statement seriously. The problem is not just the vague terms in the *definiens*—notably *economic conditions*, *mode of life*, and *culture*. Marx violated an elementary rule in using the term *classes* to define class.

AN ALTERNATIVE DEFINITION.   What other definition of class did Marx suggest? The most common answer is something like this: A class comprises all individuals and their dependents in a given social unit who occupy more or less the same position in economic relations. Even should critics grant that the definition is Marxist, there will be unending objections to some of its terms. Some critics will reject the reference to individuals, others will prefer reference to relations of production rather than to economic relations, and still others will insist on reference to social relations of production.

Because Marxists are superorganicists, they describe a class as a relation, a position, an activity, an organization, or perhaps even a culture; in brief, anything other than a population or set of individuals. They will not be swayed by the argument that empirical application of a class definition entails the notion of class membership or a boundary, which implies a set of individuals or a population.[4] But there is no mystery. When a systematic attempt is made to actually apply Marxist class terms, the outcome is usually startling, as in the case of the conclusion reached by Wright et al. (1982:710) about managers: "They are thus in a sense *simultaneously in two classes.* . . ." Wright et al. do not even confront this question: How would the situation be different if one speaks of "manager" as a position rather than "managers" as individuals?

Whatever the reactions of Marxists to the foregoing definition of class, it is far from empirically applicable. Without definitions of "economic relations" and "position" that extend to class criteria, there is no prospect of even appreciable agreement among independent investigators in identifying the number of classes in a given social unit, much less the members of each. Marx never explicitly defined economic relations or position, being content with allusions to ownership of the means of production.[5] Because of his preoccupation with capitalism, he never recognized the range of logical possibilities with regard to ownership, some of which are suggested by the following two statements. First, the means of production are owned by all who use them, by some of those who use them, or by none who use them. Second, the means of production are owned by all of those who consume the products of those means, by some of the consumers, or by no consumer. Marx scarcely gave any thought to "ownership" classes other than (1) those who own but do not use the means of production and (2) those who use but do not own the means of production. Equating class (1) with the bourgeoisie is misleading, and the same may be said of class (2) and the proletariat. For one thing, unless the term *means of production* refers to all means of production, it is ambiguous. Marx wrote as if means of production are homogeneous with regard to ownership (contemplate "the means of production"); but there are few if any societies in which all means are owned only by those who do not use them. Yet Marx never introduced a quantitative distinction in his conception of a class such as: a class is not bourgeois unless its members own more than 50 percent of the means of production. He did write as though capitalists never use a means of production; but if as organizers of production capitalists do not "use" factory buildings, the English language fails us.

OWNERSHIP VERSUS CONTROL.   Although Marx's critics argue that the relation between ownership and control changed in this century such as to invalidate Marx's interpretation of capitalism (see Wright's commentary, 1979:23, on Dahrendorf), there are three problems with that argument. The first is a confusion of conceptual issues and empirical propositions. Specifically, if corporate managers are declared a class because they control but do not own the means of production, it is not clear what Marxist proposition, if any, is refuted.

Turning to the second problem, it is pointless to argue that ownership has nothing to do with control. Some stockholders neither directly nor completely control the means of production that they jointly own; but it is grossly incorrect to suggest that no stockholder ever acts in the belief that (1) the action increases or decreases the probability of some change in the corporation's means of production and (2) the increase or decrease is desirable. True, control (direct or indirect, complete or partial) over a corporation's means of production is a matter of degree, but surely stockholders attempt more control over the corporation than do private citizens who have no affiliation whatever with the corporation. Such elementary points are overlooked in the now hoary owner-ship-control debate, because the debate is carried on as though stockholders or "legal owners" either have complete control or none at all.

The third problem with the control-not-ownership argument is that its advocates simplify control just as much as Marx oversimplified ownership. Specifically, as suggested in chapter 12, when describing control over production it is necessary to confront several questions, such as: Who controls access to the use of the means? Who controls where the means will be used? Who controls when the means will be used? Who controls how the means will be used? Who controls what the means will produce? Who controls the distribution of the products of the means? Who controls the terms and conditions under which the products of the means are used or exchanged? The questions are important because they bear on three arguments. First, all individuals who exercise more or less the same kind of control (e.g., direct versus indirect, complete versus partial) and amount of control over means of production are members of the same class. Second, such a definition of a class differs from Marx by an emphasis on control rather than ownership. And, third, a "control language" exceeds an "ownership language" with regard to empirical applica-bility (especially when considering universality), descriptive utility, and rich-ness of theoretical implications.

OTHER DIVERSE DISTINCTIONS.   Today, a bewildering variety of distinctions are invoked in defining class or in stating class criteria, all purportedly in the Marxist tradition.[6] The following list only illustrates that variety: *Anderson* (1974:50, 52): common position in the economic mode of production, separate way of life and cultural existence, conflicting and hostile interests vis-a-vis another class, social relationships and social community extending across local and regional lines, a society-wide class consciousness, political organization, producer of means of existence versus nonproducer, lives solely from the creation of value through labor versus lives from surplus value, works at fragmented and insecure job versus other, exploited versus exploiter; *Poulantzas* (1975:224–81): mental versus manual and supervisory role versus nonsupervisory role; *Wright* (1979:40): autonomy versus dependence, managerial or supervisory versus ownership, and small versus large number of employees.

Although only illustrative, the list demonstrates gross dissensus among Marxists over identification of classes and class criteria. There are two reasons. First, Marx often ignored the distinction between class attributes that are true by definition and those that are empirically contingent, with the consequence being that for more than a century Marx's followers have differed in their interpretations of his statements about class attributes.[7] Second, especially since the middle of this century, Marxists have stated criteria in order to recognize classes that cannot be distinguished readily by reference to ownership of the means of production, especially the "new middle class."

Identifying Particular Historical Classes

In describing the distinctive features of a "relational" as opposed to a "gradational" conception of class differences, Wright wrote of the former: "Classes are not labeled along a continuum from lower to upper; instead, they have names, such as: capitalist class, working class; lord, serf; ruling class, subordinate class" (1979:6). Wright makes it clear that the relational conception is Marxist but without acknowledging that the "naming" of particular historical classes has created problems. Marx himself was inconsistent when naming the classes of "capitalist" societies, and that inconsistency haunts contemporary Marxists. Why? Marxists do not identify historical classes after and as a consequence of applying a definition and related class criteria; rather, they accept existing labels (e.g., *bourgeois, patrician, proletariat*) despite their vague meaning. So it is hardly surprising that Marxists differ among themselves over class terminology.

As an illustration of the problem, contemplate Marx's statement: "wage laborers, capitalists and landlords form the three great classes of modern society resting upon the capitalist mode of production" (1909:1031). The omission of the proletariat (evidently "wage laborers" in the quote) and the implied lumping of the land-owning aristocracy with other landlords are relatively minor problems.[8] What of government employees and the self-employed? Indeed, what of categories that Marx elsewhere recognizes, such as intellectuals and the lumpenproletariat? To reply that Marx intended to recognize only the "major classes" is a dodge. The truth of the matter is that Marx departed without ever facing this question squarely: What are the classes of capitalist society, how do they differ, and why is each a class? As a consequence, when Marx recognizes a class at some point in his writing but ignores it elsewhere, one does not know what to make of it. So many of Marx's arguments suggest a two-class model, the capitalist or bourgeoisie versus the proletariat, that his occasional recognition of other classes appears anomalous. The problem survives Dahrendorf's assertion (1959:20) that Geiger refuted "unjustified objections to Marx's two-class model." If the two-class model is justified, why did Marx frequently refer to more than two classes?

Marx's inconsistencies are minor in comparison to those of contemporary Marxists. Consider some of the class designations in four widely cited books (Anderson, 1974; Poulantzas, 1975; Szymanski, 1983; and Wright, 1979), all pertaining to contemporary capitalist societies: bourgeoisie, capitalist, capitalist servant classes, commodity-producing classes, intermediate class, laboring classes, middle class, new middle class, new working class, old middle class, owning class, petty bourgeois, producing class, proletariat, propertied capitalist class, propertyless working class, ruling class, service-producing class, semiautonomous employees, small employers, traditional proletariat, traditional capitalist, traditional working class, working class, and working class proper. The contrasts become even greater in light of some terminological ambiguities. Thus, for example, Wright identifies several categories as "contradictory class location" (1979:40): top managers, middle managers, technocrats, and foremen/supervisors as located between the bourgeoisie and the proletariat; semiautonomous employees as between the proletariat and the petty bourgeoisie; and "small" employers as between the petty bourgeoisie and the bourgeoisie. Wright could not bring himself to identify those categories as classes, even though he admits (1979:26) that in a sense all class positions are "contradictory."[9] Szymanski's (1983:84–93) recognition of an intermediate sector, an excluded sector (a "class group . . . traditionally called the 'lumpenproletariat' "), and a miscellaneous category is troublesome, although refreshing for candor. Then there is the incongruity of Anderson's (1974:131) "capitalist servant class," which would include (among others) Rolls Royces chauffeurs, call girls, and some government officials and employees (although which type is unclear).

None of the three schemes provides an answer to either of the following questions as they apply to various socially recognized categories in the U.S. First, is the category a component of class composition? Second, if so, where does it fit in that composition? The military, civilian government officials, and other civilian government employees are three of several such categories.

Should Wright attempt to justify his inconsistent inclusions and exclusions (see Wright, 1978, 1979, 1985) of such categories by describing them as "outside" the capitalist mode of production, it would be a dodge (after all the categories are "in" a capitalist country). Szymanski (1983:93) is content with assigning the police to his intermediate sector, and Anderson's treatment (1974) of the three categories defies description.

Some Alternatives to a Marxist Conception of Class

Given the objections to a Marxist conception of social class, the plethora of alternatives is not surprising. However, space limitations make it necessary to treat all of the alternatives in terms of three broad categories.

THE OBJECTIVE METHOD OF CLASS DELIMITATION. When it comes to the assignment of members of a social unit (e.g., a particular city) to classes, one method is "objective" in that the perceptions of those assigned are ignored (see Broom et al., 1981:288). The method is relevant in connection with Max Weber's definition of class: "We may speak of a 'class' when (1) a number of people have in common a specific causal component of their life chances, insofar as (2) this component is represented exclusively by economic interests in the possession of goods and opportunities for income, and (3) is represented under the conditions of the commodity of labor markets" (1978:927). That definition could be quoted to question Weber's puzzling reputation in sociology as the master conceptualist. Unless one reads Weber's commentary, the definition is virtually incomprehensible; and the more one comes to understand the definition, the more glaring are some omissions. For example, even granting Weber's contention (1978:927) that a class is not a community, did he mean, as his definition suggests, that the residents of, say, Delhi and Dublin, could be members of the same class? Then there must be grave doubts about the prospect of an empirically applicable definition of "specific causal component of life chances," let alone what "represents" that component. Hence, whatever the advantages of Weber's definition over a Marxist definition, empirical applicability is not one of them. Indeed, the range of application is much more limited for Weber's definition, because it implies that classes exist only where there is a "genuine market for labor power and capital" (see Wright, 1979:9).

Most versions of the objective method treat occupation, education, or income as criteria for distinguishing classes and assigning individuals to those classes; and unless those criteria are stressed the method is not distinct from a Marxist conception of class, because "position in economic relations" is actually another (fourth) objective criterion. In any case, the delimitation of classes on the basis of occupation, education, or income is fraught with problems, one of which pertains to the occupational criterion. Because specific occupations (e.g., architect, waiter) are not classes, criteria are needed to assign specific occupations to a particular class. However, because occupational titles may have no necessary bearing on positions in economic relations, the Marxist definition of class is not relevant. But if the income or education associated with an occupation is taken as the criterion for assigning incumbents to a particular class (e.g., upper), then education or income is the class criterion, not occupations. The most common alternative is to consider an occupation's prestige as the criterion for assigning it to a particular social class, but the underlying assumptions are obscure. One possibility is to assume that (1) occupations largely determine the potential for acquiring wealth and (2) people attribute prestige largely in terms of wealth and recognize the relevance of occupations. Even so, why not assign an individual to one class or another on the basis of his or her personal prestige without considering his or her occupation?

Whatever the justification for considering occupational prestige as a class criterion, why also consider education and income? If those three variables are all closely related empirically, then it is redundant to consider more than one; but, otherwise, what is the justification for considering all three simultaneously? Moreover, given the discovery of some class correlate (e.g., a particular class has the lowest fertility), is the association due to the occupational prestige level, the educational level, or the income level of that class? To treat the three separately—as the question requires—is to imply that each individual is a member of three classes.

Whatever the level considered—occupational (prestige), educational, and/or income—designation of a particular maximum or minimum level as a class criterion reeks with arbitrariness. Sociologists speak glibly of a lower class, a middle class, an upper class, and perhaps finer distinctions (e.g., upper middle class), even though the difference between one class and another may be a matter of $1, one year of school attendance, or one "prestige point." Such arbitrariness appears inherent in the objective method of class delimitation.

SUBJECTIVE METHOD AND REFERENCE CLASSES. Interpretive sociologists are likely to argue that insofar as class membership determines an individual's behavior, it does so only through his or her identification with a particular class. The argument suggests that the most appropriate basis for class delimitation is the "subjective" method (Broom et al., 1981:289), which consists of asking social unit members a question something like this: "What is your social class?"

Even assuming that all social unit members understand the question and respond by saying something other than "I don't know," at least in some English-speaking communities there will be a bewildering variety of answers, such as: working class, average class, middle class, poor, well-off class, farmer, employee, and on and on (see studies cited in Jackman and Jackman, 1983:14–17).[10] Are "farmer" and "employee" acceptable responses? If there are 27 distinct responses, are there 27 classes in the community? Can some of the response terms be treated as synonyms? Which ones? Are these synonyms: working class, lower class, proletariat, proud-but-poor, poor employee class, laboring class? If so, why? If not, why not?

THE REPUTATIONAL METHOD AND ATTRIBUTIONAL CLASSES. Because sociologists are supposedly interested in interaction, they might see merit in this argument: an individual's interaction with other social unit members is determined not so much by his or her reference class as by the class membership attributed to him or her by others. That argument is evidently the rationale for the "reputational" method of class delimitation (Broom et al., 1981:290), which is illustrated by this question: What is the social class of (*name of a particular individual*)?

The reputational method cannot be applied readily in any community so large that any two residents selected at random are unlikely to know each other, and any rule as to "sufficient consensus" in the class identification of a particular individual is likely to be arbitrary. Again, however, the seemingly insurmountable problem is the possibility of diverse responses to the question. As in the case of the subjective method, the question need not be "open-ended," meaning that each respondent could be required to select his or her answer from a list of class labels (e.g., working class, middle class, and upper class). However, there are doubts about whether defensible rules for selecting the appropriate labels can be devised. Yet there is every reason to assume (see studies cited in Jackman and Jackman, 1983:14–17) that choice of class labels makes an appreciable difference (e.g., many more respondents will select "working class" than "lower class").

Stratification Rather Than Class?

Given the problems that haunt the conceptualization of social classes, it is no wonder that in all but Marxist circles so many sociologists now speak of stratification rather than class. The terminological change is especially understandable because the basic stratification idea is simple: in most if not all social units, some members have more of the "things" that members in general consider desirable or value. The "things" most frequently studied in stratification research are income and education.

SURMOUNTABLE PROBLEMS. The amount of stratification is typically expressed by applying some formula to the distribution of social unit members (or families or households) among a set of interval categories (e.g., annual income of less than \$10,000, \$10,000–\$19,999 . . . and more than \$99,999). Those categories are arbitrary, but they can be so detailed that there is no real problem.

To date, stratification research has been concerned almost entirely with income and education, but friendship, love, respect, and even kinship are also desired and valued. Stratification research could extend to all such phenomena, still another advantage over conventional "class" research.

THE INSURMOUNTABLE PROBLEM. Perceptions of social classes as real and qualitatively distinct supposedly have prevailed in numerous societies (e.g., England, perhaps even in this century). When that is the case, the substitution of a stratification terminology for class distinctions will ignore a crucial feature of differentiation (see Vanneman and Pampel, 1977).

The foregoing emphasis on perceptions notwithstanding, class may have a legal basis, which is a qualitative distinction. As an illustration of another "class-related" qualitative distinction, one is either an employer or one is not (with or without a legal criterion). Such distinctions are rarely considered in stratification research.

Class and Control

A class is here defined as a distinct division of members of a social unit who exercise more or less the same kind and amount of external control over human behavior. A "division" is not distinct with regard to amount of control unless it occupies one curve in what is at least a bimodal distribution (without such a distribution, one can speak of stratification but not of classes).

Although the definition is not precise, it is no more vague than any definition in the Marxist tradition.[11] Indeed, "kind and amount of external control over human behavior" is more realistic than "position in economic relations." To clarify the latter phrase, Marxists speak of the ownership of the means of production, which suggests the possibility of only two classes, propertied and propertyless. However, three labels—employers, employees, and self-employed—are alone sufficient for doubts about only two classes even in capitalist countries, let alone all social units. Most important, the "control" definition of class permits recognition of various types of classes (economic, political, cultural, etc.), which promises a way to circumvent what currently appears to be insoluble problems and irresolvable issues in identifying classes.

Despite what has been said, a control definition of class does not stand totally in opposition to the Marxist conception;[12] but Marxist labels for classes are questionable even in light of the argument made against replacing a class terminology with a stratification terminology. Briefly, it is surely doubtful whether such labels as *bourgeoisie, petty bourgeoisie, proletariat,* and *lumpen-proletariat* correspond to social perceptions in any society. There is not even evidence that those terms are used by most members of any English-speaking community. For that matter, what is one to make of glaringly divergent class labels used by Marxist writers (compare, e.g., Anderson, Szymanski, Poulantzas, and Wright) and change in choice of labels (e.g., Wright refers to "proletariat" in 1978:42 but "working class" in 1985:48)?

The extent to which humans perceive others in terms of control, including the capacity to control (power), is an empirical question yet to be answered. Nonetheless, there is no doubt that in the antebellum South the terms *master* and *slave* were socially real, nor that they are control terms. The same is true of *employer*, *self-employed*, and *employee* in Anglo-American countries. Indeed, had Marx used those three terms to identify the major classes of capitalist societies, several conceptual problems would have been avoided; and the three can be conceptualized readily in terms of control. To be sure, each "class," employers particularly, is extremely heterogenous with regard to control or anything else, but the idea that social classes can be defined so as to realize homogeneity in each class is a vast illusion (see Aldrich and Weiss, 1981). The terms *bourgeoisie* and *proletariat* promote that illusion, and *petty bourgeoisie* suggests a degree of terminological precision that is patently absurd.

STRATIFICATION AND CONTROL.   Research on income and education as bases of stratification is feasible primarily because census agencies publish enormous amounts of relevant data, but no agency gathers other than the grossest kind of control data (e.g., prison reports). Even surveys to gather data on income, educational attainment, and prestige are more feasible than research on control.

So practical considerations preclude attempts to replace measures of individual variation in income and education with measures of variation in the amount of control. Nonetheless, thinking in terms of control becomes important in connection with this question: What is the sociological significance of variation in income or education among social unit members? The answer has been suggested previously: the greater the variation, the greater the concentration of control in that social unit. The generalization's validity depends on the conception of variation, and the present conception is such that variance is greater for 0, 0, 0, 0, 20 than for 0, 2, 4, 6, 8.

Because prestige is considered desirable or valued, sociologists rightfully analyze it as a stratification variable; but they rarely recognize the connection between prestige and control. Recall evidence alluded to in a previous chapter—that the prestige of an occupation is a function of the extent to which persons in that occupation are perceived by others as having the capacity to control (power), perhaps including inanimate and biotic as well as human control.

WRIGHT ON INCOME VARIATION.   There are several ostensible alternatives to a control interpretation of income variation, one of which was given by Wright (1979) in his attempt to demonstrate that Marxist class distinctions account for much of U.S. income variation. Although obviously less conjectural than the present control interpretation and more commendable than subsequent commentary suggests, Wright's endeavour is subject to five objections.

First, Wright (1978, 1985) uses the ambiguous term *contradictory locations within class relations* ostensibly to justify recognizing categories (managers-supervisors, small employers, semiautonomous employees, petty bourgeoisie) that are patently alien to the conventional two-class Marxist schema for capitalist countries. Second, both the bourgeoisie-small employer distinction and the related criterion (ten or more employees for the bourgeoisie, in Wright, 1985:150) are blatantly arbitrary. Third, merely labeling the self-employed as petty bourgeoisie is nothing more than an obfuscation. Fourth, throughout his conceptual analysis of class, Wright frequently alludes to control but without acknowledging that it is *the* fundamental phenomenon; rather, he refers to control as some "capacity" that is "lodged in the social relations into which the individual enter," one of several impenetrable phrases in Wright's conceptualization of control (1978:24). Fifth, there is no place in Wright's explication for millionaire entertainment stars (television, movies, professional sports), and he cannot even claim that such persons inherited their wealth from bourgeois kindred.

Observe that the fourth and fifth objections are related. Had Wright not opted for an obscure structural conceptualization of control, he would have been able to describe the difference between all U.S. high-income and low-income categories in terms of control. In the case of the millionaire entertainment stars, it cannot be denied that they either control some of the behavior of multitudinous fans or play the role of strategic third parties in modulative social control, including advertising. So Wright and other Marxists strive to maintain a view of the world that has long since become a gross oversimplification at best; and as a consequence of embracing a vague structural conceptualization of control, there is no place in their schemes for various human phenomena, especially charisma and talent.

Conflict and Control

To repeat, apart from its Marxist connection, the conflict perspective has little coherence (for elaboration, see McQuarie and Murray, 1984). So describing and thinking about conflict in terms of control takes on special significance for the perspective.

Some Marxist Arguments about Conflict

Judged in terms of the frequency of wars, revolutions, rebellions, riots, and terrorism, conflict apparently varies enormously among countries and over time (see Zimmermann, 1983). How can that variation be explained? It will not do for Marxists to answer "class conflict," even though consistent with their attribution of social conflict to class conflict. Thus, the sectarian conflict in Northern Ireland can be described by Marxists as class conflict, with Protestant actions reflecting capitalist interests and Catholic actions reflecting proletarian interests. However, Marxists have never even developed a methodology for demonstrating that a particular instance of conflict stems from class interests. More serious, to speak of class conflict as inevitable is tautological. Marx and his followers define a class by reference to class conflict (or "struggle").

THE ONTOLOGY OF CLASS CONFLICT. Whatever the connection between class and class conflict, surely the amount of class conflict is not even approximately constant. Yet a formula and a procedure for expressing the amount are lacking.

Should Marxists dismiss the criticism as "positivistic," it is recognized that class conflict could be treated as a purely theoretical notion and, hence, immensurable. But Marxists do not speak of "class conflict" as though purely theoretical. For that matter, if class conflict is a purely theoretical notion, evidence can be brought to bear on arguments about it only if the term appears in premises that imply testable conclusions. Such a theory cannot have a clear logical structure if stated discursively, but Marxists appear totally committed to discursive theory construction.

THE DETERMINANTS OF CLASS CONFLICT. Even assuming that class conflict is mensurable, there is no basis to assert that class conflict explains all forms of conflict. Marxists persist in suggesting such an explanation, but they tend to ignore the extreme diversity of conflict. Even ignoring *asocial* conflict and assuming that all social conflict is either class conflict or the effect of class interests, what determines the manifestation of social conflict? Marxist conflict theory is especially ambiguous about revolution, and Marx was equivocal about violence (see Popper, 1966, and Wardlaw, 1982:23). The younger Marx apparently believed that capitalism will end only through a violent revolution (see, e.g., Marx and Engels, 1947:73–78); but he later became ambiguous (see Popper, 1966:146–65), and contemporary Marxists have virtually abandoned the subject.

But ignore the diversity of conflict and assume three things: first, some defensible measure of class conflict; second, a defensible measure of social conflict in general; and, third, a demonstration of a substantial correlation between the two measures over time and among countries. The question would then become: What determines the amount of class conflict? The Marxist answer appears to be something like this: Any economic system runs its course, and beyond some point class conflict becomes more intense. Thus, in the case of capitalism, we have Marx's law of increasing misery, according to which the proletariat's plight worsens. A long-run increase in the unemployment rate and decline in real wages furthers the class consciousness of the proletariat and prompts them to revolutionary action, ending with the violent destruction of capitalism and the advent of socialism. Hence, the answer appears to be this: Over the past two centuries class conflict has been much greater in those countries where capitalism has developed the most.

As suggested in previous chapters, there is no systematic evidence that supports the Marxist theory of conflict, and three general observations contradict it. First, the violent transition to socialism has taken place not in countries of "mature" capitalism (e.g., Great Britain) but, rather, in Russia, China, and Cuba. Second, there has been no long-run increase in the unemployment rate along with the development of capitalism, and by any reasonable criteria in at least some nonMarxist countries the standard of living of employees has increased in this century (see, especially, Popper, 1966:166–98). Third, deaths from political violence evidently reached their peak in the U.S. during 1879–1908 (see Levy, 1969:88), with no violent overthrow of capitalism and long before capitalism had run its course.

Describing and Thinking about Conflict

While a control theory of conflict is not attempted here, the notion of control has no rival in describing or thinking about conflict. The immediate argument is that conflict can be reconceptualized in terms of control.

TOWARD A RECONCEPTUALIZATION.   All theories of conflict, Marxist or otherwise, rest on a dubious conceptualization of conflict (if any at all). The notion of control provides the basis for a new definition of conflict: It is a condition in which over at least two distinct time points the behavior of each of two parties has been oriented toward reducing the effectiveness of the other party's control, and each party is aware of that orientation. So defined, conflict is never an isolated attempt to reduce the effectiveness of someone's control (a control attempt in itself); there must be more than one such attempts. Moreover, conflict is social only if each "party" consists of two or more individuals who coordinate and/or synchronize their behavior in the shared belief that it decreases the probability of effective control by the other party. On some occasions one party may seek to avoid becoming the object of effective control by the other party, as when terrorists resort to secrecy to avoid apprehension, in which case one can speak of countercontrol or resistance to control; but those terms denote a kind of control in itself, and one of the two parties may attempt to reduce the effectiveness of the other party's control over a third party. Alternatively, the goal may be to reduce the effectiveness of the other party's inanimate or biotic control, as when in a strike or civil strife the protagonists engage in property destruction.

Conflict is commonly a study in antagonisms and a test of wills, but defining conflict in terms of control makes it more than phenomenological.

Because conflict is a kind of control, it must be manifested in overt behavior, although the behavior may or may not be violent.

TOWARD A CONTROL THEORY OF CONFLICT. Defining, describing, or thinking of conflict in terms of control is a step toward a theory if only because it suggests significant questions. Consider, for example, the universal identification of war as social conflict. Thinking about war in terms of control is conducive to recognition of a factor that should be entertained in formulating a theory. Someone once corrected an explanation of war—people want it— by pointing out that people actually want not war but the very things (e.g., territory) that lead to war. While the initial explanation is naive, its correction should extend to recognition that (1) people commonly engage in war only after a decision to do so has been made by a small group of individuals and (2) the decision is rarely made without considering the prospects for victory (i.e., successful control). Accepting those two points, the decision whether or not to commence a war is improbable unless those making the decision perceive the power of the prospective opponent as less than that of their own country or tribe. The argument is not refuted by pointing to instances (e.g., Britain and Germany, France and Germany) where an approximate balance of power did not prevent war. The argument is that an extreme imbalance is a necessary condition for a low probability of a country commencing a war with a far more powerful opponent, and the history of the relation between Canada and the United States or between Belgium and France is consistent with the argument.

Boycotts, strikes, and riots are not necessarily social conflict. A boycott does not become social conflict until (1) the object of the boycott attempts to reduce the effectiveness of the boycotters' control or (2) the boycotters attempt to extend the boycott to a third party, one the first party has heretofore controlled. The same may be said of a strike, except that a strike may be a reaction to an attempt by management to reduce the control of union officials. As for riots, even if law enforcement officials attempt to control rioters, rioters do not commonly cease and recommence their rioting, let alone orient their behavior during the interval to reducing the effectiveness of official controls. A more significant theoretical consideration lies in a comparison of boycotts, strikes, and riots. A riot is much less likely to become social conflict (as defined here) because rioters tend to be less organized than are boycotters and strikers. Hence, one suggestion is that the frequency of social conflict is influenced by the probability that collective behavior will become a social movement, and some social movements are nothing less than organization for social conflict. True, whether or not a grievance gives rise to social conflict depends in part on the "mobilization of resources" by the aggrieved party; but that term is exceedingly vague, and it can best be clarified by defining it in terms of attempted control.

The pursuit of a theory by thinking of conflict in terms of control would be a less radical step than it may appear. Marx used the term *control* time and again in describing class relations, and his contemporary followers also use it for that purpose frequently (see, especially, Wright, 1978). That use is likely to increase if Marxists ever become genuinely concerned with empirical applicability, and there is a simple reason. Unless "behavioral" terms are used to define class relations, the notion can have no empirical referent.

The use of the term *control* in connection with conflict is exemplified by Collins's theory (1975) about conflict. In his 419 postulates and propositions, the term *conflict* or a derivative term appears 14 times, but the term *control* or a derivative appears 70 times.

Then there are other nonMarxist theories about conflict that could be improved by greater use of the term *control*. For example, Sorokin's theory (1937) attributes variation in the punitiveness of criminal law to variation in "ethicojuridical heterogeneity." Even though Sorokin indicates that the term really refers to divergent values, it is also clear that he thought of divergent values as generating conflict. What he fails to emphasize is the primacy of this generalization: The dominant faction (whether a class, ethnic division, or co-religionists) uses criminal law as a means to control their real or imagined opponents. However, like Durkheim's theory of punishment (especially 1949), Sorokin's theory creates the impression that criminal laws simply appear without those who enacted them perceiving any need for harsh attempts to control dissidents.

Contrary to what has been said about Coser's functional propositions, a control theory of conflict would interest functionalists, provided that they fully recognize diverse kinds and consequences of conflict. Coser failed to emphasize the possibility that once conflict comes to be manifested in persistent and widespread violence it jeopardizes societal survival. Accordingly, if it is claimed that certain kinds of control are necessary to prevent persistent and widespread violence, the claim would be a functional explanation of that kind of control and one that deserves a hearing.

The last subject—prevention of violence—transcends the interests of functionalists. It is much in keeping with one of the major questions in the sociology of control (chapter 3): What determines the efficacy of each major means of control? That question bears on a literature commonly identified as concerned with "conflict resolution." That literature is vast, extending as it does to the prevention of nuclear war. Sociologists have made few outstanding contributions to that literature, and structural sociology never will make a major contribution; but if control were taken as sociology's central notion, the field would be the natural home for the study of conflict resolution.

The most promising path to a theory lies in the possibility that certain kinds of control generate social conflict. Austin Turk has made the most extreme and important arguments along that line, one suggested by this quote: "*Control* is . . . behavior intended to establish and maintain an unequally beneficial relationship" (1982:251). Turk's blanket characterization (note the suggested imagery: control is an evil) is debatable; but there is merit in what it implies—that when control encounters resistance, it is transformed into conflict. Hence, Turk's argument can be translated into a series of statements as the foundation of a theory: (1) control is a concomitant of attempts to establish and maintain exploitative relations, (2) those attempts are especially likely to encounter resistance, and (3) resistance is either conflict in itself or conducive to it.

While Turk's arguments point the way to a control theory about conflict, there are other routes. One is suggested by Collins's argument (1975:59):

"Why is there conflict? Above all else, there is conflict because violent coercion is always a potential resource, and it is a zero-sum sort. This does not imply anything about the inherence of drives to dominate; what we do know firmly is that being coerced is an intrinsically unpleasant experience, and hence that any use of coercion, even by a small minority, calls forth conflict in the form of antagonism to being dominated."

It is not clear why conflict is necessarily a *consequence* of being coerced, but "coercion" suggests a kind of control. Moreover, if it is granted that the relation between conflict and coercion is problematical, a theory about conflict could be pursued through attempts to answer this question: What kinds of controls are especially conducive to conflict and why those kinds rather than others?

NOTES

1. For one of the rare instances of systematic research, see Markoff and Shapiro's study (1985) of consensus and conflict in France, 1789.
2. Perhaps the debate should continue, but in connection with political sociology (as in Lipset, 1985) rather than an obsession for all of the field.
3. Wright (1978:3–4) identifies class as sociology's "one independent variable"; but, without expressing wonderment, he recognizes four contending conceptions of class and refers to class as an "essentially confused concept."
4. The argument can best be stated as a question: How can research on a class be conducted without observations or data on at least some class members? In championing the superorganic conception of class, Wright (1979:20–23) ignores the question even though his major research (1979) was based on income statistics for individuals. However, a more extreme view has been expressed by Poulantzas: "The principal aspect of an analysis of social classes is that of their places in the class struggle; it is not that of the agents that compose them. Social classes are not empirical groups of individuals. . . ." (1975:17). It is as though Poulantzas never asked himself: If the members of a social class in a particular territory and time period (e.g., the London urban area, 1985) cannot be identified, how could the term possibly be construed as empirically applicable?

5. The conceptual situation is no better now, a century later. "While all Marxists see exploitation as rooted in the social organization of production, there is no agreement among them as to how the 'social relations of production' should be defined, or about what aspects of those relations are most essential for defining classes" (Wright, 1985:37).

6. Wright et al. (1982:709) acknowledge but are undaunted by the problem: "As anyone familiar with the recent history of Marxist thought will know, there is hardly a consensus among Marxists over any aspect of the concept of class."

7. Indifference to the distinction between "definitional" and "contingent" features of social classes is endemic among contemporary Marxists. Contemplate Poulantzas: "Classes exist only in the class struggle" (1975:14). One must wonder how classes can commence struggling before they are classes. In any case, Poulantzas makes the validity of this statement a logical impossibility: There have been social units and periods in which there were classes but no class struggle. Yet Poulantzas (like all other Marxists) often makes it appear that class struggle is not merely a logical (conceptual) predicate of classes.

8. According to Popper, on Marx's "own assumptions" the class structure of a capitalist society may evolve to the point that there are seven classes (1966:148).

9. Wright's ambiguities and arcane class designations are also common in his more recent works. In his most recent (1985) he appears more concerned at various places with the notion of class structure than with developing defensible bases for defining a class, identifying classes, or formulating criteria of class membership.

10. Given such diverse responses to an open-ended "class" question, it is difficult to see how any set of fixed response categories (e.g., lower class, middle class, upper class) for answers to the class question can be justified. Of course, research (e.g., Jackman and Jackman, 1983) can bear on this question: Why do individuals differ in responding to a question about class identification? But such research is not guided by a *definition* of class.

11. With a view to identifying crude approximations of classes, the control conception of class offers far more empirical applicability than does the typical version of the Marxist conception. That is the case because it can be assumed that employers, self-employed, and employees differ considerably on average with regard to control. Spaeth's findings (1985) support the control conception of class, and his research points the way to finer distinctions than employers, self-employed, and employees. Because Wright's concern (especially 1978, 1979, 1985) with the empirical applicability of class terminology exceeds that of other Marxists, it is significant that he has made extensive use of data on employers, self-employed, and employees.

12. For that matter, time and again Marx used the term *control* in his observations on classes (see, e.g., Marx and Engels, 1947:39). Wright (1985 and especially 1979) uses the term *control* as a predicate of classes or class relations more than any other term. True, he appears to identify exploitation as the defining characteristic of class relations (Wright, 1979:14–18; 1985:36), but exploitation *requires* control. For example (Wright, 1979:15): "the capacity of a dominant class to control the surplus makes it possible for members of that class to consume without producing. . . . the control over the surplus product gives the

dominant class substantial social and political power beyond purely economic concerns. . . ." Note, however, that Wright (1979:24) conceptualizes control as an attribute of a social relation, and the outcome is not just a vague definition; additionally, he ignores this question: What is the connection between control and power?

Chapter

14

Elitology

With the possible exception of formalism (chapter 11) and behavioral sociology (chapter 15), no sociological perspective is truly distinctive because of its delimitation of sociology's subject matter. Hence, if a clearly unique delimitation is necessary for a perspective, then nothing examined in Part III (chapters 9–16) qualifies. But the perspectives differ as to emphasis on this admonition: focus on the most important sociological phenomenon.

Of all the sociological perspectives, the elitogical comes the closest to exemplifying the "focus-on-the-important" admonition.[1] Described otherwise, elitologists equate the sociology of elites with the sociology of the important. Even the commendably moderate statements of Burton and Higley suggest the importance that can be attributed to elites: "What were the basic contentions of classical elite theorists? The first and best-known was that elites are an inevitable feature of all societies. . . . The second contention was that variations in elite structure and functioning are decisive for certain major political outcomes. . . . Finally, the classical theorists contended that although elite structure and functioning determine many important political outcomes, elites are not omnipotent; instead, the relationship between elites and nonelite populations is ultimately an interdependent one in which each category limits the actions that are open to the other" (1987:220).

Little attention is devoted subsequently to the validity of the contentions, and this chapter offers neither a full explication of the elitological perspective nor a thorough assessment of the validity of elite theory.[2] Comments along either line are limited to those needed to set the scene for an identification of the principal strength and weakness of the perspective.

Early Elitology

There is appreciable agreement among sociologists that Vifredo Pareto (especially 1935, 1966, 1968) is the dominant figure in the history of elite theory.[3] But Pareto's dominance is puzzling because his theories have been criticized shrilly for generations (see, e.g., Meisel, 1965), and even his champions ostensibly see no merit in many of his ideas. Perhaps numerous social scientists will pay any price for an alternative to Marx and/or subscribe to the foregoing argument about the importance of elites.

Brief Observations on Pareto's Theory of Residues and Derivations

Borkenau (1965:109) notwithstanding, Pareto's theory of elites cannot be described adequately without reference to his theory about residues and derivations. However, it would be misleading to suggest that treating the two theories as "integrated" really clarifies. There is simply no way that Pareto's ideas can be stated clearly. Even by the slack standards of sociology it is questionable to identify Pareto's ideas as a theory rather than a ramble through European history, interspersed with anecdotes and scoffs at humanitarians. But contemplate, of all people, Talcott Parsons's statement: "Either Pareto's *Treatise* is really a hodgepodge and does not contain a coherent theory at all, or the critics have failed to penetrate to the deeper levels of the work" (1965:71). Parsons concluded that "the truth is nearer the latter" (71), but only to say subsequently that "the theory of the residues . . . is not a substantive sociological theory at all, but only a conceptual framework. . . ." (76–77).

PARETO'S NOTION OF RESIDUES AND DERIVATIONS. In a bewildering variety of ways Pareto (1935) suggests that nonlogical action or conduct stems from, reflects, or is determined by "things" that he called *residues*. What did he mean by that term? The answer given by Pareto himself or his interpreters in the way of equivalent terms is astonishingly diverse, such as *instincts*, *attitudes*, *mind states*, *sentiments*, *appetites*, *tastes*, *predispositions*, *drives*, *inclinations*, and *motives*. No quote of Pareto can be identified as the correct definition of a residue. Consider this statement (Pareto, 1935:509): "Residues correspond to certain instincts in human beings, and for that reason they are usually wanting in definiteness, in exact delimitation." Although Pareto labeled his Class I residues "instinct for combinations," it appears that residues are not instincts; rather, they only correspond to certain instincts. To say that something corresponds to an instinct is not to say that it is one; and such a statement is at most only a partial definition, one that hardly clarifies.

The most astonishing feature of commentaries on Pareto is the failure to recognize the possibility that he indulged in logomachy to avoid this definition: Residues are the real causes of nonlogical action or conduct. Had Pareto formulated that definition, it would have been obvious from the outset that "things" or "classes of things" can be identified defensibly as residues, if at all, only by reference to research findings. As such, the distinction between residues and nonresidues is purely *analytical*, having the same logical status as the distinction between "things that cause crimes" and "things that do not cause crimes." Just as the latter does not justify designating any particular thing as causal, so is that the case for the distinction between residues and nonresidues. Hence, if a residue is defined as a "real cause of nonlogical action or conduct," that definition provides no a priori basis (i.e., without observations) for designating any particular event or condition as a residue.

The proposed definition of residues would not necessarily vitiate Pareto's scheme for classifying residues (some 57 classes, subclasses, or subsubclasses). Although a sympathetic critic (Finer, 1966:83) characterized the scheme as "confused and . . . bizarre," some real causes of nonlogical actions might be described as "instincts for combination," others as "persistence of aggregates," and so forth. It would depend entirely on complete definitions of those terms; but there is no basis for identifying any of Pareto's statements about any class of residues as a complete definition, and his scheme fairly reeks with arbitrariness. As a case in point, one must wonder why there is a "sex" residue but no "safety" or "hunger" residue. It is even more puzzling that in his observations on European history (1935) and in formulating the final version of his theory of elites Pareto "made do" with only two of his six major classes of residues, the instinct for combination and the persistence of aggregates. Above all, there is no evidence whatever that the terms denoting the classes, subclasses, or subsubclasses of residues are empirically applicable, meaning that independent observers could realize substantial agreement in attributing particular actions (other than those mentioned illustratively by Pareto) to some underlying particular residues.

What has been said of residues applies similarly to Pareto's notion of derivations. Commentaries on that notion identify all manner of equivalent terms, such as: *ideologies, rationalizations, myths, theories, beliefs, vital lies, explanations, and tissues of creations of imagination.* Pareto's statements scarcely provide a basis for accepting any one meaning of "derivations" to the exclusion of others. To illustrate, the first sentence of volume III (Pareto, 1935:885) suggests that "derivation" is defined on page 508 of volume II, but there we find only this: "suppose that we call the things *a*, *residues*, the things *b*, *derivations*, and the things *c*, *derivatives*." Then consider two earlier statements: "The element *a* corresponds, we may guess, to certain instincts of man, or more exactly, men, because *a* has no objective existence and differs in different individuals. . . . The element *b* represents the work of the mind in accounting for *a*" (501). Then in a footnote Pareto refers to derivations as: "the reasonings with which people try to make conduct that is non-logical seem logical" (885). However, that statement is not entirely consistent with the preceding characterization of derivations as "ways in which people try to dissemble, change, explain, the real character of this or that mode of conduct" (885).

EMPIRICAL CLAIMS. Pareto's theory of residues can be interpreted as nothing more than a classification of residues or as a scheme for assigning particular actions or types of conduct to one residue or another. If the former, one must surely wonder how the label *theory* is justified. As for the second interpretation, even if independent observers should agree in assigning a particular act or type of conduct to some class of residues, how could that assignment possibly be an explanation? Any claim to explanation would be unfalsifiable because circular. Thus, if an individual engages in an action that is attributed to Class I residues, the instinct for combination, the questions and answers would be as follows: Why did the individual engage in that action? Because of the instinct of combination. How do we know that he or she "has" the instinct of combination? Because he or she engaged in the action. That character of Pareto's residues is exemplified most clearly by his definition (1935:670) of the *neophobia* residue (a subsubtype of residues connected with sociality): "This is a sentiment of hostility to innovations that are calculated to disturb uniformities." Consistent with that definition, Pareto (1935:526) declares the residue as "prominent" in describing a case where the people drove a man out of town for raising a wolf.

Even if unfalsifiable explanations were tolerable, Pareto's sociology appears bereft of an explanation of logical action, and even his logical-nonlogical distinction is dubious. Quoting Pareto (1935:77): "Suppose we apply the term *logical actions* to actions that logically conjoin means to ends not only from the standpoint of the subject performing them, but from the standpoint of other persons who have a more extensive knowledge—in other words, to actions that are logical both subjectively and objectively in the sense just explained. Other actions we shall call *non-logical* (by no means the same as 'illogical')."

Because Pareto does not speak to several questions, the distinction promises little empirical applicability. For example, what of the relative *efficiency* of alternative means? If the question is irrelevant, then driving from Los Angeles to San Francisco via Maine would be a logical action regardless of alternative routes. Yet if only the most efficient actions are logical, how is efficiency to be reckoned without arbitrary and/or ethnocentric criteria? Then who are the "other persons" in Pareto's definition? If "everyone," no action is likely to qualify as logical. If not everyone, how can arbitrary or vague distinctions be avoided? Then what of an individual indiscriminately shooting restaurant patrons? Because a logical action need only "conjoin means to ends," why would the shooting not qualify? True, perhaps the killer sought some end beyond the deaths, but that argument only underscores the difficulty of answering this question: How are action means and ends to be distinguished and what criteria identify ultimate ends? In light of such questions it could be argued that Pareto merely used the label *nonlogical* pejoratively. In any case, what has been said of the logical-nonlogical distinction applies also to any distinction pertaining to rational, irrational, and nonrational behavior or beliefs.

Granted that humans are prone to rationalize their behavior, Pareto's purpose in introducing the notion of derivations is obscure. Merely applying the label *derivation* to some statement is not an explanation of it. Indeed, given Pareto's insistence that various derivations may "originate" in the same class of residues, why do some individuals differ as to their derivations for what appears to be the same type of action? To illustrate, if arguments (derivations) given to justify denouncement of interracial marriage originate in the persistence-of-aggregates residue, why does the content of the argument vary among individuals? It is as though Pareto invented a novel way to pose empirical questions, but only to leave them unposed. He also did not really address the theoretical question: What determines the relation between each class of derivations and each class of residues? Given Pareto's seeming indifference to such questions, it may well be that he invented the notion of derivations as a license to ridicule.

Circulation of the Elites

Time and again in various ways, Pareto (1935, 1966, 1968) argued that anything akin to a genuine political democracy neither has been realized nor ever will. Stated another way, in all political units government is dominated by elites. Pareto never made exactly that statement (see, e.g., 1935:1526), but neither version of his argument distorts. However, there is a paradox. While perhaps Pareto's most important argument, he actually devoted very little attention to its corroboration. Perhaps he believed it to be an obvious truth. In any case, Pareto is much better known for his statements about the circulation of elites than for the "how and why" of elite dominance.

THE PROCESS OF ELITE CIRCULATION. No one would question the uninformative generalization that the characteristics of governing elites (e.g., their average age, their fertility rate) change; but Pareto's claim is much more specific: sooner or later, one kind of elite comes to replace another kind in the affairs of government. Because Pareto never argued that "governing" elites are elites because they govern (if anything, just the opposite), the very idea of circulation implies two categories of elites—governing and nongoverning. The difference is not merely a matter of being in or out of office; Pareto suggested time and again that at any point in the history of a particular society the two categories tend to differ with regard to the relative prevalence of kinds of residues, especially the instinct-for-combination and the persistence-of-aggregates. Why that contrast? Pareto does not answer clearly, but the most relevant consideration appears to be certain postulated correlates of the two residues.

The persistence-of-aggregates residue prompts individuals to pursue political ends through force, and Pareto referred to such individuals as "lions." By contrast, the instinct-for-combination residue prompts individuals to pursue political ends by persuasive manipulation, and they are the "foxes" in Pareto's social zoo. Hence, if the new governing elites come into political power by force, they are lions; and the persistence-of-aggregates residue will be particularly prevalent among them. Concomitantly, so Pareto *suggested* (especially 1935:1531), by something akin to natural selection there are an inordinate number of foxes among the nongoverning elites, and the instinct-for-combination residue prevails among them.

The emphasis (*suggested*) is necessary because of various ambiguities, the most serious stemming from Pareto's failure to formulate and maintain a clear distinction between these three dichotomies: elites versus nonelites, upper stratum versus lower stratum, and higher classes versus lower classes. The problem is not just Pareto's vague conceptualization of each dichotomy. At various points (e.g., 1935:1424, 1429) he equated the upper stratum with elites and the lower stratum with nonelites, but only to write subsequently (1935:1431) of "superior elements in the lower classes" and "inferior elements in the higher classes." Accordingly, even if Pareto used "strata" terms and "class" terms as interchangeable, it appears that some upper-level individuals are nonelites, whereas nongoverning elites are in all levels; and "governing elite-lower stratum" is perhaps a logical (conceptual) impossibility. Interpretive doubts are inevitable because Pareto's conceptualization of his key term obfuscates. Moreover, Pareto never set forth a rationale (conceptual or empirical) that would preclude the possibility of circulation between governing and nongoverning elites in the upper level, even the violent displacement of the former by the latter, as in the Wars of the Roses.

Pareto also suggested that the prevailing residues among the governing elites will change if those elites permit the movement of lower-level nongoverning elites into political positions, because the residues of those elites are likely to differ from those of the governing elites. So if the lions seize power and come to share it with the foxes, eventually no particular class of residues will be truly predominant among the governing elites. Far from explicitly denying that possibility, Pareto (1935:1516–517) suggests that governing elites, whether lions or foxes, are doomed if they do not come to share power with the most able of the nongoverning elites, evidently primarily from the lower level.[4] Should the governing elites not share power, numerous able individuals accumulate among the nongoverning elites (again, evidently primarily from the lower level); and they challenge the governing elites. Hence, if the residues of the governing elites do not shift in the appropriate way, sooner or later elites of that type fall from power; and Pareto's (1935:1430) famous dictum— "History is a graveyard of aristocracies."—suggests that any particular type of governing elite will fall *sooner or later*.

SECONDARY DEFECTS. Even though Pareto evidently thought of the fall of governing elites as inevitable, at no point did he assert any maximum or minimum "lifespan," not even approximately. So even assuming that one can identify a new type of governing elite (e.g., Napoleon and all of his appointees), Pareto's circulation theory provides no basis for predicting when that type will fall.

Pareto's champions could grant that his observations on the inevitable fall of governing elites are not informative, but then argue that he at least identified the causes. That argument confuses Pareto's random observations on particular historical events with explicit and clear nomothetic propositions. There is not one explicitly identified premise or theorem in Pareto's circulation theory (1968 or 1935) in which the terms *residue* and *elites* are constituents.[5] Had Pareto stated his theory more formally, his failure to provide an empirically applicable definition of residues and criteria for determining the "residue composition" of elites (governing and nongoverning) would not have precluded tests of the theory. The "residue" terms could have appeared exclusively in the premises, with only empirically applicable terms in the theorems. Pareto eschewed that mode of theory construction, and his observations on "speculators" and "rentiers" do not make the theory testable. Because Pareto described the "speculator" as prompted by the instinct-for-combination residue and the "rentier" as prompted by the persistence-of-aggregates residue, it may appear that there is an association between the political and the economic correlates of a change in elites; specifically, speculators walk in or out along with the foxes, and the rentiers walk in or out with the lions. But Pareto did not deduce any such generalization from his theory; and even if he had, he did not define lions, foxes, rentiers, and speculators such that the definitions promise sufficient empirical applicability.

THE PRIMARY DEFECT. Even if all previous criticism were ignored, one remaining defect would in itself make Pareto's theory untestable. That defect is Pareto's definition of "elites," the most explicit and complete being: "I use the word elite . . . in its etymological sense, meaning the strongest, the most energetic, and most capable—for good as well as evil" (1968:36). The definition is *asocial* and presumes that "capabilities" can be judged apart from what social unit members consider to be desirable or undesirable behavior. Yet there is no basis to assume that any test (or measurement) of intelligence or aptitude can be devised such that it does not reflect the standards of some social units more than others. Even if such tests could be devised, the identification of any minimum "elite" score or value would be a study in arbitrariness. Hence, it is pointless to speak of elites as though they constitute an identifiable category of social unit members.

Once it is admitted that Pareto's definition of elites does not promise sufficient empirical applicability, then the governing-nongoverning distinction is lost. Of course, one may regard the present emphasis on empirical applicability as an anachronistic remnant of positivism and ask: What does the empirical applicability of the term *elites* have to do with the fact that numerous scholars have regarded the theory as interesting? Precisely because they are free to think of elites any way they choose.

Elitology's Principal Strength

Elitology's principal strength is not revealed in the impressive number of recent studies of elites, so many that one can speak of a revival of interest in the subject.[6] Several of those studies were conducted by political scientists or anthropologists; hence, elitology transcends sociology. So why are numerous social scientists attracted to the notion of elites? The question cannot be answered convincingly by pointing to any recent elite theory, let alone one that escapes the major objections to Pareto's theory. For that matter, the most conspicuous shortcoming of recent elitological studies is their atheoretical character.[7] The vast majority are largely descriptions of purported elites in a particular country or locality (see, e.g., Czudnowski, 1983; Marcus, 1983a; Moore, 1985). Nonetheless, the sheer number of recent studies reflect an awareness, however dimly, by many social scientists of elitology's principal strength. Briefly, no other perspective so clearly incorporates this argument: the study of socio-cultural phenomena is grossly incomplete without recognition of individual differences as regards ability, talent, or aptitude, and the inevitability of differential power.

Individual Differences

Sociologists often appear to deny the significance if not the very existence of extrasocial or extracultural differences among humans. Appearances to the contrary, that denial stems not just from the widespread superorganicism in sociology or the related veneration of Durkheim. Even interpretive sociologists (chapter 10) are not particularly sensitive to individual differences; after all, to emphasize the importance of "meaning" is not to imply that humans differ in any respect.

Unfortunately, the principal strength of elitology would be of questionable significance even if all sociologists should grant that numerous human differences are clearly extrasocial or extracultural. That is the case because the way humans differ (weight, height, strength, stamina, speed, coordination, etc.) are seemingly infinite, and it would be unrealistic to maintain that all differences are sociologically relevant. Although it would appear to simplify matters, nothing is really gained by speaking of ability, aptitude, or talent— the "superiority" conception of elites. The immediate question is: Superior with regard to what? Again, the possibilities appear infinite, and elitologists evidently do not agree as to which possibilities are most relevant for sociology.

Indeed, as suggested earlier, some elitologists think of human variation only in terms of power or position. Consider Field and Higley's statement: "elites are the persons who occupy strategic positions in public and private bureaucratic organizations. . . . 'elite' is not used here to designate persons allegedly distinguished by 'superior' personal traits or skills" (1980:20).

THE RELEVANCE OF CONTROL. Whatever the terminology—control ability, control aptitude, or control talent—and whatever the type or kind of control, nothing said in this book denies the significance of individual differences. Indeed, compared to other candidates for sociology's central notion (e.g., norms, organization, culture), the notion of control more nearly forces recognition of individual differences that are commonly thought of as an ability, aptitude, or talent. That is the case because control (unlike, say, social interaction or social relation) is commonly thought of in terms of success or failure.

The general point is that control could be sociology's central notion even if a particular version of elitology—one that emphasizes individual differences with regard to ability, aptitude, or talent—should become the dominant sociological perspective. That is the case if only because one can speak readily of control ability, control aptitude, or control talent. Those terms suggest an answer to this difficult question: What human differences are sociologically relevant? Any that facilitate or retard control. Thus, strength could be a relevant human difference but perhaps only in connection with coercive control.

Taking control as sociology's central notion might not result in the identification of numerous human differences as irrelevant; but it would supply a defensible criterion for judgment, something now lacking in elitology. Stating that criterion explicitly: Human differences, whatever their nature, are relevant for sociology only insofar as they have some bearing on control.

Differential Power and "Positional" Definitions

Although Pareto's definition of elites clearly suggests the "superiority" conception, many subsequent definitions (e.g., Etzioni, 1975:153) refer only to differential power. Unless one assumes that differential power necessarily stems from variation in ability, aptitude, or talent, those predispositional attributes are ignored completely by a "power" definition of elites. While such a definition does not totally undermine the principal strength of elitology, it does create problems. As suggested in chapter 3, the most conspicuous problem is the striking contrast in definitions of power and the rarity with which any definition promises sufficient empirical applicability. A less conspicuous but perhaps more intractable problem is that no power definition even suggests an answer to this question: How much power is necessary to be an elite?

Perhaps to avoid conceptual problems, elitologists have increasingly referred to positions rather than power in defining elites (see the survey of recent definitions in Burton and Higley, 1987:223). Far from avoiding conceptual problems, those references are a study in illusions.[8] Even assuming that the term *position* can be defined so that the definition promises sufficient empirical applicability, it is surely necessary to speak of elites as occupying the "top" positions or some similar designation. Otherwise, in English-speaking countries all police officers (regardless of rank) and all employers (regardless of number of employees), to mention occupants of only two positions, are elites. Yet any criterion of "top" positions is bound to be either exceedingly vague or blatantly arbitrary; and nothing is gained by the conventional dodge (see the survey in Burton and Higley, 1987:223)—allusions to institutional positions, positions of authority, or influential positions.

THE RELEVANCE OF CONTROL. To justify their studies, elitologists often claim that elites are "inevitable" (see Burton and Higley, 1987:220). In so doing they avoid this question: What constructive purpose does that claim serve unless accompanied by an empirically applicable definition of elites? The question is all the more important because evidence of "elite universality" consists of nothing more than the assertion that in all human societies occupants of some positions have more power than do occupants of other positions. Even if one accepts a "positional" definition of elites and ignores all related problems, this question would remain: Assuming that positions are present in all societies and that the positions differ significantly as to power, why is that the case? The only defensible answer is that extensive coordination and synchronization of the behavior of numerous individuals over long periods cannot be realized without leaders, dictators or otherwise. But the notion of leadership cannot be divorced from the notion of control without becoming bereft of empirical referents.

Even if elites are defined in terms of power and position, instances of human control would remain the ultimate empirical referents. Imagine someone seriously arguing that the individual who has the greatest power or who occupies the "top" position in a social unit does not engage in more successful human control than do other members. So, insofar as the term *elites* has any ultimate empirical referents, they can be described best in terms of control. However, that conclusion is not a denial of elitology's principal strength—its consistency with the argument that the study of socio-cultural phenomena is grossly incomplete without recognition of individual differences in ability, talent, or aptitude, and the seeming inevitability of differential power.

The Principal Weakness

The principal weakness of a perspective is not necessarily its most conspicuous shortcoming, and elitology is a good example. The most glaring shortcoming of that perspective is the "general poverty" of defensible theories (see Crewe, 1974:18). Even the gross defects of Pareto's "circulation" theory remain, and with few exceptions the recent outpouring of research on elites neither has been guided by nor given rise to a theory.[9] As suggested previously, virtually all of that research is little more than descriptions of putative elites in particular countries or localities. Burton and Higley's (1987:219) character- ization of the research, similar to that of Zuckerman's (1977), is even more harsh: "A large part of it focuses on readily measurable, but often quite trivial, social and educational correlates of elite status."

The commentaries by Burton, Higley, and Zuckerman are a far cry from complacency; but they do not confront this question: Does the paucity of elitological theories stem from some fundamental defect in elitology? An affirmative answer is implied by this identification of elitology's principal weakness: Far from realizing a definition of elites that is empirically applicable but not arbitrary, elitologists do not truly confront conceptual problems.

Some Conceptional Problems and Issues

The foregoing will be rejected by several elitologists, even those who bemoan the current state of their perspective. Thus, Burton and Higley describe much of recent research on elites as "a 'conceptual swamp' in which the elite concept has no agreed-upon meaning and no clearly perceived theoretical utility" (1987:237–38). To escape the swamp, Burton and Higley endorse Zuckerman's strategy (1977), which they describe as follows: "to defer further efforts to specify the concept's connotation and denotation until it has been successfully employed in theories of wide explanatory power" (238). How can a theory have explanatory power without tests of it? How can defensible tests of an elite theory be conducted without an empirically applicable definition of elites? Burton and Higley ignore those two questions. Instead, they equate Zuckerman's strategy with that of Mosca and Pareto, and they then allege (1987:238) that "progress in elite theory depends on returning to it." The argument ignores the possibility that Mosca's strategy and Pareto's strategy led to the very conceptual swamp that Burton and Higley, along with Zucker- man, now bemoan.

To be sure, an empirically applicable definition of elites is not essential for a testable elite theory, but that is the case only if the term *elites* appears in the theory's premises and not in its conclusions. Such a theory can be stated systematically only in accordance with some formal mode, and that strategy has been alien to elitology from the outset. Indeed, it is questionable for Burton and Higley (1987:237), again following Zuckerman (1977), to describe Pareto and Mosca as employing the elite concept in "sets of interrelated hypothesis." Given the extreme discursiveness of Pareto's elite theory, it distorts to allude to its constituent "hypotheses," let alone suggest that they are interrelated; and the same is true of Mosca's theory of the ruling class.

AN ILLUSTRATIVE DEFINITION.   When elitologists use the term *elites* as though it refers to an identifiable set of individuals in a particular population, an empirically applicable definition of the term is essential. Elitologists commonly use the term that way, but they are loath to recognize that their definition promises negligible empirical applicability. Examine Suzanne Keller's definition: "the term refers first of all to a minority of individuals designated to serve a collectivity in a socially valued way" (1963:4). What constitutes such a designation and who are the "designators"? What constitutes a socially valued service for a collectivity and by whose judgment? In particular, are the Afrikaners serving the Republic of South Africa in such a capacity? Did the SS serve Germany in that way? Such questions introduce value judgments, but Keller's definition cannot be applied without value judgments. If making value judgments is inevitable, then disagreements in applying Keller's definition are also inevitable.

There are distinct alternatives to Keller's definition; but only one of them appears less vague, and even in that case the appearance is misleading. The alternative equates elites with occupants of "top" positions, institutional positions, positions of authority, or positions of influence (again, see Burton and Higley's survey of definitions, 1987:223). Repeating a previous argument, insofar as a definition of those "positional" terms is empirically applicable in a particular social unit,[10] it is virtually certain to be arbitrary and couched in terms that are largely peculiar to that unit.

One thing can be said in Keller's defense: at least she formulated a definition of elites. Since then it has become fashionable, even in theoretical or conceptual works, to avoid a definition. As a case in point, Burton and Higley (1987) offer an extensive survey of definitions but stop short of offering a specific and explicit alternative; and others have seemingly abandoned attempts at a definition (see, especially, Marcus, 1983b, and Zuckerman, 1977).

CLASS AND TYPES OF ELITES.   Up to this point only one major conceptual issue in defining elites has been introduced: whether a definition should make reference to (1) "superior" individuals, (2) differential power, or (3) positions. Another issue, can be best introduced by a question: If elites are distinct from some members of the upper social class or a similar class designation, what is the difference? Unless one embraces conceptual redundancies, the inclination is to presume a difference; but it has been obscure from the outset of elitology. As Keller suggests, Pareto and Mosca used the term *elite* (or "ruling class") so as to blur the difference between its meaning and the meaning of upper social class: "They seemed to realize in principle that the two were separate entities, but confounded them in practice" (1963:12).

Avoiding conceptual redundancy is not the only consideration in contemplating the relation between elites and the upper class. Because definitions of any class are notoriously divergent and promise empirical applicability only if blatantly arbitrary (e.g., a family is "upper class" if its annual disposable income exceeds $100,000), it would be extremely questionable to use the term *upper class* in defining elites.

Regardless of any consideration pertaining to social class, if by definition elites occupy the "top" political positions, then the term *political elites* is misleading; it suggests that there are elites outside of the political sphere. Yet not even a "positional" definition necessarily limit elites to the political sphere, and such limitation raises doubts about anything akin to Pareto's distinction between governing and nongoverning elites. Moreover, insofar as Mosca's term *ruling class* is treated as equivalent to *elites*, the term is objectionable precisely because it either (1) suggests that elites are elites solely because of their political positions or (2) is hopelessly ambiguous. Perhaps most important, the vast majority of elitologists, even political scientists, recognize elites outside of the political sphere; and several elitologists have gone so far as to identify "celebrities" as elites (see Keller, 1963). Nonetheless, writers do not agree as to what other spheres should be recognized; hence, another conceptual issue is posed by this question: What type of elites other than "political" should be recognized?

The Conceptual Problem and Theory Construction

The truly intractable problem becomes obvious when examining careful research on elites, such as that conducted by John Higley and his associates (see, especially, Higley et al., 1976; Field and Higley, 1972, 1980, 1985). In one of those studies Higley et al. (1976) applied what they depicted as "elite theory" to Norway and identified national elites. The identification was guided, ostensibly, by this definition (1976:17): "In the abstract we can call *elite* those persons who individually, regularly, and seriously have power to affect organizational outcomes."

The definition reflects only the "power" conception of elites; and it ignores this question: Do elites have more power than nonelites because of their positions, some kind of superiority, or both? It is perhaps unrealistic to demand a definition that somehow avoids the issues posed by the three contending conceptions of elites or one that somehow combines them; but contemplate these terms in the definition formulated by Higley et al.: *regularly, seriously, power, affect, organizational outcomes*. Independent investigators are unlikely to realize even appreciable agreement in applying those terms.

Should Higley et al., protest that they described the procedure followed in identifying Norwegian elites, so they did. Indeed, Higley et al. deserve praise for a procedural explication that is virtually unique in elitological research; but, far from avoiding the principal weakness of elitology, the research of Higley et al., only illustrates its consequences. Although their description of the procedure followed in identifying Norwegian elites is fairly clear (very clear if judged relatively), the only rationale for that procedure is the vague definition previously examined. Consequently, the procedure was replete with what appears to be ad hoc decisions and thereby reeks with arbitrariness. Because the procedure is described in terms that apply largely if not entirely to Norway in the 1970s, it cannot be the basis for replicating the study in other places or times.

ELITES AS A CONSTRUCT.   Should the term *elite* be construed as denoting a purely theoretical notion and, hence, outside the empirical vocabulary of the social sciences, then the quest for an empirically applicable definition could be abandoned once and for all. Stating the matter another way, the term *elites* could be treated by theorists as a construct rather than a concept (see Gibbs, 1972, for an elaborate treatment of the distinction). If taken as a construct, "elites" could enter into the denotation of a property of social units, such as the *consensual unity of elites*. Even if that term could be defined so that the definition is clear and complete, the property is quantitative; and because it is difficult to imagine an empirically applicable formula, the term must be treated as a construct. Accordingly, if the term *consensual unity of elites* is used in stating a purportedly testable theory about elites, it must appear in the premises but not in the conclusions. Consider two illustrative premises. First, among countries, the greater the rural-urban homogeneity, the greater the consensual unity of elites. Second, among countries, the greater the consensual unity of elites, the less the frequency of revolutions or rebellions. Given the identification of *consensual unity of elites* as a construct, neither premise would be testable. However, if both premises are construed as asserting very close empirical relations, then by the "sign rule" (Gibbs, 1972:190–91), they imply this conclusion: Among countries, the greater the rural-urban homogeneity, the less the frequency of revolutions or rebellions. That conclusion is testable because an empirically applicable formula can be devised to express each variable.

Burton and Higley (1987) recognize that the elite could be treated as a "theoretical construct"; but they do not pursue the implications, and in his research Higley has never treated the term as though it is a construct. As a case in point, in their research Field and Higley (1980, 1985) made frequent reference to "unified elites" and used that term as denoting a property of countries. Because the property is quantitative, it can be applied empirically only by applying some formula to kinds of data stipulated by the theorist. Yet, instead of treating the term—*unified elites*—as a construct, Field and Higley (1980, 1985) classify countries with regard to the property, which is to say as though the term is empirically applicable. They do not employ any measurement procedures, and it is difficult to imagine any procedure that would not require an identification of elites (individuals) in each country. So their classification of countries is largely intuitive.

The problem is magnified by an assertion about elites in Field and

Higley's "paradigm" (1980:117): A consensually unified elite is a necessary condition for political stability. The immediate consideration is not just that distinctions as to "consensually unified," "ideologically unified elites," and "disunified elites" accentuate doubts about empirical applicability, nor that an isolated assertion hardly constitutes a paradigm or theory. Rather, given the vague definitions of the terms pertaining to elites, investigators who are aware of the assertion in question may be predisposed (unwittingly) to classify countries that have a history of political stability as having a "consensually unified elite." That possibility is all the more real because Field and Higley have not formulated objective criteria for classifying countries as to type of elite (consensually unified, ideologically unified, disunified).

Why do elitologists, such as Higley, refrain from treating *elites* and related terms (e.g., *consensual unification of elites, relative prevalence of elites*) as constructs? The question takes on added significance because, as the following illustrative list suggests, the key terms that enter into extant definition of elites denote quantitative characteristics regardless of the choice among the three contending conceptions of elites: *ability, aptitude, talent, amount of power, amount of influence, amount of control, position.* Although the last term denotes a qualitative phenomenon, in defining elites reference must be made to something like "top" positions; and that distinction introduces a quantitative consideration.

If it is granted that at least some of key terms in a definition of elites must refer to quantitative dimensions of something, there is an insoluble problem. Any definition of elites is empirically applicable only if some minimal amount of that "something" is stipulated, and any such stipulation is bound to be arbitrary. Unfortunately, the identification of elites or any related term as a construct does not really solve the conceptual problem. Even at the purely theoretical level, the distinction between elites and nonelites appears inherently arbitrary in principle; hence, it is pointless to pursue an empirically applicable definition of elites. However, if the term *elites* enters into a composite term that designates a quantitative property of social units and the latter is identified as a construct, the conceptual problem ceases to be crippling. To illustrate, examine the following premise as a restatement of Field and Higley's paradigm: Among countries, the greater the consensual unity of elites in a country, the greater the political stability of that country. If the term *consensual unity of elites* is identified as a construct, there is no need to pretend that its definition is complete or that the term can be linked to an empirically applicable formula and procedural instructions. True, the premise is not testable, but evidence can be brought to bear on it indirectly by linking it with other premises and deducing testable conclusions. Field and Higley do not employ that strategy. Again, they classify countries as either having or not having consensually unified elites, as though the term is empirically applicable in some direct sense. There is no justification whatever for such treatment of the term.

The Relevance of Control

Sociologists are more concerned with elites in the aggregate than as individuals, but the properties of such an aggregate are also properties of the larger social unit in which the elites are members, be it an organization, community, or country. Accordingly, the power conception of elites (i.e., elites have more power than nonelites) can be expressed as "power concentration," which denotes a property of a social unit, whatever the kind of power in question. After all, if social unit members do not differ as to power, how could there be elites? Similarly, when power concentration is at the maximum—only one member is perceived as having any capacity to control—how could there be more than one elite in the social unit?

One possible objection pertains to research on the correlates of "elite status," such as education, income, ideology, or social origin. Because power concentration is an aggregate property, it may appear that the correlates of elite status can be identified in a particular social unit only by comparing elites and nonelites. But if elite status is thought of as a matter of having power and a "power value" can be assigned to each social unit member or a representative sample, there is no reason why investigators cannot compute correlations between these values and the values for any other trait of individuals (e.g., annual income). Indeed, that strategy would avoid the arbitrary distinction between elites and nonelites that characterizes traditional research on correlates of elites status.

Appearances to the contrary, the strategy would not entail abandoning traditional concerns pertaining to either the "superiority" conception of elites or the "positional" conception. Definitions of elites that exemplify the latter commonly suggest that elitism is a matter of differential power. True, many elitologists evidently assume that the power of an individual stems primarily from the positions that he or she occupies, but replacing elite terminology with quantitative terms—*differential power*, *power concentration*—would promote an empirical assessment of that assumption much more than have past attempts to identify elites in terms of positions without reference to actual power values.

Just as the proposed strategy does not entail acceptance of the power conception of elites and rejection of the positional conception, neither does it entail rejection of the superiority conception. The idea that elites have special abilities, aptitudes, or talents can be perpetuated by this question: Insofar as such a trait is mensurable, what is the empirical relation among individuals between the trait values and power values? It may well be that for some or all traits the relation varies considerably from one social unit to another; if so, explanation of that variation would be a much more specific goal than elitology now has.

CONTROL, ELITOLOGY, AND THE SOCIOLOGY OF THE STATE.   Should elitologists take control as their central notion, they will be particularly suited to remedy glaring defects in sociological studies of the State. There has been a sudden increase in the popularity of those studies, but elitologists have not led the way. Rather, the most conspicuous leaders have been Marxist or neo-Marxists who came to recognize (belatedly) that the State is not simply the tail of the bourgeois dog (see Skocpol's commentary, 1980:199–201).

The most conspicuous feature of the studies is the inclination of sociologists to indulge in anthropomorphic reifications when making arguments about the State. Consider, for example, Quadagno's summary statement in a paper on welfare capitalism and the Social Security Act of 1935: "The analysis demonstrates that the state functions as a mediating body, weighing the priorities of various interest groups . . . negotiating compromises between class factions, and incorporating working-class demands into legislation on capitalist terms" (1984:632). Just as orthodox Marxists are determined to ascribe actions to social classes that only individuals can take, sociologists of various persuasions now refer to the State as though it is an actor rather than a vast and vague abstraction.

Three consequences are inevitable unless sociologists come to recognize that the term *State* is merely a label for an essentially unconceptualized set of properties of control at the macro level. First, anthropomorphic reifications of the State will continue to characterize sociological studies and perpetuate what Cassirer (1955) castigated as a myth, in a critique now seemingly unknown to contemporary sociologists. Second, sociologists will continue to write as though oblivious to problems and issues concerning the State-government distinction. And, third, sociologists will continue purported explanations of particular historical events in terms of the State, explanations that are inherently disputable (see, e.g., Wuthnow's commentary, 1985, on Swanson) because ad hoc and bereft of a defensible conceptualization the State.

What properties of control should be recognized in conceptualizing the State, including the distinction between it and "the government"?[11] The question is not simply premature for present purposes; rather, the answer should come from sociologists as they formulate theories about the State. Only three additional comments need be made. First, the notion of control will prove to be an essential tool in conceptualizing both the State and the government, especially if sociologists truly seek definitions that are empirically applicable and free of reifications. Second, compared to advocates of other perspectives, elitologists are more likely to appreciate the relevance of control notions in sociological studies of State and government. And, third, whatever its shortcomings, Pareto's distinction between governing and nongoverning elites directs attention to the endless struggle to occupy political positions, a struggle that makes sense only if the State is instrumental and more so for some people (label them elites or not) than for others.

NOTES

1. Should it be argued that the admonition is even more characteristic of Marxist sociology, with the focus being on class, the argument ignores a perennial schism among Marxists—between those who emphasize class and the materialists.

2. A full explication would counter the impression that elite theory is necessarily limited to political phenomena. It must suffice to say that the vast literature on socio-cultural change, acculturation, assimilation, and diffusion suggests this generalization: Innovations either originate among elites or come to be accepted or rejected because of reactions by elites. That generalization alone indicates how the potential scope of elite theory extends beyond political phenomena.

3. Two other principal figures in the study of elites are commonly cited (e.g., Burton and Higley, 1987:219): Gaetano Mosca and Robert Michels.

4. Again, however, Pareto's theory is a study in ambiguities. Specifically, many of his observations (e.g., 1935:1532) indicate that new governing elites tend to be lions, and other observations (e.g., 1935:1428) indicate that the only crucial considerations are the waning of Class II residues (persistence-of-aggregates) among the governing elites and the reinforcement of those residues by "tides upwelling from the lower stratum."

5. The term *elite* appears only once in the fifteen-page "Index-Summary of Theorems" (Pareto, 1935:1918), and the procedure by which the theorems were derived (if they were) is not stipulated.

6. Field and Higley (especially 1980:4–17) date the revival of interest in elites at about 1975, concomitant with a rebirth of the belief in material scarcity and growing doubts about the welfare state's viability.

7. One notable exception is John Higley's work (see, especially, Higley et al., 1976; Field and Higley, 1972, 1980, 1985).

8. Some "positional" definitions of elites create a conceptual issue by implying that social unit members who have inordinately great power over other members are not elites unless they occupy some particular position. Contemplate Field and Higley's definition: "elites are the persons who occupy strategic positions in public and private bureaucratic organizations. . . ." (1980:20). In making observations on societies in "Level 1" of development—almost all of the work force in agriculture or other kinds of "autonomous" work—Field and Higley recognize aristocracies in those societies but argue that "the absence of large-scale bureaucratic organizations in Level 1 societies meant that they did *not* contain elites in our sense of the term" (21–22). The argument contradicts one of the basic contentions of classical elite theory: "elites are inevitable features of all societies" (Burton and Higley, 1987:220).

9. The work of John Higley (see Higley et al., 1976; Field and Higley, 1972, 1980, 1985) is a particularly notable exception.

10. Consider an example of a "positional" definition of elites that promises negligible empirical applicability: "The power elite is composed of men whose positions enable them to transcend the ordinary environments of ordinary men and women; they are in positions to make decisions having major consequences" (Mills, 1959b:3). For further commentary on the defects of Mills as an "elite theorist," see Burton and Higley (1987:237).

11. Unfortunately, the question is not even addressed in Cohen and Scull's *Social Control and the State* (1983). Indeed, for all practical purposes, the contributing authors do not use the term *State* (perhaps wisely so).

Behavioral Sociology

Taken as a perspective, behavioral sociology is difficult to describe. Most behavioral sociologists are less than explicit as to the kind of explanation and the formal criteria that they prefer in assessing sociological explanations. Few of them actually identify themselves as reductionists, and it is doubtful whether even a majority would argue that explanations of sociological phenomena must be based on psychological principles. As for criteria of explanatory adequacy, most behavioral sociologists appear to be positivists, but it is as though they are unaware of marked dissensus in sociology about appropriate criteria for judging theories or explanations. So little can be said beyond this: as far as explanations are concerned, behavioral sociologists seem to prefer principles that have a large following in psychology.

Homans's Sociology and Operant Psychology

In commenting on behavioral sociology it is difficult to avoid preoccupation with George C. Homans. By character alone, he was destined to be influential.

Bringing Men Back In

Homans is an unrelenting critic of sociological perspectives, functionalism in particular. Insofar as he grants that functionalists formulated any theories at all, he denies that they have explanatory power. "Even if a statement like: 'If it is to survive, a society must possess conflict-resolving institutions,' were accepted as testable and true, it possessed (*sic*) little explanatory power. From the proposition the fact could be deduced that, given a certain society did survive, it did possess conflict-resolving institutions of some kind, and the fact was thus explained. What remained unexplained was why the society had conflict-resolving institutions of a particular kind, why, for instance, the jury was an ancient feature of Anglo-Saxon legal institutions. . . . what sociology has to explain are the actual features of actual societies and not just the generalized features of a generalized society" (Homans, 1964b:812–13).

Why is the explanatory power of functionalist theories so unimpressive? Homans's answer: Because the theories have little bearing on actual human behavior. What is the remedy? Homans argues (1964b) that it lies in "bringing men back in"; but that catchy phrase does not convey the real contention: sociology's basic explanatory principles must be psychological.

Reductionism and Other Irrelevancies

Most sociologists reject Homans's sociology because they equate it with "reductionism"; and Homans once embraced that label with such candor (1958:597) that his subsequent seeming recantation (1964b:817) is puzzling: "Nor is there any assumption here of psychological reductionism, though I used to think there was. For reduction implies that there are general sociological propositions that can then be reduced to psychological ones. I now suspect that there are no general sociological propositions, propositions that hold good of all societies or social groups as such. . . ." Why not use psychological principles to deduce sociological hypotheses or theorems that later may come to be recognized as valid propositions?

Homans's sociology is *not* based exclusively on operant psychology; he uses both operant terms (e.g., *reinforcement*) and those of economics (e.g., *cost*). That dual terminology has been stressed by Ekeh (1974:113–19), and he argued that the two do not mesh. Ekeh's extensive critique suggests that Homans should have eschewed the principles of operant psychology, because those principles supposedly apply to animals in general and, hence, ignore symbolic properties of behavior, the very ones that enable humans to relate present activities and future possibilities.

In opposing operant psychology Ekeh (1974:107) merely repeated traditional humanist arguments against behaviorism: (1) symbolic behavior is determined by a choice from probable future consequences and (2) past experiences are neither necessary nor sufficient conditions of present activities. Ekeh ignored the obvious rejoinder: Why assume that relating present activities to future possibilities and making choices accordingly are not determined by past experience?

Conceptual Issues

Homans's sociology should not be judged solely by his propositions (*infra*). In borrowing both the terminology and principles of operant psychology, he took a step toward a radical reconceptualization of sociology.

THE TERMINOLOGY GULF. Homans did not err in using only some of the key terms of operant psychology and economics, because wholesale borrowing cannot be constructive. Nor is superficiality an issue; Homans made extensive use of the borrowed terms. However, he scarcely used them to redefine any major sociological term (e.g., *norm, institution*), even though such redefinitions may well be the only way to revolutionize sociological theory.

Should Homans argue that borrowing explanatory principles is more fundamental than conceptual innovations, there would be two questions. First, how are the constituent terms of those principles and sociology's terms to be linked? Second, without that link, how can one deduce *sociological* propositions from the borrowed principles?

INSENSITIVITY TO EMPIRICAL APPLICABILITY. Assume that Homans eventually concocts rules for deducing sociological propositions from operant principles. Even so, few if any of the derived propositions would be testable, because the major terms of sociology promise negligible empirical applicability.

Homans's frequent use of sociological terms without redefinition suggests an insensitivity to the need for empirically applicable terms in a theory's conclusions or theorems. Should he propose that sociology's major terms appear only in the premises of sociological theories, is it feasible for a theory to have two sets of premises—one borrowed (in Homans's case, from psychology and/or economics) and one indigenous?

Sociology's Subject Matter

The title of Homans's best known book *Social Behavior* (1974) appears to identify sociology's subject matter, but what is "social behavior"? As Ekeh points out: "There is no full answer to that question in Homans' exchange theory. . . ." (1974:99).

Homans's failure to answer is especially troublesome because critics write as though he aims to reduce sociology's subject matter to psychology, which is quite different from granting sociology a unique subject matter and then proposing to explain it in terms of psychological principles. However, Homans invited the misinterpretation by not treating social behavior as uniquely human (see Ekeh, 1974:98 for elaboration). Whatever Homans's use of the term "*elementary* social behavior" implies about sociology's subject matter, his conceptualization of the term has become even vaguer (compare Homans 1961:2 and 1974:2).

Homans's General Propositions about Social Behavior

Few sentences in the sociological literature have received more attention than those in the following quotes (Homans, 1974:16, 22, 23, 25, 29, 37, 39).

I. *The success proposition*: "For all actions taken by persons, the more often a particular action of a person is rewarded, the more likely the person is to perform that action."

II. *The stimulus proposition*: "If in the past the occurrence of a particular stimulus, or set of stimuli, has been the occasion on which a person's action has been rewarded, then the more similar the present stimuli are to the past ones, the more likely the person is to perform the action, or some similar action, now."

III. *The value proposition*: "The more valuable to a person is the result of his action, the more likely he is to perform the action."

IV. *The deprivation-satiation proposition*: "The more often in the recent past a person has received a particular reward, the less valuable any further unit of that reward becomes for him."

V. *The aggression-approval proposition*: Va. "When a person's action does not receive the reward he expected, or receives punishment he did not expect, he will be angry; he becomes more likely to perform aggressive behavior, and the results of such behavior become more valuable to him." Vb. "When a person's action receives reward he expected, especially a greater reward than he expected, or does not receive punishment he expected, he will be pleased; he becomes more likely to perform approving behavior, and the results of such behavior become more valuable to him."

The propositions are commonly depicted as Homans's versions of operant principles, but some of the terms are alien to that brand of psychology. If Homans worded the propositions to make them fit human behavior, his departure from operant psychology was justifiable. However, whereas the first edition of *Social Behavior* (1961:12) stipulated that the propositions came from both psychology and elementary economics (see, also, Homans, 1958), the latter receives far less attention in the revised edition (1974: especially 67–68).

Whatever their origin, what do Homans's five propositions represent? One common answer—an exchange theory—is disputable. Homans expressed reluctance (1974:10) to identify the five propositions as a theory, his rationale being that social scientists use the term *theory* so pretentiously and diversely. Even if Homans did think of the five propositions and related statements as a theory, he clearly rejected (1974:56) the label *exchange theory*.

CRITICAL COMMENTARY ABOUT SUBSTANCE.   Homans's penchant for explicit propositions is unrivalled among major sociological theorists, and explicit propositions are especially vulnerable to criticism precisely because they are explicit. Hence, the defects in Homans's theorizing are readily identifiable; but until other theorists emulate Homans, criticisms of sociological theories will be little more than sheer opinion.

The first "is" in Homans's proposition I has a disturbing implication.

For any person at any time, only the frequency with which that person's previous actions have been rewarded can be known. However, had Homans used that verb form rather than the present tense, it would have suggested a contradiction between Proposition I and a statement that III and IV seem to imply: The more often in the recent past a person has received a particular reward, the *less* likely he is to perform the related action. If a person's past actions have been rewarded frequently, the reward is now less valuable for him or her (Proposition IV); hence, contrary to Proposition I, the less likely he or she is to perform the action. Had Homans used the term *reward* rather then the phrase *result of his action* in Proposition III, the contradiction would have been more obvious.

The contradiction stems from two failures: first, to maintain the distinction between the relative frequency of a reward (proportion of past actions resulting in the reward) and the absolute frequency of such rewards in the past; and, second, to clarify the conceptual link between the term *reward* and the term *valuable*. As for the first failure, the distinction is not recognized in Proposition I or IV, and a contradiction can be avoided only if one of those propositions refers to relative frequency and the other to absolute frequency. As for the second failure, it is by no means clear why "valuable" is needed. Consider, this alternative to Proposition III: The more a person perceives a given possible consequence of a contemplated action as rewarding and certain, the more likely he or she is to perform that action.

Valid or not, the alternative proposition directs attention to the absence of perceptual terms in Propositions I—IV. Their absence is justifiable only if the commission of an act is contingent less on the actor's perception of the probability of reward or punishment than on "objective" probability (e.g., the percentage of the last 50 of his or her acts that resulted in a painful consequence). Homans's avoidance of perceptual terms is consistent with operant psychology, but why make any reference at all to internal behavior? Surely "valuable" (Proposition III) and "expected" (Proposition V) do not denote overt behavior (see Mitchell, 1978:27). For that matter, unlike Skinner, Homans did not define "reward" as any consequence of behavior following an increase in the frequency of that behavior; rather, he left "reward" unconceptualized and failed to stress its social properties (the criticism applies also to Homans's use of the term *punishment*).

DEDUCTION AND LOGICAL FORM.   No major sociological theorist has devoted as much attention as Homans to the methodology of theory construction, and *Social Behavior* (1974) suffers because he evidently overlooked several methodological principles that he recognized elsewhere (e.g., 1964a, 1967). If his propositions are at least part of a theory, why are they not identified as premises, axioms, or postulates? The question is especially relevant given Homans's frequent allusions to explanation's deductive character and his insistence that a theory must explain (1964b:812). The very idea of a deductive system suggests premises and conclusions.

Homans used the term *proposition* as a generic label, but additional labels (e.g., *axioms, theorems*) are needed to clarify his theory's logical structure. Most important, why are there no explicit deductions from the propositions? Homans never prescribes particular rules of deduction (e.g., those of the classical syllogism or Boolean logic), and the logical interrelations (if any) among his five propositions are obscure. Indeed, whereas each of the first four propositions (I–IV) is contingent on a condition stipulated by one of the other propositions, the last proposition (Va or Vb) has no connection whatever with the first four.

TESTABILITY AND EMPIRICAL VALIDITY. The chief merit of Homans's theory is the explicit character of the constituent propositions. Otherwise, it is so conventionally discursive that systematic tests are inconceivable.

One characteristic of a discursive theory is that its constituent terms are not distinguished as to type (e.g., concepts, constructs). Homans does recognize "theoretical concepts," but to no purpose. Although he writes of them as "defined implicitly by the propositions in which they appear" (1974:36), it is not clear what problems are circumvented.

Judging from Homans's statement (1974:36) about value, *valuable* is the only theoretical concept in the first four propositions. In any case, the term denotes a property of internal behavior, something neither observable nor mensurable. However, like most sociologists, Homans failed to recognize that such a property can be linked to empirical referents only by asserting an epistemic correlation between it and observable events. Such assertion is the office of theory; it has nothing to do with measurement, nor is it a definition, operational or otherwise.

Homans (1974:36) merely introduces the notion of a theoretical concept, indicates that "valuable" is an instance, and refers to Braithwaite. He even ignores the implication—Propositions III and IV become tautologies (i.e., they define "valuable"). Granted Homans's point (1974:35), one that few sociologists appreciate, a tautological statement in a deductive system does not preclude synthetic conclusions; nonetheless, tautologies are untestable.

Why did Homans not identify "reward" or "rewarded" as a theoretical concept? The traditional operant definition is something like this: A reward is an event of a particular class that follows instances of a particular type of behavior with a regularity such as to cause an increase in the behavioral frequency. Homans may have been reluctant to adopt such a definition because Proposition I would become a tautology. In any case, Propositions I and II are untestable, despite Homans's cryptic suggestion that a method "could be devised" to measure the frequency of action reward (1974:33).

Homans is not criticized because some of his terms are constructs (or "theoretical concepts"), which is to say empirically inapplicable. It is doubtful whether all major terms in the premises of a testable sociological theory can be concepts (i.e., in the case of quantitative variables, terms linked directly to formulas and data instructions). Be that as it may, Homans's use of constructs did not preclude systematic tests of his theory; rather, they were precluded because he failed to (1) identify some of the terms in his propositions as concepts, (2) link those terms to formulas along with data instructions, and (3) state the propositions such that they imply at least one theorem in which the constituent variables are empirically applicable.

How could Homans's propositions be untestable if they represent his interpretation of research reports? In stating his five propositions Homans introduced terms (e.g., *valuable*) that do not appear in those reports. True, were it otherwise, the propositions could not be more general than the findings that gave rise to them; nonetheless, by no conventional logic do the propositions imply testable predictions. Hence, Homans's claim that his theory "explains" particular findings is dubious; he simply used that term loosely, a sociological tradition.

If Homans's theory cannot be tested systematically, why have many behavioral sociologists (e.g., Hamblin and Kunkel, 1977; Burgess and Bushnell, 1969) referred to the theory as the basis for their research? In no instance has a hypothesis (prediction) been derived through stipulated rules from Homans's theory. Behavioral sociologists commonly employ complex statistical techniques, but techniques do not clarify a theory's logical structure.

To be sure, many general observations can be made in support of Homans's propositions, and his references to the field studies examined in the *Human Group* (1950) are instances. Yet the findings of those studies were based on, to quote Johnson, "research weak in predictive power" (1977:57); and the logical connection between the findings and the propositions is disputable. Moreover, some general observations contradict the propositions. Thus, in formulating Proposition IV, Homans evidently did not think of a baseball pitcher throwing the ninth straight strike (let alone the 27th). If the umpire's previous strike calls were not rewarding for the pitcher, the term *reward* becomes meaningless; and surely the ninth pitch would not be less valuable. Because other exceptions abound, Homans's Proposition IV is not universally valid, not even remotely.

Still a Promissory Note

In stating his theory, Homans departed from the discursive mode only in making his five propositions explicit. Past chapter 2, *Social Behavior* (1974) wanders hither and yon, with Homans making general observations on all manner of phenomena and using virtually every major sociological term (e.g., *status, institution, conformity*). True, it appears that there is a special link between Homans's propositions and some of the subjects treated after chapter

2 (1974), notably: exchange, power, authority, sentiment, interaction, satisfaction, distributive justice, and leadership; but the link is not such that Homans formally deduces anything from his five propositions.

In focusing on "elementary" phenomena, Homans gave sociology a promissory note—that his brand of sociology can be extended to "complex" phenomena, evidently including macro, structural, and/or aggregate variables. Yet the extent to which the 1974 edition of *Social Behavior* explains more complex phenomena is debatable. Three of the five propositions in the first edition pertain to dyadic interaction; but the propositions in the revised edition are even less social, and Homans's commentary (1974:51) warrants reading. "We stated the propositions as if it made no difference where the reward of a person's action came from, whether from the physical environment or from another person. . . . the form of the propositions need not change when behavior becomes social. . . . Naturally, since the behavior of each of at least *two* persons in contact with one another is now governed by the propositions, new phenomena will emerge in the social situation that were not present when a man was alone with the physical environment. But we need no new propositions to explain the new phenomena; we need only apply the old propositions to the new given conditions. . . ." So Homans (1974) really gave sociology two promissory notes: (1) that his propositions can be extended to *at least* dyadic interaction and (2) behavioral principles can be used to explain even more complex social phenomena (e.g., institutions). Today, nearly 15 years later, even the first note remains promissory.

Although Homans writes of complex social phenomena, he appears indifferent to traditional sociological questions, such as: Why does the crime rate vary? Why does the human fertility rate vary? Why are some organizations more complex than others? But Homans does not argue that such questions are inappropriate; rather, he simply ignores them.

The Relevance of the Notion of Control

Homans notwithstanding, looking to operant psychology or economics is not an effective way to "bring men back into theory." That goal can be realized only by accepting control as sociology's central notion.

SOME CONSISTENCIES. Proposition I illustrates how Homans's arguments can be described and thought of in terms of control. Briefly, because the term *control* could be substituted for *action*, Proposition I is relevant in contemplating any basic type of control; and it also suggests an answer to this question: If some kind of control is predominant in a particular type of situation, why? Because those who attempt that kind of control perceive it as more efficacious in that situation than any perceived alternatives.

The principal consistency between adopting control as sociology's central notion and Homans's brand of sociology is that both imply endorsement of this dictum: human behavior is governed largely by its consequences. In the interest of esprit de corps, sociologists may continue to war against reductionism; but rejecting or ignoring the dictum is obstinate provincialism.

ANOTHER WAY TO BRING MEN IN. Homans's sociology is paradoxical. He clearly appreciates the purposive quality of human behavior and its importance (especially 1962); yet he selected the brand of psychology—Skinnerian—that is the most opposed to an emphasis on internal behavior. Accordingly, since control necessarily involves internal behavior, a control version of Homans's sociology would require terms that are alien to operant psychology.

Principles of control would make it possible to bring men back into sociological theory without embracing operant psychology. Reconsider the control principle of limited expertise: Because the knowledge and skills that the typical human can master are finite, he or she cannot consistently exercise effective control over an unlimited variety of objects, substances, or organisms. The principle cannot be deduced from Homans's propositions, but it does bring men back in. Yet the argument is not merely that sociological theories should be consistent with the control principle; in addition, the principle underlies the theory in chapter 6 about the division of labor, an "emergent" phenomenon. The pursuit of additional similar principles would be entirely consistent with Homans's sociology and extend it to more complex phenomena.

Other Uses of Operant Psychology by Sociologists

Homans is only one of several "operant" sociologists, but others have fared no better. Space limitations preclude more than a brief commentary on two instances.

A THEORY ABOUT SOCIAL CHANGE. The use of operant terms in analyzing sociological data creates the impression that the analysis is guided by a theory. One instance is the use of the term *reinforcement* in stating a "mathematical" theory of social change (Hamblin et al., 1973). Much of the book reports outcomes of fitting various mathematical curves, such as least-squares logistic equation and decaying exponential, to trends in numerous sets of data (e.g., annual number of automobiles produced). Each trend is identified as exemplifying one of several types of social change, such as social adaptation, binary adoption processes in cultural diffusion, and innovation.

Even ignoring the indiscriminate use of the term *social change* (as though it applies to, e.g., altitude records and number of textile workers having the "June bug" disease), Hamblin et al. present no evidence as to the empirical applicability of their definitions of types of social change. One illustration must suffice to justify doubts (1973:195): "Social adaptation is an acquisition of expertise that occurs as behaving units repetitively act upon their physical and social environments to produce reinforcers." Doubts about empirical applicability are pertinent because Hamblin et al. suggest that only one particular equation closely fits all instances of each kind (or subtype) of change (e.g., auto registration) and each type of change (e.g., use diffusion). But nothing is said to preclude the possibility that the identification of a particular data set as to type of change was ex post facto, meaning after a particular equation was found to fit better than others. Even ignoring that possibility, demonstrating that a particular equation fits better hardly explains the form of change (e.g., exponential). After all, the fit only identifies the form of change; and even if a particular equation fits some type of change (e.g., innovation) better than does any alternative, in what sense has that type of change been explained? Hamblin et al. never confront that question.

Most curiosity about social change will survive Hamblin et al., because the curve fitting exercises are uninformative. Indeed, the central question cannot be why a particular equation fits all data sets of a particular kind or type, because no equation does. Several tables (Hamblin et al., 1973:85, 93, 103, 106, 151) reveal four substantial variations in the extent to which a particular equation fits different data sets. First, for the same kind of change (e.g., annual bus registration) and the same social unit (e.g., the U.S.), the fit is much greater over some periods than others (e.g., 1928–47 versus 1948–63). Second, for the same social unit and approximately the same period, the fit is much greater for some kinds of change than others (e.g., annual U.S. movie attendance during 1936–48 versus annual U.S. malt liquor production during 1934–46), even though the kinds supposedly represent the same type of change (e.g., use diffusion). Third, for the same social unit the fit is much more uniform over several periods for some kinds of change (e.g., U.S. intercity waterway passenger miles over 1930–46, 1946–50, 1950–65) than others (e.g., U.S. bus registrations over 1928–47, 1948–63, 1963–68), even though the different kinds all supposedly represent the same type of change (e.g., use diffusion). Fourth, the fit for the same kind of change (e.g., life expectancy values) varies markedly by period and social unit (e.g., Danish males, 1953–67 versus Danish females during 1953–67 versus Norwegian males during 1953–63). Confronted with the fact that a particular equation fits some periods more than others, Hamblin et al. are content to speak of "epochs," as though that label is explanatory.

The theory in question appears formal if only because in chapter 10 (Hamblin et al., 1973) there are (identified by numerical designation) three axioms, five corollaries, seven lemmas, and twelve theorems. However, other than a cryptic reference to lemmas as "epistemic assumptions" (199), Hamblin et al. do not define those labels; and there is a multitude of unanswered questions. Because an axiom and a corollary may be alternative statements of the same equation (1973:197), why one label rather than the other? Ignoring six derivations of a theorem from a theorem, because lemmas and corollaries but not axioms enter into the derivation of some theorems, what is the logical position of the axioms? Finally, which of the axioms, corollaries, lemmas, and theorems, are analytic and which synthetic? Because Hamblin et al. (194–96) devote a section of their chapter 10 to definitions, it may appear that all axioms, corollaries, lemmas, and theorems are synthetic. Yet one quote (197) will suffice to justify doubts.

> "*Axiom 1*
> When the reinforcement contingencies for a given behavior *B* are constant over time, the rate of change in the rate of performance of that behavior d^2B/dt will be zero through time, as in the following second-order differential equation:
>
> $$\frac{d^2B}{dt} = 0$$
>
> *Corollary 1.1*
> (read Corollary 1 to Axiom 1.) By integrating the foregoing equation, when the reinforcement contingencies for a particular behavior *B* are constant over time, the rate of performance of the behavior *dB/dt* will be a constant *S* for the level of the behavioral steady state:
>
> $$\frac{dB}{dt} = S$$
>
> Axiom 1 and Corollary 1.1 are alternative statements of the first basic equation (from Chapter 2); they give the conditions under which behavioral steady states occur, even in the context of change."

Rather than a genuine empirical proposition, the first equation could be a definition, a partial definition, or criterion of "constant reinforcement contingencies." Similarly, the second equation could be a definition, a partial definition, or criterion (analytic in any event) of a "behavioral steady state."

Whether analytic or synthetic, the first quoted statement introduces a strategic term: *reinforcement*. The term could be a very important for sociology; but Hamblin et al. use it indefensibly, commencing with this definition (1973:195): "A reinforcer is any stimulus that induces positive or negative emotional reactions in people. A positive reinforcer induces a positive reaction and a negative reinforcer, an aversive reaction." Operant psychologists do not define the term *reinforcer* or *reinforcement* by reference to emotional reactions. Rather, their definitions refer to changes in the emission of overt behavior (e.g., pressing a lever), with a positive reinforcer being a stimulus that on presentation causes an emission increase and a negative reinforcer being a stimulus whose removal also causes an emission increase (see Akers, 1985:42–45; and Anderson and Willer, 1981:9–10).

The use of the term *reinforcement* by Hamblin et al. would be indefensible even if they were granted the prerogative to define the term as they have.[1] The kinds of behavior to which their data pertain are not "emotional reactions."

The connection between a reinforcer and behavior is a logical one; by definition, a reinforcer causes a change in the emission of some type of behavior. So Axiom 1 appears vacuous; it is as though someone says: When there are no changes in the cause of some behavior, the behavior will not change. Had Hamblin et al. demonstrated that an increase in instances of some particular condition is regularly followed by an increase in instances of some kind of behavior (e.g., hybrid corn adoption), then they could have justifiably inferred reinforcement. But the only relation they examine is that between a behavioral variable and time.

A CRIMINOLOGY THEORY.   There are two important features of Sutherland's theory, perhaps the best known in criminology's history. First, although commendably explicit, the nine ostensible premises (separately or together) do not imply testable predictions about crime. Second, only the sixth and the seventh premise (Sutherland and Cressey, 1974: 75–76) appear essential.
"6. A person becomes delinquent because of an excess of definitions favorable to violation of law over definitions unfavorable to violation of law.
7. Differential associations may vary in frequency, duration, priority, and intensity."

Folklore in criminology notwithstanding, systematic tests would require additional premises and definitions and formulas and data instructions. The first step is to interpret three of Sutherland's arcane terms—*definitions favorable to violation of law*, *definitions unfavorable to violation of law*, and *differential association*. The first two border on the unintelligible unless the key word— definitions—is equated with *experience*. Of course, had Sutherland used the term *experiences* rather than *definitions*, Premise 6 would appear trite (although an implicit denial of genetic determinism).

If Premises 6 and 7 were restated in terms of "experience," they would be more intelligible but no more testable, not even if the frequency, duration, priority, and intensity of differential association could be defined defensibly. Imagine someone computing eight values (four "favorable," four "unfavorable") for an individual and claiming that the values describe that individual's total favorable and unfavorable experiences toward, say, burglary. Even if there were an empirically applicable criterion for distinguishing experiences as to type (favorable versus unfavorable) and a method for describing the frequency, duration, priority, and intensity of experiences, observations would have to be made on individuals from birth onward.

In purported tests of Sutherland's theory (see, e.g., references in Akers, 1985) investigators have ignored the argument that systematic tests require (1) a restatement of the premises, (2) several definitions, (3) the stipulation of formulas, and (4) a description of requisite data. One contender for the exception is Akers's prodigious work.[2] Along with Burgess, Akers purports to have subsumed Sutherland's theory (see Akers, 1985:39–61) in the "social learning or differential association-reinforcement theory." One merit of the theory is that it reduces to seven statements (Akers, 1985:41):

"1. Deviant behavior is learned according to the principles of operant conditioning.

2. Deviant behavior is learned both in nonsocial situations that are reinforcing or discriminating and through that social interaction in which the behavior of other persons is reinforcing or discriminating for such behavior.

3. The principal part of the learning of deviant behavior occurs in those groups which comprise or control the individual's major source of reinforcements.

4. The learning of deviant behavior, including specific techniques, attitudes, and avoidance procedures, is a function of the effective and available reinforcers and the existing reinforcement contingencies.

5. The specific class of behavior learned and its frequency of occurrence are a function of the effective and available reinforcers, and the deviant or nondeviant direction of the norms, rules, and definitions which in the past have accompanied the reinforcement.

6. The probability that a person will commit deviant behavior is increased in the presence of normative statements, definitions, and verbalizations which, in the process of differential reinforcement of such behavior over conforming behavior, have acquired discriminative value.

7. The strength of deviant behavior is a direct function of the amount, frequency, and probability of its reinforcement. The modalities of association with deviant patterns are important insofar as they affect the source, amount, and scheduling of reinforcement."

Because no reference is made to punishment, Burgess and Akers evidently regard it as irrelevant or as somehow subsumed under reinforcement (contrary to several statements by Akers, 1985:44). In any case, taken individually or together the seven statements do not imply a testable prediction about behavior, criminal or otherwise. Worse, Akers (e.g., Akers et al., 1979) writes as though no empirical generalizations (axioms, postulates, propositions, transformational statements) are needed for systematic tests. Rather, he suggests that only "operational definitions" are needed.

The issue is illustrated by a report of tests (Akers et al., 1979) in which the theory is described as comprising five sets of independent variables: imitation, definitions, differential associations, social differential reinforcement, and nonsocial differential reinforcement. Because Akers et al. do not explicitly extend the seven statements to the identification of such variables, the theory is incomplete. Indeed, neither the independent variable nor the dependent variable is clearly identified (note the two phrases in Statements 6 and 7: "the probability that a person will commit deviant behavior" and "the strength of deviant behavior"). So it is necessary to assume that the dependent variable is the "frequency of deviant behavior."

Although the theory purports to explain differences among individuals, a clear logical structure requires (1) a premise linking the dependent variable to either self-reported or official deviant behavior and (2) another premise linking one of those two kinds of deviance to a formula for computing incidence measures and instructions for obtaining the requisite data. Then five premises are needed to assert an empirical relation between the dependent variable and each of the five independent variables (imitation . . . nonsocial reinforcement). Finally, at least five premises are needed to link each independent variable to some formula for computing values, along with instructions for obtaining the requisite data.

The instructions could stipulate questionnaire data, as in the case of the tests reported by Akers et al. (1979); but, contrary to what they suggest, the values computed from questionnaire data do not define or measure the independent variables. That would be the case only if a value could be construed as, say, the amount of social differential associations of the individual in question from birth onward, but the amount is unknowable for any adolescent or adult. The values derived from questionnaire data (e.g., a respondent answers a question as to whether his or her friends have encouraged him or her to use marijuana) may be correlated with the amount of social differential reinforcement, but that correlation is not a measure or a definition. Rather, it is an untestable empirical claim; as such, the claim must be asserted as part of the theory.

THE RELEVANCE OF THE NOTION OF CONTROL.   A control theory of crime or social change is not feasible at present. Nonetheless, when it comes to describing and thinking about those phenomena, a control terminology has three advantages over operant terminology.

First, a control terminology is less conducive to tautologies and vacuous claims. When using operant terminology, it is vacuous to assert that the probability of an act's repetition increases if it is rewarded, because a reward is equated with positive reinforcement and a positive reinforcer is some consequence of behavior that increases the behavior's frequency. The same argument extends to punishment: "When the events following behavior have the effect of repressing or weakening it (technically decreasing the rate at which it is emitted), we say that punishment has occurred." Akers's statement (1985:44) is consistent with operant language, but there is an implication. Accepting the operant definition, it is *illogical* to ask: Does punishing an individual for some type behavior reduce his/her subsequent emission of that behavior?

Second advantage: a control terminology's range of justified application is much greater than that of operant terminology. A justified identification of some series of events as a "reinforcer" requires convincing evidence that (1) the series would not have occurred without behavior by the organism in question and (2) the organism's subsequent emission of that behavior would not have become more frequent without the series. Those conditions are stringent, especially in a nonexperimental context. Even ignoring problems in making causal judgments, they cannot be made properly in connection with one isolated behavioral event (e.g., saying hello); rather, the term applies only to a series of events, because only then can one speak of an increase or decrease.

Third advantage: a control terminology is much more appropriate in describing or thinking about purposive or proactive behavior. From an operant viewpoint, the first instance of some type of behavior (e.g., a caged rat pressing a lever) is taken as accidental, and subsequent instances are contingent on the consequences of previous instances. But think of someone filing his or her first income tax return. Accidental? He or she will stop filing if there is no reward? All manner of other nonaccidental initial acts could be identified, and it would be misleading to reply that vicarious learning is recognized in operant principles. Few operant psychologists have done anything along that line; and when the attempt is made on the scale needed for sociology, the attractive simplicity of operant principles vanishes. Moreover, various types of human behavior are not consequences of previous similar behavior. Consider, as examples, a child's first entry into school and a baseball pitcher's departure from the mound with the bases loaded. More generally, much of human behavior is the product of interventional control. Granted that the intervenor's behavior may be governed by operant principles, that is not the case for the behavior of the object of the interventional control. Nonetheless, there is a vast overlap between control behavior and operant behavior. Even a control attempt involves overt behavior, and overt behavior alters the environment.

THE INEVITABILITY OF LOOKING OUTSIDE OF SOCIOLOGY. While the foregoing is critical of attempts to base sociological theories on operant principles, the attempts are not puzzling. As long as sociology lacks a central notion, many sociologists will look for it elsewhere. Operant psychology particularly attracts those sociologists who recognize that sociology's central notion must facilitate describing and thinking about human behavior and not just putative sociological phenomena (e.g., organizations).

What has been said of operant psychology applies to "control theory" or, more accurately, cybernetics (see references in Carver and Scheier, 1982). Although cybernetics is scarcely a theory by most standards and offers a conceptualization of control radically different from that in this book, the wonder is that more sociologists (e.g., Cadwallader, 1959) have not attempted to use the cybernetic terminology.

Exchange Theory

Most commentaries (e.g., Ekeh, 1974; Heath, 1976) identify Homans as the originator of contemporary exchange theory in sociology, but two related points are commonly ignored. First, Homans never really confronted problems and issues in defining exchange. Second, Homans (1974:56) declined to identify his major work as "exchange theory" or even to accept that term as defensible.

Conceptual Distinctions, Problems, and Issues

Although the several alternative definitions of exchange lead to quite different exchange theories (see Davis, 1975:152), with the exception of Blau (1964, 1968), the major publications on exchange theory (e.g., Ekeh, 1974; Emerson, 1972; Gergen et al., 1980; Heath, 1976; Homans, 1958, 1974; Mitchell, 1978; Willer and Anderson, 1981) suggest an astonishing indifference to conceptual problems and issues.[3] That indifference cannot be excused on the assumption that the term *reciprocity* can be used to define exchange defensibly. As Gouldner (1960:161) pointed out, numerous social scientists have emphasized the importance of reciprocity only to leave the term undefined; but Gouldner perpetuated that practice, even while granting that "few concepts in sociology . . . remain more obscure and ambiguous."

SOME ILLUSTRATIVE STATEMENTS.   One sign of a conceptual problem is the practice of either leaving the term undefined or offering a partial definition. Both practices are common in the exchange literature, and the following statements illustrate a variety of issues.

Blau: "the concept of exchange refers to voluntary social actions that are contingent on rewarding reactions from others and that cease when the expected reactions are not forthcoming" (1968:454).

Emerson: "If, in a given *situation*, the likelihood that a given organism will perform a given *behavior* is increased or maintained by a *stimulus* which is contingent upon both that act and that situation, the situation is said to be or to contain a discriminative stimulus, the behavior is called an operant, and the stimulus is named a reinforcer, all for that specific organism. Let us represent this unit as $Ax;Sy$, where x is a class of actions by organism A, S is an environmental situation, and y is a reinforcing stimulus. We understand that y is contingent upon S and x, and the recurrence of x is contingent upon y (and therefore upon S). . . . With $Ax;Sy$ clearly in mind, we can now define an exchange relation as the special case $Ax;By$, in which B is also an 'organism' in the above sense, with x as a reinforcer for B. Notice that both the contingency of x upon y and that of y upon x are now feedback processes, and each organism is a discriminated situation to the other organism" (1969:387, 388).

Homans: "the set of general propositions I shall use in this book envisages social behavior as an exchange of activity, tangible or intangible, and more or less rewarding or costly, between at least two persons" (1961:13); "interaction between persons is an exchange of goods, material and non-material" (1958:597); "we do not imply here that all social behavior—behavior in which the action of one man is a stimulus to, or reward for, the action of another—can be envisaged as a direct exchange between the two" (1974:56).

Kunkel: "While exchange always implies interaction, the reverse need not hold true" (1975:80).

Levi-Strauss: "Thus, it is always a system of exchange that we find at the origin of rules of marriage. . . . In the course of this work, we have seen the notion of exchange become complicated and diversified; it has constantly appeared to us in different forms. . . . But no matter what form it takes, whether direct or indirect, general or special, immediate or deferred, explicit or implicit, closed or open, concrete or symbolic, it is exchange, always exchange, that emerges as the fundamental and common basis of all modalities of the institution of marriage" (1969:478–479).

THREE ALTERNATIVES.   The statements indicate that social scientists use the term *exchange* in reference to three distinct phenomena—mutual actions, relations, and rules (or norms). The term *act* cannot be substituted for *mutual action* because an exchange surely requires acts by at least two individuals. Whether the acts must be perceived as rewarding, beneficial, or desirable by both parties is debatable, but most conceptual statements suggest both. In any case, must exchange be a relation or a rule in addition *to* mutual actions? Even the question's wording is controversial, because it suggests that exchange can be an isolated mutual action (compare Blau, 1964:93–97, and Anderson and Willer, 1981:14, on economic exchange). Blau's statement and Emerson's appear to be definitions of an exchange relation. Surely it is difficult to see how either definition could be applied without observations on a series of discontinuous mutual actions or interactions.

Whereas Kunkel's statement suggests that exchange is a subclass of interaction, Homans seems to equate interaction (but not social behavior) with exchange. Actually, one of many problems in defining exchange is that conceptual links among interaction, social behavior, and social action are muddled. Nonetheless, even if exchange is a subclass of interaction, that logical relation scarcely clarifies the meaning of exchange.

Levi-Strauss's statement goes beyond normative phenomena in his reference to a "system of exchange." However, because indiscriminate use has made the term *system* virtually meaningless, Levi-Strauss is interpreted as suggesting a "rule" conception of exchange. That conception is a monument to vagueness, especially in comparison to Davis's normative conception of exchange (1975).

MORE SPECIFIC ISSUES.   Limiting a definition of exchange to a mutual action, a social relation, or a rule does not avoid all conceptual issues. Elsewhere, Emerson (1972:45) formulated a definition similar to but less comprehensible than the previous quote, wherein he referred to "an organism-environment exchange relation." The phrase suggests that exchange is not limited even to animal interaction, but why define exchange so broadly?

In his extensive critique of exchange theory, Ekeh insists (1974:83) that Homans's exchange theory developed largely as a reaction not to Parsons's functionalism but, rather, to Levi-Strauss's "collectivistic social exchange theory of cross-cousin marriage." Perhaps so, but in either case Homans did battle with functionalism. Indeed, Parsons's functionalism is timid compared to the brand displayed in Levi-Strauss's book on kinship (1969); but rather than describe the debate between Homans and Levi-Strauss (especially, Homans, 1962:202–56; Levi-Strauss, 1969; Needham, 1962) as "functionalism vs. reductionism," Ekeh (1974) described it as "collectivistic vs. individualistic."

The debate between Levi-Strauss and Homans had to do with this question: Which kind of explanation—functionalist or reductionist—best explains unilateral cross-cousin marriage? That question is substantive, but there is an important related conceptual question: Who can exchange what with whom and how? Had Levi-Strauss ever confronted that question, apparently his answer would have been: Any social unit can exchange anything with any other social unit, directly or indirectly (circuitously). That answer is consistent with Levi-Strauss's notion of the generalized exchange of women, whereby (for example) the men of lineage A marry women of lineage B, the men of lineage B marry women from lineage C, and the men of lineage C marry women from lineage A.

Although largely indifferent to conceptual problems, Homans did make a noteworthy comment (1962:205–6) about generalized exchange: "It might be argued that in extending the idea of exchange in this way, Levi-Strauss has thinned the meaning out of it. Of course, some of the tribes following this rule say they exchange women for *goods*, but when Levi-Strauss talks about marriage exchange, he always means the exchange of women for *women*, whether recognized as an exchange or not." Homans failed to examine the implication of parties exchanging whether recognized *or not*. Suppose that in Chicago Jones buys gasoline from Garcia; that Garcia, but never Jones, drinks in Tamaki's tavern; that Tamaki goes to Polanski for all dental work; that Polanski has purchased all of his insurance from Schmidt; and that Schmidt regularly buys his clothes from Jones. Assuming Jones to be unaware of Garcia-Tamaki-Polanski-Schmidt relations, is he in an exchange relation with Tamaki and Polanski? Indeed, is the Jones-Garcia and Jones-Schmidt relation one of exchange? Because Levi-Strauss evidently regarded "recognition" by exchange participants as irrelevant, he suggests an affirmative answer. Yet if Jones is in an exchange relation with Tamaki and/or Polanski, he is in one with millions if not billions of others. Hence, Levi-Strauss "thinned the meaning out" of an exchange relation so much that the notion applies to virtually any two humans.

TYPES OF EXCHANGE.　The foremost conceptual issue is the preference for a narrow or broad definition of exchange (whether taken as an act, a relation, or a rule). A broad definition can be criticized as "unmanageable," meaning that no theory can explain such diverse phenomena. That criticism can be blunted somewhat by recognition of exchange types, the argument being that each type can be treated in a separate theory. Yet Blau's conceptualization (1964, 1968) is unusual in that it excludes what others would recognize as particular types of exchange. However, types of exchange have received very little systematic attention in the social science literature, and extant typologies of exchange or reciprocity (e.g., Ekeh, 1974; Foa, 1971; Sahlins, 1965, 1972) are extremely crude.

The distinction between social and economic exchange is the most common in the literature (see Blau, 1964; Ekeh, 1974; and Heath, 1976). Blau argues (1964:93–97) that social but not economic exchange (1) entails unspecific obligations, (2) creates diffuse future obligations, (3) requires trust in others to discharge their obligations, (4) engenders feelings of personal obligation or gratitude, (5) has benefits with no exact price as a quantitative medium of exchange, and (6) cannot be assessed readily in terms of extrinsic benefits apart from other relations between the parties. Such contrasts (i.e., social versus economic) may well be really a matter of degree, and Blau scarcely treats their theoretical significance.

Because social scientists seem to agree that virtually anything—tangible or intangible—can be exchanged, the "content" of exchanges plays no role in distinctions as to types. Given the sheer diversity of content (e.g., corn for feathers, diamonds for love, money for murder, etc.), it appears that instances of exchange can be described only as either balanced (neither party "gets more" than the other) or imbalanced. However the distinction be denoted (e.g., symmetrical versus asymmetrical rather than balanced versus imbalanced) and whatever the conceptual problems entailed, it is likely to endure.

Although Blau has emphasized the balanced-imbalanced distinction, he rejects (especially 1968:453) the idea of an exchange relation based on coercion; but the idea is surely defensible if it is granted that one party may perceive the other party's omission of an act as desirable. As such, contrary to Blau's example (1968:453), a gunman's threat in a holdup is an exchange (money for physical safety). Note, however, that Anderson and Willer (1981:15) castigate Blau (and all operant exchange theories) for excluding coercion, but they appear to accept Blau's denial of coercive exchange.

FORMS OF EXCHANGE. Whereas "type of exchange" refers to content, "form of exchange" refers to the number of participants and/or temporal considerations. Blau's rejection of "coercive exchange" illustrates the connection between types and conceptual issues, while the connection between forms and conceptual issues is illustrated by the debate between Homans and Levi-Strauss.

Whereas Ekeh (1974:46–56, 208–10) attempted to convey the contrast between Homans and Levi-Strauss by reference to four forms of exchange (Ekeh actually writes of "types"), at least eighteen forms should be recognized,

Table 15-1.   Diagrammatic Illustrations of Nine Forms of Exchange

Form of Exchange	Illustration
Direct-dyadic:	$A \leftrightarrow B$, $C \leftrightarrow D$, $E \leftrightarrow F$, $G \leftrightarrow H$
Indirect-octadic:	$A \to B \to C \to D \to E \to F \to G \to H \to A$
Direct-coordinative:	$(A,B) \leftrightarrow (C,D) \leftrightarrow (E,F) \leftrightarrow (G,H) \leftrightarrow (A,B)$
Indirect-coordinative:	$(A,B) \to (C,D) \to (E,F) \to (G,H) \to (A,B)$
Direct-indeterminate:	$(A,B) \leftrightarrow C$, $D \leftrightarrow E$, $(F,G) \leftrightarrow H$
Indirect-indeterminate:	$(A,B) \to C \to D \to (E,F,G,H) \to (A,B)$
Compositional:	$(A,B,C,D,E,F,G) \to H$, then $(A,B,C,D,E,F,H) \to G$

nine of which are illustrated in Table 15-1. Only nine forms are shown because each is taken to be (borrowing a version of Ekeh's distinction, 1974:51) *exclusive* exchange, meaning that each party has the relation in question with only one other party. Thus, if $A \leftrightarrow B$ signifies that A visits B, B visits A, and neither visits any other social unit member (i.e., C,D,E,F,G,H), then the A-B exchange relation *as regards visiting* is exclusive. If A and/or B visited some other members as well, the relation would be at least partially inclusive and totally inclusive if both A and B visited all other members.

Each $\to$ signifies an atemporal exchange relation. Thus, if $\leftrightarrow$ again signifies mutual visiting, there is no necessary sequence in visiting from one dyad to the next (e.g., C and D may visit before or after A and B visit). However, $\to$ signifies a sequence (e.g., B visits C only after A visits B). The spatial context of exchange is ignored here, but note that the context of each of the nine illustration could be a very small village.

All forms of exchange in Table 15-1 other than the first (direct-dyadic) entail a conceptual issue. If the indirect form is accepted as an exchange relation and internal behavior (perceptions, etc.) ignored, virtually any two humans, even residents of different countries, have an exchange relation. In any case, should it be argued that exchange involves "giving" and "receiving," the argument implies that the perceptions of the participants are relevant; and there is a major issue. Considering the second exchange form in Table 15-1, indirect-octadic, suppose that A acts toward B with no expectations whatever that H or anyone else will do what H eventually does as a consequence. If so, how could A's behavior toward B possibly be a component of an exchange relation? In other words, why would *A* act toward *B* with no basis to predict any consequence of his or her action? Skinner has argued for a narrow conception of exchange: "If I work for a company manufacturing shoes and my neighbor for a company manufacturing shirts, and if we both earn enough so that I buy a shirt and he or she a pair of shoes, we have in a sense produced something of value for each other, but there has been no direct exchange. A special opportunity to reinforce each other's behavior has been lost" (1978:9).

Even if the idea of indirect exchange is accepted, the coordinative, indeterminate, and compositional forms in Table 15-1 are controversial because of the presumption that a collectivity (two or more individuals) can exchange things with another collectivity or with an individual. The presumption is not farfetched if one thinks of mutual aid (e.g., as in "communal" crop harvesting) or of birthday parties among close friends. However, suppose that as a matter of rule and actual behavior, lineage *A* men marry only lineage *B* women, lineage *B* men marry only lineage *C* women, and lineage *C* men marry only lineage *A* women. Unless most men in each lineage coordinate and/or synchronize their behavior so as to realize such exogamous marriages, neither the rule nor the actual marriages would be exchange in light of Table 15-1.

What Is the Question?

The assumption that scientific theories are formulated to answer widely recognized research questions is alien to exchange theory. No version of that theory bears on such a question (e.g., Why does the crime rate vary?), no more than did the now defunct theory of action (Parsons and Shils, 1962).[4] For that matter, the very existence of an exchange theory is dubious. Recall that Homans declined (1974:56) to identify his work as an exchange theory. Blau stated that his monograph "may be considered as a prolegomenon of a theory of social structure" (1964:2), which is appropriate because Blau wrote a treatise wherein virtually every major sociological term is examined in connection with exchange. Another exchange theorist, Richard Emerson, has voiced a preference for "an approach, characterized by the use of certain central concepts (reward, cost, alternative, transactions, etc.), which place observations into a frame of reference called exchange" (1972:38–39). Consistent with that quote, one searches in vain among other Emerson's statements (1981 particularly) for the *specific* empirical question that led to exchange theory.

SOME POSSIBILITIES.   Sociologists commonly assume (e.g., Mitchell, 1978:1) that exchange theory was designed to answer this classical question: How is social order possible? Yet if only because the term *social order* virtually defies a comprehensible definition, any theory that purports to answer the question will be untestable. Moreover, critics of such a theory are prone to classify it as to type—reductionist, functionalist, Marxist, etc.—and assess it something like this: (1) Major premise: All type X theories are invalid. (2) Minor premise: This theory is type X. (3) Conclusion: This theory is invalid. Lest the illustration appear to be caricature, examine two statements. "Reductionism is the first fundamental fault of Homans's (and others') operant exchange theory" (Anderson and Willer, 1981:12). ". . . Homans, ironically, is not *enough* reductionist and falls into the same trap as those 'institutional' sociologists with whom he differs" (Mitchell, 1978:25).

If exchange theory does pertain to some question other than the hoary one about social order, there is only one possibility: the question is about power. Blau, Emerson, and Homans all use exchange notions to define power and to pursue theories about it. The definitions leave much to be desired. Homans's definition of power (1974:83) borders on the incomprehensible; Blau's definition (1964:115) is only partially in terms of exchange; and Emerson's conceptualization (especially 1969, 1972) resembles a bewildering house of cards, with these conceptual links: power-dependency-exchange-reinforcement.

As for the power theories, they bear not on research questions but on some theme, notably: exchange relations inevitably become unbalanced and as a consequence one party has power over the other. There are four problems with the theme. First, the inevitability of an imbalance is merely assumed. Second, to assert that exchange relations become unbalanced ignores the possibility that some commence imbalanced. Third, the theme has not given rise to a genuine tradition of research, evidently because systematic observations on exchange are difficult. Fourth, the theme is inconsistent with the inclination of many exchange theorists to ignore or belittle punishment and coercion (see Anderson and Willer's commentary, 1981:9–15), the very factors that could produce or sustain an imbalanced exchange relation.

IRRELEVANCE FOR TRADITIONAL RESEARCH QUESTIONS. Whatever the major question for exchange theorists may be (Davis, 1975:152, implies that they have none), it does not bear on traditional research questions in sociology.[5] Illustrating such questions again: Why do some marriages end in divorce? Why is political stability greater in some countries than in others?

There are doubts that exchange theory will ever bear on traditional research questions, one basis being the similarity of the following labels: exchange theory, functional theory, Marxist theory. Sociologists who regularly speak of "theory" rather than "*a* theory" or "theories" display no interest in traditional research questions.

The Relevance of the Notion of Control

The notion of control is not a substantive basis for reformulating exchange theory. Nonetheless, the notion is relevant in contemplating the conceptualization of exchange.

THE CONCEPTUAL PROBLEM. Sociologists use the term *exchange* so divergently that any empirically applicable definition is bound to appear extremely arbitrary; and there are only three options: first, continue using the term but leave it undefined; second, abandon the term; or third, adopt a radical conceptualization. The third option is advocated here; specifically to equate *exchange* with *mutual control*. Defined explicitly: Mutual control has occurred when and only when: (1) a first party has acted overtly in the hope[6] that it increases the probability of a second party responding in some particular way, (2) the first party has perceived that the second party so responded, (3) the second party responded in the hope that the response is consistent with the first party's hopes and therefore increases the probability of the first party responding in still another particular way, and (4) the second party has perceived the first party as having so responded.

The interval between an act and the response is irrelevant, although types of mutual control can be distinguished temporally (e.g., immediate versus delayed). Neither party need consist of only one individual; but if a collectivity, all members must coordinate or synchronize their behavior in the hope of a response by at least one member of the other party.

The definition can be modified readily so that it pertains to attempted mutual control, which is another argument for replacing *exchange* with *mutual control*.[7] Social and behavioral scientists scarcely use the term *attempted exchange*; and their focus on successful exchange stems from functionalism and operant psychology, both of which discourage the emphasis on internal behavior required to maintain the distinction between success and failure.

MAJOR SUBSTANTIVE ISSUES. Again, human behavior cannot be explained adequately without considering both its overt and internal components. Replacing *exchange* with *mutual control* would be consistent with that argument; but sociologists may recoil at the prospect of being inundated by diverse psychological notions—drives, motivation, attitudes, etc. The fear is realistic; but taking control as sociology's central notion would entail a consideration of only two kinds of internal behavior: (1) perceptions of behavioral consequences and (2) evaluative beliefs about those consequences. So, far from opening the door to psychology, the notion of control admits only the essential.

Still another likely reservation is that the proposed conceptual strategy appears to deny the "objective" quality of an exchange. To the contrary, because control is simultaneously internal behavior and overt behavior, mutual control has an objective quality. For that matter, the conceptual strategy does not deny what Coleman's exchange theory (see Michener et al., 1977) suggests—that exchange entails control not just in the transaction itself but power over things or events prior to the transaction. That power is defined (chapter 3) as the "perceived capacity to control" takes on special significance in connection with exchange, because that phrase identifies a necessary condition for an exchange.

Interaction

Whatever the importance of exchange, interaction could be a more strategic notion for behavioral sociology; and it can be defined with less difficulty or controversy, something like this: Interaction occurs when and only when an organism alters its behavior in response to the behavior of another organism. Accepting that definition, "social interaction" is redundant; and, unless stipulated otherwise, interaction is understood to be human behavior.

Some Potentialities

Should behavioral sociologists identify interaction as their specialty, their perspective would have greater potential. Although "human behavior" denotes a broader subject matter, a focus on interaction would promote the sociology-psychology distinction and reduce the need to be concerned with the term *social behavior* or *social action*.

CO-OPTING OTHER PERSPECTIVES. An emphasis on interaction would increase behavioral sociology's potential for absorbing other perspectives, but that emphasis would not preclude the possibility of a close tie between evolutionary theory and behavioral sociology (see Langton, 1979). For that matter, an emphasis on interaction would strengthen the link between behavioral sociology and Simmel, thereby giving the perspective a stronger tie with classical sociology.

The very name of the dominant version of interpretive sociology—symbolic interactionism—indicates the potential for a merger of that perspective and behavioral sociology. Moreover, the major figure in dramaturgical sociology, Erving Goffman (especially 1961b, 1967, 1969, and 1971), was much concerned with interaction. But the prospect of a merger is slim. Behavioral sociologists adhere to operant psychology (see, especially, Burgess and Bushnell, 1969) so rigidly that they appear hostile to interpretive sociology; and the great gulf between the two perspectives could be largely responsible (see Ekeh, 1974, and Mitchell, 1978) for exchange theory's principal defects. Yet the interpretivist epistemology borders on solipsism to the point of precluding (1) the language necessary for stating empirical generalizations that imply testable predictions and (2) tolerance of behaviorism.

Even if both behavioral sociologists and interpretivists take explanation of interactional properties as their primary goal, conceptual issues would continue to divide them. In that connection, the definition of interaction does not speak to two crucial questions. First, do the references to behavior pertain to both overt and internal behavior? Second, when someone alters his or her behavior in response to the behavior of others, is he or she necessarily aware or cognizant of the connection before, during, or after the alteration? Affirmative answers would clarify the definition and promote the integration of behavioral sociology and interpretive sociology, but behavioral sociologists are unlikely to accept those answers.

A CANDIDATE FOR SOCIOLOGY'S CENTRAL NOTION. Sociology never will have an "observational" language that can be used to describe overt human behavior without inferences. One reason is suggested by Zuriff: "Although a number of behaviorists pay lip-service to the ideal of a data language consisting solely of physical descriptions . . . in fact, no behaviorist has ever carried out this program. First, the complexity of describing even the simplest response (e.g., a smile) in this way is overwhelming. Second, the technological problems in continually measuring all the energies at sensory receptors appear practically insurmountable" (1985:38).

Consistent with Zuriff's argument, there is no defensible way to define interaction such that instances are identifiable without inferences as to internal behavior. Nonetheless, the term promises appreciable empirical applicability. There are now impressive methods for "observing" interaction, and evidence of the term's empirical applicability in research has a long history (see, especially, Bales, 1950, and Lamb et al., 1979).

A field's central notion should be denoted by a term that offers appreciable empirical applicability, but at the same time the notion must be abstract; otherwise, it cannot be used to describe and think about the field's subject matter. Few terms rival *interaction* when it comes to empirical applicability and abstractness, and for that reason alone it contends with control as candidate for sociology's central notion.

Theories of Interaction

Because a strong case can be made for identifying interaction as sociology's central notion, the paucity of a well-known theories of interaction is remarkable.[8] Indeed, there have been only approximations of an interaction theory, and only one became well-known.

EARLY HOMANS. The *Human Group* (Homans, 1950) is commonly thought of as only a step toward *Social Behavior* (Homans, 1961, 1974). However, compare the five general propositions previously considered, all from *Social Behavior* (1974), with the hypotheses that follow, each identified by a page number in the *Human Group*.

112: "If the frequency of interaction between two or more persons increases, the degree of their liking for one another will increase, and vice versa. If the interactions between the members of a group are frequent in the external system, sentiments of liking will grow up between them, and these sentiments will lead in turn to further interactions, over and above the interactions of the external system."

113: "a decrease in the frequency of interaction between the members of a group and outsiders, accompanied by an increase in the strength of their negative sentiments toward outsiders, will increase the frequency of interactions and the strength of positive sentiments among the members of the group, and vice versa."

145: "the higher a person's social rank, the wider will be the range of his interactions."

145: "a person of higher social rank than another originates interaction for the latter more often than the latter originates interaction for him."

243: "the more frequently persons interact with one another, when no one of them originates interaction with much greater frequency than the others, the greater is their liking for one another and their feelings of ease in one another's presence."

Despite Homans's dubious argument that the hypotheses can be deduced from the *Social Behavior* propositions, the hypotheses more nearly approximate a theory of interaction; and the list would be even more impressive if extended to statements that appear to be hypotheses but were not so labeled by Homans. Nonetheless, although behavioral sociology virtually commenced with the *Human Group*, that book did not attract a large following among sociologists, many of whom thought of the hypotheses as too psychological or as trivial in comparison to "grand theories." Yet in *Social Behavior* Homans turned even more to psychology and away from interaction. Homans's turn ended the first real prospect for an impressive theory of interaction since Simmel strangled himself with ideas.

A PERENNIAL NEGLECT.   It is instructive to compare two notions, interaction and culture. First off, there are no noteworthy theories about "culture." The reason is that it is difficult to think of conspicuous properties of culture, and none can be defined such as to realize empirical applicability ("complexity" and "content" hardly qualify).

What has been said of theories and culture does not apply to interaction, but conceptualizations of interaction rarely recognize formal properties. In the *Human Group*, Homans recognized frequency, duration, and order but did nothing with duration. Some other properties are obvious. Thus, one can speak of the uniqueness of interaction, meaning the proportion of instances over a given period that were between individuals who had never interacted previously.

Why have few sociologists concerned themselves with formal properties of interaction, and why is there no well-known work along that line? Perhaps the negligible interest stems from the macro interests of many sociologists and the preoccupation of others with meaning. In any event, it appears that sociologists have difficulty in describing and thinking in terms of interaction.

The Relevance of Control

What has been said previously about the relevance of control for behavioral sociology applies to interaction. However, interaction and control are contenders for sociology's central notion.

CONTROL AS INTERACTION AND VICE VERSA.   Excluding self-control, it is difficult to think of attempts at human control that do not involve interaction. Consider, for example, a hiker seeking solitude by taking a circuitous route around a campfire. That "avoidance" would not only constitute interaction but also an attempt at human control (attempted countercontrol more precisely), the latter because the hiker acted in the belief that the action reduced the probability of the campfire occupants making an attempt to communicate with him or her. Then consider an assassination attempt. The prospective victim may never be aware of the attempt; if not, he or she cannot be said to have altered his or her behavior in response to the behavior of the would-be assassin. Yet the assassin's behavior would be an attempt at control (coercive) and interaction because it is virtually certain that the would-be assassin alters his or her behavior in response to the prospective victim's behavior.

Because external human control and interaction are virtually equatable, the relation strengthens the case for taking control *or* interaction, as sociology's central notion. However, control is the more inclusive notion. Self-control, inanimate control, and biotic control are not interaction.

ADDITIONAL ARGUMENTS FAVORING CONTROL.   Some sociologists will not be impressed by the argument about self-control, inanimate control, and biotic control. Their counterargument will be that those types of control are not really "social"; hence, unlike interaction, they are outside sociology's subject matter. Even if that point were granted, external human control alone would remain more strategic for sociology than is interaction.

The principal advantage of the notion of human control is illustrated by two questions about Nazism. First, how did the Nazis interact with other Germans? Second, how did the Nazis control other Germans? The first question appears more peculiar than interesting or important. The point is not just that most sociologists are bored perhaps by the notion of interaction; additionally, the notion of control is much more in keeping with the idea of major events in human history. Thus, the passage of the Nuremberg Laws and the Night of the Long Knives were major events in Nazi Germany, but to characterize them as interaction would appear incongruous. Yet those events were indicative of the nature of Nazi control. So if a candidate for sociology's central notion must be essential to describe major events in human history, the notion of control has a real advantage over the notion of interaction.

NOTES

1. Nothing is gained by appealing to Skinner, because his conceptualizations are confusing and promise negligible empirical applicability. His definition of punishment (1974:62) is especially confusing, one reason being the implicit reference to internal behavior ("punishment is designed to remove behavior from a repertoire"), something supposedly alien to Skinner's perspective. Then consider this definition (1974:46): "A negative reinforcer strengthens any behavior that reduces or terminates it. . . ." In another publication Skinner refers to fines or imprisonment as negative reinforcers (1978:12); but it is surely difficult to see how an offender's behavior reduces or terminates either legal reaction, let alone how the reaction "strengthens" the behavior.

2. A more recent contender for an exception is the line of work commenced by Tittle et al. (1986). Although that work is promising, the present focus is on Akers and Burgess because their version of Sutherland more nearly exemplifies behavioral sociology, the use of operant principles particularly.

3. Anderson and Willer (1981) may appear to treat conceptual issues and problems; but like so many other writers on the subject, they never formulate an explicit definition of exchange.

4. The Parsonian tradition has been perpetuated by Giddens (1984) and Habermas (1984), in that both have formulated a theory which has no bearing on any particular conventional empirical question.

5. The point is especially significant when contemplating the possibility that sociologists are interested in exchange not because of a concern with the social order but because of prospects for describing and thinking about sociology's subject matter in terms of exchange. And exchange could be a candidate for sociology's central notion; but, if so, one must surely wonder why the exchange literature so rarely bears on traditional sociological questions, such as: Why does the rate of juvenile delinquency vary? Because juvenile delinquency cannot be described and thought of readily in terms of exchange, it is hardly surprising that exchange theorists have not really pursued the question. By contrast, Harriet Wilson's research findings (1980) suggests that the delinquency rate is appreciably determined by the intensity of parental control over juveniles; and viewed in the context of the deterrence doctrine (nothing less than a theory about control), any case of delinquency is a failure in the threat of legal punishment.

6. The word *hope* is used as equivalent to this phrase: behavior in the belief that (1) it increases or decreases the probability of some subsequent condition and (2) the increase or decrease is desirable.

7. The suggestion is not that instances of purported research on exchange actually have focused on *mutual control*. To the contrary, the most puzzling feature of the research is the tenuous connection between the observations (or "data") and the notion of exchange. That situation reflects the inherently nebulous character

of the notion of an "exchange of activity, tangible or intangible" (see Eve's quote of Homans, 1986:188, without real clarification of the notion).

8.   There are candidates, one having been introduced by Anderson and Willer (1981); but the premises of those candidates are obscure, and it is not even clear why they are identified as theories of "interaction."

Sociobiology

The study of hominid evolution is not a major specialty in sociobiology (see Wilson, 1975, 1978, 1980), nor is the study of age and sex as bases of the division of labor. Rather than focus on such subjects or strive for greater integration of biology and the social sciences (see Gove and Carpenter, 1982: 1–15, 289–301), sociobiologists have pursued a monstic major thesis: Human practices—institutional, cultural, organizational, or otherwise—can be explained in terms of selectivity in reproduction and concomitant differential genetic propagation.[1] The thesis is not puzzling because the application of evolutionary theory (Darwinian) to social behavior (see Barlow, 1980:3) is conducive to a preoccupation with the notion of natural selection and a narrow field of study (see Kitcher, 1985:115).

Three Arguments and an Illustration

Sociobiology's major thesis ostensibly entails three arguments. First, some humans behave such that their contribution and/or that of kindred to the gene pool exceeds that of other humans. Second, certain human practices further genetic propagation of the practitioners more than do alternative practices. And, third, practices that further genetic propagation prevail; hence, a given practice exists because it furthers genetic propagation.

To illustrate the three arguments, assume that as a consequence of a genetic mutation some men are very possessive and sexually jealous of their mates. Those men are thus inclined to impose something akin to the proscription of adultery on their mates, although not necessarily on themselves; and that behavior increases the probability that their mates will bear only their offspring. Therefore, those men who are tolerant of but faithful to a promiscuous mate contribute less to the human gene pool than do the "possessive" men, assuming that the latter exceed or equal the former in adultery, fertility, and offspring survival; and after several generations the "possessive" genetic material will have been selected to the point that it is predominant in the population's gene pool. The ultimate consequence is the "institutionalized" proscription of adultery, the product of genetic change, differential reproduction, and concomitant selectivity in genetic propagation.

The illustration is consistent with Lumsden and Wilson's statement that "those behaviors conferring the highest replacement rate in successive generations are expected to prevail throughout local populations and hence ultimately to influence the statistical distribution of cultures on a worldwide basis" (1981:99). Although the idea appears simple, its explanatory application entails several assumptions, as the proscription-of-adultery illustration suggests. Moreover, while the Lumsden-Wilson quote implies some kind of genetic determinism, elsewhere Wilson declares that "sociobiology is a discipline and not a particular theory" and that "the validity of the discipline in no way depends on a demonstration that human social behavior has a genetic basis" (1980:296). Yet Wilson attempts to depict sociobiology as both a field or discipline and a theory (see Kitcher's commentary, 1985:13), and time and again he seeks to convince readers of the very thing that supposedly need not be demonstrated. On the very page of the last quote, Wilson concludes that "the evidence appears to lean heavily in favor" of the continued existence of genetic variability and that "at least some human behavioral traits have a genetic foundation."

As the adultery illustration suggests, the "selfish gene" idea (Dawkins, 1976) is fairly clear. If some humans are more genetically disposed than others to a behavior that propagates their genes or those of genealogical kin (i.e., "inclusive fitness"), then, all things being equal, the "dispositional genes" will become more predominant in the gene pool and the behavior more common. The argument is not negated by contraception; through investing more resources in a few children a couple may propagate their genes more than they would by greater fertility. Nor is it implausible to argue that some human practices further differential genetic propagation more than do alternative practices. To supplement the adultery illustration, consider polygyny. On average, polygynous men supposedly have more offspring (see Hartung, 1982; Chagnon, 1980:551); hence, if there is a genetic change such that some men in a particular population are more genetically predisposed to polygyny than are the other men, then, all things being equal, after several generations polygyny would become common in that population.

Possible Disclaimers

The major thesis and the three arguments above are not direct quotes from any publication on sociobiology; unfortunately, that is not feasible. The problem is not just avoiding the charge of selective quotation. That charge is a strategy in refuting criticisms, and the counterstrategy cannot be extensive quotes of several sociobiologists. No sociobiologist has stated the premises of the perspective explicitly and clearly (see Trigg's comments, 1982:125, on sociobiology's "incoherence"). In those rare instances when Wilson's early statements on human sociobiology (1978) transcend the anecdotal, they are not clear and ostensibly complete, nor do they indicate unambiguously what would be relevant evidence.[2] Although sociobiologists have yet to clarify their premises,[3] they persist in statements that suggest an extreme position, as in the case of Rosenberg's argument: "scientifically acceptable explanations for human behavior are available only at the level of the heritable dispositions which it reflects or the neurological states which underlie it" (1980:159).

Sociobiologists should not seek a more moderate position by resorting to existential statements, meaning statements that claim nothing more than the existence of at least one practice, gene, or individual. Existential statements are neither informative nor falsifiable, no matter how clearly stated. If sociobiologists argue that existential statements guide research, it would be a tacit admission that they have a program rather than a theory; and if sociobiology is a program, the narrow major thesis is puzzling. Again, sociobiologists have neglected subjects that would complement sociological studies (e.g., age and sex as bases of the division of labor) and ostensibly prefer some version of genetic determinism. That preference cannot be attributed to the fact that Edward O. Wilson is a biologist. Wilson's position has not been disavowed by sociologists who champion sociobiology (e.g., Lopreato, 1984); and should sociobiologists abandon genetic determinism, their claims and underlying logic would become not just a less "bold theory" (Trigg, 1982:xii, commenting on Lumsden and Wilson, 1981) but also totally obscure.[4] Although sociologists who defend sociobiology do not refer to it as a "grand theory," they appear drawn to it because it promises unification and comprehensiveness (see, especially, Wozniak, 1984:202).

The Distinctiveness of Sociobiology

Contemporary sociobiology differs from its forerunners so much that the qualifying "contemporary" misleads. Spencer's sociology was evolutionary but vaguer than sociobiology and more Lamarckian than Darwinian (see Morris, 1983:46). Sociobiologists are less concerned with postulating some evolutionary direction for humanity than were early social evolutionists, and the latter never came closer to an explanatory mechanism than "competition."

Sociobiology even differs from earlier versions of genetic determinism, although it is no less controversial (see Caplan, 1978). One version labeled "eugenics" is now best known for the claim that most differences in human intelligence are genetically determined. Critics now commonly characterize such claims as racist rather than scientific. However, to characterize sociobiology as a "new racism" (Barker, 1982) is unfair to the many scientists who see merit in sociobiology, some of whom, such as J. B. S. Haldane, cannot be described as conservative or reactionary (see Breuer, 1982:247). For that matter, the ethical and political views of sociobiologists have no necessary bearing on the validity of their theories (see Ruse's commentary, 1979:74–89); and critics who attribute "fascist" values to sociobiologists and advocate denying them some communication medium do not recognize that they themselves are resorting to a fascist tactic: silence the opposition.

Criminology was the locus of the other "dark" side of an early interest in the biology of human behavior. From Lombroso to the present, one criminologist or another has claimed that some individuals are genetically predisposed to criminality (for a succinct survey, see Gibbons, 1982). The latest version is that men with X-Y-Y chromosomes are inclined to violent criminality (see review by Ellis, 1982). Most contemporary criminologists doubt that criminality is genetically determined; but two lines of comparisons justify further consideration of the possibility of genetic determinism: first, the criminal records of adopted children and their biological parents (see Jencks's review, 1987); and, second, the criminal records of monozygotic twins, dizygotic twins, and other siblings (see review by Ellis, 1982). However, those comparisons do not even suggest an answer to two questions (see Jencks's commentary, 1987). First, why is there enormous temporal and spatial variation in crime rates? And, second, what is the mechanism by which genetic material determines criminality?

Evidential Implications

Given sociobiology's major thesis and underlying arguments, there are two kinds of relevant evidence. Those two can best be described in connection with sociobiology's two principal propositions about human behavior.

GENETIC CORRELATES OF HUMAN PRACTICES.   The first proposition pertains to two "socio-culturally differentiated sets of individuals," meaning that only one of the two sets engages in some given human practice (cultural, institutional, or organizational). Thus, in any social unit where there are two or more forms of marriage (e.g., polygyny and monogamy), the men and women in any one conjugal form are socio-culturally differentiated. Similarly, individuals who participate in some organized religion are socio-culturally differentiated from those who do not participate.

So we have the requisite terms for sociobiology's *first principal proposition*: Given any two mutually exclusive *sets* of socio-culturally differentiated individuals, there is an asexual contrast between them with regard to the genetic materials of the members. The "asexual" qualification is necessary because sociobiologists do not point to unisexual institutions or organizations (i.e., all members or participants are of the same sex) as relevant evidence. Three other qualifications are also necessary. First, *genetic material* refers to a gene, a combination of genes, some arrangement of genes, or any quantitative property of a set of genes. Second, the contrast between the two sets of individuals may take the form of a proportion or an average, meaning that the contrast need not hold for all dyads. Third, the proposition need not hold *both* within and between social units.

Although the foregoing qualifications reduce the possibility of falsifying the proposition in question, they are necessary because sociobiologists state their arguments so vaguely that the evidential implications are obscure.[5] Thus, when sociobiologists allude to some genetic contrast as a cause of socio-cultural differentiation, it is commonly not clear whether their assertion applies only to sets of individuals in the same social unit.[6] In any case, the first principal proposition is consistent with two claims: (1) genes somehow predispose individuals to distinctive kinds of behavior and (2) some of those distinctive behaviors become human practices (i.e., widely prevalent in at least one population) because of selectivity in reproduction.

THE SECOND PRINCIPAL PROPOSITION. Even if certain genetic material does predispose individuals to distinctive behavior, that behavior will not replace alternative human practices unless the predisposing genetic condition becomes prevalent in the population's gene pool. Such change can take place only if the behavior furthers the relative reproduction of those who engage in it. So we arrive at sociobiology's *second principal proposition*: Given two mutually exclusive sets of socio-culturally differentiated individuals, average inclusive reproduction is significantly greater for one set than the other. Far from requiring stringent evidence, the proposition does not require a prediction as to which set of individuals has the higher reproductive rate.

The sociobiology literature suggests that the term *adaptation* or *inclusive fitness* should have been used in stating the proposition; but biologists tend to treat adaptation as anything that furthers fitness, and then define fitness by reference to reproduction (see, e.g., O'Donald, 1982:67).[7] The point is not just that a tautological quality creeps into statements of an association between adaptation (or fitness) and reproduction; additionally, of those terms only "reproduction" can be taken as empirically applicable.

Two questions remain. First, what is reproduction? And, second, what is inclusive reproduction? Reproduction is not just a matter of fertility and number of offspring; it is also necessary that the offspring survive long enough to reproduce. However, the measurement of reproduction requires some limiting criterion, such as number of surviving children or number of grandchildren.

The meaning of "inclusive" can best be introduced by considering homosexuality, which appears to contradict sociobiology's major thesis and underlying arguments. Even if some genetic material does predispose humans to homosexuality, the predisposition itself tends to eliminate that material from the human gene pool. Consider the question and the answer as stated by

Wilson: "How can genes predisposing their carriers toward homosexuality spread through the population if homosexuals have no children? One answer is that their close relatives could have had more children as a result of their presence" (1978:144). Wilson's elaboration indicates that close relatives of homosexuals have more children as a consequence of receiving assistance of various kinds from the homosexuals. If so, in rendering that assistance the homosexual does not increase his or her personal or individual fitness (i.e., reproduction); but the assistance could increase the homosexual's inclusive fitness (reproduction), meaning that of the homosexual and/or that of the homosexual's kin. So the notion of inclusive fitness is central for what Wilson (1978:145) calls the "kin-selection hypothesis" of homosexuality's origin.

Although sociobiologists persistently ignore it, the meaning of the term *kin* is far too ambiguous to use in what is supposedly a testable generalization. Therefore, the term *inclusive reproduction* in the second proposition refers to an individual's surviving children and those of his or her genealogical parents, brothers, sisters, uncles, aunts, cousins, nephews, and nieces. That limitation of kin is arbitrary, but arbitrariness is preferred to the uncritical way that sociobiologists use the term *kin*.

Despite their frequent reference to adaptation and inclusive fitness, in the final analysis sociobiologists must be concerned with inclusive reproduction; otherwise, they have no empirically applicable terms for predictions. Sociobiologists can argue that differential inclusive reproduction holds in the development of a human practice but not necessarily indefinitely; if so, the second proposition could be limited to "new" practices. However, should sociobiologists argue that the proposition pertains only to some human practices, the argument would convert the proposition to an unfalsifiable statement and give sociobiologists a license to search for exclusively positive evidence. If "license" appears extreme, contemplate Rosenberg's statement when arguing that sociobiology is destined to preempt the social sciences: "the theory is not committed to hereditary fixity of the current distribution of traits and dispositions [e.g., intelligence, earning power, sex roles] that we have come in ordinary life to identify and distinguish from one another. It is committed to the hereditary distribution of traits which satisfies the laws of heredity, and it individuates and distinguishes traits by appeal to whether candidates satisfy those laws. As such sociobiology is committed to the truth of the laws of heredity, and to whatever fixity those laws demand" (1980:160).

The implication is clear: sociobiology does not claim that all human practices are genetically determined or even genetically influenced; rather, if a particular practice does not conform to the laws of heredity, then sociobiologists have no interest in it. So Rosenberg would give sociobiologists a license to identify human practices that are distributed in accordance with the laws of heredity, but a license is not a theory.

If sociobiology does rest on something like the foregoing major thesis, underlying arguments, and propositions, then it has a real merit. Briefly, sociobiology offers something rivalled only by Marx's theory—the potential explanation of all human practices. But sociobiology's merit poses a dilemma. The monism underlying the merit is precisely the reason why sociobiology enjoys a following in sociology and other social sciences; and should sociobiologists deny a strong version of genetic determinism, their following is likely to decline, because without a strong version of genetic determinism sociobiology is a program rather than a theory. Sociology is so fragmented that even a program appears attractive; but, as ethnomethodology's history indicates, no brand of sociology can be sustained indefinitely by a program.

Some Other and More Specific Criticisms

Sociobiology is subject to various criticisms; and numerous negative critiques of it have been published, several by biologists (e.g., Lewontin et al., 1984). Hence, if only to indicate that sociobiology is a particularly controversial perspective, diverse criticisms are introduced briefly before identifying the principal shortcoming.

Diverse Criticisms

Sociobiology is interdisciplinary, and sociologists who identify with it (e.g., van den Berghe, Lopreato) do not necessarily subscribe to sociobiology as practiced in other fields. However, because those sociologists have yet to disavow particular versions of sociobiology, it is realistic to examine some criticisms of sociobiology in general.

THE REVIVAL OF GENETIC DETERMINISM. The nature-nurture controversy cannot be described without reference to various kinds of genetic causation. Although there is no truly conventional usage, the term *genetic determinism* is appropriate when and only when a particular kind of genetic material is necessary and sufficient for a particular type of behavior. However, genetic materials may preclude certain types of behavior; and the preclusion is genetic determinism if the following relation holds between some *class* of genetic materials, G, and some *type* of behavior, B: in all instances where G is present, B is absent; and in all instances where B is absent, G is present.

By contrast, *genetic potential* is the appropriate term when G is necessary but not sufficient for B.[8] Thus, many humans evidently cannot run a mile in less than, say, four minutes, and the reason is ostensibly at least partially genetic. Regardless of their past experiences—diet, training, etc.—some humans simply cannot run at that speed. Likewise, it appears that the vast majority of humans have the genetic potential for speaking French or robbing a liquor store, but whether they will ever actually do either is not determined by their genes.

Finally, *genetic indeterminacy* is the appropriate term when a type of behavior is such that no particular class of genetic materials is necessary or sufficient for the behavior or its preclusion. The empirical application of that term or any of the others (*determinacy, potential*) is difficult. Genes or genetic material are not observable in the ordinary sense; hence, a defensible conclusion as to the presence or absence of a particular genotype may require a complex procedure and inferences.

Most social scientists evidently believe that genetic potential is much more common than genetic determinism. However, that belief is supported primarily by general observations rather than systematic clinical or experimental evidence. Those observations can be summarized this way: given extensive instructions, ample opportunities, and various inducements, the vast majority of adult humans could perform virtually any type of act; but insofar as the act can be described in quantitative terms, there are values that only some humans can realize regardless of opportunities or inducements.

In light of the observations just summarized, the belief of social scientists about the predominance of genetic potential over genetic determinacy is surely reasonable.[9] However, social scientists who go beyond genetic potential to a belief in genetic indeterminacy are in gross error. To illustrate, there is no record of a human running 100 yards in less than eight seconds, but numerous nonhuman animals can run at that speed. Illustrating the argument another way: If anyone should believe that Lincoln's Gettysburg address had no *genetic basis*, they should try to teach a chimpanzee merely to repeat Lincoln's speech. Nonetheless, whether contrasts in the behaviors of humans (i.e., individual differences) stems from genetic differences is quite another question.

Even if all parties to the great debate should agree that genetic potential is by far the most realistic possibility for human behavior, this question would remain: Which has the most influence on human behavior, genes or the environment? The question calls for something akin to demonstrating that hydrogen has more influence than oxygen in the formation of water. Since genes appear to set limits on any kind of human behavior, they may appear more important than the environment in some absolute sense. But reconsider the possibility of some humans being genetically incapable of running a mile in less than four minutes. How important is that possibility relative to the point that some experiences can make it impossible to run at all? Nothing is gained by speaking of a "normal" environment, and any one of several diverse environments may preclude the realization of some particular genetic potential.

The foregoing distinctions have been treated at some length because many criticisms of sociobiology reduce to this: sociobiologists are attempting to resurrect the belief in genetic determinacy without any really new evidence (see commentary by Barnett, 1980, and Barkow, 1980). Sociobiologists are liable to that criticism not so much because they explicitly assert genetic determinacy; rather, they write ambiguously and rarely identify any particular environmental condition as being necessary or sufficient for some type of behavior.

THE ABUSE OF LANGUAGE. Most systematic empirical observations in sociobiology's literature pertain to nonhuman animals, and critics suggest that sociobiologists err when they generalize from those observations to humans. The criticism is somewhat misleading because no sociobiologist has argued that a valid proposition about nonhuman animals necessarily holds for humans. However, sociobiologists create the *impression* that their arguments about nonhuman animals do apply to humans; and they do it through observations on nonhuman animals and even genes that are "an orgy of ethical and economic anthropomorphisms" (Barnett, 1980:144). That usage has been stressed by critics (e.g., Sahlins, 1976:6–7; Midgley, 1980; Kitcher, 1985:184–201), and they have not exaggerated the indulgence of sociobiologists in anthropomorphism. One sociobiologist or another has used these terms to characterize the behavior of nonhuman animals: *adultery, rape, taxes, costs, patrilineal, marriage, slaves, investments, patriarch, divorce,* and *suicidal.*[10] Kitcher (1985:123) has given an illustration of a less obvious but perhaps more pernicious terminological practice among sociobiologists: "To classify (*sic*) birds as 'giving alarm calls' already suggests a function for the behavior and an evolutionary scenario."

Some items in sociobiology's literature, such as Dawkins's *The Selfish Gene*, are metaphorical in the extreme (see Midgley, 1980); but the metaphors as not merely gauche stylistic devices without consequences. They suggest that *whatever* is said about animals also applies to humans. The implications are less obvious when considering the resort of sociobiologists to unconventional definitions, especially in the case of "altruism." Early sociobiologists rightly recognized that the phenomena denoted by that term constituted a challenge to evolutionary theory. Consider a human's sacrifice of economic gain, material things, health, psychological well-being, or life itself to benefit another human. How could that sacrifice possibly propagate the altruist's genes?

Sociobiologists answer by invoking the notion of inclusive fitness, meaning the propagation of an individual's genes and/or those of his or her genealogical kin. So an animal's behavior may decrease the probability of that animal's reproduction but increase the probability of the reproduction of the animal's genealogical kin. In such a case—so the argument goes—the behavior is altruism, kin are selected, and the animal's inclusive fitness is furthered. Hence, it appears that the notions of kin selection and inclusive fitness solved the problem of altruism, but the problem was really solved by a radical redefinition of altruism. Sociobiologists came to define altruism something like this: "By an 'altruistic' trait is meant a trait which, in some sense, lowers the fitness of the individual displaying it, but increases the fitness of some other members of the same species" (Smith, 1982:29). That definition evidently applies to an animal's warning cry, because the cry alerts conspecifics and attracts the predator's lethal attention; but there is no logical connection between the conventional (lexical) definition of altruism—regard for others as a principle of action (Barnett, 1980:144)—and the notion of fitness, especially since that notion is defined clearly only by reference to reproduction.[11] Moreover, as conventionally defined, altruism involves internal behavior—intention, perception, belief, etc.—the very thing that sociobiologists are at great pains to ignore in their conceptualization of altruism (or anything else).

Sociobiologists cannot claim that their definition of altruism is superior because more empirically applicable. To apply the definition, it must be shown that the behavior in question did or did not alter reproduction probabilities as stipulated by the definition. There is not one instance in sociobiology's literature where anyone has applied the definition to human behavior through such a demonstration; rather, sociobiologists insist on a radical redefinition of "altruism" but only to use the term often in accordance with the conventional definition, and the notion of reciprocal altruism (Trivers, 1978) only complicates matters.

Glaring Omissions

Because sociobiologists apply evolutionary theory to social behavior, natural selection may well be their central notion, even though they rarely use the word *natural* (let alone, *selective survival*). However, Gould (1980:258) has argued that "other evolutionary agents—genetic drift, fixation of neutral mutations, for example"—are now granted a major role by biologists.[12] Nonetheless, some criticisms of sociobiology are puzzling, especially one that social scientists never tire of making: sociobiologists ignore socio-cultural influences on human behavior. The criticism stems from a grand illusion, particularly in anthropology and sociology—that socio-cultural phenomena are somehow distinct from human behavior. Once that illusion is abandoned, there is no basis to argue that sociobiologists ignore socio-cultural phenomena; rather, they treat the phenomena as *explananda*. That point appears so obvious that related criticisms must reflect implicit issues, one of which has been suggested by Sahlins (1976: especially 4–6). He implicitly equates sociobiology with reductionism (*inter alia*) by attributing certain views (1976:5) to Wilson: "For him, any Durkheimian notion of the independent existence and persistence of the social fact is a lapse into mysticism. Social organization is rather, and nothing more than, the behavioral outcome of the interaction of organisms having biologically fixed inclinations. There is nothing in society that was not first in the organisms."

It is just as well that Sahlins did not use the term *reductionism*,[13] because the term is unfit for purposes of communication; and Sahlins's position is clear without the term—any biological theory of socio-cultural phenomena is inadequate. Yet, far from denying that genes interact with the environment, sociobiologists would grant that the interaction is a crucial factor in evolution. However, sociobiologists rarely use the term *environment* in stating what may be a major premise, nor do they emphasize any particular environmental feature or component as a determinant of human behavior (for elaboration, see Barkow, 1980).

Sociobiologists seem to recognize nothing as mediating the interaction between genes and environment; it is as though the human body is an unthinking, unfeeling vehicle for genes (see Midgley's commentary, 1980, on the extreme case—Dawkins, 1976). Moreover, in writing about human adaptation, sociobiologists grant no significance whatever to human internal behavior, including consciousness, perception, intention, motivation, belief, or values. In that respect sociobiologists are antireductionists, a point that their "superorganicist" critics conveniently ignore.

RESORT TO GENERAL OBSERVATION. Sociobiologists commonly appear insensitive to the argument that an explanation of a particular socio-cultural phenomenon is not adequate unless it implies predictions about variation in the phenomenon. To illustrate, no explanation of polygyny is adequate unless it implies predictions about variation in the relative proportion of marriages that are polygynous or variation in the "normative" character of polygyny. Like all other socio-cultural phenomena, variation takes two forms: (1) differences among social units (e.g., countries) and (2) differences over time (e.g., feudal England versus industrial England). Sociobiologists have yet to demonstrate a correlation between variation in gene frequencies and variation in some socio-cultural feature among social units or over time, and their critics virtually deny the possibility. Consider an observation by an eminent biologist, R. C. Lewontin (quoted in Trigg, 1982:104): "Only 100 generations have passed since the Roman Republic and this time span is far too short for there to have been any major change in gene frequencies. Yet human social institutions have undergone an extraordinary change in these few generations."

Lewontin's observation could be extended at great length. Thus, are we really to believe that the Reformation stemmed from some change in gene frequencies? Are we really to believe that the prevalence of human sacrifice for hundreds of years in Middle America (Demarest, 1984) and its contemporary absence can be explained by genetic differences? The implication of such questions and Lewontin's observation do not daunt Wilson (1978:34), and it would not be constructive for Rosenberg (1980) to allege that the phenomena (e.g., the Reformation) are not "natural kinds" and, hence, cannot be explained scientifically. It is naive to assume that social scientists will abandon the questions that interest them just to embrace sociobiology (or any perspective).

Just as enormous *temporal* variation in socio-cultural phenomena raises doubt about the claims of sociobiologists, so does variation among social units—tribes, countries, etc.[14] Research on spatial variation is more feasible, but it is not even a distant prospect. So, again, critics have resorted to general observations in assessing the putative claims of sociobiology, but some of the observations are less conjectural than Lewontin's. They pertain to the emphasis of sociobiologists on kin selection and inclusive fitness. Briefly, should an animal engage in behavior that increases the probability of its kin's reproduction, that behavior furthers the propagation of the kind of genetic materials that the animal shares with its kin. As the term is used by sociobiologists, *kin* refers to genealogical relations; and genealogical kindred could be defined as any set of animals that share at least one particular kind of genetic material. However, because some 85 percent of all known genetic variation may exist in a local population (e.g., residents of a particular community) and more than 90 percent in a particular race (see Trigg, 1982:104, and Washburn, 1982:112), any stipulation of a certain minimum amount of "shared" genetic material is bound to be a dubious criterion of kin.

If kin is to be defined narrowly, one possibility lies in terms used by humans, such as *cousin*, to denote individuals who ostensibly share on the average more genetic materials in common than individuals selected at random. Note, however, that an English-speaking boy or girl refers both to his or her mother's sibling's children and to his or her father's sibling's children as "cousin"; and insofar as English-speaking individuals are inclined to aid kin (e.g., lend money to a cousin), the inclination does not appear biased maternally or paternally. So many of the kin terms of English-speaking people and related behavior are as sociobiologists would have them be (assuming substantial certainty of paternity), meaning fairly close correspondence between genealogical and social kinship. However, is there such a correspondence in all human populations? No one has been more sensitive to the importance of that question than Sahlins (1976), an eminent anthropologist. His answer is emphatically negative: "no system of human kinship relations is organized in accord with the genetic coefficients of relationship as known to sociobiologists" (57). But the point is not that social kinship diverges from genealogical kinship in the same way or to the same degree in all human populations; rather, because there is enormous variation in the social kinship systems among populations, some of them diverge more from genealogical kinship than others. For example, in some social units descent is traced only through the mother (matrilineal) and in others through the father (patrilineal); and in either case individuals act on the average much more "altruistically" toward the relations of one parent than the relations of the other parent, even though they may share no more genes with one set of relations than with the other.

It will not do for sociobiologists to argue that social kinship has nothing to do with actual altruistic behavior. As a case in point, in matrilineal social units a man is far more likely to advance the well-being of his mother's genealogical kin than his father's genealogical kin. Perhaps most important,

Sahlins (1976) points to numerous instances where close social kin are not close genealogically by any reasonable standard; and adoption as well as infanticide (see Sahlins, 1976:48–49) are not the only ways that humans may behave as though indifferent to genealogical relations. So, of all general observations, those on the divergence of genealogical kinship and social kinship most nearly discredit sociobiology.

SHOW US THE GENES. Washburn's comment (1982:113) introduces the most common criticism of sociobiology: "in the last chapter of *Sociobiology* (Wilson, 1975), genes are postulated to account for more than 25 behavioral situations. There are conformer genes, genes for flexibility, genes predisposing to cultural differences, and many others. No evidence is given for any of these. Even the altruistic genes that are central to the whole concept of kin selection are not demonstrated for human beings."

Uncritical use of the term *gene* by sociobiologists provokes such criticisms. For one thing, sociobiologists refer to genes as though they are as real as fireplugs; and, to quote Dunbar, sociobiologists "assume a genetic basis for behavior though the actual biochemistry of inheritance is seldom (if ever) known" (1982:19). Even the usual definition of a gene—"the smallest unit of hereditary information" (Breuer, 1982)—makes the application of the term to observed things conjectural. Whatever the things, how can one possibly know that they are the "smallest units" of hereditary information? Moreover, it is one thing to compile evidence that some type of human behavior is hereditary but quite another thing to identify the gene or genes that are necessary and/or sufficient for that behavior.

Even Wilson's estimate (1978:53) of 250,000 pairs of genes in a fertilized egg suggests that the term denotes a theoretical or postulated entity; and if genes are "varying sections along the DNA" (Midgley, 1980:122), any number is misleading. In any case, sociobiologists frequently use the term *gene* when they should speak of genetic material, thereby denoting any of several possibilities (a gene, two or more genes, an arrangement of genes, etc.). Terms with diverse referents are undesirable, of course; but they are more desirable than the misleading use of a term, in this case *gene* or even *genes*.

Despite the foregoing, terminology is secondary to this criticism: sociobiologists attribute human practices to genes without demonstrating the genes. Yet such criticism demands something that is currently unrealistic, and it suggests an intolerance of theoretical notions. The most advanced sciences are warehouses of terms that denote postulated entities. Thus, if one demands that all of a theory's variables refer to directly observable things or events (as opposed to observing postulated correlates), then "gravity" would have to be abandoned. Nonetheless, sociologists who defend sociobiology are now busily making the claims of Wilson obscure. Thus, Wozniak interprets sociobiologists as "*not* telling . . . that there are specific genes for specific traits" and goes on immediately to quote Wilson as asserting that sociobiology does not imply that human social behavior is determined by genes (1984:196–97). Those are two quite distinct arguments, but Wozniak never recognizes that to assert hundreds of genes determine each type of human social behavior is genetic determinism no less than the assertion that each type of human social behavior is determined by one and only one gene. Moreover, what is gained when sociobiologists explain particular instances of human behavior so as to imply genetic determinism but only to disavow it in the abstract? In any case, whether one gene or hundreds, whether genetic determinism or genetic potential, Washburn's point remains—sociobiologists have yet to demonstrate the existence of the genes that they postulate as being necessary and/or sufficient for even one particular kind of human behavior that they purport to explain, nor is there an immediate prospect of such a demonstration.

Research

With the one noted exception (sociobiologists ignore socio-cultural phenomena), all previous criticisms of sociobiology are warranted. Nonetheless, those criticisms do not emphasize the failure of sociobiologists to derive predictions from their premises about human behavior and test those predictions. The point is not just that sociobiologists frequently resort to general observations, ancedotes, and rhetoric in defending their arguments (see, e.g., Barash, 1979). Even when they do present data on particular populations, commonly the data are not used to test specific predictions deduced from their premises. The derivation of predictions (or hypotheses) is feasible only if the premises are explicit and stated in some consistent form, a mode of stating a theory that is simply alien to sociobiology (see Kitcher's commentary, 1985:16, on Wilson).

Should it appear that the foregoing exaggerates, reconsider Wilson's "kin-selection" explanation of homosexuality. At no point does Wilson recognize that the postulated process must be going on *now* and not just in the origin of homosexuality (1978:144–47). He does not even suggest that research is needed to test the generalization implied by his explanation—that "close relatives" of homosexuals have a greater number of surviving children than do close relatives of heterosexuals. In commenting on Wilson's explanation, one prominent defender of sociobiology, Joseph Lopreato (1984), does not mention Wilson's seeming indifference to systematic evidence (for an elaborate critique of Wilson on homosexuality, see Kitcher, 1985:243–52). Rather, Lopreato is content to allow that "The current sociobiological emphasis on kin selection and inclusive fitness may turn out to be excessive" (1984:218). Another defender of sociobiology in sociology, van den Berghe (1979:44), does recognize that Wilson's argument is sheer conjecture; but van den Berghe merely refers to exclusive homosexuality as "biologically puzzling." The general point is that Lopreato and van den Berghe, like Wilson, simply ignore or "comment on" phenomena that appear alien to sociobiology (e.g., in addition to homosexuality, adoption of nonkin, prostitution, and celibacy).

AN APPROXIMATION OF A TEST. Sociobiology's second principal proposition is stated such that testable predictions can be derived from it; hence, the following brief survey of illustrative research findings is oriented largely around that proposition. Should sociobiologists dismiss the proposition as a distortion, then they will have dismissed the only basis for bringing systematic evidence to bear on their arguments; and they will be obliged to answer this question: Why is the proposition a distortion and what is the alternative?

One of the very few approximations of a genuine test of sociobiology's second principal proposition was conducted by two anthropologists, Beall and Goldstein (1981). They compared the number of children ever born and number surviving in fraternal polyandrous families (the husbands are brothers) and in monogamous families, all located in Tsang village of Nepal's Limi Valley, long a Tibetan culture area. To justify the comparison, Beall and Goldstein (1981:6) quote a sociobiologist (Alexander) as stating that fraternal polyandry is "commensurate with predictions from kin selection. . . ." The argument is not just that the brothers-husbands share genes but also that polyandry furthers the amount of parental investment in child care, which in turn reduces child mortality. However, Beall and Goldstein (1981:7) report no significant difference between polyandrous and monogamous families with regard to the offspring survival rate; and for all age groups of wives except ages 30–34 the rate is greatest for monogamous families.

Because the two types of families do not differ appreciably as to child mortality, polyandry would give polyandrous husbands a reproductive advantage over monogamous husbands only if polyandrous wives are much more fertile. Beall and Goldstein report (1981:8) very little difference between the two types of families as regards average number of children ever born; and for wives over 44, those nearing completion of fertility, the average is somewhat greater for monogamy (7.8 versus 6.3). Moreover, for four of the five age groups, the average number of surviving children was greater for monogamous families.

The absence of a difference in surviving children takes on added significance because the genetic propagation of polyandrous husbands would equal that of monogamous husbands only if polyandrous wives have significantly more children. How many more depends on the number of husbands (the greater the number, the less the probability for each husband's genetic propagation). Thus, with three polyandrous husbands (all brothers), the number of surviving children must be approximately 50 percent greater than the number in a monogamous family for each polyandrous husband to have the same approximate probability of genetic propagation (or "allele transfer") as a monogamous husband. Because the mean number of surviving children was actually somewhat greater in monogamous families, polyandrous husbands had a reproductive disadvantage.

To Beall and Goldstein's credit, they consider one way that polyandry could further inclusive fitness other than through "fraternal reproduction." The reproductive disadvantage of polyandrous brothers could be offset if a much greater proportion of their sisters married and reproduced, but that does not appear to be the case; about 72 percent of the sisters of both polyandrous and monogamous husbands marry (Beall and Goldstein, 1981:9).

Sociobiology's second principal proposition is clearly inconsistent with some of the findings reported by Beall and Goldstein. Because both types of marriages are human practices, the two sets of individuals (polyandrous men or women versus monogamous men or women) are socio-culturally differentiated; but there is no significant difference between the average number of surviving children per wife or per family. Of course, sociobiologists can point out that Beall and Goldstein ignored the number of grandchildren; but should that objective be granted, sociobiological theory becomes unfalsifiable. If there is no difference with regard to number of grandchildren, then consider great-grandchildren; and if there is still no differences, then perhaps polyandrous husbands have more children out of wedlock, etc.

If the average number of surviving children is computed per husband rather than per wife or per family, then it is much greater for monogamous husbands. The difference in estimated genetic propagation is not as great; and when considering a set of individuals who are closely related genetically, comparisons with other sets should pertain to estimated genetic propagation, which includes the reproductive records of genealogical kin rather than simple reproduction (e.g., number of surviving children). Sociobiology's second principal proposition does not refer to an estimated genetic propagation because it is more difficult to compute than a reproduction measure. Moreover, in most comparisons (e.g., residents of a city who participate in organized religion versus others) a close correlation between reproduction and genetic propagation can be assumed. Be that as it may, in the case at hand it makes no difference whether reproduction or estimated genetic propagation is considered; both were much lower for polyandrous husbands.

Beall and Goldstein rightly regard their findings as refuting the claim of reproductive advantage for fraternal polyandry, but they ignore something. The reproductive disadvantage of polyandry is not so great as to insure the disappearance of a genetic predisposition to polyandry (assuming such exists), although the findings do indicate that "monogamous genes" (if such exist) will increase relative to the polyandrous genes.

Had Beall and Goldstein conducted a genuine test of sociobiology's second principal proposition rather than a vague statement by a sociobiologist about polyandry, they might have recognized that monogamy appears to further the fitness of husbands, whether measured by reproduction or estimated genetic propagation. Stated otherwise, any significant difference between monogamous and polyandrous husbands, regardless of the direction of the difference, is consistent with sociobiology's second principal proposition. However, that proposition does not hold for the wives, and the implications are unclear even in the case of husbands. Does it mean that proportion of families that are monogamous will increase if the current differences in reproduction (for husbands) holds? The arguments underlying sociobiology's major thesis surely implies that increase; and if it is not realized despite continuation of differential reproduction, there would be even more doubts about sociobiology's first principal proposition. However, monogamous families could increase (and may have been increasing for some time) because of extragenetic factors, the diffusion of Western practices in particular. So more conclusive evidence will require a historical study. If it were found that despite differential reproduction over several generations there has been no substantial change in the relative prevalence of the two types of marriages, it would be negative evidence, albeit indirectly, for sociobiology's first principal proposition. Finally, Beall and Goldstein failed to confront this question: What is the association between the marriage type of parents and that of their children? A close association could be explained socially or genetically; but if the association is insignificant, grave doubts would be raised about both explanations.

Previous speculation about monogamy's reproductive advantage indicates why the Beall-Goldstein findings are not totally inconsistent with sociobiology. However, sociobiologists cannot seize on that point and ignore this question: Given the reproductive disadvantage of polyandry, why did that marriage form ever become common in Tsang village? If the glib response is that at one time, in a different "ecological situation," polyandry had a reproductive advantage over monogamy, the answer is worse than conjecture. It would confirm a previous criticism—that sociobiologists grab at evidential straws.

DUBIOUS RESPONSES TO BEALL AND GOLDSTEIN. Beall and Goldstein's research has not resulted in sociobiology's reformulation, nor have studies been undertaken to refute them. Abernethy (1981) has criticized them for not using the average number of surviving children when estimating genetic propagation, but Goldstein and Beall (1982) show that the reproductive advantage of monogamy (for husbands) remains substantial even when children surviving is considered. As for Abernethy's argument that the "group selection model" should have been considered, Goldstein and Beall (1982) point out that sociobiologists long ago shifted from group selection (local populations or even species) to individuals and kin selection. Actually, however, sociobiologists disagree as to the relative importance of alternative types of "selection" (see, e.g., Irons, 1980; Williams, 1980), but that dissensus does not justify Abernethy's argument.

Fernandez calls for a study that would cover several generations: "With this additional time perspective Beall and Goldstein's data base allow us to argue that the 'selfish' gene—mediated by the cognition of its Tibetan carrier—is both altruistic and astute, calculating its odds over the several generations that rise into awareness during its carrier's lifespan" (1981:896). The statement makes sense only in connection with Fernandez's argument that a shift to monogamy would overpopulate the region; hence, polyandrous men increase their inclusive fitness by promoting the population's survival. As Goldstein and Beall point out (1982), Fernandez invokes two arguments that sociobiologists avoid: (1) that selectivity has some connection with consciousness and (2) that population survival can be equated with kin selection.

The unconstructive responses to Beall and Goldstein are typical. Sociobiologists simply reject reports of negative evidence rather than restate their arguments or engage in research to refute the reports. For example, Handwerker and Crosbie (1982) report findings indicating that the association between sex and dominance in an experiment involving a simulated game disappears when statistical controls for socio-cultural phenomena (e.g., expectations, esteem, resource controls) are introduced. Turke and Betzig (1983) responded by denying that the findings are inconsistent with sociobiology; but, significantly, they do not recognize the need to restate sociobiology so as to prevent more "mistakes" in identifying relevant evidence.

ANOTHER APPROXIMATION OF A GENUINE TEST. Unlike Beall and Goldstein, Chagnon's (1980) research on the Yanomamo Indians yielded evidence that is consistent with sociobiology's second principal proposition. However, the two studies are similar in that neither really tested a prediction derived from an explicit proposition.[15] Chagnon (1980:547) created the impression of such a test by this statement: "Tests of kin-selection theory require demonstrating that (1) individuals favor kin over nonkin, and among kin, favor more closely related individuals over less closely related individuals, and (2) differences in inclusive fitness . . . have something to do with patterns of preference for kin over nonkin or close kin over distant kin." There are no rules of logic by which that statement implies any of Chagnon's findings,[16] and he never specified what constitutes relevant "kin favoring," or exactly what inclusive fitness has to do with related preferences ("something to do" borders on the vacuous).

Chagnon reported (1980:558–59) that the average number of children for "related" Yanomamo spouses was 2.26, as compared to 1.92 for "unrelated" Yanomamo spouses. Moreover, for marriages in which the wife is the husband's father's sister's daughter, the average number of children was 2.19, compared to 3.24 for marriages in which the wife is the husband's mother's brother's daughter. Such differences are substantial and consistent with sociobiology's second principal proposition.

Although it is not essential to extend a test of the proposition to a prediction as to who has the greater reproduction rate, Chagnon had surprisingly little to say on the subject. Impregnating or being impregnated by genealogical kin does propagate the same kind of genetic materials, but why the difference in fertility? There is no obvious reason why a contrast in the certainty of paternity would be relevant in answering, especially since Chagnon states that reported Yanomamo paternity is "close" to actual biological paternity (1980:549).

It is unfortunate that Chagnon did not attempt to show that the type of cross-cousin marriage with the greatest fertility has been becoming more prevalent among the Yanomamo over at least two generations. Positive tests of sociobiology's second principal proposition are not evidence that some Yanomamo are more genetically predisposed to enter into that type of marriage (first principal proposition), but evidence of greater fertility for that type of marriage and an increase in its relative prevalence over generations would be indirect evidence of differential genetic predispositions.

RESEARCH WITHOUT MERIT.   When sociobiologists resort to general observations, as they often do, their arguments should not be confused with research findings. However, some research may be indefensible even though it goes beyond general observations, and the leading instances is van den Berghe and Mesher's (1980) study of royal incest.

They commence not with a statement of the premises of the sociobiological theory of inclusive fitness or kin selection but, rather, with several arguments so discursive that it is difficult to see how they could be derived from any premises. Indeed, contrary to a principle of sociobiology—selectivity in reproduction or genetic propagation has no necessary connection with consciousness—van den Berghe and Mesher (1980:304) speak of royal incest as being riskier for the queen (but there are conditions in which she "hits the fitness jackpot") and an attractive strategy for kings. Perhaps that terminology was employed to humanize sociobiology or make it more credible; in any case, there are no known rules of logic by which van den Berghe and Mesher (1980:305) move from their general arguments to the predictions that subsequently preoccupy them. They predict that royal incest is associated with hypergyny, polygyny, and patrilineal status inheritance; also (1) that royal incest is most commonly brother-sister and least commonly mother-son and (2) that royal incest between agnatic half-siblings is more frequent than that between uterine half-siblings.

Van den Berghe and Mesher admit (1980:311) that a patrilineal, polygynous monarchy is at most a necessary condition for royal incest; and they should have added that the same is also true of a highly stratified kingdom. In any case, the purported tests of the predictions are peculiar in two respects. First, of the 12 kingdoms compared, all were selected because of the presence of royal incest. Second, none of the variables considered in tests of the predictions pertain to reproduction. Elaborating on the second peculiarity, van den Berghe and Mesher use the term *fitness* repeatedly without defining it or recognizing that conventional definitions equate fitness with reproduction. Yet they (1980:301) recognize that studies of incestuous mating show that the matings do "reduce fitness through increased mortality and morbidity. . . ." True, they add that inbreeding can produce healthy offspring, but such inconclusive statements do not justify the assumption that royal incest increases fitness.[17] The point is all the more important because van den Berghe and Mesher (1980:300) describe royal incest as a "fitness maximizing strategy" if the conditions alluded to in their predictions are met, and they argue that those conditions compensate for the risk of close inbreeding. Yet the validity of their predictions has no bearing on that argument's validity, and Kitcher (1985:270–80) has demonstrated that royal incest increases inclusive fitness only under a condition that may not have obtained in the cases examined by van der Berghe and Mesher.

Having shown that the five predictions hold almost without exception for the 12 kingdoms in question, van den Berghe and Mesher then concede (1980:311) that in half of those kingdoms the royal incest strategy was "divorced from its reproductive function" (e.g., in Dahomey the incestuous offspring were excluded from royal succession). There is no recognition that the concession contradicts their argument that "royal incest is best explained in terms of the general sociobiological paradigm of inclusive fitness" (300). It is as though someone has explained the long neck of giraffes by arguing that it enables them to eat the leaves of tall plants but then to say that giraffes eat only grass.

Van den Berghe and Mesher conclude with a barrage of caveats and disclaimers, an orgy of equivocation. Consider some examples (1980:313): "Genetic predispositions are not rigidly deterministic; they allow for flexible adaptations to a wide range of ecological condition. . . . Royal incest is . . . clearly a cultural institution, one of the totality of human systems of kinship and marriage. The issue is thus not one of 'genetic determinism.' There is ample room for cultural variation and for indeterminacy of cultural adaptation. We merely claim that cultural adaptation is not random. Much of it is a response to ecological conditions external to culture, and conforms rather well to predictions derived from the simple paradigm of inclusive fitness."

RESEARCH OF QUESTIONABLE RELEVANCE. The immediate problem with Hawkes's field study (1983) of a small New Guinea community is her concern with the social and genealogical connection between individuals taken in pairs (dyads), who often help each other in routine garden tasks. That concern cannot be linked readily to sociobiological theory because such helping is not altruism as defined by sociobiologists (i.e., it does not necessarily decrease the probability of the helper's genetic propagation, nor necessarily increase that of the recipient). So Hawkes's study illustrates one reason why research on sociobiology rarely focuses on a derived prediction; sociobiology's terms are defined in such a way that they are difficult to apply.

Hawkes assigned each pair of adults to one of nine categories of social kinship relationships (e.g., father/son, father/son-in-law . . . other). She then assigned a social distance rank to each category and ascertained the proportion of pairs identified as "helpers" in each category. That arrangement of data enabled Hawkes to compute a rank-order coefficient of correlation (*rho*) among the nine categories between social distance ranks and the prevalence of helping. The correlation is substantial and statistically significant.

Having reported a very close statistical association between social kinship and helping, Hawkes (1983:357) then reports the corresponding association between helping and genetic kinship, with the latter described as the proportion of "genes identical by immediate descent." She created six categories of such proportions (.500, .250 . . . .016 or less), then assigns each pair of individuals to one of those categories, and then computed the proportion of pairs in each category identified as helpers. Given that data arrangement, she then computed the correlation (*rho*) among the six categories between the rank of genetic connection (.500 ranked 1) and the rank of the proportion of pairs identified as helpers. *Rho* is positive for all three kinds of pairs but statistically significant (.05 level) only for heterosexual pairs.

Up to this point Hawkes's findings are summarized by one of her conclusions (1983:353): "Social evaluations rather than straight genetic facts order patterns of interaction." That statement appears to contradict sociobiology, but Hawkes denies the contradiction by purporting to demonstrate a very close association between social kinship and genealogical kinship. The demonstration takes the form of a comparison of seven social kinship categories, with a social distance rank and a value representing the "average proportion of genes identical by immediate descent" (Hawkes, 1983:357) for each category. For all three kinds of pairs (men, women, heterosexual), the correlation (*rho*) between social distance and proportion of genes is 1.00. However, there are so many problems that only a brief treatment of the most important is feasible. All crucial questions about social kinship categories (Why these rather than others?) and the social distance scale are left unanswered. Hawkes's failure to describe how pairs of individuals were categorized is especially troublesome. Because the categories are described in English terms, how could a pair of individuals be assigned to a particular "social" category (e.g., Uncle/Nephew) without considering their genealogical relation?

Another conspicuous problem is manifested in Hawkes's own statement (1983:354):

"This test attends to 'consanguineal' categories only. The in-law categories introduce a complicating factor, since in-laws, while genetically unrelated to each other, may as 'coparents' or 'coancestors' have genetic kin in common and so acquire fitness benefits from mutual aid. (These are logistic rather than theoretical problems. The 'altruism' of spouses is no embarrassment to kin selection theory.)"

Such ill-disguised equivocation would make comment largely superfluous, but the equivocation is not peculiar to Hawkes. What passes for theory in sociobiology is so ambiguous that researchers must decide what is relevant evidence, and they have a virtual license to interpret research findings as they see fit and make whatever general observations they deem relevant.[18] Consider just one of Hawkes's general observations (1983:359): "If a Binumarien man has a genetic full sister who has married into a neighboring community, his sister and her children belong to an enemy group. Yet within his own community there are individuals who are genetically so distant from his as to be effectively nonkin. If, by contrast, a Binumarien woman has married in from elsewhere, she lives with and cooperates in everyday activities with individuals who, excepting her own children, are not genetic kin, while her natal community is the enemy of these people whom she helps. All this appears as a contradiction to kin selection principles only so long as precise calculations of genetic relations are assumed to be the characteristics organizing sociability."

RESEARCH WITHOUT PREMISES. Hartung (1982:1) tested a fairly specific hypothesis—"humans tend to transmit wealth to male descendants where polygyny is possible"—with data from the Standard Cross-Cultural Sample and Murdock's *Ethnographic Atlas*. While it is difficult to see the connection between the hypothesis and Hartung's report of a positive association between "bride-price" and polygyny, that is not the case for his reported positive association between polygyny and male inheritance. The latter association is impressive; but at no point does Hartung derive the hypothesis from premises, nor can it be derived from sociobiology's two principal propositions, its major thesis, or the underlying arguments. True, Hartung viewed his hypothesis as having something to do with sociobiology; and in commenting on it he states what could be taken as one of sociobiology's premises: "It [his hypothesis] does assume that if a pattern of behavior causes people to produce more descendants who also follow that pattern, the behavior will eventually come to predominate—or be naturally selected" (1982:1). However, Hartung immediately followed that statement with another that raises serious doubts as to the assumption's bearing on selectivity in reproduction or genetic propagation: "This should hold regardless of the mechanism of transmission of the behavior from parents to children." In any case, there are no rules of logic (e.g., the classical syllogism, Boolean) by which Hartung's hypothesis can be deduced from any of his other statements.

The ambiguous logical status of Hartung's hypothesis is especially unfortunate because the data used to test it pertain to a question that sociobiologists tend to ignore: Why do socio-cultural phenomena vary among social units? At first glance, Hartung's findings appear to answer the question as it applies to polygyny. Specifically, polygyny is present only where male inheritance is present. However, Hartung's hypothesis and his statements about it suggest that polygyny is necessary and perhaps even sufficient for male inheritance, which is to say that variation in marriage form explains variation in the rules of inheritance. Accordingly, neither Hartung's arguments nor his findings answer this question: Why is polygyny *normative* only in some units? The question is all the more important because Hartung (1982:1) argues that his hypothesis follows from "considering the difference in within-sex variance in reproductive success between males and females . . . and the fact that in polygynous societies multiple wives are acquired by men who can afford them." Hartung's hypothesis cannot be deduced from that statement, nor does the statement answer this question: If polygyny is a consequence of greater male success in reproduction (because his investment is less than the female), why is polygyny normatively proscribed in some social units?

SOME CONVENTIONAL DODGES. Sociobiologists not only fail to test formally derived hypothesis; they also deny the relevance of research findings reported as being contrary to sociobiology. Two examples must suffice.

As indicated previously, Sahlins's critique focused on what may well be the most important argument in sociobiology, that pertaining to kin selection.[19] Sociobiologists are particularly sensitive to Sahlins's claim (1976) that there are glaring discrepancies between social and genealogical kinship; but for reasons never made explicit, sociobiologists in anthropology have sought to refute Sahlins largely through observations on matrilineal kinship systems, the avunculate in particular (see, e.g., Greene, 1978). Perhaps that focus is suggested because the idea of a man investing more resources in his sister's children than his own appears alien to kin selection. In any case, the only merit of the focus is that it may lead sociobiologists to recognize that their argument must generate predictions about variation in socio-cultural phenomena. Thus, granted that polygyny increases the inclusive fitness of husbands (i.e., more offspring and, hence, more genetic propagation), why is polygyny not universal? Similarly, why are some kinship systems matrilineal, others patrilineal, and still others bilineal? A partial answer to the last question has been suggested in publications (e.g., Greene, 1978) that question Sahlins. Stating the argument briefly: In social units where wives engage in extramarital relations frequently, a husband can further his inclusive fitness more by investing his resources in his sister's children. Hence, uncertainty in paternity gives rise to a matrilineal kinship system and the avunculate (or so some commentators, such as Kurland, 1979, seem to suggest), but not because of the perceptions of the participants. All that one need postulate is that some men are genetically predisposed to invest in their sister's children, and selection does the rest.

The "uncertain paternity" argument deserves consideration because it at least implies an explanation of the presence of the matrilineal system and the avunculate in some social units but not others; and there is some evidence (see, e.g., Greene, 1978) of an association among social units between the promiscuity of women and a matrilineal kinship system, including the avunculate. However, even if that association does hold, it does not refute Sahlins. The reason is suggested by this question: Even in a patrilineal social unit where no wife is an adultress, why would husbands invest much more resources in paternal relatives than maternal relatives when there is no difference in the genetic coefficients of those relations? The general point has been stated more cogently by Kitcher: "given starting assumptions that are *no less plausible* than those favored by Alexander and Kurland, we can argue that the avunculate does *not* maximize the inclusive fitness of the men and women who engage in it" (1985:301).

Silk's (1980) findings on adoption in Oceania indicate that Sahlins (1976) overlooked the commonly close genealogical relation (other than biological paternity) between adopters and adoptees in Oceania. Nonetheless, surely Silk knows of social units (English-speaking in particular) where such adoption is not even typical;[20] and if there is no genealogical relation between adopter and adoptee, how could the adoption possibly further the inclusive fitness of the adopter? If the answer is that adoption is along ethnic or racial lines, it is a dodge to equate race and kin or ethnicity and kinship; and that point is sufficient reason in itself for doubts about van den Berghe's application (1981) of sociobiology's putative principles to the "ethnic phenomenon." In any case, van den Berghe's general observations and commentaries on the phenomenon are a far cry from a theory that implies testable predictions.

SOME PUZZLES.   The research findings do not warrant a categorical rejection of sociobiology's second principal proposition. However, there has been all too little research, one reason being the failure of sociobiologists to make the proposition explicit; and some of the positive findings are puzzling. In particular Chagnon (1980:553) reports that the average number of offspring for Yanomamo "headmen" is more than twice that of other males over age 34. Because the two sets of individuals are socio-culturally differentiated, the finding is consistent with the sociobiology's second principal proposition; and sociobiology's first principal proposition implies that some Yanomamo men are more genetically predisposed than others to become headmen. But if the genetic material that so predisposes becomes more prevalent (as a consequence of the reproduction rate of headmen), how could more than a few members of the population possibly become headmen? The increase in the relative prevalence of that genetic material in the Yanomamo gene pool will be checked?

How? Why? Is the number of headmen constantly increasing among the Yanomamo? That possibility is suggested by Chagnon's report (1979) of frequent village fissioning among the Yanomamo, but he did not emphasize the "spread of headmen genetic material" in his observations on that fissioning. For that matter, unless one assumes that villages can proliferate indefinitely among the Yanomamo, there must be limits as to the manifestations of the "headman genotype," even granting its existence; and one must wonder why such a volume of village fissioning is not even remotely universal. Similarly, if the "constant fighting over women and sex" among the Yanomamo makes "a great deal of sense when considered in terms of Hamilton's theory of inclusive fitness" (Chagnon, 1979:87), why is such behavior not conspicuous among all other peoples, even all other nonliterate peoples?

Essentially the same questions apply to Irons's report (1980) of a much greater reproductive rate for wealthy Yomut Turkmen. If some Yomut are more genetically predisposed than others to acquire wealth and if the disposing genetic material becomes more prevalent in the gene pool as a consequence, what would prevent virtually all of the population (at least the males) from becoming wealthy? But because wealth is first and foremost a relative matter, how could even the majority become wealthy?

Irons's findings (1980) are all the more puzzling when compared with numerous reports of much higher reproduction rates for the "lower class" in high-energy countries. The contrast suggests that the wealthy are selected in some environments but the poor in others. If so, there is nothing in sociobiology theory that even suggests why, let alone a designation of the other environmental conditions that determine the "direction of class selection."

Control and Sociobiology

Assume that eventually there is a great deal of systematic research on sociobiology's two principal propositions. Regardless of the outcome, the proposal to make control sociology's central notion would not entail anything akin to a categorical rejection of sociobiology. Indeed, if some tests of the second principal proposition are negative, the notion of control offers a way to reformulate the proposition so as to identify the conditions in which it may be valid.

The Control Imperative

The relevance of the notion of control for sociobiology is suggested by Skinner's statement: "We often overlook the fact that human behavior is also a form of control. That an organism should act to control the world around it is as characteristic of life as breathing or reproduction. A person acts upon the environment, and what he achieves is essential to his survival and the survival of the species" (1974:189).

SEXUAL INTERCOURSE AND CONTROL.   Given the connection between fitness and reproduction, it is hardly surprising that sociobiologists commonly write as though impregnation is the ultimate human concern, although all the while denying the relevance of consciousness and any related internal behavior. Even so, no one impregnates any one without exercising control, call it seduction, rape, prostitution, mutually enjoyable sex, or what have you. Moreover, although sexual intercourse requires interpersonal control, humans engage in all manner of attempts *to control those interpersonal controls*. Consider the legal punishment of forcible rape. Even if there is a genetic disposition to rape,[21] the extent to which individuals are selected for the genetic material in question depends on the kind, extent, and effectiveness of attempts to prevent rapes. So if there is a genetic predisposition to rape, we have an inconspicuous possibility of "culture selecting for genes" (for others, see Livingstone, 1980).

It is difficult to imagine sociobiologists denying that sexual intercourse requires human control or that control has a genetic basis, but there is an inconspicuous implication. What if humans were initially selected for capacity to control other humans for sexual pleasure rather than procreation? In the absence of contraception, that selection alone would insure the genetic propagation of the "control genes." Continuing the argument, accessible and effective contraceptive devices or practices (inanimate or biotic control in either case) may have initiated another massive selection process, this time favoring those who are genetically predisposed to avoid contraception. If so, what are the implications for the long-run future trend in human fertility? The argument does not extend to an answer, but it indicates how introducing the notion of control into sociobiology gives rise to significant questions.

THE MEDIATION OF GENES AND THE ENVIRONMENT.   Sociobiologists often write as though genes and the environment interact without anything intervening, but it is ludicrous to suggest that genes "do" anything to the environment. Indeed, genetic materials influence human behavior largely through *determining* the capacity or incapacity for inanimate, biotic, and human control.[22] Should anyone doubt the genetic basis of the capacity for control, they should attempt to teach a chimpanzee to pilot an aircraft, grow corn, or drill an infantry platoon. However, to say that genetic material determines the capacity to control is not to say that it determines human behavior. Genetic material largely limits human behavior, and that relation stems primarily from the genetic determination of the capacity to control. What humans control or do not control, how they control, and to what ends are determined by the interaction of genes, experience, and extrahuman features of human environments. To express the argument in terms other than control, such as "closed vs. open behavioral programs" or the "capacity to make choices" (see Freeman, 1980:200–1), is to invite ambiguity.

Still another argument has to do with something that sociobiologists rarely stress—survival is necessary for reproduction. Perhaps sociobiologists view mortality as far less problematical than fertility, but no human contributes to the gene pool unless he or she survives until puberty; and a great deal of genetic selection must have taken place in human history when surviving until puberty was far more problematical than reproducing. An extension of the argument would be all too speculative, but there is no speculation entailed in this assertion: Human survival depends on the amount, kind, and effectiveness of human control over the environment—animals, plants, other humans, and inanimate things (including physiographic factors, such as protection from the cold). If that point is granted and it is further granted that impregnation of humans is a matter of human control, then the greatest selectivity in the history of human genetic materials has always been in connection with the capacity to control. Wilson made a similar argument this way: "genes promoting flexibility in social behavior are strongly selected at the individual level" (1975:549). However, control is a much more precise notion than is flexibility.

Should Sociobiology Be Refuted

Should sociobiology be overturned by tests of propositions, the findings are not likely to be uniformly negative; hence, the challenge will lie in this question: What kinds of human practices are more nearly determined or influenced genetically through selectivity in reproduction? The question is complex; but this control principle (16–1) is at least a partial answer: To the extent that a human practice entails or has some bearing on controls over the environment, it is genetically determined or influenced through selectivity in reproduction.

The extent to which a human practice entails or has some bearing on control over the environment is not necessarily obvious; and the numerical expression of "extent" will be difficult. So, at least initially, the principle must be taken as nothing more than a guide for research. Nonetheless, the requisite research can be illustrated readily.

The illustrative research (Kitahara, 1982) stemmed from an experiment and general observations on two reactions of animals to menstrual odor: aggression by carnivores and omnivores, but inquisitive avoidance by herbivores. Kitahara recognized that for people who survive largely through hunting (a kind of biotic control over the environment) it is very important to come near game animals without being noticed and to avoid provoking dangerous animals. If animals respond to menstrual odors as indicated, the probability of a successful and safe hunt would be increased by not only excluding menstruating women from the hunt but also all men who have been in contact with those women. Wittingly or unwittingly, strict menstrual taboos reduce such contacts. Hence, so Kitahara reasoned, there should be a direct association among social units between the strictness of the taboos and the predominance or extent of hunting. Kitahara used two scales, one pertaining to the strictness of menstrual taboos and the other pertaining to the predominance or extent of hunting, both already prepared for numerous "societies" in the HRAF or cross-cultural files. The two scales are positively associated to a conventional level of statistical significance.

Because Kitahara's research is taken as only illustrative, it is not necessary to consider the quality of the data and the adequacy of the research design. All that need be said further is that the same association does not hold among pastoralists, in which case one of the scales pertains to the predominance-extent of animal domestication. That finding is not surprising because success in the kinds of biotic control attempted by pastoralists rarely requires stealth.

More important than the quality of the data or the design, Kitahara's research suggests how human practices pertaining to environmental control may be selected (in the genetic sense) without postulating intention on the part of the participants. It is reasonable to assume that early hunting people who did not practice strict and effective menstrual taboos were not successful in their attempts at biotic control, and they became extinct or survived by turning to other means of sustenance. While the process could operate without any participant being aware of the connection between the taboos and success in hunting, the taboos themselves and the hunting are control behavior nonetheless.

BEYOND THE PRINCIPLE.   The notion of control is relevant for sociobiology beyond drawing distinctions as to kinds of human practices. As suggested previously, there is every reason to assume that genetic material determines the *capacity* for control and limits human behavior through that determination. Now examine four questions. First, to what extent do differences between the behavior of humans and the behavior of other animals reflect corresponding differences in the capacity for control? Second, how much do humans and human populations differ as to the capacity for control? Third, what laws govern the heritability of the capacity for control? And fourth, what is the association between differences among humans or human populations as regards control and differences as regards reproduction?

Those four questions are not pursued by sociologists or other social scientists, but that is precisely the point. Not even the harshest critic of sociobiology is likely to deny the importance of the questions, but only sociobiologists have interests and skills suited for the pursuit of the questions. Indeed, the principal merit of sociobiology is its potential contribution toward answering this question: How is biology relevant in the scientific study of human behavior? Only a very dogmatic social or behavioral scientist would deny that biology is somehow relevant; but it will not do (see Gove, 1987) to castigate sociobiologists for having given an inadequate answer to the question: How is biology relevant in the scientific study of human behavior? Their answer is inadequate because couched in terms of a narrow genetic determinism, which is the principal shortcoming of sociobiology. The question is answered here this way: the biological characteristics of humans determine their behavior insofar as those characteristics limit the human capacity for control. If sociobiologists accept that answer, it will further the principal merit of their perspective and reduce its shortcomings.

NOTES

1. Initially, van den Berghe (1975, 1978) was content largely to demonstrate the relevance of various biological variables for sociology, but more recently he appears inclined to accept a version of sociobiology akin to that of Edward O. Wilson, a biologist. All in all, sociologists could have best remedied their indifference to and ignorance of genetics by following Eckland's lead (1967) rather than that of Wilson. There are even fairly recent treatments of the relevance of biology for the social sciences that are far more realistic than the views of Wilson or his disciples (see, particularly, Gove, 1987; Wallace, 1983; Baldwin and Baldwin, 1981; Jencks, 1980; and Langton, 1979).

2. Sociological versions (e.g., Ellis, 1977; Lopreato, 1984; van den Berghe, 1981) neither clarify sociobiology's premises nor offer testable propositions. Consider what Lopreato identifies as a "provocative" hypothesis: "sociocultural behavior is at least in part causally rooted in biology. . . ." (1984:18). Provocative or not, the hypothesis is so ambiguous that idiosyncratic tests are inevitable. Moreover, Lopreato's version of sociobiology, though erudite, is inordinately anecdotal. It comprises general observations on literally hundreds of subjects seemingly unrelated other than sequence (e.g. territoriality, the urge to victimize, the need for vengeance), laced with references to Pareto but not with testable propositions. There are occasional allusions to explanation, but the writing is so discursive that the premises cannot be identified with confidence. For example, one section of the chapter on ascetic altruism is designated as an explanation (Lopreato, 1984:222–28); but it comprises nothing more than meandering general observations on reciprocal favoritism, conformity, hierarchy, social approval, self-deception, and the idea of the soul. The chapter ends with two conclusions, one identified (Lopreato, 1984:233) as *overall*: "If there is validity to the argument of this chapter, especially to the functions assigned to self-deception and the soul, *then it is entirely possible to have genuinely altruistic behavior WITHOUT altruistic genes.*" Only general observations and nothing remotely resembling genetic research or even systematic data are offered to support the conclusion; and the same is true of the second conclusion: "I conclude by suggesting the law that *organisms have evolved a tendency to maximize their inclusive fitness, but the tendency is reducible by self-deception*" (235).

3. Examine Barash's Central Theorem of Sociobiology: "insofar as a behavior in question represents at least some component of the individual's genotype, then that behavior should act to maximize the inclusive fitness of the individual concerned" (1980:211). Whatever the premises from which the theorem was derived, there is no immediate prospect for demonstrating that a given behavior does or does not "represent at least some component of the individual's geno-

type." For that matter, does "should" mean "will," "does," or neither? So Barash's reference (1980:211) to the theorem as "testable" is grotesque, especially since he does not even suggest a test procedure. Kitcher provides the appropriate summary: "To test a theory it is important to formulate it. Lucky expositors can state the theories they expound by quoting the authors. Lumsden and Wilson do not lend themselves to this kind of treatment. There is a common tendency, even among those who hail the theory as a major new intellectual departure . . . to describe the mathematical formulations as opaque, even unintelligible. Perhaps this is one reason why Lumsden and Wilson have been able to dismiss many of their critics as failing to address the substance of their work. If the substance is guarded by densely packed equations, bristling with ferocious symbolism, reviewers may be forgiven for seeking topics elsewhere" (1985:350). Kitcher's references are to Lumsden and Wilson's *Genes, Mind, and Culture* (1981).

4. "Without a commitment to 'genetic determinism' pop sociobiology may be full of sound and fury, but it signifies nothing" (Kitcher, 1985:18).

5. Kitcher recognizes the charge of "untestability" made by many critics of sociobiology (1985:58) and identifies the central theme of his book as: "The dispute about human sociobiology is a dispute about evidence" (8). However, he immediately muddies the water by vilifying the notion of falsifiability without offering a real alternative (58–59).

6. The problem is exacerbated because, as a careful reading of Dawkins (1982) will indicate, it is not at all clear what sociobiologists take to be the "unit of selection"—group, species, kin, individuals, genes, or alleles.

7. In one succinct statement, Warner unwittingly reveals the analytic or conceptual character of seemingly synthetic (empirically contingent) propositions about adaptation, fitness, and reproduction: "Adaptations are those traits that convey the highest fitness (measured in terms of numbers of descendants or numbers of copies of a gene passed on) out of an array of possible alternative traits" (1980:153). Dunbar's sophisticated attempt (1982) to solve the conceptual problem (i.e., to define adaptation, fitness, and reproduction such that they are distinct) is more nearly a demonstration that the problem defies solution; and one must wonder what Kitcher's equating fitness with a "measure of the propensity to leave offspring" accomplishes (1985:52). In any case, Barash's definition is indicative of the outcome when an attempt is made to define adaptation without reference to fitness or reproduction: "Adaptation . . . refers to the ability of a living thing to function well in its environment" (1979:18–19).

8. There is no appropriate label to identify the case where G is sufficient but not necessary for B, nor to identify the genetic potential for precluding behavior, as when B is never present when G is present, or G is always present when B is absent but in some instances B is present when G is present.

9. Jencks acknowledges that even geneticists "often argue that while genes do not 'determine' phenotypes, genes do 'set limits' on phenotypes" (1980:732). Yet he seems to harbor misgivings about the argument, his ostensible rationale being that "we know virtually nothing about the limits genes place on specific phenotypes. . . ." (733). True, but Jencks does not point to any body of knowledge as justifying a stronger version of genetic determinism.

10. Sociobiologists do strive to mitigate their predilection for anthropomorphism, as in the case of Barash: "Of course, our genes don't think, much less plan strategies. But they act as though they do" (1979:25). Actually, the indulgence of sociobiologists in anthropomorphic expressions is no more grotesque than that of the superorganicists in the social science when they speak of society or culture as "doing" this or that.

11. "The insect killed by the queen of the colony as it fertilizes her eggs is, in Wilson's parlance, behaving altruistically. . . . But when 'altruism' is used indifferently to characterize unconscious instinctual behavior and voluntary sacrifice by a creature conscious of the nature of death, it is not scientific information . . . that we are receiving. It is, I fear, an object lesson in the abuse of words" (Frankel, 1982:47).

12. Gould's point should not be construed as implying that all biological explanations of human behavior are evolutionary. To the contrary, there are at least two nonevolutionary kinds of biological explanations (Mazur, 1978).

13. The suggestion is not that Sahlin's attribution of reductionism to sociobiology is a distortion, if only because van den Berghe (1982:14–15) defends reductionism and Ellis (1977:57) castigates antireductionism in making arguments for sociobiology. However, Sahlins fails to acknowledge that sociobiologist are at one with Durkheim in their indifference if not hostility to an emphasis on internal behavior (e.g., intention, beliefs).

14. Note, however, that Wilson's statement raises grave doubts as to what the claims of sociobiology really are: "The evidence is strong that almost all differences between human societies are based on learning and social conditioning rather than on heredity" (1978:48). Perhaps Wilson made the statement to appear moderate; but if his statement is valid, why bother with sociobiology?

15. The two questions—What are the premises of sociobiology? and What predictions do those premises imply?—cast doubt also on the claim that female infanticide increases inclusive fitness (see Kitcher's critique, 1985:315–29).

16. The point is particularly relevant in contemplating Chagnon's claim that an ax fight he observed among two Yanomamo groups was such as to increase inclusive fitness (briefly, in this case, kindred are more prone to side with each other in fights). Kitcher's assessment (1985:307–15) of Chagnon's observations creates doubts as to their relevance.

17. The same ambiguity haunts Shepher's attempt (1983) to explain the incest taboo from the perspective of sociobiology. For an elaborate critique of the preoccupation of sociobiologists with incest, see Kitcher (1985).

18. Illustrations abound in the literature. Consider Daly and Wilson's (1982) report that of 508 Detroit homicides the offender-victim relation was consanquineal (genealogical kin) in 38 or 6.3 percent of the cases. Daly and Wilson write as though those numbers corroborate sociobiology, but that conclusion stems from an ad hoc standard rather than a derived prediction.

19. Although Sahlins is an anthropologist, many anthropologists ostensibly see great merit in sociobiology (see, e.g., Chagnon and Irons, 1979).

20. Of 38 states in the U.S. for which there are statistics on 1975 adoption petitions granted (National Center for Social Statistics, 1977:7), in no state was the percentage of petitioners classified as "other relative" (i.e., other than one or

both of the child's natural or biological parents) greater than 23, and in ten states the percentage was less than 5. Indeed, given that the percentage of petitioners classified as "unrelated to the child" varied from 16 (Alabama) to 97 (Massachusetts), it is pointless to deny enormous variation in the genealogical relation between adopters and adoptees.

21. "Perhaps human rapists, in their own criminally misguided way, are doing the best they can to maximize their fitness" (Barash, 1979:55).

22. A control terminology would not replace evolutionary terminology (e.g., *adaptation, favorable traits*); rather, the former would be used to clarify the latter. The need for clarification is commonly overlooked not just by many biologists but also by social scientists who rightly see merit in evolutionary theory (see, e.g., Langton, 1979:300).

Two Special Subjects

Unfortunately, a candidate for a field's central notion can be assessed thoroughly only through extensive attempts to use it. Those attempts should be made by professionals having varied interests, because they know where the shoe pinches. But no one is likely to make the attempt unless convinced that the candidate is deserving. This book extols the merits of control as a candidate for sociology's central notion, and little more can be done beyond encouraging sociologists to describe and think about their subject matter in terms of control. The point is not just that the fate of any proposed central notion hinges on attempts to use it; additionally, no sociologist has the expertise for a competent assessment of the candidate in all sociological specialties (e.g., deviance, stratification, collective behavior).

Given what has just been said, the book could have ended with chapter 16. Chapters 1–16 are sufficient for sociologists to understand the book's two principal arguments: first, maximum coherence in a scientific field requires a central notion; and, second, control could be sociology's central notion. However, even ignoring those two arguments, control deserves far more attention than sociologists have devoted to it.

The immediate pivotal question for the "sociology of control," one pursued throughout chapter 17, is this: What is the efficacy of any given means of control? The question is pivotal because few sociologists would think of control as important if they believed that control attempts are only rarely efficacious (see Sieber, 1981, on social intervention), and they surely would be even less inclined to accept control as sociology's central notion.

One argument against more policy-relevant work in sociology is that such work is bound to benefit some humans, the affluent in particular, more than others. The argument is understandable; but it is difficult to imagine sociologists seriously extending the argument beyond the idea of policy-relevance to human concerns in general, even though much of sociology often appears strangely removed from human concerns. In particular, contemporary sociologists devote little attention to the idea of freedom, despite evidence that the idea has been a perennial human concern for centuries. Accordingly, if it is granted that sociology should bear on humans concerns, the question becomes: How can the notion of control be used to describe and think about freedom? That question is examined at length in chapter 18. The examination is not entirely independent from the argument that control could be sociology's central notion, but the relation between freedom and control warrants study apart from arguments about a central notion.

Chapter

17

Future Work on the Efficacy of Control

Whether or not control becomes sociology's central notion, this question is pivotal: Given some particular means of control, what is its efficacy? Eventually, the second efficacy question—What determines the efficacy of a given means of control?—will become more important; but an answer will require efficacy estimates for a given means of control under various conditions, and each estimate will bear on the first efficacy question. So the first question is more immediate; but it is important also because of its connection with this version of the "efficacy" principle of control (17–1): Given alternative means of control as perceived by social unit members, the greater the efficacy of a particular means, the greater the relative frequency with which the members employ it. If valid, the principle is relevant when explaining variation among social units in the relative frequency of some type of control attempt. In any case, if sociologists aspire to have an impact on human history, it will be through a focus on control efficacy rather than chattering about praxis.

Some Issues Concerning the Efficacy Principle

Many sociologists appear reluctant to emphasize the purposive quality of human behavior, not in light of formal criteria of explanatory adequacy but, rather, because of a dogmatic antireductionism. Hence, they will be skeptical about the efficacy principle, and therein lies two issues.

First Issue

The efficacy principle does not explain any particular act or type of act, nor does it answer a "why" question about individual differences, such as:

Why do some people rob banks? The principle answers only questions about alternative means, such as: Why do more bank robbers use a gun than a knife? The efficacy principle is relevant because those questions are of this general form: Why this means rather than another?

IRRELEVANCE OF THE RATIONALITY ARGUMENT. Although the term *rational* does not appear in the efficacy principle, critics will insist that the principle assumes "rationality." It will not do to reply that some human behavior is rational; rather, the notion of rationality is intolerably vague, and an empirically applicable definition of rational behavior or belief is bound to be arbitrary.[1] That would not be the case if the definition could be limited to the notion of effectiveness; but it would be indefensible to ignore the notion of efficiency, and contending efficiency criteria appear infinite.

One likely counterargument: Nonetheless, the efficacy principle presumes rationality because it suggests that choices are made so as to maximize the benefit/cost ratio. Such terminology alone is objectionable. The key terms—*choices, cost, benefit*—are commonly used by those who take the notion of rationality seriously (e.g., Heath, 1976); but to use those terms in a definition is to insure negligible empirical applicability. Furthermore, effective control is a matter of the would-be controller's perception; and efficiency criteria are always relative to the conservation of things that the would-be controller perceives as desirable, perhaps including beliefs about "technological" threats to jobs or occupations (see Hanisch, 1980). Definitions of rationality are especially ambiguous with respect to perception, possibly in an attempt to avoid conceptual issues. For example, if rational behavior is defined as simply goal-oriented behavior and the crucial perception is made by the actors, then virtually all of human behavior is rational and the rational-irrational distinction has no real consequences.[2] As for efficiency, the immediate issue in stipulating a rationality criterion is the identity of the "perceiver"; but, whoever, recognizing only one efficiency dimension (time, energy, pain reduction, etc.) would be arbitrary.

The Second Issue

An army of sociologists (e.g., Empey, 1984) has pursued this question: How is social order possible? That question and the efficacy question are competitors; and the choice between them is not a superficial issue because in a field without a central notion, or even accepted theories, a pivotal question provides the only basis for coherence.

A GHASTLY QUESTION. Despite its longevity, the order question is indefensible.[3] For one thing, it suggests that social order is something like a universal constant; but think of instances of extreme civil strife, one outstanding case in 1986 being Lebanon. If the illustration is disputable because its relevance depends on the definition of social order, that is another reason to reject the "order" question. Even if an empirically applicable definition could be formulated, numerous sociologists are likely to reject it. While some sociologists use the term *social order* to denote uniformities in behavior (e.g., average or typical behavior), others use it to denote conformity to putative norms. To illustrate, if all Americans should shoplift each time they enter a store, then behavioral order would be at a maximum; but normative order would be at a minimum, assuming a putative norm that proscribes shoplifting. So the two conceptions are not necessarily compatible, and there is an insoluble problem in either case. Although sociologists refer to social order as though it is a qualitative property, even casual observations indicate that it is quantitative; but there is no prospect of a measurement procedure.

Should it be claimed that social order is a purely theoretical notion and, hence, not empirically applicable, sociologists do not use the term that way. Indeed, they are inclined to assess a theory in light of what it seems to imply about social order, especially whether order is based on consensus or conflict. Such assessments reflect a blatant indifference to the need for systematic tests.

A SINGULAR MERIT. The order question's only merit is that it directs attention to one of the most conspicuous features of human behavior: perhaps in all social units there are periods in which behavior patterns are markedly stable over time. Now contemplate a connection between control efficacy and behavioral uniformity over time. Why do individuals tend to employ the same means of control again and again? Because they perceive it as efficacious. That answer suggests another control principle (17–2): The more a control means is perceived as efficacious, the less likely its abandonment.

The principle does not deny the relevance of socialization. Humans do learn how to control, but are we to assume that socialization agents emphasize ineffective means? Some means of human control are taught because they are effective, and to learn a language is to master an instrument of control and to become vulnerable to control (see Fowler et al., 1979).

The Efficacy of Law

Sociology currently has little impact on policy, whether that of governments or terrorists. Greater concern with control would make applied sociology more respectable (see Rossi, 1980) and further sociology's policy relevance. An emphasis on law would be especially strategic, and the argument goes beyond the conventional identification of law as a means of social control.[4] The identification is disputable because it runs contrary to a sociological tradition established by Sumner (1906:55–57)—a persistent denial of the efficacy of law (but see Ball et al., 1962). That tradition discourages research on this question: How efficacious is law as a means of control? Compelling evidence of negligible efficacy would have enormous policy implications, but a conceptual problem must be confronted before undertaking the requisite research.

Conceptions of Law

The major schools of jurisprudence—analytical jurisprudence, legal realism, and natural law theory—are distinguished primarily by their definitions of law. The contrasts are illustrated subsequently, but note preliminarily that the English language blurs the distinction between *a* law and law. Whatever "law" may be, it includes "laws"; hence, any definition of law implies or presupposes some definition of *a* law, which is the primary concern here.

Because of space limitations, several conceptual strategies must be slighted or ignored entirely. For example, Friedman and Macaulay (1977:829) define a legal system as a "set of sub-systems which, for one reason or another, people choose to call 'legal.' " Should their strategy be extended to defining a law, then laws would be peculiar to English-speaking countries. Such a definition would be worthless in the debate over the universality of law (Hoebel, 1968), and to assume that in all languages there is a term equivalent to "a law" merely relegates the problem to lexicographers. For that matter, Friedman and Macaulay's strategy is dubious even for Anglo-American countries, because it assumes consensus among English-speaking people in identifying laws.

ANALYTICAL JURISPRUDENCE AND THE COERCIVE CONCEPTION OF LAW. The following four definitions make coercive enforcement the essential feature of law or a law.

Austin: "a law is a command which obliges a person or persons, and obliges *generally* to acts or forebearances of a *class*. . . . A Command is distinguished from other significations of desire . . . by the power . . . of the party commanding to inflict an evil or pain in case the desire be disregarded. . . . The evil . . . is frequently called a *sanction*. . . . . . . Every positive law . . . is set . . . by a sovereign individual or body, to a member or members of the independent political society wherein its author is supreme" (1954:24, 14, 15, 350).

Weber: "An order will be called . . . *law* if it is externally guaranteed by the probability that physical or psychological coercion will be applied by a *staff* of people . . . to bring about compliance or avenge violation" (1978:34).

Hoebel: "A social norm is legal if its neglect or infraction is regularly met, in threat or in fact, by the application of physical force by an individual or group possessing the socially recognized privilege of so acting" (1968:28).

Kelsen: "Law is the primary norm, which stipulates the sanction. . . . . . . If 'coercion' in the sense here defined is an essential element of law, then the norms which form a legal order must be norms stipulating a coercive act, i.e. a sanction" (1945:61, 45).

Such emphases on coercion elicit vigorous objections. Thus, Hart (1961) points out that people may heed laws out of a sense of obligation rather than fear of punishment. Even so, it hardly follows that no one is ever deterred; and, in any case, a coercive definition of a law implies no efficacy claim. So Hart demands something that no definition provides—answers to empirical questions (see Gibbs, 1968, for elaboration).

Legal realists reject the "formalism" of analytical or positivistic jurisprudence and its preoccupation with normative phenomena to the neglect of actual behavior (for elaboration, see Lempert and Sanders, 1986:215). Such criticism of Austin and Kelsen is justified; but a coercive definition does not imply that laws necessarily constitute a logical system or emanate from a sovereign, and the definitions of Hoebel and Weber do refer to actual behavior.

In light of a coercive definition, laws have no necessary connection with justice, ethics, or morality (see Weinreb, 1978), for the definition makes a law's content irrelevant. Consider Nazi Germany's infamous Nuremberg Laws, which threatened Jews with punishment for, among other things, practicing certain professions. The threats were coercive, but to identify them as "laws" suggests a neutrality that natural law theorists reject. Because definitions are not demonstrably true or false, the issue cannot be resolved.

Using the term *norm* or *rule* in defining a law reduces the definition's empirical applicability because either term is a study in conceptual problems. Coercive definitions would be improved by identifying laws as a subclass of "statements that imply an evaluation of a type of behavior." That inelegant phrase promises greater empirical applicability than does norm or rule.

Hart (1961) rightly points out that a coercive definition is especially questionable when extended beyond criminal law. Some statutes provide instructions for but do not prescribe such actions as entering into marriage, disposing of property, or adopting. Such "enabling functions" are not trivial, and to argue that the actions in question create a sanction potential borders on logomachy. It is more realistic to recognize that some laws are intended to facilitate particular types of behavior without prescribing them, and only interference with that facilitation elicits a coercive threat.

Turning to more specific criticisms, with what frequency must a statement be enforced coercively to be a law? Austin and Kelsen provide no answer; Hoebel's term "regularly" is unrealistic if it means all instances; and Weber did not stipulate a *minimum* probability (surely he did not mean any probability whatever), let alone how probability is to be reckoned.

Coercive definitions neither attribute normative consensus to laws nor speak of legitimacy. Critics reject the implication—that legitimacy stems from laws; but if legitimacy is something more than normative consensus, its meaning is intolerably vague, a point ignored by Weberians and natural law theorists. Yet to depict a law as necessarily accepted by at least the majority of those to whom it applies is ethnocentric. Nonetheless, coercive definitions do ignore a feature of putative laws—rare coercive resistance to or coercive retaliation for their enactment or enforcement. While a defensible criterion of "rare" is wanting, the feature warrants recognition.

LEGAL REALISM. The central argument of legal realists is suggested by the following statements.

Holmes: "The prophecies of what the courts will do in fact, and nothing more pretentious, are what I mean by the law" (1897:461).

Llewellyn: "This doing of something about disputes . . . is the business of law. And the people who have the doing in charge, whether they be judges or sheriffs or clerks or jailers or lawyers, are officials of the law. *What these officials do about disputes is . . . the law itself* . . . the theory that rules decide cases seems for a century to have fooled not only library-ridden recluses, but judges" (1960:12, 1934:7).

Frank: "Rules, whether stated by judges or others, whether in statutes, opinions or text-books by learned authors, are not the Law, but are only some among many of the sources to which judges go in making the law of the cases tried before them. . . . The law . . . consists of decisions, not of rules. If so, then whenever a judge decides a case he is making law" (1930: 127–28).

Advocates of analytical jurisprudence dismiss Holmes by arguing that laws create courts, and he did leave many questions unanswered. Whose prophecy constitutes "law"? If a prophecy stems from recognition of some uniformity in court rulings, why the uniformity? Because a uniformity suggests something that constrains judges, what is that "something" if not laws?

Unlike Holmes, later legal realists spoke of decisions, not prophecies. However, do all decisions of a judge qualify as laws? If not, what kind of decision? Should an American judge sentence a convicted tax evader to execution, the sentence would be a decision; but would it be a law? If legal realists argue that the sentence would be appealed and overruled, why the prediction?

The legal realists' conception of law is difficult to apply outside Anglo-American jurisdictions. If a definition of courts or judges is to apply universally (including the possibility of their absence in some social units), it must refer to the enforcement of laws; but legal realists imply that laws can be identified only after courts and judges are identified. They ignore the problem by limiting their observations to Anglo-American judges and courts; indeed, they appear preoccupied with case law and appellate decisions.

NATURAL LAW THEORY. Members of still another jurisprudential school seem to argue that a positive law (a law actually decreed or enacted enforced) is not really a law unless consistent with "natural law." That argument has been debated for centuries, and definitions of natural law intensify the debate. They are so divergent that a short list could mislead. Legal scholars have recognized eight meanings of natural law, but in a well-known work Patterson lists six: "1. Any critical or constructive theory of legal valuation, or of the ideals of law. . . . 2. The use of reason in the making and administration of law. . . . 3. Principles of human conduct that are discoverable by 'reason' from the basic inclinations of human nature, and that are absolute, immutable and of universal validity for all times and places. . . . 4. A theory of natural rights based upon a supposed 'state' of nature, a prepolitical society, and a supposed social compact in which men conferred limited powers on a political government, and in so doing reserved natural rights. . . . 5. Norms of human conduct discoverable by experience and observation as prevalent and useful among different peoples. . . . 6. The capacity to perceive, or any intuitive perception of 'justice' or 'equity' in concrete situations" (1953: 333–34).

Patterson's list excludes the will, command, or design of a supreme being, recognition of which makes definitions of natural law even more divergent. However, the issues are not limited to divergent meanings. Critics depict the notion of natural law as metaphysical, and no well-known definition suggests defensible criteria for identifying *particular* instances. Consider, the "universality" criterion, akin to numbers 3 and 5 in Patterson's list. If natural law comprises only norms that are present in all societies, the definition would be fairly clear; but few if any specific putative norms appear to be universal.

Lon Fuller's (1969) eight *desiderata* of law could lead to an empirically applicable definition of natural law: (1) general, (2) promulgated, (3) clear, (4) free of contradictions, (5) not retroactive, (6) does not demand the impossible, (7) appreciable constancy over time, and (8) congruent with official actions. Fuller (1969:96) characterized his work as a "procedural version of natural law"; and his *desiderata* scarcely constitute even a partial definition of positive law, especially given Fuller's statement that "law is the enterprise of subjecting human conduct to the governance of rules" (106). Many such enterprises lack some of Fuller's *desiderata*, and to argue that an enterprise is not law without all eight *desiderata* would merely extend a seemingly sterile debate.[5] The alternative interpretation is that Fuller's *desiderata* imply this empirical proposition: To the extent that a law (positive) lacks the *desiderata*, compliance is reduced. Yet Fuller's disciples do not identify his argument as an efficacy proposition.

Even if Fuller's work should lead to an empirically applicable definition of natural law, the debate would continue. The paramount issue is the insistence that an evaluative statement cannot be a law unless consistent with natural law (see, e.g., Olivecrona, 1971:23); hence, critics regard any definition of natural law as value judgement about what positive laws should and should not be. So there is no prospect for resolving the issue.

A Control Conception of a Law

Problems in defining a law may defy solution. The term *law* is not needed to focus theory and research on certain quantitative variables, such as the frequency of coercive enforcement of evaluative statements and the frequency of coercive resistance; but since social scientists and legal scholars would reject abandoning the term, there is no realistic choice other than modifying extant definitions of a law so as to blunt some criticisms. However, the ultimate justification of a definition is its use in widely accepted theories, and there is a dilemma. Definitions are needed to formulate a theory; and the dilemma is especially acute in sociology, where there are no accepted theories. Here we have another advantage of a central notion; it serves as a rationale, one less stringent than appealing to accepted theories, in choosing among alternative definitions.

To propose that law be defined in terms of control is not radical because of the maxim that law is a means of social control. Unfortunately, however, the maxim does not suggest an answer to this question: How does law differ from other means of social control? The following definition is consistent with the maxim and implies an answer to the question: A statement is a law in a particular social unit if and only if: (1) the majority of at least one socially recognized category of members (e.g., a legislative body but perhaps a category with only one member) have made or endorsed the statement publicly; (2) the statement implies an evaluation of some *type* of human behavior; (3) all members of at least one other socially recognized category (e.g., the police) have by public statements or other actions consistently indicated an intention to promote, facilitate, prevent, punish, revenge, or rectify such behavior by any member of at least one other socially recognized category of members (e.g., juveniles); (4) the intention extends to the use of unlimited coercion given coercive resistance or coercive retaliation; and (5) no socially recognized category of members is collectively engaged in such coercive resistance or coercive retaliation.

LAW AND SOCIAL CONTROL. All putative laws are social control as conceptualized in Chapter 3. In particular, whether construed as a command, a directive to legal officials, or a prediction, a criminal statute is attempted referential social control by those who enacted or decreed it (the first party), for the statute implies reference to what a third party (judges, police officers) should or will do given some type of act by any member of at least one category of members (second parties). Likewise, Hart's "secondary rules" as components of law pertain to *three* parties; and such rules are evaluations of conduct, with those opposing or interfering with their administration being subject to punishment backed by coercive threats.

Along with legal realists, assume that law is found only in the actual behavior of officials. Even so, no judge imposes a sentence or awards damages without regard to promoting general deterrence, catering to public opinion, currying the favor of elites, and/or placating complainants. So a third party is involved, and any court order is referential social control because it implies reference to what other officials will do should the order be violated.

Now reconsider laws's "enabling functions," such as legal instructions for entering into marriage. While it distorts to say that people follow those instructions to create a sanction potential, the instructions are not formulated or followed without some belief about eventual behavior control. Specifically, compliance with legal instructions in a legally permissive actions furthers the influence of those who comply. Both the second and the third party in social control may be indefinite categories; and those persons (e.g., legislators) who formulate such legal instructions are the first party in modulative social control, with one goal being the prevention or resolution of disputes.[6] The crucial point is that attempts at prevention are made by increasing the influence of certain categories of potential third parties.

The control definition indicates the sense in which law differs from extralegal means of social control. It is not just coercion, although one must wonder why natural law theorists and even legal realists balk at emphasizing coercion. If they argue that coercion is only a necessary feature of a law, the belief is consistent with the present definition, according to which a law necessarily also involves three parties. The triadic requirement blunts Hart's allegation (1961) that a coercive definition does not distinguish law from the acts of a gunman. The typical gunman does engage in control but not *social* control. For that matter, since a gunman does not command types of behavior for potentially infinite individuals, the gunman's behavior is not a law even ignoring the triadic requirement (a consideration Hart ignored).

The contrast between the proposed control definition of a law and that preferred by natural law theorists cannot be described readily because they appear indifferent to this question: What distinguishes laws from norms or rules in general (e.g., customs, mores)? However, such indifference is not peculiar to natural law theorists (see, e.g., Malinowski, 1959; Ehrlich, 1936).

The Efficacy of Criminal Law

There are two noteworthy features of the only major line of sociological work on criminal law, which pertains to deterrence. First, some of the independent variables—properties of statutory or actual punishments—are controlled by officials (e.g., legislators); hence, the potential impact of deterrence research on penal policy is considerable. Second, the potential has not been realized, perhaps in part because horrendous evidential problems have precluded conclusive findings.

SOME COMPLEXITIES. Bentham's version (1962) of the deterrence doctrine is extremely discursive. It actually suggests two theories, one about specific deterrence (the deterrent impact of punishment on those who have been actually punished) and one about general deterrence (the deterrent impact of punishment threats on those who have not been punished). Evidence bearing on one type of deterrence has no necessary bearing on the other; and the same is true of a less conventional distinction, between absolute and restrictive deterrence. In the latter case the fear of punishment does not prompt offenders to refrain from criminality *entirely*; rather, they curtail their criminal activity to reduce apprehension risk and/or punishment severity. Subsequent observations ignore the absolute-restrictive distinction, and specific deterrence is examined in chapter 18.

Attempts to reduce the deterrence doctrine to one proposition (e.g., certain, severe, and swift punishments deter crime) ignore more than types of deterrence. As many as 12 properties of legal punishments could be relevant (Gibbs, 1986); and it is imperative to maintain two distinctions: (1) between objective and perceptual properties and (2) between statutory and actual punishments.

Unless deterrence is defined so as to emphasize fear of punishment, it cannot be distinguished from several nondeterrent mechanisms that prevent crimes (Gibbs, 1975:57–93). One is "incapacitation," where an actual punishment makes it difficult if not impossible for an offender to repeat the offense (e.g., safecrackers cannot practice their craft readily in prison). Such distinctions can be ignored in stating a theory about the *general preventive effects* of legal punishments, but legislators are attracted to deterrence because it promises inexpensive crime prevention. What could be cheaper than merely threatening punishment? But if punishments prevent crimes only through incapacitation, a low crime rate will be very costly (see Currie, 1985:81–101).

Finally, the deterrence doctrine does not assert that the crime rate is determined solely by legal punishments. Hence, when testing propositions about general or specific deterrence, relevant extralegal etiological conditions (e.g., perhaps unemployment, social condemnation of criminality, rewards for criminal activity) should be controlled.

EVIDENTIAL PROBLEMS. All of the foregoing complexities create serious evidential problems in deterrence research apart from the reliability of data (see, especially, Zedlewski, 1983). For all practical purposes, none of the problems have been solved or avoided in any deterrence study.

Space limitations permit only four additional observations on evidential problems. First, conventional crime data are such as to preclude recognition of the general-specific and absolute-restrictive distinctions. Second, no study has considered more than two of the 12 possibly relevant properties of legal punishments, and perceptual properties (e.g., the severity of statutory punishments as perceived by potential offenders) have been totally excluded in research comparing political units (e.g., states). Third, a defensible research design that controls for nondeterrent preventive mechanisms has not been realized. And, fourth, in many studies no attempt was made to take relevant extralegal conditions into account, and there are no truly accepted theories about the etiology of crime to guide the identification of conditions (but see Piliavin et al., 1986, on rewards; and Erickson and Gibbs, 1978, on social condemnation).

PRINCIPAL FINDINGS: A BRIEF SUMMARY. Because of evidential problems, the findings provide at most only limited support for the general deterrence argument. Very few of the correlations between average or median length of prison sentences served and crime rates among American states are significant; and for no type of crime is the correlation significant at all time points (e.g., 1960, 1970, 1980). There is no compelling evidence that controls for extralegal conditions result in an inverse relation between punishment severity and the crime rate, and recent findings (Paternoster and Iovanni, 1986) do not indicate even a statistically significant association among individuals between the perceived severity of legal sanctions and frequency offense.

Only one finding is indicative of general deterrence: a fairly consistent negative correlation among states, metropolitan areas, and cities between the objective certainty of arrest or incarceration (the proportion of reported crimes that resulted in such punishment) and the crime rate. While no type of crime has proven to be a consistent exception, the evidence is debatable for three reasons. First, since "number of crimes" is the rate's numerator but the certainty measure's denominator, critics allege that the negative correlation is a statistical artifact; and the issue stands unresolved. Second, it has been argued that an increase in the crime rate causes a decrease in punishment's objective certainty (the "overload" hypothesis); and longitudinal findings in the form of lag correlations are often not consistent with the cross-sectional findings. Third, the frequently reported inverse relation among individuals between the perceived certainty of legal punishment at T_2 and the frequency of self-reported offenses over T_{1-2} came to be questioned once researchers considered perceptions at T_1 and the frequency of self-reported offenses over T_{1-2} as self-reported at T_2 (see Gibbs, 1986, for some references).

A LARGER ISSUE. Conclusive findings are most unlikely without major methodological innovations,[7] but sociologists should not abandon deterrence research. Conclusive findings in any policy-relevant research may be difficult to realize, and deterrence investigators perhaps have an advantage in being aware of evidential problems.

But why assume that conclusive deterrence findings (whatever they are) would alter penal policy? As a case in point, the U.S. trend toward longer prison sentences commenced some 15 years ago despite several published reports of no significant inverse relation among American states between length of prison sentences and crime rates. So it appears that sociologists must become more "active" (see Whyte, 1986:556) for their findings to influence policy, but that strategy is consistent with treating control as sociology's central notion.

Some Other Varieties of Law

There is an astonishing paucity of even speculative books on the efficacy of noncriminal law (see Allott, 1980, and Jones, 1969). For that matter, there are numerous books on the sociology of law in which efficacy is not recognized as posing a major question (e.g., Aubert, 1983), and Black (1972) has castigated concern with legal effectiveness. Most telling, in the subject headings (17 pages) for the *Index to Legal Periodicals* (1983–84), the word *Eskimos* appears but not *efficacy*, *effectiveness*, or *efficiency*.

TORT LAW AND DISPUTE SETTLEMENT. Although the deterrence doctrine applies to tort law (but see Keenan and Rubin, 1982), deterrence research has not extended to torts. That lacuna is unfortunate but understandable. While judgments against tort defendants could be the basis for computing severity measures, no agency compiles statistics on tort incidence; and the number of court cases is not an incidence measure. As for gathering unofficial data, there are horrendous problems. So tort law must be considered in some context other than deterrence.

The emphasis on dispute settlement in legal anthropology and by legal realists suggests that law's essential function is to settle disputes.[8] Hence, rather than assess the deterrent efficacy of tort law, attention could be shifted to its efficacy in dispute settlement. Yet few findings bear even remotely on this question: Do disputes become violent without legal intervention? Sherman and Berk (1984) report that during 1981–82 repetition of a domestic assault in Minneapolis became less likely if the alleged offender (mostly spouses) was arrested rather than admonished or ordered to vacate the premises for eight hours. The finding pertains to legal dispute settlement but in connection with criminal law and specific deterrence rather than tort law and general deterrence.

In light of adjudication costs and delays, critics suggest that the American legal system is inefficacious in dispute settlement, and throughout U.S. history various communal or interest groups have commonly resorted to extralegal means of dispute settlement (see Auerbach, 1983). Yet evidence will remain inadequate without systematic comparisons of the efficacy of law relative to that of extralegal means. In one of the very few relevant publications, Sarat described his findings concerning small claims litigation by conventional adjudication and arbitration (less formal but not strictly extralegal) this way: "almost four times as many of the arbitrated cases facilitated the continuance of the parties' relationship" (1976:369).

CONTRACT LAW AND DISPUTE SETTLEMENT. Because the difficulties in estimating incidence are greater for contract violations than for torts, there is scarcely even any indirect evidence on the efficacy of contract law. That evidence is nothing more than estimates of the frequency of contracts.

In reporting extremely rare research on the frequency of contracts, Macaulay (1963) reached two conclusions after interviewing 68 Wisconsin businessmen and lawyers. First, few interviewees reported a business transaction through an ostensible contract. And, second, law suits for alleged breaches of contract appear extremely rare. Both conclusions indicate that most business executives view contract law as ineffective and/or inefficient.

REGULATORY LAW. In 1952 Justice Jackson asserted that the "rise of administrative bodies probably has been the most significant legal trend in the last half-century" (Freedman, 1978:3). So why the paucity of research on the efficacy of what may well be the wave of the future?[9] Because the difficulties are so formidable.

A defensible procedure for estimating violations is wanting just as much for regulatory law as for contract or tort law, and there are even greater problems when defining regulatory law (see, especially, Noll, 1985:9,71,111; Stone, 1982:7–34; and Thompson and Jones, 1982:8–21). In jurisprudential literature the term *administrative law* is commonly used as though everyone knows what it denotes, or as though designations of particular agencies, boards, bureaus, tribunals, or commissions are substitutes for a definition. Many of those designations appear inconsistent with the suggestion that administrative law has to do with "government intervention in the economy, through regulation" (Rabin, 1979:1). Consider that suggestion in connection with references made in a treatise on administrative law (Freedman, 1978:4) to the Civil Service Commission, Interstate Commerce Commission, Federal Trade Commission, Selective Service Commission, Tennessee Valley Authority, Securities and Exchange Commission, Internal Revenue Service, National Labor Relations Board, National Aeronautics and Space Administration, and Environmental Protection Agency. It distorts to attribute regulatory activities to NASA and TVA, especially activities similar to those of the SEC or the FTC. No doubt, each title does denote an administrative agency, and each was created by administrative law; but there is a rationale for recognizing regulatory law as a type of administrative law—only *some* administrative agencies regulate sectors of the economy.

The problem is commonly exacerbated by definitions like that of Breyer and Stewart's: "Administrative law consists of those legal rules and principles that define the authority and structure of administrative agencies, specify the procedural formalities that agencies employ, determine the validity of particular administrative decisions, and define the role of reviewing courts and other organs of government in their relation to administrative agencies" (1979:10). The definition ignores regulatory activities per se, but are we to conclude that, for example, SEC regulations are not laws?

Equating administrative law in general with regulations issued to control production and/or consumption is objectionable (see commentary by Barry and Whitcomb, 1981:3). Moreover, a careful conceptualization would be needed to distinguish (1) contemporary control of Britain's economy and control in medieval Britain and (2) regulatory law and sumptuary law.

Unfortunately, conceptual clarification will not reveal the efficacy of regulatory law, and systematic research on the subject (as distinct from studies of postulated "effects" of regulation, such as those published in the *Journal of Law and Economics*) has been negligible.[10] One of many difficulties stems from the need to assess two contending strategies for promoting compliance with regulation—disincentives and incentives (for other but similar distinctions, see Richardson, 1987).[11] The disincentive strategy is akin to criminal law because the targets are threatened with a loss for failure to comply. By contrast, the incentive strategy awards compliance, such as tax reductions for installing devices in manufacturing that lower air pollution. Although enforcement is more difficult in the disincentive strategy, the incentive strategy's range of application is narrower.

Two Concluding Arguments

The most conspicuous feature of efficacy research is its limitation to criminal law and horrendous problems regardless of the type of law.[12] Those features preclude an informative conclusion.

THE MAJOR LACUNAE. Deterrence research has been narrow, with the typical study limited to a few types of crime and one type of punishment. Hence, researchers have not really taken up this question: What is the efficacy of the legal system taken as an entity? Stating the matter another way, should the legal system disappear, what would be the consequences?

Research has been concerned virtually exclusively with marginal deterrence, such as the difference in the amount of deterrence produced by, say, the threat of ten years of imprisonment rather than five, or an objective imprisonment certainty of, say, .75 rather than .25. In the case of nonmarginal deterrence, the contrast is between some threat of punishment and none whatever. The latter situation obtains only when the behavior in question (e.g., smoking) has been legal for several generations. The related argument is that most citizens are deterred, if at all, not by accurate knowledge of possible penalties and their objective certainty but, rather, by the belief that the behavior in question entails *some* risk of *some* punishment. That possibility can be assessed only through research on "nonmarginal deterrence," by comparing the frequency of some type of behavior in two jurisdictions, one where the behavior is criminal and one where it has not been criminal for several generations, or frequency before and after criminalization (e.g., Nichols's survey, 1982:67, indicates 20–40 percent safety belt usage rates before legislation and 70–90 percent after). Should someone object that such research would only demonstrate the obvious, they have wittingly or unwittingly endorsed the deterrence doctrine.

CONTROL IN ANY CASE.   There are two reasons why sociologists may not recognize the connection between research on the efficacy of law and the proposal to make control sociology's central notion. First, they rightly identify law as a macro phenomenon but erroneously think of control as inherently micro. Second, Durkheim has led sociologists to view laws as purely symbolic, because he habitually described laws as flowing from the collective conscience through the unwitting acts of faceless legislators, meaning as though the laws were neither enacted nor enforced with a view to controlling someone.

Some sociologists will grant both the importance of law and its control character but denigrate efficacy research by suggesting that it serves some establishment. But why does "the establishment" support so little of the very research that supposedly benefits it? Arguments by Marxist criminologists are especially puzzling. For example, Quinney denounced deterrence research as "a defense of punishment applied in order to protect a late capitalist social order" (1976:415). Since most deterrence findings question the efficacy of American criminal law, how does the research defend punishment? Be that as it may, Marxists frequently suggest that capitalists use criminal law to control dissidents, and the suggestion tacitly attributes validity to the deterrence doctrine.

The Efficacy of Extralegal Means of Control

Although sociologists traditionally doubt the efficacy of law, they have done even less research on the efficacy of extralegal control.[13] It is as though they either are unaware that much of human interaction is attempted control or incuriously assume that the attempts are efficacious. Even a defensible typology of means of extralegal control is wanting. Since a defensible typology is beyond this book, the subsequent survey considers only a few broad spheres where extralegal controls are conspicuous and pose noteworthy issues.

Terrorism

In attempting to prevent terrorism, officials often go beyond deterrence to incapacitation and prelusive social control, especially surveillance (e.g.,

408 / Control: Sociology's Central Notion

planting informants in politically active groups) and exclusionary means (e.g., elimination of dissidents). Those prelusive measures are commonly illegal, and erosion of the rule of law takes on added significance in light of Gurr's report (1983) of only four terrorist episodes or campaigns in East Germany, Yugoslavia, Bulgaria, Czechoslovakia, Hungary, Poland, Rumania, USSR, and Cuba over 1961–71, far less than the number reported for liberal democracies (e.g., 27 for Italy).[14] So, insofar as the terrorism rate varies inversely with the effectiveness of preventive measures, the most effective measures are employed in countries where police practices are ostensibly the least restrained by the rule of law (see Wilkinson, 1986:10). In any case, terrorism prevention has become a virtually global concern, especially since the advent of international terrorism; and the efficacy of alternative preventive measure is only one of many issues (see, e.g., Bakhash, 1986; O'Brien, 1986; and Wilkinson, 1986). All that can be said of those issues (e.g., the extent to which terrorism prevention requires a diminution of the rule of law) is that they can be described in terms of control. Space limitations preclude more than observations on terrorism's efficacy, a subject that has received far less attention than has the efficacy of measures to prevent terrorism.

CONCEPTUALIZATION. Definitions of terrorism are divergent and controversial, but space limitations preclude treatment of conceptual problems and issues. It must suffice to modify Wardlaw's careful definition: "political terrorism is the use, or threat of use, of violence by an individual or a group, whether acting for or in opposition to established authority, when such action is designed to create extreme anxiety and/or fear-inducing effects in a target group larger than the immediate victims with the purpose of coercing that group into acceding to the political demands of the perpetrators" (1982:16).

There are three objections to Wardlaw's definition. First, rather than expect the "target group" to accede, terrorists may seek to provoke governmental measures so repressive that the regime loses public support and falls in a popular revolution. Second, terrorism differs from a civil war in that terrorists rely on secrecy as to personal identity, concealment of location, and/or some immunity from conventional military attack; and they do not attempt a permanent territorial defense. Third, even when terrorists are government officials and controlled by the highest political authority (see Duvall and Stohl, 1983), their actions go unacknowledged by themselves and/or their superordinates.

The most controversial issue pertains to actions by government officials to create "extreme anxiety and/or fear inducing effects in a target group larger than the immediate victims." If such actions constitute terrorism, as Wardlaw's definition surely indicates (also see Walter, 1969), why would the infliction of clearly legal punishments to deter potential offenders not be terrorism? The question is commonly ignored in conceptualizations of terrorism, perhaps in dim recognition that much of criminal justice would be terrorism.

THE EFFICACY OF TERRORISM.   Writers who question terrorism's efficacy far outnumber those who grant it even occasional limited success, but defensible judgments depend on the "failure criterion." Consider Laqueur's assertion that "There is no known case in modern history of a small terrorist group seizing political power. . . ." (1977:221). That assertion may be valid without the "small" qualification; but Laqueur concedes that terrorism has resulted in political changes,[15] and it is questionable to deny that terrorism contributed to Algerian independence and the Irish Free State.

Even if the terrorist's ultimate goal is a regime's overthrow, there are intermediate goals; and often, because of a strategic mistake, achieving an intermediate goal precludes the ultimate goal. In the classic case, Uruguay's Tupamaros (following Carlos Marighela's *Minimanual of the Urban Guerilla*) sought to provoke the government to such extreme repressive measures that it would fall in a popular revolution; and the strategy succeeded so well that a liberal democracy was replaced by a right-wing regime, one that crushed the Tupamaros and remained in power (see Wardlaw, 1982:37–38). So terrorism's efficacy should be assessed not by simple success-failure criterion but by several quantitative criteria, such as amount of publicity received and number of successful operations (e.g., airplane seizures and assassinations).

A CASE OF INDIFFERENCE TO TERRORISM.   Sociologists have contributed little to the extensive literature on terrorism, but not because terrorism is a dull subject. As Stohl, a political scientist, aptly described it: "Political terrorism is theater. It is drama of the highest order. Violence, death, intimidation, and fear are its ingredients" (1983:1) Nor can sociologists readily dismiss terrorism as unimportant. The global annual number of deaths attributable to terrorism averaged nearly 300 over 1968–84 (Segaller, 1986:3); and although the monetary cost of attempts to prevent terrorism defies computation, some idea is suggested by one estimate of the cost of screening passengers at U.S. airports as $194,200,000 over 1973–76 (see Wardlaw, 1982:58).

So why have so few sociologists studied terrorism? Perhaps because many of them believe that research on terrorism contributes to the defeat of noble causes. But since terrorists come in such diverse stripes, how could all of their causes be noble?

OTHER QUESTIONS.   While questions about terrorism are not limited to efficacy (terrorism prevention or terrorist goals), others—such as the "why" of variation in incidence—can be thought of in terms of control. However, consider one of several additional questions: What is the empirical relation between terrorism and revolution?

In warning about reliance on repressive measures to counter terrorism, Wardlaw implies (1982) that dictatorships emerge when the "rule of law" is abandoned to prevent terrorism. So another question: To what extent does terrorism result in the departures from the rule of law?

Advertising

Because advertising is a major industry, the related extensive literature is hardly surprising. However, over many years few books in that literature have been reviewed in a major sociology journal.

THE PROMOTION OF INDIFFERENCE.   Although the literature on advertising is predominantly "applied," many of the books are either reports of systematic research or genuinely theoretical (see, e.g., Fulop, 1981; Reuijl, 1982). None of the authors are sociologists,[16] and Michael Schudson's *Advertising, the Uneasy Persuasion* (1984) is neither a research report nor theoretical.

One of Schudson's ostensible goals was to create the impression that advertising is ineffective, largely by reference to a few research findings, such as (1984:3): "on average, less than 25 percent of a television audience can remember an ad they saw on television the day before, even when prodded with various clues." Never mind that a television advertisement could prompt viewers to buy a product after they cease to remember it. Nor never mind that effectiveness is a matter of degree; and no one assumes that (1) all potential consumers are exposed to each advertisement, *or* (2) that all of those exposed buy the product as a consequence, *or* (3) that the advertisement prompted those exposed to switch brands and purchase more of that type of product, *or* (4) that those who bought as a consequence of the advertisement will remain loyal to the brand indefinitely, etc., etc.[17] Finally, because advertising efficacy is a question both of degree and of kind, it could be that some advertising increases total consumption without significant brand switching.

Although Schudson might deny having failed to recognize that advertising effectiveness is a matter of degree, he did create the impression of some criterion of minimal effectiveness (e.g., more than 25 percent of the viewers must remember an advertisement). Moreover, one of his qualifications results in this convolution (1984:4): "This does not mean that the ads are ineffective. . . . television ads may be powerful precisely because people pay them so little heed that they do not call critical defenses into play. . . . But why do most people most of the time tune out advertisements? Because, to put it simply, advertising is propaganda and everyone knows it."

All in all, Schudson is extremely ambiguous about efficacy, as this statement (1984:3) illustrates: "Advertisements ordinarily work their wonders, to the extent that they work at all, on an inattentive public." More important, Schudson never suggests that social or behavioral scientists should aspire to a rigorous assessment of advertising efficacy. That omission and Schudson's ambiguity about efficacy were totally ignored in the book's review (*American*

Journal of Sociology, July, 1985, 159–61); hence, both the book and its review will further sociological indifference to advertising's efficacy.

If sociologists eschew a rigorous assessment of advertising's efficacy, what should they do? Schudson does suggest an answer (1984:11, 240): "National consumer product advertising is the art form of bad faith: it features messages that both its creators and its audience know to be false and it honors values they know to be empty. . . . Nonprice advertising often promotes bad values, whether it effectively sells products or not." So Schudson appears content to pass moral judgment on advertising.

THE ULTIMATE EFFICACY QUESTION. Schudson does not cite any of several careful reports (e.g., Reuijl, 1982) of a significant positive association between a measure of advertising volume and a measure of sales volume. Worse, while acknowledging the evidential problems in efficacy research, he did not encourage their solution; and devising efficacy measures call for methodological aptitudes that many sociologists possess.

Insofar as Schudson goes beyond moralizing, he is interested in advertising as a cultural phenomenon (an art form, to use his own words), not as attempted control. Nonetheless, advertising offers unrivalled opportunities for research on the efficacy of control. Viewed crassly, the total estimated expenditure on American advertising in 1980 of more than $55 billion (Albion and Farris, 1981:xi) is indicative of the potential research resources. Should it be argued that the research would promote the interest of the affluent and powerful, whose interests are promoted by declining to assess advertising's efficacy?[18] The question becomes more important in light of another one ignored in reviews of studies of advertising (e.g., Draper, 1986): What impact would the definitive analysis of advertising's efficacy have on its volume?

Control at the Micro Level

The control targets in terrorism and advertising are commonly indefinite categories, a characteristic of control at the macro level. Psychotherapy, everyday interaction, and socialization are treated in this chapter section as illustrations of predominantly micro control.

PSYCHOTHERAPY. Their protestations notwithstanding, psychiatrists, psychoanalysts, clinical psychologists, and counselors (even Rogerians) regularly engage in control attempts; and there are two questions for the sociology of control. First, what are the distinctive characteristics of control attempts by psychotherapists? Second, how efficacious are those attempts?

Since mid-century the reliability of psychiatric diagnosis has been questioned to the point of implying that the terms *neurosis* and *psychosis* defy empirically applicable definitions. The same is even more true of generic labels, such as mental illness or emotional disorder. Indeed, there are sociologists (e.g., Scheff, 1984) and even psychiatrists (e.g., Szasz, 1974) who suggest that mental illness is a myth. Although the debate appears sterile, no efficacy question about psychotherapy can be pursued thoroughly without confronting the conceptual issues and problems.

Critics of the "disease model" of mental illness depict the mentally ill as having waltzed through life merrily until a psychiatrist pounces on them with that label and forthwith deprives them of their liberty. That picture ignores individuals who come to psychotherapists and describe *themselves* as tormented. Given their self-reported state, it is not puzzling that those individuals seek help, relief, a cure, etc. More specifically, they (1) want to alter some recurrent features of their overt or internal behavior, (2) solicit the control of persons to whom they attribute expertise, and (3) perceive their solicitation as voluntary. The control they solicit is henceforth designated as "petitionary." It is a subclass of "consensual" control, which also includes (for example) much of control of one's spouse or friends.

Some psychiatrists are not regularly engaged in petitionary control; rather, in the name of treatment they control individuals who did not solicit it. Why? Commonly because a legal official (rightly or wrongly) has authorized placing such individuals under a psychiatrist's control in a coercive context. Such "impositional" control is a subclass of coercive contextual control, along with (for example) armed robbery. Of other subclasses, the most important is the carceral because the pertinent question is this: How does a psychiatrist's impositional control in a mental hospital differ from a prison guard's control? Nothing is gained by replying that psychiatrists treat patients. The term *treatment* or *therapy* is subject to diverse interpretations. Literally hundreds of therapy modes have been identified (APA Commission on Psychotherapies, 1982:5), and the control exercised over mental hospital patients may not be obviously different from the control exercised over convicts. There is only one crucial but not obvious difference; impositionalists claim expertise in transforming human behavior without actual use of coercion (despite the context, evidently), and that claim is sanctioned by those who authorize the control (e.g., legislators attribute expertise to psychiatrists).

So psychotherapy is petitionary or impositional control, but in either case possibly involving inanimate control, including psychopharmacology. The definition is very broad; but psychotherapy cannot be defined adequately by reference to some distinctive treatment mode, and experts either stop short of an explicit definition (see, e.g., APA Commission on Psychotherapy, 1982) or offer a virtually incomprehensible definition (see Herron and Rouslin's survey, 1982:2–3). Finally, any list of occupational titles (e.g., psychiatrist, counselor, etc.) would be arbitrary; and even if psychotherapy could be defined justifiably as "that which psychotherapists provide," the definition would apply only in English-speaking social units.

What is psychotherapy's efficacy? For various reasons (see Garfield,

1984, and APA Commission on Psychotherapy, 1982), there is nothing approaching an incontrovertible estimate, not even for a particular therapist-patient population (e.g., a sample of Boston psychiatrists "treating" diagnosed ambulatory schizophrenics in 1986). Moreover, there are no prospects of defensible estimates as long as efficacy judgments entail the problem of defining and identifying the mentally ill (i.e., if psychotherapy is defined by reference to mental illness). That problem can be ignored if the present conceptualization of psychotherapy is accepted. For sociological purposes, the question in each case of psychotherapy becomes: To what extent was the attempted control a success?

Sociologists should never purport to judge psychotherapy's efficacy by their own perceptions. For any instance the question is: To what extent do the psychotherapist and the other interested party perceive the hoped-for behavioral change as having been realized? The other interested party is the individual who initiated the psychotherapy, a "voluntary" patient, the recipient's guardian, or an official who ordered the therapy. The initiation itself is attempted control, but modulative social control if made by someone other than the recipient, and attempted self-control through external human control if made by the recipient.

The prescribed basis for judging success-failure is largely alien to conventional assessments of psychotherapy's efficacy since about 1940; but the rationale is not just that sociologists have less expertise in such matters than do some psychiatrists or psychologists, such as Hans Strupp (1984). The kind of control that psychotherapists attempt is influenced by their perceptions of past successes and failures, but whether a particular mode of psychotherapy becomes conventional may depend appreciably on the success-failure perceptions of other interested parties (for illustrative research, see Lebow, 1983).

Should sociologists recoil at the complexity of research on psychotherapy's efficacy, conventional research (see APA's Commission on Psychotherapy, 1982) is simpler only because problems and issues are ignored. As to the research's importance, the U.S. mental health "industry" operated during 1980 at an estimated cost of $14 billion (McGuire, 1981:13), and yet conventional psychotherapy is such that perhaps no more than two percent of Americans needing therapy can receive it (Kiesler, 1984:361–62).

EVERYDAY INTERACTION.   Although most of everyday interaction is proximate control, sociologists rarely study interaction in any direct sense; and control has never been the central notion. The scientific literature that bears on proximate control, especially the efficacy question, is largely limited to social psychology, even though the practitioners rarely use the term *control* (see, e.g., Weimann, 1982; Bickman, 1974).

Witty commentators have suggested that Skinner's experimental animals controlled him, and to his credit Skinner recognized (1983:267) the humor as well as some partial validity. Yet the suggestion touches on the reason why operant psychology is a far cry from the sociology of control. Skinner's protestations (e.g., 1978:16) notwithstanding, operant psychology's principles stemmed largely from experiments with nonhuman animals; but that point is different from the shrill rejection of operant psychology by the likes of Koestler and Chomsky (see references in Skinner, 1983). Nonetheless, operant psychology's principles are too narrow for the sociology of control. Far from demonstrating otherwise, Homans's use (1974) of operant psychology illustrates its limits; and Skinner's voluminous writings on human control (see, e.g., 1983, 1978, 1974, 1971) are largely rhetoric and casual reflection.

"Behavior modification" offers more to sociology than does operant psychology, precisely because it is focused on the control of human behavior.[19] Granted the difficulties in generalizing beyond situations where behavioral modification is attempted, the practice of behavior modification should be a distinct component of sociology's subject matter; and the practitioners have already examined their effectiveness in considerable detail (e.g., Matson and DiLorenzo, 1984; Krasner, 1982). While effectiveness depends appreciably on the specific method employed and the kind of behavior, it is generally far from impressive (see, especially, Foa and Emmelkamp, 1983), especially in the modification of putative deviance, such as drug addiction, alcoholism, and homosexuality. An attempt to explain the unimpressive results would bear on the second major question for the sociology of control (What determines the efficacy of control attempts?) and is not directly relevant for present purposes.

There is a purely practical reason why the sociology of control must go far beyond operant psychology and behavior modification. If only because of limited resources, sociologists must answer questions about control in connection with what are conventional subjects of study in the field. Hence, the immediate question is this: What kinds of control are predominant in everyday interaction? The answer for most social units is "commands and requests." Requests may be more common, but commands are strategic in sequential control.

Not even a focus on the efficacy of commands would insure continuity in research, and the problem transcends limited resources. The research should pertain to conventional sociological phenomena. Two illustrations of alien research, both by social psychologists, must suffice. First, there is Bickman's field study (1974) of responses by pedestrians to commands given by individuals in different uniforms (e.g., a pedestrian is commanded by a "milkman" to move from a bus stop). Second, Milgram (1974) reported an experiment in which paid research volunteers inflicted what they perceived as severe electrical shocks on someone (who feigned suffering pain) at the command of a person dressed as a scientific investigator. Although both studies pertain to proximate control's efficacy, the findings are limited to rare social situations.

Sociological research on proximate control's efficacy should focus on either commands in employment-work situations or requests between friends.

Although such commands and requests are common, sociological research on them is rare. Sociologists evidently assume that the effectiveness of commands in employment-work situations or requests of a friend is not problematical (but see Hamilton and Biggart, 1985). They never inquire whether the relations in question require effective proximate control. Yet the proposed research is feasible. One possibility is the solicitation of responses from community residents to questions something like these: When did you last ask a friend to do something and the friend refused? What did you ask? What were the circumstances? Similar questions could be asked about the last successful request. Both superordinates (e.g., managers) and subordinates in employment contexts would be asked questions about commands last obeyed and last disobeyed.[20] The difference between the dates of most recent "successes" and "failures" would permit crude estimates of command-request effectiveness in various conditions.

SOCIALIZATION. The indifference of sociologists to conceptual problems is manifested in their definitions of "socialization," but writers in other disciplines also appear indifferent. The most relevant illustrations are four essays on socialization in the *International Encyclopedia of the Social Sciences* (Sills, 1968-XIV:543–62), none of which treat conceptual problems or issues (see also Hargreaves, 1985). The first author, a psychologist, does not even define socialization. The second author, an anthropologist, alludes to definitions without identifying any major problems or issues. The third author, a political scientist, defines "political socialization" but does not suggest a generic definition. Finally, the sociologist defines socialization generically but not adult socialization, the essay's subject.

As the subsequent definitions indicate, the term *socialization* is a conceptual monstrosity; and the definitions are typical.

Brim: "In the simplest terms, one can say that through socialization the individual acquires the culture of his group or groups" (1968:555).

Greenstein: "Narrowly conceived, political socialization is the deliberate inculcation of political information, values, and practices by instructional agents who have been formally charged with this responsibility" (1968:551).

Mortimer and Simmons: "For the group, socialization is a mechanism through which new members learn the values, norms, knowledge, beliefs, and the interpersonal and other skills that facilitate role performance and further group goals. From the perspective of the individual, socialization is a process of learning to participate in social life" (1978:422).

Wentworth: "Socialization is the activity that confronts and lends structure to the entry of nonmembers into an already existing world or a sector of that world. . . ." (1980:85).

The quotations illustrate four reasons why definitions of socialization (even the most recent and most thoughtful: Long and Hadden, 1985:42) commonly offer negligible empirical applicability . First, a reference to process, activity, or mechanism with some vaguely designated outcome (e.g., "the individual acquires the culture of his group or groups") makes virtually any human event an instance of socialization. Second, definitions of a type of socialization (e.g., political) and the recognition of multiple perspectives (e.g., group versus individual) are not adequate substitutes for a generic definition. Third, the use of extremely abstract terms (e.g., *culture*) in defining socialization invites all manner of interpretation. And, fourth, a reference to "new members" without indicating when socialization ceases is objectionable.

Given what has been said, it is not surprising that sociologists appear unconcerned with assessing socialization's effectiveness. Indeed, in light of the typical definition of socialization, there are no successes or failures. Rather, it either happens or does not happen; and given the vague definitions of socialization, it is difficult to imagine socialization not happening.

The following definition reflects a concern with empirical applicability: socialization is any instance of attempted external human control, wherein the would-be controller perceives the kind of attempt (1) as appropriate because the object of the attempt has been a member of a particular social unit less than some relative or absolute period recognized by the would-be controller and (2) as increasing or decreasing the probability of at least one particular kind of behavior by the object in a potentially unlimited series of subsequent situations. Space limitations permit recognition of only one issue. Although the definition encompasses more than control attempts by official agents, it excludes the acquisition of behavior patterns through imitation, emulation, or any unilateral learning process.

Because the notion of socialization is relevant for virtually all sociological subfields (see commentary on the notion's importance by Long and Hadden, 1985), various efficacy studies could be undertaken; but one illustration must suffice. Harriet Wilson's rarely cited research on juvenile delinquency (1980) is relevant despite her seeming avoidance of reference to socialization or control. For each of 120 randomly selected families in a British city Wilson assessed the parental supervision of juvenile boys. Her scale ranged from 0 (very strict parental supervision) to 7 (very lax), with the component values compiled from responses to a few simple questions posed in interviewing the mother (e.g., two points toward "laxness" if the boy's mother reported no rules about the boy telling his mother where he goes).

Wilson computed three delinquency values for each boy: one from the local law enforcement records (official incidence), another from the boy's answer to questions (self-reported delinquency), and still another from misbehavior reports by teachers. Those values entered into a delinquency rate for each of three categories of families: strict parental supervision (0–1 on the parental supervision scale), intermediate (2–3), and lax (4–7).

The delinquency rate was much greater for lax supervision families than strict supervision families, with the ratio being about seven times greater in one comparison (Wilson, 1980:230). Moreover, the difference holds (1) for all types of rates; (2) for comparisons made within each of three "social handicap" categories of families—low, moderate, severe; and (3) for the inner city as well as suburbs (but limited to "difficult housing estates"). Indeed, variation in parental supervision is associated with much greater variation in delinquency rates than is variation in social handicap (a distinction akin to social class), area (inner city versus suburbs), or criminal history of parents.[21] The findings are all the more noteworthy because Wilson's parental supervision scale is very crude; but it does pertain to socialization as control, and it is significant that one of the few other instances of systematic research on socialization (Cook-Gumperz, 1973) also pertained to control.

Wilson's research has been ignored totally by sociologists, leaving it to a political scientist, James Q. Wilson (1983), to make arguments consistent with her findings. Why are sociologists seemingly reluctant to argue that parental supervision prevents delinquency? First, because they are enamored with superorganic notions and structural variables; hence, they wish to speak of anomie or class as causing delinquency.[22] Second, they view Wilson's findings as supporting a conservative position, and even she expressed concern that her study might be identified as "positivist criminology" (1980:203).

The Efficacy of Inanimate and Biotic Control

Even if sociology's research resources would permit the hundreds of needed descriptive studies of inanimate and biotic control, a focus is needed to formulate theories. All that can be done here is identify promising lines of efficacy research.

Inanimate Control

Research on inanimate control's efficacy should focus on technological efficiency. Again, virtually all of inanimate control is the creation, use, or maintenance of technological items; and efficiency appears to be technology's most important property (but complexity is a contender).

MORE CORRELATES OF TECHNOLOGICAL EFFICIENCY. Because the possible correlates of technological efficiency are seemingly infinite, the theory in chapter 6 is very narrow. It could be expanded by formulating additional axioms and/or postulates. However, the most strategic work will pertain to the empirical validity of Postulate 6-1, which asserts a direct relation between technological efficiency and inanimate energy use. The immediate doubt stems from recognition that technological efficiency may be a function of several variables in addition to inanimate energy use, such as the efficiency of inanimate energy converters (e.g., turbines).

The situation is more complicated than suggested in chapter 6. As recognized there, a close direct relation between technological efficiency and inanimate energy use may not hold when comparing "tribes," because such populations use relatively little inanimate energy and yet their tools differ appreciably (see Oswalt, 1976). However, there may be a problem even when comparing contemporary countries. International variation in computer use is one cause for doubt, because computers contribute to over-all technological efficiency (especially temporal efficiency) but in use require little inanimate energy per capita.

Why devote so much attention to postulated *mensurable* correlates of technological efficiency? Consider one alternative—additional axioms concerning the *theoretical* correlates. Those axioms would expand the theory's scope, but it would be a disaster if Postulate 6-1 is empirically invalid (contrary to evidence in chapter 6). If so, because technological efficiency would be a construct in each additional axiom, all theorems deduced (in part) from the new axioms will be invalid.

THE EFFECTIVENESS OF INANIMATE CONTROL. Automobiles do run, there are machines that can pump water, and electricity is generated by turbines. However, even though for most kinds of inanimate control the question is efficiency rather than effectiveness, the latter should not be slighted.

What technological developments will be necessary for voyages to other solar systems? The question takes on added significance now that all other planets appear lifeless. In any case, the question implies an assessment of current human technology—that it is ineffective for space travel over enormous distances. The same can be said of the current technology of weather control.

THE QUESTION OF PERCEPTION. Efficiency has been treated as though unrelated to the perceptions of those who use the technological items, which is not the case. While the time and human energy conserved can be measured without reference to such perception, they are efficiency criteria only on the assumption that humans value such conservation. Moreover, time and human energy are not the only efficiency criteria that deserve attention.

The global proliferation of environmental protection agencies suggests the emergence of a new criterion of technological efficiency. Because large amounts of pollution come from the creation or use of technological items, the concern with pollution reduction could become the major impetus of technological change. Paradoxically, the most relevant sociological specialty, human ecology, is not known for work on environmental problems; but there have been a few major sociological works (e.g., Dunlap and Catton, 1979; and Catton, 1980), and recent publications on "risk" (e.g., Perrow, 1984) are also relevant.

Just as grim prophecies of an eventual genuine energy crisis have gone unheeded, so have warnings about technological change, automation especially, producing unemployment. Nonetheless, a technological item's impact on employment is a possible efficiency criterion, even though commentators may not use the term *efficiency* in assessing that impact. The argument is not altered by granting that the association between technological change and employment remains debatable, and sociologists should not abandon the question to economists.

The Efficacy of Biotic Control

When shooting at an animal, the hunter is attempting biotic control; and he or she is likely to perceive the attempt as a failure if the animal is not immobilized. Such perceptions pertain to the *effectiveness* of biotic control, but *efficiency* pertains to the amount of valued conservations in attempting biotic control.

THE EFFICIENCY OF FOOD PRODUCTION.   Slash-and-burn agriculture in certain parts of Mexico once yielded some 2,000 kilograms of corn per hectare (nearly 2.5 acres), an amount equal to approximately 6,901,200 kilogram calories (kcal) of energy (Pimentel, 1980:5). The production required 1,144 hours of labor and about 589,160 kcal of human energy (all numbers are per hectare unless indicated otherwise). So for every kcal of human energy expended in corn production (primarily planting, hoeing, and harvesting), about 11.7 kcal were realized. That "caloric efficiency ratio" (11.7) appears impressive, but it represents gross efficiency because two things are ignored: (1) the human, animal, and inanimate energy expended in creating, distributing, and maintaining the tools and seed and (2) the inanimate and animal energy used directly in production. Little more than human energy was expended directly in the corn production, and the energy invested in the tools and seeds was about 53,178 kcal per hectare (16,570 for axes and hoes, 36,608 for the seeds). So *net* caloric efficiency, which takes into account all forms of energy expended, directly or indirectly, was 6,901,200/642,338, a ratio of 10.7.

The small difference between the two ratios, gross (11.7) and net (10.7), indicates that very little inanimate energy was used in Mexican corn production. By contrast, the gross caloric efficiency of American corn production in 1975 (see Pimentel, 1980:10) was about 3,431.7 per hectare, meaning that every calorie of human energy expended directly in corn production generated about 3,432 food calories. However, the net caloric efficiency ratio was only about 2.9. The contrast (3,431.7 versus 2.9) is enormous because, in addition to the 5,580 kcal of human energy expended directly, some 6,526,491 kcal (virtually all inanimate) were expended in machinery, fossil fuels, electricity, irrigation, transportation, fertilizers, insecticides, and herbicides.

Because the American gross caloric efficiency ratio exceeds Mexico's for numerous types of food production, the percentage of the economically active regularly engaged in animate industries (agriculture, forestry, fishing, and hunting) is much greater in Mexico. So the comparison supports the theory in chapter 7, which implies an inverse relation between percentage of the economically active (labor force) in animate industries and inanimate energy use per capita.

GENETIC ENGINEERING.   Even cautious assessments of genetic engineering's future (especially Zimmerman, 1984) suggest that it could result in an enormous increase in the efficiency of food production, the virtual eradication of cancer, a reduction in the need for organ transplants, and an unprecedented decline in human mortality. The ultimate change would be the lengthening of the life span (see Stableford, 1984:94–107) through reduction of totipotency loss in the nuclei of human cells, thereby arresting or reversing the aging process. However, genetic engineering is a fountain of prospective issues. Two examples must suffice. Genetic engineering could lead policymakers to anticipate such enormous increases in food production that they cease considering "overpopulation." More important, genetic engineering is likely to have all manner of *unintended* consequences, which may or may not pose the greatest danger, depending on its military uses (see Dickson, 1986).

Sociologists are likely to underestimate the experience required to become knowledgeable about even isolated aspects of genetic engineering; but the expertise problem would be diminished by an exclusive concern with genetic engineering's efficacy, because the success-failure judgments would not be made by sociologists. Advanced graduate students in genetics, microbiology, or biochemistry could be employed to survey scientific publications and tabulate success-failure frequencies in particular lines of genetic engineering, with tabulations for a sample of countries over the last three quinquennial years (e.g., 1975, 1980, 1985). Because a greater proportion of "failures" are likely to go unpublished, the data would be supplemented by a survey of a random sample of scientists regularly engaged in genetic engineering, with the interviews designed to elicit success-failure reports.

Given defensible success-failure tabulations in at least one particular line of genetic engineering (e.g., creating insect resistant plants), the research would become more in keeping with the interests and methodological skills of sociologists and expand the scope the sociology of science. Although there is no theory on genetic engineering's efficacy, numerous possible antecedent correlates of the success/failure ratio can be identified. For example, governmental regulation could be so stringent that it reduces the success/failure ratio, but corporate ventures in genetic engineering probably increases the ratio by discouraging high risk projects.

THE CONTROL OF HUMAN BIRTHS.   After centuries, no theory provides a defensible explanation of variation in human fertility rates. No one should be puzzled, nor wonder why the theories imply so little about control of fertility rates. Most well-known theories are "structural" in that they describe variation in the fertility rate as a function of such variables as percent of women economically active, per capita income, degree of urbanization, and age composition. Those variables cannot be manipulated readily (if at all) by legislation; hence, even if valid, structural theories do not identify feasible means for controlling fertility rates. As for the validity, the statistical association between structural variables and fertility rates provides no basis for even approximately accurate predictions. "Not infrequently, relationships are found to differ not only in magnitude but even in direction in different settings and at different times" (Bongaarts and Potter, 1983:1). Why do structural theories offer so little? Because they ignore the proximate determinants of births (see comments by Bongaarts and Potter, 1983), all of which can be described in terms of control. Thus, sterility commonly can be altered, if at all, only by somatic control (e.g, surgery); an induced abortion is successful somatic control; and individuals may refrain from or curtail sexual intercourse in the belief that it decreases the probability of becoming pregnant or impregnating.

Space limitations permit only a few observations on the relation between birth control and variation in fertility rates. An age-sex adjusted fertility rate may be largely a function of three values, each pertaining to some birth control device or practice (BCDP) resorted to by at least one population member during the 21 months before the end of the birth enumeration period of one year. The first value, P, is the proportion of fecund and sexually active members who resorted to a BCDP at least once; M is the maximum effectiveness of that BCDP, the greatest proportion of potential conceptions that can be prevented if the device or practice is used or followed in some specified way; and R is the regularity with which those who use the BCDP do so approximately in that specified way. Although the P, M, and R values would have to be crude estimates (see, e.g., Pratt et al., 1984), over-all preventive effectiveness (Oe) can be expressed as: $Oe = PMR$.

Although sociologists are not trained to design birth control devices or practices, they can conduct surveys, compute the P, M, and R values, and subsequently examine the relation between Oe measures and fertility rates. One goal should be an assessment of the relative importance of birth control means as determinants of fertility rates, which would complement Keyfitz's (1971) analysis of logical possibilities. Another goal would be pursued in research where (1) P and R values are the *dependent* variables and (2) the independent variables pertain to programs for promoting sexual restraint, contraception, or abortion. The P and R values would be analyzed with a view to answering this special question: What determines the efficacy of such programs?

Because structural theories do not emphasize the importance of birth control, their policy implications are negligible.[23] Yet the theories seem to assume that fertility is effectively controlled at the individual level. Contemplate two illustrative questions. First, how could even a great change in an individual's income influence his or her fertility if he or she neither has nor comes to have control over becoming pregnant or impregnating? Second, without such control, how could unemployment reduce that individual's fertility?

Even if variation in birth control does determine all fertility variation, control of the fertility rate requires programs to promote or discourage sexual intercourse, contraception, and/or abortion. Yet many demographers evidently assume that such programs are irrelevant because they are rare and/or inefficacious. That assumption is becoming increasingly dubious (see, e.g., Tsui and Bogue, 1978; Freedman, 1979); nonetheless, much of the demographic research has little bearing on birth control. That feature of research is all the more important because the hoary debate over the desirability of population growth (see, e.g., Lieberson, 1986) is largely bootless if fertility rates are uncontrollable.

A SPECIAL PROBLEM.   Although general observations suggest that technology determines the features of biotic control, thousands of studies will be needed to analyze the relation thoroughly. The point is illustrated by one of the few systematic studies of the efficiency of technological items in hunting. Hames (1979) examined the kilograms of game killed per hunting hour over a 216-day period in two tribal populations, both occupying a neotropical forest in the Upper Orinoco. One population hunted primarily with bows; the other primarily with shotguns. Hames's comparisons extended to individuals who hunted with a bow at times and with a shotgun at other times. In zones near a village, game taken was about 231 percent more for shotgun hunting. That contrast holds approximately for hunters using a shotgun and the same hunters using a bow; but hunting in distant zones yielded greater game weight regardless of weapon, meaning that biotic control's efficiency depends on technology and procedure.

The study illustrates why such efficacy research must be very limited. Enormous resources would be needed to consider all technological items and all kinds of biotic control in even one small population; hence, the efficacy of total biotic control must be treated as a purely theoretical notion.

Failures in Attempts at Control, Institutions, and Organizations

What sociologists identify as "institutions" are abstractions from patterned control attempts. When there are multiple participants in patterned human behavior, some participants may be "regular" in that they repeat their behavior, while others are transitory. The repetitive behavior of regular participants is the context in which the participants, regular and/or transitory, attempt to control other participants, regular and/or transitory. To illustrate, the Anglo-American trial is an institution characterized by regular and transitory participants, but all principal participants in slavery are "regular," and all participants in a debutante ball may be transitory.

What has been said of institutions applies to organizations, except there is no organization in which all participants are transitory. Nonetheless, in both cases the notion can be described in terms of control and perhaps so defined. While the description of something in terms of control is not an explanation, it facilitates explanation because it bears on the "how" question, which must be confronted to answer the "why" question. Moreover, it is not even claimed that all control attempts in institutions or organizations are successful. Otherwise, the efficacy of control would not be problematical; and if all attempts at control in institutional or organizational contexts were successful, control efficacy could not be relevant in explaining why some contexts disappear. For that matter, the efficacy of some particular kind or means of control must be assessed always relative to alternatives. Consider the American criminal justice system. Each year millions are not deterred by the threat of legal punishment; hence, by an absolute standard the system is grossly ineffective (see, e.g., Zeisel, 1982). But what is the *relative* efficacy of each alternative?

Some institutions and organizations would not exist without control failures. Thus, each crime is a failure in attempted control; and if failures were not inevitable, criminal courts would be inexplicable. As for civil law, prospective litigants rarely initiate a law suit if their demands are met, and demands are control attempts.

The few brief illustrations are not an adequate substitute for extensive and systematic research. Such research is far beyond this monograph, but it is feasible to make some general observations on revolutions and religion.

Revolutions and Rebellions

The enormous attention devoted by sociologists to revolutions has not yielded a defensible theory, and other social scientists have fared no better. Even a claim of progress would be disputable.

CONCEPTUAL PROBLEMS AND ISSUES. Barrington Moore reportedly believed that only four revolutions have occurred, whereas Pitirim Sorokin identified more than a thousand (see Russell's commentary, 1974:57). Such disagreement is hardly surprising. In defining *revolution* sociologists commonly ignore various distinctions, such as political versus nonpolitical and violent versus nonviolent. Those distinctions entail conceptual issues over which reasonable sociologists differ; but often sociologists largely ignore the issues (see, e.g., Goldstone, 1982), and the hoary practice of defining a revolution by reference to the overthrow of a politically dominant social class insures negligible empirical applicability.

Because this book is not a treatise on revolutions, no full-scale attempt is made even to identify conceptual problems and issues (see Kotowski, 1984). For that matter, no claim is made that subsequent definitions solve even most conceptual problems or resolve the issues.

Attempted rebellion: the existence within a territorial unit of the synchronization and coordination by multiple individuals of their public and potentially lethal acts, or their threats of such violence, in the belief that the action increases the probability of one or more other individuals ceasing to have superordinate political power in that territorial unit.

Attempted revolution: an attempted rebellion in which one goal of the superordinate rebel or rebels at some point is the permanent termination of the political power of a socially recognized category of individuals (e.g., all members of the "nobility") in that territorial unit and not just the political power of a set of particular individuals.

SOME DEFECTS OF THEORIES.   Theorists (see Russell's survey, 1974:8) often emphasize the people's "state of mind," as when it is asserted that a short-run decline in intense relative deprivation of the masses leads to revolution. That emphasis is conducive to untestable theories because any collective "state of mind" is a theoretical notion, and a focus on the masses, the rebels, or the revolutionaries ignores the regime's countercontrol strategy/tactics. That focus is so conventional that Russell (1974:10) made this complaint but without recognizing Charles Tilly as an exception: "it is often regarded as reactionary even to stress the importance of the regime and armed forces."

Perhaps two theories are needed—one about the causes of attempted revolutions or rebellions and another pertaining to conditions that determine success or failure. Yet some sociologists will resist that strategy, as indicated by Stinchcombe's statement: "Explaining who won, and why, is primarily a problem of military science, not of social science" (1965:170). The statement ignores the possibility that many potential rebels or revolutionaries remain nothing more because they perceive little chance of success, and the same argument applies to the seeming indifference of sociologists to outcomes of strikes (a recent exception: Ragin et al., 1982).

If rebellions and revolutions are conceptualized as attempts, the regime's characteristics (resources, countercontrol tactics, etc.) become especially relevant. Evidence has been compiled by Russell (1974) in an analysis of seven successful and seven unsuccessful rebellions. Of the successful, in no case is the armed forces disloyalty score less than 10.5, whereas for four of the seven unsuccessful rebellions that score is zero. So appreciable military loyalty appears sufficient but not necessary (a distinction Russell ignores) for a failed rebellion against an indigenous government, and Russell's observations suggest that military loyalty is influenced by the strategy and tactics of both the regime and the rebels. To conclude, improved theories can be realized by viewing rebellions or revolutions and opposition to them as attempts at control on a massive scale, and the same argument applies to social movements (see, especially, McAdam, 1983).

Religion and Magic

One of numerous problems in defining religion (see Bloch, 1985) is the distinction between religion and magic. Consider Malinowski's statement: "We have taken for our starting-point a most definite and tangible distinction: we have defined within the domain of the sacred, magic as a practical art consisting of acts which are only means to a definite end expected to follow later on; religion as a body of self-contained acts being themselves the fulfillment of their purpose" (1948:68). Far from clarifying the distinction, the statement is scarcely intelligible.

In defining religion, social scientists use terms that create problems; thus, Malinowski followed Durkheim in using the term *sacred*, which promises negligible empirical applicability. Moreover, the term is conducive to vacuous claims, such as Durkheim's assertion that religion is the veneration of society (see Parsons' statement in Swanson, 1960:15). Such conceptual problems are ignored in Geertz's essay (1968) on the anthropological study of religion and in Bellah's essay (1968) on the sociology of religion; indeed, neither author defines religion.

No claim is made that the following definitions promise appreciable empirical applicability, and it is recognized that even the feasibility of distinguishing between religion and magic is debatable (see Hammond, 1970). The definitions are stated only to indicate the general meaning of the terms *religion* and *magic* as used here.

A *religion* is a unique set of beliefs pertaining to the existence of supernatural beings and the related overt behavior, if any, that stems from or reflects that belief.

Magic is any belief in the existence of some impersonal supernatural force and at least one distinctive type of overt behavior that stems from or reflects that belief.

One reason for doubts about the empirical applicability of both definitions pertains to the term *supernatural*. Treating the term as primitive will not do, but conventional definitions merely mix synonyms (e.g., miraculous) and uninformative phrases (e.g., above or beyond nature).

SOME CONSPICUOUS DEFECTS IN THEORIES.   The study of religion illustrates why the pursuit of a theory is unproductive without prior articulation of a defensible question. Not one of the well-known theories on religion (see surveys in Geertz, 1968, and Bellah, 1968) can be tested systematically, and that defect partially stems from the questions that theorists have pursued.

The earliest anthropological theory is conventionally attributed to Edward Tylor (1920: I, II). His theory is often reduced by commentators to one simple argument, something like this: religion originated as animism. The theory is far more complex than the reduction suggests; but it is a theory about the origin of religion, as are several subsequent theories. Such theories cannot be tested because they pertain to something that took place long before recorded history. Accordingly, no question about the origin of religion is defensible because the answer and any assessment of it are bound to be conjectural. Malinowski's commentary on Tylor's theory is illustrative: "it made early man too contemplative and rational" (1948:2).

If Durkheim's observations (especially 1965) on religion suggest any empirical generalization about variable features of religions, it is this: a society's structural features determine the features of its religion. So variation in social structure supposedly causes variation in religion; but the generalization implies no prediction about the space-time association between any particular structural feature and any particular feature of religion.

Swanson's *The Birth of the Gods* (1960) is not a validation of Durkheim. The research is most commendable; and it gave rise to an intriguing proposition (1960:64): Monotheism or recognition of a high god appears only in tribes or societies having three or more types of sovereign groups ranked hierarchically. Although Swanson's findings support the proposition, there is no logic by which his proposition can be deduced from Durkheim's statements (1965).

CONTROL, RELIGION, AND MAGIC. Descriptions of religious practices commonly emphasize their propriational or supplicatory character, which suggests that the practices are attempts to control supernatural beings. But the suggestion raises two questions. First, why did humans come to believe that supernatural beings exist and exercise control? Second, why do humans attempt to control supernatural beings? The first question is answered by the "agency" argument: Humans came to perceive themselves as controlling so many kinds of events that they could not conceive of uncontrolled events; hence, recognition of events uncontrolled by observable beings led humans to postulate control by unobservable beings.[24] The second question's answer: Humans attempt to control all events that they perceive as influencing their individual or collective well-being; hence, evidence of their inability to control such events directly leads humans to attempt control indirectly, through supernatural beings.

Only the second question's answer suggests a generalization: The more members of an isolated social unit perceive themselves as having the capacity for direct control over events that they perceive as influencing their individual or collective well-being, the less the intensity of religion in that social unit. The relation is actually too complicated to express as a simple proposition. For one thing, an event (e.g., an earth tremor) is relevant only to the extent that population members perceive it as important, with perceived determinants of life or death being paramount. Moreover, the relevant perceptions of individuals pertain not just to what they personally can and cannot control, what they regard as important, etc., but to all humans.

Although the generalization illustrates how some institutions stem from control failure (no failures, no religion), it is not testable if only because there are no known social units that have been isolated throughout each member's life. Isolation is important because nonmembers could influence the perceptions of members as to what humans can control directly (i.e., without supernatural intervention). However, isolation can be treated as a matter of degree, and the relation between the generalization's two principal variables should become less problematical as the social units become more isolated. Even so, a procedure for measuring the principal variables cannot be formulated at present, which is to say that they are constructs. The generalization is thus an axiom, and two postulates are needed to link the constructs with concepts. One possibility: The *greater* the variation in age at death, the *less* do members of an isolated social unit perceive themselves as having the capacity for direct control over events that they perceive as influencing their individual or collective well-being. While the mortality phrase can be taken as a concept, there is no postulate that links the construct "intensity of religion" to a concept;[25] and until that postulate is formulated, evidence cannot be brought to bear even indirectly on the axiom.

The axiom is not truly novel. Numerous observations by anthropologists, commencing with Tylor, suggest a connection between religion and control. Thus, Malinowski argued that nonliterate peoples resort to magic in coping with "the domain of the unaccountable and adverse influences" (1948:12). Consider his observation on the Trobriand Islands: "in Lagoon fishing, where man can rely completely upon his knowledge and skill, magic does not exist, while in the open-sea fishing, full of danger and uncertainty, there is extensive magic ritual to secure safety and good results" (14).

Malinowski's argument pertains to magic, and he provides no rationale for extending it to religion. However, the control argument can be extended to magic. The first step is this distinction: to perceive no capacity whatever for control is one thing, but to perceive control as *problematical* is another. The latter perception is crucial for magic; and the generalization is this: The more do members of an isolated social unit perceive success as problematic in their attempts at direct control over events that they perceive as influencing their individual or collective well-being, the greater the reliance of the members on magic.

All qualifications of the first generalization (axiom) apply to the second, and both are untestable for the same reasons. However, for illustrative purposes, consider the second generalization in connection with Gmelch's research (1980). His observations on the prevalence of "superstitious" beliefs among baseball players indicate that pitchers are especially superstitious, as are all players with regard to hitting. Assuming some relation between superstitious behavior and magic, Gmelch's observations appear consistent with the second generalization. Pitchers appear obsessed with control and are inclined to view it as problematical, and the same is true of players with regard to hitting but not fielding. However, because there is no logic by which the second generalization alone implies Gmelch's observations, the connection is only suggestive. The same is true also of the connection between the general argument leading up to the generalizations and the conclusion reached by Hyams et al.: "The results of this study do support the central hypothesis that subjects with a more internal locus of control report less anxiety about death than their peers who have a more external locus of control" (1982:180). However, that conclusion is all the more only suggestive unless one assumes that internal locus of control pertains to the perceived capacity for control over events or things, while external locus of control pertains to control vulnerability or belief in fate; but the notion of "control locus" is actually very vague when it comes to the nature of the internal-external distinction.

Even if the rational-irrational distinction were defensible, an identification of all facets of religion as irrational would be unwarranted. Although robotic sociology does not encourage recognition of it, religion can be used in external human control, especially referential and modulative social control. The latter use is illustrated by Pope's report (1942) that factory owners in a North Carolina mill town supplemented the income of fundamentalist preachers, ostensibly in recognition that the preachers stressed conservative values in communicating with congregation members, many of whom were millhands.

In the case of referential control, the first party makes reference to a third party, someone who the second party presumably respects, values, fears, loves, admires, or hates. If the presumption is valid, the second party may be influenced by what the first party says about the third party; and only in the case of referential control can the third party be a supernatural being. If the second party believes in the being's existence and regards the first party's reference as credible, the first party in effect speaks to the second party through the supernatural being. The significance of such use of religion should be obvious, but monotheism is advantageous for first parties who regularly use religion in referential control. Unity and coherence in messages from some unobservable world are more feasible and exclusive if there is only one supernatural being.

Returning to Swanson's proposition, if there is an association between three-or-more levels of social organization and monotheism, why does it hold? Recall an assertion made in chapter 3: social control is more effective than proximate control and even sequential control when it comes to controlling large numbers. Because the three-or-more level of social organization is virtually certain to be associated with a fairly large population, the use of social control probably is especially prevalent at that level.

A "control" interpretation of Swanson's proposition anticipates questionable cases, such as the polytheism of the Aztecs and ancient Rome. For a people initially threatened with subjugation and subsequently bent on conquest, the adoption (more nearly co-optation) of alien gods offers numerous advantages. For that matter, the extent that leaders must resort to social control to subjugate other peoples depends on their military resources.

So the control interpretation of religion does what a structural interpretation cannot do—it explains the relation asserted in Swanson's proposition and anticipates questionable cases. But the argument is not ad hoc. Any space-time association between structural features is inherently problematical because it holds only through attempts at control. One brief illustration must suffice. If there is a direct relation among social units between population size and any feature of human control, it is not even approximately invariant. The efficacy of an attempt to control all population members depends not on their number but also on, among other things, the technology of communication.

In reacting to the foregoing, critics are likely to make this argument: The observations imply that religion was created deliberately for human control. More than a simple denial is needed. The origin of monotheism may have had nothing to do with facilitating human control; and it may have become fairly prevalent through selective survival of monotheistic elites, which is to say that in certain unidentified conditions monotheistic elites have a survival advantage. However, if so, the survival advantage stems from the use of monotheistic religion in human control by the elites, even granting that monotheism may facilitate such control only in as of yet unidentified conditions.

NOTES

1. Lest the frequent condemnation of arbitrary definitions appear whimsical, arbitrary definitions are not likely to gain acceptance; and they reduce the predictive accuracy of the theories in which they are employed. That argument is not negated by granting that arbitrariness is a matter of degree.

2. Paradoxically, in a four-volume work on sociology's "theoretical logic," Alexander treats rationality as central for social theory (1982-I:72), while at the same time ostensibly recognizing (1982-I:72–90) that the notion is a conceptual swamp (Schutz, 1970, is illustrative). The adherence of sociologists to the rational-irrational distinction is all the more puzzling because there are obvious alternatives. Thus, Klandermans (1983) invokes the distinction to describe the major contrast between resource mobilization theory (emphasis on rationality) and the older social movement theories (emphasis on irrationality). Yet it would be more informative to describe resource mobilization theory as emphasizing the instrumental character of social movements and deemphasizing their expressive character. True, social movement theorists, even the synthesizers (e.g., Feree and Miller, 1985), scarcely use a control terminology; but until they do any theory is likely to be a grab bag of vague, disconnected generalizations and a

bewildering melange of research findings (see *Social Research*, Winter, 1985). Even the term *resource mobilization* is indicative of the thirst of sociologists for an arcane language, one as far removed from actual human behavior as possible.

3.   Alexander (1982-I:90–112) encourages pursuit of the "order problem," despite this earlier (1982-I:xiv) lament: "contemporary sociology seems to have forgotten nothing and learned nothing new."

4.   Although the present focus is on the efficacy of law, the ultimate concern is not just with the efficacy of legislative attempts to control human behavior but also attempts to control the behavior of legislators; and the exemplar of a study that does both is Burstein's work (especially 1985).

5.   Note Fuller's indifference to coercion as a feature of law.

6.   Labor relations legislation cannot be described readily as creating an "enabling function" of law; nonetheless, it is modulative social control and illustrates how legislators *may* attempt to limit the influence of a potential third party, labor or management in this case.

7.   Field experiments (Berk et al., 1985) and a combination of experimental and observational research (Stafford et al., 1986) are promising.

8.   Although the efficacy of some laws may be judged in terms of promoting rather than preventing certain types of behavior, the distinction is not always obvious; and some laws are neither proscriptive nor prescriptive. For example, although various statutes and court rulings can be construed as directions for entering into a legally valid marriage, legislators and judges do not seek to promote the marriage of everyone without regard to any consideration (e.g., age, physical condition), some of which are recognized statutorily.

9.   Zald's article (1978) is perhaps the best-known of a very limited number of publications by sociologists that bear on regulation (in the sense that the term is used in jurisprudence). Perhaps it is significant that Zald does not explicitly subscribe to the counteraction-of-deviance conception of social control.

10.   One reason is the popular wisdom that big business has "captured" regulatory agencies and that such capture has been documented (for contrary evidence and commentary, see Freitag, 1983). In any case, most research on regulatory law do not bear directly on the efficacy question (see, e.g., *Law and Contemporary Problems*, Winter-Spring, 1979; and for the closest approximation to an exception, see *Law and Human Behavior*, September, 1983).

11.   Still another difficulty is that an assessment of the efficacy of regulatory law may require that investigators look beyond compliance by the immediate target, as when attention focuses on changes in smoking rates subsequent to some regulation of cigarette advertising.

12.   The most immediate problem is the need to assess both effectiveness and efficiency; and the preoccupation of economist with efficiency notwithstanding, the importance of the distinction is not limited to regulatory law.

13.   For that matter, some relevant research may not be recognized as bearing on the efficacy question. Thus, it is not obvious that Gerber and Short's study (1986) of the public controversy concerning the marketing of infant formula in less developed countries really pertains to the efficacy of allegative and referential social control. Similarly, neither Luckenbill's study (1982) of the compliance

of robbery victims nor the study of Heritage and Greatbatch (1986) on applause reactions to political speeches are likely to be recognized readily as efficacy research.

14. The few reported cases for Marxist countries may reflect the reluctance of Marxist officials to publicize terrorism campaigns; but not reporting may well be an attempt at control, because prospective terrorists can be discouraged by the impression that they would be acting alone.

15. Wilkinson (1986:5) identifies only three clear-cut "instances of political terrorism *per se* succeeding in realizing strategic or long-term aims," all three being in opposition to British forces: Palestine, 1945–47; Suez Canal Zone in the early 1950s; and Cyprus, 1955–59. He then says: "the track record of terrorism as a weapon for overthrowing indigenous autocracy, liberal democracy and totalitarianism is abysmal."

16. Sociologists seem to see only one alternative to condemning advertising— depicting it as offering employment opportunities for sociologists (see, e.g., Smith, 1983).

17. Like Schudson, most casual commentaries suggest that advertising is ineffective; but in reviewing recent books, Draper states: "the tendency to belittle the effectiveness of advertising has gone too far" (1986:14).

18. The question is conveniently ignored when advertising is treated as though simply a component of the "culture of capitalism." Even when advertising is described in connection with social control (e.g., Ewen, 1976:259), only rarely do the writers suggest theoretical or research questions. One of Draper's conclusions is an exception: "Editorial influence is not . . . the heart of advertising's impact on the mass media, which it shapes instead by shaping the way the press and television define their own markets" (1986:17).

19. Skinner (e.g., 1978:10) maintains that behavior modification is limited to changing behavior through positive reinforcement, but it appears clearly arbitrary to exclude modification of human behavior through (for example) implanting electrodes, psychotropic drugs, and aversive conditioning. In any case, behavior modification is not the more conventional label for what has been designated (chapter 3) as proximate control; rather, behavior modification is proximate control undertaken in the belief that it permanently increases or decreases the probability of a change in someone's behavior.

20. Should critics denigrate research on such questions as trivial, they will have ignored its bearing on the putative power of the capitalist over the proletariat. Far from explaining that power, Marx took it for granted, thereby establishing a tradition. Edwards's study (1979) and Burawoy's study (1979) are relevant; but their observations on control in the workplace are all casual and general to answer the paramount question: What is the efficacy of alternative means of control in that context? Likewise, in attempting to explain "worker attachment," Halaby (1986) does not emphasize the bearing of his study on this question: What determines the efficacy of attempts at control? What has been said of Edwards, Burawoy, and Halaby applies all the more to observations by Clegg and Dunkerley (1980) on control and organizations (again, though, primarily companies or corporations).

21. Wilson's findings clearly indicate that lax supervision of boys is much more common in families identified as "severe social handicap." Wilson found also that boys are substantially more likely to be delinquent in families where a parent has a criminal history; but lax supervision of children is much more characteristic of families where a parent has a criminal history (see, especially, Wilson, 1980:228). Those two conclusions are all the more important because of two things suggested by the "subcultural" and "conflict" perspectives: first, in large capitalist social units (e.g., Chicago), vast numbers of individuals oppose the values expressed in the criminal code; and, second, as parents those individuals encourage their children to violate laws. If such a "Fagin" view of criminality is valid, parental control over juveniles is irrelevant in explaining variation in delinquency, among individuals or populations.

22. The commitment of sociologists to such notions is reflected in the staying power of Merton's theory of anomie (1957). It is one of the two best known theories on deviance (including crime and delinquency), even though after nearly 50 years there has never been a defensible test of it. If only because the notion of anomie is so far removed from actual human behavior, it is hardly surprising that Merton's theory is so intractably untestable. True, Sutherland's notion of differential association is not superorganic or structural, and yet the theory (Sutherland and Cressey, 1974) has a staying power equal to that of Merton's. Nonetheless, there is no emphasis in Sutherland's theory on the purposive quality of human behavior; "differential association" simply happens or does not happen. Note, however, that until one can measure the exposure of individuals from birth onward to "definitions" favorable and unfavorable to crime, purported tests of Sutherland's theory will be dubious (but see Tittle et al., 1986, for a promising line of work). For a more extensive commentary on the two theories—Merton's and Sutherland's—see Gibbs (1985).

23. The suggestion is not that structural theories or macro research on differential fertility be abandoned; rather, the real need is for theories and research that combine structural variables, birth control programs, birth control practices, and socio-economic characteristics of individuals (or families) in attempts to explain variation in individual fertility when the individuals reside in different countries (for a similar argument, see Nardi, 1981). Although still rare, such multilevel work is becoming more common (see, e.g., Entwisle and Mason, 1985); but that work tends to slight birth control practices.

24. Skinner's argument is particularly relevant: "Man's first experience with causes probably came from his own behavior: things moved because he moved them. If other things moved, it was because someone else was moving them, and if the mover could not be seen, it was because he was invisible" (1971:7).

25. It is doubtful that the construct reduces to something like "belief in the existence of a god"; and it may prove necessary to change the construct from "intensity of religion" to "supernatural intensity," with supernatural beliefs pertaining to everything that is loosely identified as religion, magic, sorcery, witchcraft, thaumaturgy, superstition, spiritualism, or animism.

Control and Freedom

If sociologists do anything well, it is their contribution to liberal education (for elaboration, see Nettler, 1980); and since much of liberal education is an increasing awareness of human concerns, sociology's central notion must further that awareness. So we reach the final major claim: control is the ultimate human concern.

The Notion of Freedom as a Contender

During the past three centuries several famous orations or publications in the West have suggested that freedom is the ultimate human concern. Hence, freedom and control may be both antithetical and contenders.

Major Issues

"Freedom is one of the most obscure and ambiguous terms not only of philosophical but also of political language" (Cassirer, 1955:361). The conceptualization of freedom in terms of control will clarify and reveal that freedom is a zero-sum game. A person has a duty to act if he or she perceives omission as increasing the probability of a punitive reaction (including undesired interference), and a person has a duty to refrain from acting if he or she perceives commission as increasing that probability. Conversely, an act is a privilege if and only if the actor perceives neither its omission nor its commission as increasing the probability of a punitive reaction. So absolute freedom for more than one social unit's member is a logical impossibility.[1] No act can be a privilege for anyone unless everyone else is under a duty not to react punitively. Yet to speak of avoiding a punitive reaction or to say that one is restrained from reacting punitively is to speak of control (countercontrol or otherwise).

Outside of carceral contexts (e.g., prisons), anticipated consequences probably determine perceptions of freedom more than does the physical possibility of acts. Typically, adults can commit all manner of acts, provided they accept the possible consequences. Humans think of freedom largely in terms of responses to acts, perhaps because other (asocial) consequences and sheer physical possibilities are similar for everyone (*beyond human control*). However, reactions as sanctions are not the only consideration. If perceiving a risk of an undesirable response makes one unfree to act, then one is not merely unfree to commit crimes; in addition, the perceived risk of becoming a crime victim reduces freedom. Thus, if a person refrains from walking city streets in fear of becoming a robbery victim, he or she is not free; but no one thinks of robbery as a sanction.

Even when a physical obstacle can be overcome, the perceived risk of some undesirable consequence (e.g., lacerations) reduces freedom. However, the argument does not limit the reduction of freedom to conditions that make acts physically impossible (e.g., walking through a stone wall). Humans may anticipate the actions of other humans and interfere. Interference is control, whether perceived as punitive or not; but no one is likely to think of interference as reducing freedom if it has been perceived as desirable (e.g., a pedestrian is pulled from the path of a rapidly moving vehicle). So, to summarize, freedom is a matter of the perceived consequences of action, including the physical possibility or impossibility of goal attainment.

AN IDEOLOGICAL ISSUE.   Frank Parkin's observation introduces a rarely recognized paradox: "The great promise contained within the heart of Marxism is not merely that of a classless future, but of a society in which the highest aspirations for liberty will find fulfillment. Marxism does not differ from other and earlier traditions of socialist thought in the importance it attaches to the combined package of equality and freedom, nor in the conviction that one hardly makes sense without the other" (1979:176). So freedom appears as much a capitalist value as a Marxist value,[2] but statements about freedom in both Marxist countries and capitalist countries are most debatable.

According to the Marxist critique, in capitalist countries gross economic inequalities preclude freedom. Such inequalities do preclude equalities in opportunities, but individuals who have no opportunities have equal opportunities. Thus, granted that gross economic inequality is absent among the Kalahari hunters, none of them have the opportunity to drill deep wells. So Marxists err in implying that economic equality or even equal opportunity assures freedom. Nevertheless, apologists for capitalism do not emphasize that goals require opportunities. Thus, to say that an American family with an annual income less than $15,000 is free to take world cruises constitutes a cruel joke.

Just as Marxists dismiss the idealization of freedom in capitalist countries as a bourgeois sham, critics of communism claim that various freedoms are absent in Marxist countries (e.g., to publish without governmental censorship, to travel abroad freely). Above all, Marxist regimes are charged with contempt for the rule of law, but social scientists and even specialist in jurisprudence are prone to write on "Marxism and the rule of law" rather than "Marxist regimes and the rule of law" (see, e.g., Mandel, 1986).

The allegation that Marxist regimes make a mockery of freedom is no longer blunted by the argument that the regimes reflect a seige mentality. The Russian revolution took place more than three generations ago, but freedom did not flourish once the revolutionary trauma ceased. Indeed, in the case of China Mao sought to renew the trauma as a "cultural revolution."[3] Finally, evidence of substantial income and/or privilege differences in Marxist countries (see literature cited in Turner, 1986:108–13) creates doubts about the extent of equality of opportunity. It is as though a people gave up the prospect of freedom to realize equality of opportunity, only to end with neither. Hence, Marx's rarely quoted prophecy (1963:174) is grotesque: "Does this mean that after the fall of the old society there will be a new class domination culminating in new political power? No."

Freedom and Control

An individual is free to the extent that he or she perceives himself/ herself as capable of control, be it inanimate, biotic, or human (including countercontrol, immunity from human control). The argument is best stated as a question: How could an individual perceive himself or herself as free even though bereft of any control capacity and totally vulnerable to control?

PREVIOUSLY RECOGNIZED PROBLEMS.   If freedom is defined in terms of control, the previously recognized conceptual problems are reduced substantially. Reconsider the argument that the freedom to take a world cruise is a cruel joke for the impecunious, meaning that freedom without opportunity is a contradiction. Defining freedom in terms of control (including power) clarifies the relation between freedom and opportunity. The impecunious do not perceive themselves as capable of exercising the control over others necessary to take a world cruise. Yet one may anticipate changes in control capacity, and the prospect of an increase probably makes the discrepancy between freedom and opportunity more tolerable than critics of the notion of freedom recognize.

Much of what has been said about opportunity also applies to the distinction between physical possibility and impossibility, but the bearing of that distinction on power can be described even more precisely. Recall that a control attempt is overt behavior in the hope that it increases or decreases some probability. Accordingly, to believe that some condition is physically impossible is to believe that the probability of realizing that condition cannot be increased.

Finally, anticipation of interference reduces freedom, and avoiding such interference is countercontrol. Imagine someone describing themselves as free but unable to prevent anyone's actions.

Freedom to Communicate

The only well-known typology of fundamental freedoms was suggested by Franklin Roosevelt, in an address on January 6, 1941. Therein (1946:266) Roosevelt identified the first of four freedoms as speech and expression. It is reidentified here as the freedom to communicate.

Major Issues

Communication freedom varies enormously. The variation among social units largely reflects contrasts in opportunities—radios, television sets, and newspapers per capita. However, within a social unit, freedom to communicate is largely contingent on access to facilities, which is determined by a member's skills in inanimate control (constructing, operating, and maintaining communication instruments) or by his or her human control.

The argument is not contradicted by any observation pertaining to "ownership" because ownership is a control matter. Moreover, while communication facilities in Marxist countries are not "privately owned," access to them requires human control, just as it does in nonMarxist countries. Accordingly, it is not surprising that capitalist ideologues praise the freedom to communicate; they know full well that access to communication facilities is extremely limited. Marxist ideologues recognize that in capitalist countries freedom to communicate particularly serves the interests of the wealthy; but they avoid this question: Where does the typical citizen have the greatest access to communication facilities—in a Marxist country or in a capitalist democracy?

Unless a punitive reaction to a communication is interference (undesired, of course), the communicator has already realized his or her immediate goal. So interference more nearly negates communication freedom, and it is usually indicative of a gross imbalance in coercive power. Because governmental agents are especially likely to succeed when interfering with communication, it is not surprising that the first amendment of the U.S. Constitution identifies Congress as a threat to communication freedom. But communication freedom is also diminished by the punitive reactions of private persons. If an individual cannot be fired or denied employment because he or she has expressed controversial opinions, employers have less "freedom of association."[4] Indeed, if punitive reactions to communicative acts were totally eliminated, libel and slander suits would end.

Freedom's zero-sum quality is conspicuous in communication. It is a relational phenomenon, and attempts to communicate commonly fail unless the "targets" are under a duty to listen or look. Such a duty is alien to countries where the rule of law prevails, and in those countries various laws (e.g., those pertaining to privacy, disturbing the peace) in effect proscribe involuntary communication. However, there is no explicit proscription in the U.S. Constitution (but in the case of privacy, see Gavison, 1980), and in totalitarian regimes, including Orwell's *1984*, punitive reactions to communication avoidance are manifestations of a highly organized control system.

Control and Communication

There is a close connection between human control (external) and communication in that the latter often appears essential for the former, which makes communication freedom all the more important. More obvious, perhaps, the control of communication reduces communication freedom.

COMMUNICATION IN CONTROL.   Noncoercive proximate control and sequential control are studies in communication because of the predominance of commands, requests, threats, promises, and offers as means. Communication is no less an invariant feature of social control. Whatever the type (referential, etc.), the first party must communicate something to the third party and/or the second   party.

Although arguments about the relative importance of the various means of control are premature, note two contrasts between communication and coercion. First, to the extent the state monopolizes coercion, communication is virtually the exclusive means of control in nongovernmental spheres. Second, communication appears more efficacious than coercion in controlling large numbers.

CONTROL OF COMMUNICATION.   Granted communication's importance, there is no fundamental distinction between attempts to control it and attempts to control other behavior. Virtually any kind of proximate, sequential, or social control can be employed to silence someone or to prompt them to communicate.

Technology largely determines only what is possible in communication, and what one can communicate with impunity is commonly perceived as unrelated to technology. Nonetheless, the connection between technology and communication control becomes conspicuous when an innovation makes it possible to interrupt communication solely and directly through inanimate control. Of the few such innovations, radio "jamming" is the most conspicuous; but even it has played a major role in communication control only in the Cold War.

Control of communication has taken one of two directions in this century—regulatory agencies in democracies and government monopolies elsewhere. Although monitoring telephone calls and mail is a strategic kind of prelusive control in a few countries, the most conspicuous communication control pertains to the mass media, especially the electronic modes. "The new communication technologies have not inherited all the legal immunities that were won for the old. When wires, radio waves, satellites, and computers became major vehicles of discourse, regulation seemed to be a technical necessity" (Pool, 1983:1).

Control over mass media is commonly described in terms of a trichotomy: governmental ownership, governmental regulation, or private. However, those terms denote only undisclosed properties of control, and the most relevant consideration in connection with freedom is the concentration of communication control. Even if a defensible concentration measure could be devised, it would be extremely difficult to obtain the requisite data; nonetheless, virtually any measure would be an improvement over the usual trichotomy. Concentration of communication control is a matter of degree, not a trichotomy; and private ownership does not preclude a degree of concentration comparable to that resulting from government regulation.

The Future of the Concern

Of all freedoms, concern with communication may prove the most time bound. Freedom to communicate became a major Western concern during the Enlightenment, and the concern flourished with the idealization of democracy. However, since World War I communication freedom has been jeopardized, particularly by Marxist and fascist regimes. Those events evidently prompted the prophecy in Orwell's *1984*, Huxley's *Brave New World*, and Zamjiatin's *We* of an end to communication freedom. While that prophecy may prove unrealistic, there are at least two threats to communication freedom.

THE MONOLITHIC THREAT. The global evolutionary trend toward greater socio-cultural differentiation (especially in the economic sphere) appears conducive to mass media pluralism. However, while pluralism flourished in Germany after World War I, the Nazis ended it; and the Russian revolution did not result in greater communication freedom once Stalin came to power. But there is no paradox if it is assumed that authoritarians, fascists or Marxists, perceive socio-cultural differentiation and concomitant pluralism as a threat.

To assume that a monolithic mass media prevails only in fascist or Marxist countries is a comforting illusion. The monolithic threat is an integral feature of capitalist countries because publishing or broadcasting can be both lucrative and a means for political control. Owners and managers of publishing or broadcasting firms have abundant opportunities for referential and allegative social control, with potential voters as the third party and candidates as the second party. Such control has implications beyond election outcomes. To the extent that politicians perceive owners and managers of mass media facilities as influencing the electorate, politicians are vulnerable to control. Moreover, the owners and managers can further an ideology by selective promotion of political careers, a kind of modulative social control that is less conspicuously self-serving than direct means (e.g., editorials criticizing labor leaders).

The most conspicuous trend for American mass media in this century has been the sharp decline in the per capita number of newspaper publishers. That decline indicates greater concentration of control, but a concentration measure alone is not sufficient. An increase in the ideological homogeneity of those who control communication is no less indicative of a decline in freedom to communicate.

Regardless of concentration or ideological homogeneity, in non-Marxist countries the consequences of a monolithic trend depend on regulatory agencies. Unless regulatory agencies (e.g., the FCC) maintain the "fairness" doctrine, an increase in the ideological homogeneity of those who control broadcasting facilities could have even greater electoral consequences. That *possibility* does not interest sociologists because of the widespread belief that regulatory agencies are controlled by the very industries that the agencies supposedly regulate, but systematic sociological research on the amount of independent control exercised by those agencies has never been undertaken.

THE TECHNOLOGICAL THREAT.   Commencing with movable type (an inanimate control innovation), technological change has made mass communication possible; and in that sense it has expanded communication freedom. However, mass communication requires facilities, the complexity of which limits their number and makes them inaccessible to most citizens. So technological change has increased communication freedom but also increased the concentration of communication control.

Ignoring Bell's wretched invention, technological change has yet to result in a substantial reduction of a seldom recognized freedom—avoidance of communication. Immemorially, here or there humans have been threatened with punishment for failing to attend propaganda ceremonies, but defiance is a physical possibility. While some coercive devices (e.g., a cell) make it virtually impossible for the coerced to avoid communication, their use on a massive scale is not feasible. Fortunately, authoritarians lack what they need— an implantable electronic device that makes it impossible to avoid auditory and/or visual communication; but, unfortunately, biotechnology may eventually give authoritarians what they need (see Stableford, 1984:136–57, 184).

Freedom of Association

Although treated here as fundamental, association is not among Roosevelt's four freedoms (1946:266), one of which, "freedom of every person to worship God in his own way," is treated here as largely dependent on communication and association. Yet identifying particular freedoms as fundamental is secondary to describing and thinking about them in terms of control.

Major Issues

Defining any kind of freedom generates conceptual issues. Moreover, one may grant the reality of some freedom but then deny its significance; and since contemporary sociologists devote so little attention to freedom, they may well doubt the significance of even associational freedom.

CONCEPTUAL MATTERS. Few Americans have a real opportunity to associate with the President, but lack of opportunity is distinct from physical impossibility. Whereas the latter permanently and totally eliminates freedom, lack of opportunity may be transitory and commonly translates as "difficult." Nonetheless, physical possibility, opportunity, and freedom can be all thought of in terms of power, the perceived capacity to control.

Since "associating" entails acts (e.g., kissing), it is those acts that one is free or unfree to commit or omit. Hence, one can speak of the freedom of association as distinct from acts if and only if this condition obtains: X can omit or commit at least one type of act with or toward Y without a punitive reaction, but X cannot omit or commit the same type of act with or toward Z without a punitive reaction. As such, X is free to associate with Y but not with Z. Humans associate with each other through acts; but the evaluation of an act is virtually always contingent on the actor's identity and/or the act object, and freedom of association is limited to such contingent acts. If a social unit member can commit a particular type of act toward any other member without risking a punitive reaction, the freedom pertains to the act, not to an association. To illustrate, sexual intercourse is virtually always an associational freedom because a punitive reaction is contingent on the age and sex of the partners.[5] If there are no risks regardless of the partners, it is sexual freedom rather than freedom of sexual association; and a punitive reaction regardless of the partners precludes sexual freedom.

SOCIOLOGICAL DISINTEREST. The reason for the seeming disinterest of sociologists in freedom of association is suggested by this epigram: economics is all about why individuals make choices; sociology is all about why individuals have no choices to make. Yet many philosophers will view sociologists as naive if they reject the notion of freedom (see Wallace's commentary, 1983:481–85) on the ground that it implies free will and denies determinism (see, e.g., Sankowski, 1980). Moreover, associational freedom is a fundamental human concern, and sociologists are inviting extinction if they ignore such concerns. True, citizens of Western democracies often appear little concerned, but they simply take freedom of association for granted. It can be taken for granted only because of the laws and charters of those countries (e.g., the U.S. Constitution proclaims the "right" of people to assemble peaceably).

Concern with freedom of association will grow if sociologists ever truly confront the fate of dissidents in Marxist or fascist countries. Granted that American foreign policy promotes freedom's extinction in the name of anti-communism, to praise Marxist or fascist regimes is another contribution to freedom's extinction. However, Americans need not look elsewhere to appreciate the fragility of associational freedom. It was jeopardized during the McCarthy era and is currently diminished by statutes pertaining to subversive organizations.

Association and Control

Insofar as sociology's subject matter is human interaction and social relations, both external human control and association are in the field's mainstream. Moreover, the success of attempted external human control commonly depends on the prior association between the parties.

ASSOCIATION AND PROXIMATE CONTROL.   There is no connection between association and proximate control when a command is given as a punitive threat (e.g., a store clerk obeys a gunman's order). By contrast, prior association is relevant when an employer commands an employee or when someone makes a request of a friend.

The suggestion is not that attempts at proximate control are somehow external to social relations, and the point bears on the failure of sociologists to realize a definition of a social relation that is empirically applicable but does not reek with arbitrariness. A definition in terms of power (the perceived capacity to control) is a possible solution. Two individuals, X and Y, have a social relation if and only if (1) both X and Y perceive X has having some power over Y and/or (2) both X and Y perceive Y as having some power over X.

ASSOCIATION, ORGANIZATION, AND SEQUENTIAL CONTROL.   Although *organization* is one of sociology's major terms, it is a thicket of conceptual problems. Those problems are not solved by the distinction between an entity (i.e., an organization) and a process (e.g., as in "organization occurs"), nor by an interactional definition. Although the term *interaction* promises substantial empirical applicability, it cannot be used to define an organization without stipulations of kinds and frequencies that are inherently arbitrary.

The prospects are quite different if the definition of an organization is couched in terms of social relations, as previously defined. An organization consists of a set of three or more individuals such that (1) each individual has a social relation with at least two others and (2) each individual perceives one of them or a subset of them as having unique powers over all others. An individual has a unique power if he or she is perceived by all set members as the only member having the capacity to control all others to at least one end in at least one context. Assume that X, Y, and Z are linked in an inclusive network of social relations (i.e., no fourth individual is linked to at least two of them). Then assume that all three perceive (1) Y as having the capacity to control X's diet but not Z's, (2) Z as having the capacity to control Y's sexual behavior but not X's, (3) X as having the capacity to control Y's dress but not Z's, and (4) X as the only member having the capacity to control the work behavior of both Y and Z. As such, X has a unique power. As for a "subset of individuals," the term is used to recognize that a board, committee, council, or tribunal may be perceived as having the unique power in question. Whatever the subset's title, the control capacity attributed to them must pertain to "representational control" (chapter 2).

Because power is the perceived capacity for any type of control, sequential control is not a defining characteristic of an organization. Nonetheless, sequential control takes place so rarely outside of an organization that for all practical purposes the connection between them is not problematical. Moreover, it appears that the ratio of sequential to proximate control tends to increase as organizational size increases.

ASSOCIATION AND REFERENTIAL SOCIAL CONTROL.   Typically, when the first party makes reference to a third party in communicating with the second party, he or she assumes some social relation between the second and third parties. So a study of referential control approximates an inventory of important associations in the social unit.

The relative frequency of each type of external human control is assumed to be a postcedent correlate of one or more of these social unit properties: (1) *size*, meaning number of members; (2) *social differentiation*, the sheer number of status categories, including organizations; and (3) *normative consensus,* the extent to which members agree in their evaluations and/or expectations of conduct. Although the last two properties are constructs, there is a basis for empirical generalizations about the relation (cross-sectionally and longitudinally) between those properties and "control ratios," with each ratio expressing the relative frequency of two types of control.

If there is absolute normative consensus, proximate control is successful because all commands or requests are perceived by participants as justified. That argument extends to an empirical generalization about the ratio of instances of referential social control to instances of proximate control (RSC/PC ratio) over some period (e.g., a month). Because the efficacy principle implies that the most efficacious type of control is employed the most frequently, we have Axiom 18-1: The greater a social unit's normative consensus, the less the unit's RSC/PC ratio.

While additional axioms could be formulated about other ratios with

PC as the denominator (e.g., the ratio of allegative social control to proximate control or ASC/PC), only the RSC/PC ratio is closely related to normative consensus. There may be no instances of other types of social control (e.g., prelusive) long after a decline in normative consensus; hence, the other ratios (e.g., ASC/PC) may be zero despite variation in normative consensus. Stated otherwise, once proximate control commences to decline, referential social control is the first to increase. Even when normative consensus is less than necessary for predominantly effective commands or requests, it may be enough for the first party to make a credible and compelling reference to a third party's evaluations of conduct. To illustrate, according to Kluckhohn and Leighton, the Navaho admonish other tribal members this way: "If you don't tell the truth, your fellows won't trust you. . . ." (1962:297). Without considerable normative consensus, the second party would not perceive the reference to the third party (fellows) as credible, nor be moved by it.

ASSOCIATION AND ALLEGATIVE SOCIAL CONTROL.   In attempting such control the first party necessarily communicates something about the second party to the third party. That communication may be anything about the second party—what he or she has done, is doing, will do, or may do; what someone has done to or with him or her; what someone will do to him or her, etc. However, successful allegative control is more likely when there is a social relation between the second and third party, which makes the third party more inclined to respond.

If normative consensus declines indefinitely, referential social control (RSC) eventually decreases because it becomes too ineffective; and if the social unit's size increases, allegative social control (ASC) is the first alternative to increase substantially. However, normative consensus may decline so much that the typical first party cannot make a credible reference to the social unit's members as a collectivity. Even so, superordinates—parents, clan heads, etc.—continue to evaluate the conduct of their subordinates; and superordinates are strategic third parties in allegative social control, with their subordinates as second parties. Although a second party may not heed a command or request by an equal, he or she is likely to obey a superordinate's direct order. Hence, the first party often attempts to elicit such an order by appealing to the superordinate's normative standards and/or self-interest. First parties turn all the more to allegative control if the social unit's size increases as normative consensus declines. When size increases, status categories tend to emerge and the superordinate/subordinate distinction become more strategic. So we have Axiom 18-2: The greater a social unit's normative dissensus and size, the greater the unit's ASC/RSC ratio.

ASSOCIATION AND VICARIOUS SOCIAL CONTROL.   A substantial increase in vicarious social control requires an enormous increase in the social unit's normative dissensus and size. Assume that a hunting-gathering band has become a huge tribe; but for the sake of simplicity assume only two lineages, X and Y, each with only three members. If $Y1$ is the head of lineage Y, than any lineage X member can attempt to control $Y2$ or $Y3$ through allegative social control, with $Y1$ as the third party. Likewise, any lineage Y member can attempt to control $X2$ or $X3$ through allegations made to $X1$ (lineage X head). However, such attempts will be effective only insofar as a head of a lineage shares evaluations of conduct with members of other lineages.

Now assume that a tribal member perceives the need for lineage cooperation in, say, warfare. If normative dissensus precludes an effective appeal to tribal welfare (referential control), allegative control is not a realistic alternative because the lineage heads have no superordinate. So the threat of punishment in deterrent vicarious social control comes to be the only feasible way to control all tribal members.

Control through punishment backed by coercion is especially likely to follow a permanent settlement of a social unit's territory by invaders, a sequence that results in a larger social unit and normative dissensus. Those changes make allegative control less effective, but a military conquest is not necessary for a substantial increase in vicarious control. Even if normative consensus remains unchanged, a social unit's size may increase so much that no first party can control all members through allegations about them to superordinates (e.g., lineage heads). Because control of all members through direct commands is even less feasible, eventually the commands pertain to categories of acts and persons; and related punishments are imposed to promote general deterrence (normative consensus has declined so much that only the threat of physical pain motivates all social unit members). So allegative social control (ASC) declines relative to vicarious social control (VSC); and the primary antecedent correlates are identified in Axiom 18-3: The greater a social unit's size and normative dissensus, the greater the unit's VSC/ASC ratio.

ASSOCIATION AND MODULATIVE SOCIAL CONTROL. To the extent that the State monopolizes legal coercion by violence (Weber, 1978:314), that condition creates a problem for nongoverning elites. They cannot use violence without risking retaliation; hence, they increasingly resort to modulative social control. One illustration must suffice. Even if capitalists control the State, they do not use violence to sell commodities. Competition prevents that use, but it does not prevent capitalists from attempting control through advertising. When a commodity owner purchases time or space in some mass medium, he or she uses the influence (expertise) of the medium's personnel, just as the owner does when turning to an advertising agency. In either case, it is modulative social control.

The foregoing argument is summarized by a postulate (18–2) about vicarious social control (VSC) and modulative social control (MSC): The greater a social unit's size, the greater the unit's MSC/VSC ratio. The postulate (so labeled because "size" is treated as a concept) does not imply that modulative social control replaces vicarious social control, or even that the former is an alternative to the latter. That is the case even though as a social unit's size, internal social differentiation, and normative dissensus increase, human control through general deterrence tends to becomes less effective. A large social unit makes it difficult for officials to apprehend offenders, with the consequence being a decline in the certainty of legal punishment; and the decline in normative consensus lessens public support for severe penalties. Nonetheless, in virtually all countries general deterrence is one aim of criminal justice (Morris, 1966:631); and evidence of the ineffectiveness of rehabilitation programs (see, e.g., Lipton et al., 1975) may create doubts about alternatives to a deterrent penal policy. In any case, modulative social control thrives not as an alternative to general deterrence but because the State has deprived private first parties of the use of punishment backed by the threat of coercion in attempting large-scale human control.

ASSOCIATION AND PRELUSIVE SOCIAL CONTROL.   As a social unit's size increases, those who attempt large-scale control commonly find it beyond their resources without answers to two questions. First, of all social unit members, who should be controlled the most? Second, what is the most effective means of control for any given member category (e.g., juveniles)? Limited resources also may prompt the first party to exclude certain categories from particular spatial-social contexts (e.g., entry into a country, membership in an organization) and thereby avoid the subsequent need to control them. When the first party commences using a third party to answer the two questions or to exclude people from certain contexts, it is prelusive social control.

The argument concerning the conditions that give rise to prelusive social control (PSC) can best be summarized in an axiom pertaining to its relative frequency and that of all other types of human control (OTHC). The axiom (18–4) is: The greater a social unit's size, social differentiation, and normative dissensus, the greater the unit's PSC/OTHC ratio. Prelusive social control is not an alternative to other types of human control; rather, the former becomes common only because of conspicuous problems with the latter (e.g., identifying relevant potential strategic third parties in social control).

TOWARD COMPLETION OF THE THEORY.   Of all variables considered, only "social unit size" is a concept. All others—normative consensus or dissensus, social differentiation, and each control ratio (e.g., ASC/RSC)—are constructs. Because constructs cannot be linked directly to referential formulas, no testable statements can be deduced from the premises (the axioms and the postulate). So future formulations must add the premises and temporal quantifiers needed to derive testable statements, but the present premises

446 / Control: Sociology's Central Notion

do demonstrate how social unit size, social differentiation, and normative consensus can be thought of in terms of control.

Because the conceptualization of control (chapter 3) purports to be empirically applicable, identification of the control ratios (e.g., RSC/ASC) as constructs may appear strange. Given incidence figures for the various control types (e.g., PC, RSC) in a particular social unit over some period, the ratios could be computed readily. However, the ratios are constructs because the requisite research resources alone preclude incidence figures for even a few social units. So the goal must be postulates that connect each control ratio (as a construct) with a concept. To illustrate, it could be assumed that among nonMarxist countries there is a direct relation between the ratio of modulative social control to vicarious social control (i.e., MSC/VSC) and another ratio, the number of individuals employed in the advertising to the number employed in law enforcement. The latter ratio, a concept, can be an empirically applicable formula because it can be applied to census data.

Control and Association

Many previous observations appear to have no bearing on associational freedom; but not in light of this question: Why are people concerned with freedom of association? Because they dimly perceive the connection between it and control.

It is not claimed that individuals often enter into or terminate associations to avoid or realize control, and it should be recognized again that citizens of various nonMarxist democracies (e.g., Sweden, Great Britain, the United States) appear rarely concerned with associational freedom. However, the rarity means only that those citizens lead, politically speaking, a very sheltered life. In those countries control over controls, especially the rule of law, are such that freedom of association is taken for granted.

The future of the concern depends on the type of country. Without a turn to the rule of law in a Marxist or fascist country, concern with freedom of association will continue to rival concern with freedom of communication as the source of dissidence. In democracies, concern with freedom of association will increase only if that freedom is jeopardized by departures from the rule of law. Yet Huxley's *Brave New World* serves to remind how thoroughly freedom of association can be eliminated. Even more than Orwell, Huxley appreciated how humans can be too controlled by controlling their associations. The road to a real *Brave New World* will be a long one, paved with seemingly benign governmental actions. An American instance is governmental proscription of travel to particular countries on the grounds that the visit would be dangerous. It is as though Americans have been told: You can have neither liberty nor death.

Freedom from Deprivation

When President Roosevelt (1946:266) tacitly identified "freedom from want" as fundamental, he knew when an idea's time had arrived. The Great Depression forced Americans to appreciate freedom *from* as well as freedom *to*.

Major Issues

Because want is a less social notion than is deprivation, all further references are to freedom from deprivation. Sociologists are unrealistic if they allow their aversion to reductionism to make them indifferent to deprivation, thereby surrendering the subject to economists and psychologists.

CONCEPTUALIZATION. Deprivation is a desire to resemble some other humans with regard to some material or nonbehavioral biotic condition of life, coupled with the belief that the contrast is neither justified nor immutable. It is not merely the longing for something; it is also (1) recognition that others possess what is wanted and (2) denial that the difference is warranted.

Not all wants are deprivations; one may desire something (e.g., immortality) without invidious comparisons. However, unless deprivation pertains to material or *nonbehavioral* biotic conditions, freedom from it cannot be distinguished from freedom of communication or association.

REDUCTIONISM. Although sociologists speak often of relative deprivation, there is no major sociological theory or line of research on the subject; and the reason is obvious. Many sociologists deny interest in psychological phenomenon, evidently including even perceptions of human differences, the ostensible rationale being that such concern leads to reductionism. Whatever the rationale for antireductionism, the present argument is not that freedom from deprivation explains anything; rather, if such freedom varies substantially among social units and/or over time, that variation calls for explanation.

Should sociologists disavow interest in freedom from deprivation, it would reflect an indifference to fundamental human concerns. Most humans make invidious comparisons in connection with material things, and much of human behavior is oriented toward the acquisition of food, clothing, and shelter. Correlatively, sociologists are interested in capitalism, socialism, and communism; and the advocates of each make claims about the system's efficacy for maximizing freedom from deprivation. Most important, those who aspire to political control will fail if they ignore the human concern with freedom from deprivation. Demagogues rarely ignore that concern, and their use of the "deprived" to control others has been a perennial ingredient of human history.

Freedom from Deprivation and Control

There is a vast literature on major kinds of deprivation, notably those pertaining to hunger, housing, and health. No attempt will be made to describe that literature; rather, the subject is limited to control and freedom from deprivation.

INEQUALITY OF ACCESS TO NATURAL RESOURCES. Insofar as sociologists have anything to say about deprivation, they suggest that it stems from inequality (see Milner's survey, 1987). Evidence requires the identification of relevant inequalities, and the most obvious candidate is access to natural resources. One relevant comparison would be between a hunting-gathering unit and some agricultural unit in which land is privately owned by Anglo-American standards. The assumption would be much greater equality of access to natural resources in the hunting-gathering unit; hence, deprivation should be much greater in the agricultural unit because of a greater concentration of wealth (see Angle, 1986:303). Although anthropologists commonly label hunting-gathering peoples as egalitarian, they have yet to undertake a systematic comparison of social units as regards the extent of deprivation. The outcome might appear so predictable that the research need not be undertaken, but equality of access to natural resources is merely equality of opportunity.

Evidence that deprivation is reduced by equal access to natural resources would suggest a connection between control and deprivation. Equality of access requires *no control* over any members' hunting, fishing, forestry, and mining. As for the differential skills (e.g., in hunting) that result in an unequal distribution of personal possessions or prestige, those skills are nothing less than effective biotic, inanimate, or human control.

Now think of social units where natural resources are privately owned by Anglo-American standards. An empirically applicable definition of ownership or property requires at least implicit reference to human control. Thus, it makes no sense to say that someone owns a particular space if no one risks punishment, regardless of previous behavior (e.g., soliciting permission), by repeatedly moving across or using the space; and the threat of punishment to prevent use of natural resources is an attempt to control behavior.

SLAVERY, SERFDOM, EMPLOYMENT, AND UNEMPLOYMENT. Human inequalities stemming from differential skills in inanimate or biotic control appear minuscule compared to those stemming from differential capacities for human control. The master-slave relation is an extreme instance of inequalities in power, but the extent to which slavery generates deprivation is less obvious.

Scholars have applied the term *lord-serf* to extremely diverse human relations, and descriptions of a serf are commonly oversimplifications. Thus, Cohen (1978:65) describes the serf as, unlike the slave or proletarian, owning some of "his labor power" and "the means of production that he uses." The immediate problem is that the term *owning* denotes only some unidentified control phenomena. That problem also haunts definitions of a slave, but Cohen's description does not even imply control over the serf by a lord.

All major features of the lord-serf relation or the master-slave relation can be described in terms of control. Even the argument that lords and slave masters are bound by law suggests that their control is somehow limited.

If employment is the expenditure of human energy on a regular and contractual basis in return for something valued, then it differs from slavery and serfdom; and Marx correctly identified "wage labor" as a distinguishing feature of capitalism. He also formulated the best known argument for assuming that the employer-employee relation generates inequality and ensuing deprivation. However, the terms *bourgeoisie* and *proletariat* contribute nothing to the assumption; and it is puzzling why Marxists do not speak simply of employers and employees. In any case, while Marxists never tire of suggesting that Marx explained the power differential, the explanation is not explicit. In particular, granted that employers use State agents to protect their property, in practice they do not also use them to force employees to work.

The subject is all the more puzzling because Marx argued that owners of labor power and owners of money "meet in the market, and deal with each other on the basis of equal rights. . . ." (1906-I:186). Although the nature of that exchange is disputable, in the workplace employers do control employees; and that control is the salient consideration. The difference varies over time and space; but the variation does not refute two arguments: (1) that the employer-employee relation generates deprivation and (2) the relation is a control relation, whatever the relevance of "worker attachment" (Halaby, 1986).

Contrary to Marx's law or theory of increasing misery (see Popper, 1966:166–92, and Lebowitz, 1977–78), there is no systematic evidence of a decline in the real wages of employees in nonMarxist countries over this century. Just the opposite; most evidence indicates a substantial increase, and it is even debatable whether employer-employee income inequality has increased.[6] For that matter, inequality does not have a special relation to capitalism (see Turner, 1986:16), nor has the trend of income inequality been even approximately the same in capitalist countries (see, e.g., Hanneman, 1980); and Marxism has not ushered in equality where it has triumphed. Whether or not there is a "new class" in Marxist countries, various reports indicate enormous variation in the standard of living within Marxist countries (see literature cited by Turner, 1986:108–13). Income variation is probably greater in the U.S. and many other nonMarxist countries (see Gorin, 1980), but by any convention the median standard of living is greater in the U.S. than in Marxist countries.

Nonetheless, Marxists can make some irrefutable arguments about capitalist inequalities. Despite the relatively high median American family income, millions of families live far below the official poverty level; and despite decades of minimum wage legislation, the annual income of many American employers is more than a hundred times that of some of his or her employees. Capitalist ideologues respond something like this: Freedom of communication and association is desirable, but no system can assure freedom from deprivation without a stagnant economy. Similar sophistry is exhibited by contemporary Marxist ideologues, who are sensitive to freedom from deprivation but not freedom of communication and association. So one ideologue's fundamental freedom is another's folly, and "committed" sociologists excoriate one folly but tolerate others.

Control and Deprivation

Nothing is gained by identifying slavery, serfdom, employment, and unemployment as "structural" sources of deprivation. It is not some "structure" but, rather, differentials in effective control that generate deprivation. The connection is all the more real in that inequality and ensuing deprivation may be promoted as a means of control.

A RUDIMENTARY MEANS. Considered as a distinct means of control, the promotion of deprivation is fairly rare. Even if convicts deplore their material condition (e.g., the food) and are thus deprived, imprisonment also sharply reduces freedom of association and communication. All pains of imprisonment may appear deprivational; but, again, unless freedom of deprivation is defined in terms of material or biotic conditions, it is not distinct.

Deprivation promotion is rudimentary even in the case of fines. The imposition of a fine could promote deprivation, and that legal punishment is virtually global. Yet the maximum fine is commonly so low as to create serious doubts about its deterrent efficacy, and there is reason to doubt the significance of the sharp increase in the use of fines as legal punishment among many Western European countries during the 19th century. Fines did not become the most strategic legal punishment for felonies, and the abandonment of forfeiture of estates as a legal punishment was a step away from deprivation promotion.

The promotion of deprivation has never been a major means of legal or extralegal control, and there is no conspicuous trend in that direction. True, during this century parents in some countries have come to rely less on corporal punishment (see, e.g., Ziegert, 1983) and perhaps more on reduction in monetary allowance, but the promotion of deprivation appears to be rare. The rarity is puzzling, especially in the case of countries characterized by ever increasing consumption. So the argument goes, to be bereft of material possessions in a consuming society is akin to civil death; hence, even the threat of dispossession should be an effective means of human control. Yet there is a contrary argument: the proliferation of material things makes each one less valued.

USING THE DEPRIVED. Throughout history, "the poor" have been a significant third party in social control. The point is not the usual one made in critiques of contemporary capitalism—the welfare state is a vast regulation of the poor (see, e.g., Cohen and Scull, 1983, and Piven and Cloward, 1971).[7] The poor's plight is even worse than the critiques suggest. Far from being content to control the poor, some elites use them to control other elites.

From ancient Greece to the present, numerous charismatic leaders have incited the poor either to attack the leader's political opponents or destroy the opponents' property. Such actions are social control even when the third party is a mob. When a first party incites a mob, the mob's "influence" is violent; but it is also social control when the first party seeks the votes of the poor by attributing their plight to the first party's political opponents. Huey Long was a master of that kind of control, whereas Franklin Roosevelt excelled in describing the poor such as to sway affluent voters.

The Future of the Concern

If the "poor are always with us," then the use of the deprived as a means of social control (Higgins, 1980) may never cease. However, the future of freedom from deprivation is linked with several perennial issues.

THE GHOST OF MALTHUS. The previous emphasis on perception does not implicitly deny the possibility of a very close connection between objective conditions and deprivation, but it could be that acute deprivation prevails only when there is extreme inequality and the per capita amount of material possessions has reached a very low level. If so, Malthus's ghost points to unprecedented increases in deprivation, perhaps globally.

Malthusian theory was rejuvenated by the energy crisis in the 1970s and the global population explosion after World War II. That explosion prompted Malthusians to forecast even more global poverty, but they have not been the only grim futurists since World War II. In the sixties "environmentalists" commenced prophesying a vast ecological crisis, with depletion of natural resources and pollution at irreversible, catastrophic levels. The environmentalists are more pessimistic than Malthusians, because not even zero-population growth rates would necessarily prevent some of the anticipated disasters.

Malthusians and environmentalists deny the possibility of a technological "quick fix," one common presumption being that the net energy yield in petroleum production will approach the negative level before an efficient alternative can be exploited. Nor do they see a real prospect for technological innovations that continuously increase food production commensurate with population growth rates. By contrast, critics of the "doomsters" depict humanity as standing on the threshold of technological wonders, with enormous leaps in food production. Certain economists (e.g., Simon and Kahn, 1984, and Wattenberg and Zinsmeister, 1985) are especially optimistic, even without presuming technological miracles. They argue that the market mechanism is sufficient if left uncontrolled.

There can be no conclusive assessment of the claims made by doomsters or their critics. The world's population is expanding rapidly in terms of absolute numbers despite a decline in the fertility rate *circa* 1975–85 (see Tsui and Bogue, 1978; Lieberson, 1986), and in the late eighties there is some evidence that the decline has ended. So prophecies of mass starvation and global ecological crises are hardly grotesque in the absence of major innovations in inanimate control and/or biotic control (genetic engineering especially). Such control innovations cannot be anticipated merely by extrapolating current trends. The immediate need is a far-reaching technological theory, but it is not being really pursued by sociologists. What with no effective replacements of Ogburn (e.g., 1964), Cottrell (e.g., 1955), or Form (e.g., 1972) on the horizon, sociological interest in technology appears to be declining; and a revival is unlikely unless control becomes the field's central notion.

Granted that the recent decline in the global population growth rate was only from about 2 percent to about 1.7 percent (Lieberson, 1986:37) and the possible end of the decline, there is at least one basis for optimism: billions of humans still do not use effective contraception methods. However, because social scientists with demographic interests have been preoccupied more with presumed structural determinants of fertility rates than with birth control, no theory answers two crucial questions. First, under what condition are governmental agencies or nongovernmental organizations most likely to launch and maintain a program to reduce a country's fertility rate? And, second, what determines a program's efficacy? Before the child limitation program in China (see Greenhalgh and Bongaarts, 1987), most demographers ostensibly presumed that such programs are too ineffective to warrant serious attention (Tsui and Bogue, 1978, are two exceptions). The China program may have altered their thinking, but answers to the two questions are needed for defensible speculation about the future of human fertility. Nothing would promote answers more than taking control as sociology's central notion.

DEPRIVATION PROMOTION IN MARXIST COUNTRIES. In all Marxist countries the first victims of the proletariat dictatorship have been the freedoms of communication and association. If freedom is a bourgeois notion, one must wonder why it is extolled in constitutions of Marxist states and why Marxists speak tirelessly of human liberation (again, see Parkin's commentary, 1979:176). As for the argument that the oppressiveness of Marxist regimes reflects the authoritarianism of Marx and/or Lenin (see Lovell's commentary, 1984), it strains credulity to suppose that a leader's character determines a regime's features more than sixty years later. One alternative argument is that the integration of various kinds of freedom precludes an enormous increase or decrease in only one. Extending the argument, in Marxist regimes the extreme concentration of control over production-consumption and cultural activities precludes a free market of ideas. Countries known for socialism-sans-Marx (e.g., Sweden) may appear to be exceptions, but not if the concentration and intensity of controls over production-consumption and cultural activities are less than in Marxist countries.

The apparent rarity of public protest in Marxist countries is indicative of fairly effective control, but it is disputable to attribute that effectiveness solely to coercion. In addition, extensive economic controls in Marxist regimes enable officials to threaten dissidents with deprivation. Party officials ultimately determine who will work, when, with whom, in what position, at what income, and promotion opportunities. In particular, Soviet officials can deprive an individual of his or her "work book" (labor record), thereby making it difficult for him or her to secure another position; and by controlling admissions to universities and other training facilities, officials can make an individual permanently ineligible for various jobs or positions (see Hollander, 1982:332). So, of Marxist countries, at least the U.S.S.R. is an exception to a previous generalization—that deprivation promotion is a rare means of human control. The reason is best expressed by Shatz: "Soviet society is far more tightly controlled by the state than imperial society ever was, not just by police methods such as surveillance, residency restrictions, and the passport system, but economically and even psychologically by the government's exclusive 'ownership' of the economy, the educational system, and virtually all occupations" (1980:172).

FUTURE OF DEPRIVATIONAL PROMOTION IN AMERICA.   Any governmental program that contributes to a citizen's material well-being is a potential means of human control, because the beneficiaries are confronted with the threat of deprivation for criminal or even dissident acts (see Rosenthal, 1983). Hence, welfare programs have special control implications in countries where, unlike Marxist regimes, governmental regulation of the economy is not such as to threaten dissidents with deprivation. The U.S. is a case in point. Most American voters and legislators appear disenchanted with the "welfare state," but it is unlikely that welfare programs will cease to be potential deprivational means of control. Lest that prospect appear grossly unrealistic, consider a recent illustration. When numerous draft-eligible males refused to register for Selective Service in 1982, Congress acted to bar them from federal student aid. However, an even greater use of deprivational threats is contingent on an anticipated continuation of a particular welfare program.

If life expectancy continues to increase without a substantial increase in the average retirement age, federal legislators will become even more reluctant to terminate Social Security. Yet, providing the elderly with benefits is one thing, while providing them unconditionally is quite another. A criminal record does not preclude Social Security benefits, and various ideological dissidents are current recipients. But what would happen if the ratio of recipients to economically active individuals continues to increase and there is an ideological witch hunt even more virulent than that in the 1950s? As the questions suggest, it would be rash to conclude that Social Security can never make deprivational threats a common means of human control, such as making Social Security benefits for parents contingent on their children's conduct.

What has been said of the Social Security applies also to freedom and welfare programs in general (see *Journal of Social Policy*, April, 1982). Hopefully, Americans will balk at converting welfare programs into deprivational threats; but capitalist ideologues are likely to emphasize "control dangers" in arguing against welfare programs, which in itself is a control attempt.

Freedom from Fear

When speaking in January, 1941, of freedom from fear, President Roosevelt (1946:266) "translated it into world terms" as requiring global disarmament. That translation reflected widespread fear of war. Because of nuclear weapons and two generations of continuous international tension, the fear of war may well be greater now than in 1941. But far from limited to war, fear is so pervasive that freedom from it may well be the most fundamental freedom.

Few sociologists explicitly attribute importance to fear; and if they refrain because fear is psychological, it is another manifestation of antireductionism. To emphasize the ubiquity and importance of concern with freedom from fear is not to imply an explanation of human behavior; but as long as sociologists describe and think of social phenomena as somehow removed from human fears, their work will be divorced from the world as humans perceive it.

Fear and Control

Intensity of fear is partially contingent on the amount of control over whatever is feared. That relation is especially conspicuous in "phobic behavior," which is a failure in self-control, meaning a failure to overcome the diffuse fear known as anxiety. However, the connection between self-control and fear is not emphasized subsequently, because it would elicit the aversion of sociologists to "psychologizing."

CRIMINAL VICTIMIZATION. Evidence that a multitude of Americans frequently fear crime (see Currie, 1985) cannot be readily dismissed as "psychological" and, hence, alien to sociology's subject matter. Many sociologists have conducted research on that fear (see DuBow et al., 1979), one of few instances in which sociologists have taken a human concern seriously. Most of them have either estimated the prevalence of the fear of crime or identified some characteristics (e.g., age, sex, race) of the most fearful. The ostensible behavioral correlates of the fear should be the ultimate concern of sociologists; and it appears that the increase in fear has been associated with: (1) an enormous jump in the sales of security equipment, including guns; (2) an unprecedented increase in private security personnel; and (3) a multitude of changes in lifestyles, such as avoiding street walking after dark (see, e.g., Skogan and Maxfield, 1981).

Such correlates are indicative of attempts to prevent criminal victimization, a form of countercontrol (see Lavrakas and Lewis, 1980); and fear of crime may be accentuated by personal failures (e.g., a locked house is burglarized) or vicarious failures (e.g., a neighbor's house is burglarized despite an alarm system). Yet failure in crime prevention is not just a personal matter. Durkheim notwithstanding, legislators prescribe punishments to prevent crime; therefore, any crime is a failure of that vast control enterprise known as criminal justice.

Although the relation between fear of crime and the true crime rate remains debatable, it would tax credulity to deny any connection between increase in that fear over the past 25 years and the publicized rise in the official crime rate. Then there is evidence that the relation between fear of crime and victimization is hardly "irrational" (see Skogan, 1987). Finally, if Americans did not perceive criminality as *controllable*, the "crime problem" would not have become a political issue (see, e.g., Cohen, 1985; Currie, 1985; and Pepinsky, 1980).

The foregoing arguments suggest a control principle (18-1): If all conditions are perceived as approximately likely and harmful, the intensity of fear of a particular condition varies inversely with the perceived capacity to control that condition. That principle could guide sociological research on all kinds of fear (for evidence justifying the qualifying phrase in the principle as it applies to crime, see Warr and Stafford, 1983).

HUMAN MORTALITY. Various general observations suggest that most humans fear death and perceive it as unpreventable. Accordingly, control principle 18-1 implies that death is feared intensely because of the perceived incapacity to control it, but variation in that intensity among social units is the real concern.[8] Because the capacity to control is also the capacity to predict accurately, the incapacity to predict accurately is assumed conducive to perceptions of control incapacity (even granting that humans cannot control all that they can predict accurately, such as planetary movement). So great variation in age at death is taken (1) as indicative of an incapacity to predict when individuals will die and (2) as reducing perceptions of the human capacity to control death. That conclusion, along with control principle 18-1, suggests this potentially testable proposition: The more social unit members differ with regard to age at death, the more intense the fear of death in that social unit.

The proposition has a special implication for high-energy countries, where (1) age at death is now far less problematic than two centuries ago because somatic control innovations (especially public heath measures) have reduced the death rate of children enormously, (2) future innovations (e.g., cancer therapy) are most likely to reduce various leading causes of death among the elderly, and (3) genetic engineering is most likely to expand the human lifespan. For at least a generation, failure in those controls will be fairly common; hence, age at death may become more problematical. If so, the proposition anticipates an intensification of fear of death.

THE PROSPECTS OF ECOLOGICAL CRISES.   Over recent decades, the prospect of a vast ecological crisis has become a global fear. The following are illustrative possibilities: (1) a global temperature increase with catastrophic consequences because of carbon-dioxide concentration in the atmosphere; (2) massive loss of life (human and nonhuman) from toxic waste accumulation; (3) irreversible deforestation and concomitant desertification; (4) soil erosion that jeopardizes the earth's food supply; (5) extinction of lake life and stunted forests from acid rain; and (6) a lethal increase in ultraviolet light concomitant with deterioration of the ozone layer, something caused by human use of chemicals.

Catastrophic forecasts are often made contingent on continued global population growth, but many are described as virtually certain. In any case, the grim prophecies of environmentalists (see Council on Environmental Quality and the Department of State, 1980–81) have not gone unchallenged, especially in *The Resourceful Earth* (Simon and Kahn, 1984). Because distinguished scientists are found in both camps, an appeal to authority is feckless when assessing the prospect of an ecological crisis; but even if it were otherwise, sociologists have little expertise to offer. A greater interest in inanimate and biotic control is needed to further the expertise of sociologists and breathe new life into a now moribund but relevant sociology subfield, human ecology.

PROSPECTS OF NUCLEAR WAR.   Consistent with control principle 18-1, fear of nuclear war may become the most intense in humanity's history, although it is currently less of a concern or problem for Americans (see Schuman et al., 1986) than was suggested by Tyler and McGraw (1983). Despite passionate pleas for peace, throughout the world people commonly perceive themselves as totally incapable of preventing a nuclear war (but see Tyler and McGraw, 1983). The fear is all the more intense because of the perceived potential destructiveness of nuclear war; but that consideration is recognized by one of the qualifications of control principle 18-1 (that pertaining to harm), and the other qualification (perceived likelihood) suggests a reason why Americans are not more fearful (Schuman et al., 1986). However, the idea of perceived capacity to control extends to the consequences of nuclear war; and scientists increasingly identify consequences (e.g., a "nuclear winter") that are beyond control, which increases fear.

Sociologists will not go far beyond their limited contributions (see, e.g., *Sociological Quarterly*, Fall, 1985) to the vast literature on nuclear war (e.g., Zuckerman, 1985) and control strategies (e.g., Bundy et al., 1986) until they cease their preoccupation with meaning as an end in itself or with structural variables. True, no proposed strategy has reduced the prospects of nuclear war, but that depressing recognition is all the more reason for sociologists to participate.

Control and Fear

Freedom from fear is more frequently jeopardized by human control than is any other freedom, and the reason is simple. Would-be controllers often attempt to induce or heighten the experience of fear. Most of the attempts are punitive, but the specific means are extremely varied.

A BRIEF CONCEPTUALIZATION. If punishment is defined as any act that results in a pain or discomfort by at least one human being, the definition makes internal behavior irrelevant; and a multitude of anomalies ensue. Thus, should a motorist accidentally injure a pedestrian, it would be punishment.

Such anomalies can be avoided only by this "control" definition: Punishment is an overt act undertaken in the belief (1) that it increases the probability of some human experiencing pain or discomfort and (2) that the increase is desirable. Even that definition ignores the internal behavior of the act's object, but it can be recognized in distinguishing types of punishment.

SPECIFIC DETERRENCE. So defined, punishment is always attempted control; and a would-be controller may act in the belief that the act will alter or maintain only the targets' internal behavior. However, when humans punish in a successful attempt to control the punished individual's overt behavior, it is specific deterrence.

There is now an extensive literature in psychology on experimental work with punishment, but no one has integrated that work and specific deterrence research on criminality (for a step in that direction, see Gray et al., 1985). The separation is unfortunate if only because in recent decades experimental findings contradict Skinner's early conclusion (see Axelrod and Apsche, 1983) that punishment is an ineffective means of controlling behavior. Yet the findings on specific deterrence and criminality (see two surveys: Currie, 1985; and Gibbs, 1986) appear largely consistent with Skinner's conclusion. With few exceptions (e.g., Berk and Newton, 1985), the findings indicate either no relation or a direct relation among individuals between the presumptive severity of legal punishments and subsequent official recidivism. Nonetheless, virtually all of the research has been indefensible. There is a fairly substantial direct relation between number of previous arrests and severity of punishment on last conviction; hence, those most inclined to repeat an offense (with or without punishment) are most likely to be punished severely once convicted. The only solution is randomization of legal punishments, but judges understandably balk at imposing severe punishments randomly. In the few instances where punishments have been randomized, most findings have not indicated any specific deterrence (the virtually unique exception is Sherman and Berk, 1984); but contrasts in the presumptive severity of the punishments have not been substantial.

Still another shortcoming: investigators have ignored several possibly relevant properties of legal punishments, concentrating on presumptive severity (i.e., magnitude). Other properties, even perceived severity, have been ignored because the research was not guided by an explicit theory that confronts this question: Why would punishing an individual for an act decrease the probability of him or her repeating the act? The argument must be that punishment increases the object's (1) perception of punishment certainty and/or (2) perception of punishment severity. Yet not one specific deterrence study has examined changes in perceived certainty or perceived severity (the research by Bridges and Stone, 1986, is relevant but flawed because they did not examine actual change in perceptions before and after punishment).

Future of the Concern with Freedom from Fear

Although humans may come to enjoy more freedom from fear, some fears are likely to haunt humanity forever. If so, fear will never cease to be used in human control.

OLD AND NEW FEARS.   Contemplate the possible escalations of a perennial fear. Assume that genetic engineering eventually eliminates all deaths from "old age"; then imagine what the fear of accidents, homicide, and suicide would become. Conjecture, to be sure, but a field's central notion should stimulate conjectures.

Numerous scientists, social critics, and politicians have voiced concern that experimental genetic engineering will produce new life forms (bacterial or viral) that are unexpectedly conducive to human morbidity if not mortality, or forms that compete all to effectively with humans in the food quest. Nothing akin to that fear has been realized (see Zimmerman, 1984:141–77); but, sooner or later, genetic engineering will have unanticipated consequences. The inevitability of unanticipated consequences may appear to undermine the importance of control itself, but no one engages in genetic engineering accidentally. For that matter, *anticipated* (planned) consequences of genetic engineering may pose serious issues and perceived dangers. The possible military use of genetic engineering (along with "biotechnology" in general) is a constant danger (see, e.g., Stableford, 1984: 176–80), and it is already a major concern in international negotiations pertaining to weapons control (see Dickson, 1986). Moreover, the scene is being set for organizations to use "genetic screening" when identifying the eligibility of individuals for insurance or employment; and should genetic criterion become the basis for employment and/or promotion, genetic research will have provided the foundation for a caste system resembling Huxley's *Brave New World*. Indeed, those who advocate using genetic engineering to produce superhumans seem to ignore the implication—the simultaneous creation, in effect, of an "inferior" race. Sociologists need not leave the investigation of such issues to journalists; and the investigation should extend to this question: What will be the direction and effectiveness of attempts to control genetic engineering through law (see Harlow, 1986, and Fogleman, 1987)?

THE CRISIS OF CRIME CONTROL. An anticipated condition is far less conjectural if described as an extension of some trend, such as the soaring official crime rate since the 1950s. Granted that even enormous further increases will not destroy social order, should the current seeming reversal of the trend be temporary, fear of crime could become so intense that Americans abandon the rule of law, commencing with preventive detention.

Fear of crime is accentuated by perceptions of failures in attempts at crime prevention. Numerous Americans long ago abandoned the rehabilitation *ideal*, in part because of surveys (e.g., Lipton et al., 1975) that raised serious doubts about the effectiveness of conventional rehabilitation programs. Yet the kinds of legal punishments (e.g., imprisonment) and related properties (e.g., minimum level of objective certainty) necessary to reduce the crime rate are unknown, and there is a host of related ethical and political issues (see, e.g., Cohen, 1985; Currie, 1985; and Pepinsky, 1980). Even assuming that the deterrence doctrine is valid, Americans are likely to regard the cost of reducing the crime rate through deterrence as prohibitive (see Phillips and Votey, 1981), and the same is true of incapacitation.

Law-and-order advocates in the U.S. appear to be shifting their emphasis from deterrence to retribution. The retributive doctrine is easier to defend than rehabilitation, deterrence, or incapacitation, because it really makes no empirical claims. However, the doctrine leaves far too many questions unanswered to be a basis for penal policy (see Gibbs, 1978), and Americans are now discovering the staggering cost of long, mandatory prison sentences (see Currie, 1985).

Rehabilitation, deterrence, incapacitation, and retribution are virtually the only bases for criminal justice policy, which suggests that humans are not imaginative in answering this question: What is the appropriate response to criminality? Answers by sociologists have not been imaginative (see Currie's extensive commentary, 1985), and that is likely to be the case until control becomes the field's central notion.

Conclusion

As suggested previously, sociologists now virtually ignore the notion of freedom (but see Bovone, 1985).[9] Perhaps they believe that the subject belongs to social philosophy, but sociology's central notion should facilitate describing and thinking about sociology's marginal as well as mainline subject matter. The pivotal question for future studies of freedom should be this: If freedom is a zero-sum game, why do social units ostensibly differ as to the amount of freedom? The tentative answer is that humans are concerned more with avoiding being controlled than with controlling (interfering with or reacting punitively to the acts of others in particular).

In this and preceding chapters, there are several instances where describing and thinking about phenomena in terms of control have not yielded a theory or even a redefinition of a major sociological term. Although it would be unrealistic to demand instant theories or conceptualizations, that argument should not become a crutch in defending control as a candidate for sociology's central notion. Whatever the candidate, most sociologists in each specialty (stratification, deviance, etc.) must conclude that describing and thinking about phenomena in terms of the notion facilitate theories and conceptualizations more than do contenders; and that is the claim made for control.

Finally, recall the two principal arguments. First, maximum coherence in a scientific field requires a central notion, meaning a notion that can be used to describe and think about all or virtually all of the field's subject matter. Second, control could be sociology's central notion. One may accept the first argument but reject the second, and rejection of the first argument renders the second moot. Although the primacy of the first argument is recognized, it has been slighted in this book only because little is gained by examining the idea of a central notion in the abstract.

NOTES

1.   The argument is relevant in assessing Rawls's first principle: "Each person is to have an equal right to the most extensive total system of equal basic liberties compatible with a similar system of liberty of all" (1971:302).

2.   Contemplate Alexander's claim: "The central problem in Marx's work, all agree, is the relation between freedom and necessity" (1982-II:11).

3.   Granted, in virtually all so-called communist countries the Marxist regimes did not deprive people of political freedom because they did not have it to lose (in the case of Russia, see Shatz, 1980). But that consideration does not make the

praise of freedom by officials in Marxist regimes any less hypocritical; and the implied suggestion—Marxist regimes have only perpetuated the oppression that gave rise to them—is surely a paradox. For that matter, the history of Czechoslovakia contradicts the argument that a Marxist regime is oppressive only in countries where political freedom was never a tradition.

4. Should a court rule that one can be fired or denied employment for expressing opinions, the ruling would imply that association freedom take precedence over communication freedom. However, a court ruling may imply that persons do not have the same freedoms, and early in this century the Supreme Court supplied an illustration by striking down statutes that forbid an employer to discharge an employee for joining a union (Lempert and Sanders, 1986:182). The rationale—such statutes abrogate an employer's freedom of contract—implies ascendancy of an employer's freedom of association over that of an employee. The more general point is that virtually any court ruling or legislative action implies an answer to this question: Who shall be free to do what to whom with impunity?

5. Unless there are defensible inferences as to the perceptions of the participants, it should be understood that social or behavioral scientists (as observers) are speaking of *presumptive* freedom, control, or power.

6. In commenting on Habermas, van den Berg (1980:454) observes that such criticisms of Marx are now accepted even by advocates of "critical theory." However, a survey of the relevant evidence would not convince such defenders of Marx as Lebowitz (1977–78), who argues that capitalism produces new needs that are not met by wage increases.

7. In the typical study of the relation between welfare or social security and social control, the latter is construed so broadly, if not left undefined, that it becomes a grab-bag notion (see Armour and Couglin's survey, 1985).

8. Because the voluminous observations of Aries (1981) on death are so discursive and ambiguous, they may or may not be construed as suggesting enormous variation in fear of death. Despite praise of Aries in sociological reviews, his book should prompt sociologists to entertain this question: How does sociology differ from history and philosophy?

9. The same cannot be said for several of the major figures in sociology's history. Alexander (1982) has argued convincingly that Marx, Durkheim, Weber, and Parsons were very much concerned with freedom; but Simmel's interest in the notion (especially 1978) was perhaps even keener.

References

Abernethy, Virginia. 1981. Comments on Tibetan fraternal polyandry. *American Anthropologist* 83 (December) 895.

Abrahamson, Mark. 1978. *Functionalism*. Englewood Cliffs, N.J.: Prentice-Hall.

Adams, Richard N. 1982a. *Paradoxical harvest*. New York: Cambridge University Press.

———. 1982b. The emergence of the regulatory society. Pp. 137–63 in Gibbs, 1982a.

———.1975. *Energy and structure*. Austin: University of Texas Press.

Akers, Ronald L. 1985. *Deviant behavior*, 3d ed. Belmont, Calif.: Wadsworth.

——— et al. 1979. Social learning and deviant behavior. *American Sociological Review* 44 (August):636–55.

Albion, Mark S., and Paul W. Farris. 1981. *The advertising controversy*. Boston: Auburn House.

Alcorn, Paul A. 1986. *Social issues in technology*. Englewood Cliffs, N.J.: Prentice-Hall.

Aldrich, Howard, and Jane Weiss. 1981. Differentiation within the United States capitalist class. *American Sociological Review* 46 (June):279–90.

Alexander, Jeffrey C. 1982, 1983. *Theoretical logic in sociology*, 4 vols. 1982-I and II, 1983-III and IV. Berkeley: University of California Press.

Allott, Antony N. 1980. *The limits of law*. London: Butterworth.

Anderson, Bo, and David Willer. 1981. Introduction. Pp. 1–21 in Willer and Anderson, 1981.

Anderson, Charles H. 1974. *The political economy of social class*. Englewood Cliffs, N.J.: Prentice-Hall.

Angle, John. 1986. The surplus theory of social stratification and the size distribution of personal wealth. *Social Forces* 65 (December): 293–326.

Anthony, E. James. 1980. Psychoanalysis and environment. Pp. 201–39 in Greenspan and Pollock, 1980-III.

APA Commission on Psychotherapies. 1982. *Psychotherapy research.* Washington, D.C.: American Psychiatric Association.

Argyle, Michael. 1980. The laws of looking. Pp. 65–74 in Spradley and McCurdy, 1980.

Aries, Philippe. 1981. *The hour of our death.* New York: Knopf.

Armour, Philip K., and Richard M. Couglin. 1985. Social control and social security. *Social Science Quarterly* 66 (December):770–88.

Aubert, Vilhelm. 1983. *In search of law.* Totowa, N.J.: Barnes and Noble.

Auerbach, Jerold S. 1983. *Justice without law.* New York: Oxford University Press.

Austin, John. 1954. *The province of jurisprudence determined.* London: Weidenfeld and Nicolson.

Axelrod, Robert. 1984. *The evolution of cooperation.* New York: Basic Books.

Axelrod, Saul, and Jack Apsche, eds. 1983. *The effects of punishment on human behavior.* New York: Academic Press.

Bacharach, Samuel B., and Edward J. Lawler. 1976. The perception of power. *Social Forces* 55 (September): 123–34.

Bakhash, Shaul. 1986. Reign of terror. *New York Review of Books* 33 (August 14): 12–13.

Baldwin, John D., and Janice I. Baldwin. 1981. *Beyond sociobiology.* New York: Elsevier.

Bales, Robert F. 1950. *Interaction process analysis.* Cambridge, Mass: Addison-Wesley.

Ball, Harry V. et al. 1962. Law and social change. *American Journal of Sociology* 67 (March):532–40.

Barash, David P. 1980. Predictive sociobiology. Pp. 209–26 in Barlow and Silverberg, 1980.

———. 1979. *The whisperings within.* New York: Harper and Row.

Barber, Bernard. 1956. Structural-functional analysis. *American Sociological Review* 21 (April):129–35.

Barbour, Ian G. 1980. *Technology, environment, and human values.* New York: Praeger.

Bargatzky, Thomas. 1984. Culture, environment, and the ills of adaptationism. *Current Anthropology* 25 (August-October):399–406.

Barker, Martin. 1982. *The new racism.* Frederick, Md.: University Publications of America.

Barkow, Jerome H. 1980. Sociobiology. Pp. 171–97 in Montagu, 1980.

Barlow, George W. 1980. The development of sociobiology. Pp. 3–24 in Barlow and Silverberg, 1980.

———, and James Silverberg, eds. 1980. *Sociobiology.* Boulder, Colo.: Westview.

Barnes, Barry. 1974. *Scientific knowledge and sociological theory.* London: Routledge and Kegan Paul.

Barnett, S. A. 1980. Biological determinism and the Tasmanian native hen. Pp. 135–57 in Montagu, 1980.

Barry, Donald D., and Howard R. Whitcomb. 1981. *The legal foundations of public administration.* St. Paul: West.

Baumgartner, M. P. 1985. Law and the middle class. *Law and Human Behavior* 9 (March):3–24.

Bealer, Robert C. 1979. Ontology in American sociology. Pp. 85–106 in Snizek et al., 1979.

Beall, Cynthia M., and Melvyn C. Goldstein. 1981. Tibetan fraternal polyandry. *American Anthropologist* 83 (March):5–12.

Beetham, David. 1981. Michels and his critics. *Archives Europeennes de Sociologie* 22 (no. 1):81–99.

Bell, Richard Q., and Lawrence V. Harper. 1977. *Child effects on adults.* Hillsdale, N.J.: Lawrence Erlbaum Associates.

Bellah, Robert N. 1968. The sociology of religion. Pp. 406–14 in Sills, 1968-XIII.

Bentham, Jeremy. 1962. *The works of Jeremy Bentham,* vol. 1. New York: Russell and Russell.

Berger, Joseph et al., eds. 1974. *Expectation states theory.* Cambridge, Mass.: Winthrop.

Berger, Peter L., and Thomas Luckman. 1966. *The social construction of reality.* Garden City, N.Y.: Doubleday.

Berk, Richard A., and Phyllis J. Newton. 1985. Arrest and wife battery. *American Sociological Review* 50 (April):253–62.

————— et al. 1985. Social policy experimentation. *Evaluation Review* 9 (August): 387–429.

————— et al. 1983. Prisons as self-regulating systems. *Law and Society Review* 17 (no. 4):547–86.

Berkowitz, S. D. 1982. *An introduction to structural analysis.* Toronto: Butterworths.

—————. 1980. Structural and non-structural models of elites. *Canadian Journal of Sociology* 5 (Winter):13–30.

Bernard, Thomas J. 1983. *The consensus-conflict debate.* New York: Columbia University Press.

Beyer, Janice M., and Harrison M. Trice. 1979. A reexamination of the relations between size and various components of organizational complexity. *Administrative Science Quarterly* 24 (March):48–64.

Bickman, Leonard. 1974. The social power of a uniform. *Journal of Applied Social Psychology* 4 (January-March):47–61.

Bierstedt, Robert, ed. 1969. *A Design for Sociology.* Philadelphia: American Academy of Political and Social Science, Monograph 9.

Birnbaum, N. 1955. Monarchs and sociologists. *Sociological Review* 3 (July): 5–23.

Black, Donald, ed. 1984a. *Toward a general theory of social control,* 2 vols. New York: Academic Press.

—————. 1984b. Social control as a dependent variable. Pp. 1–36 in Black, 1984a-I.

—————. 1984c. Crime as social control. Pp. 1–27 in Black, 1984a-II.

—————. 1976. *The behavior of law.* New York: Academic Press.

—————. 1972. The boundaries of legal sociology. *Yale Law Journal* 81 (May): 1086–100.

Blake, Judith, and Kingsley Davis. 1964. Norms, values, and sanctions. Pp. 456–84 in Faris, 1964.

Blankstein, Kirk R., and Janet Polivy, eds. 1982. *Self-control and self-modification of emotional behavior.* New York: Plenum.

Blau, Judith R., and Peter M. Blau. 1982. The cost of inequality. *American Sociological Review* 47 (February): 114–29.

Blau, Peter M. 1977. *Inequality and hetrogeneity*. New York: Free Press.

———, ed. 1975a. *Approaches to the study of social structure*. New York: Free Press.

———. 1975b. Introduction. Pp. 1–20 in Blau, 1975a.

———. 1968. Interaction: social exchange. Pp. 452–58 in Sills, 1968-VII.

———. 1964. *Exchange and power in social life*. New York: Wiley.

———, and Joseph E. Schwartz. 1984. *Crosscutting social circles*. New York: Academic Press.

——— et al. 1984. Intersecting social affiliations and intermarriage. *Social Forces* 62 (March):585–606.

Bloch, Maurice. 1985. Religion and ritual. Pp. 698–701 in Kuper and Kuper, 1985.

Blumer, Herbert. 1969. *Symbolic interactionism*. Englewood Cliffs, N.J.: Prentice-Hall.

Bohra, Kayyum A., and Janak Pandry. 1984. Ingratiation toward strangers, friends, and bosses. *Journal of Social Psychology* 122 (April):217–22.

Boissevain, Jeremy. 1985. Networks. Pp. 557–58 in Kuper and Kuper, 1985.

Bongaarts, John, and Robert G. Potter. 1983. *Fertility, biology, and behavior*. New York: Academic Press.

Borkenau, Franz. 1965. A manifesto of our time. Pp. 109–14 in Meisel, 1965.

Boudon, Raymond. 1982. *The unintended consequences of social action*. New York: St. Martin's Press.

———. 1981. *The logic of social action*. London: Routledge and Kegal Paul.

Bovone, Laura. 1985. The problem of freedom in contemporary German sociology. *Sociological Theory* 3 (Fall):76–86.

Bredemeier, Harry C. 1955. The methodology of functionalism. *American Sociological Review* 20 (April):173–80.

Brenner, Charles. 1975. Affects and psychic conflict. *Psychoanalytic Quarterly* 44 (January):5–28.

Breuer, Georg. 1982. *Sociobiology and the human dimension*. Cambridge, England: Cambridge University Press.

Breyer, Stephen G., and Richard B. Stewart. 1979. *Administrative law and regulatory policy*. Boston: Little, Brown.

Bridges, George S., and James A. Stone. 1986. Effects of criminal punishment on perceived threat of punishment. *Journal of Research in Crime and Delinquency* 23 (August):207–39.

Brim, Orville G., Jr. 1968. Adult socialization. Pp. 555–62 in Sills, 1968-XIV.

Brinberg, David. 1979. An examination of the determinant of intention and behavior. *Journal of Applied Social Psychology* 9 (November-December): 560–75.

Brooks, Harvey. 1980. Technology, evolution, and purpose. *Daedalus* 109 (Winter):65–81.

Broom, Leonard et al. 1981. *Sociology*, 7th ed. New York: Harper and Row.

Brubaker, Rogers. 1985. Book review. *Social Forces* 64 (December):509–11.

Buckley, Walter F. 1967. *Sociology and modern systems theory*. Englewood Cliffs, N.J.: Prentice-Hall.

Bukharin, Nikolai. 1925. *Historical materialism*. New York: International Publishers.

Bundy, McGeorge et al. 1986. Back from the brink. *Atlantic* 258 (August):35–41.

Burawoy, Michael. 1979. *Manufacturing consent*. Chicago: University of Chicago Press.

Burgess, Robert L., and Don Bushell, Jr., eds. 1969. *Behavioral sociology*. New York: Columbia University Press.

Burke, Peter. 1980. *Sociology and history*. London: George Allen and Unwin.

Burns, Tom. 1958. The forms of conduct. *American Journal of Sociology* 64 (September):137–51.

Burstein, Paul. 1985. *Discrimination, jobs, and politics*. Chicago: University of Chicago Press.

Burt, Ronald S. 1982. *Toward a structural theory of action*. New York: Academic Press.

Burton, Michael G., and John Higley. 1987. Invitation to elite theory. Pp. 219–38 in G. William Domhoff and Thomas R. Dye (eds.), *Power elites and organizations*. Beverly Hills, Calif.: Sage.

Buss, David et al. 1987. Tactics of manipulation. *Journal of Personality and Social Psychology* 52 (June):1219–29.

Cadwallader, Mervyn L. 1959. The cybernetic analysis of change in complex organizations. *American Journal of Sociology* 65 (September):154–57.

Campbell, Bernard G. 1976. *Humankind emerging*. Boston: Little, Brown.

Cancian, Francesca. 1960. Functional analysis of change. *American Sociological Review* 25 (December):818–27.

Caplan, Arthur L., ed. 1978. *The sociobiology debate*. New York: Harper and Row.

Carlton, Eric. 1977. *Ideology and social order*. London: Routledge and Kegan Paul.

Carpenter, G. Russell. 1982. The social control of biology. Pp. 281–87 in Gove and Carpenter, 1982.

Carrier, David R. 1984. The energetic paradox of human running and hominid evolution. *Current Anthropology* 25 (August-October):483–89.

Carroll, Glenn R. 1985. Concentration and specialization. *American Journal of Sociology* 90 (May):1262–83.

Carver, Charles S., and Michael F. Scheier. 1982. Control theory. *Psychological Bulletin* 29 (July):111–35.

Cassirer, Ernst. 1955. *The myth of the state*. Garden City, N.Y.: Doubleday.

Catton, Bruce. 1981. *Reflections on the civil war*. Garden City, N.Y.: Doubleday.

Catton, William R., Jr. 1980. *Overshoot*. Urbana: University of Illinois Press.

Cawte, John. 1974. *Medicine is the law*. Honolulu: University Presses of Hawaii.

Chagnon, Napoleon A. 1980. Kin-selection theory, kinship, marriage and fitness among the Yanomamo Indians. Pp. 545–71 in Barlow and Silverberg, 1980.

———. 1979. Mate competition, favoring close kin, and village fissioning among the Yanomamo Indians. Pp. 86–144 in Chagnon and Irons, 1979.

———, and William Irons, eds. 1979. *Evolutionary biology and human social behavior*. North Scituate, Mass.: Duxbury Press.

Chodorow, Nancy J. 1985. Beyond drive theory. *Theory and Society* 14 (May): 271–319.

Choldin, Harvey M. 1978. Urban density and pathology. *Annual Review of Sociology* 4 (annual):91–113.

Cicourel, Aaron V. 1973. *Cognitive sociology*. Baltimore: Penguin Books.

———. 1964. *Method and measurement in sociology*. New York: Free Press.

Clarke, Simon. 1981. *The foundations of structuralism*. Brighton, England: Harvester Press.

Clegg, Stewart, and David Dunkerley. 1980. *Organization, class and control*. London: Routledge and Kegan Paul.

Cohen, G. A. 1978. *Karl Marx's theory of history*. Princeton, N.J.: Princeton University Press.

Cohen, Lawrence E., and Marcus Felson. 1979. Social change and crime rate trends. *American Sociological Review* 44 (August):588–608.

Cohen, Stanley. 1985. *Visions of social control*. Cambridge, England: Polity Press.

———, and Andrew Scull, eds. 1983. *Social control and the state*. New York: St. Martin's Press.

Coleman, James S. 1986. Social theory, social research, and a theory of action. *American Journal of Sociology* 91 (May):1309–35.

Collins, Randall. 1986. Is 1980s sociology in the doldrums? *American Journal of Sociology* 91 (May):1336–55.

———, ed. 1983. *Sociological Theory, 1983*. San Francisco: Jossey-Bass.

———. 1975. *Conflict sociology*. New York: Academic Press.

Conrad, Geoffrey W., and Arthur A. Demarest. 1984. *Religion and empire*. Cambridge, England: Cambridge University Press.

Cook-Gumperz, Jenny. 1973. *Social control and socialization*. London: Routledge and Kegan Paul.

Coser, Lewis A. 1956. *The functions of social conflict*. New York: Free Press.

Cottrell, Fred. 1955. *Energy and society*. New York: McGraw-Hill.

———. 1951. Death by dieselization. *American Sociological Review* 16 (June):358–65.

Council on Environmental Quality and the Department of State. 1980–81. *The global 2000 report to the president*. Washington, D.C.: U.S. Government Printing Office.

Crewe, Ivor. 1974. Introduction. Pp. 9–51 in Ivor Crewe (ed.), *Elites in western democracy*. New York: Wiley.

Crews, Frederick. 1986. In the big house of theory. *New York Review of Books* 33 (May 29):36–42.

Currie, Elliott. 1985. *Confronting crime*. New York: Pantheon.

Czudnowski, Moshe M., ed. 1983. *Political elites and social change*. DeKalb: Northern Illinois University Press.

Dahl, Robert A. 1982. *Dilemmas of pluralist democracy*. New Haven, Conn.: Yale University Press.

———. 1968. Power. Pp. 405–15 in Sills, 1968-XII.

Dahlitz, Julie. 1983. *Nuclear arms control*. London: George Allen and Unwin.

Dahrendorf, Ralf. 1959. *Class and class conflict in industrial society*. Stanford, Calif.: Stanford University Press.

———. 1958. Out of utopia. *American Journal of Sociology* 64 (September): 115–27.

Daly, Martin, and Margo Wilson. 1982. Homicide and kinship. *American Anthropologist* 84 (June):372–78.

Davies, Nigel. 1984. Human sacrifice in the old world and the new. Pp. 211–26 in

Elizabeth H. Boone (ed.), *Ritual human sacrifice in Mesoamerica*. Washington, D.C.: Dumbarton Oaks Research Library and Collection.

Davis, John. 1975. The particular theory of exchange. *Archives Europeennes de Sociologie* 16 (no. 2):151–68.

Davis, Kingsley. 1959. The myth of functional analysis as a special method in sociology and anthropology. *American Sociological Review* 24 (December): 757–72.

———, and Wilbert E. Moore. 1945. Some principles of stratification. *American Sociological Review* 10 (April):242–49.

Dawkins, Richard. 1982. Replicators and vehicles. Pp. 45–64 in King's College Sociobiology Group, 1982.

———. 1976. *The selfish gene*. New York: Oxford University Press.

Deak, Istvan. 1984. How guilty were the Germans? *New York Review of Books* 31 (May 31):37–42.

DeFleur, Lois B. 1982. Technology, social change, and the future of sociology. *Pacific Sociological Review* 25 (October):403–17.

DeFleur, Melvin L. et al. 1984. *Sociology*, 4th ed. New York: Random House.

Demarest, Arthur A. 1984. Overview. Pp. 227–43 in Elizabeth H. Boone (ed.), *Ritual human sacrifice in Mesoamerica*. Washington, D.C.: Dumbarton Oaks Research Library and Collection.

Demerath, N. J., III, and Richard A. Peterson, eds. 1967. *System, change, and conflict*. New York: Free Press.

Denzin, Norman K. 1987. The death of sociology in the 1980s. *American Journal of Sociology* 93 (July):175–80.

Dhingra, Harbans H. 1983. Patterns of ownership and control in Canadian industries. *Canadian Journal of Sociology* 8 (Winter):21–44.

Dickson, David. 1986. Gene splicing dominates review of weapons pact. *Science* 244 (October 10):143–45.

di Leonardo, Micaela. 1979. Methodology and the misinterpretation of women's status in kinship studies. *American Ethnologist* 6 (November):627–37.

Dillon, Richard G. 1980. Violent conflict in Meta' society. *American Ethnologist* 7 (November):658–73.

DiTomaso, Nancy. 1982. "Sociological reductionism" from Parsons to Althusser. *American Sociological Review* 47 (February):14–28.

Dore, Ronald P. 1961. Function and cause. *American Sociological Review* 26 (December):843–53.

Douglas, Jack D. 1967. *The social meanings of suicide*. Princeton, N.J.: Princeton University Press.

Draper, Roger. 1986. The faithless shepherd. *New York Review of Books* 33 (June 26):14–18.

Dubin, Steven C. 1986. Artistic production and social control. *Social Forces* 64 (March):667–88.

DuBow, Fred et al. 1979. *Reactions to crime*. Washington, D.C.: National Institute of Law Enforcement and Criminal Justice.

Dunbar, R. I. M. 1982. Adaptation, fitness and the evolutionary tautology. Pp. 9–28 in King's College Sociobiology Group, 1982.

Duncan, Marvin, and Kerry Webb. 1980. *Energy and American agriculture*. Kansas City: Federal Reserve Bank.

Dunlap, Riley E., and William A. Catton, Jr. 1979. Environmental sociology. *Annual Review of Sociology* 5 (annual):243–73.

Dunsire, Andrew. 1978. *Control in a bureaucracy*. New York: St. Martin's Press.

Durkheim, Emile. 1965. *The elementary forms of the religious life*. New York: Free Press.

———. 1951. *Suicide*. New York: Free Press.

———. 1949. *The division of labor in society*. New York: Free Press.

———. 1938. *The rules of sociological method*. Chicago: University of Chicago Press.

Duvall, Raymond D., and Michael Stohl. 1983. Governance by terror. Pp. 179–219 in Stohl, 1983.

Dye, Thomas R. 1983. Who owns America. *Social Science Quarterly* 64 (December): 862–70.

Eckland, Bruce K. 1967. Genetics and sociology. *American Sociological Review* 32 (April):173–94.

Edgerton, Robert B. 1985. *Rules, exceptions and social order*. Berkeley: University of California Press.

Edmondson, Ricca. 1984. *Rhetoric in sociology*. London: Macmillan.

Edwards, Richard. 1979. *Contested terrain*. New York: Basic Books.

Ehrlich, Eugen. 1936. *Fundamental principles of the sociology of law*. New York: Russell and Russell.

Ekeh, Peter P. 1974. *Social exchange theory*. Cambridge, Mass.: Harvard University Press.

Ellis, Lee. 1982. Genetics and criminal behavior. *Criminology* 20 (May):43–66.

———. 1977. The decline and fall of sociology, 1975–2000. *American Sociologist* 12 (May):56–66.

Emerson, Richard M. 1981. Social exchange theory. Pp. 30–65 in Morris Rosenberg and Ralph H. Turner (eds.), *Social psychology*. New York: Basic Books.

———. 1972. Exchange theory. Pp. 38–87 in Joseph Berger et al. (eds.), *Sociological theories in progress*, vol. 2. Boston: Houghton Mifflin.

———. 1969. Operant psychology and exchange theory. Pp. 379–405 in Burgess and Bushell, 1969.

———. 1962. Power-dependence relations. *American Sociological Review* 27 (February):31–41.

Emerson, Robert M., and Sheldon L. Messinger. 1977. The micro-politics of trouble. *Social Problems* 25 (December):121–34.

Empey, LaMar T. 1984. How is social order possible? *Sociological Perspectives* 27 (July):259–80.

Entwisle, Barbara, and William M. Mason. 1985. Multilevel effects of socioeconomic development and family planning programs on children ever born. *American Journal of Sociology* 91 (November):616–49.

Erickson, Maynard L., and Jack P. Gibbs. 1978. Objective and perceptual properties of legal punishment and the deterrence doctrine. *Social Problems* 25 (February):253–64.

Ervin, Delbert J. 1987. Interdependence and differentiation as components of the division of labor. *Social Science Quarterly* 68 (March):177–84.

Etzioni, Amitai. 1975. *A comparative analysis of complex organizations*, rev. ed. New York: Free Press.

———. 1968. Social control. Pp. 396–402 in Sills, 1968-XIV.

Evans-Pritchard, E. E. 1977. *Witchcraft, oracles and magic among the Azande.* Oxford, England: Clarendon Press.

Eve, Raymond A. 1986. Children's interpersonal tactics in effecting cooperation by peers and adults. Pp. 187–208 in Patricia A. Adler and Peter Adler (eds.), *Sociological studies in child development.* Greenwich, Conn.: JAI Press.

Ewen, Stuart. 1976. *Captains of consciousness.* New York: McGraw-Hill.

Fallding, Harold. 1963. Functional analysis in sociology. *American Sociological Review* 28 (February):5–13.

Fallows, James. 1986. The Japanese are different from you and me. *Atlantic* 258 (September):35–41.

Fararo, Thomas J., and John Skvoretz. 1986. E-state structuralism. *American Sociological Review* 51 (October):591–602.

Faris, Robert E. L., ed. 1964. *Handbook of modern sociology.* Chicago: Rand McNally.

Felson, Richard B. 1981. Self- and reflected appraisal among football players. *Social Psychology Quarterly* 44 (June):116–26.

Feree, Myra M., and Frederick D. Miller. 1985. Mobilization and meaning. *Sociological Inquiry* 55 (Winter):38–61.

Fernandez, Renate L. 1981. Comments on Tibetan polyandry. *American Anthropologist* 83 (December):896–97.

Field, G. Lowell, and John Higley. 1985. National elites and political stability. Pp. 1–44 in Moore, 1985.

———. 1980. *Elitism.* London: Routledge and Kegan Paul.

———. 1972. *Elites in developed societies.* Beverly Hills, Calif.: Sage.

Finer, S. E. 1966. Introduction. Pp. 1–91 in Pareto, 1966.

Fischer, Claude S. 1982a. *To dwell among friends.* Chicago: University of Chicago Press.

———. 1982b. What do we mean by 'friend'? *Social Network* 3 (April): 287–306.

——— et al. 1977. *Networks and places.* New York: Free Press.

Foa, Edna B., and Paul M. G. Emmelkamp, eds. 1983. *Failures in behavior therapy.* New York: Wiley.

Foa, Urich G. 1971. Interpersonal and economic resources. *Science* 171 (January 29):345–51.

Form, William H. 1972. Technology and social behavior of workers in four countries. *American Sociological Review* 37 (December):727–38.

Fogleman, Valerie M. 1987. Regulating science. *Environmental Law* 17 (Winter): 183–273.

Foss, Dennis C. 1977. *The value controversy in sociology.* San Francisco: Jossey-Bass.

Foucault, Michel. 1977. *Discipline and punish.* New York: Pantheon Books.

Fowler, Roger et al. 1979. *Language and control.* London: Routledge and Kegan Paul.

Frank, Jerome. 1930. *Law and the modern mind.* New York: Bretano's.

Frankel, Charles. 1982. The social sciences cannot be unified with biology. Pp. 45–52 in Wiegele, 1982.

Freedman, James O. 1978. *Crisis and legitimacy*. Cambridge, England: Cambridge University Press.

Freedman, Ronald. 1979. Theories of fertility decline. *Social Forces* 58 (September):1–17.

Freeman, Derek. 1980. Sociobiology. Pp. 198–219 in Montagu, 1980.

Freeman, Howard E. et al., eds. 1983. *Applied sociology*. San Francisco: Jossey-Bass.

Freeman, Linton C. 1984. Turning a profit from mathematics. *Journal of Mathematical Sociology* 10 (nos. 3–4):343–360.

Freidman, Lawrence M., and Stewart Macaulay. 1977. *Law and the behavioral sciences*, 2d ed. New York: Bobbs-Merrill.

Friedrichs, Robert W. 1970. *A sociology of sociology*. New York: Free Press.

Freitag, Peter J. 1983. The myth of corporate capture. *Social Problems* 30 (April): 480–91.

Freud, Sigmund. 1953–74. *The standard edition of the complete psychological works of Sigmund Freud*, 24 vols. London: Hogarth.

Freudenburg, William R. 1986. The density of acquaintanceship. *American Journal of Sociology* 92 (July):27–63.

Frisbie, W. Parker, and Clifford J. Clarke. 1979. Technology in evolutionary and ecological perspective. *Social Forces* 58 (December):591–613.

Fuller, Lon L. 1969. *The morality of law*, rev. ed. New Haven, Conn.: Yale University Press.

Fulop, Christina. 1981. *Advertising, competition and consumer behavior*. New York: Holt, Rinehart and Winston.

Gabe, Jonathan, and Susan Lipshitz-Phillips. 1984. Tranquilizers as social control? *Sociological Review* 32 (August):524–46.

Gamson, William A. et al. 1982. *Encounters with unjust authority*. Homewood, Ill.: Dorsey Press.

Garnsey, Elizabeth. 1981. The rediscovery of the division of labor. *Theory and Society* 10 (May):337–58.

Garfield, Sol L. 1984. Psychotherapy. Pp. 295–304 in Williams and Spitzer, 1984.

Garfinkel, Harold. 1967. *Studies in ethnomethodology*. Englewood Cliffs, N.J.: Prentice-Hall.

Gavison, Ruth. 1980. Privacy and the limits of law. *Yale Law Journal* 89 (January):421–71.

Geertz, Clifford. 1973. *The interpretation of cultures*. New York: Basic Books.

———. 1968. Religion. Pp. 398–406 in Sills, 1968-XIII.

Gellner, Ernest. 1985. Soviets against Wittfogel. *Theory and Society* 14 (May): 341–70.

Gendron, Bernard. 1977. *Technology and the human condition*. New York: St. Martin's Press.

Gerber, Jurg, and James F. Short, Jr. 1986. Publicity and the control of corporate behavior. *Deviant Behavior* 7 (no.3):195–216.

Gergen, Kenneth J. et al., eds. 1980. *Social exchange*. New York: Plenum.

Gibbons, Don C. 1982. *Society, crime, and criminal behavior*, 4th ed. Englewood Cliffs, N.J.: Prentice-Hall.

Gibbs, Jack P. 1986. Deterrance theory and research. Pp. 87–130 in Gary B. Melton (ed.), *The law as a behavioral instrument*. Lincoln: University of Nebraska Press.

———. 1985. The methodology of theory construction in criminology. Pp. 23–50 in Robert F. Meier (ed.), *Theoretical methods in criminology*. Beverly Hills, Calif.: Sage.

———, ed. 1982a. *Social control*. Beverly Hills, Calif.: Sage.

———. 1982b. Law as a means of social control. Pp. 83–113 in Gibbs, 1982a.

———. 1982c. Testing the theory of status integration and suicide rates. *American Sociological Review* 47 (April):227–37.

———. 1982d. Evidence of causation. *Current Perspectives in Social Theory* 3 (annual):93–127.

———. 1981. *Norms, deviance, and social control*. New York: Elsevier.

———. 1978. The death penalty, retribution and penal policy. *Journal of Criminal Law and Criminology* 69 (Fall):101–14.

———. 1975. *Crime, punishment, and deterrence*. New York: Elsevier.

———. 1972. *Sociological theory construction*. Hinsdale, Ill.: Dryden.

———. 1968. Definitions of law and empirical questions. *Law and Society Review* 2 (May):429–46.

———, and Harley L. Browning. 1966. The division of labor, technology, and the organization of production in twelve countries. *American Sociological Review* 31 (February):81–92.

———, and Walter T. Martin. 1959. Toward a theoretical system of human ecology. *Pacific Sociological Review* 2 (Spring):29–36.

Giddens, Anthony. 1984. *The constitution of society*. Berkeley: University of California Press.

———. 1981. *A contemporary critique of historical materialism*, vol. 1. Berkeley: University of California Press.

Gmelch, George. 1980. Baseball magic. Pp. 316–26 in Spradley and McCurdy, 1980.

Goffman, Erving. 1974. *Frame analysis*. Cambridge, Mass.: Harvard University Press.

———. 1971. *Relations in public*. New York: Basic Books.

———. 1969. *Strategic interaction*. Philadelphia: University of Pennsylvania Press.

———. 1967. *Interaction ritual*. Garden City, N.Y.: Anchor Books.

———. 1963. *Behavior in public places*. New York: Free Press.

———. 1961a. *Asylums*. Garden City, N.Y.: Anchor Books.

———. 1961b. *Encounters*. Indianapolis: Bobbs-Merrill.

Golding, Robert. 1982. Freud, psychoanalysis, and sociology. *British Journal of Sociology* 33 (December):545–62.

Goldstein, Melvyn C., and Cynthia M. Beall. 1982. Tibetan fraternal polyandry and sociobiology. *American Anthropologist* 84 (December):898–901.

Goldstone, Jack A. 1982. The comparative and historical study of revolutions. *Annual Review of Sociology* 8 (annual):187–207.

Goode, William J. 1978. *The celebration of heroes*. Berkeley: University of California Press.

———. 1973. *Explorations in social theory*. New York: Oxford University Press.

Goodenough, Ward H. 1970. *Description and comparison in cultural anthropology*. Chicago: Aldine.

Gorin, Zeev. 1980. Income inequality in the Marxist theory of development. *Comparative Social Research* 3 (annual):147–74.

Gould, Stephen J. 1980. Sociobiology and the theory of natural selection. Pp. 257–69 in Barlow and Silverberg, 1980.

Gouldner, Alvin W. 1985. *Against fragmentation*. New York: Oxford University Press.

————. 1973. *For sociology*. New York: Basic Books.

————. 1970. *The coming crisis of western sociology*. New York: Basic Books.

————. 1960. The norm of reciprocity. *American Sociological Review* 25 (April): 161–78.

Gove, Walter R. 1987. Sociobiology misses the mark. *American Sociologist* 18 (Fall):258–77.

———— and G. Russell Carpenter, eds. 1982. *The fundamental connection between nature and nurture*. Lexington, Mass.: D. C. Heath.

Grabosky, Peter N. 1984. The variability of punishment. Pp. 163–89 in Black, 1984a-I.

Grandjean, Burke D. 1974. The division of labor, technology, and education. *Social Science Quarterly* 55 (September):297–309.

Granovetter, Mark. 1983. The strength of weak ties. Pp. 201–33 in Collins, 1983.

Gray, Louis N. 1985. Observational and experiential effects in probability learning. *Social Psychology Quarterly* 48 (March):78–85.

Greene, Penelope J. 1978. Promiscuity, paternity, and culture. *American Ethnologist* 5 (February):151–59.

Greenhalgh, Susan, and John Bongaarts. 1987. Fertility policy in China. *Science* 235 (March 6):1167–72.

Greenspan, Stanley I., and George H. Pollock, eds. 1980. *The course of life*, 3 vols. Washington, D.C.: U.S. Government Printing Office.

Greenstein, Fred I. 1968. Political socialization. Pp. 551–55 in Sills, 1968-XIV.

Griffin, Larry J. et al. 1986. Capitalist resistance to the organization of labor before the New Deal. *American Sociological Review* 51 (April):147–67.

Griffith, W. I., and L. N. Gray. 1985. A note on the "social law of effect." *Social Forces* 63 (March):1030–37.

Gurr, Ted R. 1983. Some characteristics of political terrorism in the 1960s. Pp. 23–49 in Stohl, 1983.

Habermas, Jurgen. 1984. *The theory of communicative action*, vol. 1. Boston: Beacon Press.

Hadley, Trevor R., and Theodore Jacob. 1976. The measurement of family power. *Sociometry* 39 (December):384–95.

Hagan, John, and Celesta Albonetti. 1982. Race, class, and the perception of criminal injustice in America. *American Journal of Sociology* 88 (September): 329–55.

Halaby, Charles N. 1986. Worker attachment and workplace authority. *American Sociological Review* 51 (October):634–49.

Halfpenny, Peter. 1983. A refutation of historical materialism? *Social Science Information* 22 (no. 1):61–87.

Hallett, Jean-Pierre. 1965. *Congo kitabu*. New York: Fawcett.

Hallpike, C. R. 1977. *Bloodshed and vengeance in the Papuan mountains*. Oxford, England: Clarendon Press.

Hamblin, Robert L., and John H. Kunkel, eds. 1977. *Behavioral theory in sociology.* New Brunswick, N.J.: Transaction Books.

Hamblin, Robert L. et al. 1973. *A mathematical theory of social change.* New York: Wiley.

Hames, Raymond B. 1979. A comparison of the efficiencies of the shotgun and the bow in neotropical forest hunting. *Human Ecology* 7 (September): 219–52.

Hamilton, Gary G., and Nicole W. Biggart. 1985. Why people obey. *Sociological Perspectives* 28 (January):3–28.

Hammond, Dorthy. 1970. Magic. *American Anthropologist* 72 (December):1349–56.

Hampson, Sarah E. 1985. Attribution theory. P. 52 in Kuper and Kuper, 1985.

Handwerker, W. Penn, and Paul V. Crosbie. 1982. Sex and dominance. *American Anthropologist* 84 (March):97–104.

Hanisch, Ted. 1980. The idea of a macro job-killer. *Acta Sociologica* 23 (no. 4): 279–86.

Hannay, N. Bruce, and Robert E. McGinn. 1980. The anatomy of modern terminology. *Daedalus* 109 (Winter):25–53.

Hanneman, Robert A. 1980. Income inequality and economic development in Great Britain, Germany, and France: 1850 to 1970. *Comparative Social Research* 3 (annual):175–84.

Hargreaves, David J. 1985. Socialization. Pp. 775–76 in Kuper and Kuper, 1985.

Harlow, Ruth E. 1986. The EPA and biotechnology regulation. *Yale Law Journal* 95 (January):553–76.

Harris, Marvin. 1979. *Cultural materialism.* New York: Random House.

———. 1977. *Cannibals and kings.* New York: Random House.

———. 1964. *The nature of cultural things.* New York: Random House.

Hart, H. L. A. 1961. *The concept of law.* Oxford, England: Clarendon Press.

Hartung, John. 1982. Polygyny and inheritance of wealth. *Current Anthropology* 23 (February):1–8.

Hawkes, Kirsten. 1983. Kin selection and culture. *American Ethnologist* 10 (May):345–63.

Heath, Anthony. 1976. *Rational choice and social exchange.* London: Cambridge University Press.

Heilbroner, Robert L. 1983. The problem of value in the constitution of economic thought. *Social Research* 50 (Summer):253–77.

Heise, David R. 1979. *Understanding events.* New York: Cambridge University Press.

Hempel, Carl G. 1965. *Aspects of scientific explanation.* New York: Free Press.

———. 1959. The logic of functional analysis. Pp. 271–307 in Llewellyn Gross (ed.), *Symposium on sociological theory.* Evanston, Ill.: Row, Peterson.

Heritage, John, and David Greatbatch. 1986. Generating applause. *American Journal of Sociology* 92 (July):110–57.

Herman, Edward S. 1981. *Corporate control, corporate power.* London: Cambridge University Press.

Herron, William G., and Sheila Rouslin. 1982. *Issues in psychotherapy.* Bowie, Md.: Robert J. Brady.

Higgins, Joan. 1980. Social control theories of social policy. *Journal of Social Policy* 9 (January):1–23.

Higley, John et al. 1976. *Elite structure and ideology*. New York: Columbia University Press.

Hill, Stephen. 1981. *Competition and control at work*. Cambridge, Mass.: MIT Press.

Hirschi, Travis. 1969. *Causes of delinquency*. Berkeley: University of California Press.

Hobhouse, L. T. et al. 1930. *The material culture and social institutions of the simpler peoples*. London: Chapman and Hall.

Hoebel, E. Adamson. 1968. *The law of primitive man*. New York: Atheneum.

Hogan, Richard. 1985. The frontier as control. *Theory and Society* 14 (January): 35–51.

Hollander, Paul. 1982. Research on Marxist societies. *Annual Review of Sociology* 8 (annual):319–51.

Hollingsworth, Rogers. 1984. The snare of specialization. *Bulletin of the Atomic Scientists* 40 (June/July):34–37.

Holmes, Oliver Wendell. 1897. The path of the law. *Harvard Law Review* 10 (March): 457–78.

Homans, George C. 1975. What do we mean by social structure? Pp. 53–75 in Blau, 1975a.

———. 1974. *Social behavior*, rev. ed. New York: Harcourt, Brace, Jovanovich.

———. 1967. *The nature of social science*. New York: Harcourt, Brace and World.

———. 1964a. Contemporary theory in sociology. Pp. 951–77 in Faris, 1964.

———. 1964b. Bringing men back in. *American Sociological Review* 29 (December):809–18.

———. 1962. *Sentiments and activities*. New York: Free Press.

———. 1961. *Social behavior*, 1st ed. New York: Harcourt, Brace and World.

———. 1958. Social behavior as exchange. *American Journal of Sociology* 63 (May):597–606.

———. 1950. *The human group*. New York: Harcourt, Brace and World.

Houts, Marshall. 1972. *King's X*. New York: Morrow.

Huber, Joan. 1979. Comment. *Sociological Quarterly* 20 (Autumn):591–603.

Humphries, Drew, and David F. Greenberg. 1984. Social control and social formation. Pp. 171–208 in Black, 1984a-II.

Hyams, Nanci B. et al. 1982. Differential aspects of locus of control and attitudes toward death. *Social Behavior and Personality* 10 (no. 1):177–82.

Irons, William. 1980. Is Yomut social behavior adaptive? Pp. 417–63 in Barlow and Silverberg, 1980.

Isajiw, Wsevolod W. 1968. *Causation and functionalism in sociology*. New York: Schocken.

Itoh, Makoto. 1978. The formation of Marx's theory of crisis. *Science and Society* 42 (Summer):129–55.

Jackman, Mary R., and Robert W. Jackman. 1983. *Class awareness in the United States*. Berkeley: University of California Press.

Janowitz, Morris. 1975. Sociological theory and social control. *American Journal of Sociology* 81 (July):82–108.

Jencks, Christopher. 1987. Genes and crime. *New York Review of Books* 34 (August 17):33–41.

———. 1980. Heredity, environment, and public policy reconsidered. *American Sociological Review* 45 (October):723–36.

Johanson, Donald C. and Maitland A. Edey. 1981. *Lucy*. New York: Simon and Schuster.

————, and T. D. White. 1979. A systematic assessment of early African hominids. *Science* 203 (January):321–30.

Johnson, Harry M. 1985. Norms. P. 560 in Kuper and Kuper, 1985.

Johnson, Miriam M. 1982. Fathers and 'feminity' in daughters. *Sociology and Social Research* 67 (October):1–17.

Johnson, Weldon T. 1977. Exchange in perspective. Pp. 49–90 in Hamblin and Kunkel, 1977.

Jones, Harry W. 1969. *The efficacy of law*. Evanston, Ill.: Northwestern University Press.

Kang, Gay E. 1979. Exogamy and peace relations of social units. *Ethnology* 18 (January):85–99.

Katz, Daniel, and Robert L. Kahn. 1978. *The social psychology of organizations*, 2d ed. New York: Wiley.

Keenan, Donald C., and Paul H. Rubin. 1982. Criminal violations and civil violations. *Journal of Legal Studies* 11 (June):365–77.

Keller, Suzanne. 1983. Celebrities as a national elite. Pp. 3–14 in Czudnowski, 1983.

————. 1963. *Beyond the ruling class*. New York: Random House.

Kelsen, Hans. 1945. *General theory of law and state*. Cambridge, Mass.: Harvard University Press.

Kerbo, Harold R., and L. Richad D. Fave. 1983. Corporate linkage and control of the corporate economy. *Sociological Quarterly* 24 (Spring):201–18.

Keyfitz, Nathan. 1971. How birth control affects births. *Social Biology* 18 (June): 109–21.

Kiesler, Charles A. 1984. Psychotherapy research and top-down policy analysis. Pp. 360–66 in Williams and Spitzer, 1984.

King's College Sociobiology Group. 1982. *Current problems in sociobiology*. Cambridge, England: Cambridge University Press.

Kitahara, Michio. 1982. Menstrual taboos and the importance of hunting. *American Anthropologist* 84 (December):901–3.

Kitcher, Philip. 1985. *Vaulting ambition*. Cambridge, Mass.: MIT Press.

Klandermans, Bert. 1984. Mobilization and participation. *American Sociological Review* 49 (October):583–600.

Klausner, Samuel Z., ed. 1965. *The quest for self-control*. New York: Free Press.

Kluckhohn, Clyde, and Dorthea Leighton. 1962. *The Navaho*. Garden City, N.Y.: Natural History Library.

Knoke, David, and James H. Kuklinski. 1982. *Network analysis*. Beverly Hills, Calif.: Sage.

Koepping, Klaus-Peter. 1983. The limitations of network analysis for the study of value systems. *Sociologus* 33 (no. 2):97–130.

Kotowski, Christopher M. 1984. Revolution. Pp. 403–51 in Sartori, 1984.

Krasner, Leonard. 1982. Behavior modification and social control. Pp. 115–32 in Gibbs, 1982a.

Krislov, Samuel. 1982. The politics of control and the control of politics. Pp. 57–81 in Gibbs, 1982a.

Kuhn, Alfred and Robert D. Beam. 1982. *The logic of organization*. San Francisco: Jossey-Bass.

Kuhn, Thomas S. 1970a. Reflections on my critics. Pp. 231–78 in Lakatos and Musgrave, 1970.

———. 1970b. *The structure of scientific revolutions*, 2d ed. Chicago: University of Chicago Press.

Kunkel, John H. 1975. *Behavior, social problems, and change*. Englewood Cliffs, N.J.: Prentice-Hall.

Kuper, Adam, and Jessica Kuper, eds. 1985. *The social science encyclopedia*. London: Routledge and Kegan Paul.

Kurland, Jeffrey A. 1979. Paternity, mother's brother, and human sociality. Pp. 145–80 in Chagnon and Irons, 1979.

Lacy, Michael G. 1985. Apparent and genuine affluence. *Sociological Perspectives* 28 (April):117–43.

Laibman, David. 1984. Modes of production and theories of transition. *Science and Society* 48 (Fall):257–74.

Lakatos, Imre, and Alan Musgrave, eds. 1970. *Criticism and the growth of knowledge*. London: Cambridge University Press.

Lake, Laura M. 1982. *Environmental regulation*. New York: Praeger.

Lamb, Michael E. et al., eds. 1979. *Social interaction analysis*. Madison: University of Wisconsin Press.

Landes, David S. 1986. To have and have not. *New York Review of Books* 33 (May 29):46–49.

———. 1983. *Revolution in time*. Cambridge, Mass.: Harvard University Press.

———. 1969. *The unbound Prometheus*. London: Cambridge University Press.

Lane, Jan Erik, and Hans Stenlund. 1984. Power. Pp. 315–402 in Sartori, 1984.

Langton, John. 1979. Darwinism and the behavioral theory of sociocultural evolution. *American Journal of Sociology* 85 (September):288–309.

Laqueur, Walter. 1977. *Terrorism*. Boston, Mass.: Little, Brown.

Laumann, Edward O. et al. 1983. The boundary specification problem in network analysis. Pp. 18–34 in Ronald S. Burt and Michael J. Minor (eds.), *Applied network analysis*. Beverly Hills, Calif.: Sage.

———, and Franz U. Pappi. 1976. *Networks of collective action*. New York: Academic Press.

Lavrkas, Paul J., and Dan A. Lewis. 1980. The conceptualization and measurement of citizens' crime prevention behavior. *Journal of Research in Crime and Delinquency* 17 (July):254–72.

Leakey, Richard E. 1982. *Human origins*. New York: Dutton.

———, and Roger Lewin. 1978. *People of the lake*. Garden City, N.Y.: Anchor Press/ Doubleday.

Leavitt, Gregory C. 1986. Ideology and the materialist model of general evolution. *Social Forces* 65 (December):525–53.

Lebow, Jay L. 1983. Client satisfaction with mental health treatment. *Evaluation Review* 7 (December):729–52.

Lebowitz, Michael A. 1977–78. Capital and the production of needs. *Science and Society* 41 (Winter):430–47.

Lefcourt, Herbert M. 1984. New directions in research with the locus of control construct. *Psychological Studies* 29 (January):107–11.

Lefebvre, Henri. 1968. *Dialectical materialism*. London: Jonathan Cape.

Lemert, Edwin M. 1972. *Human deviance, social problems, and social control*, 2d ed. Englewood Cliffs, N.J.: Prentice-Hall.

Lempert, Richard, and Joseph Sanders. 1986. *An invitation to law and social science*. New York: Longman.

Lenski, Gerhard E. 1975. Social structure in evolutionary perspective. Pp. 135–53 in Blau, 1975a.

Lenski, Gerhard, and Jean Lenski. 1987. *Human societies*, 5th ed. New York: McGraw-Hill.

———. 1974. *Human societies*, 2d ed. New York: McGraw-Hill.

Lester, David. 1984. *Gun control*. Springfield, Ill.: Charles C. Thomas.

Levinson, David. 1979. Population density in cross-cultural perspective. *American Ethnologist* 6 (November):742–51.

Levi-Strauss, Claude. 1969. *The elementary structures of kinship*. Boston: Beacon Press.

Levy, Howard S. 1966. *Chinese footbinding*. New York: Walter Rawls.

Levy, Marion J., Jr. 1968. Functional analysis. Pp. 21–29 in Sills, 1968-VI.

Levy, Sheldon G. 1969. A 150-year study of political violence in the United States. Pp. 84–100 in Hugh D. Graham and Ted R. Gurr (eds.), *The history of violence in America*. New York: Praeger.

Lewontin, Richard C. 1977. Caricature of Darwinism. *Nature* 266 (March):283–84.

——— et al. 1984. *Not in our genes*. New York: Pantheon Books.

Lieberson, Jonathan. 1986. Too many people? *New York Review of Books* 33 (June 26):36–42.

Liebow, Elliot. 1967. *Tally's corner*. Boston: Little, Brown.

Lipset, Seymour M. 1985. *Consensus and conflict*. New Brunswick, N.J.: Transaction Books.

Lipton, Douglas et al. 1975. *The effectiveness of correctional treatment*. New York: Praeger.

Livingstone, Frank B. 1980. Culture causes of genetic change. Pp. 307–29 in Barlow and Silverberg, 1980.

Llewellyn, K. N. 1960. *The bramble bush*. New York: Oceana.

———. 1934. The Constitution as an institution. *Columbia Law Review* 34 (January):1–40.

Long, Theodore E., and Jeffrey K. Hadden. 1985. A reconception of socialization. *Sociological Theory* 3 (Spring):39–49.

Lopreato, Joseph. 1984. *Human nature and biocultural evolution*. Boston: Allen and Unwin.

Lovell, David W. 1984. *From Marx to Lenin*. Cambridge, England: Cambridge University Press.

Luckenbill, David F. 1982. Compliance under threat of severe punishment. *Social Forces* 60 (March):811–25.

Lumley, Frederick E. 1925. *Means of social control*. New York: Century.

Lumsden, Charles J. and Edward O. Wilson. 1981. *Genes, mind, and culture*. Cambridge, Mass.: Harvard University Press.

Macaulay, Stewart. 1963. Non-contractual relations in business. *American Sociological Review* 28 (February):55–67.

Mahler, Vincent A. 1980. *Dependency approaches to international political economy.* New York: Columbia University Press.

Malinowski, Bronislaw. 1959. *Crime and custom in savage society.* Paterson, N.J.: Littlefield, Adams.

———. 1955. *Sex and repression in savage society.* New York: Meridian Books.

———. 1948. *Magic, science and religion and other essays.* Boston: Beacon Press.

———. 1944. *A scientific theory of culture, and other essays.* Chapel Hill: University of North Carolina Press.

———. 1926. Anthropology. Pp. 131–40 in *Encyclopedia Britannica*, Supplementary Volume 1. London: Encyclopedia Britannica.

Mandel, Michael. 1986. Marxism and the rule of law. *University of New Brunswick Law Journal* 35 (annual):7–33.

Manderscheid, Ronald W. et al. 1982. A stochastic model of relational control in dyadic interaction. *American Sociological Review* 47 (February) 62–75.

Marcus, George E., ed. 1983a. *Elites.* Albuquerque: University of New Mexico Press.

———. 1983b. Elite as a concept, theory, and research tradition. Pp. 7–27 in Marcus, 1983a.

Markham, William T. et al. 1984. Measuring organizational control. *Human Relations* 37 (April):263–94.

Markoff, John, and Gilbert Shapiro. 1985. Consensus and conflict at the outset of revolution. *American Journal of Sociology* 91 (July):28–53.

Marsden, Peter V. 1987. Core discussion networks of Americans. *American Sociological Review* 52 (February):122–31.

Marsh, Robert M. 1971. The explanation of occupational prestige hierarchies. *Social Forces* 50 (December):214–22.

Martindale, Don. 1979. Ideologies, paradigms, and theories. Pp. 7–24 in Snizek et al., 1979.

———, ed. 1965. *Functionalism in the social sciences.* Philadelphia: American Academy of Political and Social Sciences, Monograph No. 5.

Marx, Gary T. 1974. Thoughts on a neglected category of social movement participants. *American Journal of Sociology* 80 (September):402–42.

Marx, Karl (and Frederick Engels). 1975. *Collected works.* New York: International Publishers.

———. 1963. *The poverty of philosophy.* New York: International Publishers.

———. 1926. *The eighteenth brumaire of Louis Bonaparte.* London: George Allen and Unwin.

———. 1906, 1907, 1909. *Capital*, 3 vols.: 1906-I, 1907-II, 1909- III. Chicago: Kerr.

——— and Friedrich Engels. 1947. *The German ideology*, Parts 1 and 3. New York: International Publishers.

Masterman, Margaret. 1970. The nature of a paradigm. Pp. 59–89 in Lakatos and Musgrave, 1970.

Matson, Johnny L., and Thomas M. DiLorenzo. 1984. *Punishment and its alternatives.* New York: Springer.

Mayhew, Bruce H. 1984. Baseline models of sociological phenomena. *Journal of Mathematical Sociology* 9 (no. 4):259–81.

———. 1981. Structuralism versus individualism: Part II. *Social Forces* 59 (March): 627–48.

———. 1980. Structuralism versus individualism: Part I. *Social Forces* 59 (December):335–75.

Maynard, Douglas W., and Thomas P. Wilson. 1980. On the reification of social structure. *Current Perspectives in Social Theory* 1 (annual):287–322.

Maze, J. R. 1983. *The meaning of behavior*. London: George Allen and Unwin.

Mazur, Allan. 1978. Biological explanation in sociology. *Sociological Quarterly* 19 (Autumn):604–13.

McAdam, Doug. 1983. Tactical innovation and the pace of insurgency. *American Sociological Review* 48 (December):735–54.

McDonald, Neil A. 1965. *Politics*. New Brunswick, N.J.: Rutgers University Press.

McFarland, Andrew S. 1969. *Power and leadership in pluralist systems*. Stanford, Calif.: Stanford University Press.

McGuire, Thomas G. 1981. *Financing psychotherapy*. Cambridge, Mass.: Ballinger.

McHugh, Peter. 1968. *Defining the situation*. Indianapolis: Bobbs-Merrill.

McQuarie, Donald. 1977–78. A further comment on Karl Popper and Marxian laws. *Science and Society* 41 (Winter):477–84.

———, and Martin Murray. 1984. Conflict theory. *Current Perspectives in Social Theory* 15 (annual):201–23.

Mehta, Surinder K. 1964. Some demographic and economic correlates of primate cities. *Demography* 1 (no. 1) 136–47.

Meisel, James H., ed. 1965. *Pareto and Mosca*. Englewood Cliffs, N.J.: Prentice-Hall.

Mele, Alfred R. 1985. Self-control, action, and belief. *American Philosophical Quarterly* 22 (April):169–75.

Merry, Sally E. 1984. Rethinking gossip and scandal. Pp. 271–302 in Black, 1984a-I.

Merton, Robert K. 1975. Structural analysis in sociology. Pp. 21–52 in Blau, 1975a.

———. 1957. *Social theory and social structure*, rev. ed. New York: Free Press.

Messner, Steven F. 1982. Poverty, inequality, and the urban homicide rate. *Criminology* 20 (May):103–14.

———, and Kenneth Tardiff. 1986. Economic inequality and levels of homicide. *Criminology* 24 (May):297–317.

Michels, Robert. 1959. *Political parties*. New York: Dover.

Michener, H. Andrew et al. 1977. Social exchange. *American Sociological Review* 42 (June):522–35.

Micklin, Michael, and Harvey M. Choldin, eds. 1984. *Sociological Human Ecology*. Boulder, Colo.: Westview.

Midgley, Mary. 1980. Gene-juggling. Pp. 108–34 in Montagu, 1980.

Milgram, Stanley. 1974. *Obedience to authority*. New York: Harper and Row.

Mills, C. Wright. 1959a. *The sociological imagination*. New York: Oxford University Press.

———. 1959b. *The power elite*. New York: Oxford University Press.

Milner, Murray, Jr. 1987. Theories of inequality. *Social Forces* 65 (June):1053–89.

Mirkovic, Damir. 1980. *Dialectic and sociological thought*. Ontario: Diliton.

Mirowsky, John, and Catherine E. Ross. 1983. Paranoia and the structure of powerlessness. *American Sociological Review* 48 (April):228–39.

Mitchell, Jack N. 1978. *Social exchange, dramaturgy and ethnomethodology.* New York: Elsevier.

Mizruchi, Ephraim H. 1983. *Regulating society.* New York: Free Press.

Molotch, Harvey L., and Deirdre Boden. 1985. Talking social structure. *American Sociological Review* 50 (June):273–88.

Montagu, Ashley, ed. 1980. *Sociobiology examined.* New York: Oxford University Press.

Moore, Gwen, ed. 1985. *Studies of the structure of national elite groups* (vol. 1 of *Research in Politics and Society*). Greenwich, Conn.: JAI Press.

Morgan, Lewis H. 1964. *Ancient society.* Cambridge, Mass.: Harvard University Press.

Morris, Norval. 1966. Impediments of penal reform. *University of Chicago Law Review* 33 (Summer):627–56.

Morris, Richard. 1983. *Evolution and human nature.* New York: Seaview/Putnam.

Morris, William, ed. 1969. *The American heritage dictionary of the English language.* Boston: Houghton Mifflin.

Mortimer, Jeylan T., and Roberta G. Simmons. 1978. Adult socialization. *Annual Review of Sociology* 4 (annual):421–54.

Mount, Ferdinand. 1982. *The subversive family.* London: Jonathan Cape.

Mouzelis, Nicos. 1984. On the crisis of Marxist theory. *British Journal of Sociology* 35 (March):112–21.

Mukerji, Chandra. 1983. *From graven images.* New York: Columbia University Press.

Mulkay, M. J. 1971. *Functionalism, exchange and theoretical strategy.* New York: Schocken.

Nagel, Ernest. 1961. *The structure of science.* New York: Harcourt, Brace & World.
———. 1956. *Logic without metaphysics.* New York: Free Press.

Nagel, Jack H. 1975. *The descriptive analysis of power.* New Haven, Conn.: Yale University Press.

Nardi, Bonnie A. 1981. Modes of explanation in anthropological population theory. *American Anthropologist* 83 (March):28–56.

National Center for Social Statistics. 1977. *Adoptions in 1975* (Report E–10[1975], DHEW Publication no. [SRS] 77–03259). Washington, D.C.: Department of Health, Education, and Welfare.

Needham, Rodney. 1962. *Structure and sentiment.* Chicago: University of Chicago Press.

Nettler, Gwynn. 1980. Sociologists as advocate. *Canadian Journal of Sociology* 5 (Winter):31–53.

Nichols, James L. 1982. *Effectiveness and efficiency of safety belt and child restraint programs.* Springfield, Va.: National Technical Information Service.

Nisbet, Robert A. 1969. Comment on Smelser's paper. Pp. 30–35 in Bierstedt, 1969.
———, and Robert G. Perrin. 1977. *The social bond,* 2d ed. New York: Knopf.

Nolan, Patrick D. 1983. Status in the world economy and national structure and development. *International Journal of Comparative Sociology* 24 (nos. 1–2): 109–20.

————. 1979. Size and administrative intensity in nations. *American Sociological Review* 44 (February):110–25.

Noll, Roger G., ed. 1985. *Regulatory policy and the social sciences*. Berkeley: University of California Press.

O'Brien, Connor C. 1986. Thinking about terrorism. *Atlantic* 257 (June):62–66.

O'Donald, Peter. 1982. The concept of fitness in population genetics and sociobiology. Pp. 64–85 in King's College Sociobiology Group, 1982.

Ogburn, William F. 1964. *On culture and social change*. Chicago: University of Chicago Press.

Olivecrona, Karl. 1971. *Law as fact*, 2d ed. London: Stevens.

Oliver, Ivan. 1983. The 'old' and the 'new' hermeneutic in sociological theory. *British Journal of Sociology* 34 (December):519–53.

Oppenheim, Felix E. 1961. *Dimensions of freedom*. New York: St. Martin's Press.

Oswalt, Wendell H. 1976. *An anthropological analysis of food-getting technology*. New York: Wiley.

Parens, Henri. 1980. Psychic development during the second and third years of life. Pp. 459–500 in Greenspan and Pollock, 1980–1.

Pareto, Vilfredo. 1968. *The rise and fall of the elites*. Totowa, N.J.: Bedminster Press.

————. 1966. *Sociological writings*. New York: Praeger.

————. 1935. *The mind and society*, 4 vols., continuous pagination. New York: Harcourt, Brace.

Parkin, Frank. 1979. *Marxism and class theory*. New York: Columbia University Press.

Parsons, Talcott. 1980. The law and social control. Pp. 60–68 in William M. Evan (ed.), *The sociology of law*. New York: Free Press.

————. 1965. Pareto's central analytical scheme. Pp. 71–88 in Meisel, 1965.

————. 1951. *The social system*. New York: Free Press.

————, and Edward A. Shils, eds. 1962. *Toward a general theory of action*. New York: Harper and Row.

Paternoster, Raymond, and Leeann Iovanni. 1986. The deterrent effect of perceived severity. *Social Forces* 64 (March):751–77.

Patterson, Edwin W. 1953. *Jurisprudence*. Brooklyn: Foundation Press.

Pepinsky, Harold E. 1980. *Crime control strategies*. New York: Oxford University Press.

Perrow, Charles. 1984. *Normal accidents*. New York: Basic Books.

Pfeffer, Jeffrey, and Gerald R. Salanick. 1978. *The external control of organizations*. New York: Harper and Row.

Phillips, Llad, and Harold L. Votey, Jr. 1981. *The economics of crime control*. Beverly Hills, Calif.: Sage.

Pike, Kenneth. 1967. *Language in relation to a unified theory of the structure of human behavior*, 2d ed. The Hague: Mouton.

Piliavin, Irving et al. 1986. Crime, deterrence, and rational choice. *American Sociological Review* 51 (February):101–19.

Pimentel, David. 1980. *Food, energy and the future of society*. Boulder: Colorado Associated University Press.

————, and Marcia Pimentel. 1979. *Food, energy and society*. New York: Wiley.

Pitcher, Brian L., and Sung Young Hong. 1986. Older men's perceptions of personal control. *Sociological Perspectives* 29 (July):397–419.

Pitts, Jesse R. 1968. Social control. Pp. 381–96 in Sills, 1968-XIV.

Piven, Frances F., and Richard A. Cloward. 1971. *Regulating the poor.* New York: Random House.

Plekhanov, G. V. 1947. *In defence of materialism.* London: Lawrence and Wishart.

——. 1940. *Essays in historical materialism.* New York: International Publishers.

Polhemus, Ted, and Lynn Procter. 1978. *Fashion and anti-fashion.* London: Thames and Hudson.

Pool, Ithiel de Sola. 1983. *Technologies of freedom.* Cambridge, Mass.: Harvard University Press.

Pope, Harrison G. 1985. Psychopharmacology. Pp. 670–71 in Kuper and Kuper, 1985.

Pope, Liston. 1942. *Millhands and preachers.* New Haven, Conn.: Yale University Press.

Pope, Whitney, and Barclay D. Johnson. 1983. Inside organic solidarity. *American Sociological Review* 48 (October):681–92.

Popper, K. R. 1966. *The open society and its enemies,* vol. 2, 5th ed. London: Routledge and Kegan Paul.

——. 1957. *The poverty of historicism.* Boston: Beacon Press.

——. 1940. What is dialectic? *Mind* 49 (October):403–26.

Porpora, Douglas V. 1983. On the prospects for a nomothetic theory of social structure. *Journal for the Theory of Social Behavior* 13 (October):243–64.

Poulantzas, Nicos. 1975. *Classes in contemporary capitalism.* London: New Left Books.

Power, Richard. 1984. Mutual intention. *Journal for the Theory of Social Behavior* 14 (March):85–102.

Pratt, William D. et al. 1984. Understanding U.S. fertility. *Population Bulletin* 39 (December):1–42.

Psathas, George, ed. 1973. *Phenomenological sociology.* New York: Wiley.

Punch, Maurice, ed. 1983. *Control in the police organization.* Cambridge, Mass.: MIT Press.

Quadagno, Jill S. 1984. Welfare capitalism and the Social Security Act of 1935. *American Sociological Review* 49 (October):632–47.

Quinney, Richard. 1976. Book review. *Contemporary Sociology* 5 (July):414–18.

Rabin, Robert L. 1979. *Perspectives on the administrative process.* Boston: Little, Brown.

Ragin, Charles. 1983. Theory and method in the study of dependency and international inequality. *International Journal of Comparative Sociology* 24 (nos. 1–2): 121–36.

—— et al. 1982. Major labor disputes in Britain, 1902–1938. *American Sociological Review* 47 (April):238–52.

Rawls, John. 1971. *A theory of justice.* Cambridge, Mass.: Harvard University Press.

Reuijl, Jan C. 1982. *On the determination of advertising effectiveness.* Boston: Kluwer-Nijhoff.

Richardson, Genevra. 1987. Strict liability for regulatory crime. *Criminal Law Review* 1987 (May):295–306.

Richter, Maurice N., Jr. 1982. *Technology and social complexity*. Albany: State University of New York Press.

Ridgeway, Cecilia, and Joseph Berger. 1986. Expectations, legitimation, and dominance behavior in task groups. *American Sociological Review* 51 (October): 603–17.

Ridley, Jasper. 1984. *Henry VIII*. London: Constable.

Ritzer, George. 1979. Toward an integrated sociological paradigm. Pp. 25–46 in Snizek, 1979.

———. 1975. *Sociology*. Boston: Allyn and Bacon.

Rock, Paul. 1973. *Making people pay*. London: Routledge and Kegan Paul.

Rohner, Ronald P., and Evelyn C. Rohner. 1981. Parental acceptance-rejection and parental control. *Ethnology* 20 (July):245–60.

Roosevelt, Franklin D. 1946. *Nothing to fear*. Boston: Houghton Mifflin.

Rosenberg, Alexander. 1980. *Sociobiology and the preemption of social science*. Baltimore: Johns Hopkins University Press.

Rosenthal, Uriel. 1983. Welfare state or state of welfare? *Comparative Social Research* 6 (annual):279–97.

Ross, E. A. 1901. *Social control*. New York: Macmillan.

Rossi, Ino, ed. 1982. *Structural sociology*. New York: Columbia University Press.

Rossi, Peter H. 1980. The presidential address: the challenge and opportunities of applied social research. *American Sociological Review* 45 (December): 889–904.

Rothbaum, Fred et al. 1982. Changing the world and changing the self. *Journal of Personality and Social Psychology* 42 (January):5–37.

Rothschild-Whitt, Joyce. 1979. The collectivist organization. *American Sociological Review* 44 (August):509–27.

Ruse, Michael. 1979. *Sociobiology*. Dodrecht, Holland: D. Reidel.

Russell, Bertrand. 1938. *Power*. New York: Norton.

Russell, D. E. H. 1974. *Rebellion, revolution, and armed forces*. New York: Academic Press.

Sahlins, Marshall. 1976. *The use and abuse of biology*. Ann Arbor: University of Michigan Press.

———. 1972. *Stone age economics*. Chicago: Aldine-Atherton.

———. 1965. On the sociology of primitive exchange. Pp. 139–236 in Michael Banton (ed.), *The relevance of models for social anthropology*. London: Tavistock.

Sankowski, Edward. 1980. Some problems about determinism and freedom. *American Philosophical Quarterly* 17 (October):291–99.

Sarat, Austin. 1976. Alternatives in dispute processing. *Law and Society Review* 10 (Spring):339–75.

Sartori, Giovanne, ed. 1984. *Social science concepts*. Beverly Hills, Calif.: Sage.

Scheff, Thomas J. 1984. *Being mentally ill*, 2d ed. New York: Aldine.

Schein, Edgar H. 1956. The Chinese indoctrination program for prisoners of war. *Psychiatry* 19 (May):149–72.

Schelling, Thomas C. 1984. *Choice and consequence*. Cambridge, Mass.: Harvard University Press.

Schneider, Louis. 1975. *The sociological way of looking at the world*. New York: McGraw-Hill.

Schrag, Clarence. 1982. Book review. *Contemporary Sociology* 11 (July):414–16.

Schudson, Michael. 1984. *Advertising, the uneasy persuasion*. New York: Basic Books.

Schuman, Howard et al. 1986. The perceived threat of nuclear war, salience, and open questions. *Public Opinion Quarterly* 50 (Winter):519–36.

Schutz, Alfred. 1970. The problem of rationality in the social world. Pp. 89–14 in Dorthy Emmet and Alasdair MacIntyre (eds.), *Sociological theory and philosophical analysis*. New York: Macmillan.

———. 1967. *The phenomenology of the social world*. Evanston, Ill.: Northwestern University Press.

Schweitzer, Arthur. 1984. *The age of charisma*. Chicago: Nelson-Hall.

Sciulli, David. 1986. Voluntaristic action. *American Sociological Review* 51 (December):743–66.

Scott, John. 1986. *Capitalist property and financial power*. Brighton, England: Wheatsheaf.

Scott, John F. 1971. *Internalization of norms*. Englewood Cliffs, N.J.: Prentice-Hall.

Scott, W. Richard. 1987. *Organizations*, 2d ed. Englewood Cliffs, N.J.: Prentice-Hall.

Searle, John R. 1983. *Intentionality*. Cambridge, England: Cambridge University Press.

Secher, H. P. 1962. Introduction. Pp. 7–23 in Weber, 1962.

Seeman, Melvin. 1983. Alienation motifs in contemporary theorizing. *Social Psychology Quarterly* 46 (September):171–84.

———, and Teresa E. Seeman. 1983. Health behavior and personal autonomy. *Journal of Health and Social Behavior* 24 (June):144–60.

Segaller, Stephen. 1987. *Invisible armies*. New York: Harcourt Brace Jovanovich.

Shatz, Marshall. 1980. *Soviet dissent in historical perspective*. London: Cambridge University Press.

Shaw, William H. 1978. *Marx's theory of history*. Stanford, Calif.: Stanford University Press.

Sheleff, Leon S. 1975. From restitutive law to repressive law. *Archives Europeennes de Sociologie* 16 (no. 1):16–45.

Shepher, Joseph. 1983. *Incest*. New York: Academic Press.

Sherman, Lawrence W., and Richard A. Berk. 1984. The specific deterrent effects of arrest for domestic assault. *American Sociological Review* 49 (April):261–72.

Shils, Edward, and Michael Young. 1953. The meaning of the coronation. *Sociological Review* 1 (December):63–81.

Sieber, Sam D. 1981. *Fatal remedies*. New York: Plenum.

Silk, Joan B. 1980. Adoption and kinship in Oceania. *American Anthropologist* 82 (December):799–820.

Sills, David L., ed. 1968. *International encyclopedia of the social sciences*, 17 volumes. New York: Macmillan.

Silverman, Martin A. 1980. The first year after birth. Pp. 147–75 in Greenspan and Pollock, 1980-I.

Simmel, Georg. 1978. *The philosophy of money*. London: Routledge and Kegan Paul.

———. 1950. *The sociology of Georg Simmel*. New York: Free Press.

Simon, Julian L., and Herman Kahn. 1984. *The resourceful earth.* New York: B. Blackwell.

Simpson, Richard L. 1985. Social control of occupations and work. *Annual Review of Sociology* 11 (annual):415–36.

Sites, Paul. 1975. *Control and constraint.* New York: Macmillan.

———. 1973. *Control.* New York: Dunellen.

Skinner, B. F. 1983. *A matter of consequences.* New York: Knopf.

———. 1978. *Reflections on behaviorism and society.* Englewood Cliffs, N.J.: Prentice-Hall.

———. 1974. *About behaviorism.* New York: Knopf.

———. 1971. *Beyond freedom and dignity.* New York: Knopf.

Skocpol, Theda. 1980. Political response to capitalist crisis. *Politics and Society* 10 (no. 2):155–201.

———. 1979. *States and social revolution.* London: Cambridge University Press.

Skogan, Wesley G. 1987. The impact of victimization fear. *Crime and Delinquency* 33 (January):135–54.

———, and Michael G. Maxfield. 1981. *Coping with crime.* Beverly Hills, Calif.: Sage.

Smelser, Neil J. 1969. The optimum scope of sociology. Pp. 1–21 in Bierstedt, 1969.

Smelt, Simon. 1980. Money's place in society. *British Journal of Sociology* 31 (June):204–23.

Smith, A. Emerson. 1983. Consumer and advertising research. Pp. 189–99 in Howard A. Freeman et al. (eds.), *Applied sociology.* San Francisco: Jossey-Bass.

Smith, Adam. 1952. *An inquiry into the nature and causes of the wealth of nations.* Chicago: William Benton.

Smith, J. Maynard. 1982. The evolution of social behavior. Pp. 29–44 in King's College Sociobiology Group, 1982.

Snizek, William E. et al., eds. 1979. *Contemporary issues in theory and research.* Westport, Conn.: Greenwood Press.

Sorokin, Pitirim A. 1975. *Hunger as a factor in human affairs.* Gainesville: University Presses of Florida.

———. 1947. *Society, culture, and personality.* New York: Harper.

———. 1937. *Social and cultural dynamics,* vol. 2. New York: American Book Co.

South, Scott J., and Steven F. Messner. 1986. Structural determinants of intergroup association. *American Journal of Sociology* 91 (May):1409–30.

Spaeth, Joe L. 1985. Job power and earnings. *American Sociological Review* 50 (October):603–17.

Spector, Paul E. 1986. Perceived control by employees. *Human Relations* 39 (November):1005–16.

Spiro, Melford E. 1982. *Oedipus in the Trobriands.* Chicago: University of Chicago Press.

Spradley, James P., and David W. McCurdy, eds. 1980. *Conformity and conflict,* 4th ed. Boston: Little, Brown.

St.Aubyn, Giles. 1983. *The year of three kings: 1483.* New York: Atheneum.

Stableford, Brian M. 1984. *Future man.* New York: Crown.

Stafford, Mark C. et al. 1986. Modeling the deterrent effects of punishment. *Social Psychology Quarterly* 49 (December):338–47.

Staples, William G. 1987. Technology, control, and the social organization of work at a British hardware firm, 1791–1891. *American Journal of Sociology* 93 (July):62–88.

Stehr, Nico, and Volker Meja, eds. 1984. *Society and knowledge.* New Brunswick, N.J.: Transaction Books.

Stein, Leonard I. 1967. The doctor-nurse game. *Archives of General Psychiatry* 16 (June):699–703.

Steward, Julian H. 1955. *Theory of culture change.* Urbana: University of Illinois Press.

Stinchcombe, Arthur L. 1983. *Economic sociology.* New York: Academic Press.

———. 1965. Social structure and organizations. Pp. 142–93 in James G. March (ed.), *Handbook of organizations.* Chicago: Rand McNally.

Stohl, Michael, ed. 1983. *The politics of terrorism,* 2d ed. New York: Marcel Dekker.

Stoller, Robert J. 1980. A different view of oedipal conflict. Pp. 589–602 in Greenspan and Pollock, 1980-I.

Stone, Alan. 1982. *Regulation and its alternatives.* Washington, D.C.: Congressional Quarterly Press.

Strube, Michael J., and Carol Werner. 1985. Relinquishment of control and Type A behavior pattern. *Journal of Personality and Social Psychology* 48 (March): 688–701.

Strupp, Hans H. 1984. The Vanderbilt psychotherapy research project. Pp. 235–45 in Williams and Spitzer, 1984.

Stryker, Sheldon. 1981. Symbolic interactionism. Pp. 3–29 in Morris Rosenberg and Ralph H. Turner (eds.), *Social psychology.* New York: Basic Books.

Sumner, William G. 1906. *Folkways.* New York: Dover.

Suppe, Frederick, ed. 1977. *The structure of scientific theories,* 2d ed. Urbana: University of Illinois Press.

Susskind, Charles. 1973. *Understanding technology.* Baltimore: Johns Hopkins University Press.

Sutherland, Edwin H., and Donald R. Cressey. 1974. *Criminology,* 9th ed. Philadelphia: Lippincott.

Suttles, Gerald D., and Mayer N. Zald, eds. 1985. *The challenge of social control.* Norwood, N.J.: Ablex.

Swann, William B. et al. 1981. Curiosity and control. *Journal of Personality and Social Psychology* 40 (April):635–42.

Swanson, Guy E. 1960. *The birth of the gods.* Ann Arbor: University of Michigan Press.

Swidler, Ann. 1986. Culture in action. *American Sociological Review* 51 (April): 273–86.

Szasz, Thomas S. 1974. *The myth of mental illness,* rev. ed. New York: Harper and Row.

Szymanski, Albert. 1983. *Class structure.* New York: Praeger.

Tallman, Irving. 1984. Book review. *Social Forces* 62 (June):1121–22.

Tannenbaum, Arnold S. et al. 1974. *Hierarchy in organizations.* San Francisco: Jossey-Bass.

Tanner, Nancy M. 1981. *On becoming human.* Cambridge, England: Cambridge University Press.

————, and Adrienne Zihlman. 1976. Women in evolution, Part I. *Signs* 1 (Spring):585–608.

Thomas, William I., and Dorthy S. Thomas. 1928. *The child in America.* New York: Knopf.

Thompson, Fred, and L. R. Jones. 1982. *Regulatory policies and practices.* New York: Praeger.

Thoresen, Carl E., and Michael J. Mahoney. 1974. *Behavioral self-control.* New York: Holt, Rinehart and Winston.

Tisdall, Paul. 1981. *In search of human origins.* Toronto: Canadian Broadcasting Corporation.

Tittle, Charles R. et al. 1986. Modeling Sutherland's theory of differential association. *Social Forces* 65 (December):405–32.

Tolpin, Marian, and Heinz Kohut. 1980. The disorders of the self. Pp. 425–42 in Greenspan and Pollock, 1980-I.

Trigg, Roger. 1982. *The shaping of man.* Oxford, England: Basil Blackwell.

Trivers, Robert L. 1978. The evolution of reciprocal altruism. Pp. 189–226 in T. H. Clutton-Brock and Paul H. Harvey (eds.), *Readings in sociobiology.* San Francisco: W. H. Freeman.

Tsui, Amy O., and Donald J. Bogue. 1978. Declining world fertility. *Population Bulletin* 33 (October):1–55.

Turk, Austin T. 1982. Social control and social conflict. Pp. 249–64 in Gibbs, 1982a.

Turke, Paul W., and L. L. Betzig. 1983. Testing sociobiological theory. *American Anthropologist* 85 (June):409–11.

Turner, Bryan S. 1986. *Equality.* London: Tavistock.

Turner, Jonathan H., and Leonard Beeghley. 1981. *The emergence of sociological theory.* Homewood, Ill.: Dorsey Press.

————, and Alexandra Maryanski. 1979. *Functionalism.* Menlo Park, Calif.: Benjamin/Cummings.

Tyler, Tom R., and Kathleen M. McGraw. 1983. The threat of nuclear war. *Journal of Social Issues* 39 (no. 1):25–40.

Tylor, Edward B. 1920. *Primitive culture,* 2 vols. London: John Murray.

United Nations. 1980. *Compendium of social statistics, 1977.* New York: United Nations.

————. 1979. *Yearbook of international trade statistics, 1977,* vol. 1. New York: United Nations.

————. 1976. *World energy supplies, 1950–1974.* New York: United Nations.

————. 1973. *Demographic yearbook, 1972.* New York: United Nations.

————. 1967–75. *Statistical yearbook,* each year 1966–74. New York: United Nations.

Van Dam, Heiman. 1980. Ages four to six—the Oedipus complex revisited. Pp. 573–87 in Greenspan and Pollock, 1980-I.

Van den Berg, Axel. 1980. Critical theory. *American Journal of Sociology* 86 (November):449–78.

Van den Berghe, Pierre L. 1982. Bridging the paradigms. Pp. 13–28 in Wiegele, 1982.

————. 1981. *The ethnic phenomenon.* New York: Elsevier.

————. 1979. *Human family systems.* New York: Elsevier.

————. 1978. *Race and racism.* New York: Wiley.

————. 1975. *Man in society*. New York: Elsevier.

————. 1963. Dialectic and functionalism. *American Sociological Review* 28 (October):695–705.

————, and Gene M. Mesher. 1980. Royal incest and inclusive fitness. *American Ethnologist* 7 (May):300–17.

Vanneman, Reeve, and Fred C. Pampel. 1977. The American perception of class and status. *American Sociological Review* 42 (June):422–37.

Veblen, Thorstein. 1898. Why is economics not an evolutionary science? *Quarterly Journal of Economics* 12 (July):373–97.

Wagner, Helmut R. 1973. The scope of phenomenological sociology. Pp. 61–87 in Psathas, 1973.

Waite, Robert G. L. 1977. *The psychopathic god*. New York: Basic Books.

Walker, A. et al. 1986. 2.5 Myr *Australopithecus boisei* from west of Lake Turkana, Kenya. *Nature,* 322 (August):517–22.

Wallace, Walter L. 1983. *Principles of scientific sociology*. New York: Aldine.

Walter, Eugene V. 1969. *Terror and resistance*. New York: Oxford University Press.

Ward, Lester F. 1903. *Pure sociology*. New York: Macmillan.

Wardlaw, Grant. 1982. *Political terrorism*. Cambridge, England: Cambridge University Press.

Warner, Robert R. 1980. The coevolution of behavioral and life-history characteristics. Pp. 151–88 in Barlow and Silverberg, 1980.

Warr, Mark, and Mark Stafford. 1983. Fear of victimization. *Social Forces* 61 (June):1033–43.

Washburn, S. L. 1982. Human behavior and the behavior of other animals. Pp. 95–117 in Wiegele, 1982.

Waste, Robert J., ed. 1986. *Community power*. Beverly Hills, Calif.: Sage.

Wattenberg, Ben, and Karl Zinsmeister. 1985. *Are world population trends a problem?* Washington, D.C.: American Enterprise Institute for Public Policy Research.

Weber, Max. 1978. *Economy and society*, 2 vols., continuous pagination. Berkeley: University of California Press.

————. 1962. *Basic concepts in sociology*. New York: Greenwood Press.

Weimann, Gabriel. 1982. Dealing with bureaucracy. *Social Psychology Quarterly* 45 (September):136–44.

Weinberg, Martin S., and Colin J. Williams. 1975. *Male homosexuals*. New York: Penguin Books.

Weinreb, Lloyd L. 1978. Law as order. *Harvard Law Review* 91 (March):909–59.

Weinstein, Jay. 1982. *Sociology/technology*. New Brunswick, N.J.: Transaction Books.

Weiss, Gerald. 1973. A scientific concept of culture. *American Anthropologist* 75 (October):1376–413.

Wellman, Barry. 1983. Network analysis. Pp. 155–200 in Collins, 1983.

Wenke, Robert J. 1980. *Patterns in prehistory*. New York: Oxford University Press.

Wentworth, William M. 1980. *Context and understanding*. New York: Elsevier.

White, Leslie A. 1975. *The concept of cultural systems*. New York: Columbia University Press.

———— (with Beth Dillingham). 1973. *The concept of culture*. Minneapolis: Burgess.

————. 1959. *The evolution of culture*. New York: McGraw-Hill.

————. 1949. *The science of culture*. New York: Grove Press.

————. 1948. The definition and prohibition of incest. *American Anthropologist* 50 (July-September):416–35.

White, Lynn, Jr. 1962. *Medieval technology and social change*. Oxford, England: Clarendon Press.

Whyte, William F. 1986. On the uses of social science research. *American Sociological Review* 51 (August):555–63.

————. 1955. *Street corner society*, 2d ed. Chicago: University of Chicago Press.

Wiegele, Thomas C., ed. 1982. *Biology and the social sciences*. Boulder, Colo: Westview.

Wiley, Norbert. 1985. The current interregnum in American sociology. *Social Research* 52 (Spring):179–207.

————. 1979. The rise and fall of dominating theories in American sociology. Pp. 47–79 in Snizek et al., 1979.

Wilkinson, Paul. 1986. Terrorism versus liberal democracy. Pp. 3–28 in William Gutteridge (ed.), *The new terrorism*. London: Mansell.

Willer, David, and Bo Anderson, eds. 1981. *Networks, exchange and coercion*. New York: Elsevier.

Williams, B. J. 1980. Kin selection, fitness and cultural evolution. Pp. 573–87 in Barlow and Silverberg, 1980.

Williams, Janet B. W., and Robert L. Spitzer, eds. 1984. *Psychotherapy Research*. New York: Guilford Press.

Williams, Kirk R. 1984. Economic sources of homicide. *American Sociological Review* 49 (April):283–89.

Williamson, Joel. 1984. *The crucible of race*. New York: Oxford University Press.

Wilson, Edward O. 1980. A consideration of the genetic foundation of human social behavior. Pp. 295–306 in Barlow and Silverberg, 1980.

————. 1978. *On human nature*. Cambridge, Mass.: Harvard University Press.

————. 1975. *Sociobiology*. Cambridge, Mass.: Harvard University Press.

Wilson, Harriett. 1980. Parental supervision. *British Journal of Criminology* 20 (July):203–35.

Wilson, James Q. 1983. Raising kids. *Atlantic* 252 (October):45–56.

Winkler, Karen J. 1984. Applied sociology now overshadows the theoretical in much of Europe. *Chronicle of Higher Education* 29 (September 5):17.

Winner, Langdon. 1977. *Autonomous technology*. Cambridge, Mass.: MIT Press.

Woodward, Susan L. 1983. Book review. *American Journal of Sociology* 88 (January):810–12.

Wozniak, Paul R. 1984. Making sociobiological sense out of sociology. *Sociological Quarterly* 25 (Spring):191–204.

Wright, Erik O. 1985. *Classes*. London: Verso.

————. 1979. *Class structure and income determination*. New York: Academic Press.

————. 1978. *Class, crisis and the state*. London: New Left Books.

———— et al. 1982. The American class structure. *American Sociological Review* 47 (December):709–26.

Wrong, Dennis H. 1979. *Power*. New York: Harper and Row.

Wuthnow, Robert. 1985. State structures and ideological outcomes. *American Sociological Review* 50 (December):799–821.

Yates, Aubrey J. 1980. *Biofeedback and the modification of behavior*. New York: Plenum.

Zald, Mayer N. 1978. On the social control of industries. *Social Forces* 57 (September):79–102.

Zedlewski, Edwin M. 1983. Deterrence findings and data sources. *Journal of Research in Crime and Delinquency* 20 (July):262–76.

Zeisel, Hans. 1982. *The limits of law enforcement*. Chicago: University of Chicago Press.

Ziegert, Klaus A. 1983. The Swedish prohibition of corporal punishment. *Journal of Marriage and the Family* 45 (November):917–26.

Zihlman, Adrienne L. 1978. Women in evolution, Part II. *Signs* 4 (Autumn):4–20.

Zimmerman, Burke K. 1984. *Biofuture, confronting the genetic era*. New York: Plenum.

Zimmermann, Ekkart. 1983. *Political violence, crises, and revolutions*. Boston: G. K. Hall.

Zuckerman, Alan. 1977. The concept of political elite. *Journal of Politics* 39 (May):324–44.

Zuckerman, Lord. 1985. The prospects of nuclear war. *New York Review of Books* 32 (April 15):21–26.

Zuriff, G. E. 1985. *Behaviorism*. New York: Columbia University Press.

Name Index

Subject Index